The Legal Defense of Pathological Intoxication

THE LEGAL DEFENSE OF PATHOLOGICAL INTOXICATION

With Related Issues of Temporary and Self-Inflicted Insanity

LAWRENCE P. TIFFANY
and
MARY TIFFANY

Q

QUORUM BOOKS
New York • Westport, Connecticut • London

Library of Congress Cataloging-in-Publication Data

Tiffany, Lawrence P.
The legal defense of pathological intoxication : with related issues of temporary and self-inflicted insanity / Lawrence P. Tiffany and Mary Tiffany.
p. cm.
Includes bibliographical references.
ISBN 0-89930-548-2 (lib. bdg. : alk. paper)
1. Drunkenness (Criminal law)—United States. 2. Criminal liability—United States. 3. Alcoholism—United States.
I. Tiffany, Mary. II. Title.
KF9243.T54 1990
345.73'04—dc20
[347.3054] 89-49429

British Library Cataloguing in Publication Data is available.

Library of Congress Catalog Card Number: 89-49429
ISBN: 0-89930-548-2

First published in 1990

Quorum Books, 88 Post Road West, Westport, CT 06881
An imprint of Greenwood Publishing Group, Inc.

Printed in the United States of America

The paper used in this book complies with the Permanent Paper Standard issued by the National Information Standards Organization (Z39.48-1984).

10 9 8 7 6 5 4 3 2 1

Copyright Acknowledgments

The authors and publishers gratefully acknowledge permission to reprint from the following:

A. GOLDSTEIN, THE INSANITY DEFENSE (1967), reprinted by permission of Yale University Press.

A. Lewis, *Psychological Medicine*, in PRICE'S TEXTBOOK OF THE PRACTICE OF MEDICINE 1172 (1966), and N. MORRIS & C. HOWARD, STUDIES IN CRIMINAL LAW 62 (1964), reprinted by permission of Oxford University Press.

ABA, CRIMINAL JUSTICE MENTAL HEALTH STANDARDS, Standard 7-6.1 (1984).

AMERICAN PSYCHIATRIC ASSOCIATION: DIAGNOSTIC AND STATISTICAL MANUAL OF MENTAL DISORDERS, THIRD EDITION, REVISED. Washington, D.C., American Psychiatric Association, 1987.

Andrulonis, Donnelly, Glueck, Stroebel & Szarek, *Preliminary Data on Ethosuximide and the Episodic Dyscontrol Syndrome*, 137 AM. J. PSYCHIAT. 11, 12. Copyright 1980, The American Psychiatric Association. Reprinted by permission.

Automatism or Unconsciousness as Defense to Criminal Charge, 27 A.L.R.4th 1067 (1984), reprinted by permission of The Lawyers Co-operative Publishing Company, Rochester, New York.

Bach-y-Rita, Lion, Climent & Ervin, *Episodic Dyscontrol: A Study of 130 Violent Patients*, 127 AM. J. PSYCHIAT. 11. Copyright 1971, The American Psychiatric Association. Reprinted by permission.

Bach-y-Rita, letter to the editor, 128 AM. J. PSYCHIAT. 660-661. Copyright 1971, The American Psychiatric Association. Reprinted by permission.

Blair, *The Medicolegal Aspects of Automatism*, 17 MED., SCI. & LAW 167 (1977), and Knox, *Epileptic Automatism and Violence*, 8 MED., SCI. & LAW 96 (1968), reprinted by permission of Chiltern Publishing.

Coid, *Mania A Potu: A Critical Review of Pathological Intoxication*, 9 PSYCHOL. MED. 709 (1979), Cambridge University Press, publishers.

Cook, *Act, Intention, and Motive in the Criminal Law*, reprinted by permission of The Yale Law Journal Company and Fred B. Rothman & Company from *The Yale Law Journal*, Vol. 26, pp. 645 - 663.

Desai, *Complex Partial Seizures*, 30 AM. FAM. PHYS. 158, 159 (1984), is reprinted from the 1984 issue of *American Family Physician*, published by the American Academy of Family Physicians.

Glasgow, *The Anatomy of Automatism*, 64 N.Z. MED. J. 491 (1965), reprinted by permission of the author and the publisher.

GOODMAN & GILMAN'S, THE PHARMACOLOGICAL BASIS OF THERAPEUTICS (A. Gilman, L. Goodman, T. Rall & F. Murad eds. 7th ed. 1985), reprinted by permission of Macmillan Publishing Co.

Gunn, *Epileptic Homicide: A Case Report*, 132 BR. J. PSYCHIAT. 510 (1978), reprinted by permission of The British Journal of Psychiatry.

Harding, *Sane and Insane Automatism in Australia: Some Dilemmas, Developments and Suggested Reforms*, 4 Int'l J. L. & Psychiat. 73 (1981), reprinted by permission of Pergamon Press.

Henry, *Positive Spike Discharges in the EEG and Behavior Abnormality*, in EEG AND BEHAVIOR 315, 316 (G. Glaser ed. 1963), and Thompson, *Acute and Chronic Alcoholic Conditions*, in 2 AMERICAN HANDBOOK OF PSYCHIATRY 1208-1209 (1959), reprinted by permission of Basic Books, Inc., of Harper & Row Publishers.

KOLB, L., MODERN CLINICAL PSYCHIATRY. Philadelphia, W.B. Saunders Co., 7th ed., 1968 and 9th ed. 1977. Reprinted by permission.

LEVIN, J. AND FOX, J., MASS MURDER 31 (1985), reprinted by permission of Plenum Press.

Lewis, Pincus, Shanok & Glaser, *Psychomotor Epilepsy and Violence in a Group of Incarcerated Adolescent Boys*, 139 AM. J. PSYCHIAT. 882. Copyright 1982, The American Psychiatric Association. Reprinted by permission.

MACDONALD, J., PSYCHIATRY AND THE CRIMINAL 245 (3d ed. 1976), and G. THOMPSON, THE PSYCHOPATHIC DELINQUENT AND CRIMINAL 115 (1953), courtesy of Charles C Thomas, Publisher, Springfield, Illinois.

Maletzky, *The Alcohol Provocation Test*, 39 J. CLIN. PSYCHIAT. 403 (1978), and Stevens, *Psychiatric Aspects of Epilepsy*, 49 J. CLIN. PSYCHIAT. 49 (1988), reprinted by permission of Physicians Postgraduate Press.

MODEL PENAL CODE (Proposed Official Draft). Copyright 1962 by the American Law Institute. Reprinted with the permission of the American Law Institute.

MODEL PENAL CODE (Tent. Draft No. 4). Copyright 1955 by the American Law Institute. Reprinted with the permission of the American Law Institute.

MODEL PENAL CODE (Tent. Draft No. 9). Copyright 1959 by the American Law Institute. Reprinted with the permission of the American Law Institute.

MODEL PENAL CODE AND COMMENTARIES. Copyright 1980 by the American Law Institute. Reprinted with the permission of the American Law Institute.

MODEL PENAL CODE AND COMMENTARIES. Copyright 1985 by the American Law Institute. Reprinted with the permission of the American Law Institute.

Paulsen, *Intoxication as a Defense to Crime*, 1961 U. ILL. L. FORUM 1, 17, reprinted by permission of The Board of Trustees of the University of Illinois.

Perr, *Pathological Intoxication and Alcohol Idiosyncratic Intoxication—Part I: Diagnostic and Clinical Aspects*, 31 J. FOR. SCI. 806 (1986); Perr, *Pathological Intoxication and Alcohol Idiosyncratic Intoxication—Part II: Legal Aspects*, 31 J. FOR. SCI. 812 (1986). Extracted with permission, from the JOURNAL OF FORENSIC SCIENCES, July 1986, copyright American Society for Testing and Materials, 1916 Race Street, Philadelphia, PA 19103.

Pincus, *Can Violence be a Manifestation of Epilepsy?*, 30 NEUROLOGY 304 (1980), reprinted by permission of the author and the publisher.

Reprint with permission from *A Dictionary of Words About Alcohol* by M. Keller, M. McCormick & V. Efron. Copyright 1982 by Journal of Studies on Alcohol, Inc., Rutgers Center of Alcohol Studies, New Brunswick, N.J.

Reproduced, with permission, from J. Hughes and W. Wilson, eds., EEG AND EVOKED POTENTIAL IN PSYCHIATRY AND BEHAVIOR (Stoneham, MA: Butterworth Publishers, 1984).

Skelton, *Alcohol, Violent Behavior, and the Electroencephalogram,* 63 S. MED. J. 465 (1970), reprinted by permission of the publishers.

Terrell, Letter: *Behavioral Dyscontrol Associated With Combined Use of Alprazolam and Ethanol,* 145 AM. J. PSYCHIAT. 1313 (1988), reprinted by permission of the American Psychiatric Association.

Victor, *The Pathophysiology of Alcoholic Epilepsy,* 46 RES. NERV. MENT. DIS. 431 (1968), reprinted with permission of the publisher.

Yudofsky, S.C., Silver, J.M.: *Psychiatric Aspects of Brain Injury: Trauma, Stroke and Tumor,* in PSYCHIATRIC UPDATE: AMERICAN PSYCHIATRIC ASSOCIATION ANNUAL REVIEW, Vol. 4. Edited by Hales, R.E. and Frances, A.J. Washington DC, American Psychiatric Press, 1985, pp. 142-158.

Every reasonable effort has been made to locate the owners of copyright materials in this book, but in some instances this has proven impossible. The publishers will be glad to receive information leading to more complete acknowledgments in subsequent printings of the book, and in the meantime extend their apologies for any omissions.

To Eric and Julie,
law and medicine
and other shared and promising ventures.

Contents

Preface

Our involvement with the subject of pathological intoxication actually began in 1965 when a criminal defense attorney called to ask if any information was available on the subject. He had a client who had gone on a Sunday afternoon picnic with his wife in Denver's City Park and, after drinking a few beers with lunch, he had repeatedly run over her with his car in the park before a number of witnesses. Little material was accessible then and the attorney had to use what could be gleaned from the Model Penal Code and the meager psychiatric literature on the subject at the time.

Despite repeated returns to the subject over the next several years, little more became available. We returned to the task now and then, once to write a Master's level paper and more than once to try to pull together what was known in the form of a law review article, but each time the data seemed too sparse. Due as much to improved research methods (now also more commonly available) as to expanded information on both the legal and medical sides of the question, this time the effort went to closure.

The book is an in-depth study and analysis of a phenomenon that is not yet well integrated into the criminal law of defenses. To a substantial extent, it is aimed at the judge, lawyer or mental health practitioner who is involved in the practice of criminal law. There is also a great deal here that is essentially theoretical and hopefully it will be of benefit to other criminal law researchers and writers as well, particularly with reference to personal fault on the part of the actor as a limitation on the availability of this defense (or others). This is not the final word on the subject; indeed, in the legal literature, it is nearly the first. The coverage, however, is quite thorough and should equip the litigator with both the medical background knowledge and our best reflections on the legal implications they entail.

The research recounted here was made accessible to us partly by means of computer data base research techniques and inter-library loan programs. Mary Younger and David Burrows of the University of Denver College of Law library, headed by Barbara Greenspahn, deserve special mention in that connection as does Bette Jean Ingui who directs her own commercial research-assistance service in Denver. Her services were made possible by a small grant from the Hughes Research Fund which is operated by the College of Law.

Over the life of this project, the work has received attention of a number of students at the law school. Bob Richards helped launch the effort long ago. Madeline Caughey made early contributions to some of its foreign literature components. Celeste Gamache and Christine Chauche helped more recently in the final editing stages. Their responsibilities were frequently tedious and always poorly compensated and we wish to acknowledge their contributions.

Colleagues Frank Jamison, Ved Nanda and Ed Richards listened and commented well and earned our indebtedness. A special expression of appreciation is due William A. Beaney who, at the time of this writing, is Acting Dean (for the second time) at the University of Denver College of Law. Bill provided critical support of this particular effort at important times and we are both grateful that Bill has been our friend for many years and that he has provided support in consequential ways not measured by this work.

Lawrence P. Tiffany
Mary Tiffany
Denver, Colorado
April 27, 1990

1

Introduction

Pathological intoxication, also called pathological reaction to alcohol, is essentially a temporary psychotic reaction, often manifested by violence, which is triggered by consumption of alcohol by a person with a predisposing mental or physical condition. That condition may be temporal lobe epilepsy, traumatic brain damage, metabolic disturbances or a variety of other factors. One technique used to confirm the existence of this condition involves the use of the EEG and alcohol provocation in the laboratory setting. This phenomenon occurs infrequently but often with devastating effects when it does. Pathological reaction to alcohol is the one alcohol psychosis for which chronic alcoholism is not a necessary condition.[1] All other alcohol-related mental illness presupposes alcoholism as a pre-condition.[2]

The phenomenon of pathological intoxication has been an enigma to the law for over a century, even before the problem was medically identified as early as 1869.[3] After extensive review of the medical, legal and interdisciplinary literature, our conclusion is that pathological intoxication is coextensive with neither a discrete medical diagnostic category nor with any single category of established legal defenses. Obviously it does not follow from those two observations that pathological intoxication "does not exist" as some have claimed or that it is not of defensive relevance. Pathological intoxication is real, often disastrously so, and it provides a potentially significant defense in many serious cases more frequently than presently supposed. We believe that pathological

---

1. Banay, *Pathologic Reaction to Alcohol*, 4 QRTLY J. STUD. ALCOH. 580 (1944).

2. The others listed in AMERICAN PSYCHIATRIC ASSOCIATION, DIAGNOSTIC AND STATISTICAL MANUAL OF MENTAL DISORDERS 127-133 (3d ed. rev. 1987), (hereinafter cited as DSM-III-R), include alcohol withdrawal delirium, alcohol hallucinosis, alcohol amnestic disorder (Korsakoff's psychosis) and dementia.

DSM-I was published in 1952, DSM-II in 1968, DSM-III in 1980 and DSM-III-R in 1987. We will use the short citation form throughout the book.

3. Krafft-Ebing, 27 DTSCH. Z. STARZNEIK. 444 (1869).

intoxication is best thought of as consisting of three paradigms. The abnormal reaction is triggered by consumption of alcohol or other drug by a person with (1) a mental disease or defect, (2) a physical disability or recent trauma, either involving the brain or (3) who is alcohol sensitive, temporarily or permanently. Depending upon which is involved, and that is sometimes problematical, these three types of pathological intoxication respectively fit most logically within the defenses of insanity, automatism and intoxication. In our opinion, whether the defense succeeds or fails should turn on the actor's culpability in contributing to the abnormal mental state. The doctrine of "voluntary intoxication" is stretched by some courts and statutes to serve that fault finding function for want of a more explicit fault limiter which applies to all defenses, including insanity and automatism. Neither the facts nor the law will, of course, prove to be entirely so exact, but the categories will serve to advantage moderately well and they facilitate understanding an area that can become quite complex and enigmatic without at least a modicum of order being imposed.

THE ISSUES ASSOCIATED WITH PATHOLOGICAL INTOXICATION

The central medical position developed here is that the affliction historically known both medically and legally as pathological intoxication is a phenomenon which encompasses a variety of relatively definable underlying predisposing conditions, usually physiological in nature, and in which alcohol consumption serves as the precipitating cause of the reaction. It typically results in a temporary psychotic condition and frequently in violent behavior. The position developed on the legal side is that such conduct usually is best dealt with under the insanity defense when the underlying cause is a condition fairly described as a "mental disease or defect," under the defense of automatism when it is more clearly physical in nature so that it does not seem appropriate to classify the condition as legal insanity, and as involuntary intoxication in the event of a case of inadvertent intoxication. In addition, we develop the idea that the level of success of each defense should turn upon the actor's degree of awareness of personal susceptibility to such a reaction. A minority of courts, however, have treated drinking as "fault" on the part of the actor sufficient to eliminate these defenses, while we believe the level of the actor's awareness should be the relevant fault factor.

Present usage shows some preference for the expression "pathological reaction to alcohol" over the term "pathological intoxication," although the terms are usually treated as though they were technically interchangeable. The most common terminology employed by courts and psychiatrists is "pathological intoxication." While others have used the phrase "complicated intoxication," "pathological alcoholic intoxication" (to differentiate it from other toxic agents), "pathological drunkenness"[4] or more recently "atypical intoxication," we prefer the term "pathological reaction to alcohol," as originally coined by Krafft-Ebing when he provided the first clinical description of the phenomenon. The most recent version of the American Psychiatric Association's Diagnostic and Statistical Manual, DSM-III-R, now uses the expression "alcohol idiosyncratic intoxication"[5] where it originally used "pathological intoxication."[6] It has perhaps more often been referred to as pathological intoxication, but that term is descriptively misleading: Pathological reaction to alcohol is not intoxication at all if "intoxication" is taken to mean drunkenness. The same point has been made by others. English and Finch[7] took the position that the phrase "pathological intoxication" perhaps ought not to be used "since it indicates that the alcohol itself is of major importance, while in reality the underlying psychological problems are merely brought to the fore by the alcohol." We believe in most cases it is actually an underlying physical problem, but the point is the same: Alcohol is only the catalyst. That fact alone has misled some courts and has contributed to a confusing legal response to the problem in criminal cases and undoubtedly other types of cases as well, legal and medical. The major problem with the use of the other terms is their use of the word "intoxication" which is deceptive in an important way. As our discussion of symptomatology will emphasize, pathological reaction to alcohol does not necessarily involve any of the typical symptoms of alcohol intoxication. Perhaps it would not be unduly confusing to note that we think it accurate to conceive of pathological reaction to alcohol as a type of pathological intoxication because pathological intoxication need not involve alcohol as the inducing chemical, although it usually is what is involved. But we will simply use the terms interchangeably.

Such an abnormal reaction to alcohol or other drug should be a valid defense to resulting criminal charges, at least under some restricted circumstances such as when the actor was not given cause to know of the possible reaction. What is remiss on the legal side of the question is, in general terms, twofold: The defense is not presented adequately by defense counsel because they do not understand what they are dealing with and, secondly, partly as a result of that, the defense is badly misperceived and therefore is also misanalyzed and mistrusted by some courts. The result is not only the tragedy of the original occurrence, often a homicide or serious assault, but the compounding aftermath of treating

---

4. Blair, *The Medico-Legal Problems of Pathological Alcoholic Intoxication: An Illustrative Case*, 9 MED., SCI. & LAW 94, 96 (1969).

5. DSM-III-R at 128-29.

6. AMERICAN PSYCHIATRIC ASSOCIATION, DIAGNOSTIC AND STATISTICAL MANUAL OF MENTAL DISORDERS (1952).

7. O. ENGLISH & S. FINCH, INTRODUCTION TO PSYCHIATRY 449 (3d ed. 1964).

the result of involuntary action as criminal and punishing a person through our criminal courts who, if unaware of the condition, is actually blameless. The "fault" found by those courts is the mere act of drinking alcohol; our position is that fault should not turn on an act of the defendant but upon awareness of the probable outcome of that conduct. Most courts agree.

It should be emphasized at the outset that pathological intoxication is in fact a generic term which may encompass a relatively wide variety of specific, medically recognized pathologies. For example, it is clearly related to traumatic brain damage and psychomotor epilepsy. Still, medical disagreement is limited largely to nomenclature and etiology and medical literature rarely questions its existence per se.

The symptoms of ordinary intoxication are familiar to everyone:

> The essential feature of this disorder is maladaptive behavioral changes due to recent ingestion of alcohol. These changes may include aggressiveness, impaired judgment, impaired attention, irritability, euphoria, depression, emotional lability, and other manifestations of impaired social or occupational functioning. Characteristic physiologic signs include slurred speech, incoordination, unsteady gait, nystagmus, and flushed face.
>
> The diagnosis is not made when there is evidence that the amount of alcohol ingested was insufficient to cause intoxication in most people, as in Alcohol Idiosyncratic Intoxication....[8]

By pathological reaction to alcohol or pathological intoxication we do not mean the existence of bodily or mental conditions which lead a person to become intoxicated more quickly or more heavily than is normal for that person or any other person similarly situated, a condition that is sometimes referred to as alcohol sensitivity. Temporary conditions, such as not eating or fatigue or even emotional state, can cause a person to become more intoxicated with less alcohol. But these differences relate simply to quantitative variations in the rate of becoming intoxicated or the degree of intoxication. Pathological reaction to alcohol is a qualitatively different event. It does not result in drunkenness at all; it results in a temporary psychosis.

Beyond that medical and physiological premise which will be explored in detail later, the second major question is the legal analysis that is appropriate for the trial of persons who experience pathological intoxication and are charged with a crime for harm caused. The law has

---

8. DSM-III-R at 127.

a complicated and sometimes confusing classification scheme of defenses, and part of the task is to fit this defense within that design, a task somewhat akin in its complexity and ambiguity to the task of fitting pathological intoxication into existing psychiatric classification methods. Absent recognition of an entirely new category of defense, the questions will resolve themselves into whether, if the defense is to be recognized at all, it will fall within the existing categories of (1) legal insanity;[9] (2) involuntary act (automatism); (3) involuntary intoxication; (4) voluntary intoxication; (5) lack of *mens rea* as to the crime charged; or (6) diminished capacity or related doctrines.

As we understand the medical facts, the case is clearly one of temporary legal insanity or, with some reservation, involuntary act, subject to the limitation in both cases that the defendant did not know that a violent or otherwise abnormal reaction might be the result of drinking alcohol. The legal tension surrounding its proper classification will occur not only because of concern on the part of judges about false claims made to insulate the actor from the legal consequences of ordinary intoxication but from the fact that the legal structure basically now provides that a person who successfully defends on the ground of involuntary act is acquitted outright while the person found not guilty by reason of insanity is also acquitted but is then subject to civil commitment. At the same time, courts sometimes have difficulty classifying cases of pathological intoxication as "legal insanity" because of the uncertainty whether there is a "mental disease or defect" involved and the defendant is left trying to defend the case on an inappropriate plea if he pleaded not guilty by reason of insanity where that is required, instead of simply pleading not guilty, as one would in defending on the ground of involuntary act. There is also the confounding concept of "temporary insanity" which suggests even civil commitment may be inappropriate if the reason for confinement is to treat the patient. Abstention from alcohol may be the only treatment needed; it may also be the only treatment available.

Criminal law has typically allowed, but does not require, a jury to reduce what is referred to as a "specific intent" crime[10] to a so-called

---

9. Unless the context indicates otherwise, "insanity" will refer to the defendant's mental condition at the time of the conduct charged. The issue of pathological reaction to alcohol will rarely be a matter for challenging competency to stand trial. *But see* State v. Fox, 112 Ariz. 375, 542 P.2d 800 (1975) (in a case of possible pathological intoxication, the case was remanded to determine the defendant's competency to stand trial).

10. Much ado has been made of this term used at common law, and varying definitions have been offered which need not detain. *See, e.g.*, Note, *Alcohol Abuse and the Law*, 94 HARV. L. REV. 1660, 1683 (1981), and authorities cited therein. It seems sufficient to define a specific intent crime as a crime which requires a culpable mental state of intent with respect to any required *actus reus* result element. A "general intent" crime is any other crime, that is, one which has no result requirement, or which, if it does have a result requirement, can

"general intent" crime if such a lesser, included offense exists when the defendant was drunk at the time of the crime. This sometimes even means allowing a jury to obviate the possibility of the death penalty in a case charged as murder in the first degree by reducing the conviction to murder in the second degree. The "reality" of this device is obviously open to question. More recently, the law has invented the doctrine called diminished capacity which shares with the specific versus general intent distinction the task of avoiding more serious convictions (and the death penalty) when relatively stringent rules regarding the defense of legal insanity would otherwise prevent any mitigation. In addition, the law has rediscovered the ancient principle that a person cannot be found guilty of a crime unless his conduct is deemed to be at least in part voluntary, now often referred to as the automatism defense when it is based on unconsciousness on the part of the defendant. For centuries, the law has also drawn a distinction between voluntary and involuntary intoxication, and that distinction is still not clearly understood by some courts.

We raise these general questions regarding the state of the art in medical research regarding alcohol, and in the state of the art in handling defenses based in part on the defense of use of alcohol to indicate briefly the complexity of the problems involved, because it is on top of these that we raise the additional problem of pathological reaction to alcohol. Even when the problem of pathological intoxication is adequately researched and presented in court, it must be offered against an uncertain body of legal doctrine, involving enormous jury discretion. On top of all that, there will be cases which will be difficult to classify either because of the murkiness of some of the boundaries on the medical side, or confusion and ambiguity on the legal side, all exacerbated by the fact that what we are talking about is in any event not intoxication (drunkenness) or insanity in the usual longer term sense of that idea.

On the legal side, we will argue that once the appropriate medical facts are proven at trial, only one real quandary need remain because one of two dispositions may be more appropriate. One outcome is that the defendant was legally insane at the time of his act and therefore is entitled to an acquittal but is also subjected to possible "treatment"

---

be committed with a *mens rea* of less than intent, e.g., recklessness.

It is also noted that "courts often eschew theoretical distinction and look to public policy for guidance in classifying crimes as requiring specific or general intent." *Note* at 1684. Assault is the most frequent example because, to the extent it is defined as attempted battery, it is clearly a specific intent crime. Yet to so hold would mean that intoxication would be a defense. Thus, assault is frequently held to be only a general intent crime. On the other hand, if assault actually means battery, then it may well be a general intent crime. *See also* Burke, *The Defense of Voluntary Intoxication: Now You See It, Now You Don't*, 19 IND. L. REV. 147 (1986).

incarceration in a state hospital. The other view, appropriate in a different class of case, is that the defendant, in legal contemplation, committed no relevant voluntary act at all and should therefore be acquitted outright without further state intervention.

This conundrum exists because the two legal concepts of "insanity" and "involuntary act" are not entirely mutually exclusive; they can and do overlap, and pathological intoxication often is such a case. That common ground can be seen in one especially pertinent example: the disparate responses by the courts to the defense of "automatism." Some courts treat automatism as a claim of involuntary act which may be raised like any other defense at trial of the case, while other courts take the position that if automatism is to be raised as a defense, at least in a case involving a mental disease, it must be raised under the special procedures universally provided for raising the insanity defense, procedures which, for example, require special pleading on the part of the defense and which also provide at least the important possibility of civil incarceration if the defendant prevails on that special plea of not guilty by reason of insanity. Yet there is no agreement on what constitutes a "mental disease," the concept that is the exclusive hallmark of the insanity defense. What is important here is that states avoid a "pleading trap" set for defense counsel; counsel should know whether a special plea of insanity is required or not. Obviously, a legitimate defense ought not to be lost because the law of the jurisdiction is so problematic that the defense lawyer is required to guess.

Confined to this narrow conceptualization of the issue, the procedural, legal question is quite straightforward: Must the defense plead not guilty by reason of insanity, or will a simple plea of not guilty suffice to allow presentation of the medical evidence supporting the defense of pathological reaction to alcohol and allow the question to be submitted to the jury under appropriate instructions? In most states, the defendant may plead both not guilty and not guilty by reason of insanity, but that hardly helps in presenting a straightforward defense.

Pathological reaction to alcohol clearly exists, clearly results in a temporary (but possibly recurrent) psychotic condition and clearly should result in a successful defense to a criminal charge when the defendant was unaware of the possible result of drinking alcohol, that is, as long as the temporary "insanity" or the "involuntary act" was an unexpected event to him. Just as certainly, some appellate cases in the United States reject one or more of these points. Mental irresponsibility as a defense is getting more complex. The more we learn about the human mind and human emotions, the more claims are made that a particular person should not be held criminally responsible even if we have the concession that they ought to be subject to close state control in any event and perhaps even subjected to civil commitment. It seems increasingly probable that much, but not all, seriously deranged and dangerous behavior will, in the end, be found to have biological concommitants beyond our present ability to diagnose much less do anything about. But exactly as the defensive claims increase, public tolerance decreases, leading to efforts to limit or even abolish the defenses. The tension seems to vary little over time. Judges tend to respond to individual cases where it is often obvious to everyone closely involved that something is seriously wrong with the defendant, but the public responds more to the cases which draw more attention. This is the closer case, the contested one. The public and therefore legislative bodies also tend to respond to the plight of the victim and are upset when a brutal crime is uncovered and an insanity plea is successfully entered, an extremely rare event. On top of that, both sides are predisposed to mistrust psychiatrists and juries. If we are right at all about where medical research will take us, the tension is a more or less permanent condition.

We would have supposed at the outset that there would be a fundamental disagreement between "law" and "psychiatry" over the pathological intoxication issue. This is not the case. There are psychiatrists whose clinical experience and research support the concept, and most courts recognize it as a defense. But there are also courts which badly mistreat it, and there are psychiatrists who in some sense virtually deny its existence. The opposition camps, however, are not joined in their objections. The courts which show some reluctance to recognize it by and large simply misconstrue it as ordinary alcohol intoxication, which it is not, and the psychiatrists who oppose it do so largely but not entirely on nosologic grounds; it just does not fit into their own intellectual scheme of things concerning the human mind. Its existence as a phenomenon, nonetheless, is beyond serious contention, as we will chronicle.

There is one further confounding legal factor which deserves attention. If the concept of pathological reaction to alcohol improves its footing in our law of excuses relating to criminal responsibility, it is likely to be at least partially because of the remarkably influential effort by the American Law Institute in their Model Penal Code which has facilitated the adoption of new criminal codes in about forty states over the past two decades, about half of which have been heavily influenced by the Model Penal Code.[11]

Several points with respect to that effort are especially pertinent here. The states have been persuaded to adopt as the prevailing insanity test the Model Penal Code's "substantial capacity" test in place of the right-wrong (*M'Naghten*) test, which had predominated in this country for over a century. More importantly for our purposes, the drafters of that code were equally effective in gaining adoption of their statutory

11. AMERICAN LAW INSTITUTE, 1984 ANNUAL REPORT 20.

intoxication defense. That provision was basically a clarification and restatement of the pre-existing common law and then-existing state law. Within the same Model Penal Code section on intoxication is a definition of what they designate "pathological intoxication." While adopted in few states, it is a problem in several important ways. First, it tends to identify the clinical phenomenon as a kind of (possibly unexpected) excessive intoxication (drunkenness) instead of a psychotic reaction to alcohol having nothing to do with getting drunk. Secondly, they awkwardly drafted the section in such a way that if the defendant knew he was susceptible to such a reaction the reaction is defined legally as not having occurred. This is simply bad drafting in not separating the questions of what occurred medically from the question of legal responsibility for it. However, the former view, equating pathological reaction to alcohol with unexpected drunkenness, will contribute to the confusion of the courts in trying to sort out, on the one hand, pathological reaction to alcohol from, on the other hand, getting more drunk than might have been expected given the amount of alcohol consumed. Some of the states which have adopted the general provisions based on the Model Penal Code regarding intoxication and criminal responsibility have also unfortunately adopted this particular subsection. More states may use it for guidance.

As noted above, the new "official" psychiatric nomenclature for pathological intoxication or pathological reaction to alcohol is "Alcohol Idiosyncratic Intoxication," which is defined in part as follows:

> The essential feature of this disorder is a marked behavioral change—usually to aggressiveness—that is due to the recent ingestion of an amount of alcohol insufficient to induce intoxication in most people. There is usually subsequent amnesia for the period of intoxication. The behavior is atypical of the person when not drinking—for example, a shy, retiring, mild-mannered person may, after one weak alcoholic drink, become belligerent and assaultive.
>
> This disorder has also been called "pathological intoxication."[12]

Alcohol idiosyncratic intoxication is classified in DSM-III-R under a heading of "Alcohol-Induced Organic Mental Disorders.[13] We will deal with this formulation in greater detail later. Perhaps it would suffice here to point out that it is misleading in its suggestion that the actor is intoxicated, and it is simply wrong in its insistence that the amount of alcohol is a diagnostic sine qua non.

---

12. DSM-III-R at 128-29.
13. DSM-III-R at 127.

On the legal side we will argue that pathological reaction to alcohol should be recognized as a medical, not a criminal, problem for all those defendants who lacked awareness that, for them, consumption of alcohol in any amount, large or small, was a dangerous act in itself—a sufficient predicate for denying the defense to them, but only to them.

The phenomenon of pathological reaction to alcohol literally has been treated in six different ways by the courts. Each has strengths and weaknesses as to its appropriateness. Automatism, or involuntary act, commends itself because it is logical: True cases of pathological intoxication or pathological reaction to alcohol, particularly those which are psychomotor epilepsy or some other form of epilepsy triggered by alcohol, clearly involve automatic behavior either during the ictal stage or the immediate post-ictal stage. One manifestation of epilepsy is an excessive neuronal discharge within the central nervous system. During a seizure there may be an abrupt change in behavior, roughly coincident with automatism, and this period is referred to as ictal behavior. The longer periods between attacks are referred to as interictal periods, a period of normal behavior. Thus, the automatism is temporary. The problem with the use of the automatism defense is the disposition of the defendant because an outright acquittal will follow, and for this reason we would not expect the defense to be favored in these cases.

The very expression "pathological intoxication" operates like a Rorschach test on the courts; most see pathology, but many see intoxication. But even within the legal concept of intoxication, there are two subcategories: voluntary intoxication, which has only very limited defensive utility (though better than nothing from the defense perspective) and involuntary intoxication which, if it also reaches the level of insanity, will be treated as a possible complete defense. The problem with involuntary intoxication as the defense theory (or the court's theory) is that it is just as inappropriate as the voluntary intoxication category; it assumes a case in which the actor was indeed intoxicated but became so involuntarily or unknowingly. Neither is true in archetypal cases of pathological reaction to alcohol: If the actor was intoxicated at all, it is quite beside the point because the defendant will have been just as psychotic (insane) whether he was intoxicated or not and whether the actor was unaware will, of course, depend upon the particular case. Pathological reaction to alcohol is a psychotic reaction to alcohol, usually attributable to some underlying organic defect of the brain which may or may not be clearly diagnosed but which is clear enough based on other evidence. And it is for this reason that we believe that insanity is the appropriate defense category, not only because of the logic of it, which it shares with the automatism approach, but because of the disposition alternatives which exist in the court which are lacking in the involuntary act approach. On the other hand, there may be no "mental disease" in the case.

A few of the cases have also dealt with pathological intoxication as an excuse in the sense of defeating a showing by the state of the requisite *mens rea* of the crime charged against the defendant either as a general *mens rea* defense or a defense of diminished capacity. While this is no more inappropriate in the instance of pathological intoxication than it is with any other psychological impairment that renders cognitive capacity dysfunctional, it poses the same difficulty as exists in other areas of overlap between insanity and other defenses. Finally, we introduce the notion that perhaps it would be appropriate in some cases to try the matter under Model Penal Code-based statutes allowing for reduction of murder charges to manslaughter upon a showing by the defense of "extreme mental or emotional disturbance for which there is reasonable explanation or excuse."[14]

The case law discussed later makes one point amply clear: It will require both a medical expert and skillful defense counsel to invoke successfully the defense of pathological reaction to alcohol in a criminal case whether it goes to trial or not, and each needs to understand the other if they are to prevail in persuading both a judge that appropriate instructions to the jury should be given by the court and also a jury to apply them to facts adequately and lucidly elicited at trial. It will be even more common to encounter the need to persuade the prosecutor and possibly the state expert witnesses that pathological intoxication is what was actually involved in order to facilitate a negotiated disposition of the case.

The legal position expressed in this book is quite straightforward but intricate to develop. First, pathological intoxication should not be treated as voluntary intoxication in all cases because that tends to beg the question regarding voluntariness and because it is not intoxication in the usual sense in any event. We will discuss some cases in which the court essentially identifies drinking alcohol as the fault on the part of the actor. Thus, pathological intoxication, being triggered by consumption of alcohol, would never be a defense, and that seems wrong to us. If the matter is litigated as one of legal insanity, automatism, or involuntary intoxication, as we suggest, the defense in improper cases will fail in any event, and we have devoted considerable effort to demonstrate that.

If we were writing on a clean slate, we would also say that it usually should not be treated as involuntary intoxication because it is not in its classical formulation inebriation at all. Because this approach, some cases, if successful, result in the wrong disposition: outright release. But the Model Penal Code will undermine this view. Despite the advances shown in the dominant line of cases, which recognize that the fault limitation on this defense should focus on the actor's awareness of the

14. MODEL PENAL CODE § 210.3(1)(b) (Proposed Official Draft 1962).

probable outcome of drinking in his or her condition, to take the matter only into involuntary intoxication does not resolve the critical issues on the other side of the balance between the defendant's rights and the public interest. It is only treated as involuntary intoxication by the Model Penal Code and some courts because they were not sure a mental disease was involved and because they were not used to thinking of insanity law having a fault limitation built into it as intoxication law does in its distinction between voluntary intoxication and involuntary intoxication. Treatment of some of these cases as voluntary or involuntary intoxication, depending upon the fault limiter, though not as pathological intoxication, is appropriate when no underlying disease is involved such as in a case of mixing prescription medicines or receiving a blow to the head while already intoxicated.

Third, pathological intoxication usually should not be treated as automatism, or involuntary act, because of the disposition problem and the fact that it is often due to what the courts might classify as a disease of the mind. Automatism should be limited, as the English have done, to those cases in which disease of the mind is not involved (because of the disposition issue), although the categorization is not as easy as one might desire. This is not to advocate elimination of the automatism defense or even restriction of its recognition; rather the idea is that automatism due to mental disease should be required to be pleaded and defended as a form of insanity, which it is, under the procedural rules associated with the insanity defense. Most courts do appreciate the fact that pathological intoxication ought to be governed by insanity law, although there is still a modest line of cases which insists that it is only voluntary intoxication. What is not clear is how many courts require its treatment this way. Because of our procedural rules, defense attorneys tend to control the defense decision, not the courts.

A few psychiatrists are aligned with the attitude that pathological intoxication does not exist or ought not to. As to the former objection, we will present what is known about the subject of pathological intoxication. Based on this we think that any reasonable person would come to the same conclusion we have reached: From a phenomenological perspective, there is no reasonable doubt that pathological intoxication is real. From the second perspective, whether it ought to exist, the objection is only that pathological intoxication is not a primary disease, but represents a set of discernable symptoms reflective of other problems with the individual. With this we agree, but challenge its relevance as an objection to what is essentially a forensic concept.

There is no medical treatment for pathological reaction to alcohol per se; one must either treat and resolve or control the underlying condition or the person cannot drink or both. It is in this sense that pathological intoxication is not a primary disease, but is a symptomatic manifestation of a disease or defect of the brain (or mind). An analogy might be made, for example, in the observation that seizures are not a disease either, but only a manifestation of one or more underlying conditions. In the same vein pathological intoxication, like insanity itself as a general concept, is a forensic concept. But like the concept of automatism, there is no war between the legal perspective and the mental health perspective. As with automatism, the mental health expert needs to know more to decide how to treat, and the courts will need to know more to decide how to handle the responsibility question. It is of some significance to the courts that the reaction was caused by brain damage, though that will be of central interest to the mental health professional. Conversely, it is presumably of no interest to the mental health practitioner that the patient drank knowing of prior adverse and extreme reactions, while that fact will be crucial in the courts. Also on the legal side, it is important to remember, in the context of a defense that smacks of "temporary insanity" that the reaction is temporary, but the underlying condition sometimes is not. The same phenomenon underlies both perspectives; one simply branches out professionally to a different focus at the treatment point or the decision regarding responsibility.

Treatment of pathological intoxication as negating a requisite *mens rea*, diminished capacity, under any of its variants or under the "heat of passion" defense, should not be precluded and need not be reserved for marginal cases of pathological intoxication or other forms of temporary insanity, although they may have more utility in marginal cases, marginal in the sense of fault in some way causing the condition or where the condition was not sufficient to establish legal insanity or automatism in any event. In these cases, the fault limiter will operate with the culpability defense. The requirement in "heat of passion" cases under modern legislation will additionally require that the "extreme emotional disturbance" have a "reasonable explanation or excuse." Finally, marginal cases of pathological intoxication can be accounted for in sentencing, marginal again meaning either in terms of the degree of reaction suffered or in terms of the degree of fault involved in drinking while aware in the first instance.

Many pathological intoxication cases will typically be treated as insanity with the qualification that insanity is not a defense if it is self-induced with sufficient fault on the part of the actor. This will require something the legislatures have not provided for and which the courts are not used to handling: the need to establish a fault limiter in insanity cases just as the courts have done in intoxication cases and other defenses such as necessity, self-defense and duress. Not only is this the most accurate characterization of pathological intoxication within existing legal categories of defenses, it also provides the latitude needed for a fitting disposition: evaluation followed by treatment while confined or release under certain conditions which could also include a treatment regimen. It is important to note that other than conviction for the crime charged, this is the only way of dealing with a person who, while not guilty of the offense charged, is nevertheless potentially dangerous. The insanity defense as the proper place to deal with pathological intoxication requires, in addition, that pathological intoxication be recognized as a "mental disease or defect" or whatever similar limitation exists within the state's restrictions on the insanity defense. Since pathological intoxication is essentially the triggering of an underlying condition by the use of alcohol, this is readily possible, as we demonstrate in detail in the case of psychomotor epilepsy and more perfunctorily with other conditions.

One of our major conclusions is that pathological intoxication belongs to a genre that can best be described as temporary brain disorders. It is not a group of cases in which the defendant has probably fared well because of the suspicion of fraud generated by such a claim in which it would appear the defendant gets off too easily: Temporary insanity appears to be almost too good a defense, and so does automatism, especially since it, unlike insanity, will not usually be accompanied by civil commitment. But a generalized skepticism is no excuse for treating as common drunks and criminals those defendants who do have a legitimate claim to exoneration on the grounds of a temporary brain malfunction when they bear no responsibility for that condition.

Cases of pathological reaction to alcohol, by definition, involve people who have been drinking. The broader category may or may not involve alcohol but may instead involve something as commonplace as mixing two drugs which were not intended to be mixed or a spontaneous attack of temporal lobe epilepsy. The feature these cases have in common is the temporary nature of the resultant mental incapacity. These people do not fit the popular image of mental patients who undergo long-term commitment and, hopefully, treatment. Pathological intoxication happens to be the better known of these cases, but legally it is the broader category that ought to be of concern as well. The fact that alcohol consumption is the triggering mechanism in most of these cases of temporary brain disorder, hence, pathological intoxication, is a fortuity of biology and a function of the extensiveness of alcohol consumption. Even so, those cases indisputably circumscribe the genre and prescribe much of the judicial treatment of it. It is because of this that its consideration commands most of the analysis in this monograph. But we do give some attention to the other cases as well in the interests of what a medical practitioner might refer to as differential diagnosis.

AN EXEMPLARY CASE

People v. Higgins, decided 30 years ago by the New York Court of Appeals, is an exemplary case of pathological intoxication in a number of respects.[15] The defendant was convicted of murder in the first degree and sentenced to death. The case was obviously well tried. The experts devoted significant time to the case, which is not the unvarying norm judging by the reported cases, and it is one of the very rare cases in which the defendant won an evidence sufficiency appeal in this context. That, however, may be in part at least attributable to the allocation of the burden of proof on the insanity issue to the state, which was then the rule in New York.

The defendant pleaded not guilty with a specification of insanity, which is roughly equivalent to today's insanity plea. The court held in a majority decision by Judge Froessel that the burden on the insanity issue was not sustained by the people and reversed the conviction. The decision was four for reversal on evidence sufficiency grounds. The concurring judge joined in the reversal mainly on the ground that an intoxication instruction should have been given even though not requested by the defense. Two of the majority judges also would have voted for reversal solely on the intoxication instruction ground. Two judges dissented, one with an opinion. On the issue of evidence sufficiency, the court divided 4-3.

The defendant had been drinking heavily. He gave a ride in his car to a woman he knew slightly, but they were not previously involved. They parked and began to engage in sexual activity in the back seat of his car. She said she wanted to get some more drinks, creating the impression that they would have intercourse later. Evidently at that point the defendant picked up a hammer and hit her on the head 19 times. He removed her from the car and after placing her on the sidewalk, still alive, went home and went to sleep. She was found and died in a hospital that night. The following morning he threw in the trash the hammer, her shoes and purse left in the car and purchased and installed new seat covers for the car.[16]

The defendant testified that when she said "No, not yet", he suddenly felt dizzy and started shaking. His next recollection was screeching brakes and shouts as he was driving on the wrong side of a street later that night. He remembers then removing her from the car. He assumed he had done something wrong and so disposed of the evidence, and he lied at first to the police regarding his whereabouts that night after seeing an account of the crime in the newspapers. He assumed he had done it.[17]

Several witnesses testified that the defendant had prior fits, and in all they described nine of them in detail. Prior to all but two or three of these he had been drinking and generally had not eaten. Most of the

---

15. People v. Higgins, 5 N.Y.2d 607, 186 N.Y.S.2d 623, 159 N.E.2d 179 (1959).
16. *Higgins* at 610-12, 186 N.Y.S.2d at 625-27, 159 N.E.2d at 180-81.
17. *Higgins* at 611, 186 N.Y.S.2d at 625, 159 N.E.2d at 181.

prior incidents sound like grand mal seizures but not all of them. Some may have been psychomotor (temporal lobe) seizures, and they appear to be mixed as to alcohol involvement or not. In several of these instances, he struck out violently, "swinging like a fighter" at people in one of them. He would generally start shaking and striking out and then would go into a grand mal seizure. In one prior incident he broke out of a strait jacket during a seizure.[18]

Three experts with outstanding credentials testified for the defense.[19] All the standard tests they administered were negative except for hyperinsulism and brain damage. Because they suspected epilepsy despite the test results, the experts undertook an alcohol-provocation test to see if alcohol would provoke an epileptic seizure. One would testify that: "'There are many epileptics who will get spells most [sic] or only after alcohol.'"[20]

While the case was not tried expressly in terms of pathological intoxication, despite the evidence of alcohol involvement on the part of the defendant, it is now clearly established that alcohol can trigger an attack of psychomotor epilepsy. Indeed, it is somewhat ironic that the defendant may have garnered the necessary votes on appeal because the trial court did not *sua sponte* instruct the jury on the relevant law of intoxication. The dissent, on the other hand, thought that "Defense counsel minimized the drinking and at no time alluded to intoxication for the very good reason, no doubt, that such a claim might well have diverted the attention of the jury and jeopardized acceptance of the key defense based on the epileptic seizure...."[21] Notice that the court treated the drinking and the epileptic attack as unconnected events.

He was fitted for an EEG examination during this alcohol activation test. In all he was administered about 6 ounces of whiskey, mixed with sugar and orange juice, over a thirty-minute period of time. Nine minutes after the second three ounces he had a seizure. The reaction was so violent, the EEG leads came off and four officers could not hold him down; he was eventually handcuffed to a chair. His pupils dilated and their reaction was sluggish. One expert testified that this condition could not be simulated.[22] He could not communicate for about half an hour. After this episode, he had amnesia for the period of the violent part of the test and for the 30 minute period following the reaction.[23]

---

18. *Higgins* at 612-14, 186 N.Y.S.2d at 627-28, 159 N.E.2d at 181-82.

19. *Higgins* at 614, 186 N.Y.S.2d at 628, 159 N.E.2d at 182.

20. *Higgins* at 623, 186 N.Y.S.2d at 636, 159 N.E.2d at 187.

21. *Higgins* at 633, 186 N.Y.S.2d at 644, 159 N.E.2d at 193-94. The concurring opinion objected: "The prosecution's claim that the defendant is concluded [sic] by the deliberate action taken by his counsel is untenable." *Higgins* at 630, 186 N.Y.S.2d at 641, 159 N.E.2d at 191.

22. *Higgins* at 623, 186 N.Y.S.2d at 635, 159 N.E.2d at 187.

23. *Higgins* at 614-15, 186 N.Y.S.2d at 628-29, 159 N.E.2d at 182-83.

One of the experts described the reaction as a grand mal seizure combined with a "spell of rage, of furor."[24] This expert described the usual three forms of epilepsy, grand mal, petit mal and psychomotor, but classed this case as a fourth type which was called "hypothalamic epilepsy."[25] It is characterized by furor attacks, and he noted that the thalamus also is involved with emotional reactions. He testified that partial amnesia is possible in this type of epileptic seizure and that skillful movements are possible during the attack. In response to hypothetical questions, each expert testified that in his opinion the defendant was insane at the time of the homicide. One of the experts further testified that in his opinion "hyperinsulism" (hypoglycemia) had triggered an epileptic attack "which did not take the convulsive form."[26] The state's rebuttal expert witnesses never saw the defendant.[27] One said he did not know whether the defendant had a seizure at the time of the attack, and the second said that the defendant did not have an epileptic attack and was sane.

Since the state had the burden of proof on the insanity issue and since all five experts, defense and state, had agreed that a person is legally insane during an epileptic attack of the sort described here, the state had to prove beyond a reasonable doubt that the defendant was not having an attack at the time of the homicide. The state relied only on the admittedly coordinated efforts of the defendant and the partial memory he exhibited. Both state experts testified that the recall exhibited by the defendant was inconsistent with a seizure.[28] But the defense witnesses testified that during the furor stage of a seizure the defendant could have picked up a hammer even though he would not be capable of doing so throughout the seizure attack. Further, skillful movements had been evident in the defendant's prior attacks. The court also relied upon one of their own earlier cases, *Barber*,[29] which "recognized that an individual was capable of committing a homicide during an epileptic furor attack, and that the defense of insanity 'was one most proper to be urged, and required most deliberate and careful consideration.'[30]...The Barber case involved a *violent assault* upon two persons, followed by a burning of the house in which they lay helpless, resulting in the death of one of them....This court unanimously reversed the conviction of murder in the

24. *Higgins* at 615, 186 N.Y.S.2d at 629, 159 N.E.2d at 183.

25. The term was first used in Gibbs & Gibbs, *Electroencephalographic Evidence of Thalamic and Hypothalamic Epilepsy*, 1 NEUROL. 136 (1951).

26. *Higgins* at 616, 186 N.Y.S.2d at 630, 159 N.E.2d at 183.

27. *Higgins* at 616, 186 N.Y.S.2d at 630, 159 N.E.2d at 183-84. This is all too common in the cases.

28. *Higgins* at 617, 186 N.Y.S.2d at 630-31, 159 N.E.2d at 184.

29. People v. Barber, 115 N.Y. 475, 22 N.E. 182 (1889).

30. *Barber* at 489-90, 22 N.E. at 187. *See also* People v. Magnus, 92 Misc. 80, 155 N.Y.S. 1013 (1915).

first degree and ordered a new trial"[31] and took notice that "the weight of the evidence supports the view that defendant was physically capable of picking up the homicide weapon and inflicting the deadly blows upon decedent during an epileptic furor attack."[32] The court totally dismissed as of any evidentiary value the defendant's efforts at concealing his involvement with the attack.

There was another piece of information not admitted into evidence. The defense experts had also conducted a sodium amytal (truth serum) test, which is not normally considered truly reliable. During this test, the defendant described the speech of the victim just prior to the attack. He quoted her as saying "Tommy, why are you shaking? What's wrong with you? Are you sick?" "You're talking crazy. You're talking nonsense. What's wrong with you?" He reported no response. This lends extraordinary corroboration although neither the experts nor the court purported to rely upon it much.[33]

The fact that the conduct involved was motiveless is a powerful proof in pathological intoxication cases and, in the court's opinion, that was the case here; the state simply speculated regarding some motives of sexual rejection (the evidence was to the contrary)[34] and that the defendant was motivated by his desire to prevent the victim from telling his fiancée. The court said only that this "does not strike us as plausible...."[35]

There are any number of these cases which we will discuss later specifically dealing with problems of proof, but one of the points we want to make here, and why we went into such detail, is that the proof of the connection between epilepsy and violence is overwhelming unless the defense experts were lying about the alcohol provocation test results. It may be true that all of the exact physiological causes are yet to be identified, but that is true of most mental diseases. The fact is that more is known here than is usually the case. Despite established, contrary positions, the controversy regarding epilepsy and violence is its degree, not its reality. Further, the epileptic research almost systematically excludes the combined effects of various forms of epilepsy and alcohol when they address the question of the relationship between epilepsy and violence. Perhaps it is thought of only as alcohol and violence by these researchers just as some courts are wont to do.[36] Thus, one answer to the grand objection to pathological reaction to alcohol as a concept, that it is not a disease, is answered in many cases like *Higgins* by proof that

---

31. *Higgins* at 619, 186 N.Y.S.2d at 632, 159 N.E.2d at 185.
32. *Higgins* at 619, 186 N.Y.S.2d at 632, 159 N.E.2d at 185.
33. *Higgins* at 622, 186 N.Y.S.2d at 635, 159 N.E.2d at 187.
34. *Higgins* at 623-24, 186 N.Y.S.2d at 636, 159 N.E.2d at 188.
35. *Higgins* at 624, 186 N.Y.S.2d at 636, 159 N.E.2d at 188.
36. *See, e.g.*, Evilsizer v. State, 487 S.W.2d 113 (Tex. Crim. App. 1972).

there is indeed an underlying disease. But, of course, this proof will not always be possible.

A BRIEF WORD ON THE CONTENTS AND ORGANIZATION OF THE BOOK

Especially in the first half, the text relies heavily on medical authorities of various fields including psychiatry and some of the biological sciences. This is necessary because our reading of the cases and secondary legal literature indicated, to no one's surprise, that the lawyers handled the legal side of the issues presented in pathological intoxication cases with adeptness roughly in proportion to their evident understanding of the medical facts with which they were confronted. Cases in which the defense was weakly presented are often cases in which there simply was nothing to work with from the outset, but there are as often cases in which insufficient evidence of the right sort was presented when the facts suggested that more should have been available if the attorney knew what it was he or she was actually after. A number of the cases appear to involve attempts to get a retrial on the basis of "newly discovered" evidence. Most of those are in fact cases of "newly discovered" medicolegal theory (pathological intoxication) when the facts were known all along and their significance was seen too late. It is equally evident that courts who are not educated by the attorney on the concept of pathological intoxication have a natural bent to perceive the case presumptively as a matter of another drunk who got into serious trouble. They see so many cases of intoxicated defendants in the trial courts and appellate tribunals that it may be difficult for anyone in that role to regard these cases as presenting profoundly different issues.

Those are some of the reasons for undertaking this task. We have tried to make available to the judge and the attorney what there is on pathological intoxication in both medical and legal literature, pro and con. Our own views will be clear enough. In some instances we had some difficulty obtaining the materials, and many foreign materials were never found in translated form. We think it would be difficult for attorneys to do this on their own, especially given the lack of leisurely pursuit time the typical practitioner has available in the average criminal case. This led to the inclination to be rather inclusive in the amount of medical literature presented. At least if one is driven to Index Medicus or the Mental Health Abstracts, there will be something to start with and perhaps discussions with expert witnesses will be facilitated as well. There is occasional need to provide dictionary definitions of medical terminology. We hope this expedites reading more than it rankles.

The organization runs along these lines. The first half of the book is mostly medical, Chapters 2 through 5. The second half is largely legal,

Chapters 6 through 10. Chapter 2 presents the original starting point, clinical observations that provided the take-off for the modern medical literature. Much of it is still quite useful. With application of EEG technology to the problem by a number of researchers, some of whom are forensic psychiatrists, the nature of the evidence supporting the existence of pathological intoxication became more sophisticated. Those studies are presented in Chapter 3. The writings of those who doubt the existence of pathological (few in number) and those who doubt the utility of the concept (a somewhat larger number) are discussed in Chapter 4. The next chapter deals with one major component of pathological intoxication, psychomotor epilepsy partly to rebut the arguments made by the doubters and partly to provide detailed information on the one form of pathological intoxication that has received the most attention and is the most likely to be encountered.

Chapters 6 through 9 take up special questions that the defense presents when tried as insanity, automatism, involuntary intoxication or diminished capacity or equivalent doctrines. Each has its own peculiar strengths, weaknesses and problems, and their adaptability to pathological intoxication will, to some extent, depend on the facts at hand and the jurisdiction in which the question arises. In each of these law chapters, we give some background on the general law of the defense involved more to make sure the writers and the readers are on the same wave length than out of a desire to present a national black letter treatment of each area although that sometimes is the outcome.

Once the medical case can be made, and the defense strategy decided upon, Chapter 10 then is perhaps the most critical for the litigator. We think this is where most cases are actually won or lost. It does no good if the court or jury is persuaded of the validity of the medical foundation for the defense and agrees that the facts are properly litigated under whatever branch of criminal law defenses the case is tried if, in the end, they see the defendant as having been at fault in bringing about the situation to begin with. Yet it is here that the law is the least clear. We have taken the liberty of trying to classify the cases along lines that should prove useful in an attempt to understand exactly what fault in this context means, for, as we said, it is critical in so many cases. Chapter 11 is the conclusion.

It is evident that the text is not written as a traditional treatise in which the categories of discourse are essentially bestowed in advance. The literature is too unsettled for that. At the same time, we will, of course, be disappointed if what we believe was diligent examination has left much unearthed.

2

Clinical Evidence of Pathological Intoxication

THE EARLY CLINICAL WRITERS

The syndrome of pathological reaction to alcohol was first identified in 1869 by Krafft-Ebing,[1] who delineated the clinical signs as entailing abnormal behavioral responses, deliriums, hallucination and illusions, most often depressive and paranoid in nature, causing great apprehension and fear. He said that pathological intoxication resembles an acute delirium in which incidental emotional factors may produce a fit of rage leading to a desire for destruction. A convulsion may occur at the height of the episode, and this is similar to epileptoid excitement. There is partial or total amnesia for the events.

Krafft-Ebing emphasized the underlying pathological condition of the brain including residual effects of a disease or an injury to the brain. This was mentioned first in his list of predisposing conditions for pathological intoxication.[2] He also inferred that other factors such as psychosis, severe neurosis, typhoid, chronic circulatory disturbances, meningeal changes of chronic alcoholism and epilepsy might play an important role. He said that the condition of the patient at the time of the drinking episode was more important than the quantity or quality of alcohol consumed. In his writings in 1897,[3] Krafft-Ebing summarized the following criteria applicable to pathological intoxication:

1. The quantity of alcohol has no relation to the effect, since organic and accidental factors operate to modify the reaction. (Most of the early writers take the same position, but there had been a persistent, albeit sometimes merely careless,

---

1. Banay, *Pathologic Reaction to Alcohol*, 4 QRTLY J. STUD. ALCOH. 580, 582 (1944), citing Krafft-Ebing, 27 DTSCH. Z. STARZNEIK. 444 (1869).

2. Others which have been dropped over the years are physical exertion, excessive smoking and sexual over-activity.

3. R. KRAFFT-EBING, LEHRBUCH DER PSYCHIATRIE (1897).

emphasis on the amount of alcohol as being of diagnostic value. This issue will recur throughout.)

2. The timing of the attacks is peculiar. They do not often occur at the height of intoxication but rather in the earlier stages of drinking or well after drinking has stopped.

3. There is a distinct difference in quality from simple intoxication. The perception of the environment is distorted by the presence of more or less well organized delirium, as manifested by illusions and hallucinations, complete suspension of self-awareness, manic outbursts accentuated by instinctive drives rather than conscious[4] or purposeful motivations, and terminal fits of rage and irresistible desire for destruction.

4. Marked congestion of the brain, pulsating carotids, rapid pulse, flushed complexion, and congested and shining eyes are present.

5. Movements are not coordinated. Under the influence of cerebral irritation, movements become strong and energetic, and the muscles are capable of extraordinary performances.

6. There is amnesia[5] for the entire period.[6]

These diagnostic criteria and hypotheses (or conjectures) regarding etiology will endure remarkably well over the next century. Bowman and Jellinek,[7] writing in 1941, examined the ancient question "whether abnormal drinking is a symptom or a disease",[8] and more specifically "in the case of alcoholic mental disorders is drinking itself etiological or symptomatic?"[9] More importantly for our purposes they considered also the more specific question addressed here: whether a nonalcoholic psychosis can be precipitated by alcohol.[10]

---

4. "'Consciousness' means a sense of awareness of self and of the environment, and, phylogenetically, it probably represents the most highly developed and complex process or [sic; for?] organizing and handling experience." McCaldon, *Automatism*, 91 CAN. MED. ASS'N J. 914 (1964), citing A. NOYES & L. KOLB, MODERN CLINICAL PSYCHIATRY 8 (5th ed. 1960).

5. Amnesia may be due to failure in registration, retention or recall. McCaldon, *Automatism*, 91 CAN. MED. ASS'N J. 914, 915 (1964). Anterograde amnesia refers to that period which occurs following the precipitating trauma. Retrograde amnesia refers to loss of memory for events occurring before the precipitating trauma. TABER'S CYCLOPEDIC MEDICAL DICTIONARY 65 (C. Thomas ed. 14th ed. 1981).

6. Banay at 583.

7. Bowman & Jellinek, *Alcoholic Mental Disorders*, 2 QRTLY J. STUD. ALCOH. 312 (1941). At the time of the publication of this summary of prior studies, Bowman was a Professor of Psychiatry, New York University College of Medicine and Director, Division of Psychiatry, Bellevue Hospital, and Jellinek was an Associate Professor, Applied Physiology, Yale University.

8. Bowman & Jellinek at 313.

9. Bowman & Jellinek at 313.

10. Bowman & Jellinek at 316.

In the course of their discussion of the various opinions existing at the time regarding the proper classifications of acute reactions to alcohol, the authors discuss the concept of pathological intoxication.[11] They also attempted a rough estimate as to the number of occurrences of pathological reaction to alcohol: Based on another author's data compiled earlier, Bowman and Jellinek estimate that "pathological intoxication constituted 8 to 9 per cent of all first admissions for alcoholic psychoses and consequently less than 1 per cent of all cases of alcoholism."[12]

They express a preference for the term "pathological reaction to alcohol" over "pathological intoxication" as Krafft-Ebing also initially proposed because "the condition commonly referred to as pathological intoxication largely lacks the characteristic toxic symptoms"[13] of ordinary alcohol intoxication such as slurred speech and motor incoordination. They also point out that the term "pathological intoxication" "originates in forensic considerations" and is not meant to be of psychiatric classificatory relevance but instead is "a concession to the general opinion that all intoxications do not constitute mental disturbances in the sense of the responsibility concept of criminal law...."[14]

In defining pathological reaction to alcohol, Bowman and Jellinek drew attention to another critical point constantly missed by some courts and other writers: While acknowledging that cases had been reported of pathological reaction to alcohol occurring on the basis of small amounts of alcohol (as well as large amounts), the authors stress that

> this condition [of pathological reaction to alcohol] should not be confused with alcohol intolerance, in which small quantities bring about disproportionately strong reactions without qualitatively abnormal features. This warning is especially important since some textbooks, in the endeavor to make concise statements, have defined pathological intoxication as intoxication following the ingestion of small quantities of alcohol.[15]

The clinical picture summarized from the earlier literature included "blind rage and confusion, with usually complete amnesia for the condition," which "is all independent of the amount of alcohol consumed" with a duration of a "few minutes to a few hours."[16]

---

11. Bowman & Jellinek at 322.
12. Bowman & Jellinek at 323.
13. Bowman & Jellinek at 323.
14. Bowman & Jellinek at 323.
15. Bowman & Jellinek at 323. *See also* H. HAGGARD & E. JELLINEK, ALCOHOL EXPLORED 228 (1946) *and* Frame, *Alcoholism: Some Medico-Legal Aspects*, 2 J. FOR. MED. 151 (1955).
16. Bowman & Jellinek at 324.

By this time there already was general agreement regarding the existence of pathological reaction to alcohol and in distinguishing it from ordinary intoxication. The "chief distinguishing factor between pathological intoxication and ordinary intoxication [is] the absence of ataxia and speech disturbances in the former."[17] But matters were not so clear regarding the diagnostic criteria to be used to distinguish pathological intoxication from other acute alcoholic psychoses. At least one earlier writer believed that "diagnosis [is] greatly validated if the patient's history showed previous pathological intoxications and also, especially, if there had been head trauma or syphilis."[18] Summarizing the clinical picture, Bowman and Jellinek conclude:

> Various forms of pathological intoxication have been described by different authors and numerous classifications of this disorder have been proposed, but only the form designated originally as "epileptoid pathological intoxication" is regarded at present by a majority of psychiatrists as genuine pathological intoxication.[19]

Opinions varied regarding the etiology of pathological intoxication. While it was first thought to require a "psychopathic personality," the absolutism of that had been rejected and "[e]xclusive views are not held at present [the early 1940's] by any investigator."[20] Recurrent etiological factors reported are brain traumata, epilepsy and hypoglycemia or a related process. All of these are still important.

It was recognized that pathological reaction to alcohol is not constant even in patients presumably permanently predisposed. Separate research efforts by both Bonhoeffer[21] and Binswanger[22] to provoke pathological reaction to alcohol were unsuccessful even in patients who had previously experienced the reaction. The same lack of success was encountered in patients with brain injuries even though some of them had previously subjectively complained that since the injury, alcohol "went to their heads." The researchers involved in these efforts concluded that some other factor or factors must be required as well.[23]

> In recapitulation it may be stated that pathological intoxication, or preferably the pathologic reaction to alcohol, in

---

17. Bowman & Jellinek at 325.
18. Bowman & Jellinek at 325.
19. Bowman & Jellinek at 326.
20. Bowman & Jellinek at 326.
21. K. BONHOEFFER, DIE AKUTEN GEISTESKRANKHEITEN DER GEWOHNHEITSTRINKER (1901).
22. Binswanger, 152 Z. GES. NEUROL. PSYCHIAT. 703 (1935).
23. Bowman & Jellinek at 327.

> contrast to other alcoholic psychoses is not a disturbance of chronic alcoholism but occurs as a direct effect of drinking—frequently of very small quantities of alcohol—and is distinguished from acute intoxication qualitatively rather than quantitatively. Predominantly this disturbance occurs in psychopathic personalities who, even in the absence of drinking, show unprovoked fits of rage. It is not, however, a constant reaction in these personalities, but requires special conditions, such as temporary dysphorias and perhaps temporary hypoglycemic states, which may be occasioned by exhaustion or illness. In these states it may also occur in nonpsychopathic personalities. The occurrence of pathological intoxication in persons suffering from brain injury is also dependent on temporary specific conditions.[24]

A few years later, Banay,[25] focusing on pathological reaction to alcohol, provided a more detailed critique of prior studies which ranged from 1869 up until his article was published in 1944. What follows is an approximately chronological synopsis of the major works reviewed and summarized by Banay. We will leave aside most of the psychiatric or psychological theories underlying some of the prior writings that are of little relevance here, but many of these summaries by Banay of early writings are important because the works have as yet to be translated into English and so are generally inaccessible to American courts.

After Krafft-Ebing[26] made the original diagnosis which has been summarized above, Heilbronner,[27] writing in 1901, also stressed that pathological intoxication is qualitatively different from ordinary intoxication and that it "may be the result of moderate use as well as abuse of alcohol."[28] Emphasis is placed on the frightening or threatening visual and auditory hallucinations which accompany an attack. Onset is sudden, its duration short, and it is followed by amnesia. He gave an example of a man returning with friends from a picnic at which all had been drinking but who were not drunk. The man fell onto the bed of the

---

24. Bowman & Jellinek at 327-28.

25. Banay, *Pathologic Reaction to Alcohol,* 4 QRTLY J. STUD. ALCOH. 580 (1944). Banay was Lecturer in Criminal Psychopathology, College of Physicians and Surgeons, Columbia University. The article is subtitled "I. Review of the Literature and Original Case Reports" and refers to a "second part....to be published in a forthcoming issue of this Journal," the second part dealing with "a synthesis of the clinical picture and an analysis of diagnostic and differential diagnostic criteria", Banay at 581. Evidently this second article was never published.

26. R. KRAFFT-EBING, LEHRBUCH DER PSYCHIATRIE (1897); Krafft-Ebing, 27 DTSCH. Z. STARZNEIK. 444 (1869).

27. Heilbronner, 48 MUNCH. MED. WSCHR. 962 (1901).

28. Banay at 583.

wagon and thrashed about in a violently defensive manner until he hurt someone with a knife who was trying to help him. They placed him in a shop and he regained his composure but had amnesia for the episode.

As predisposing factors Heilbronner mentions epilepsy, hysteria, mental deficiency, head injuries, habitual intoxication and "a state of constitutional inferiority." He also mentions sexual exhaustion and emotional changes as in fright, anxiety or quarrels.

Bonhoeffer[29] felt that any reaction to alcohol other than normal intoxication should be classed as pathological intoxication. He differentiated two types, one of which was called "delirious" and manifested by anxiety, delusions and faulty orientation. He thought this form occurred only in the case of confirmed inebriates. The other form was called "epileptoid" and was characterized by motor agitation and rage often leading to homicide or suicide. Etiological factors reported were epilepsy, hysteria, skull injuries and in the case of "psychopaths and inebriates...a temporary state of exhaustion."[30] Banay quotes Bonhoeffer: "'The brain injured by chronic use of alcohol reacts differently to alcohol than the healthy brain.'"[31]

Krafft-Ebing's original work was also elaborated on by Cramer.[32] The opinion was expressed that absence of pupillary reflexes is corroborative of the diagnosis of pathological reaction to alcohol, but their presence does not exclude the diagnosis. He noted that amnesia could as well be caused by ordinary drunkenness. He also differentiated pathological intoxication from alcohol intolerance. (In another early study, the researcher still thought in 1921 that pathological reaction to alcohol was alcohol sensitivity.[33]) Voss[34] stressed that alcoholic twilight states should not be confused with pathological reaction to alcohol. Ziehen[35] stressed hostile hallucinations and severe motor actions. He, too, mentions retardation of pupillary reflexes. Branthwaite[36] noted that congenital defectives become disorderly and violent on small amounts of alcohol. He does not refer to this as pathological intoxication, however. Stapel[37] also reported that pupillary reflex abnormalities are more pronounced than in ordinary intoxication.

Writing in 1912, Schroeder[38] noted that alcohol may play the role

---

29. K. BONHOEFFER, DIE AKUTEN GEISTESKRANKHEITEN DER GEWOHNHEITSTRINKER (1901).

30. Banay at 585.

31. Banay at 585.

32. Cramer, 13 MSCHR. PSYCHIAT. NEUROL. 56 (1903).

33. Schultze, 20 MEDIZINISCHERS KLINIK 581 (1921). *See also* Jones, *Medical Aspects of Chemical Tests for Intoxication*, 8 CLEV.-MARSHALL L. REV. 228 (1959).

34. Voss, 31 ZBL. NERVENHEILK 678 (1908).

35. G. ZIEHEN, PSYCHIATRIE FUR AERZTE UND STUDIERENDE (4th ed. 1911).

36. Branthwaite, in ANNUAL REPORT FOR 1909 OF THE INSPECTOR UNDER THE INEBRIATES ACT (1911).

37. Stapel, 29 MSCH. PSYCHIAT. NEUROL. 216 (1911).

38. Schroeder, *Intoxikationspsychosen*, in HANDBUCH DER PSYCHIATRIE 180 (G.

of agent provocateur so that the amount of alcohol is relatively unimportant. The usual signs of intoxication are missing. Both physiological and transitory, psychic factors may play a role in bringing on an attack, and Schroeder thought that their role may account for the failure to induce pathological reaction to alcohol experimentally. Among the physiological factors which may predispose, Schroeder mentioned skull injury, carbon monoxide poisoning, arteriosclerosis, syphilis and brain damage due to prolonged alcohol abuse. He suggested the term "transitory alcoholic psychosis."

Busch[39] believed that head injuries led to alcohol sensitivity but not to pathological intoxication. Siebert[40] thought that pathological reaction to alcohol as described by Krafft-Ebing, pathological intoxication as described by Cramer, twilight states discussed by Voss, and complicated intoxication used by Ziehen, all cited above, were the same phenomenon.

In contrast to what Banay called typical pathological reaction to alcohol, Bing and Schonberg,[41] writing in 1925, described atypical pathological reaction to alcohol cases which involved overactivity and ridiculous behavior, gaiety and expansive ideas. They also indicated that some industrial poisons (especially benzine) may provoke a state identical to pathological intoxication.

Meggendorfer[42] agreed with Bonhoeffer's dual classification. Two points were added: He was of the opinion that there was some memory of the episode but that it disappeared quickly, like a dream. Secondly, he believed that sexual offenses were common in this condition but take the form of exhibitionism or homosexuality rather than sexual assaults on women.

Seelert[43] added hypoglycemia to the list of possible causes and stated that there were certain hypoglycemic conditions which were indistinguishable from pathological reaction to alcohol. He also noted that hypoglycemia may occur without diabetes but is traceable to physiological problems such as brain injuries, severe liver ailments and tumors of the pancreas. He questioned the existence of psychopathologic factors in pathological reaction to alcohol and stressed the need for research into organic causes. He also added "the possibility of sudden changes of vasomotor tone."[44] Binswanger[45] evidently thought that

---

Aschaffenburg ed. 1912).

39. Busch, 24 J. PSYCHOL. NEUROL. 101 (1918).

40. Siebert, 38 NEUROL. ZBL. 610 (1919).

41. Bing & Schonberg, 55 SCHWEIZ. MED. WSCHR. 157 (1925).

42. Meggendorfer, *Intoxikationspsychosen*, in 7 HANDBUCH DER GEISTESKRANKHEITEN (O. Bumke ed. 1928).

43. Seelert, *Zur Frage der Entwicklungsbedingungen des Pathologischen Rausche*, 86 MSCHR. PSYCHIAT. NEUROL. 191 (1933).

44. Banay at 589.

45. Binswanger, 152 Z. GES. NEUROL. PSYCHIAT. 703 (1935).

underlying psychological abnormalities in combination with any amount of alcohol could cause pathological reaction to alcohol.

Pathological reaction to alcohol was divided into two groups by Binder,[46] (1) complicated (quantitatively abnormal) intoxication; and (2) pathologic (qualitatively abnormal) intoxication, with the latter further subdivided into (a) twilight form and (b) delirious form. Fear and delusions characterize this type and may lead to maniacal outbursts. Pupils are often paralyzed, and tendon reflexes are diminished. Bleuler, noted for his earlier pioneering work on dementia praecox (schizophrenias), writing in 1937[47] agreed with two others that the delirious form of pathological reaction to alcohol belongs to the abortive form of delirium tremens.[48]

Having summarized the works of others, Banay added his own thoughts on the implications of these reports for the administration of criminal justice: "A clear appreciation of the relationship between alcohol and crime can be achieved only when the nature of the pathologic reaction to alcohol is fully understood."[49] The overview he provided is interesting:

---

46. Binder, 35 SCHWEIZ. ARCH. NEUROL. PSYCHIAT. 209 (1935).

47. E. BLEULER, LEHRBUCH DER PSYCHIATRIE (6th ed. 1937).

48. Delirium tremens is said to be the serious result of alcoholism over a long period of time. It may be attributable to nutritional deficiencies, themselves attributable to alcohol consumption. Whatever the mechanism, long-term alcohol use has affected the brain. It often occurs at the end of a long drunken period and is associated with withdrawal rather than concurrent intoxication. It occurs three to four days, or even a week, after last ingesting alcohol. Thompson offers this description of the actual clinical manifestations:

> Myoclonic jerkings of the extremities, head, and neck, and generalized weakness with profuse sweating occur. There is a true delirium, with impairment of all intellectual functions, spotty or partial amnesia, confusion, disorientation, and partial impairment of attention, perception, and comprehension are prominent. Partial contact with environment usually remains, and the patient may be able to discuss his illness with the physician. Visual hallucinations are almost always present and are described as vague shadows or forms which are frightening and often produce panic....Auditory hallucinations may occur but are less frequent than in acute alcoholic hallucinosis....In delirium tremens there may be several days of prodromal [premonitory] symptoms such as irritability, insomnia, anorexia, general restlessness, tremors of fingers and face, and slurred speech. There may be excessive perspiration and dilation of the pupils....The patient's mood varies from depression to fear, extreme excitability, and even silliness at times. Memory is impaired, particularly for recent events, and, during the height of the illness, disorientation may be complete. The patient's retentive ability is markedly impaired, and there are extreme defects of insight and judgment.

Thompson, *Acute and Chronic Alcoholic Conditions*, in 2 AMERICAN HANDBOOK OF PSYCHIATRY 1208-09 (S. Arieti ed. 1959).

49. Banay at 581.

> Chronic alcoholism is a necessary condition for all the alcoholic psychoses save one. This exception is the pathologic reaction to alcohol, more frequently but less appropriately referred to as pathological intoxication. This shortest of all alcoholic mental disorders may develop in an occasional drinker of fairly moderate or even rather small quantities of alcoholic beverages, but it may also occur as an atypical reaction in a chronic alcoholic. The fact that the pathologic reaction to alcohol is clearly differentiated from acute alcoholic intoxication and that nevertheless this definitely psychotic manifestation is not a consequence of habitual excessive drinking places this condition in a position of special interest and significance.[50]

INTERNATIONAL WORKS AND STANDARD TEXTS

There are many works published on pathological intoxication or pathological reaction to alcohol from other countries, although some involve only implicit recognition of the concept such as including it as a diagnostic category.[51] But many are of considerable value in establishing both the general existence of the entity and providing support for various details regarding it. While most of these are not available in English, most are summarized in English abstracts, which make it relatively clear that the virtual consensus on its existence is worldwide. While we have obtained a few translations, for most articles we have only summary abstracts which are relied upon here.

---

50. Banay at 580.

51. Hudolin, *Complicaciones Agudas del Alcoholismo* (Acute Complications of Alcoholism), ARCH. BIOL. MED. EXP. 132 (Supp. 3, 1969), substantially reprinted in ALCOHOL AND ALCOHOLISM (R. Popham ed. 1970) (classification and quantification of hospital admissions to psychiatric hospitals in Croatia, including "pathological states of inebriation"); Paraire, Juillet, Delivre & Lefevbre, *Problems de Toxicophilie Chez les Jeunes Adultes au Stade des Obligations Militaires* (Problems of Drug Addiction in Young Adults at the Time of Military Duty), 128 ANN. MED.-PSYCHOL. 93 (1970) (one category designated "pathological"); Pollner, *A Koros Reszegseg Fogalma es a Hazai Gyakorlat* (The Concept of Pathological Intoxication and Its Application in Our Country), in TANULMANYOK AS ALKOHOLIZMUS PSZICHIATRIAI KOVETKEZMENYCIROL (Results of Psychiatric Studies on Alcoholism) 65 (I. Tariska, G. Gereby & G. Kardos eds. 1969) (from Budapest, Hungary); Huszar & Ir'anyi, *Typusos es Atypusos Reszegsegi Allapotok Elkulonitesenek Elmeszakertoi Problemai* (The Differentiation of Typical and Atypical States of Intoxication According to Expert Opinion), 20 IDEGGYOGY. SZLE BP. 202 (1967) (includes discussion of differential diagnosis of pathological intoxication); Strauss, *Las Tosicofrenias Alcoholicas en la Republica de Panama* (Alcoholic Psychoses in the Republic of Panama), 13 BOL. ASS'N MED. NAC. PANAMA 65 (1950) (tabulation of first admissions to a hospital for alcohol-related reasons, including pathological intoxication).

Prior to World War II, it almost appeared that pathological reaction to alcohol, or pathological intoxication, was a "European diagnosis."[52] Now, most American reports are confined to Anglo-American studies and reports, but this is due to the general unavailability of translations of reports and studies done in other countries, largely European at that time, of known relevance and not because pathological reaction to alcohol has become an "American diagnosis." This does mean, however, that some detailed data are omitted for want of a translation.

Morozov, Kachayev and Lukacher[53] of The Serbskii Central Scientific Research Institute of Forensic Psychiatry in Moscow, trying to make the clinical content of pathological intoxication more precise, studied the conditions which contribute to its origin. Their first study, reported in 1973, compared the results of neurological examinations of 105 persons who were diagnosed as having committed unspecified criminal acts during a period of pathological intoxication to the same examination of 110 persons who had also committed unidentified criminal acts during ordinary intoxication.

Of the 105 patients who committed an offense in the state of pathological intoxication, 90.5 percent had a history of some organic disease of the brain, chiefly of traumatic etiology; 76 had closed brain trauma with loss of consciousness prior to the event, 1 person had some kind of electrical trauma, 6 had neurological infections and 2 had been exposed to carbon monoxide poisoning. In these 85 individuals there was a change in the neurological status. In the group of 110 persons identified as having committed their offenses during ordinary intoxication, 49.9 percent were reported to have central nervous system changes. Thus, the frequency of pre-existing brain damage was almost twice as high in the pathological intoxication group compared to the ordinary intoxication group (90.5% to 49.9%).

Based on their own research and a review of existing literature, it was also noted that "the authors assume that one of the reasons for the development of states with twilight consciousness which is characteristic of pathological intoxication is a rapid increase of intracranial pressure due to alcohol consuming, with a hypertensive syndrome in the past."[54] What may be most critical is not the existence of intracranial pressure but the adaptation of the brain to rapid changes in that pressure. It was suggested that in the presence of the "hypertension syndrome," "alcohol intake causes further increase in the intracranial pressure which may

---

52. Banay at 580.

53. Morozov, Kachayev & Lukacher, *On the Pathogenesis of Pathological Intoxication*, 73 ZHURNAL NEUROPATHOLOGII PSITHIATRII 1196-99 (1973). Our discussion of this research report is based on translations we commissioned of the original work published in Russian.

54. Morozov, Kachayev & Lukacher at 1196 (abstract).

precipitate the emergence of twilight disorders of consciousness."[55] It was also proposed that when there is some evidence of pathological intoxication, an effort should be made to examine the spinal cord fluid to determine whether there is abnormal pressure.

Soviet law already recognizes pathological intoxication as a defense to criminal charges[56] but does not recognize ordinary intoxication as a defense, and Soviet scientists routinely make the diagnosis of pathological versus ordinary intoxication for purposes of trying to determine its etiology, while some English and American psychiatrists are still disputing its existence.[57]

In 1974, the following year, the authors reported on a second study[58] of 103 subjects who also committed offenses thought to be during a period of pathological reaction to alcohol. The examinations of these subjects again were compared to examinations conducted on 250 subjects believed to have committed offenses during ordinary intoxication. In the pathological intoxication group, 90 percent were found to have moderate organic changes in the central nervous system, mostly of

---

55. Morozov, Kachayev & Lukacher at 1198.

56. KOMMENTARII K UGOLOVNOMU KODEKSU RSFSR 25 (I. Severin ed. 1980) (COMMENTARIES TO THE CRIMINAL CODE OF THE RSFSR). While ordinary intoxication does not excuse, pathological intoxication, by special statutory provision, does. *See also* W. BUTLER, SOVIET LAW 264 (1983); Osakwe, Book Review, 59 TUL. L. REV. 858, 870-71 (1985). "Section 12 of the Criminal Code states that a person who commits a crime in a state of intoxication shall not be freed from criminal responsibility" but that "Section 12 does not apply to (1) the mentally ill who committed a crime while in a state of intoxication..., and (b) to pathological intoxication, i.e., a short-lasting, rare acute psychosis occurring suddenly in connection with the consumption of even a small amount of alcohol. Such persons are subject to compulsory medical treatment under Sections 11, 58-61 of the RSFSR Criminal Code...." Hearings on Reform of the Federal Criminal Laws, Before the Subcomm. on Criminal Laws & Procedures of the Senate Judiciary Comm., 92nd Cong., 2d Sess., pt. 3, subpt. C, at 2929 (1972).

See also Hearings at 2551, based on the CRIMINAL CODE OF THE PEOPLE'S REPUBLIC OF BULGARIA, April 2, 1968:

> [G]uilt may be excluded in the following three situations: namely, when there is (a) mental retardation; (b) permanent mental disturbance; and (c) temporary mental disturbance, and as a result thereof, the perpetrator was in such a mental condition that he could not comprehend the criminality of his conduct or conduct himself in conformity with the requirements of law. The last category of temporary mental disturbance may be the result also of alcoholic or other drug intoxication, i.e., a case of a pathological alcoholic intoxication. However, the doctrine excludes "normal drinking (getting drunk) of alcohol" as a defense.

57. *See* Rozhnov, *Alcoholism and Other Drug Addictions,* in FORENSIC PSYCHIATRY 343, 346-56 (referred to as "Pathologic Inebriation") (G. Morozov & I. Kalashnik eds. M. Vale trans. 1970) (originally published as SUDEBNAIA PSIKHIATRIIA in 1967 by a research group at the Serbskii Central Scientific Research Institute of Forensic Psychiatry).

58. Morozov, Kachayev & Lukacher, *Characteristics of Forensic Psychiatric Examination of Pathological and Simple Alcohol Intoxication,* 17 SUDEBNO-MEDITSINSKAIA EKSPERTIZA 51 (April-June 1974). Our discussion of this research report is based on translations we commissioned of the original work published in Russian.

traumatic origin. Such CNS changes were also found in 48 percent of the ordinary intoxication group, but they were not only less frequent, they are reported as milder changes as well.

The authors noted that in earlier writings, Sukharova had stated that the onset of pathological intoxication has to do with increased intercranial pressure, resulting from the rapid and spasmodic increase of pressure, and Vyazemsky had suggested that the rapidity of development with sharp changes in cerebrospinal fluid pressure reduces the compensatory abilities of the brain, impeding recovery, causing a decompensation of cerebral activity, resulting in a psychotic state.[59] It should be noted that in acute alcoholic intoxication (drunkenness), the cerebrospinal fluid pressure increases. In this study, the cerebrospinal fluid pressure was determined in 26 of the pathological intoxication group and in 30 ordinary intoxication subjects. All 26 of the pathological intoxication group had elevated spinal fluid pressure, while only one of the ordinary intoxication group had slightly increased pressure, findings consistent with the first report in 1973. The pressure was increased significantly in the pathological intoxication group both when supine and seated, while in the ordinary intoxication cases, the two measurements were reported to be normal in all but one case. EEG's were also administered to a sample from each group, and abnormalities were found more pronounced in the pathological intoxication group.

Morozov had earlier served as editor of *Forensic Psychiatry* while director of the Serbskii Institute, where this research was undertaken. That volume "represents an authoritative Soviet statement on the basic principles of this important subject."[60] Within that volume, Rozhnov summarized the state-of-the art regarding pathological intoxication (translated as "pathological inebriation"). It was stated that pathological intoxication is a "temporary" pathologic condition but that opinions on both the etiology and clinical picture of pathological intoxication were "very contradictory and extremely varied."[61] It is noted that

> S.S. Korsakov and V.P. Serbskii, toward the end of the last century, very clearly described the clinical picture of pathologic inebriation.
>
> In their view, pathologic inebriation was a condition that, although associated with the use of alcohol, was qualitatively different from simple inebriation. They regarded it as

---

59. Morozov, Kachayev & Lukacher, *Characteristics of Forensic Psychiatric Examination of Pathological and Simple Alcoholic Intoxication*, 17 SUDEBNO-MEDITSINSKAIA EKSPERTIZA 51 (April-June 1974).

60. Bazelon, *Introduction*, in FORENSIC PSYCHIATRY viii (G. Morozov & I. Kalashnik eds. M. Vale trans. 1970).

61. Rozhnov at 346.

> a brief, acute, mental disorder with all the peculiar features of such a state and with a pathologic, active symptomatology in the form of hallucinatory and delusional experiences with a characteristic, profound disorder of consciousness and resultant aberrant behavior. The condition was regarded as absolute and indisputable grounds for relieving a person of legal responsibility for any crime committed while in such a state.
>
> With further study of the clinical features of pathologic inebriation, its definition was narrowed, and the psychopathologic symptoms and the dynamic principles of this psychotic condition became more precisely delineated.[62]

The relative rarity of the condition was noted,[63] and it is emphasized that pathological intoxication differs from ordinary intoxication qualitatively, not quantitatively: "The modern concept of pathologic inebriation is based on its qualitative distinction from simple inebriation. It is wrong to regard pathologic inebriation as merely a more severe degree of inebriation. Instead, it is a brief psychotic state in which alcohol is only one (albeit the main one) of many possible causal factors."[64] A somewhat different view of amnesia is presented:

> It should not be thought that everything experienced during pathologic inebriation is totally forgotten. In our description of simple drunkenness, we stressed that, in severe states, partial or even total amnesia is not only possible but is usually the rule. In contrast, in pathologic inebriation morbid experiences may be retained in memory. Most often these recollections are fragmentary and patchy. Persons who have been in a state of pathologic inebriation generally remember the main content of pathologically distorted experiences of fear and foreboding regarding assault from companions and explain their aggressive actions as protection or self-defense.[65]

Others have recognized the additional differentiation from ordinary intoxication manifested by the absence of the usual signs of drunkenness. Rozhnov also underscores this telling distinction:

---

62. Rozhnov at 346-47.

63. "The number of persons who commit crimes in a state of pathologic inebriation is very low and, in proportion to the number of legally responsible offenders, constitutes only a few tenths of a percent." Rozhnov at 347.

64. Rozhnov at 347.

65. Rozhnov at 349-50.

> The complete preservation of motor functions is a characteristic sign of pathologic inebriation. In contrast to the state in simple drunkenness, motor coordination is good; and equilibrium and the ability to move, run, and jump quickly are preserved. The impetuousness and agility of pathologically inebriated persons in attack or flight are striking to others. In cases in which simple drunkenness gives way to pathologic inebriation, it is instructive to hear from witnesses who have observed the person in both conditions how sharp and striking was the change in his movements, the impression being one of an abrupt reversion to sobriety.[66]

It seems fair to assume from the description of the actor as transforming from simple intoxication to pathologic intoxication that more than a minimal amount of alcohol may have been involved. It was asserted that pathological intoxication "develops a short time after intake of alcohol, independently of the dose or strength of the alcohol. Cases are described of pathologic inebriation arising after consumption of very small quantities of grape wine as well as of large amounts of strong beverages."[67] Indeed, in an illustration provided of a case of pathological reaction to alcohol, the amount consumed was identified as "0.5 liter of vodka."[68] It is emphasized that "pathologic inebriation, like every psychotic state, arises independently of the wishes and will of the person experiencing it. The person is not able to evoke the condition voluntarily, whereas simple drunkenness is the direct consequence of alcohol consumption and is completely dependent on the quality and quantity of the beverage consumed; for example, an increase in the amount of wine consumed inevitably results in an intensification of the inebriated state."[69] On the other hand, the author does not attach much significance to the termination by deep sleep, so often mentioned, noting that this may also be characteristic of ordinary intoxication if the intoxication was great enough.[70]

While it is alluded to by only a few other sources, Rozhnov made an observation that might be useful in litigation. Rozhnov noted an additional unusual clinical aspect of the actor's behavior while in a state of pathological intoxication:

> such persons act in silence; if they speak at all it is very little. The speech of such persons is very characteristic: it is

66. Rozhnov at 350.
67. Rozhnov at 348.
68. Rozhnov at 353.
69. Rozhnov at 356.
70. Rozhnov at 350-51.

> extremely brief. Words are uttered fragmentarily, often in the form of orders; sometimes individual words are repeated several times as commands. These may be either threats or, on the contrary, cries for help. These isolated utterances are so incomprehensible that they give the impression of a foreign language or a nonsensical muttering or repetition of unrelated syllables.[71]

Pathological intoxication is described, as others have done, as of two sorts: epileptoid and delusional (or hallucinatory-paranoid).

> The psychotic state in epileptoid pathologic inebriation closely resembles an epileptic twilight state. A sharply altered consciousness, which changes the person's entire behavior, is predominant. Proper orientation is lost; and an extremely strong psychomotor excitation sets in, accompanied by an affect of uncontrollable rage or anger, which leads to extraordinarily destructive actions and aggressive behavior, with subsequent total amnesia of everything that has occurred. Sometimes this state is somewhat modified to a less chaotic motor excitation with a predominance of automatic, stereotypic movements and behavior.[72]

In the delusional form, "pathologic inebriation usually refers to a state in which delusional ideas and disorder in perception, with illusory and hallucinatory experiences, occur. Disorders of consciousness also appear, as in the epileptoid form, although they are usually not as deep."[73] This may explain the different descriptions of the degree of amnesia. The violence of the resulting conduct and its motivelessness are both also noted, evidently in reference to both types identified.[74]

A variety of conditions of the person is thought to contribute to susceptibility; the author mentions overfatigue, undernourishment, infectious diseases, emotional agitation, anxiety and fear. Rozhnov notes, despite the apparent emphasis on factors that are more transient than those listed by other researchers, that

> [s]ome authors are inclined to regard ordinary, severe inebriation in psychopaths or persons with craniocerebral trauma or epilepsy as pathologic inebriation. However, it must be borne in mind that in such people the atypical

71. Rozhnov at 349.
72. Rozhnov at 351.
73. Rozhnov at 351.
74. Rozhnov at 355-56.

> characteristics and gravity of the inebriation, which result from the heightened susceptibility of their brains to alcohol, are, in the overwhelming majority of cases, a constant factor that always gives the same general pattern to the picture of pathologic inebriation. The uniqueness of inebriation in such persons is so evident that its characteristics are well known to both the victims themselves and their associates.[75]

While we agree, of course, that the actor's awareness of his or her condition ought to be "borne in mind," that awareness cannot actually influence the diagnosis of pathological intoxication. The actor's awareness of prior abnormal effects of alcohol should and likely will have an effect on the legal determination of responsibility for resulting crimes because the actor may have knowingly brought on the reaction. But that question is better kept separate from the question of the existence of the alcohol reaction phenomenon. As we will discuss in some detail later, the drafters of the Model Penal Code took the same direction.

Rozhnov hypothesized that while "[s]everal external and internal factors must concur to produce pathologic inebriation," and "[a]lthough the possibility of repeated pathologic inebriation in the same person cannot be rejected on theoretical grounds, there is, nevertheless, no description of incontestable recidivism in the psychiatric literature."[76] In some of the literature we will discuss, such reactions have been noted in a laboratory setting in the context of alcohol activation procedures. The observation may result from Rozhnov's disinclination to treat cases of known predisposition to abnormal reaction to alcohol as instances of pathological intoxication; cases such as epilepsy and brain injury, which are mentioned. As such, his may be more a comment on the actor's legal liability than on medical ability to replicate the reaction.

More recent studies assume the established existence of pathological intoxication and attempt to take the research further. One study attempted to distinguish between "semiconscious forms of pathological intoxication" and "classical pathological intoxication."[77] Ochernal and Szewczyk[78] also reported on their efforts to distinguish pathological intoxication from other forms of abnormal intoxication. Pionkowski,

---

75. Rozhnov at 347-48.

76. Rozhnov at 348.

77. For the most recent, *see, e.g.*, Lange, *Die "Dammerige" Form des krankhaften Alkoholrausches, ihre Kennzeichnenden Besonderheiten und ihre Abweichungen von den "klassischen" pathologischen Rauschformen* (The "Semiconscious" Form of Pathological Innebriatation [sic], Its Characteristics, and How It Differs from "Classical" Pathological Forms of Inebriation), 39 PSYCHIAT. NEUROL. MED. PSYCHOL. 193 (1987).

78. Ochernal & Szewczyk, *On the Problem of Abnormal Alcoholic Intoxication in Forensic and Psychiatric Judgments*, 30 PSYCHIAT. NEUROL. MED. PSYCHOL. 365 (1978).

Wojdyslawska and Patura[79] also differentiated between two forms of pathological intoxication depending upon their assessment of its etiology:

> The authors analysed [sic] 54 case histories and forensic psychiatric opinions concerning men who were described as having committed unlawful acts while in the state of pathological intoxication with alcohol. It was determined that mental disturbances encountered in this kind of intoxication can be divided into two groups—depending on the origin of pathology. a) In psychoses, mental defects and epilepsy with dementive changes or character disorders, alcohol either intensifies existing psychotic symptomes [sic] (and other existing mental disturbances), or provokes the appearance of psychotic symptomes [sic] which were absent during the time immediately preceeding [sic] alcohol intake—while the external symptomes [sic] remain typical to a normal alcohol intoxication. b) In cases of organic brain syndromes, without clearly defined mental disturbances and in epilepsy without dementive or characterological changes alcohol can cause: intensification of alcohol intoxication symptomes [sic]—even after a small dose of alcohol, severe consciousness disturbances, paranoidal states, unprovoked agressiveness [sic] with a high degree of agitation, etc., while conserving the external appearance of normal alcohol intoxication. Pathological intoxicatio [sic] with alcohol was most commonly diagnosed in persons with character disturbancies [sic] and encephalopaties [sic]—without steady, well defined mental disturbances.[80]

Stuchlik[81] reported on the recognition of pathological intoxication under Czechoslovakian laws as involving a disturbance of consciousness accompanied by sudden excitation entailing a loss of judgment, which acquits on the grounds of irresponsibility under Czechoslovakian laws if not repeated. Racz[82] similarly reported on the Hungarian Supreme Court's creation of a new category of defense under the Hungarian Penal Code denominated "abortive pathological alcoholism," which falls between the previous two categories of simple intoxication and pathological

---

79. Pionkowski, Wojdyslawska & Patura, *Upojenie Alkoholowe na Podlozu Patologicznym* (*Pathological Intoxication with Alcohol*), 9 PSYCHIAT. POL. 161 (1975).

80. Pionkowski, Wojdyslawska & Patura at 166 (authors' summary). *See also* Turunen, (Acute Alcohol-Induced Psychic Disturbances), 88 DUODECIM 310 (1972).

81. Stuchlik, *Soudne Psychiatricky Vyznam Paticke Opilosti* (Significance of Pathological Intoxication in Forensic Psychiatry), 66 CSL. PSYCHIAT. 289 (1970).

82. Racz, *Legfelsobb Birosag Elvi Allasfoglalasa az Abortiv Pathologias Reszegsegrol* (The Position of the Supreme Court on Abortive Pathological Alcoholism), 1 ALKOHOLOGIA, BP. 36 (1970).

alcoholism. While it allows mitigation of punishment, it is more suggestive of alcoholism as a defense than pathological intoxication. Cozzo,[83] on the other hand, noted the distinction between qualitatively atypical alcohol intoxication and acute alcohol intoxication and labels the former pathological alcohol intoxication.

Legal responsibility is part of the focus of two other articles. Michel[84] stressed that pathological intoxication is qualitatively different from other forms of intoxication, consisting of a twilight or confusional state regarded as legal insanity. In one of its forms, it is equated to abortive acute alcoholic delirium. Ir'anyi[85] defined pathological intoxication as a transitory psychosis caused by alcohol and thought that in a first case it could mitigate a crime. Included are case histories illustrating the difficulties of diagnosis. The epileptoid type of pathological intoxication is also mentioned.

The importance of amnesia is stressed in one study by Konuma,[86] who includes amnesia in the definition of pathological intoxication. It is argued that pathological intoxication is usually accompanied by physical or emotional illness and results in impulsive behavior inappropriate to the circumstances.

Sipkovenski[87] described pathological intoxication as involving a temporary disorder of consciousness accompanied by the absence of pupillary reactions to light and weakened muscular reflexes, recognized as a special nosological entity which provides grounds for excluding punishment. Pathological intoxication is also specifically described as a special nosological entity of the acute effects of alcohol in which neither constitutional characteristics nor lasting morbid personality changes play an etiological role. Etiological factors include psychological and physical traumas in combination with even small amounts of alcohol. Clinical signs include loss of pupillary reflex but retained speech and motor

---

83. Cozzo, *Considerazioni Sulle Psicosi da Intossicazione Alcoolica Acuta e Sulle Psicosi da Intolleranza All'alcool* (Remarks on Psychosis Due to Acute Alcohol Intoxication and on Psychosis Due to Alcohol Intolerance), 39 LAV. NEUROPSICHIAT. 451 (1966).

84. Michel, *Le Probleme de la Responsabilite Penale dans les Differentes Formes de L'Ivress Ethylique* (The Problem of Penal Responsibility in Different Forms of Alcohol Intoxication), 4 REV. ALCSME 181 (1957).

85. Ir'anyi, *Die Gerichtsarztliche Beurteilung des Pathologischen Rausches* (Medicolegal Evaluation of Pathological Intoxication), 18 PSYCHIAT. NEUROL. MED. PSYCHOL. (Leipz.) 267 (1966).

86. Konuma, *Some Topics in Forensic Psychiatric Studies on Offences During Drunkenness*, 4 JAP. J. STUD. ALCOH. 6 (1969).

87. Sipkovenski, *Nozoloskoj Problematici Patoloskog Pijanstva* (On the Nosological Problems of Pathological Drunkenness), 8 ALKOHOLIZAM, BEOGRAD 5 (1968). *See also* Schipkowensky, *Zur Klinik des Pathologischen Rausches* (On Clinical Aspects of Pathological Intoxication), 159 ZBL. GES. NEUROL. PSYCHIAT. 21 (1960), who characterizes pathological intoxication as a well-defined nosological entity. We assume these are the same author.

coordination. It leads to crimes of violence and should be differentiated from ordinary intoxication for penological purposes.

Venzlaff[88] argued that pathological intoxication defined as small quantities causing a pathological reaction is not reasonable and that underlying factors must come into play such as organic brain disease or extreme fatigue. Anchersen[89] discussed "relative unconsciousness" brought on by pathological intoxication. Small doses of alcohol can lead to meaningless violence and assaults not typical for the actor, usually followed by complete amnesia. He stressed that blackouts suffered by alcoholics should be differentiated from the unconsciousness associated with pathological intoxication.

A very important point is made by Rommeney.[90] He acknowledged that the concept of pathological intoxication is apparent, but he also pointed out that not all unusual forms of intoxication are violent or even criminal. The professional concern expressed is that there remains a tendency to make a diagnosis based heavily on the resulting violent crimes committed, whereas finer aberrations, which are as important psychopathologically as the more expansive actions, are hardly considered. We strongly suspect this remains true today. Much of what is known results from research and diagnoses which are heavily concentrated in the context of criminal cases where there is a focus on the extreme case. Expensive, publicly-funded diagnostic resources are not typically expended on marginally criminal conduct. Most, although not all, psychiatrists whose research and writing are reported on here probably would not feel uncomfortable with the label of forensic psychiatrist. Another major source of descriptive material regarding pathological intoxication is gleaned from appellate cases and reported trial testimony of forensic psychiatrists, and those tend to be the (legally) more important cases. The entire field, in a sense, is based on retrospective studies. The anomaly is discovered by happenstance, and that happenstance is often a violent crime. While this does not affect the legitimacy of the concept, it does shade its content if our speculations are true.

While there are large variations in the opinions expressed in the writings summarized here — variations regarding etiology and diagnostic criteria and classificatory schema regarding acute alcohol reactions in general — there obviously is substantial common ground. One point needs to be stressed, and that is the first point made by Banay: Patholog-

---

88. Venzlaff, *Die "Pathologischen" Alkoholreaktionen-Atiologie, Klinik and Forensisch-Psychiatrische Beurtelung* (The "Pathological" Alcohol Reactions; Etiology, Clinical Diagnosis and Forensic-Psychiatric Assessment), 47 MED. WELT 2623 (1965).

89. Anchersen, *Rettspsykiatriske Problemer i Forbindelse Med Sovn og Vissthetsforstyrreiser* (Legal Psychiatric Problems Related to Sleep and Modifications of Consciousness), 87 TIDSSKR. NORSKE LAEGEFOREN 1796 (1967).

90. Rommeney, *Ungewohnliche Formen des Alkoholrausches* (Unusual Forms of Alcohol Intoxication), 41 DTSCH. Z. GES. GERICHTL. MED. 277 (1952).

ical reaction to alcohol is not necessarily associated with an *alcoholic* psychosis, although some of the earlier writers failed to make this differentiation.

There is further agreement that pathological intoxication is dissimilar to ordinary intoxication, or drunkenness. Skelton put it this way:

> Alcohol intoxication has long been associated with a decrease in inhibition and overt expression of aggressive and sexual behavior, ranging from mild assertiveness or flirtation to assault or rape. Individuals with personality disorders of the antisocial, emotionally unstable, or aggressive type are particularly prone to impulsive, aggressive behavior when intoxicated. However, their behavior is characteristically an exaggeration of previous personality traits. They are usually aware of their behavior or, if not, the period of amnesia is consistent with the level of intoxication. In these disorders the aberrant behavior is not accompanied by changes in the electroencephalogram.[91]

There are a dozen or so older articles which are included in the accompanying note, and we have included them out of a sense of aesthetic completion and to facilitate future researchers, not because we have had access to them.[92]

---

91. Skelton, *Alcohol, Violent Behavior, and the Electroencephalogram*, 63 S. MED. J. 465 (1970).

92. Profous, (Problems of Pathological Drunkenness and Pathological Effects in Tipsyness in Forensic Psychiatric Practice), 70 CESK. PSYCHIATR. 29 (1974); Reckel, (Pathological Intoxication in Forensic-Psychiatric Evaluation of Alcoholic Intoxication), 151 ARCH. KRIMINOL. 65 (1973); Lustig, *Uber Alkoholismusprobleme in Sowjetischer und europaischer Sicht* (Problems of Alcoholism in Soviet and European Views), 115 WIEN. MED. WSCHR. 400 (1965) (discussing the criminal defense of pathological intoxication in the Soviet Union); Hirschmann, *Zur Kriminologic der akuten Alcoholpsychosen* (The Criminology of Acute Alcoholic Psychoses), 6 KRIMINALBIOL. GEGENWARTSFR. 55 (1964) (alcohol is only one of many factors acting together which cause pathological intoxication); Csiky & Ander, *Reszegseg, Koros Reszegseg es Beszamithatosag orvosi Szempontbol* (Intoxication, Pathological Intoxication and Responsibility from the Medical Point of View), 6 ORV. SZLE 415 (1960); Rakhal'skii, *O Svoyeobraznykh Pskhoticheskikh Sostoyaniyakh pre Alkogol'noi Intoksikatsii* (On Atypical Psychotic States in Alcohol Intoxication), 57 ZH. NEVROPAT. 1299 (1957); Julius & Bohacek, (The Alcoholic Psychoses in Forensic Psychiatry), 1 NEUROPSIHIJATRIJA, ZAGREB 21 (1953); Rauch, *Zur Behandlung der akuten Alkoholvergiftung* (The Treatment of Acute Alcohol Poisoning) 45 MED. KLINIK 1348 (1950); Tobben, *Ein Beitrag zur Forensischen Bedeutung des Pathologischen Rausches* (A Contribution to the Forensic Significance of Pathological Intoxication), 33 D.Z. GES-GER M. 103 (1940); Ciafardo, *Delito en Estado de Inconsciencia por Embriaguez Pathologica en un Degenerado* (Crime in the State of Unconsciousness from Pathological Intoxication in a Degenerate), 2 R. PSIQT. CRIMINOL. 625 (1937); Wachkoly, *Zur Kasuistik des Pathologischen Alkoholrausches* (Toward a Formal Ethical Theory of Pathological Alcohol Intoxication), 11 BEITR. GER. M. (1931); Decsi, *Beitrag aur Forensischen Bedeutung der*

There have since been numerous references to pathological intoxication or pathological reaction to alcohol in the medical or medicolegal literature, some of it rather cursory,[93] some quite useful.

Pathologischen Rauschzustande (Contribution to the Forensic Significance of the State of Pathological Intoxication), 29 PSYCHT. NEUR. WSCHR. 37 (1927); Herschmann, *Totschlag im Pathologischen Rausch* (Manslaughter in Pathological Intoxication), 69 ARCH. KRIMINOL. 115 (1917); Raecke, *Zur Lehre vom Pathologischen Rausche* (Toward a Theory of Pathological Intoxication), 53 VJSCHR. GER. M. 49 (1917); Monkemoller, *Der Pathologische Rauschzustand und Seine Forensische Bedeutung* (The Pathological Intoxication State and Its Forensic Significance), 59 ARCH. KUMANTHROP. 120, 193 (1914); Claude, *Sur le Diagnostic des Formes Larvees de l'Epilepsie Alcoolique at des Crises Psycho-Motrices de l'Ivresse Pathologigue; son Importance Medico-Legale* (On the Diagnostics of the Early Forms of the Epileptic Alcoholic and of the Psychomotor Seizure of Pathological Intoxication; Its Medical-Legal Importance), 40 PROGR. M. PAR. 497 (1912); Kuten, *Der Pathologische Rausch* (Pathological Intoxication), 4 M. KLIN. 1369 (1908); Schenk, *Der Pathologische Rausch* (Pathological Intoxication), 26 D. MED. ZTG. 657 (1905); Oswald, *Gutachten uber einen Fall von Pathologischen Rauschzustand* (Expert Opinion on a Case of Pathological Intoxication Condition), 10 ARZTE. SACHVERST ZTG. 223 (1904); Ritter, *Ueber die Forensische Bedeutung des Normalen und Pathologischen Rausches* (On the Forensic Significance of Normal and Pathological Intoxication), 13 MSCHR. PSYCHT. NEUR. 36 (1903); Mayet, *Les Differentes Formes Anentales de l'Ivresses Alcoolique; Ivress Normale; Ivresses Abnormales; Peudo-Ivresses Pathologigues,* 16 PROV. M. 74 (1902).

93. WORLD HEALTH ORGANIZATION, ALCOHOL-RELATED DISABILITIES (G. Edwards, M. Gross, M. Keller, J. Moser & R. Room eds. 1977) had this definition of "pathological alcohol reaction" which is based on WORLD HEALTH ORGANIZATION, MANUAL OF THE INTERNATIONAL STATISTICAL CLASSIFICATION OF DISEASES, INJURIES, AND CAUSES OF DEATH (1977): "*Includes* acute psychotic episodes induced by relatively small amounts of alcohol. These are regarded as individual idiosyncratic reactions to alcohol, not due to excessive consumption and without neurological signs of intoxication. *Excludes* simple drunkenness." WHO at 54 (emphasis in original).

See TABER'S CYCLOPEDIC MEDICAL DICTIONARY 415 (C. Thomas ed. 14th ed. 1983), which defines pathological reaction to alcohol as "An exceedingly severe reaction to ingestion of alcohol, esp.[sic] to small amounts. Manifested by irrational violent behavior followed by exhaustion, sleep, and loss of recall of the event. Patient may not be intoxicated."; O. ENGLISH & S. FINCH, INTRODUCTION TO PSYCHIATRY 449 (3d ed. 1964) (pathological intoxication is "the sudden onset of a relatively severe behavior reaction which is brought on by a mild to moderate intake of alcohol."); J. CAVANAGH & J. MCGOLDRICK, FUNDAMENTAL PSYCHIATRY 426 (1958) ("Pathological Intoxication is an acute alcoholic psychosis in which the individual reacts to the ingestion of even small amounts of alcohol with violence, delusions, or hallucinations. It is usually followed by a profound sleep and amnesia for the attack."); H. DAVIDSON, FORENSIC PSYCHIATRY 330 (1952) (pathological intoxication is "An excessive reaction to moderate amounts of alcohol; a period of frenzy precipitated by drinking, for which the subject subsequently has amnesia. Also called *mania a potu.*")

See also L. KOLB, NOYES' MODERN CLINICAL PSYCHIATRY 642 (9th ed. 1977); Chafetz, in COMPREHENSIVE TEXTBOOK OF PSYCHIATRY 1341 (A. Freedman, H. Kaplan & B. Sadeck eds. 2d ed. 1975); R. Kelley, P. Solomon & H. Emmanuel, in HANDBOOK OF PSYCHIATRY 415 (P. Solomon & V. Patch eds. 1974); L. HINSIE & R. CAMPBELL, PSYCHIATRIC DICTIONARY 410 (4th ed. 1970); R. MCNICHOL, THE TREATMENT OF DELIRIUM TREMENS AND RELATED STATES 76 (1970); I. BATCHELOR, HENDERSON AND GILLESPIE'S TEXTBOOK OF PSYCHIATRY 407 (10th ed. 1969); L. HINSIE & R. CAMPBELL, PSYCHIATRIC DICTIONARY (3d ed. 1960); H. WEIHOFEN, MENTAL DISORDER AS A CRIMINAL DEFENSE 126 (1954); A. NOYES, MODERN CLINICAL PSYCHIATRY 221 (2d ed. 1939); Meyer, *Alcohol as a Psychiatric Problem,* and Pollock, *The Prevalence of Mental Disease Due to Alcoholism,* in ALCOHOL AND MAN 293, 345 (H. Emerson ed. 1935); W. EAST,

Keller and McCormick defined the concept — pathological alcohol reaction, pathological intoxication — as follows:

> [a]n extraordinarily severe response to alcohol, especially to small amounts, marked by apparently senseless violent behavior, usually followed by exhaustion, sleep and amnesia for the episode. Intoxication is apparently not always involved, and for this reason *pathological reaction to alcohol* is the preferred term. The reaction is thought to be associated with exhaustion, great strain, or hypoglycemia, and to occur especially in people poorly defended against their own violent impulses. HAGGARD & JELLINEK (1942): "This violent reaction to alcohol has little, if anything, in common with [alcohol] intoxication. It is not ordinary intoxication occurring in an individual with extremely low tolerance to alcohol. There are none of the common symptoms of drunkenness: there is no flushing of the face, no staggering, and no slurring of speech. This peculiar reaction, which usually takes the form of furor, occurs in normal persons under exceptional conditions...."
>
> The phenomenon is sometimes classed among the alcoholic psychoses. The American Psychiatric Association's *Diagnostic and Statistical Manual: Mental Disorders* (1952) requires classification under 'acute brain syndrome, alcohol intoxication' where there is no apparent preexistent mental disorder, and where there is, classification under the diagnosis of the underlying condition.[94]

In a later edition of this work,[95] the second paragraph was changed to:

> The phenomenon is sometimes classed among the alcoholic psychoses. The American Psychiatric Association's DSM-II (1968) classified it as an 'acute brain syndrome manifested by psychosis after minimal alcohol intake,' and in DSM-III (1980) it is named idiosyncratic alcohol intoxication.

AN INTRODUCTION TO FORENSIC PSYCHIATRY IN THE CRIMINAL COURTS (1927); H. MAUDSLEY, RESPONSIBILITY IN MENTAL DISEASE (1906).

94. M. KELLER & M. MCCORMICK, A DICTIONARY OF WORDS ABOUT ALCOHOL 150 (1968).

95. M. KELLER, M. MCCORMICK & V. EFRON, A DICTIONARY OF WORDS ABOUT ALCOHOL 189 (2d ed. 1982).

CONCLUSION

The etiology and symptomatology of pathological reaction to alcohol may be summarized as follows: Pathological reaction to alcohol is not intolerance to alcohol. The amount of alcohol consumed is irrelevant. Brain damage or prior disease affecting the brain may be predisposing factors, and pathological reaction to alcohol may be related directly or indirectly to the conditions associated with diabetes. Pathological reaction to alcohol is qualitatively distinct from both intoxication and other alcohol-related psychoses. An outburst of rage and senseless violence is characteristic of the reaction. Onset is sudden, duration is brief, albeit sometimes violent, and is followed by sleep and amnesia. The amnesia may be total or partial. The reaction of the person is colored by fear or anxiety, rage, strong motor releases, often explosively violent, with corresponding misunderstanding and disorientation to the situation, confusion, delusions or distorted perceptions of the environment sometimes to the point of hallucinations. Automatic behavior results. There is an absence of motor incoordination, slurred speech and diplopia (blurred vision) which characterize ordinary alcohol intoxication. There may be an absence of pupillary reflexes. While the absence of pupillary reflexes is useful in making the diagnosis, neither their presence nor absence is, taken alone, determinative as indeed might be said of most of the criteria. The episode lasts for a short time, a few hours to a day, and terminates in deep sleep. The amount of alcohol ingested is irrelevant; it can be great or small. The strong and purposeful motor behavior may be one of the most important diagnostic factors because of the contrast between it and the slurred speech and general incoordination which characterize a state of intoxication, although speech may be abnormal in other ways. The factor of critical significance is the absence of the ordinary signs of intoxication. The presence of other precipitating factors is suspected, explaining the inability to induce pathological reaction to alcohol consistently in experimental settings.

The frequency of the occurrence of pathological reaction to alcohol is difficult to estimate. Abortive delirium tremens is often diagnosed as pathological intoxication, and this leads to an over-estimate. Sometimes the pathological reaction is so brief that the subject never reaches the hospital, or jail, leading to an under-estimate. Reported cases of pathological intoxication are probably less than 1 percent of all admissions for acute and chronic alcoholism to any type of hospital. Binswanger found that the average age of patients with pathological intoxication was thirty-one years of age.[96] This is more than ten years younger than the

---

96. Bowman & Jellinek, *Alcoholic Mental Disorders*, 2 QRTLY J. STUD. ALCOH. 312, 324

average age of all alcoholic admissions. The difference is related to the fact that pathological reaction to alcohol is not a manifestation of chronic alcoholism. And it should be emphasized that we are describing psychomotor or temporal lobe epilepsy (complex, partial seizures), not epilepsy involving seizures of the convulsive type.[97]

(1941).

97. On the latter, in relation to alcohol, alcoholism, pre-existing head injury and convulsive seizures, see Victor, *The Pathophysiology of Alcoholic Epilepsy*, 46 RES. NERV. MENT. DIS. 431 (1968).

3

Experimental Evidence of Pathological Intoxication: Alcohol Provocation and the EEG

The terms "alcohol provocation test" and "alcohol activation test" are synonymous but used two ways in the research literature relating to pathological intoxication, sometimes to refer to an attempt in a controlled setting to induce actual behavioral signs of an attack of pathological reaction to alcohol and more commonly to designate an attempt to trigger the brain wave abnormalities associated with pathological intoxication. It can, of course, mean both.

Alcohol provocation has been used from the earliest times,[1] since it has been obvious to researchers that one way to understand more fully pathological reaction to alcohol is to experimentally provoke it under laboratory conditions. While failure to provoke it would not prove it did not exist, perhaps such experiments could be useful to establish its exact nature. Later, when the technology became available, researchers investigated the relationship between psychomotor epilepsy[2] and pathological reaction to alcohol by administration of the electroencephalogram (EEG).[3]

---

1. *See, e.g.*, Kantorovich & Constantinovich, *Effect of Alcohol in Catatonic Syndromes: Preliminary Report*, 92 AM. J. PSYCHIAT. 651 (1935); Newman, *Alcohol Injected Intravenously: Some Psychological and Psychopathological Effects in Man*, 91 AM. J. PSYCHIAT. 1343 (1935).

2. Psychomotor seizures were evidently first described in Gibbs, Gibbs & Lennox, *Epilepsy: A Paroxysmal Cerebral Dysrhythmia*, 60 BRAIN 377 (1937).

3. The earliest effort we have found trying to measure alcohol-induced pathological reaction with the EEG is in Greenblatt, Levin & DiCori, *The Electroencephalogram Associated with Chronic Alcoholism, Alcoholic Psychosis and Alcoholic Convulsions*, 52 ARCH. NEUROL. PSYCHIAT. 290 (1944).

"About 75 years ago [1874], an English scientist, Caton, discovered the fact that electrical activity was one of the phenomena of the brains of living animals...." Spirer, *Biochemistry as a Defense*, 4 MIAMI L.Q. 1, 2 (1949). The development of the EEG evidently goes back to about 1924. Walton, *Some Observations on the Value of Electroencephalography in Medico-Legal Practice*, 31 MEDICO-LEGAL J. 15 (1963); Note, *The Legal Problems of Epilepsy*, 29 TEMP. L.Q. 364, 373 (1956); Berger, *Uber das Elektrenkephalogramm dan Menschen*, 87 ARCH. FOR. PSYCH. 527 (1929).

The role of the EEG in both crime research and litigation, criminal and civil,[4] is quite significant.[5] While there is relatively little in the law review literature on the subject, much of it focusing on the problem of defining death,[6] many appellate cases involve EEG examinations, beginning in the late 1950's,[7] and the use of the device could become more prevalent and powerful as interpretation of electroencephalograms becomes more sophisticated through computer-processed statistical analysis.[8]

> October, 1938: "In 1928, Dr. Hans Berger of Jena reported that it is possible to show and record a quite strange electrical rhythm of the human brain. Borrowing a vacuum tube, Berger built an amplifier powerful enough to magnify weak electric impulses a millionfold. This powerful amplifier, in the hands of Berger and later of many others, has disposed of the old, static picture of the brain. Today, a motion picture of the true, the dynamic brain can be exhibited. And already features of this cinema are being practically applied to common but heretofore completely baffling medical problems, such as epilepsy, man's fitful malady."

Scientific American 12 (Oct. 1988). *See also* O. ENGLISH & S. FINCH, INTRODUCTION TO PSYCHIATRY 497 (3d Ed. 1964); F. GIBBS & E. GIBBS, ATLAS OF ELECTROENCEPHALOGRAPHY 7-8 (1941); Adrian & Matthews, 57 BRAIN 355 (1934).

4. Investigation of post-traumatic epilepsy is one of the common uses, *see, e.g.*, Walton, *Some Observations on the Value of Electroencephalography in Medico-Legal Practice*, 31 MEDICO-LEGAL J. 15, 30-33 (1963), but investigation of other results of head injuries are also common. Walton at 33-34.

5. *See, e.g.*, Mednick, Volavka, Gabrielli & Itil, *EEG (Electroencephalogram) as a Predictor of Antisocial Behavior*, 19 CRIMINOLOGY 219 (1981); Mandelzys & Marceau, *Relationship of Violence to Alpha Levels in a Biofeedback Training Paradigm*, 37 J. CLIN. PSYCHOL. 202 (1981). These are just examples of what is in print.

6. *See, e.g.*, Smith, *Legal Recognition of Neocortical Death*, 71 CORNELL L. REV. 850 (1986); Comment, *Artificial Nutrition and the Terminally Ill: How Should Washington Decide?* 61 WASH. L. REV. 419 (1986); Note, *Toward an Ohio Natural Death Act: The Need for Living Will Legislation*, 46 OHIO ST. L.J. 1019 (1985). *But see* SOUTHERN EEG SOCIETY, ELECTROENCEPHALOGRAPHY AND THE LAW (1968), (moot trial proceedings on two cases).

7. *See, e.g.*, People v. Higgins, 5 N.Y.2d 607, 186 N.Y.S.2d 623, 159 N.E.2d 179 (1959).

8. *See, e.g.*, BRAIN ISCHEMIA: QUANTITATIVE EEG AND IMAGING TECHNIQUES (G. Pfurtscheller, E. Jonkman, & F. Lopes da Silva eds. 1984) (based on the International Symposium on Quantitative EEG and Imaging Techniques in Brain Ischemia, Austria, 1983) ["Quantification of the EEG (qEEG), by way of computer analysis, has opened up new possibilities for the evaluation of slight EEG changes which may accompany cerebrovascular insufficiency." BRAIN ISCHEMIA at vii]; RHYTHMIC EEG ACTIVITIES AND CORTICAL FUNCTIONING (Proceedings of the International Symposium on Event-Related Changes in Cortical Rhythmic Activities. Behavioural Correlates. Austria, 1979) (G. Pfurtscheller, P. Buser & F. Lopes da Silva eds. 1980); THE ALPHA SYLLABUS (B. Brown & J. Klug eds. 1974); RECENT ADVANCES IN CLINICAL NEUROPHYSIOLOGY (L. Widen ed. 1967); Denno, *Human Biology and Criminal Responsibility: Free Will or Free Ride?* 137 U. PA. L. REV. 615, 633-39 (1988).

See also, EEG AND BEHAVIOR (G. Glaser ed. 1963), especially Henry, *Positive Spike Discharges in the EEG and Behavior Abnormality* at 315, *and* Glaser, Newman & Schafer, *Interictal Psychosis in Psychomotor-Temporal Lobe Epilepsy: An EEG-Psychological Study* at 345. Both of these chapters contain extensive bibliographical listings and reproductions of illustrative EEG's.

The terms "psychomotor epilepsy" and "temporal lobe epilepsy" are viewed as synonymous by most writers. "Psychomotor epilepsy" was the older term coined by the early clinicians, and "temporal lobe epilepsy" came more into vogue with evidence of the particular part of the brain involved, the existence of which was made possible by the advent of the development and widespread use of the EEG as a diagnostic and research tool. It has even been suggested[9] that the term "temporal lobe epilepsy" be used when the patient was identified by scalp EEG criteria and that "psychomotor epilepsy" be used when the patient was identified largely on the basis of clinical observations and manifestations of the disorder. The idea was to foster more uniformity of patient selection to facilitate cross-study comparisons lest there be some difference in the groups. Nevertheless, as we indicated, most writers do not draw the distinction, and we will treat the terms as having identical denotations. More recently, it is referred to as a complex partial seizure of temporal lobe origin (CPS/TL).[10]

One manifestation of epilepsy is an excessive neuronal discharge within the central nervous system. During a seizure there may be an abrupt change in behavior, and this is referred to as ictal behavior. An ictus is a sudden attack or convulsion, and the time of attack is called the ictal period. The longer periods between attacks are referred to as interictal periods. This ictal period and perhaps periods just preceding and following it are periods of unconsciousness, and the resulting condition is one form of automatism.

> With the advent of electroencephalography about 40 years ago, the temporal lobe origin of most of these seizures was documented and the term "temporal lobe epilepsy" came into use. The term "partial seizures" was introduced by Gastaut to denote seizures that arise from a part of the brain. Partial seizures were divided into two main categories: simple partial seizures, in which consciousness is not impaired, and complex partial seizures, in which consciousness is impaired either at the onset or at some point during the seizure. Some partial seizures may become secondarily generalized. The term "temporal lobe epilepsy" has been discarded because these

---

Others seem less sanguine regarding the future of the EEG technology. "[R]ather like each new drug, brain-wave recording has oscillated from early lack of interest (when its possibility was first reported) to tremendous enthusiasm to downright skepticism and finally to a grudging acceptance that it does have a role to play, though uncertainty still exists as to the nature of that role." A. SMITH, THE MIND 102-03 (1984).

9. R. MONROE, EPISODIC BEHAVIORAL DISORDERS 96-97 (1970).

10. *See, e.g.*, Hermann, Wyler & Richey, *Epilepsy, Frontal Lobe, and Personality*, 22 BIOL. PSYCHIAT. 1055 (1987).

> seizures may also originate from the orbital surface of the frontal lobe and the limbic system.[11]

Nevertheless, it is also believed that "Nearly 90 percent of patients with complex partial seizures have the type characterized by psychomotor symptomatology."[12] Because the writers and the research discussed often span the time the terminology was being revised, we will often use the nomenclature of the writer to avoid confusion.

THOMPSON

Thompson was of the opinion that with electroencephalography came the "objective" evidence that would augment the clinical evidence so long in existence, but so long viewed with great caution by the legal profession,[13] and would advance it to such an extent that the question of the existence of the phenomenon of pathological intoxication could be laid to rest and attention could focus on whether it was the essential cause of the crime.[14] While activation techniques had been used earlier, notably with a drug called metrazol,[15] it was known that it would not only activate cerebral electrical seizures in a large number of known epileptics, it would also do so with nonepileptic control subjects in about 15 percent of the cases. Since it was claimed that alcohol was the precipitating factor in the cases studied, it was logical to use it as the activator.[16] It had been observed as early as 1941 that "apparently in man, alcohol precipitates convulsive attacks only in those who are subject to seizures."[17]

Thompson's summary of the situation as of 1963 is of particular interest:

> The disease [here called "acute pathological alcoholic intoxication"] occurs usually in previously brain-injured individuals or

---

11. Desai, *Complex Partial Seizures,* 30 AM. FAM. PHYS. 158, 159 (1984).
12. Desai at 160.
13. Smith, *Medico-Legal Facets of Epilepsy,* 31 TEX. L. REV. 765 (1953).
14. Thompson, *The Electroencephalogram in Acute Pathological Alcoholic Intoxication,* 28 BULL. L.A. NEUROL. SOC. 217 (1963). *See also* Ellington, *The Electroencephalogram and Criminal Responsibility,* 3 J. FOR. MED. 115 (1956), which compares the efficacy of the EEG in detection of epilepsy and organic diseases in contrast to their utility in detecting functional mental diseases.
15. Kaufman, Marshall & Walker, *Metrazol Activated Electroencephalography,* 26 J. NERV. & MENT. DIS. 476 (1947); Kaufman, Marshall & Walker, *Activated Electroencephalography,* 58 ARCH. NEUROL. & PSYCHIAT. 533 (1947).
16. Kershman, *Syncope and Seizures,* 12 J. NEUROL., NEUROSURG. & PSYCHIAT. 25 (1949).
17. Lennox, *Alcohol and Epilepsy,* 2 QRTLY J. STUD. ALCOH. 1 (1941).

> those who have had brain disease or other organic abnormality. The disease or traumatic process is usually in frontal or temporal lobes or their connections with the thalamus. The afflicted individual exhibits an abnormal behavior response to inhibition [sic, imbibition?] of relatively small amounts of alcohol. This amount of alcohol ordinarily would have only minor effects on the average person. Total or partial amnesia follows....
>
> During the period of amnesia the afflicted individual carries out behavior that is automatic. To the unaware observer the behavior may appear consciously motivated. In this and in almost all other respects the disorder is identical with psychomotor epilepsy....The only difference is that in pathological alcoholic intoxication the attack is precipitated by the irritant effect of alcohol; in psychomotor epilepsy the attacks occur spontaneously....Explosively violent behavior is typical and occurs frequently, although it is not necessary to the diagnosis.[18]

He also pointed out that trauma is not the only source of the brain lesions,[19] which appear to be the cause of the reaction, but that they can as well be degenerative, infectious, neoplastic,[20] congenital, chemical or hormonal,[21] and he said that "it is not the nature of the lesion but its location in the brain that determines the defect."[22]

> In an afflicted individual, alcohol alone does not, at all times, precipitate attacks. This peculiarity is used frequently by district attorneys in their attempts to secure criminal convic-

---

18. Thompson, *The Electroencephalogram in Acute Pathological Alcoholic Intoxication,* 28 BULL. L.A. NEUROL. SOC. 217 (1963). *See also* Jones, *Medical Aspects of Chemical Tests for Intoxication,* 8 CLEV.-MARSHALL L. REV. 228, 232 (1959): "A violent form of intoxication, *mania a potu,* may result from the consumption of small amounts of alcohol in persons suffering from epilepsy, cerebral arteriosclerosis, previous cerebral trauma and mental instability." Jones cites IMRIE, ACUTE ALCOHOL POISONING IN EMERGENCIES IN GENERAL PRACTICE 376-83 (1957).

There is a suggestion by the court in People v. Murtishaw, 48 Cal. 3d 1001, 258 Cal. Rptr. 821, 773 P.2d 172 (1989), that Thompson used a combination of alcohol and barbiturates for the EEG test, but no details are provided. Normally, alcohol is used alone.

19. A "lesion" is a rather general term denoting a "circumscribed area of pathologically altered tissue" or an injury or wound to an area. TABER'S CYCLOPEDIC MEDICAL DICTIONARY 809 (C. Thomas ed. 14th ed. 1981).

20. "A new and abnormal formation of tissue, as a tumor or growth. It serves no useful function, but grows at the expense of the healthy organism." TABER'S CYCLOPEDIC MEDICAL DICTIONARY 941 (C. Thomas ed. 14th ed. 1981). The term includes both benign and malignant tumors.

21. Thompson, *The Electroencephalogram in Acute Pathological Alcoholic Intoxication,* 28 BULL. L.A. NEUROL. SOC. 217, 218 (1963).

22. Thompson at 218.

> tions. It is well known that fatigue by-products and emotional stress may add to the susceptibility of the patient, just as these factors may initiate seizures in the epileptic patient.[23]

Several kinds of EEG abnormalities are associated with pathological intoxication: (1) localized spiking (usually in the temporal or frontal lobe); (2) high-voltage slow-wave bursts (also usually in the temporal or frontal lobe at 2 to 6 cycles per second); and (3) spike- and slow-wave mixtures, again in localized bursts.

> All persons with the above electroencephalographic findings do not have pathological intoxication or psychomotor epilepsy. Neither do all persons who have these clinical syndromes have these electroencephalographic findings. A person may have psychomotor epilepsy or pathological alcoholic intoxication or both, and have a normal prealcohol electroencephalogram and a normal alcohol-activated electroencephalogram.[24]

The pattern most often associated with psychomotor epilepsy and behavioral disorders is the 14 and 6 cycle-per-second positive spiking.[25] Charles Henry[26] provided a summary of the literature in 1963. He stated: "My task is to present the material dealing with that curiously complex configuration in the electroencephalogram only approximately described as 6 and 14/sec. positive spiking...." The literature was reviewed from Gibbs & Gibbs,[27] which was the first report of the 6 and 14 cycle-per-second positive spiking phenomenon, up through the literature to 1963. The year following their first report, Gibbs and Gibbs made a further report:

> The following year saw only a single major publication, but it received very wide distribution since it was Chapter 13 of Volume 2 of the second edition of Gibbs and Gibbs' *Atlas.*[28]

---

23. Thompson at 218.

24. Thompson at 219. Normal alcohol-influenced EEG's are discussed in Kelley & Reilly, *EEG, Alcohol, and Alcoholism*, in EEG AND EVOKED POTENTIALS IN PSYCHIATRY AND BEHAVIORAL NEUROLOGY 55, 64 (J. Hughes & W. Wilson eds. 1983). "Evoked potentials, or evoked responses, are recordings of CNS [central nervous system] electrical activity after a brief sensory stimulation in any modality." Kelley & Reilly at 63.

25. J. MACDONALD, PSYCHIATRY AND THE CRIMINAL 227 (3d ed. 1976).

26. Henry, *Positive Spike Discharges in the EEG and Behavior Abnormality*, in EEG AND BEHAVIOR 315 (G. Glaser ed. 1963).

27. Gibbs & Gibbs, *Electroencephalographic Evidence of Thalamic and Hypothalamic Epilepsy*, 1 NEUROL. 136 (1951).

28. Gibbs & Gibbs, *Thalamic and Hypothalamic Epilepsy*, in 2 ATLAS OF ELECTROENCEPHALOGRAPHY 329 (1952).

> The electrographic features were expanded [from their first report the year before] and illustrated and the number of cases increased to 427. They pointed out that psychiatric disorder was more common in this positive-spike group than with any other type of epilepsy except the anterior and mid-temporal lobe focal disturbance, with the main feature being a behavioral disturbance. Again there was a very long list of associated clinical complaints with some emphasis on pain, parethesias,[29] and rage attacks; as in their first paper, they mentioned the unique fact that four of these patients had committed murder. Etiology remained uncertain except that 21 per cent of the patients had experienced severe head trauma and another 9 per cent encephalitis.[30]

Henry noted that "In 1953 Schwade and colleagues[31] reported two cases of murder in teenage boys with 6 and 14/sec. positive spiking and stated that they had similar EEG abnormality on 46 cases with impulsive amnestic behavior. The case of (probable multiple) homicide is a vivid example of the clinical behavior exhibited by some of these patients. The authors clearly indicate their assumption of a causal relationship between the inferred thalamic disorder and its electrographic and clinical expression."[32]

> An exhibit from Schwade and Geiger[33] dealt with over 500 children and young adults with clinical histories of impulsive violent behavior, all showing 14 and 6/sec. positive spiking in their EEGs. Presumably this is the same series of cases reported more extensively the following year[34] as 453 cases between 1.5 and 18 years of age, including five "bizarre, impulsive-compulsive" murderers.[35]

---

29. A sensation of numbness, prickling or tingling. TABER'S CYCLOPEDIC MEDICAL DICTIONARY 1049 (C. Thomas ed. 14th ed. 1981).

30. Henry, *Positive Spike Discharges in the EEG and Behavior Abnormality,* in EEG AND BEHAVIOR 315, 316 (G. Glaser ed. 1963).

31. Schwade & Geiger, *Matricide with Electroencephalographic Evidence of Thalamic or Hypothalamic Disorder,* 14 DIS. NERV. SYST. 18 (1953); Schwade & Otto, *Homicide as a Manifestation of Thalamic or Hypothalamic Disorder with Abnormal Electroencephalographic Findings,* 52 WIS. MED. J. 171 (1953).

32. Henry at 317.

33. Schwade & Geiger, *Behavior Disorders of the Impulsive-Compulsive Type with Consistent Abnormal EEG Findings,* 7 ELECTRO-ENCEPH. CLIN. NEUROPHYSIOL. 473 (1955).

34. Schwade & Geiger, *Abnormal Electroencephalographic Findings in Severe Behavior Disorders,* 17 DIS. NERV. SYST. 307 (1956).

35. Henry at 318.

Henry summarized numerous other studies which tended to reach much the same conclusions as the earlier work,[36] but there was awareness all along that the studies were retrospective and failure to use controls had become the norm. Even the studies which purported to use control groups obtained those subjects from the patients referred to the researchers,[37] but when such limited controls were used the relationship between the EEG abnormalities and aggressive behavior both diminished and became more complex. Still, the reports continued to come in:

> Stehle[38] reported 30 cases with the positive spike discharge, all showing severe aggressive behavior and affective defect; the behavior of two patients resulted in death of a family member, two others severe physical injury, and two suicide attempts, plus other examples of extreme property damage....Schwade and Geiger[39] related this type of discharge to the "irresistible impulse"....[40]

Monroe also underscored that these 6 and 14 cycles-per-second patterns are of importance

> because of the alleged behavioral manifestations of impulsive rage and homicidal reaction, irresistible impulses, and other episodic symptoms supposedly associated with this EEG abnormality....The autonomic symptoms associated with 14 and 6 positive spikes appear epileptoid in that they appear abruptly, are of transitory nature, and disappear equally precipitously. The behavioral episodes, although impulsive and explosive, are usually characterized by a skilled, well-

---

36. Much of the reported literature at the time of this summary provided only clinical observations, but many of the reports are as persuasive as the later experimental evidence. *See, e.g.*, Walker, *Murder or Epilepsy?* 133 J. NERV. & MENT. DIS. 430 (1961), providing the medical and behavioral background, including an eventual autopsy, of a patient with an abnormal left temporal lobe who had killed his wife and could not recall the event. The court psychiatrist and the hospital staff agreed that he had committed the motiveless killing in a postictal automatism, and he was committed. There is no mention of alcohol involvement in the case. Walker also reported on another patient he had examined who "while committed to an institution for delinquents, encountered a smaller boy he had never seen before and drowned him in a nearby stream. He told his story without any sign of remorse or emotion. He had a 14 and 6 pattern in his electroencephalogram." Walker at 435.

37. Walter, Colbert, Goegler, Palmer & Bond, *A Controlled Study of the Fourteen- and Six-per-Second EEG Pattern*, 2 ARCH. GEN. PSYCHIAT. 559 (1960).

38. Stehle, *Thalamic Dysfunction Involved in Destructive-Aggressive Behavior Directed Against Persons and Property*, 12 ELECTROENCEPH. CLIN. NEUROPHYSIOL. 264 (1960).

39. Schwade & Geiger, *Severe Behavior Disorders with Abnormal Electroencephalograms*, 21 DIS. NERV. SYST. 616 (1960).

40. Henry at 324.

> planned and coordinated behavior. This sets these episodes apart from the usual psychomotor automatism and "furors" that might appear as ictal or postictal phenomena. Hughes[41] reports that in the group of 14 and 6 positive spike patients, 90 percent had clinical manifestations of behavior disorders and/or autonomic dysfunctions. However, most observers do not feel that the 14 and 6 abnormality per se is an ictal phenomenon, that is, a manifestation of concomitant excessive neuronal discharge.[42]

The same pattern has been found by others as well to be associated with extreme violence, including murder.

> Although it is risky to generalize from individual cases, it may be significant that Gibbs[43]...reports that the four murderers from his epileptic series all had positive spikes. Eleven other childhood or adolescent homicidal acts occurring in patients with 14 and 6 abnormalities have been reported in the literature, including several instances of matricide.[44]...It has been remarked that these murders were usually committed with little or no motivation. However, it is quite obvious that evaluations regarding motivation would require rather detailed clinical contact with the subject, which is not usually indicated in the reports. Perhaps it would be a more cautious statement to say that homicidal acts were committed without obvious motivation. It is probably significant that the victim often is a member of the family. However, in several reported cases the victim has been a total stranger.[45]

As to this latter point, let us add that if a person is engaged in truly senseless and motiveless violence, it is probable that the person attacked would be among those who are most frequently around the actor, his family.

Most of the research reviewed above takes this approach: If one starts with abnormal EEG's, what abnormal behavior is associated with that, rather than what abnormal EEG's are found when you start with abnormal behavior. Monroe also considered the research which

---

41. Hughes, Gianturco & Stein, *Electro-Clinical Correlations in the Positive Spike Phenomenon*, 13 ELECTROENCEPH. CLIN. NEUROPHYSIOL. 599 (1961).
42. R. MONROE, EPISODIC BEHAVIORAL DISORDERS 133 (1970).
43. 2 F. GIBBS, ATLAS OF ELECTROENCEPHALOGRAPHY (1952).
44. Schwade & Geiger, *Severe Behavior Disorders with Abnormal Electroencephalograms*, 21 DIS. NERV. SYST. 616 (1960).
45. R. MONROE, EPISODIC BEHAVIORAL DISORDERS 137-38 (1970).

addressed the converse issue and points out that the complexities are compounded in this effort:

> A particularly pertinent study is that of Stafford-Clark[46]...who reported on EEG records of prisoners charged with murder. He found that the EEG was much more likely to be abnormal in those prisoners who committed motiveless murders, or who were psychotic at the time of the murder, when compared with those subjects whose homicidal act was accidental or those whose acts were premeditated. Murder associated with sexual offenses fell somewhere in between these two groups.[47]

There is another point that is accented in this extensive report by Monroe. He discussed activation procedures and defined activation as referring to "any procedure or manipulation, either physiologic, psychologic, or pharmacologic, utilized to elicit latent EEG abnormalities in order to reduce the number of false negatives, and at the same time (this has been less well studied) without significantly increasing the number of false positives."[48] While other drugs are used in activation procedures, most notably alpha-chloralose, his analysis of the literature mentions no instances of the utilization of alcohol as an activating agent. Although this is generally an accurate depiction of the research literature, it mysteriously fails to take account of the studies reported on here which do use alcohol-activation techniques. In fact, alcohol involvement with epileptics and violence is notably missing from the entire book. In later research, Monroe does tie alcohol to the "dyscontrol syndrome," which he describes as associated only to some degree to epilepsy,[49] and this will be discussed in a later chapter.

Thompson stresses that neither the presence nor the absence[50] of

---

46. Stafford-Clark & Taylor, *Clinical and EEG Studies of Prisoners Charged with Murder*, 12 J. NEUROL., NEUROSURG. & PSYCHIAT. 325 (1949).

47. R. MONROE, EPISODIC BEHAVIORAL DISORDERS 162-63 (1970).

48. R. MONROE, EPISODIC BEHAVIORAL DISORDERS 177 (1970).

49. Monroe, *Episodic Behavioral Disorders and Limbic Ictus*, 26 COMP. PSYCHIAT. 466, 472 (1985).

50. EEG's will not identify all cases of psychomotor epilepsy. *See, e.g.*, J. MACDONALD, PSYCHIATRY AND THE CRIMINAL 225 (3d ed. 1976). MacDonald estimates that from 5 to 40 percent of those with epilepsy will not show EEG abnormalities associated with psychomotor epilepsy, depending upon the thoroughness of the examination. It has been noted also in Hughes, *The Medicolegal EEG*, in EEG AND EVOKED POTENTIALS IN PSYCHIATRY AND BEHAVIORAL NEUROLOGY 366 (J. Hughes & W. Wilson eds. 1983) that "A normal EEG pattern cannot, of course, guarantee that seizures will not occur...." *See also* Courjon, *Apport de l'Exploration Fonctionelle du System Nerveux dans le Diagnostic et le Pronostic des Traumatismes Craiens Recents*, 70 ACTA NEUROL. BELG. (1970); Marshall & Walker, *The Value of Electroencephalography in the Prognostication and Prognosis of Post-Traumatic Epilepsy*,

these EEG abnormalities can be taken alone as conclusive in either direction,[51] for not all cases of pathological reaction to alcohol will exhibit these abnormalities, nor does their presence conclusively demonstrate the existence of the disease.[52] In his judgment, a majority of those exhibiting pathological intoxication will also exhibit these abnormalities on the EEG. But he notes that the EEG "does not make the diagnosis."[53] "It is of paramount importance to recognize that any competent and unbiased neurologist or psychiatrist can make the diagnosis of Acute Pathological Alcoholic Intoxication without the benefit of the electroencephalographic findings."[54]

Thompson maintained for years that pathological intoxication and psychomotor epilepsy seizures were indistinguishable. In 1953 he argued the point.

> The close relationship between the psychopathic personality, psychomotor epilepsy, and pathological intoxication has been described. It should be pointed out that some persons who are entirely normal when not under the influence of alcohol may develop psychomotor attacks identical with psychomotor epilepsy when a small amount of alcohol is imbibed. This, of course, is the syndrome of pathological intoxication. There is no way to distinguish pathological intoxication and psychomotor epilepsy in these cases as they are simply terms describing the same thing, namely, the individual who because of disturbed engramme function becomes a psychopath under the influence of a small amount of alcohol.[55]

---

2 EPILEPSIA 138 (1961).

51. Another study indicated that definite spike-, sharp-wave or slow-wave foci were present in a total of 92 percent of the sample studied, 6 percent had ill-defined foci and 2 percent showed no focus. Six percent showed a temporal lobe focus in the absence of any clinical attacks of temporal lobe epilepsy. Six percent of sleep recordings were positive when one or more routine EEG's had been negative. Currie, Heathfield, Henson & Scott, *Clinical Course and Prognosis of Temporal Lobe Epilepsy,* 94 BRAIN 173, 179 (1971).

52. *See also* Kotani, *EEG Studies on Endogenous Psychoses and Alcohol Intoxication,* 12 BULL. OSAKA MED. SCH. 303 (Supp. 1967).

53. Thompson, *The Electroencephalogram in Acute Pathological Alcoholic Intoxication,* 28 BULL. L.A. NEUROL. SOC. 217, 219 (1963). *See also* R. MCNICHOL, THE TREATMENT OF DELIRIUM TREMENS AND RELATED STATES 76 (1970): "Skull x-rays and an EEG are helpful in making the correct diagnosis."

54. Thompson, *The Electroencephalogram in Acute Pathological Alcoholic Intoxication,* 28 BULL. L.A. NEUROL. SOC. 217, 219 (1963).

55. G. THOMPSON, THE PSYCHOPATHIC DELINQUENT AND CRIMINAL 115 (1953). *See also* Thompson, *Relationship of Sexual Psychopathy to Psychomotor Epilepsy and Its Variants,* 121 J. NERV. & MENT. DIS. 374 (1955); G. THOMPSON, ALCOHOLISM 467 (1956); Thompson, *The General Practitioner and the Dangerous Patient,* 11 G.P. (KANSAS CITY) 59 (1955).

See also Pincus & Tucker, *Violence in Children and Adults: A Neurological View,* 17 J. AM. ACAD. CHILD PSYCH. 277 (1978) (pathological intoxication is associated with brain

He later stated that

> [t]his interesting association of some cases of psychopathic personality with psychomotor epilepsy and pathologic alcoholic intoxication [pathological intoxication] indicates that pathologic alcoholic intoxication and psychomotor epilepsy may be the same disease under two different names. In the one case (psychomotor epilepsy) psychomotor epileptic attacks simply occur spontaneously; in the other (pathological intoxication), psychomotor attacks occur under the stimulus of alcohol.[56]

At this point, in 1956, Thompson had reached the following conclusions:

> 1. Pathological alcoholic intoxication can be established by psychiatric examination as a well-defined diagnostic category.
> 2. The electroencephalogram is of great value as objective evidence in studies of these cases.
> 3. Pathological alcoholic intoxication constitutes alcoholic insanity and legal recognition of this fact should be established by legislative action.
> 4. "Alcohol electroencephalograms" can be of assistance, but should be used only under careful psychiatric supervision.
> 5. Great care should be exercised so that "responsible" criminals cannot hide behind an apparent but false diagnosis of pathological alcoholic intoxication.[57]

He also characterized the situation which is still somewhat true today:

> One psychiatric syndrome that is not well defined in its relationship to legal responsibility...is that known as pathological alcoholic intoxication. Frequently, it is difficult to establish this diagnosis in the minds of judges and juries. It is only recently that this disorder has become a well-established and well-known psychiatric syndrome. The greatest difficulty involved in the entire problem is to convince the legally-trained mind that such a condition exists. First one must overcome the general skepticism that is a product of legal thinking. Nothing is true unless it can be proved

---

damage, epilepsy, retardation and psychosis).

56. Thompson, *Legal Aspects of Pathological Intoxication (Alcoholic Insanity)*, 2 J. SOC. THEORY 182, 184 (1956).

57. Thompson at 187.

> legally. Medicine must provide objective evidence for what it knows to be true clinically.
>
> Gradually medicine has provided the objective evidence that the law has required. Pathological alcoholic intoxication is now a legal as well as a medical entity.[58]

After review of some of the earlier works of Marinacci, Thompson again stated his conception of the phenomenon of pathological intoxication.[59] He still stressed the small amount of alcohol which can trigger the reaction[60] and put considerable importance on the "high correlation between a history of previous brain injury and the later occurrence of pathological intoxication."[61] Summarizing one of Marinacci's studies, Thompson observed that

> Many similarities have been found in the electroencephalograms of these two groups of patients [psychomotor epilepsy and pathological intoxication]. Of these, the six-per-second pattern is found most frequently in both groups....This is the psychomotor-seizure pattern, and it occurs with a high degree of frequency also in cases of acute pathological intoxication.[62]

In his 1963 article,[63] Thompson provided additional case reports, and each of them involved a final trial court disposition in Los Angeles. In the first case report, a 33-year-old man had been treated in a state hospital having been diagnosed as "emotionally unstable" from alcohol consumption. He had a history of blackouts. There was no history of brain injury. On this occasion he drank several martinis at a hotel bar. His last recollection was of ringing door bells at rooms in the hotel and of the victim opening her door to him; she was a person he knew casually, a 78-year-old woman. He hit her and attempted to rape her. He remembered lying on the floor and walking down the stairs. During the attack, he also took money from her purse. "The resting electroencephalogram (before alcohol) showed occasional sharp waves coming from the left anterior temporal area. Following his ingestion of two ounces of alcohol many spikes and slow waves were seen coming from the left

---

58. Thompson at 182.

59. Thompson, *Acute and Chronic Alcoholic Conditions*, in 2 AMERICAN HANDBOOK OF PSYCHIATRY 1203, 1210 (S. Arieti ed. 1959).

60. Thompson at 1210, 1212 (two or three drinks in the first statement; five drinks in the latter case history).

61. Thompson at 1210.

62. Thompson at 1211.

63. Thompson, *The Electroencephalogram in Acute Pathological Alcoholic Intoxication*, 28 BULL. L.A. NEUROL. SOC. 217 (1963).

anterior temporal lead."[64] "[The case] illustrates abnormal pre-alcohol electroencephalogram and temporal lobe spiking with alcohol activation."[65] He was tried by a court and found legally insane at the time of the offense.

In another case report by Thompson, the 50-year-old defendant shot and killed his son-in-law and wounded his step-daughter in one incident. He had been cleaning his rifle before the shooting. He claimed alcohol had not been a problem but had four arrests for intoxication. At the time of the killing, he had consumed several beers and perhaps some small amount of whiskey. He had a history of severe head injury[66] and a previous concussion.

> The electroencephalographic examination revealed no abnormalities until alcohol activation was done. This showed isolated right frontal and temporal spikes and slow waves. The clinical diagnosis was chronic brain syndrome with mental impairment due to trauma and acute pathological alcoholic intoxication....He was considered legally insane at the time of the offense and mentally ill but legally sane at the time of the examination. His trial by jury resulted in a reduction of the charge of murder to a verdict of involuntary homicide and dismissal of the charge of assault with attempt to commit murder.[67]

MARINACCI

Thompson was obviously influenced by the work of Marinacci, which was first published in 1955, and he cited several of the cases Marinacci had reported, one of which follows:

> A 21-year-old newsboy drank two bottles of beer within a half-hour. Shortly afterward while driving his car he struck and killed a pedestrian. He stated he had no memory of driving for a distance of 200 feet before striking the victim. All studies of the patient were normal, including a routine

---

64. Thompson at 220.

65. Thompson at 219.

66. Consumption of alcohol by a person with a history of serious head injury is one of the most commonly encountered example of pathological intoxication. For still another example, *see* Glasgow, *The Anatomy of Automatism*, 64 N.Z. MED. J. 491, 493-94 (1965). *See also* Victor, *The Pathophysiology of Alcoholic Epilepsy*, 46 RES. NERV. MENT. DIS. 431 (1968) *and* Victor, *The Role of Alcohol in the Production of Seizures*, 4 MOD. PROBL. PHARMACOPSYCHIAT. 185 (1970).

67. Thompson at 223.

> electroencephalogram. A test electroencephalogram was taken after a twelve-ounce bottle of beer was administered. No abnormality appeared during a recording of twenty minutes. Then a second bottle of beer was given the patient and fifty-five minutes after the first drink a short petit-mal seizure discharge appeared. The patient had no clinical manifestations. In view of this electroencephalographic evidence the patient was placed on probation....[68]

These cases were selected from 60 adults,[69] aged 18 to 65, who were referred to the Los Angeles County Hospital, Department of Electroencephalography who

> were referred for electroencephalographic studies, when their clinical courses suggested this possibility, or when it was alleged that alcohol had been the cause of a temporary loss of consciousness, episodes of confusion, abnormal behavior, trance-like or fugue states, automatism, destructive rage, or even major convulsions. Some of these episodes were of legal significance because they had resulted in automobile accident, fatal stabbing or shooting, strangulation, sadistic murder, or some other antisocial behavior.[70]

The examination was designed to determine whether the patient was "suffering from an epileptic seizure or some other abnormal cerebral state which rendered him unconscious of his environment, making his acts automatic and without volition, depriving him of reason so that he was unaware of the wrongfulness of his acts and unable to comprehend the nature and the quality of his acts...."[71] The patients were given pre- and post-alcohol EEG's. The amount of alcohol varied from between 2 and 4 bottles of beer or 2 to 6 ounces of liquor. The same form of alcohol was used that evidently precipitated the problem in the first instance. In

---

68. Thompson, *Legal Aspects of Pathological Intoxication (Alcoholic Insanity)*, 2 J. SOC. THEORY 182, 185 (1956). This case is also reported in Marinacci, *The Electroencephalogram in Forensic Alcoholism*, 20 BULL. L.A. NEUROL. SOC. 177 (1955). Dr. Marinacci is identified as being from the Departments of Electroencephalography, at the Hospital of the Good Samaritan and the Los Angeles County Hospital and the University of Southern California School of Medicine.

69. Marinacci at 178-79.

70. Marinacci, *A Special Type of Temporal Lobe (Psychomotor) Seizures Following Ingestion of Alcohol*, 28 BULL. L.A. NEUROL. SOC. 241, 243 (1963). The statement of referral criteria is taken from a later report on this series of patients, but the report in the text at this point is from the 1955 report.

71. Marinacci, *The Electroencephalogram in Forensic Alcoholism*, 20 BULL. L.A. NEUROL. SOC. 177, 179 (1955).

33 of the 60 cases, the EEG remained normal. "Of the twelve patients who showed seizure discharges after administration of alcohol, only two patients had normal pre-alcoholic tracings. On the ten remaining patients a degree of abnormality or instability was definitely present."[72]

Here is one of the cases reported by Marinacci:

> A 29-year-old male had a normal history prior to a head injury which he had incurred while in the service in 1945. His record revealed that he had been unconscious for two days following the injury. Examination at that time revealed a bloody spinal fluid.
>
> Before his head injury the patient had been able to tolerate up to five highballs without ill effects. Following the injury, however, a moderate amount of alcohol induced abnormal behavior, which at the time went unrecognized for its true significance. This behavior took the form of belligerence, even to the point of insulting his superior officers. Following formal charges, the patient was court martialed, and subsequently discharged dishonorably from the service.
>
> In May 1951 after he had had a few drinks at a bar in downtown Los Angeles, the patient left and went a few doors down the street where he ordered a soft drink. Observers stated that he had a strange look in his eyes. Suddenly, he then drew a revolver which he fired four times; the fourth shot struck the proprietor in the leg....
>
> The patient stated that he found himself in custody about four hours later and at the time denied all knowledge of the incident....[An EEG examination was requested by the court.]
>
> The routine electroencephalographic tracing [reproduced in the article] showed normal activity. A tracing after ingestion of alcohol [also reproduced] was taken more or less continuously. Two ounces of whiskey were given every 30 minutes for a total of two doses. Ninety minutes after the first dose, a short seizure discharge of 4-7 c/s waves and single spikes appeared, most outstanding in the bitemporal area. Clinically, the patient was very much confused....[A]fter about an hour, his behavior returned to normal.[73]

In still another case,

72. Marinacci at 180.
73. Marinacci at 186-87.

> A 34-year-old male was a moderate social drinker and prior to the episode in question had suffered no ill effects from drinking. In March 1950, he was involved in an automobile accident and sustained an ecchymosis [bruise] of the right frontal area. There was a temporary loss of consciousness. Subsequently, he began to suffer severe headaches. In October 1950 following a highball, the patient experienced a period of confusion. In February 1951, he drank five highballs. That afternoon he found himself in custody of the police charged with manslaughter. It was noted that following the drinking bout (the patient claimed no memory of this interval) he had acted as though he was "loco." He began to shoot his gun aimlessly, and by accident one of the bullets fatally injured a passing pedestrian.
>
> The routine electroencephalogram [reproduced in the report] showed no diagnostic abnormality. The next day a natural sleep tracing likewise showed no seizure discharges. Following this two ounces of whiskey were given by mouth. The patient was encouraged to go to sleep, and no abnormality appeared in the tracing. Two more ounces of whiskey were given at the end of the 30 minutes. About 75 minutes after the first dose of whiskey, long runs of 4-6 c/s waves with positive spikes were recorded from the bitemporal areas, more so on the right. [The tracing is reproduced in the report.] As this activity was recorded, the patient started to move and the recording had to be terminated. The patient was confused and began to take off his clothes. He was disoriented and obviously out of contact with his surroundings. After one hour, his behavior returned to normal. The tracing showed seizure discharges in the bitemporal area, more so on the right, which were consistent with his psychomotor behavior.[74]

Hollender, a critic of the concept of pathological intoxication, will later claim with specific reference to this case that "the segment of the EEG reproduced to support this interpretation, however, was not convincing."[75] Hollender did not comment on the other five EEG's also reproduced in the study's report.[76]

---

74. Marinacci at 185-86.

75. Hollender, *Pathological Intoxication — Is There Such an Entity?* 32 J. CLIN. PSYCHIAT. 424 (1979).

76. Hollender evidently made reference only to the reporting of this case by Thompson, *Acute and Chronic Alcoholic Conditions*, in 2 AMERICAN HANDBOOK OF PSYCHIATRY 1211-12 (S. Arieti ed. 1959).

In 1963, Marinacci published the second report of his study of a larger number of these patients, relating temporal lobe (psychomotor) epilepsy to pathological intoxication via the EEG,[77] in which he stated the problem in these terms:

> During the attacks of a form of epilepsy designated as psychomotor, the victim acts automatically and does not remember what takes place. During an attack his behavior may become violent, resulting in destruction of property and injury to others, but he may not be aware of his loss of consciousness and that his actions are due to the ingestion of alcohol. The problem, therefore, is to determine whether the individual has actually experienced alcohol temporal lobe epilepsy.[78]

It was Marinacci's belief that when such outbursts of rage are actually psychomotor seizures triggered by alcohol, the actor is often labeled a drunkard and the correct diagnosis is missed. "These attacks are now called psychomotor seizures, and are synonymous with temporal lobe epilepsy."[79]

Marinacci now had studied 402 such adults, and this report stated that it included only those who had no electrical seizure discharges on the screening test. They were then given alcohol orally in quantities of about 2 to 4 drinks. "The same form and amount of alcoholic beverage was used which had presumably precipitated the abnormal state." If both of these statements are correct, it would mean that none of the patients referred, or studied, had actually consumed large amounts of alcohol or that a reaction was seen before the comparable amount was consumed. They were then administered post-alcohol EEG's.

---

77. Marinacci, *A Special Type of Temporal Lobe (Psychomotor) Seizures Following Ingestion of Alcohol,* 28 BULL. L.A. NEUROL. SOC. 241 (1963). His previous study is reported in Marinacci, *The Electroencephalogram in Forensic Alcoholism,* 20 BULL. L.A. NEUROL. SOC. 177 (1955), reprinted in G. THOMPSON, ALCOHOLISM (1956).

78. Marinacci, *A Special Type of Temporal Lobe (Psychomotor) Seizures Following Ingestion of Alcohol,* 28 BULL. L.A. NEUROL. SOC. 241 (1963).

79. Marinacci at 242.

The results may be summarized as follows:

402 patients/referrals
Post-alcohol EEG's and clinical observations:
347 (86%)—No abnormalities
55 (14%)—Anterior temporal lobe spiking
Clinical observations of the 55:
18—automatic (psychomotor) episodes (4.5% of sample)
21—mental confusion
16—no signs

Marinacci concluded that 18 patients of the 402 involved in the study (4.5%) "had definite alcoholic temporal lobe seizures. The confusion manifested by 21...patients could have been the result of intoxication."[80] Marinacci also provided more detailed summaries of pathological intoxication cases. Here is one of them.

> A 27-year-old male had been perfectly normal until the age of 23 years, when a craniocerebral injury resulted in a right temporal skull fracture and an associated period of unconsciousness. Subsequently, following the ingestion of even a minor amount of alcohol he became belligerent, confused, and destructive. On one occasion, the patient had two cocktails five minutes before he walked into a liquor store to purchase additional liquor. On being refused the sale of the liquor he went into a rage, and the salesman attempted to subdue him. The patient picked up a knife from the counter and stabbed the salesman several times. He was overcome by several bystanders before the police arrived. The salesman was dead on the arrival of the ambulance. An alcohol-activation electroencephalogram was requested by the public defender. The routine study...showed generalized instability and isolated short spikes in the right anterior temporal area (region of the skull fracture). Following alcohol-activation, profuse spikes were recorded in the right anterior temporal area with spreading to the right parietal and temporal areas....[81]

Marinacci, like Thompson and others,[82] emphasized that the EEG

---

80. Marinacci at 244.
81. Marinacci at 246-47.
82. Also in 1963, Walton described the same phenomenon as those reported by Thompson and Marinacci. Walton, *Some Observations on the Value of Electroencephalography in*

results must be integrated into the entire clinical picture[83] and he tried to establish diagnostic criteria:

> The following five criteria should be considered: (1) There should be a previous history of a lesion involving the temporal lobes. (2) There should be a history of previous psychomotor episodes following the ingestion of alcohol. (3) There must be no logical or specific motive (premeditation) for the crime. (4) The history must be suggestive of episodes of temporal lobe dysfunction, by amnesic episodes (sleep-walking, fugue states), psychomotor attacks, olfactory, gustatory, dreamy states, or visual and auditory hallucinations. (5) The alcohol-activation electroencephalogram must produce spike seizure discharges and appropriate associated clinical manifestations....[84]

Apparently not all of these are to be considered essential to establishing pathological reaction to alcohol since Thompson did not even consider the EEG to be essential. How, for example, does one prove a previous history of a lesion involving the frontal lobe? The existence of a brain lesion would become critical to the establishment of pathological reaction to alcohol in those cases in which the reaction results from psychomotor epilepsy. Those resulting from adult trauma seem to be the

---

Medico-Legal Practice, 31 MEDICO-LEGAL J. 15 (1963). He recounted a case of a man accused of murder who had no history of epilepsy or any other serious illness. The man claimed amnesia for the time of the killing. After ingesting alcohol to the point of "clinical signs of intoxication," the man's EEG, which had been normal to that point, "did suggest a distinct possibility that there was a focus of epileptic discharge in the left temporal lobe, though they were by no means diagnostic." Walton at 23:

> In comment upon this case, I would say that the only evidence in favour of a diagnosis of epilepsy was the EEG finding, and I would not personally have felt that this was sufficiently clear-cut for one to argue that this man had committed his crime in an epileptic attack. On the other hand, this case does approximate closely to [sic] that described by Hill, Sargant and Heppenstall (1943) and it seems clear that some kind of alteration in this man's physiological state occurred as a result of the ingestion of alcohol, which almost certainly diminished his responsibility for his actions and which was mirrored by a focal abnormality appearing in the EEG.

The reference is to Hill, Sargant & Heppenstall, *A Case of Matricide*, LANCET 526 (1943).

Walton is identified as "Neurologist, Newcastle General Hospital and Newcastle Regional Hospital Board; Physician in Neurology, Royal Victoria Infirmary, Newcastle upon Tyne.

83. Failure to do so no doubt accounts for part of the variability in assessing correlates of brain disease and abnormal brain waves elicited on the EEG. The point has also been made by V. MARK & F. ERVIN, VIOLENCE AND THE BRAIN 137 (1970).

84. Marinacci at 244.

easiest to prove,[85] but those associated with birth trauma are also common.[86] Evidently the existence of lesions was stressed in this statement of criteria only because that was the focus of the author's summary of prior research on this question; in one of his own later methods of classification, it was only one of four:

> This clinical picture [of "the alcoholic form of psychomotor seizures"[87]] has divided itself into groups as far as their etiology is concerned: (1) those developing from birth, (2) those incident to trauma to the head, usually contre-coup,[88] (3) those incident to variable lesions, and (4) an idiopathic[89] group.[90]

Marinacci also reported on one of the subjects who demonstrated both abnormal EEG and clinical signs of psychomotor (temporal lobe) epilepsy. The woman was 23 at the time of the study and at the age of 19 she had been hit in the head with a baseball bat and was unconscious for two days as a result. She had been charged with murder for beating her child to death. Marinacci concluded, as did the court, that the criteria were satisfied: "(1) there was a history of previous trauma, (2) there was evidence of psychomotor seizures following the ingestion of alcohol, (3) there was lack of motive for the crime, and (4) re-production of psychomotor seizures following the ingestion of alcohol for alcohol-activation electroencephalogram."[91] This summary only roughly tracks the five criteria set out earlier. For example, in this instance there was no direct proof of a lesion; that is a matter of inference from the EEG itself as well as the previously suffered head injury.[92]

---

85. Courville, *Traumatic Lesions of the Temporal Lobe as the Essential Cause of Psychomotor Epilepsy*, in TEMPORAL LOBE EPILEPSY (M. Baldwin & P. Bailey eds. 1958).

86. Malamud, *Psychiatric Disorder With Intracranial Tumors of Limbic System*, 17 ARCH. NEUROL. 113 (1967); Malamud, *Psychiatric Symptoms and the Limbic Lobe*, 22 BULL. L.A. SOC. NEUROL. PSYCHIAT. 131 (1957).

87. Marinacci & Von Hagen, *Alcohol and Temporal Lobe Dysfunction: Some of Its Psychomotor Equivalents*, 3 BEHAV. NEURO-PSYCHIAT. 2, 3 (1972).

88. A contrecoup injury is "an injury to parts of the brain located on the side opposite that of the primary injury, as when the frontal and temporal lobes of the brain are forced against the irregular bones of the anterior portion of the cranial vault as a result of a blow on the back of the head." TABER'S CYCLOPEDIC MEDICAL DICTIONARY 330-31 (C. Thomas ed. 14th ed. 1981).

89. Pertaining to a condition without clear pathogenesis, or a disease without a recognizable cause. TABER'S CYCLOPEDIC MEDICAL DICTIONARY 706 (C. Thomas ed. 14th ed. 1981).

90. Marinacci & Von Hagen at 3 (citations omitted).

91. Marinacci, *A Special Type of Temporal Lobe (Psychomotor) Seizures Following Ingestion of Alcohol*, 28 BULL. L.A. NEUROL. SOC. 241, 248-49 (1963).

92. Smith has provided some data on the frequency of serious head injuries: "One price of an increasingly mechanized society is the rising incidence of damage to the head....Figures from the United States, where such [road] accidents are the greatest cause of death and injury

Two cases reported by Marinacci and Von Hagen involved a female.[93] The overwhelming majority of cases of pathological reaction to alcohol, as claimed in court or as measured in the lab, have been of males, but much of the latter is due to sample selection. One source indicated that epilepsy of all sorts was slightly more common among males "probably because of the greater frequency of head trauma in the male both at birth and in adult life,"[94] but a later report[95] indicates an insignificant difference in temporal lobe epilepsy distribution by gender. In a study of 666 patients diagnosed as having features of temporal lobe epilepsy, 52.5 percent were females, and that figure held fairly constant through various age discriminations.[96]

Marinacci concluded:

> Predisposition to abnormal cerebral states appears to be involved in bringing [about?] temporal lobe seizures....Factors which may be responsible for stimulating or lowering the convulsive threshold include drugs, alcohol, toxic substances, emotional states, fatigue and other chemical and physiological factors. Pre-existing organic lesions especially, whether they be vascular, neoplastic, infectious, traumatic, or congenital, may serve as contributing elements. But even after all the above factors have been considered, it must be concluded that in some individual cases electrical temporal lobe seizure discharges are activated following the intake of alcohol which

---

to people under thirty-five, suggest that three-quarters of these accidents involve injuries to the head. The World Health Organization states that the head injury proportion varies between 50 per cent and 80 per cent in different countries (as against 10-40 per cent for chest injuries). What is not known is how much the brain has suffered in all this injury." A. SMITH, THE MIND 246 (1984). Smith also discusses war wounds, which appear regularly in the reported cases of pathological intoxication, Smith at 249-52, and boxing as a source of head injuries is discussed in Smith at 252-55.

Boxing as a source of head injury is not mentioned in the literature as much as we would expect, but then there are a lot fewer boxers than, for example, drivers and passengers in automobile crashes. *See, e.g.*, Perr, *Pathological Intoxication and Alcohol Idiosyncratic Intoxication—Part II: Legal Aspects,* 31 J. FOR. SCI. 812, 813 (1986); Bach-y-Rita, Lion, Climent & Ervin, *Episodic Dyscontrol: A Study of 130 Violent Patients,* 127 AM. J. PSYCHIAT. 11, 12 (1971). Data is also provided in Yudofsky & Silver, *Psychiatric Aspects of Brain Injury: Trauma, Stroke and Tumor,* 4 PSYCHIATRY UPDATE 142 (1985), discussed in more detail in Chapter 5, *infra.*

93. In the other reported case involving a female, the incident involved a person with a history of head injury who had a visual hallucination causing her to swerve her car, killing a passenger. Marinacci & Von Hagen at 10.

94. L. KOLB, NOYES' MODERN CLINICAL PSYCHIATRY 262 (7th ed. 1968).

95. Currie, Heathfield, Henson & Scott, *Clinical Course and Prognosis of Temporal Lobe Epilepsy,* 94 BRAIN 173, 175 (1971).

96. Currie, Heathfield, Henson & Scott at 176.

> can be considered a special type of temporal lobe (psychomotor) seizures.[97]

Thus, pathological reaction to alcohol is thought to be, at least in major part, a manifestation of psychomotor epilepsy released by alcohol in persons predisposed to such seizures. A person may drink to intoxication on one occasion yet on another suffer pathological intoxication. In some patients with temporal lobe dysfunction or psychomotor epilepsy, alcohol may precipitate a mild psychomotor seizure or release latent hostile paranoid behavior. The amount of alcohol required varies.

In their 1972 article, Marinacci and Von Hagen reviewed some of the research related to brain lesions as one cause of temporal lobe epilepsy (now also temporal lobe dysfunction).[98] They noted that:

> often-times, only a small amount of alcoholic beverage may definitely and distinctly alter the clinical picture of the seizures so as to thrust a medicolegal and a quasi-criminal element into a problem already complex. This problem has been simplified by the use of an alcohol activated electroencephalogram. It has been in continuous use by the writer since 1948.[99]

The authors note that much of the prior research seemed to overlook the role played by alcohol:

> Among the numerous investigators who have dealt with the problem of psychomotor attacks, occasional mention has been made that in some cases the attacks seem to be precipitated by indulgence in alcohol. In these cases, the influence of alcohol in precipitating the attack, or that such seizures presented any unusual features, especially those leading to legal complications, seems to have escaped the notice of such writers.[100]

As we analyze the chronological development in these areas, it may not be overly simplistic to observe that what essentially appears to have occurred is that those studying pathological intoxication have been led back through the obvious involvement of alcohol in search of underlying causes such as psychomotor epilepsy in which attacks are both triggered

---

97. Marinacci, *A Special Type of Temporal Lobe (Psychomotor) Seizures Following Ingestion of Alcohol*, 28 BULL. L.A. NEUROL. SOC. 241, 249 (1963).

98. Marinacci & Von Hagen, *Alcohol and Temporal Lobe Dysfunction: Some of Its Psychomotor Equivalents*, 3 BEHAV. NEURO-PSYCHIAT. 2 (1972).

99. Marinacci & Von Hagen at 3.

100. Marinacci & Von Hagen at 4.

and perhaps worsened by alcohol use, and those researchers who have focused on psychomotor epilepsy have often simply missed the effects of alcohol on the disease they studied. This point is made clear in later material dealing directly with psychomotor epilepsy.

In the cumulative forensic experience of Marinacci and Von Hagen, of the 800 persons or so they have examined who were accused of antisocial acts associated with alcohol, about 13 percent showed abnormal EEG's induced by one ounce of alcohol taken every fifteen minutes until a maximum of four ounces was consumed.[101]

In the Marinacci and Von Hagen report, the authors note that "The amount of alcohol required to produce such behavior is quite variable and only a very small amount is necessary *in some patients*."[102] In one of the case histories given, the amount consumed before the shooting of his victim was 12 to 15 Scotch and sodas.[103] The alcohol activation test showed "that alcoholic drinks produced a definite left temporal lobe dysfunction."[104] The defendant had amnesia for the period of most of the drinking and the killing, had a history of a serious head injury inflicted at birth and had previously experienced auditory and visual hallucinations. He had more or less consistently been violent when drinking, and it was the belief of the authors that his conviction rested on the fact that the "jury felt that the patient was aware of the fact that alcoholic drinks produced an abnormal brain function and that he had knowledge of his low threshold for alcohol."[105]

The link between pathological intoxication and head injury, particularly damage to the temporal lobe, has been mentioned by numerous writers and researchers. Mark and Ervin discuss the point:

> Head injuries in growing children, adolescents, and adults are very likely to damage the undersurface of the frontal lobe and the tips of the temporal lobe—in other words, those parts of the limbic brain that lie closest to the bones of the skull. Normally, brain and bones are separated from each other by a cushion of fluid and a tough membrane. But if the head is struck hard enough, or if the body suddenly hits the ground with some force, the frontal and temporal lobes may be jarred against the base of the skull. The resulting damage to the brain stem is indicated by the loss of consciousness. It often

---

101. Marinacci & Von Hagen at 11.

102. Marinacci & Von Hagen at 11 (emphasis added). Earlier in the same article the authors said: "It should be mentioned that the severity of the attack is not always dependent upon the amount of alcohol taken on that occasion." Marinacci & Von Hagen at 6.

103. Marinacci & Von Hagen at 7.

104. Marinacci & Von Hagen at 7.

105. Marinacci & Von Hagen at 7.

> happens, however, that when the brain stem recovers and consciousness returns, the injured person undergoes a period of uninhibited, aggressive, and combative behavior. Most severe head injuries produce fairly widespread damage, so that it is difficult to ascribe altered behavior to the dysfunction of a certain brain area, but studies of patients with injuries known to involve chiefly the temporal lobe indicate that these patients tend to be inappropriately combative—that is, they show the effects of limbic dysfunction.[106]

The authors also discuss viral infections,[107] brain tumors[108] and similarly associated brain damage with the possible development of violent conduct.[109]

The amount of alcohol administered in this clinical study by Marinacci and Von Hagen was described as 100 ml of 45 percent alcohol in three to five minutes (on an empty stomach). That is 3.2 ounces of alcohol of about the strength of whiskey, or about two drinks. In the Maletzky study, discussed later, much more alcohol was needed to provoke pathological reaction to alcohol. That preoccupation with small amounts of alcohol, possibly induced by careless descriptions of pathological reaction to alcohol in many texts, may in part explain the negative results in the next study summarized. But we know that small amounts are often enough:

> A 27-year-old Negro male suffered a head injury in Vietnam in 1965 as the result of a helicopter crash. He was unconscious for an unknown length of time, regaining consciousness in a military hospital. While still a hospital patient he went on leave to Saigon. While there, he became intoxicated and thereafter became belligerent and argumentative so that he was taken into custody by the military police. While in jail he became destructive for which he claimed amnesia. He was returned to the hospital for further medical care. Five months

---

106. V. MARK & F. ERVIN, VIOLENCE AND THE BRAIN 57 (1970). *See also* R. MCNICHOL, THE TREATMENT OF DELIRIUM TREMENS AND RELATED STATES 76 (1970) ("Most patients suffering from this condition have a background of serious head injury, with or without convulsions or temporal lobe epilepsy."). The relationship between head injury, "brain damage" and the EEG is considered in the context of the expert witness in Hughes, *The Medicolegal EEG,* in EEG AND EVOKED POTENTIAL IN PSYCHIATRY AND BEHAVIORAL NEUROLOGY 361, 365-67 (J. Hughes & W. Wilson eds. 1983).

107. Mark & Ervin at 57-58.

108. Mark & Ervin at 58-59.

109. Encephalitis has also been mentioned as implicated along with head injury. Cohen, *Pathological Intoxication,* 10 DRUG ABUSE NEWSLETTER 1 (1981), reprinted in S. COHEN, THE ALCOHOLISM PROBLEMS: SELECTED ISSUES (1983).

> after the injury, he began to notice episodes of a foul odor. At first it was faint but increased in intensity. With this odor he also began having hallucinations of an unpleasant sense of taste which began with a smacking of his lips. These episodes of disagreeable odors and tastes were rather short, lasting only a few seconds at a time. On other occasions he would experience a "dreamy state" where unfamiliar faces appeared to be in the middle of a burst of flames. The patient was returned to the States and finally received a medical discharge from the Army. Prior to going to Vietnam he married a woman with three children by a previous marriage, and with whom he had one child, now two years old. While intoxicated he became very abusive toward his wife and all four children. On one occasion he was ejected from his home by his wife who became frightened by his behavior. He then walked down the street, and apparently while having a psychomotor seizure, started a fight with some acquaintances. He was struck on the head with a piece of lumber but was able to stagger toward a gas station where he bought a gallon of gasoline. It was alleged that he took the gasoline to his home and threw it over the four children asleep in bed. He then set fire to the bedclothes, causing the death of all four children. When the police arrived, they found the man in a confused state and because of his crime, [he] was taken into custody. After recovering from his state of intoxication, he claimed amnesia for the entire episode, having no recollection of anything that took place after he became intoxicated until he found himself in jail.
>
> The Court appointed a team of medical examiners, including a psychiatrist, who requested an alcohol activated electroencephalogram. The routine electroencephalogram was found to be normal, but after alcohol activation (2 oz), the tracing showed spikes and slow wave activity in both anterior and mid-temporal regions. As the result of these findings of a temporal lobe dysfunction, the patient was committed to an institution for the criminally insane.[110]

The occurrence of olfactory, gustatory and auditory hallucinations or aurae as well as the lip-smacking are all associated with temporal lobe epilepsy as, of course, is head injury. It should also be noted that the alcohol activation test involved only two ounces of alcohol and although

---

110. Marinacci & Von Hagen, *Alcohol and Temporal Lobe Dysfunction: Some of Its Psychomotor Equivalents*, 3 BEHAV. NEURO-PSYCHIAT. 2, 8 (1972).

it did not trigger a violent reaction, that is the point of undertaking this type of examination.

Fear is also a common feature of pathological reaction to alcohol, and this has been described by a number of writers. One of the case studies reported by Marinacci and Van Hagen accented the prominence of this, and the case also illustrates the influence of witnesses who can verify the actor's state of automatism at the time of the offense to clearly link his conduct to his disease.

> A 34-year-old man, an officer of the law, was involved in an automobile accident in March 1950 and sustained an ecchymosis of the right frontal area....
>
> Prior to the accident, he had been able to consume two or three highballs without ill effects. Following the accident he not only developed a severe headache when drinking but could not tolerate alcohol as before, becoming confused, argumentative, and somewhat hostile. [On several subsequent occasions he suffered minor episodes of confusion and hostility.]....
>
> Finally, at 10:30 one morning in February 1951, he went into a bar and had five highballs in rapid succession. While at the bar, he imagined the place to be full of enemies, all with the intention of harming him. He called the F.B.I. on the phone and reported the place to be over-run with spies. He became aggressive and using his revolver, tried to herd the people to one end of the room, firing two shots in the process. One shot went wild, the other fatally injuring a passing pedestrian. He found himself in custody charged with murder by 3:00 that afternoon. The patient claimed amnesia for the period beginning at about 10:30 that morning until 3:00 that afternoon. An officer, on interviewing the people at the bar, found that most all agreed that the man was more crazed than drunk, was out of contact with his surroundings and had a glassy stare. The main symptom was his great fear and hostility.
>
> Prior to the trial, the judge appointed a board of medical examiners to evaluate the prisoner, and an alcohol activated electroencephalogram was ordered. The routine electroencephalogram was normal, but after the administration of 3 ounces of alcohol, seizure discharges originated from both anterior and mid-temporal areas. The seizure discharges consisted of paroxysmal theta and spike activity....
>
> The Medical Board concluded that the patient, while in the line of duty, sustained brain damage to the temporal lobes as demonstrated by the electroencephalogram which showed

> psychomotor seizures. These seizures were apparently precipitated by the alcoholic drinks....The patient was placed on probation,[111] and followed with routine electroencephalograms at six-month intervals for twelve years. During this period he abstained from alcoholic beverages and there were no recurrences of abnormal behavior.[112]

By the time of the publication of these case studies, the criteria for diagnosis of "temporal lobe dysfunction syndrome" were reduced to three: "(1) there should be a history of a lesion, usually traumatic, which may involve one of the temporal lobes, (2) there should be a history of typical psychomotor episodes following the ingestion of alcohol and (3) the ingestion of alcohol should activate temporal lobe seizure discharges in the electroencephalogram."[113]

Marinacci and Von Hagen also draw a factual distinction that will become the critical legal point in court once pathological intoxication becomes more fully understood:

> In examining approximately 800 of these [temporal lobe dysfunction] cases for the courts, it has been our observation that the judges and juries are lenient to the first offenders who claim that alcohol altered their consciousness which resulted in the antisocial act or alleged crime. However, judges as well as the Courts [sic, juries?] do feel that many chronic offenders have knowledge that alcohol has a bad effect on their mental behavior. Therefore, they are looked upon as dangerous to society. Alcoholic drinks to these individuals are equivalent to a loaded gun. It is apparent that many of them know the bad effect alcohol has on their behavior, but nevertheless take a chance in the hope of getting by with it, until a criminal act ensues.[114]

ZAKOWSKA-DABROWSKA AND STRZYZEWSKI

Zakowska-Dabrowska and Strzyzewski[115] reviewed the previous

---

111. *But see* A. BENNETT, ALCOHOLISM AND THE BRAIN 31 (1977), where the author summarized Marinacci's results and indicated they were confirmed by his own work, but he also said that his experience demonstrated that juries are not prone to believe such testimony. However, he gave no indication whether the murder cases he mentioned involved defendants who were previously aware of the existence of a serious problem with alcohol. *See also* Bennett, *Mental Disorders With Temporal Lobe Epilepsy*, 26 DIS. NERV. SYST. 275 (1965).

112. Marinacci & Van Hagen at 8-9.

113. Marinacci & Van Hagen at 11.

114. Marinacci & Van Hagen at 10.

115. Zakowska-Dabrowska & Strzyzewski, *Value of Experimental Administration of*

attempts to induce pathological reaction to alcohol. "The interest in experimental administration of alcohol grew with the development of electroencephalography. For example, 60% of the cases of so-called pathological intoxication studied by Hoff and cited in this study showed irregularities on the routine EEG recording.[116] Under the influence of alcohol administered by mouth, the percentage of these irregularities increased to 75%." As the researchers note, it was this approach that strengthened the connection between pathological intoxication and epilepsy.[117]

> Marinacci and coworkers stressed the importance of alcohol activation in cases in which pathological intoxication is suspected. After administration of alcohol, in 12 cases out of 60, Marinacci found bioelectrical discharges typical of epileptic attacks. At the same time, 7 of the individuals showed during the test such clinical symptoms as convulsions, automatism or significant impairment of consciousness. Whenever such epilepsy-like discharges are produced on the EEG after the administration of alcohol, "the doctor is justified in expressing the opinion that alcohol was the factor responsible for the impairment of consciousness" concluded Marinacci.[118]

The authors point out that Bonhoeffer[119] was skeptical of this approach because many other factors contribute to a pathological reaction to alcohol; thus it is not certain that "alcohol administered under experimental conditions could bring about a pathological reaction." This is a valid concern only to a point: It merely means that the absence of a reaction will not prove the negative proposition. All subsequent researchers have recognized this point. The authors cite another study in which the point is also made. In that study, in only four cases of

---

Alcohol in the Diagnosis of So-Called Pathological Intoxication, 3 PSYCHIAT. POLSK. 565 (1969). We rely here in part on a translation we commissioned of this article.

116. Zakowska-Dabrowska & Strzyzewski at 565, citing Hoff, 36 Medizimisches Klinik 1425 (1954).

117. G. THOMPSON, ALCOHOLISM (1956); Thompson, *The Electroencephalogram in Acute Pathological Alcoholic Intoxication,* 28 BULL. L.A. NEUROL. SOC. 217 (1963). *See also* Thompson, *Acute and Chronic Alcoholic Conditions,* in 2 AMERICAN HANDBOOK OF PSYCHIATRY 1203 (S. Arieti ed. 1959).

118. Zakowska-Dabrowska & Strzyzewski at 565-66, citing, inter alia, Marinacci, *A Special Type of Temporal Lobe (Psychomotor) Seizures Following Ingestion of Alcohol,* 28 BULL. L.A. NEUROL. SOC. 241 (1963). The data, however, are from Marinacci's earlier sample. His 1963 report involved 402 subjects. It is not clear why the earlier, smaller sample is the only one reported on in the summary of prior studies.

119. Bonhoeffer, 6 Deutsche Klinik 540 (1906). Other work by this author is also discussed in Chapter 2.

pathological intoxication was she able to detect "changes in the bioelectrical activity of the brain."[120]

In the Zakowska-Dabrowska & Strzyzewski study, the subjects were 63 males aged 18 to 60, all referred to the clinic in Poznan for a court-ordered examination, having committed criminal acts while intoxicated. Preliminary examinations and psychological tests revealed that 46 of the 63 subjects showed symptoms of organic damage to the central nervous system, an extraordinary 73 percent. Based on clinical observations, the manner of committing the crimes involved and the condition of the accused at the time of the crime, they were placed in three subclasses defined as (1) pathological intoxication (evidently partly on the basis of reported blackouts[121]) (n=6), (2) atypical intoxication "due to organic factors" (n=5) and (3) simple intoxication (n=52). Prior to the administration of alcohol, 11 of the 52 given the EEG test from the normal intoxication group showed clearly abnormal EEG's,[122] but none from the other two categories did so.

Alcohol intake was described as follows: "[I]n the course of 3-5 min., the individuals drank, on empty stomachs, 100 ml of 45% alcohol." Forty-five minutes later, the EEG's were administered. "Following alcohol intake, the [total] number of EEG's showing pathological bioelectrical activity increased to 34. Thus, the administration of alcohol by mouth led in 23 cases to the detection of pathological traits that did not show up on the preliminary EEG records." However, "in this number, patients from all three subcategories were represented." Of the original six who were classified as "so-called pathological intoxication" cases, none showed pre-administration of alcohol EEG abnormalities but five showed such abnormalities post-alcohol administration. In the simple intoxication group of 52 subjects, 11 showed pre-administration irregularities and 26 showed post-administration irregularities. None were of "paroxysmal character." Only slight intoxication was shown by any of the subjects.

In the form originally reported, the researchers concluded that the appearance of increased abnormal EEG was not statistically significant in the differences manifested as between the original three groups. Since "abnormalities of this type often appear on EEG records obtained with a 10-20 electrode system...no significant diagnostic conclusions should be

---

120. Zakowska-Dabrowska & Strzyzewski at 566, citing Fleszar-Szumigajowa, 13 Psychiatria Sad i Kryminat (Archives of Court [Forensic] Medicine) 23 (1961).

121. "Blackout" is used in a number of research reports and cases but may be used in two different ways, and the sense intended is not always made clear. "Blackout" refers to amnesia not associated with a loss of consciousness, but the term is also often used in connection with automatism, which involves not only amnesia but loss of conscious control as well.

122. The authors describe the EEG test as "An 8 channel apparatus of East German make....It had a 10-20 electrode system employing standard surface (skin) and deep (needle) lead-offs."

drawn from them."[123] "[T]he usefulness of this [alcohol activation EEG test] method in determining the nature of alcoholic intoxication at the time of crime is doubtful. This conclusion disagrees with those of other authors."[124]

The difficulty of drawing conclusions from this study derives from the groups compared: Two of the three groups combined, the important two for our purposes, contained only 11 people, 6 in one and 5 in the other. We would doubt that statistically significant results could be expected with numbers of that size.

That problem is independent of the questions raised regarding the initial classification which differentiated these two groups from each other and both from the group consisting of simple intoxication cases. Even more problematic is the number of the subjects showing symptoms of organic damage to the central nervous system. Like so many of these studies, one always wishes more information had been provided. Notably missing here and in the work by Morozov,[125] for example, is a description of the crimes for which the men had been arrested. Were they crimes of violence? Were they obviously motivated or apparently "senseless"? Did the men show signs of obvious intoxication at the time of the offenses? How exactly was the subclass of pathological intoxication created? What selection criteria led to the clinical referral in the first place that resulted in such an abnormal group as measured by the incidence of central nervous system damage (73% of the entire sample)?

Pathological reaction to alcohol is not an ordinary or common event, from all that can be gleaned from the literature. We would suppose that the chances of provoking it in a true case are problematical, and the chances go down dramatically with tests run on doubtful cases, to begin with. For example, in another reported case in the Zakowska-Dabrowska & Strzyzewski study, a person had been accused in a criminal case of committing homosexual acts (while intoxicated), and a clinical test was undertaken. While intoxicated, the accused made overtures toward his male nurse, and the researcher, at least, took this as conclusive proof that

---

123. Zakowska-Dabrowska & Strzyzewski at 568.

124. Zakowska-Dabrowska & Strzyzewski at 568 (footnotes omitted). Some of the cited works are 2 AMERICAN HANDBOOK OF PSYCHIATRY (S. Arieti ed. 1959) [this is probably a citation to Thompson, *Acute and Chronic Alcoholic Conditions,* found in that volume]; Marinacci, in G. THOMPSON, ALCOHOLISM (1956); Marinacci, *A Special Type of Temporal Lobe (Psychomotor) Seizures Following Ingestion of Alcohol,* 28 BULL. L.A. NEUROL. SOC. 241 (1963); Thompson, *The Electroencephalogram in Acute Pathological Alcoholic Intoxication,* 28 BULL. L.A. NEUROL. SOC. 217 (1963); G. THOMPSON, ALCOHOLISM (1956).

125. Morozov, Kachayev & Lukacher, *Characteristics of Forensic Psychiatric Examination of Pathological and Simple Alcohol Intoxication,* 17 SUDEBNO-MEDITSINSKAIA EKSPERTIZA 51 (April-June 1974).

he had indeed committed the offenses charged.[126] Pathological reaction to alcohol is a bit more elusive.

BACH-Y-RITA, ET AL.

Bach-y-Rita, Lion and Ervin[127] suggested the propositions they were trying to test:

> The clinical histories of several Massachusetts General Hospital patients with symptoms of pathological intoxication prompted us to investigate whether the outbursts were primarily due to alcohol, to induced seizures, to a reaction to emotionally stressful situations, or, more realistically, to the way in which these complex factors interacted.[128]

Only ten male patients, aged 25 to 35, were selected. Each had previously entered the psychiatric emergency room with a complaint of violence under the influence of alcohol, and all had thereafter been diagnosed as cases of pathological intoxication. Unfortunately, the authors provide little in the way of describing why they had been so diagnosed. Violence and alcohol are indicated as was previous experience involving visual hallucinations.

Effort was made to place the men in a relaxed setting where they were intravenously administered 150 to 300 cc of a 25-percent solution of ethanol. They were not told that alcohol was being infused, and interestingly, only one became subjectively aware that alcohol was involved. Two other patients were also involved in the experiment, each with a history of temporal lobe seizures and each with temporal lobe depth electrodes previously surgically implanted in the amygdaloid region, which were used in the experiment.

---

126. As reported in Zakowska-Dabrowska & Strzyzewski, *Value of Experimental Administration of Alcohol in the Diagnosis of So-Called Pathological Intoxication*, 3 PSYCHIAT. POLSK. 565 (1969).

127. Bach-y-Rita, Lion & Ervin, *Pathological Intoxication; Clinical and Electroencephalographic Studies*, 127 AM. J. PSYCHIAT. 698 (1970):

> At the time this paper was written Drs. Bach-y-Rita and Lion were research fellows in psychiatry, Harvard Medical School...and clinical research fellows and acting assistant residents in psychiatry, Massachusetts General Hospital....- Dr. Bach-y-Rita is currently director of inpatient services, Marin Community Mental Health Center...San Rafael, Calif. Dr. Lion is staff psychiatrist, department of neuropsychiatry, U.S. Naval Hospital, Philadelphia, Pa.; and Dr. Ervin is associate clinical professor in psychiatry, Harvard Medical School and psychiatrist, Massachusetts General Hospital.

128. Bach-y-Rita, Lion & Ervin at 699.

Both of these latter two patients showed an increase in abnormal EEG activity after administration of the alcohol. But the ten men previously diagnosed as having suffered an attack of pathological intoxication showed no abnormality in their EEG's and no "behavior arousal,"[129] although all showed the usual signs of intoxication such as slurred speech and other incoordination. In short, no seizures were initiated. The researchers were inclined to believe that the absence of any reaction was attributable to the calm environment they created and that this difference served to distinguish earlier research which had found a reaction, such as the study done by Marinacci.[130] The authors evaluated that study:

> Marinacci gave various types of beverages to 402 patients. Fifty-five showed anterior temporal lobe spiking on their electroencephalograms (EEG's) during alcohol administration, and 18 [of the 55] showed concomitant changes in mental status that the author described as "psychomotor episodes."-...No attempt was made to control for other variables that might contribute to producing a seizure—e.g., the social setting (presence of physicians or technicians) in the lab....[131]

In differentiating the lack of abnormal response in their sample compared to the responses detected in the earlier study, the authors stated while "our results appear contradictory to those of Marinacci, [this] is not a necessary interpretation" because "emotion can play [a role] in triggering temporal lobe seizures, and it appears that these two factors (alcohol and affect) combined (as may have occurred in Marinacci's experiments) can provoke a seizure."[132] In further explaining his interpretation of the etiology of pathological intoxication, Bach-y-Rita said:

> For a patient to experience this syndrome, factors other than a few drinks are necessary. This is one of the points we made in our paper. The observation that several factors must converge to elicit the syndrome means that a patient may, on one occasion, ingest alcohol to the point of acute alcoholic intoxication and, on another, suffer pathological intoxication after the ingestion of a minimal quantity of alcohol.[133]

---

129. Bach-y-Rita, Lion & Ervin at 700.

130. Marinacci, *A Special Type of Temporal Lobe (Psychomotor) Seizures Following Ingestion of Alcohol*, 28 BULL. L.A. NEUROL. SOC. 241 (1963).

131. Bach-y-Rita, Lion & Ervin at 698 (citations omitted).

132. Bach-y-Rita, Lion & Ervin at 702.

133. Bach-y-Rita, in a letter to the editor, 128 Am. J. Psychiat. 660-61 (1971).

To further the judgment that it was the absence of anxiety in the testing situation that differentiated their EEG results from Marinacci's, the authors pointed out that

> We noticed, however, that many of the pathological intoxication episodes occurred when these patients were in situations that could be interpreted as threats to their sexual identity. One man, for example, would get into a fight in a bar whenever someone referred to him as a "queer"; another purposely struck up friendships with homosexuals in taverns but would become assaultive when intimacies reached a peak. It is interesting that such patients drank in those public places where they were most likely to encounter homosexuals and persisted in this behavior while vehemently upholding their own identities as "men." It appeared that increased ambivalent homosexual strivings triggered panic states that took the form of assaultive behavior in these individuals.[134]

It would appear that a rather expansive definition of pathological intoxication was used to identify these men in the first place as having suffered an attack of pathological reaction to alcohol. As we noted at the outset, it would be useful if more data were provided on what led to the selection of the sample studied. Repeated occurrences of the same violent reaction to what the actor consciously perceived as provocation does not qualify as "motiveless" violence.

The amount of alcohol used in the Bach-y-Rita, Lion and Ervin study translates roughly into three or four drinks. But we would suspect not the small amount of alcohol as the reason for the failure to find any effect, but the small sample size, and most importantly, the criteria by which the small sample of ten men were selected in the first place: The two case histories described simply do not appear to us to have involved pathological reaction to alcohol cases, to begin with. Furthermore, in Marinacci's largest sample, reactions were clearly detected in only 18 of 402 cases, or 4.5 percent. The sample in this study was only ten. The role of affect in triggering a pathological reaction to alcohol is an interesting thesis, but we do not believe this study could shed any light on it at all.

To digress a moment on one point: A case study reported in 1970[135] by Skelton illustrates the variability from subject to subject in the amount of alcohol sufficient to trigger a reaction. In this case in a motiveless killing, the defendant shot his friend at the end of considerable drinking for a good part of the day. The first clinical observation was

---

134. Bach-y-Rita, Lion & Ervin at 701.

135. Skelton, *Alcohol, Violent Behavior, and the Electroencephalogram*, 63 S. MED. J. 465 (1970).

made after ingestion orally of six ounces of 95 percent ethyl alcohol (perhaps nine or ten drinks). The EEG was normal. In a second test with the same amount of alcohol, the EEG was abnormal when it was traced at the same time as abnormal behavioral changes that occurred.[136] Skelton noted that "increasingly such episodes are considered to be instances of psychomotor epilepsy released by alcohol in persons predisposed to such seizures."[137] He noted that his findings were consistent with "the impression of a seizure disorder released by alcohol."[138]

The following year, Bach-y-Rita, Lion, Climent and Ervin reported on another study which involved 130 patients with complaints relating to assaultive or destructive behavior.[139] Their primary point was that neither psychiatric nor neurological approaches should be used exclusively for diagnosis or management but that both were needed. The authors classified their patients by chief complaint. Seven of the 130 came in with a diagnosis of temporal lobe epilepsy, 30 had seizure-like outbursts and 25 were classified as meriting "the diagnosis of pathological intoxication."[140] Later interviews with 50 of the 130 turned up 29 instances of possible prior brain insult or epilepsy, and 79 received EEG examinations with 37 showing abnormalities. Thirteen of 123 patients had undiagnosed temporal lobe epilepsy. They also noted that if "seizure occurred in the depth of the temporal lobe, the abnormal activity was usually not visible at surface recording sites. This would imply that some temporal lobe epileptics are read as normals on the clinical EEG report."[141] Specific figures were not given as to how many of the pathological intoxication patients were also psychomotor epilepsy cases. No alcohol activation tests were reported.

It might be useful here to underscore one point made by these researchers: Emotional factors may well play a role in the triggering of pathological reaction to alcohol. Several of the early writers refer to this factor, and one suspects, albeit at something of an intuitive level, that the matter is not so simple as the equation: Alcohol plus brain injury always equals pathological intoxication.

> Human behavior, violent or peaceful, is always the product of *brain-environment* interaction. Neither of these two influences can solely determine behavior; but many sociologists and

---

136. Skelton at 466.

137. Skelton at 465.

138. Skelton at 466.

139. Bach-y-Rita, Lion, Climent, & Ervin, *Episodic Dyscontrol: A Study of 130 Violent Patients*, 127 AM. J. PSYCHIAT. 1473 (1971). The additional researcher, Climent, was a Clinical Fellow and Chief Resident in Psychiatry, Boston City Hospital.

140. Bach-y-Rita, Lion, Climent & Ervin at 1475.

141. Bach-y-Rita, Lion, Climent & Ervin at 1476.

> some neurologists talk and act as if this were so. This dualistic view, which states that behavior is generated *either* by the environment *or* by the brain, impedes any rational approach to the understanding and treatment of violent individuals.[142]

It is this dichotomous thinking that is counter-intuitive and objectionable. Simple two-way interaction is not very probable. As Mark and Ervin asserted, "Our past environment, once it is past, is no longer a sociological phenomenon. It is imbedded in our brain and its use is dependent on the function or malfunction of the cerebral tissue."[143] Thus, one would not be surprised to find when all the findings are finally in on pathological intoxication that emotions triggered by past or present (mis)perceptions (as, for example, of threats to self) play a role.

The authors similarly conclude:

> Violence was then viewed as a symptom not solely psychogenic in origin or due to brain dysfunction or a product of social disorganization, but as resulting from the interplay of all three factors. Within this context, our practice of diagnosis and therapy has not always been consistent. In some cases we have been content with a psychodynamic explanation of the patient's violent behavior, while in others we have assumed that brain dysfunction has played the major role. In still others, as just mentioned, there was evidence of both.[144]

MALETZKY

Based on the work summarized here, Maletzky suggested this definition of pathological intoxication: "[a]n acute brain syndrome manifested by psychotic behavior after alcohol intake, and characterized by delusions, hallucinations, disorientation with or without inappropriate expressions of rage, prolonged sleep following the episode, and amnesia for the episode thereafter."[145]

Maletzky studied "[s]ubjects with a history of violent or psychotic behavior while under the influence of alcohol"[146] who were given a 25-percent alcohol solution. Maletzky concluded: "Based on electroencepha-

---

142. V. MARK & F. ERVIN, VIOLENCE AND THE BRAIN 138 (1970) (emphasis in original).

143. Mark & Ervin at 141 (emphasis omitted).

144. Bach-y-Rita, Lion, Climent & Ervin at 1474.

145. Maletzky, *The Diagnosis of Pathological Intoxication*, 37 QRTLY J. STUD. ALCOH. 1215, 1227 (1976).

146. Maletzky at 1215.

lograms, blood alcohol concentrations and behavioral observations, the results confirm the probable existence of a discrete syndrome of pathological reaction to alcohol without reference to the amount of alcohol consumed."[147]

The population from which the actual sample derived consisted of persons who had a history of either violent or bizarre behavior while under the influence of alcohol. Twenty-two patients were selected from that pool using the following criteria: (a) more than one episode of violent or bizarre behavior under the influence of alcohol; (b) the absence of such behavior when sober; (c) amnesia for the prior episodes; and (d) the *absence* of neurological disorder based on either history, neurological examination and EEG, i.e., pre-infusion EEG's had to be normal or they were excluded from the study. Two persons were excluded with abnormal EEG's in an attempt to exclude those who might trigger an epilepsy-alcohol reaction, but it was not clear that a surface EEG was capable of completely accomplishing that exclusion.

The 22 patients were predominately white (20) and all male. Marital status varied (15 married). Mean age was 26.1. In non-exclusive categories, they were further described as follows:

> All viewed their [prior] episodes as foreign and distasteful. Nonetheless, 6 had a history of alcohol addiction as defined by the National Council on Alcoholism criteria,[148] 16 had used alcohol excessively and seemed headed for addiction, 12 had a history of legal difficulties when drinking, and 10 were referred by court authorities for investigation because of violent crimes committed under the influence of alcohol. Six had histories of significant head trauma, 14 had family histories of alcoholism and 3 had family histories of epilepsy. Almost all reported prolonged sleep following the [previous] violent episodes.[149]

The alcohol infusion took place in a lounge-like hospital room and was videotaped. The subjects were accompanied by two psychiatric technicians throughout the experimental procedures. The subjects were not told it was alcohol that was infused. The amounts infused ranged from 400 to 1,200 cc, the mean was 980. It had been planned to use 1,200 on all, but the behavior of 12 made that impossible. Approximately 50 cc of the 25-percent solution used in the study would equal a can of beer or a shot of whiskey so that the amounts ranged from 8 to 24 drinks. Intake

---

147. Maletzky at 1215.

148. Nat'l Council on Alcoholism, Criteria Committee, *Criteria for the Diagnosis of Alcoholism*, 129 AM. J. PSYCHIAT. 127 (1972).

149. Maletzky at 1217-18.

was at 200 cc an hour approximating drinking a drink or a can of beer at a rate of about four drinks an hour.[150] Blood alcohol levels were determined hourly, and readings ranged from 0.095 to 0.275 with a mean of 0.191 around the point of most critical behavioral reactions. Drunk driving is around 0.10 to 0.15 by current standards, for a familiar basis of comparison. EEG changes occurred in 15 of the 22 subjects. "These usually took the form of generalized slowing and disorganization of the pattern with occasional sharp waves in the temporal or occipital regions..." but not all of the subjects with EEG changes also displayed behavioral changes. "Two with no behavior change besides normal intoxication manifested abnormalities of the EEG, while two with psychotic behavior change had no EEG alteration, again raising the question of surface recording specificity for behavioral changes."[151] Maletzky concluded that "EEG's were varying and not helpful. The sharp waves seen were never organized sufficiently to suggest an epileptic attack. Intracortical recording, however, might well have produced a more striking record."[152]

According to Maletzky, the reactions of the patients could be readily categorized along the lines of the authors who are summarized by Banay, thus seemingly reinforcing the studies which are debunked by May and Ebaugh, whose paper we will discuss in the next chapter.[153] "Behavior changes resembling a psychotic state were observed in 15 of the 22 subjects while under the influence of alcohol."[154] The behavioral results may be summarized as follows:

No. of Subjects	*Category*	*Description of Category*
9	Violent	Inappropriate rage
4	Psychotic	Hallucinations, delusions, and distortions
2	Mixed	Components of both the above
7	Normal	Alcohol intoxication alone, such as slurred speech

An example of each of these categories is provided: One in the violent category attacked an attendant for no reason; one in the psychotic category spoke to the furniture as though to members of his family and one in the mixed category verbally responded to a technician who had said nothing, then attacked him.

150. Maletzky at 1219 n.2.

151. Maletzky at 1220.

152. Maletzky at 1226 (footnote omitted).

153. May & Ebaugh, *Pathological Intoxication, Alcoholic Hallucinosis, and Other Reactions to Alcohol: A Clinical Study,* 14 QRTLY J. STUD. ALCOH. 200 (1953).

154. Maletzky at 1220.

The Maletzky study is subject to two limitations which he assessed himself: It is an uncontrolled, observational study. Obviously if one is to study behavioral reactions, the appropriate method is observation. The point rather is that the observations would be more trustworthy if a control group was also observed in the study when the observer did not know which was which, and observers ought to be used who are not aware of the nature of the groups observed.

These are the main conclusions of the author regarding his behavioral observations:

> From our observations, we would propose a continuum of reactions to alcohol, rather than a sharply demarcated state of PI [pathological intoxication]....Nonetheless, the pathological states, when present, were striking and merited the designation "psychotic." Even the aggression seen was clearly unrealistic and dysfunctional; subjects struck out at those trying to help them, imagined threats in neutral stimuli, and exhibited blind rage, attacking everything which lay in their path and exposing themselves to considerable danger. Usually, but not always, these states were superimposed on normally intoxicated behaviors such as ataxia. Occasionally, however, a subject manifested psychotic behavior without the slightest evidence of intoxication. A witness to a crime, at such a point, would be blind to the etiological agent, alcohol.[155]

Specifically regarding the May and Ebaugh study, discussed later, Maletzky concludes that his study does not support their objection to the diagnosis of [pathological intoxication] as a redundancy or their position that alcohol merely triggers, or disinhibits, already existing personality or neurological defects, noting that the men in his study had no history of psychotic or violent behavior in a sober state. But we see no particular conflict; while it is true that his study does not support their opinion, it does not refute it either. Nothing in the study eliminates the possibility, for example, that underlying but undetected brain damage could be triggered by alcohol consumption. His description of the sample indicates that 6 of the 22 had a history of significant head trauma, but we were not provided with information regarding the behavioral reaction of this subgroup. In other words the same "debate" alluded to earlier will continue to exist, all being irrelevant to forensic concerns: The disagreement identified relates only to whether pathological intoxication is a "valid" diagnosis, but the "validity" turns on the use to be made of

155. Maletzky at 1225-26.

it—criminal responsibility or treatment alternatives. Surely, Maletzky has provided extremely valuable evidence regarding the need to recognize pathological reaction to alcohol as a defense to criminal responsibility when the defendant was unaware of the condition, whether or not his study tracks the exact cause of the malady, which it surely does not. In short, that is an irrelevant argument regarding etiology, not a denial of the symptomatology with which the law ought to concern itself.

Maletzky concludes that the "behavior of the pathologically intoxicated appeared qualitatively different not only from normal intoxication, but also from their own behavior when sober."[156] For legal purposes, that is a terribly important point, and its actual occurrence is what matters, not how psychiatrists chose to classify it. Maletzky himself goes beyond psychiatry to observe: "Certainly such a state cannot be employed to defend all violent behavior under the influence of alcohol."[157] What matters legally is whether the defendant was aware of the likelihood of the reaction. Every person in this particular study had a history of this kind of reaction. At the same time, the reaction initially must have been a surprise to the actor.

Maletzky was aware that his results might be at variance with the observations made by Bach-y-Rita, Lion and Ervin,[158] and he attributed the difference to the amount of alcohol involved while Bach-y-Rita, Lion and Ervin themselves attribute their failure to make observations similar to previous studies to the theory that pre-existing stress was both

---

156. Maletzky at 1226. Many other writers have stressed the same qualitative distinction between normal intoxication and pathological intoxication, but the following abstract presents an unusual measure of it. While we have not obtained a translation of the following article, the results are interesting.

> When a person is drunk to the extent that he cannot be wakened, the services of a physician are imperative. In such cases the physician must attempt to neutralize the narcotic effects of alcohol by means of analeptica [CNS stimulants], such as coramine and cardiazol. The basic dose of 5 cc. of coramine in 25-per-cent solutions and 4 cc. of cardiazol in 10-per-cent solution were injected in 14 unconscious patients with severe alcohol poisoning. In all cases the injection produced sneezing and in most cases vomiting within a few minutes. There were no complications. The same medication was attempted in 2 cases of pathological intoxication without success. It is concluded that in pathological intoxication alcohol is only a means of releasing abnormal reactions in the brain and that the condition is not an intoxication in the usual sense of the word.

11 QRTLY J. STUD. ALCOH. 316 (1950), abstract of Rauch, *Zur Behandlung der akuten Alkoholvergiftung*, 45 MED. KLINIK 1348 (1950).

It was also reported in Teixeira, 19 REV. MED. PARANA 194 (1950), that in pathological intoxication cases, the blood alcohol level does not reflect the clinical state of intoxication.

157. Maletzky at 1226.

158. Bach-y-Rita, Lion & Ervin, *Pathological Intoxication; Clinical and Electroencephalographic Studies*, 127 AM. J. PSYCHIAT. 698 (1970).

necessary and absent in their subjects. But, as Maletzky pointed out, there was no particular stress involved in his clinical setting not present also in the earlier study. What varied was the amount of alcohol, Maletzky using three or four times as much as that used by Bach-y-Rita, Lion and Ervin. Concerning etiology, Maletzky also suspects a relationship "to temporal lobe epilepsy and to other syndromes of violence."[159]

On the other hand, it should be emphasized that the Maletzky study excluded those persons who had a "neurological disorder based on history, neurological examination, and EEG."[160] One would suppose that part of his dramatic results are attributable to the larger amount of alcohol he used in the activation experiment. Presumably it would be even more dramatic if persons of known neurological disorder had not been excluded from the study.

Maletzky also observed, regarding the amount of alcohol necessary to pathological reaction to alcohol, that only one author of the 14 cited by Banay[161] (Branthwaite from England, whom he called Braithwaite) alluded to the amount of alcohol as having any significance.[162] But in

---

159. Maletzky at 1227 (footnotes omitted).

160. Maletzky at 1217.

161. Banay, *Pathologic Reaction to Alcohol,* 4 QRTLY J. STUD. ALCOH. 580 (1944).

162. Maletzky at 1215. The reference is to Branthwaite, in ANNUAL REPORT FOR 1909 OF THE INSPECTOR UNDER THE INEBRIATES ACT (1911). There is another thesis in the literature which as yet has not received much investigation, and that is that it may not be alcohol which, entirely at least, is responsible for the reaction: It may be the particular substances found in different alcohol drinks which may trigger an allergic reaction. Quirk, *Treatment For Epileptic Alcoholism,* 7 ONTARIO PSYCHOL. 36 (1976). Marinacci did replicate the same general type of alcohol that the actor claimed precipitated the original attack. Marinacci, *A Special Type of Temporal Lobe (Psychomotor) Seizures Following Ingestion of Alcohol,* 28 BULL. L.A. NEUROL. SOC. 241, 243 (1963). Quirk hypothesizes:

> One problem in understanding these cases [alcohol ingestion frequently followed by epileptiform behavior] is that, although chemical triggers for epilepsy are not unknown, it seems unlikely that a general agent such as alcohol would serve effectively as a trigger for epilepsy and one does not usually think of epilepsy as a disorder primarily induced by exogenous chemical means. Moreover, it frequently seems to be true that in such cases a particular type of alcohol will serve best as the epileptic trigger. Perhaps a more elegant means is available for understanding alcohol as an epileptogenic trigger than merely thinking of the alcohol as a specific chemical triggering agent. Exogenous substances tend to have another type of irritative effect on the body. They tend more frequently to have an allergic inflammatory effect. Although allergic reactions are most frequently recognized as affecting the skin and the respiratory tract, perhaps because these systems are more readily observed than other bodily systems, there seems to be no particular reason why allergic responses might not just as easily affect other bodily systems. Indeed, there is some reason to believe that allergic reactions do not affect the central nervous system....

Quirk at 36.

any event, Branthwaite's reference was to "congenital defectives" in reformatories, and he said that these persons had a marked intolerance to alcohol so that even small amounts of alcohol made them disorderly and violent.[163]

Two years later, in 1978, Maletzky reported on a related study.[164] In this study, the 57 subjects[165] were 49 males and 8 females drawn from three groups of patients: (1) those referred for diagnosis after committing a crime, usually of violence and usually under the influence of alcohol (37 males, 1 female); (2) those referred for therapeutic purposes related to excessive drinking (9 males, 5 females); and (3) those referred to determine if alcohol provoked "either seizure-like behavior or focal epileptic change in their electroencephalograms"[166] (2 males, 3 females). In contrast to the previous report, in this study Maletzky makes no mention of an exclusion criterion based on known or suspected pre-existing neurological abnormalities or abnormal preinfusion EEG's, probably due to the nature of the referrals who served as the subjects of the report. "Videotape review added additional observations by a group of psychiatrists and psychologists following the actual test."[167]

The alcohol infused was 20 percent at a rate of 200 cc per hour, and the total amount ranged from 350 to 2,000 cc, or from about 3 to 4 drinks up to 20 drinks. Maletzky points out that the exact relationship between intravenous injection of alcohol and oral consumption is not known.[168]

Regarding pathological intoxication, Maletzky reports that while some subjects did progress to aggressiveness without violence (13 of the 57),

> Nonetheless, a certain number of Ss (N=37, all male) demonstrated a bizarre and violent reaction to alcohol in varying amounts, consisting usually of a suspicious and hostile misperception of neutral stimuli. Among such Ss, grossly inappropriate behavior, frequently of a violent nature, was observed, occasionally at relatively low BAL's [blood-alcohol levels]....[S]uch reactions usually took the form of inappropriate rage, hallucinations, delusions and disorientation.[169]

The 37 of the total of 57 subjects who manifested the described reactions are not related in the report to the referred groups, nor is any

---

163. Banay at 587.
164. Maletzky, *The Alcohol Provocation Test*, 39 J. CLIN. PSYCHIAT. 403 (1978).
165. The subjects did not include the 22 reported on in the first study. Maletzky at 403.
166. Maletzky at 403.
167. Maletzky at 407.
168. Maletzky at 407.
169. Maletzky at 409.

other information provided other than gender. More importantly, perhaps, is the fact that the "N=37" is extraordinarily high. Is it actually possible that it is due to selection of a highly relevant group and that the open-ended amount of alcohol achieves such high results? That would be 65 percent. Only 9 of 22 instances of violent rage were reported in the earlier study in which the subjects had been selected precisely because pathological intoxication was suspected. The answer appears to be that Maletzky did not consider all 37 of these reactions to be pathological intoxication. In his discussion, he refers to the fact that "some few of our Ss actually suffered the syndrome of pathological intoxication, and were rendered psychotic at certain BAL's...."[170] But the exact number he considered to be instances of pathological intoxication is not specifically reported.[171]

Of the total sample, 27 had pre-infusion as well as post-infusion EEG's administered. Five of these had been specifically referred to determine if alcohol provoked an abnormal EEG. "In all 5 some sharp waves, particularly in the temporal regions, were determined."[172] As to the other 20, "EEG changes were seen in 15 of the remaining 20 Ss, usually taking the form of generalized slowing and disorganization of pattern, with only occasional spiking of temporal or occipital regions."[173] The 20 were not identified by category except that they exclude the 5 specifically referred for these purposes.[174] Part of the interest in this Maletzky study is the fact that observations were made as well of "normal intoxication." Here is the general observation:

> Thus, many high tolerance Ss with long drinking histories show very few behavioral changes associated with alcohol intake until they reach very high BAL's, while several others show extreme behavioral changes at varying BAL's, including those whom we felt demonstrated pathological intoxication. Many of these latter could become psychotic and violent *before* manifesting signs of intoxication, such as discoordination or slurred speech.[175]

As Maletzky also observes: "It takes very high BAL's to produce standard signs of intoxication in these high tolerance Ss, yet they may, at even lower levels, manifest aggression and loss of control."[176] What is

---

170. Maletzky at 410.
171. The abstract appearing in 39 Qrtly J. Stud. Alcoh. (Abstracts) (1978) reports the number 37 as actually instances of pathological intoxication.
172. Maletzky at 410.
173. Maletzky at 410.
174. Maletzky at 410.
175. Maletzky at 409.
176. Maletzky at 409.

not shown, of course, is whether those who demonstrate an appearance of not being intoxicated while having high BAL's nevertheless are significantly impaired mentally thus creating the possibility that "explosive violence" by such a person might be misconstrued as violence by a nonintoxicated person.

THE NEW TECHNOLOGY

There are new technologies being developed, computer assisted tomography (CAT), magnetic resonance imaging (MRI), positron emission tomography (PET) and magnetoencephalography (MEG), which integrate aspects of biophysics and computer sciences and hold promise of improving the power of detection of organic or functional brain abnormalities which will improve upon the precision and completeness with which the EEG can detect them.[177] Magnetoencephalography measures the magnetic field generated by intracellular electrical currents within the brain, while the EEG records the electrical potentials within the brain. Current research efforts usually record the two together for comparison purposes, and the extent to which the MEG method will supplant the EEG is now known as yet. The equipment will have to be studied further, refined and made available in more patient locations before its full power is known. Epilepsy research already heads the list of applications of MEG, primarily to increase the precision of identifying the location of the source of the abnormal electrical activity.[178] Other

---

177. *See, e.g.*, Fenwick, *The Inverse Problem: A Medical Perspective*, 32 PHYS. MED. BIOL. 5 (1987), discussing computer-assisted tomography (CAT), magnetic resonance imaging (MRI), positron emission tomography (PET) and magnetoencephalography (MEG).

178. Sutherling, Crandall, Darcey, Becker, Levesque & Barth, *The Magnetic and Electric Fields Agree with Intracranial Localizations of Somatosensory Cortex*, 38 NEUROL. 1705 (1988). "Precise localization of essential cortex is important in surgical treatment of partial epilepsy, brain neoplasms, and vascular malformations....There have been recent advances in noninvasive localization by the combined use of the magnetoencephalogram (MEG) and electroencephalogram (EEG), which give complementary information for identification of somatosensory cortex, localization of the seizure focus, and detection of interictal spikes." Sutherling, Crandall, Darcey, Becker, Levesque & Barth at 1705 (citations omitted); Gordon, Sloggett, Harvey, Kraiuhin, Rennie, Yiannikas & Meares, *Magnetoencephalography: Locating the Source of P300 via Magnetic Field Recording*, 23 CLIN. EXP. NEUROL. 101 (1987); Rose, Sato, Smith, Porter, Theodore, Friauf, Bonner & Jabbari, *Localization of Magnetic Interictal Discharges in Temporal Lobe Epilepsy*, 22 ANN. NEUROL. 348 (1987); Rose, Smith & Sato, *Magnetoencephalography and Epilepsy Research*, 238 SCIENCE 329 (1987); Weinberg, Brickett, Robertson, Harrop, Cheyne, Crisp, Baff & Dykstra, *The Magnetoencephalographic Localisation of Source-Systems in the Brain: Early and Late Components of Event Related Potentials*, 4 ALCOHOL 339 (1987); Sato & Smith, *Magnetoencephalography*, 2 J. CLIN. NEUROPHYSIOL. 173 (1985); Hari & Antervo, *Comparison of Magneto- and Electroencephalographic Techniques in Event-Related Response Research—A Brief Survey*, in *Behavioral Neuroscience in Scandinavia*, SCAND. J. PSYCHOL. 170 (Supp. 1, 1982); Cuffin & Cohen, *Comparison of the*

techniques include magnetic resonance imaging[179] and positron emission tomography.[180]

"Recent advances in brain imaging techniques have led to increased interest in pathophysiological brain changes in epilepsy. Magnetic resonance imaging (MRI) is one such technique which is noninvasive, avoids the use of radiation and is well tolerated by patients."[181] Much of the benefit is expected to derive from the fact that in some cases of

---

Magnetoencephalogram and Electroencephalogram, 47 ELECTROENCEPH. CLIN. NEUROPHYSIOL. 132 (1979); Hughes, Cohen, Mayman, Scholl & Hendrix, *Relationship of the Magnetoencephalogram to Abnormal Activity in the Electroencephalogram*, 217 J. NEUROL. 79 (1977). Each of these articles has extensive bibliographic material of a more expansive scope.

179. Henriksen, Mogelvang & Thomsen, *Magnetic Resonance in Clinical Physiology*, 8 CLIN. PHYSIOL. 541 (1988); Mander, Weppner, Chick, Morton & Best, *An NMR Study of Cerebral Oedema and Its Biological Correlates During Withdrawal From Alcohol*, 23 ALCOH. & ALCOHOLISM 97 (1988); Conlon & Trimble, *Magnetic Resonance Imaging in Psychiatry*, CAN. J. PSYCHIAT. 702 (1987). The relationship between epilepsy and psychosis is discussed, and the authors conclude:

> Whether psychiatrists like it or not, brain imaging seems to be here to stay. MRI has a selective potential to contribute to the investigation of both, the structure and function of the brain....[T]he precise niche of MRI in the study of psychiatric illness has not yet been firmly established. Nevertheless, MRI promotes further understanding of clinically observable conditions, thereby challenging the traditional boundaries of mental disorders.

Conlon & Trimble at 709. *See also* Kitaguchi, Kobayashi, Tobimatsu, Goto & Kuroiwa, *Computed Tomography and Magnetic Resonance Imaging in a Young Patient with Wernicke's Encephalopathy*, 234 J. NEUROL. 449 (1987).

180. Positron emission tomography works by "measuring the local tissue concentrations of injected positron-emitting isotope..." Johnson, Adinoff, Bisserbe, Martin, Rio, Rohrbaugh, Zubovic & Eckardt, *Assessment of Alcoholism-Related Organic Brain Syndromes with Positron Emission Tomography*, 10 ALCOH. CLIN. EXPER. RES. 237, 238 (1986). Brain metabolism varies with its activity, and its metabolism can be measured by detecting the decay of injected isotopes. "Already PET scans are proving useful in the diagnosis of schizophrenia, manic-depression, and other psychiatric conditions." R. RESTAK, THE BRAIN 249 (1984).

See also Volkow, Mullani, Gould, Adler, Guynn, Overall & Dewey, *Effects of Acute Alcohol Intoxication on Cerebral Blood Flow Measured with PET*, 24 PSYCHIAT. RES. 201 (1988) (measurements of regional cerebral blood flow (rCBF) with positron emission tomography indicated that high doses of alcohol increased blood flow to the right temporal and the prefrontal cortex); Hemmingsen, Vorstrup, Clemmesen, Holm, Tfelt-Hansen, Sorensen, Hansen, Sommer & Bolwig, *Cerebral Blood Flow During Delirium Tremens and Related Clinical States Studied with Xenon-133 Inhalation Tomography*, 145 AM. J. PSYCHIAT. 1384 (1988); American College of Nuclear Physicians & Society of Nuclear Medicine, *Positron Emission Tomography: Clinical Status in the United States in 1987*, 29 J. NUCL. MED. 1136 (1988); Kessler, Partain, Price & James, *Positron Emission Tomography: Prospects for Clinical Utility*, 22 INVEST. RADIOL. 529, 530 (1987) (estimate of the rate of seizures in the United States is 0.6%); Leenders, Gibbs, Frackowiak, Lammertsma & Jones, *Positron Emission Tomography of the Brain: New Possibilities for the Investigation of Human Cerebral Pathophysiology*, 23 PROG. NEUROBIOL. 1 (1984).

181. Conlon, Trimble, Rogers & Callicott, *Magnetic Resonance Imaging in Epilepsy: A Controlled Study*, 2 EPILEP. RES. 37 (1988).

epilepsy, including complex partial seizure disorder cases, gross anatomical lesions are often lacking and other means of detecting the abnormality may be ineffective.

A COMMENTARY ON THE STUDIES

As Kelley and Reilly summarized in 1983: "Thus, the literature does support the concept that certain people with abnormal EEGs, a history of head trauma, or epilepsy may be more susceptible to the effects of alcohol both behaviorally and in terms of EEG changes."[182] We should point out that the prevalence of the use of the EEG and its ability to detect psychomotor epilepsy may over-emphasize the role of psychomotor epilepsy in pathological intoxication in contrast to the clinically observed, and mostly older cases, where the cause was less discernable.

The researcher must use either very large numbers, or one must begin with a highly selected population to precipitate pathological intoxication in the laboratory-like setting; randomly selected populations will not display pathological intoxication in modest population numbers. Even a person clearly susceptible will not with any reliability display symptoms on command, although there are many reported cases in which this did in fact occur. The experimental population must be selected on relevant criteria, not just drunks or even hospitalized drunks as appears to be the case in the May and Ebaugh work discussed in the next chapter. In fact one would do well to exclude known alcoholics because many psychoses are associated with that disease which have nothing to do with pathological reaction to alcohol.

Is pathological intoxication susceptibility acquired or inherited? Both are involved, just as they are in the case of psychomotor epilepsy, but most case histories of persons susceptible to pathological intoxication indicate that head injury is the single most common cause.

There has never been a reported attempt to replicate the research design of any prior researcher; there are only opportunistic and retrospective designs. To cite one obvious omission as an example, the same population which is found in one study to test positive for pathological intoxication in a research setting has never been studied twice. Nor are control groups compared to the patient group.

There is something of an understandable, but misleading, focus in the literature on crimes of violence, just as there is with small amounts of alcohol. Certainly, the dramatic case is the one in which after a few drinks the actor engages in extraordinarily brutal conduct. It will be

---

182. Kelley & Reilly, *EEG, Alcohol, and Alcoholism,* in EEG AND EVOKED POTENTIALS IN PSYCHIATRY AND BEHAVIORAL NEUROLOGY 55, 57 (J. Hughes & W. Wilson eds. 1983).

unfortunate, however, if such extreme occurrences are thought to be necessary to a finding of pathological reaction to alcohol. The point is that given the necessary underlying condition, any amount of alcohol can lead to automatic behavior, and during automatic behavior, the actor is capable of any kind of conduct. If it is not criminal, we may never hear of it. If it is dramatically criminal, the chances go up that it will be reported. If it is merely "criminal" of a mundane sort, "indecent exposure," for example, it is very apt to get lost. In many of the reported cases, the actor engages in undramatic behavior, and only happenstance produces an accurate diagnosis, or any at all.[183]

Blair reports such a case.[184] The defendant was charged with breaking and entering with intent to commit a felony, larceny here. He was a middle-aged male with a good war record, no history of prior involvement either with the law or alcoholism. After two double whiskeys, he was found at night in the office of the factory at which he had worked for ten weeks. When asked what he was doing in there, he said he was testing the security systems. He claimed amnesia for the episode. The author made a diagnosis of pathological intoxication which was accepted by the court. The defendant's background did contain self-reported instances of amnesia, but the diagnosis appears to have been made primarily on the basis of the relatively small amount of alcohol in combination with the rather strange crime, strange for this individual.

The mythology is perpetuated and compounded when pathological intoxication is described in dramatic terms alone so that the drama is taken for diagnosis: "Pathological intoxication is a severe reaction to the ingestion of alcohol. It is characterized by a precipitous and almost maniacal response to a comparatively small amount of alcohol."[185] That is an eye-catcher, but it is also misleading: The points rather should be that the amount of alcohol is of no diagnostic value and automatic behavior results, and that can be anything.

Kolb provides a description of a case which makes the point that the amount of alcohol may not necessarily be limited to small amounts and that the actor does not necessarily commit grossly violent crimes:

---

183. Prosaic cases are often described in the nonlegal literature. *See, e.g.*, Gunn & Fenton, *Epilepsy, Automatism, and Crime*, LANCET 1173 (June 1971) (probable epileptic seizure involving smashing a window). Driving offenses are also frequently reported as having arisen from epileptic attacks, but most of these cases are pure epilepsy, not pathological intoxication; that is, no alcohol is reported as involved in most of them. *See, e.g.*, Walton, *Some Observations on the Value of Electroencephalography in Medico-Legal Practice*, 31 MEDICO-LEGAL J. 15, 25-27 (1963), where the author discusses a number of other types of cases and provides details of one driving offense, including the relevant EEG tracings.

184. Blair, *The Medico-Legal Problems of Pathological Alcoholic Intoxication: An Illustrative Case*, 9 MED., SCI. & LAW 94 (1969).

185. R. CATANZARO, ALCOHOLISM: THE TOTAL TREATMENT APPROACH 103 (1968).

> N.W., aged 28, was seen in jail while awaiting trial on a charge of drunkenness and disorderly conduct. The patient's father had committed suicide as he was about to be sent to a hospital for mental diseases. The patient himself was described as being a friendly but quick-tempered and restless individual whose marriage had terminated in early divorce. He was said never to have been particularly alcoholic, but one July 4 he celebrated the holiday by drinking two bottles of beer and a glass of wine. Soon afterward he attempted to fling himself down an 80-foot embankment and was so greatly excited that he was taken to the police station for the night. The next morning he had no recollection of the affair. Ten months later the patient called late one afternoon to see friends who invited him to sample what they considered choice varieties of whiskey and gin. He accepted their invitation and drank somewhat more heavily than usual. Soon after leaving the home of his friends he was observed by a police officer to be acting strangely. As the officer spoke to him he attacked him. While the officer was calling for help, the patient disappeared. About 15 minutes later two women were startled to see a strange man thrust his head through a closed window of their living room and shout, "Help! Murder!" It was the patient, who then ran on to another house where he rang the doorbell insistently. As the occupant answered the summons he again screamed, "Murder!" and ran to the street once more, where he broke the windshields and headlights of several parked automobiles and tore out the seats and pulled parts from other cars. At this point he was seized and taken to the police station where, on awakening the following morning, he had no recollection of his experiences of the previous night.[186]

Is this a case of pathological intoxication? It is understandable why some authorities would like to limit pathological intoxication to those cases in which the actor drank only amounts small enough that one could fairly conclude that he could not have been merely intoxicated (drunk) and hence his behavior could safely be attributed to something else. We do not know the exact amount consumed, however, and it may well have been enough to make "N.W." drunk. Strange, even illegal, behavior and amnesia are characteristics of a drunken spree as well as pathological intoxication. Kolb clearly believes this was a case of pathological intoxication, but just as clearly it would take more evidence than that

186. L. KOLB, NOYES' MODERN CLINICAL PSYCHIATRY 196-97 (7th ed. 1968).

presented here. This is why it is so important to know more: Did he have a history of brain injury or epilepsy? Were his physical signs typical of the drunk, as in slurring his speech, moving with an unsteady gait and so on?

One thing quite extraordinary about this incident is that it came to anyone's attention who had even heard of pathological intoxication much less to one in a position to make such a diagnosis. We strongly suspect that this accounts for the predominance of murder and serious assault cases in most of the legal literature; appellate cases represent a strongly biased sample if the relevant universe is pathological reaction to alcohol.

4

Quasi-Nosologic Reservations Regarding Pathological Intoxication: What Do the Doubters Doubt?

In 1953 May and Ebaugh presented a critical assessment of pathological intoxication:[1] "It is generally accepted that among the reactions to alcohol there should be included an entity which has been dignified by the name 'pathological intoxication,' a somewhat redundant designation since intoxication can hardly be considered a normal psychological event."[2] That observation sets the tone of their article. Of course, in one sense, intoxication is not a normal state; but it is hardly an unusual one. More to the point is not whether intoxication is a normal psychological event but whether there is a category of abnormal as well as normal intoxication, a category so abnormal that it is not even intoxication but rather an abnormal state triggered by alcohol consumption. That is why the term "*pathological* intoxication" is used.

The authors are extremely skeptical regarding the existence of pathological reaction to alcohol. Their characterization of the existing literature of the time (1953, prior to the modern EEG studies reported on in Chapter 3) was as follows:

> Critical study of the various descriptions of pathological intoxication tends to create the suspicion that a naive and credulous belief in the magic powers of alcohol and the diagnostic value of amnesia has [sic] resulted in a blending of the symptoms and characteristics of different reaction types to create an entity that bears more relation to legendary composite figures such as the minotaur and the centaur than to clinical reality....[I]t seems that any person who exhibits

---

1. May & Ebaugh, *Pathological Intoxication, Alcoholic Hallucinosis, and Other Reactions to Alcohol: A Clinical Study,* 14 Qrtly J. Stud. Alcoh. 200 (1953). May was an Assistant Clinical Professor of Psychiatry, University of Colorado School of Medicine, and Ebaugh was a Clinical Professor of Psychiatry at the same school.

2. May & Ebaugh at 200.

> antisocial behavior, especially violence, under the influence of alcohol may fairly be classified under pathological intoxication.[3]

It should be pointed out that by the time of this statement, condemnatory of all that had gone before, the 1952 Diagnostic and Statistical Manual had included the following description of pathological intoxication:

> "Pathological intoxication" may cause difficulty in proper diagnosis. When, without apparent preexisting mental disorder, there is a marked behavioral or psychotic reaction with an acute brain syndrome after minimal alcoholic intake, the case will be classified here [under acute brain syndrome, alcohol intoxication]. When a preexisting psychotic, psychoneurotic or personality disorder is made more manifest after minimal alcoholic intake, the case will be classified under the diagnosis of the underlying condition.[4]

Both the DSM and May and Ebaugh turn the sufficient cause, minimal alcohol intake, into a critical diagnostic element of pathological reaction to alcohol, and then to compound matters, May and Ebaugh essentially say they do not believe it. Their own investigation leads them to the conclusion that there is

> no justification for the use of pathological intoxication as a special diagnostic term, either on the basis of reaction to minimal amounts of alcohol or on the basis of an allegedly specific clinical picture. In short, both the concept and the term should be abandoned, and reactions to alcohol should be classified on a more specific and logical basis.[5]

Thus, the grand objection to pathological intoxication may be that it is descriptive of a set of symptoms rather than a disease. Is that not true of many medical phenomena? What is the underlying cause of diabetes? Of clinical depression? Or asthma? They "exist," and as we have shown, so does pathological intoxication. The objection may only be to the use of pathological intoxication "as a special diagnostic term...."

And again, the literature dating back to Krafft-Ebing in 1869 has stressed that the amount of alcohol was not of diagnostic value, not that minimal amounts were required to establish a diagnosis. And most

---

3. May & Ebaugh at 200-01.
4. DSM-I.
5. May & Ebaugh at 202.

careful writers since have taken the same position. They do later acknowledge that the amount of alcohol is not important, but for some oddly antagonistic reason, they refer to that fact, well-known even when they wrote their article in 1953, as an "admission."[6] If the objection is only to the term as a diagnostic category, what could turn on the amount of alcohol involved?

They do the same thing with amnesia as part of the pathological intoxication picture. Much of the research has treated the associated amnesia as either partial or total for the episode. But that hardly underlies the tone set for the report of their project:

> Amnesia, although often admitted to be inconstant or partial, occupies such a prominent part in the description that it is apparently justifiable to classify as "pathological intoxication" the condition of a man who committed a crime under the influence of alcohol, made a detailed confession and then subsequently claimed that he could not remember what had happened, or indeed almost any instance of ingestion of alcohol followed by antisocial behavior with subsequent claim of amnesia.[7]

But that is only a slight misreading of the literature by May and Ebaugh mixed in with more than a little hyperbole. Meggendorfer is cited in that passage, and he does indeed take the position that the associated amnesia may be partial in the sense that memory of a dream fades with time.[8] May and Ebaugh did not, of course, have access to the later studies reported in the previous chapter, but that fact is sometimes lost to those later writers who did but who persist in quoting the most cynical of the passages from May and Ebaugh because of the colorful and metaphorical passages it contains. May and Ebaugh report that they undertook an inquiry themselves on the subject, albeit a review of hospital files. The effort was to study not pathological intoxication but the classification methods used by others and to propose how they would have done it instead, and their conclusion will be that they would not have classified any of the cases as pathological intoxication, which is, of course, what they would have said before they read the files.

> A review was made of the records of all cases of *alcoholism*, with or without psychosis, admitted to the Colorado Psycho-

---

6. May & Ebaugh at 201.
7. May & Ebaugh at 201 (citation omitted).
8. Banay, *Pathologic Reaction to Alcohol*, 4 QRTLY J. STUD. ALCOH. 580, 589 (1944), summarizing Meggendorfer, *Intoxikationspsychosen*, in 7 HANDBUCH DER GEISTESKRANKHEITEN (O. Bumke ed. 1928).

> pathic Hospital between February 1925 and January 1952. Two supplementary studies were made of the records of other types of patients admitted to the hospital over the same period: (1) Those diagnosed as having an obsessive-compulsive neurosis. This was intended to clarify the relationship, if any, between this type of disorder and alcohol intoxication. (2) Those classified as "criminal cases," i.e., persons charged with a criminal offense who had entered a plea of insanity. This group was selected because of the known relationship between crime and alcohol (28 per cent of this series were either drunk at the time of the crime or had been drinking to excess for some time before it) and because of the medicolegal significance attached to the diagnosis of pathological intoxication. There was no overlapping between this latter series and the other two, for criminal cases are diagnosed either sane or insane without further definitive diagnosis.[9]

We have provided some information on Korsakoff's psychosis[10] and alcoholic hallucinosis[11] in the footnotes. Evidently based on the original

---

9. May & Ebaugh at 202 (emphasis added).

10. Korsakoff's psychosis is a disorder resulting from chronic alcoholism and a vitamin deficiency. Marcus & Coulston, *Water-Soluble Vitamins: The Vitamin B Complex and Ascorbic Acid,* in GOODMAN & GILMAN'S, THE PHARMACOLOGICAL BASIS OF THERAPEUTICS 1551, 1554 (A. Gilman, L. Goodman, T. Rall & F. Murad eds. 7th ed. 1985). Apparently, it is the frequent residual of recovery from Wernicke's disease, delirium tremens or acute alcoholic hallucinations. "Wernicke's syndrome is an additional serious consequence of alcoholism and thiamine deficiency....Wernicke's syndrome may be accompanied by an acute global confusional state that may also respond to thiamine. Left untreated, Wernicke's encephalopathy frequently leads to a chronic disorder in which learning and memory are impaired out of proportion to other cognitive functions in the otherwise-alert and responsive patient....[Korsakoff's psychosis] is characterized by confabulation...." Marcus & Coulston at 1554. The principal characteristics are extreme memory defects and confabulation. There is less introspection and judgment. Amnesia for recent events is characteristic. It often seen in chronic alcoholics, but it is also seen in cases of head injury, subarachnoid bleeding, arteriosclerosis and even toxic psychosis. *See also* Martin, Adinoff, Weingartner, Mukherjee & Eckardt, *Alcoholic Organic Brain Disease: Nosology and Pathophysiologic Mechanisms,* 10 PROG. NEURO-PSYCHOPHARMACOL. & BIOL. PSYCHIAT. 147 (1986). Johnson, Adinoff, Bisserbe, Martin, Rio, Rohrbaugh, Zubovic & Eckardt, *Assessment of Alcoholism-Related Organic Brain Syndromes with Positron Emission Tomography,* 10 ALCOH. CLIN. EXPER. RES. 237 (1986), view it as synonymous with alcoholic amnestic disorder, which itself is a type of organic brain syndrome. *See also* Keller, *A Lexicon of Disablements Related to Alcohol Consumption,* in ALCOHOL-RELATED DISABILITIES 23 (G. Edwards, M. Gross, M. Keller, J. Moser & R. Room eds. 1977).

11. Alcoholic hallucinations develop gradually during the drinking history of the person. The usual manifestation is the occurrence of auditory hallucinations. The reaction of the individual may become violent because of the threatening content of the hallucinations, and he may try to defend himself from them. An unusual aspect is that throughout the illness, it is possible that the person's mental faculties to stay seemingly normal. Visual hallucinations may also occur but are more rare. The illness can last for a long period of time, as long as

diagnoses, their population consisted of the following categories and numbers:

Pathological intoxication	41
Delirium tremens	208
Korsakoff's psychosis	27
Alcoholic hallucinosis	99
Acute alcoholism with psychosis	17
Chronic alcoholism with psychosis	340
Chronic alcoholism, no psychosis	1,289
"Criminal cases"	1,120
Obsessive-compulsive neurosis	185
TOTAL	3,326

We assume that the first seven categories were from the "alcoholism" sample and that the last two were the supplemental samples. There were 41 instances of previously diagnosed cases of pathological intoxication, all from the initial "alcoholism" category, and no instances of previously diagnosed cases of pathological intoxication in the "criminal" category, presumably because those cases were not further diagnosed originally. As to the amount-of-alcohol question, the authors state:

> In none of our cases was there any reliable evidence that symptoms had arisen as the result of the ingestion of alcohol in amounts that would be expected to have little or no effect on the average individual; in fact, in all cases the patient had been drinking heavily for at least a few hours and usually for periods of days, months or years.[12]

Now that, of course, is a reference to the entire population, the vast majority of whom had been admitted diagnosed as alcoholics. What the drinking pattern was for those originally diagnosed as having suffered an attack of pathological intoxication is not given. May and Ebaugh then give support to what the literature had said in the first place before May and Ebaugh themselves set up the straw man of "small amount" as being of diagnostic significance or even of necessity:

> It would seem logical to eliminate entirely all reference to the amount of alcohol consumed, and to differentiate only between those cases in which the symptoms appear to be precipitated by the ingestion of alcohol and which may

---

three to four months. Some evidently doubt its existence as a specific entity. Because it is very similar to schizophrenia, some say it is schizophrenia developing in a drinker.

12. May & Ebaugh at 204.

> properly be classified as "acute brain syndrome, alcohol intoxication," [under the DSM of the time] and those cases in which the symptoms do not appear to be precipitated by the use of alcohol, and where alcohol is either a secondary or an unimportant factor.[13]

Undeniably, the literature supports this view; in fact, it is all the clinical literature had ever supported, although perhaps we are only finding fault with the DSM's language of "small amount of alcohol."[14] Citing several earlier writers, only one of whom actually supports the position,[15] the authors state their opinion that:

> there is no justification for continuing to believe in the existence of pathological intoxication as a special diagnostic category. It is a diagnostic catch-all, and difference of opinion as to its symptomatology may be attributed to failure to distinguish between the various reaction types. In all of our patients whose symptoms appeared as a result of alcohol intoxication, it was possible to classify the symptomatology in terms of the predominant reaction type without using the term pathological intoxication, without inventing any new terms and without any greater difficulty than is encountered in attempting to classify *any other psychiatric disorder.*[16]

This statement requires more discussion, but first let us turn to the chore the authors undertook. "As it is neither practicable nor necessary to include detailed case histories to illustrate all the different types of reaction to alcohol, the following summaries have been chosen to illustrate points relevant to the problem of pathological intoxication."[17]

There follow 36 case summaries classified according to how the authors would make their retrospective diagnosis, based on the files, and according to a "scheme of reference"[18] they propose. The authors state that the "summaries have been chosen to illustrate points relevant to the

---

13. May & Ebaugh at 204.
14. DSM-III-R at 129.
15. Fleming, *A Psychiatric Concept of Acute Alcoholic Intoxication*, 92 AM. J. PSYCHIAT. 89 (1935). The basis for the conclusion is not provided except that the author establishes elsewhere in the article that there is a wide variety of types of moods and behavior accompanying the broad category of drunkenness. The connection between inconstancy of normal intoxication on the one hand and pathological intoxication on the other is not made clear. It seems probable that Fleming assumed it was just another variety of drunkenness. If so, he does not support the viewpoint.
16. May & Ebaugh at 205 (emphasis added).
17. May & Ebaugh at 206.
18. May & Ebaugh at 206.

problem of pathological intoxication," but there is no indication that any of the cases presented are drawn from the cases previously categorized as pathological intoxication. It appears they were not. But why draw a sample of 3,326 cases, 41 of which may have involved pathological reaction to alcohol, and then "prove" the nonexistence of pathological intoxication of 36 non-pathological intoxication cases? The illustrations provided evidently were designed to demonstrate episodically that "senseless violence" can occur outside the category of pathological reaction to alcohol, that is, by drunks, and that cases of amnesia also can occur without pathological intoxication and that amnesia can be faked as well. Not surprisingly, no cases are classified by the researchers as pathological intoxication.

It is difficult to see what this "investigation" was supposed to prove or disprove. Not one of the 36 cases discussed involved psychomotor (temporal lobe) epilepsy. Indeed, there is no mention made in any of the cases of any sort of pre-existing brain damage. It is not possible to tell whether there were none, whether they were all missed, whether May and Ebaugh would not classify them as pathological intoxication if they were present or whether they did not look for them. What is well established in this report is that the combination of violence while intoxicated followed by amnesia and sleep does not establish pathological intoxication. No one disagrees.

On the other hand, does this study disprove the existence of pathological intoxication as we have described the existing research? A study that does not even deal with psychomotor epilepsy could hardly do so unless the implicit position was taken (it certainly was not made expressly) that in such a case, the case should more properly be classified as psychomotor epilepsy. But what of the other brain damage cases? If the authors also believed that these would be valid diagnostic categories and that the consumption of alcohol can and does trigger violence in such persons (followed by amnesia and prolonged sleep after the episode), then our argument is reduced to nosological semantics in the pejorative sense of that word. Can it be that May and Ebaugh are only arguing about the proper domain of psychiatry? Surely, one would not have to read all those files to make the point that physical brain damage is not within the province of psychiatry, if that is the point.

A previous piece by Fleming written in 1935 is cited, and they acknowledge their agreement with a statement made there:

> In a brief reference to "pathological intoxication" he presents, without further elaboration, a point of view with which we are in complete agreement: "Largely as a response to practical needs of forensic psychiatry, unusual and widely divergent symptoms in *drunkenness* have been dubiously grouped

> together into the hypothetical syndrome—pathological intoxication."[19]

The attitude of the authors reflects the one expressed in two earlier articles by still another author, Lewis, that the cases taken as pathological intoxication are actually only manifestations of the obvious point that "alcohol may release varying types of reaction according to the personality."[20] The case studies of May and Ebaugh then "demonstrate" that conclusion based on a population largely consisting of committed alcoholics and "criminal cases."

The aim here is not to quarrel with the retrospective, from-the-files diagnosis made of each of the cases presented. But we do, however, dispute the notion that presenting 36 cases which are not pathological reaction to alcohol cases demonstrates that pathological reaction to alcohol does not exist.

Apart from the point that the rigor of either the methodology or the explanation of it is woefully inadequate to support the sweeping language used in other parts of the paper, a theme is introduced more or less clearly for the first time: The needs of psychiatrists in making a diagnosis for purposes of establishing treatment will vary from the needs of the criminal justice system in making decisions regarding responsibility. The law uses terms such as "diminished capacity" and "legal insanity" and even lack of *mens rea* and involuntary act. No one suggests that the medical profession adopt such language or concepts or judgmental labels for purposes of diagnosis and treatment. Thus, when it is argued that "pathological reaction to alcohol" or "pathological intoxication" exists or does not exist, the central point that always must be kept in mind is: for what purpose? This, one supposes, is the underlying point of the article and, of course, it takes no study to support it. One does not "treat" pathological intoxication per se, and that is part of the nosology problem. While the symptoms vary no more than they usually do with a mental disease, the underlying causes do vary significantly, but the significance of that variability is to those who treat, not those who judge. The concept therefore has utility in the relative uniformity of those symptoms from a forensic perspective, particularly because they differentiate normal intoxication from pathological intoxication on a nonjudgmental basis, leaving the question of fault to be determined on other grounds.

Two different decision structures exist for two different, if related, purposes, and they derive from different, albeit overlapping, premises. If

---

19. May & Ebaugh at 205, citing Fleming, *A Psychiatric Concept of Acute Alcoholic Intoxication*, 92 AM. J. PSYCHIAT. 89 (1935) (emphasis added).

20. May & Ebaugh at 205. The references are to Lewis, *Psychiatric Resultants of Alcoholism: Alcoholism and Mental Disease*, 2 QRTLY J. STUD. ALCOH. 293 (1941) and Lewis, *Personality Factors in Alcoholic Addiction*, 1 QRTLY J. STUD. ALCOH. 21 (1940).

the argument is about the label, it is not worth anyone's time. But if the May and Ebaugh thesis is that their classification of files demonstrates that there are not cases in which alcohol can trigger a temporary, violent, psychotic reaction, known or unknown to the actor, it will obviously take more than arguments to support the view. If, instead, their point was that some cases classified as pathological intoxication by someone else at an earlier time (with first-hand information) is not the way they would classify the case retrospectively, so be it. And so what. But it is not even clear in the report that this much disagreement exists. If we are arguing about the facts, their article provides no new ones, much less contradictory ones; and if we are arguing about what to call relevant facts, the simple truth is that we have no need to agree on one.[21]

The same sort of objection to the words has been recorded by MacDonald:[22] After quoting the language of May and Ebaugh regarding the "magic powers of alcohol," he states flatly that "The term *pathological intoxication* should be abandoned in favor of more accurate clinical diagnosis."[23] It is interesting that having concluded that epilepsy may be a more appropriate diagnosis in some cases now classed as pathological intoxication, in his discussion of epilepsy, MacDonald notes the possibility that there might be a relationship between alcohol and epileptic seizures. But he does not give it a name.

Cohen has made similar arguments.[24] "A wide variety of bellicose disturbances that happen to occur in connection with drinking are randomly grouped together by some clinicians as pathological intoxication. These include psychomotor epilepsy, delirium tremens, violence resulting from drunkenness and certain dissociation states." But if pathological reaction to alcohol is partly, or even perhaps largely, temporal lobe epilepsy (now known as complex partial seizures) triggered by alcohol, its legal status as a defense would be significantly different than if it were only a case of a spontaneous seizure. Indeed, the distinction would appear to be of profound medical importance as well. The same author goes on to conclude that "this condition represents a rare, but real diagnostic entity that can be sorted out from the other states

---

21. Comment, *Legal and Psychiatric Concepts and the Use of Psychiatric Evidence in Criminal Trials,* 73 CALIF. L. REV. 411 (1985) (authored by Peter R. Dahl).

22. "Professor of Psychiatry, University of Colorado School of Medicine; Director of Forensic Psychiatry[,] University of Colorado Medical Center; Psychiatrist to the District Courts of Colorado." J. MACDONALD, PSYCHIATRY AND THE CRIMINAL iii (3d ed. 1976).

23. J. MACDONALD, PSYCHIATRY AND THE CRIMINAL 244 (3d ed. 1976). The same language is used in MacDonald, *Alcoholism and Drug Addiction,* 21 OHIO ST. L.J. 96, 103-04 (1960). It is also debunked in MacDonald, *Alcoholism as a Medicolegal Problem,* 11 CLEV.-MARSHALL L. REV. 1, 39 (1962).

24. Cohen, *Pathological Intoxication,* 10 DRUG ABUSE & ALCOHOLISM NEWSLETTER 1, 3 (June 1981).

mentioned."[25] Thus, the concern expressed by Cohen is a call for accurate diagnoses.

The American Psychiatric Association also defined "pathological intoxication" in DSM-II (as they had in the first edition) as follows: "When without apparent pre-existing mental disorder, there is a marked behavioral or psychotic reaction with acute brain syndrome after minimal alcoholic intake, the case will be classified here. When a pre-existing psychotic, psychomotor or personality disorder is made more manifest after minimal alcohol intake, the case will be classified under the diagnosis of the underlying condition."[26] By this, the term "pathological intoxication" is deliberately made rather generic and contingent on how much is known. If a pre-existing condition of psychomotor epilepsy is known, that will be the classification, whereas if it is present but not known, the case will be classified as pathological intoxication. This seems to be the gist of MacDonald's objection to the use of the term; to a certain extent, it is necessarily a confession of ignorance regarding the cause of the symptoms. Along similar veins, the term "pathological intoxication" has been criticized on the grounds that it "indicates that the alcohol itself is of major importance, while in reality the underlying psychological problems are merely brought to the fore by the alcohol."[27] But pathological intoxication requires both, and therefore both are important. MacDonald says:

> Aggressive behavior and amnesia may have an epileptic origin. Following severe head injury there may be greatly reduced tolerance to alcohol associated with behavioral reaction. The possibility of a short-lived delirious reaction with bizarre behavior should not be overlooked. *Even* small quantities of alcohol may temporarily release a schizophrenic reaction or exacerbate the symptomatology in cases of ambulatory or pseudo-neurotic schizophrenia. The association of amnesia, violence and alcohol does not justify diagnosis of the dubious hypothetical syndrome, pathological intoxication.[28]

But that is an objection made from the perspective of a person involved with treatment where the psychological cause is paramount in importance, not from the perspective of decision making regarding criminal responsibility, where symptomatology is of predominant importance, whatever its "ultimate" cause may be. The definition and

---

25. Cohen at 3.
26. DSM-II § 291.6, at 26.
27. O. English & S. Finch, Introduction to Psychiatry 449 (3d ed. 1964).
28. J. MacDonald, Psychiatry and the Criminal 245 (3d ed. 1976) (emphasis added).

identification of a "problem" are determined by the methodology used to define it, and that in turn derives from one's needs to respond to it. The medical profession's understanding, then, of pathological reaction to alcohol is likely to be from a perspective of diagnosis and treatment, and this depends on the sub-branch of medicine. The legal perspective is likely to be one of assessing responsibility, and in that context, for example, the actor's state of mind in contributing to the condition is likely to be central. Neither has done too well in some areas. For example, one of the additional, presumably more precise, diagnoses that should replace a diagnosis of pathological intoxication, according to MacDonald, is "sociopathy,"[29] which Pincus has carrying with it "the hopelessness of therapeutic nihilism."[30] In the DSM-III-R,[31] the statement is made:

> Axis III permits the clinician to indicate any current physical disorder or condition that is potentially relevant to the understanding or management of the case. These are the conditions listed *outside the mental disorders section of ICD-9-CM.*[32] In some instances the condition may be etiologically significant (e.g., a neurologic disorder associated with Dementia); in other instances the physical disorder may not be etiologic, but important in the overall management of the case (e.g., diabetes in a child with Conduct Disorder).

Is it actually possible that all May and Ebaugh were saying is that pathological intoxication is not a valid *psychiatric* diagnosis, just, presumably, as diabetes is not? Is that all the argument is about? If the perspective is limited to that taken by psychiatry, then pathological intoxication is nothing but underlying personality predispositions released by alcohol. And if that is true, then one might fairly argue that what is left must be classified according to a scheme of things, which leaves out any case in which the underlying etiology is physical in nature. That, it would appear, is what May and Ebaugh are doing. Thus, when they say that "it was possible to classify the symptomatology in terms of the predominant reaction type without using the term pathological intoxication, without inventing any new terms and without any greater difficulty than is encountered in attempting to classify *any other psychiatric disorder*,"[33] they evidently quite literally mean that the diagnosis does

29. MacDonald at 244.

30. Pincus, *Can Violence Be A Manifestation of Epilepsy?* 30 NEUROL. 304, 305 (1980). Pincus is identified with the Department of Neurology, Yale University School of Medicine, New Haven, Connecticut.

31. DSM-III-R at 18 (emphasis added).

32. The reference is to WORLD HEALTH ORGANIZATION, INTERNATIONAL CLASSIFICATION OF DISEASES—CLINICAL MODIFICATION (9th rev. 1977).

33. May & Ebaugh at 205 (emphasis added).

not (in their judgment) belong to psychiatry. It is only in what we might call the jurisdictional sense that they are arguing that "it" (pathological intoxication) "does not exist." The attack on pathological intoxication on the grounds that it is not within the province of psychiatry because it has an essentially physical origin is not, obviously, an attack upon its scientific validity; it is simply an acknowledgment of an inability to deal with the cause of the reaction. But to discredit pathological intoxication because it "belongs" in neurology or epileptology or some other branch of medicine is condescending frivolity.

A system of classification has no meaning at all without a referent or a reason for existence. It is important to determinations of responsibility that the actor was psychotic at the time. Leaving aside a defendant's culpability in bringing about the condition, it matters not what species of psychosis is involved or what its ultimate cause may be. It is enough that the reaction occurred. A judicial fact finder would take note of that fact and would do so without concern for the ultimate cause. A generic label covering those cases adequately diagnosed, and those which are not, is useful in the legal system. As the drafters of the Model Penal Code put it: "There is substantial dispute among physicians whether 'pathological intoxication' is a *distinct* clinical entity. Yet the term seems the best to employ for legal purposes in describing a grossly abnormal reaction to alcohol, without respect to the medical reason for the reaction."[34]

A psychotic reaction to alcohol ought to have a bearing on criminal responsibility whether or not psychiatrists can classify the precise underlying conditions bringing about the reaction. Their ignorance ought not be laid at the doorstep of the defendant. The degree of requisite precision varies with the context of its use, treatment or responsibility. Further, and worse, if the desire of psychiatrists of the May and Ebaugh persuasion is merely to eschew professional responsibility for what they believe to be a syndrome that wholly or partly derives from some other field such as neurology, and hence would tarnish psychiatry, it would have been better had they said s, because that is not the way they are always read.

Thus, May and Ebaugh ought to be read as concerned exclusively with the purity of explicit psychiatric nosology predicated on an unspoken assumption regarding the jurisdictional exclusivity of psychiatry. Others obviously do not share this conception of the scope of psychiatry. The question remains whether pathological reaction to alcohol which has no discernable physiological basis ought to be called pathological intoxication or not. But the law cannot wait for these jurisdictional niceties to be resolved by whatever political means they are

---

34. MODEL PENAL CODE § 2.08 comment 7 at 12 (Tent. Draft. No. 9, 1959) (emphasis added).

eventually resolved; these are real cases in our courts, and they need sensible responses now.

Marinacci and Von Hagen wrote a passage that prophetically touches upon the concern here:

> Doctor William G. Lennox,[35] the grand old man in the field of the convulsive disorders, called the psychomotor epilepsies "a cross-roads, the meeting ground for the various disciplines and research minded investigators" of the Neurological Sciences. Whether the final designation of this disorder be "psychomotor epilepsy," to give a bow to the clinicians, or "temporal lobe seizures," to recognize the contributions of the neurosurgeons, is of little moment, because any term will be bound to overlook all the nonclinical scientists—the physiologist, neuropathologist, and the neurochemist, to say nothing of the more limited electroencephalographers or what else.[36]

Still the detractors persist. In 1979, Coid published a "critical review of pathological intoxication"[37] in which he expressed considerable skepticism regarding the nosological value of the concept of pathological reaction to alcohol. This was his conclusion:

> Behavior which fits descriptions of PI [sic] following alcohol intake but which is apparently not understandable in either the light of forensic assessment *or the present framework of psychiatric practice,* has been described in the literature. However, the need for a diagnostic category to span the gap between murder committed when drunk and the range of the McNaughten Rules cannot justify the manufacture of a fictitious label which, furthermore, risks shifting the responsibility away from the individual to an assumed cerebral disease or to an unwarranted power of the drug itself. Although the concept of PI has survived from the last century, it may well be that with further research there is now sufficient diagnostic understanding to allocate many states of supposed PI to more appropriate categories. Meanwhile, the present inflexible and unsupported criteria would appear to have rendered such a nosological entity obsolete.[38]

---

35. Lennox, *Phenomena and Correlates of the Psychomotor Triad,* 1 NEUROL. 357 (1951).

36. Marinacci & Von Hagen, *Alcohol and Temporal Lobe Dysfunction: Some of Its Psychomotor Equivalents,* 3 BEHAV. NEURO-PSYCHIAT. 2 (1972).

37. Coid, *Mania A Potu: A Critical Review of Pathological Intoxication,* 9 PSYCHOL. MED. 709 (1979). Dr. Coid was at the Maudsley Hospital, London, at the time of publication.

38. Coid at 718 (emphasis added).

The title of Coid's article includes the old term "mania a potu," which is another term for pathological intoxication used in some of the older texts.[39] There appears to be more shift in the nomenclature of pathological intoxication than in the phenomenological reality of the event. Cohen, discussed earlier, also said:

> Pathological intoxication, or alcohol idiosyncratic intoxication as it is called in DSM III, is a rather infrequent condition. But when a case is seen, it remains in the memory of those nearby because of the impressive panic or rage reactions. An older name for the disorder is *mania a potu*. This term should be discarded because it has also been used in connection with the delirium tremens.[40]

No new research was reported in the Coid article, but some of the literature to that date were reviewed. The argument is again partly nosological, on what the events should be called, and concern that the concept of pathological intoxication actually overlaps existing diagnostic categories which are deemed adequate. But Coid goes even further and questions the events themselves.

Coid is overly taken with the existence of many inadequate descriptions handed down in various texts over the years. It is obvious that many of these are poorly stated, brief descriptions, often just inaccurate, what lawyers would disparagingly call "black letter law." For example, he quotes from one textbook where pathological intoxication is described as

> The acute effects of a single dose of alcohol on either the well-known phenomena of intoxication, or on excitement (mania a potu) sometimes with clouding of consciousness. The excitement is commoner in people with cerebral trauma, arterio-sclerosis, epilepsy or unstable hysterical personality, and in them may lead to acts of violence; rarely it may occur in normal persons who have taken alcohol when they were exhausted or upset.[41]

But one cannot deny the existence of an event on the grounds that someone else's description of it is not to one's liking. Coid cites the ICD-

---

39. *See, e.g.*, H. DAVIDSON, FORENSIC PSYCHIATRY 330 (1952); W. STODDART, MIND AND ITS DISORDERS (1921).

40. Cohen, *Pathological Intoxication*, 10 DRUG ABUSE & ALCOHOLISM NEWSLETTER 1 (June 1981).

41. Lewis, *Psychological Medicine*, in PRICE'S TEXTBOOK OF THE PRACTICE OF MEDICINE 1172 (1966).

9-CM, which defines "pathological drunkenness." It "Includes acute psychotic episodes induced by relatively small amounts of alcohol. These are regarded as individual idiosyncratic reactions to alcohol, not due to excessive consumption and without neurological signs of intoxication."[42] It is this idiosyncratically determined reaction to alcohol, in the sense of an obscure or unknown cause, which is stressed in the latest version of the DSM (DSM-III-R) and which earlier had disturbed May and Ebaugh.

Coid admits that the ICD definition (that only a small amount of alcohol is of diagnostic value) is of unknown origin and refuted in the Maletzky study[43] even though it is repeated throughout the summary literature.[44] He then faults the concept of pathological intoxication because clinical studies have failed to confirm that the event can be precipitated by a small amount of alcohol. The Maletzky study is dismissed on the ground that it was uncontrolled. Coid also says that "there is no study based on eye-witness accounts or experimental evidence that 'small' quantities of alcohol have ever induced the condition." Surely the works of Marinacci and Thompson, among others, would qualify.

In his discussion of the clinical signs of pathological reaction to alcohol, Coid gives little credence to the consistent observations that pathological reaction to alcohol differs from normal intoxication in that the usual signs of drunkenness are lacking because pathological reaction to alcohol is not intoxicated behavior at all. As to the etiology of pathological intoxication, Coid makes the curious observation that

> despite the fact that PI should not in itself be affected by social factors, no study has ever excluded this possibility, nor has evidence been presented that extensive investigations have been carried out to identify underlying organic illness.[45]

Bach-y-Rita made a point of the social factors, as have others, including Thompson. As to the second point, we will shortly provide considerable evidence of organic illness as underlying the concept of pathological intoxication, but we have already reviewed the extensive works by Marinacci and Thompson and numerous others regarding psychomotor epilepsy and traumatic brain damage as important contributors. Coid included a section on "organic brain damage, epilepsy and the

---

42. WORLD HEALTH ORGANIZATION, INTERNATIONAL CLASSIFICATION OF DISEASES— CLINICAL MODIFICATION § 291.4 (9th rev. 1977).

43. Coid at 710; Maletzky, *The Alcohol Provocation Test*, 39 J. CLIN. PSYCHIAT. 403 (1978).

44. *See, e.g.*, D. HENDERSON & R. GILLESPIE, TEXTBOOK OF PSYCHIATRY (1969); Keller, *A Lexicon of Disablements Related to Alcohol Consumption*, in ALCOHOL-RELATED DISABILITIES 23 (G. Edwards, M. Gross, M. Keller, J. Moser & R. Room eds. 1977); Keller, *A Lexicon of Disablements Related to Alcohol Consumption*, in WORLD HEALTH ORGANIZATION, ALCOHOL-RELATED DISABILITIES (No. 32, 1966).

45. Coid at 712.

EEG."[46] He cited Lishman[47] for the observation that individuals can be subject to a sudden explosion of violent conduct following relatively minor provocations and notes that Lishman attributes this to "increased sensitivity to the effects of alcohol, an exacerbation of previous personality traits, or an entirely new phenomenon."[48] He also mentioned the 1974 Morozov study summarized earlier.[49]

With respect to temporal lobe epilepsy, he adverts to the studies by Skelton, Marinacci (in 1963), Zakowska-Dabrowska and Strzyzewski, and Bach-y-Rita, all summarized in detail earlier. He is unimpressed with any of the evidence. In a particular reference to Thompson's work, he states:

> he believed that there was a high incidence of previous brain injury, along with degenerative[,] infectious, neoplastic and congenital aetiologies, but he provided little evidence for his assertions. He described specific EEG abnormalities of 3 types....At the same time he pointed out that the EEG does not establish the diagnosis since not all patients with the above findings had PI or psychomotor epilepsy; nor did he state that all persons with the clinical symptoms have such electroencephalographic findings.[50]

In Coid's conclusion, he states that "the possibility that PI is an epileptic phenomenon induced by alcohol has been extensively examined without being confirmed."[51] Even his own selective summary does not support that statement.

Whatever assessment one makes of Coid's reservations regarding pathological reaction to alcohol as an entity, it is clear that his objections rest on grounds other than those of May and Ebaugh. The latter seem simply to exclude the case from consideration if there is an underlying physical cause, while Coid seems to deny that the existence of physical causes has been established, and in this we have already tried to show that he is wrong. A good part of the next chapter will be devoted to the question as well, partly because of statements like Coid's. It might be instructive to read Coid's critique of the May and Ebaugh assessment of the evidence as well as the reverse. They do not agree on why they disagree with pathological intoxication.

---

46. Coid at 713.
47. W. LISHMAN, ORGANIC PSYCHIATRY (1978).
48. Coid at 713.
49. Morozov, Kachayev & Lukacher, *Characteristics of Forensic Psychiatric Examination of Pathological and Simple Alcohol Intoxication*, 17 SUDEBNO-MEDITSINSKAIA EKSPERTIZA 51 (April-June 1974).
50. Coid at 714.
51. Coid at 718.

But of paramount importance for the law is to distinguish between the professional purposes and therefore the psychiatrist's needs in diagnosing and treating abnormal behavioral problems and the law's need to make decisions regarding responsibility. Even Bach-y-Rita, et al, prior to describing their own study, began by observing that "Despite a broad clinical consensus on the manifestations of this disordered behavior pattern, its existence *as a definable syndrome is still controversial*."[52] Coid seems to want to deny even this much.

Hollender[53] debunks pathological intoxication on somewhat different grounds. Hollender recites two cases which he believes were wrongly diagnosed as pathological intoxication, and it is difficult to disagree (or agree) with him. He evidently would prefer that one case be diagnosed as hysterical psychosis[54] or dissociative state. The 22-year-old patient drank a single bottle of malt liquor at a party. He became agitated, and in a rage after returning home, he pushed members of his family around, destroyed some furnishings and ran into the street in his underwear, where he preached from the top of a car. Four emergency personnel who responded were unable to control him physically. Eventually he just gave up in a dazed state to the police and eventually fell into a deep sleep in a hospital, where he was examined the next morning by one of the authors of whom Hollender is critical.[55]

There was there no history in this case of brain injury or epilepsy. No EEG abnormalities were found, but alcohol activation evidently was not employed. Hollender equates the episode, nevertheless, to what the members of the New Guinea Bena Bena tribe call an attack of *negi negi*, or victimization by malevolent ghosts, which he believes to be hysterical psychosis.[56] Perhaps of more importance than Hollender places on it is the fact that the patient reported one prior incident of the same sort, violence directed at friends in the service following the drinking of wine. That episode ended with the same type of terminal sleep. This had occurred two years earlier, and he still had amnesia for that episode as well.

The authors in the original report diagnosed the case as pathological intoxication. They were aware of the objections posed by May and Ebaugh that "from the standpoint of theoretical ego psychology, alcohol

---

52. Bach-y-Rita, Lion & Ervin, *Pathological Intoxication: Clinical and Electroencephalographic Studies*, 127 AM. J. PSYCHIAT. 698 (1970) (emphasis added).

53. Hollender, *Pathological Intoxication—Is There Such an Entity?* 32 J. CLIN. PSYCHIAT. 424 (1979).

54. Hollender at 426. *See also* Hollender & Hirsch, *Hysterical Psychosis*, 120 AM. J. PSYCHIAT. 1066 (1964).

55. Hollender, *Pathological Intoxication—Is There Such an Entity?* 32 J. CLIN. PSYCHIAT. 424, 425 (1979). Kosbab & Kuhnley, *Pathological Intoxication*, 15 PSYCHIAT. OP. 35, 36 (1978).

56. Citing Langness, *Hysterical Psychosis in the New Guinea Highlands: A Bena Bena Example*, 28 PSYCH. 258 (1965).

intoxication produces defects in ego function with release of underlying conflicts; these conflicts may be accentuated or provoked by coincident environmental psychological stimuli."[57] But they argue

> that while underlying aspects of personality defects may well be crucial contributing factors, or even a sine qua non of the condition, they should nevertheless not necessarily be regarded as a priori causative elements in the PI syndrome. If this were so, one would have to postulate that a far greater number, if not the majority of all patients with such underlying personality defects and deficiencies in ego functioning, would react to alcohol in such a specifically pathological sense. Obviously, this is not the case, nor has it been supported by empirical observation or statistical data.[58]

Based on their own review of the literature, Kosbab and Kuhnley speculated as follows:

> Stress, as a contributing factor,[59] appears to be at least of hypothetical importance. The stress reaction perhaps may be seen as a temporary, more or less transient, pathological excitation of the pituitary-adrenal system, which then is aggravated and accentuated by the psychologically disinhibiting elements inherent in alcohol consumption. This also would, to some extent, explain why certain individuals will experience pathological reactions to alcohol on some occasions, but not in all instances of alcohol intake. In other words: we may be dealing with a pathological exaggeration of the "fight-or-flight" reaction as a culmination of a complex interplay of underlying personality structure, predisposing stress, and a peculiar trigger function of alcohol, one of its metabolites, or, conceivably, some specific "contaminating" constituents in certain commercially processed alcoholic beverages. This latter aspect would open up the interesting question of whether an allergic component may be present in some instances.[60]

---

57. May & Ebaugh, *Pathological Intoxication, Alcoholic Hallucinosis, and Other Reactions to Alcohol: A Clinical Study*, 14 QRTLY J. STUD. ALCOH. 200, 226 (1953).

58. Kosbab & Kuhnley at 37.

59. The reference here is to Bach-y-Rita, Lion & Ervin, *Pathological Intoxication: Clinical and Electroencephalographic Studies*, 127 AM. J. PSYCHIAT. 698 (1970).

60. Kosbab & Kuhnley at 38. *See also* Quirk, *Treatment For Epileptic Alcoholism*, 7 ONTARIO PSYCHOL. 36 (1976), who also hypothesizes that the reaction could be due to other substances found in alcoholic drinks.

In the other case, Hollender reports a newspaper article about a man who drove his van into a bridge, killing himself, after breaking the windows out of his house. There is no indication the death was not accidental. Newspaper speculation was that he passed out from blood loss from the cuts he had obtained while tearing up his house. No one even diagnosed this case as pathological intoxication or even referred to it. In brief, the title of this piece is a good deal more ambitious than the evidence.

Hollender makes the observation that: "In more than a cursory review of the literature, I did not find a single report of a case of pathological intoxication in a woman."[61] Actually, there are a number of them, and we have previously discussed how their numbers are reduced by case selection methods. Marinacci and Von Hagen report some, one of which we have also previously discussed.[62]

One gets the sense in reading some of these opinions of psychiatrists that perhaps they are skeptical in part because they have never seen a case of pathological reaction to alcohol. But it is a matter of numbers. The phenomenon we are discussing is an unusual incident, but it is extremely significant when it does occur. Even the average police officer will probably never be involved in a gunfight. One of us has been teaching criminal law and criminal procedure for 25 years and has been at the scene of numerous homicide investigations but has never seen a murder. Yet murder is common. But with some of the objections, the impression is that they will never encounter a case of pathological intoxication because it does not fit some scheme of classification related to abnormalities of the human mind.

The Diagnostic and Statistical Manual of the American Psychiatric Association (DSM-III, 1980), which is relied upon in the Perr articles discussed next, is as follows in full:

> 291.40 Alcohol Idiosyncratic Intoxication.
> The essential feature is a marked behavioral change—usually to aggressiveness—that is due to the recent ingestion of an amount of alcohol insufficient to induce intoxication in most people. There is usually subsequent amnesia for the period of intoxication. The behavior is atypical of the person when not drinking—for example, a shy, retiring, mild-mannered person may, after one weak drink, become belligerent and assaultive. During the episode the individual seems out of contact with others.

---

61. Hollender, *Pathological Intoxication—Is There Such an Entity?* 32 J. CLIN. PSYCHIAT. 424, 426 (1979).

62. Marinacci & Von Hagen, *Alcohol and Temporal Lobe Dysfunction: Some of Its Psychomotor Equivalents*, 3 BEHAV. NEURO-PSYCHIAT. 2 (1972).

This disorder has also been called "Pathological Intoxication." [It was called pathological intoxication in DSM-II.]

Age at onset. No information.

Course. The change in behavior begins either while the individual is drinking or shortly thereafter. The duration is quite brief, and the condition ceases within a few hours. The individual returns to his or her normal state as the blood alcohol level falls.

Prevalence. Apparently extremely rare.

Complications. The individual may do harm to himself or herself or to others.

Predisposing factors. A small percentage of individuals with this disorder have been reported to have temporal lobe spikes on an electroencephalogram after receiving small amounts of alcohol. Although the reports are still anecdotal, it is thought that people with brain damage lose "tolerance" for alcohol and behave abnormally after drinking small amounts. The types of brain injury most often associated with this syndrome are from trauma and encephalitis. The loss of tolerance may be temporary or permanent. It is also reported that individuals who are unusually fatigued or have a debilitating physical illness may have a low tolerance for alcohol and respond inappropriately to small amounts.

Differential diagnosis. Other exogenous agents, especially barbiturates and similarly acting substances, may occasionally cause abrupt changes in behavior. Temporal lobe epilepsy, during the interictal period, may be associated with fits of destructive rage. In Malingering, the individual may wish to avoid responsibility for aggressive behavior, claiming that it occurred while he or she was intoxicated from a small amount of alcohol.

Diagnostic criteria for Alcohol Idiosyncratic Intoxication

A. Marked behavioral change, e.g., aggressive or assaultive behavior that is due to the recent ingestion of an amount of alcohol insufficient to induce intoxication in most people.

B. The behavior is atypical of the person when not drinking.

C. Not due to any other physical or mental disorder.

This description is not significantly changed in DSM-III-R, but it is even further from the mark than the earlier versions quoted above.

Perr[63] in 1986 reviewed part of the medical literature relating to

63. Perr, *Pathological Intoxication and Alcohol Idiosyncratic Intoxication—Part I:*

pathological reaction to alcohol.[64] He notes what he believes to be varying clinical descriptions and disagreements about the "causes" of the phenomenon and quotes extensively from the criticism voiced previously by Coid and Hollender. With no explanation as to why, except perhaps his contention that "The practice of psychiatry requires meticulous attention to the use of words in an exact, uniform, and unambiguous fashion,"[65] he concludes that "If the concept [of pathological intoxication] is to be retained, then it probably should be restricted as it is in DSM-III to conditions arising with minimal intake—one or two drinks—at a level insufficient to cause drunkenness in a person who characteristically does not drink and who behaves in a way out of keeping with prior modes of functioning."[66] We have no difficulty with the restriction to unusual behavior, but the insistence on "one or two drinks" as a limiting criterion is simply not supported by the medical literature. There is obviously a sense of caution operating here which will eliminate some cases of what psychiatrists like to call "malingering." It is equally clear, however, that there is no justification for telling a jury something adverse to a criminal defendant's case that simply has no support in the existing research or clinical observations. Indeed the weight of the evidence supports the antithesis. The "one or two drinks" rule would make diagnosis easier and surer but at a high cost of inaccuracy, and it is not the psychiatric profession that it is proposed pays the cost. It is as though forensic psychiatrists think it is part of their professional responsibility to help courts and juries avoid unjustified acquittals even if it means convicting innocent people by misrepresenting the state of their own art.

In a companion piece, Perr points out, with reference to a refinement he proposes between *a* pathological intoxication and *the* pathological intoxication, a distinction that eludes us: "This distinction, based on amount of intake of alcohol, may be arbitrary, but it is an essential consideration in the effort to have uniformity and consistency in diagnosis."[67] Deliberate inaccuracy of diagnoses in criminal cases is an exorbitant sacrifice for verbal purity.

> Since it [pathological intoxication] is being used in statutes [New Jersey's then-existing version of the Model Penal Code's section on involuntary and pathological intoxication], psychia-

---

Diagnostic and Clinical Aspects, 31 J. FOR. SCI. 806 (1986); Perr, *Pathological Intoxication and Alcohol Idiosyncratic Intoxication—Part II: Legal Aspects,* 31 J. FOR. SCI. 812 (1986). (Hereinafter cited as Perr, Part I and Perr, Part II.) Perr is an M.D. and J.D and currently a professor of psychiatry, Rutgers Medical School.

64. Much is left out. For example, the studies by Marinacci and the extensive writings of Thompson are both omitted, as is all of the foreign literature.

65. Perr, Part I at 806.

66. Perr, Part I at 810.

67. Perr, Part II at 817.

> trists may appropriately use the term in medicolegal situations. But they should do so narrowly and in strict conformance with the requirements of DSM-III. No therapeutic purpose is gained by using PI otherwise, and the practice of adopting alcohol idiosyncratic intoxication in all future reports would help to create a more uniform usage within the profession.[68]

The "uniform usage" desired by Perr can only be a reference to verbal replacement of pathological intoxication with "alcohol idiosyncratic intoxication" and hardly addresses what he sees as untoward variations in its description. Secondly, the admonition to psychiatrists to use the term only "narrowly" sounds like a professionally imposed rule of strict construction applied to criminal defenses, which is wholly unjustified. And the reason is clear: "no *therapeutic* purpose is gained by using PI otherwise." Thus, we have a classic instance of the tensions created between psychiatry and law on this issue. The needs of the legal system to take account of behavioral phenomenon interferes with the "uniform usage" sought in psychiatry for *therapeutic* purposes. It would be interesting to know how widespread this attitude is in the psychiatric profession and in the courtroom.

In the second piece,[69] Perr describes the following case. The source of the description is not reported, but the events given are as follows:[70]

> Before the adoption of the Model Penal Code rule in New Jersey in 1979, a 29-year-old policeman went to a wedding, had an unknown amount of alcohol—apparently six to seven glasses of whiskey, and was noted to be intoxicated. Afterwards he went to a bar; from that point he had no recollection.
>
> Later that night—about 4 a.m.—he went "berserk" at home, shooting up his own home with his parents fleeing into the night. His father was awakened by a crash of breaking glass and found his son rambling, smashing furniture, babbling, and so forth. The son went to the cellar and started shooting up the basement, and during this period he called a policeman friend and spoke of people being against him, taking his enemies with him, being deserted, hostages, morphine, and so forth in a disorganized and incoherent fashion.

68. Perr, Part I at 810.
69. Perr, Part II.
70. Perr, Part II at 813-14.

> The police were called and when he appeared armed on the lawn, he was shot in the legs and was brought to the hospital with a traumatic fracture of the left ankle. He awakened 4 h later in a clearly lucid condition, asking what happened and why he was in a hospital; he thought that he had been in an automobile accident. Drug screening was negative, as was the electroencephalogram (EEG) and neurological examination. Diagnosis at the hospital was toxic exogenous encephalopathy. He had no hangover; a psychiatrist who saw him a month later made a diagnosis of PI.
>
> The subject had no prior psychiatric history, no difficulty in functioning, and a modest alcohol history. Periodically he would have up to six drinks in an evening; there was no history of any type of misbehavior. His associates reported that when he drank he was never nasty or giddy. He was a poor driver, not well coordinated, and had trouble remembering routes.
>
> He had a history of two possible concussions in automobile accidents. He also had been a boxer several years earlier and had fought extensively.
>
> On examination, he was pleasant, affable, cooperative, without any apparent psychopathology. He was a high school graduate; on the Wechsler Adult Intelligence Scale (WAIS), he had a verbal score of 133, performance score of 94 (full scale: 117). In view of the great disparity, he was referred for neuropsychological testing, which reflected right tempero-parieto-occipital malfunction and some left auditory nerve deafness. EEG was normal.
>
> The picture was one of bizarre and destructive behavior, hallucinations, paranoid expressions, amnesia with rapid recovery and no sequelae.
>
> The only issue as to a diagnosis of PI was the apparent intake of at least a moderate amount of alcohol—beyond any minimal intake level. He was charged with assault with a deadly weapon, but was found not guilty by reason of insanity and released. (He was also removed from the police force and advised to avoid alcohol—in view of his history and evidence of right-sided brain damage.)

It seems that Perr does not disagree with the disposition of this case, but his two articles will doubtless be counted, as we do, among the literature critical of the pathological reaction to alcohol defense.[71] The

71. He also presents two other cases of which he is critical.

fact is that except for the insistence on "one or two drinks" as a limitation, he appears to think justice was done by acquitting a person on the defense of not guilty by reason of insanity who "committed" assault with a deadly weapon and who went "berserk" (his term) after consumption of a considerable amount of alcohol.

This case is followed by Perr's observation that "Crucial, however, is the current requirement that the amount of alcohol be insufficient to produce intoxication in most people."[72] Several pages earlier, in the "Diagnostic and Clinical Aspects" piece, he had concluded that

> Most important is the recommendation that acute rage reactions, no matter how unclearly motivated, in associations with significant alcohol intake should no longer be classified as pathological intoxication, an expression that should be allowed to die through deliberate neglect. As review of the legal aspects demonstrates, this is not a picayune matter, but one which has significant social import.[73]

We now have an entirely new basis of objection, and it purports to concern itself with no more than the amount of alcohol consumed although the author seems ambivalent even on that limitation. The concept of pathological reaction to alcohol is criticized for the lack of precise uniformity over the years or across different writers even within the same time frame. But that is true of psychiatric nosology in general. The criticism of the concept of pathological intoxication by psychiatrists on the grounds that it lacks precision seems fatuous.[74]

In another sense, all that is involved here is whether pathological reaction to alcohol is a disease or a symptom of some other disease or defect. In a case of claimed pathological intoxication, a psychiatrist may find that the actor was nonpsychotic and sober, psychotic or merely intoxicated. So too the legal system provides for findings of sane and sober, merely intoxicated ("voluntary intoxication") or legal insanity (also encompassing "involuntary intoxication" except for the disease requirement). The condition of extreme drunkenness bears all the hallmarks of psychosis or legal insanity, although it has been deliberately excluded from those categories in both psychiatry and law.[75] The law excludes it because the actor is responsible for his own condition, and, in a sense, psychiatry excludes it for very similar reasons: The actor was responsible, and a disease was not responsible for the behavior. While insanity law

---

72. Perr, Part II at 813.

73. Perr, Part I at 810-11.

74. L. Coleman, The Reign of Error (1984); W. Winslade, The Insanity Plea: The Uses and Abuses of the Insanity Defense (1983).

75. This is discussed in more detail in Chapter 6 on Insanity.

may assume the existence of some underlying disease, the jury is never, or rarely, told they must either identify the underlying disease or convict.[76] Thus the law is content to conclude that the actor was insane without troubling to determine whether the ultimate cause was an identifiable disease. What difference could it make as long as the insanity was not brought on through the fault of the actor? Indeed, it is not clear that psychiatric nosological classifications add anything to a lay person's attitude toward responsibility. Often it is the very inexplicability of many of the pathological intoxication "stories" that lends the most credence to the defendant's claim. That, for example, is why motivelessness is so important in deciding whether it is an authentic case.

Psychiatrists, on the other hand, can hardly be content to conclude that their patient was insane. While the idea is not as meaningless as they sometimes claim, it is not useful to them to carry out their professional charge. The question is, what is wrong with the patient and what course of treatment regimen is thereby indicated? What separates law and psychiatry is the need of psychiatry to define with particularity the disease involved, just as the law must concern itself with what crime is charged, a matter rarely of concern to the psychiatrist outside the realm of forensic psychiatry. Of course, in the context of a criminal trial, the defendant is not the patient of the expert witness and there is no expectation of a treatment program that will be based upon that diagnosis. Trial court diagnoses are diagnoses not subject to revision as treatment progresses and more is known.

Part of the dispute with this psychiatric camp is whether pathological intoxication is a disease or a set of symptoms of some other disease. It may readily be conceded that it is a set of symptoms without giving away anything. Does the law really care whether in one case it was the product of limbic epilepsy and in another of temporal lobe epilepsy?[77] Or that the experts cannot find an organic cause? Or for that matter, whether it was the result of traumatically induced brain damage not amounting to epilepsy? It does help to make the responsibility decision if this is known, but it is not essential; it only helps to exclude those cases in which the defendant is lying.

There is a converse difference in the focus of law and psychiatry. The law should, and usually does, place great weight on whether the actor was aware that alcohol might trigger a reaction such as the one leading to criminal charges in the case. But surely, awareness or not of a condition does not affect the existence of the condition or the existence, for that matter, of the disease. Psychiatry will look largely to the

---

76. 1 W. LAFAVE & A. SCOTT, SUBSTANTIVE CRIMINAL LAW 440 (1986).

77. Indeed, it was not long until the nomenclature was changed to "complex partial seizures" because it was later discovered that not all seizures had their origin in the temporal lobe. Desai, *Complex Partial Seizures*, 30 AM. FAM. PHYS. 158 (1984).

existence of the clinical reality of a disease because it needs to respond to the disease. The law will look largely for fault underlying the behavior because it needs to respond to the conduct of the accused.

Of course, being intoxicated is not a disease and does not alone indicate the presence of any disease. By the same token, having consumed enough alcohol to be considered intoxicated under normal circumstances does not preclude the existence of a disease which might explain the inordinate response to drinking. And it is this point which is overlooked or more likely rejected in the DSM's insistence, embraced by Perr, on small amounts of alcohol consumption being not only of diagnostic value, which it can be, but as a sine qua non of having an underlying disease which caused the behavior in question. In short, they have excluded too much out of a sense of caution, and the DSM has done so in the face of considerable evidence to the contrary.

The three main organizations involved, the American Medical Association, the American Psychiatric Association and the World Health Organization, have not classified mental disorders relating to alcohol in the same way. Keller provides this summary:

> (1) In the American Medical Association's *Standard Nomenclature of Diseases and Operations* (1961), (a) under Acute Brain Disorders: Acute Brain Syndrome, alcohol intoxication, with two subcategories, Acute hallucinosis and Delirium tremens; (b) under Chronic Brain Disorders: Chronic brain syndrome associated with intoxication [Korsakoff's psychosis,[78] Wernicke's encephalopathy[79]]; Chronic brain syndrome, alcohol intoxication, with reaction when known [alcoholic deterioration, etc.].
>
> (2) In the American Psychiatric Association's *Diagnostic and Statistical Manual* (1968), (a) under Psychoses Associated with Organic Brain Syndromes:—Alcoholic psychosis; Delirium tremens; Korsakov's psychosis (alcoholic); Other alcoholic hallucinosis; Alcohol [sic] paranoid state (Alcoholic paranoia); Acute alcohol intoxication; Alcoholic deterioration; Pathological intoxication; Other [and unspecified] alcoholic psychosis; (b) under Non-psychotic Organic Brain Syndromes:—Non-psychotic organic brain syndrome with alcohol (simple drunkenness).
>
> (3) In the World Health Organization's *International Classification of Diseases* (1977) under Alcoholic psychoses: Chronic alcoholic brain syndrome. (Other states classified as

---

78. Now known as Alcohol Amnestic Disorder. DSM-III-R at 98.
79. Now known as Delirium. DSM-III-R at 98.

> organic psychotic include Delirium tremens; Korsakov's psychosis, alcoholic; Alcoholic dementia, other; Alcoholic hallucinosis, other; Pathological drunkenness;[80] Alcoholic jealousy; Alcoholic mania; Alcoholic psychosis, not otherwise specified.)[81]

How, then, is one to assess the evidence presented above with the objections of MacDonald, May and Ebaugh, Coid, Hollender and Perr? The answer may be quite fundamental: Paradigms have anomalies, and it is often repeated demonstration of the anomalies that has challenged the paradigms. Kuhn has shown this in the world of science,[82] and Banay, in his discussion of pathological intoxication, has noted that "In the history of medicine, atypical forms of disease have sometimes contributed toward the understanding of the typical forms."[83] Dahl[84] takes the Kuhn analysis as appropriate not only to psychiatry but to law as well. But this is paradigm by metaphor. Kuhn is not just describing adaptive responses by a field of expertise as Dahl's analogy suggests. Kuhn's analysis is about disciplines which have developed significant scientific explanatory and predictive powers.[85] There is no general theory of law; it is a complex set of techniques to govern and seldom makes any pretense to the contrary. In the end, law is nothing more than a method to foster the monopolization of the use of force by governments and, within that political framework, to achieve its goals.

Perhaps Kuhn's theory could be argued in the context if not of law, then psychiatry. But to assume that the officially available diagnostic categories are scientifically derived is unequivocal nonsense. That is why three summaries of them are reproduced. We would argue that Kuhn's thesis applies only to the hard sciences where the concept of a paradigm makes empirical sense; that is not the case in psychiatry, although other areas of medicine such as neurology would better qualify. What scientific breakthrough or even research led to the medical profession labeling alcoholism a disease?[86] That was a political-therapeutic decision dictated

---

80. WORLD HEALTH ORGANIZATION, INTERNATIONAL CLASSIFICATION OF DISEASES 180 (9th rev. 1977) defines "Pathological drunkenness" as "Acute psychotic episodes induced by relatively small amounts of alcohol. These are regarded as individual idiosyncratic reactions to alcohol, not due to excessive consumption and without conspicuous neurological signs of intoxication. Excludes: simple drunkenness."

81. M. KELLER, M. MCCORMICK & V. EFRON, A DICTIONARY OF WORDS ABOUT ALCOHOL 62 (2d ed. 1982). The []'s are in the DICTIONARY. The DSM cited is DSM-II, which was revised again in DSM-III. The "pathological drunkenness" referred to in the WHO publication is their term for pathological intoxication.

82. T. KUHN, THE STRUCTURE OF SCIENTIFIC REVOLUTIONS (1962).

83. Banay, *Pathologic Reaction to Alcohol*, 4 QRTLY J. STUD. ALCOH. 580 (1944).

84. Comment, *Legal and Psychiatric Concepts and the Use of Psychiatric Evidence in Criminal Trials*, 73 CALIF. L. REV. 411, 418-19 (1985) (authored by Peter R. Dahl).

85. *See, e.g.*, J. GLEICK, CHAOS (1987).

86. The American Medical Association declared alcoholism a disease in 1956. *See* S. Rep.

by the realities of the behavioral symptoms and the desire to do something about them, which required federal funding, while waiting for someone "scientifically" to define it. One article has put that matter correctly: "'[D]isease' theorists sought to eliminate the stigma attached to alcoholism, in order to make it easier to justify provision of treatment to problem drinkers." The author refers to this as winning a "polemical battle."[87] But we do not say this to denigrate the movement but to identify it as a political one, not a scientifically generated one.[88] If we had waited for scientific purism, the drunk tank and "revolving door"[89] would still be the rule. Dahl's premise is that "the law is a social enterprise and psychiatry a scientific one."[90] That is an aspiration, not reality. Szasz has remarked that "psychiatry is a form of social engineering. It should be recognized as such."[91] We doubt that argument in these terms can be fruitful.

As we understand Kuhn, it would suffice to observe that anomalies require paradigms and psychiatry does not have one. The "volatility"[92] of psychiatry is notorious. Kuhn suggests that the disagreements reflected in the psychiatric literature may be even more fundamental. While he is speaking of social sciences more broadly, it was his idea that what differentiated them from the physical sciences was the very concept of a paradigm.[93] For science to operate successfully, there must first be a substantial agreement on some fundamentals. In this sense, psychiatry is pre-scientific; "[Psychiatry] is the softest of the soft sciences, psychiatrists disagree on key concepts and their conclusions and analyses turn on their own value judgments."[94] There is no reason for any court to rely on the presence or the absence of discrete categories in deciding upon the existence of mental illness and in making decisions regarding responsibility. In its best light, it would appear that the grand objection is that pathological intoxication is a syndrome, not a disease, and perhaps that it is a "questionable" one at that because of the unjustified insistence of one group of psychiatrists on a nonintoxicating amount of alcohol to

---

No. 93-208, 93d Cong., 2d Sess. 4, *reprinted in* 1974 U.S. Code Cong. & Ad. News 3039, 3042. *See also* Nemerson, *Alcoholism, Intoxication, and the Criminal Law*, 10 CARDOZO L. REV. 393 (1988).

87. Note, *Alcohol Abuse and the Law*, 99 HARV. L. REV. 1660, 1662 (1981).

88. Note at 1662.

89. D. PITTMAN & C. GORDON, THE REVOLVING DOOR (1958).

90. Dahl at 414.

91. T. SZASZ, LAW, LIBERTY AND PSYCHIATRY: AN INQUIRY INTO THE SOCIAL USES OF MENTAL HEALTH PRACTICES vii (1963).

92. Comment, *Legal and Psychiatric Concepts and the Use of Psychiatric Evidence in Criminal Trials*, 73 CALIF. L. REV. 411 (1985) (authored by Peter R. Dahl).

93. Kuhn defined paradigms as "universally recognized scientific achievements that for a time provide model problems and solutions to a community of practitioners." T. KUHN, THE STRUCTURE OF SCIENTIFIC REVOLUTIONS x (1962).

94. Kadish, *The Decline of Innocence*, 26 CAMBRIDGE L.J. 273, 277 (1968).

satisfy their concern with "malingering." At worst, the grand objection is simply an anti-alcohol stance, if not in a moral sense, then in the sense that its consumption is a competing explanation for behavior.

We would assume that the ordinary utility of alternative nosological schema in medicine, as is certainly true in law, would vary with the purpose for which they are created. This book, for example, takes the phenomenon of pathological reaction to alcohol and tries to trace backwards toward its etiology using medical categories, and forward toward the responsibility question using legal criteria commonly found in criminal cases. There is no reason to suppose they would coincide, given such diverse purposes in the creation of the categories, to begin with. The same is true not just across disciplines but within them as well. Diseases are classified different ways for different purposes. For example, epilepsy is classified in many ways.[95]

What is needed on the medical side is a more systematic effort to deal with interactions involving alcohol in combination with other known medical conditions; its significance is correspondingly disparaged, most often by omission. There are important exceptions, but most literature on temporal lobe epilepsy, for example, does not discuss alcohol. Most medical literature that deals with alcohol deals with alcoholism, not with its potentiation capacity in connection with other drugs or other conditions of the mind. The criminal law, on the other hand, tends to over-focus on alcohol when it is involved in a defense to a criminal charge, and there is a tendency to treat it as equivalent to fault irrespective of the actor's awareness of the potential unusual effects it, as a drug, might have on his behavior. On both sides, the reason is clear enough. Both tend to deal with the norm to the exclusion of exceptional situations, and in some instances a few of the authorities on both sides tend to want to deny even the existence of exceptional situations, though most do not. But there is simply too much evidence to continue to do so. We have no argument with the position that medicine needs to better understand just exactly what has occurred in a case of pathological intoxication so it can be avoided and the underlying cause dealt with. So, too, law needs to recognize that it does occur and deal with the responsibility ramifications of that, presumably in terms of the actor's awareness or fault in creating the situation. Neither observation justifies the attitude that "it does not exist."

Indeed, it would even appear late in the scheme of things to be drawing unadorned dichotomies between law and "medicine." As but one of numerous examples of differing approaches within the broad category of medicine, consider the perspectives of psychiatry and neurobiology.

---

95. Desai, *Complex Partial Seizures*, 30 AM. FAM. PHYS. 158 (1984), provides an overview of the latest classification plan.

The following passages written by Konner are obviously written from the perspective of behavioral biology, but the point for our purposes would be the same:

> The most prominent modern theorist of the nature of the "soul" was Sigmund Freud, a neurologist by training and, at least until his middle years, by inclination. Through the 1880's, he was involved in such enterprises as brain anatomy, clinical neurology, and investigations of the psychotropic and other medicinal effects of cocaine. It was only in the 1890's that he began to write on psychology per se; by this time he was over thirty-five and well known as a medical scientist—a fact that undoubtedly helped make possible his leadership in his newly adopted field. A reading of his papers of the early 1890's leaves a strong, often surprising impression that Freud was completely conversant with the neuroanatomical and neurophysiological knowledge of the day and seemed satisfied with the possibility of accounting for much of the human mind by reference to it....
>
> In subsequent years, Freud made a variety of transformations in many of these concepts and replaced his anatomical conception of the structure of the human soul with various others of a more metaphoric nature. Many of his later contributions were of the greatest importance, both clinically and scientifically, and must not be minimized or even slighted. Nevertheless, it is a pity that he did not continue to follow in an active way the developments relevant to the neurobiology of emotion during the last four decades of his life and attempt to relate them to his growing, flowering theory. If he had, it would perhaps not now be as difficult as it is to bridge the gap between psychoanalysis and neurobiology—a difficulty that arises in part from the fact that few practitioners of either discipline share with Freud the inclination and ability to follow both.[96]

The matter is, of course, a good deal more complex than that, and one would want to include other disciplines such as neuroethology and psychopharmacology. What is clear here is that whatever conflicts of perspective exist, it is not a division between "law and medicine" or even "law and psychiatry," although that is closer.

---

96. M. KONNER, THE TANGLED WING: BIOLOGICAL CONSTRAINTS ON THE HUMAN SPIRIT 130, 136 (1982).

5

Pathological Intoxication as either Induced Psychomotor Epilepsy or the Episodic Dyscontrol Syndrome

As we saw in the previous chapters, psychomotor epilepsy is obviously a major component of the phenomenon of pathological intoxication, and in the first part of this chapter we will take a more detailed look at what is known about the origins and manifestations of psychomotor epilepsy, particularly in relation to crime and violence without any concern for the involvement of alcohol as a triggering mechanism, which was the focus of Chapter 3. The second part of this chapter will also explore the relationship between pathological intoxication and the episodic dyscontrol syndrome, for they share some attributes, and it will consider both psychomotor epilepsy and pathological intoxication in a broader context of ongoing contemporary research and diagnoses involving violence and brain malfunctioning. In summary, psychomotor epilepsy is part of pathological intoxication, and pathological intoxication and psychomotor epilepsy are both part of the broader concept of episodic dyscontrol syndrome. The final section of the chapter takes up some special matters of proof.

PSYCHOMOTOR EPILEPSY (COMPLEX PARTIAL SEIZURES)

We have tried to show that the grand objection to pathological intoxication is the insistence by a few psychiatrists that the concept is nosologically objectionable because it is symptomatic of other, underlying mental diseases. That view is of little concern to the legal system so long as the dispute remains within the realm of psychiatry and does not invade the courtroom. There also is a general skepticism displayed, largely and curiously by the same writers, which challenges the very existence of pathological intoxication as a phenomenon. This doubt finds much of its expression in advocacy of the position by these psychiatrists that there should be an insistence on only a small amount of alcohol before such a diagnosis is made. The two objections are somewhat contradictory in the sense that there is both an insistence that the diagnosis of pathological intoxication be based on only a small quantity of alcohol and that a small amount of alcohol cannot have such an effect. How plausible is it that alcohol in combination with some underlying disease is actually the meaning of pathological intoxication? We think it is accurate, and so we have tried to identify the most likely candidates, and among those, psychomotor epilepsy is seemingly paramount in terms of its frequency. What is psychomotor epilepsy? Is it associated with violence? These are some of the questions addressed in this section. Mark and Ervin, in their classic treatise on violence and the brain address the first question:

> What is epilepsy? Epilepsy itself is not a disease. It is a symptom of brain dysfunction and electrical disorganization within the brain. This disorganization is manifested inside the brain as a very noticeable electrical discharge marked by an increase in both amplitude and frequency of the brain waves. The discharges may occur in various parts of the brain (such as the temporal lobe) or in the entire brain. Behavioral symptoms occasionally occur in relation to certain kinds of epileptic spells, such as temporal lobe seizures; but behavioral symptoms also occur between attacks and cannot be distinguished electrically by the inadequate tools that we now use to record brain wave disturbances.[1]

Konner, in his remarkable tour de force of modern biological research related to human behavioral biology, outlines the scope of research as of several years ago:

> The short-term physiological causes of aggressive behavior, unknown until a few years ago, have now become a subject of active study. Inroads have come from investigators in neuroethology, physiological psychology, psychopharmacology, and most controversially, neurosurgery. The latter has produced both knowledge and controversy in this area for the same reason: the recent use of a type of neurosurgical practice called "psychosurgery" in the treatment of violent epileptic fits. The vast majority of cases of severe epilepsy are characterized by seizures involving massive but uncoordinated muscle contractions, dangerous only to the seizure victim. In a very small percentage, the seizure is directed outward and can result in violent attacks on another person....[2]

---

1. V. MARK & F. ERVIN, VIOLENCE AND THE BRAIN 60 (1970).

2. The same social concern is expressed in Lion, *Medical Treatment of Violent Individuals*, in VIOLENCE AND THE VIOLENT INDIVIDUAL 343 (J. Hays, T. Roberts & K. Solway eds. 1981).

> By the 1950's it was known that lesions of the hypothalamus—the basal brain structure that is the "hub" of the limbic system—could produce violent behavior in rats in the laboratory. Different hypothalamic lesions could reduce violent behavior, and stimulation of appropriate regions of the intact hypothalamus, using implanted electrodes, could either increase or reduce such behavior. These findings were consistent with both the central role postulated for the hypothalamus in the limbic system and the central role postulated for the limbic system in the emotions. Earlier still, it had become evident that other limbic system structures played an important role in aggression.[3]

Epilepsy can be classified in different ways,[4] the utility of which depends upon the purpose of the classification.[5] In the broadest terms of classification by origin, the terms "idiopathic" on the one hand and either "primary" or "symptomatic" on the other designate simply those without an identified cause (idiopathic) and those with known causes (primary or symptomatic) such as "trauma, neoplasm, infection, developmental abnormalities, cerebrovascular disease, or various metabolic conditions."[6] Classified in terms of the type of seizure involved, complex partial seizures, as distinct from generalized seizures, those that are focalized and local, are the phenomena most closely associated with pathological intoxication. It has been suggested that the term "temporal

---

The focus of the concern was the "possible psycho-surgical intervention with violent individuals, including members of racial minorities and prisoners." Lion at 345. *See also* D. SHUMAN, PSYCHIATRIC AND PSYCHOLOGICAL EVIDENCE 89 (1986).

3. M. KONNER, THE TANGLED WING: BIOLOGICAL CONSTRAINTS ON THE HUMAN SPIRIT 188-89 (1982). *See also* Malamud, *Psychiatric Disorder with Intracranial Tumors of Limbic System*, 17 ARC. NEUROL. 113 (1967). Malamud's research indicated that most destructive lesions in the hypothalamic area, lesions which are identified with aggressive behavior and "rage reactions," are neoplastic in quality. The following also essentially support the report by Malamud: Killefer & Stern, *Chronic Effects of Hypothalamic Injury: Report of a Case of Near Total Hypothalamic Destruction Resulting from Removal of a Craniopharyngioma*, 22 ARC. NEUROL. 419 (1970); Reeves & Plum, *Hyperphagia, Rage, and Dementia Accompanying a Ventromedialhypothalamic Neoplasm*, 20 ARC. NEUROL. 616 (1969). *See also* Alpers, *Relation of the Hypothalamus to Disorders of Personality: Report of a Case*, 38 ARC. NEUROL. PSYCHIAT. 291 (1937). For a capsulized review of the broader topic of "violence and the brain", see Goldstein, *Brain Research and Violent Behavior*, 30 ARC. NEUROL. 1 (1974).

4. Comm'n on Classification of Terminology of the Int'l League Against Epilepsy, *Proposal for Revised Clinical and Electroencephalographic Classification of Epileptic Seizures*, 22 EPILEPSIA 489 (1981).

5. *See, e.g.*, Holmes, *How to Evaluate the Patient After a First Seizure*, 83 POSTGRAD. MED. 199 (1988).

6. Rall & Schleifer, *Drugs Effective in the Therapy of the Epilepsies*, in GOODMAN & GILMAN'S, THE PHARMACOLOGICAL BASIS OF THERAPEUTICS 446 (A. Gilman, L. Goodman, T. Rall & F. Murad eds. 7th ed. 1985).

lobe epilepsy" be discarded because the seizures originate as well in the frontal lobe and from the limbic system.[7] However, it is believed that the vast majority of cases of "complex partial seizures" have psychomotor symptomatology.[8] One description of the characteristics of this type of epilepsy is:

> Attacks of confused behavior, with impairment of consciousness, with a wide variety of clinical manifestations, associated with bizarre generalized EEG activity during the seizure but with evidence of anterior temporal lobe focal abnormalities even in the interseizure period in many cases....[9]

"The EEG amply demonstrates that seizures are associated with abnormal and sometimes massive electrical discharges in the brain and serves as the basic method of differential diagnosis of the epilepsies."[10] The same authors put the frequency of epilepsy in general at 3 to 6 per 1,000 population.[11] Attacks may be triggered in a variety of ways:

> physiological changes that cannot in themselves cause seizures may trigger the focus or facilitate spread of abnormal electrical activity to normal tissue. Among such factors are changes in blood glucose concentration, blood gas tensions, plasma pH, and electrolyte composition of extracellular fluid; endocrine changes, fatigue, emotional stress, and nutritional deficiencies may also contribute. Many factors can interact to precipitate seizures in a brain predisposed by injury or inherited defect....[12]

---

7. Desai, *Complex Partial Seizures*, 30 AM. FAM. PHYS. 158, 159 (1984).

8. Desai at 160. *See also* Stevens, *Psychiatric Aspects of Epilepsy*, 49 J. CLIN. PSYCHIAT. 49, 50 (1988):

> The old-fashioned term "temporal lobe epilepsy" is readopted here. The newer term "complex partial seizure,"...refers to any seizure that commences focally with a complex aura or is manifest by automatism associated with loss of consciousness. Temporal lobe epilepsy on the other hand refers to all seizures of temporal lobe origin, including those seizures that commence with primary sensory phenomena originating in the temporal lobe. Since the vast majority of the literature about psychiatric disorders and epilepsy is concerned with temporal lobe epilepsy or psychomotor seizures, I have used these terms in this review, recognizing that only 80% to 90% of temporal lobe epilepsy starts in the temporal lobes and that fewer than half of temporal lobe seizures are manifest only as complex partial seizures.

9. Rall & Schleifer at 447.

10. Rall & Schleifer at 446.

11. Rall & Schleifer at 446, citing Hauser, *Epidemiology of Epilepsy*, 19 ADV. NEUROL. 313 (1978).

12. Rall & Schleifer at 448-49.

"Of the varieties of epilepsy which begin in or are confined to a particular part of the brain, the most important with regard to impulsive or violent behavior is temporal lobe epilepsy...."[13] Linkage of pathological intoxication and epilepsy, partly explored in Chapter 3, suggests the usefulness of some further exploration of the plausibility that, in many cases, the pathological intoxication phenomenon is a psychomotor or other type of seizure triggered by and perhaps even exacerbated by alcohol.

Temporal lobe epilepsy, it would appear, is not much better defined than is pathological reaction to alcohol.[14] Another source describes it as:

> A recurrent paroxysmal [sudden, acute] disorder of cerebral function characterized by sudden, brief attacks of altered consciousness, motor activity, or sensory phenomena. Convulsive seizures are the most common form of attacks, but any recurrent seizure pattern is considered epilepsy.[15]

A neurologist provides more descriptive detail:

> Psychomotor seizures are suspected when aberrant behavior is inappropriate; sometimes purposeless, stereotyped, and repetitive; and associated with confusion, typical automatisms (such as swallowing), typical subjective alterations (mood change, anxiety, gustatory-olfactory hallucinations, deja vu, dreamlike states, feelings of unreality, macropsia[16], or micropsia), impaired memory for the events of the episode, and postictal depression. Not every patient manifests all of these during a psychomotor attack, and it is not clear what the minimal criteria for diagnosis are.
>
> Fortunately, the diagnosis of psychomotor epilepsy is usually not difficult, despite the lack of a completely satisfactory definition. When the diagnosis is unclear, the presence of major motor or grand mal seizures, the history of undisputed brain damage, typical EEG abnormalities, or the response to therapy may influence clinical appraisal.[17]

---

13. V. MARK & F. ERVIN, VIOLENCE AND THE BRAIN 60 (1970). An extensive bibliography, compiled as of 1970, is found at 65-68.

14. Weinberg, *Epilepsy and the Alternatives For a Criminal Defense*, 27 CASE W. RES. L. REV. 771, 773-75 (1977).

15. TABER'S CYCLOPEDIC MEDICAL DICTIONARY 490 (C. Thomas ed. 14th ed. 1981). *See also* 3 LAWYERS' MEDICAL CYCLOPEDIA, § 17.9, at 15, 18-19, § 22.13, at 379, 385 (1970); H. MERRITT, A TEXTBOOK OF NEUROLOGY 753-63 (4th ed. 1967); GREEN & STEELMAN, EPILEPTIC SEIZURES (1956).

16. "Condition in which objects look larger than they really are." TABER'S CYCLOPEDIC MEDICAL DICTIONARY 848 (C. Thomas ed. 14th ed. 1981).

17. Pincus, *Can Violence Be a Manifestation of Epilepsy?* 30 NEUROL. 304, 305 (1980).

The scope and tenor of the debate in that context sound like a replay of the discussion regarding pathological reaction to alcohol: "Most doctors have come to agree that epilepsy should not even be considered a 'disease,' but rather a collection of symptoms."[18] Weinberg states: "The justification for this change [from disease to symptoms] appears to be that since the cause, form, and severity of epileptic seizures can be so diverse and dissimilar, the title 'epilepsy' can be retained only as a generic term for the manifestations which may evidence the condition."[19] Indeed, in the recent past, epilepsy was usually referred to as a "functional" disease, that is without a demonstrable pathology, rather than organic,[20] but it is now clear that the underlying cause is organic.[21] The enhanced precision of diagnosis is largely attributable to the routine use of the EEG as a diagnostic tool[22] even though EEG examinations, especially surface examinations, will miss the abnormalities as they do in cases of pathological reaction to alcohol. The importance of the EEG in this context is due to the almost definitional inevitability of the presence of abnormal electrical impulses from the brain. Indeed, the particular part of the brain involved accounts for much of the variability in the symptomatology of epilepsy.[23]

The underlying causes of epilepsy are numerous in the extreme,[24] yet most cases of epilepsy may still be classed medically as "idiopathic," which means that the cause is not identified. According to Restak "The most common cause of hippocampal damage is loss of normal oxygen supply due to a difficult birth and delivery. A brief period of *anoxia* (lack of oxygen) wreaks its greatest damage to the hippocampus.[25] The great

---

Pincus was with the Department of Neurology, Yale University School of Medicine at the time this article was published.

18. Weinberg at 774, citing L. KOLB, NOYES' MODERN CLINICAL PSYCHIATRY 259 (7th ed. 1968); Rose, *Criminal Responsibility and Competency as Influenced by Organic Disease*, 35 MO. L. REV. 326, 343-44 (1970).

19. Weinberg at 774 n.24.

20. W. DORLAND, THE AMERICAN ILLUSTRATED MEDICAL DICTIONARY (22d ed. 1951).

21. M. BLINDER, PSYCHIATRY IN THE EVERYDAY PRACTICE OF LAW § 24(h), at 103 (1973).

22. Blinder at 103. The pioneering work in the area is found in Gibbs, Gibbs & Lennox, *Electroencephalographic Classification of Epileptic Patients and Control Subjects*, 50 ARC. NEUROL. PSYCH. 111 (1943); Gibbs, Gibbs & Lennox, *Cerebral Dysrhythmias of Epilepsy*, 39 ARC. NEUROL. PSYCH. 298 (1938).

23. Weinberg at 776.

24. One medical writer has listed 67 possible causes, B. ALPERS, CLINICAL NEUROLOGY (5th ed. 1963).

25. *See also* Walton, *Some Observations on the Value of Electroencephalography in Medico-Legal Practice*, 31 MEDICO-LEGAL J. 15, 29 (1963), describing a case that gave rise to considerable diagnostic difficulty over a period of years until the child involved told authorities that "when he was noisy and difficult his mother quietened [sic] him by attaching a rubber pipe to the gas-tap and putting it in his mouth."

majority of patients with *idiopathic epilepsy* (where the cause is unknown) suffered at birth from anoxia that damaged the hippocampus."[26] Idiopathic epilepsy as a diagnosis will undoubtedly decrease as a proportion of all cases[27] as diagnostic techniques improve; it is after all but an acknowledgment of uncertainty as to the specific pathology involved when a diagnosis is based on other factors such as behavioral manifestations.[28] Some epileptics show seizure discharges in the mesocortical areas. "The resulting psychomotor epilepsy can, on occasion, mimic acute schizophrenia down to the smallest detail. Some investigators who have studied schizophrenia via implanted EEG electrodes have even reported abnormal spike discharges in these areas, the distinctive EEG trademark of epilepsy."[29] In cases in which the cause is known, brain damage, either congenital or due to head injury or disease such as neurosyphilis, is a numerically leading cause. A 1971 study of 666 patients with temporal lobe epilepsy indicated definite etiological factors in only 25 percent of the cases reviewed. About half of these were attributable to tumors, and about half were due to head injury. The rest were spread over a variety of factors accounting for a small proportion of the total cases.[30] "Head injuries can predispose to the development of epilepsy; with penetrating wounds the risk may be as high as 30 to 40%."[31]

There are three main types of seizures associated with the disorder of epilepsy, but only one is of concern here. Each type of malady has its

---

> A defence offered to the charge in this case was that this child was, in fact, an epileptic and that his condition had nothing to do with the coal-gas poisoning. It is, however, well recognized that one of the important causes of temporal lobe epilepsy is a focal abnormality arising in one or other temporal lobe as a result of anoxia. The sequence of the EEG changes in this child's case left one in no real doubt that the early abnormalities were not those of epilepsy, but that the succession of records and the changes which had occurred in them were compatible with, and indeed strongly suggestive of, repeated cerebral insults leading eventually to the development of organic changes in the temporal lobes, giving rise to clear-cut localized epileptic discharge arising in these areas. It was not, of course, possible to exclude with certainty the possibility that this child had temporal lobe epilepsy as a result of birth injury, but there was no suggestion of this in his earlier recordings and the interpretation given above, though by no means conclusive, seemed much more probable on the EEG evidence.

26. R. RESTAK, THE BRAIN 209 (1984).

27. Weinberg at 777 nn.43, 44.

28. *See also*, Semenov, *Epilepsy*, in FORENSIC PSYCHIATRY 231 (G. Morozov & I. Kalashnik eds. M. Vale trans. 1970).

29. R. RESTAK, THE BRAIN 291 (1984).

30. Currie, Heathfield, Henson & Scott, *Clinical Course and Prognosis of Temporal Lobe Epilepsy*, 94 BRAIN 173, 180-82 (1971). *See also* B. ALPERS, CLINICAL NEUROLOGY (5th ed. 1963).

31. Rall & Schleifer, *Drugs Effective in the Therapy of the Epilepsies*, in GOODMAN & GILMAN'S, THE PHARMACOLOGICAL BASIS OF THERAPEUTICS 446, 469 (A. Gilman, L. Goodman, T. Rall & F. Murad eds. 7th ed. 1985).

own distinctive EEG pattern. Grand mal seizures are the best known because of their dramatic, obvious manifestations. The patient falls down and goes into contractions of the entire voluntary muscle system.[32] The second major type is called petit mal, in which there is a transient interruption of the stream of consciousness for usually less than a minute.[33] Grand mal and petit mal seizures can, of course, be involved in criminal cases as, for instance, involuntary manslaughter charges based on automobile crashes in which a seizure may have been involved. In addition, it is known that one type of seizure may change into another type.[34]

Psychomotor epilepsy, later more commonly referred to as temporal lobe epilepsy (and now subsumed under complex partial seizures), in which the focal point of the abnormal electrical discharge is the temporal lobe of the brain, is the third type, and it is the type associated by both Marinacci and Thompson[35] as well as others such as Skelton[36] with pathological reaction to alcohol. Some writers include a fourth type called epileptic furor attacks,[37] although most would subsume that category under psychomotor epilepsy.[38] As we have seen, their view is that while most often the onset of any attack in cases of epilepsy is spontaneous, alcohol also is a pervasive triggering mechanism and that essentially many or even most instances of pathological intoxication are actually cases of psychomotor epilepsy where the agent responsible for the seizure is alcohol.

Psychomotor epilepsy is that type of epilepsy "in which transient mental disturbances replace the typical convulsions." It is characterized "by automatic, stereotyped movements which are reflections of disordered and confused psychic functioning." Gibbs, who suggested the adoption of the term in 1937 described it in these terms: "hallucinations, bizarre visceral sensations, feelings of depersonalization, sudden feeling of panic and impending catastrophe, distortions of bodily or spatial perceptions, loss of consciousness without convulsive movements, amnesia episodes, and automatic behavior."[39]

---

32. L. KOLB, NOYES' MODERN CLINICAL PSYCHIATRY 262-63 (7th ed. 1968).

33. Kolb at 264-66. *See, e.g.*, People v. Decina, 2 N.Y.2d 133, 157 N.Y.S.2d 558, 138 N.E.2d 799 (1956). But these are not our main interest here. Those types of seizures are outlined in more detail in Weinberg, *Epilepsy and the Alternatives for a Criminal Defense*, 27 CASE W. RES. L. REV. 771 (1977).

34. Semenov, *Epilepsy*, in FORENSIC PSYCHIATRY 231 (G. Morozov & I. Kalashnik eds. M. Vale trans. 1970).

35. These and similar studies are discussed in Chapter 3.

36. Skelton, *Alcohol, Violent Behavior, and the Electroencephalogram*, 63 S. Med. J. 465 (1970).

37. *See, e.g.*, B. MALOY, NERVOUS AND MENTAL DISEASES 268 (1935).

38. L. KOLB, NOYES' MODERN CLINICAL PSYCHIATRY 263 (7th ed. 1968); Walker, *Murder or Epilepsy?* 133 J. NERV. & MENT. DIS. 430, 431 (1961), (referring to a case classified by him as psychomotor epilepsy as illustrating "the modern version of a case of epileptic furor").

39. Gibbs, Gibbs & Lennox, *Epilepsy: A Paroxysmal Cerebral Dysrhythmia*, 60 BRAIN 377

More recently, temporal lobe epilepsy was described as resulting in "such seizures [as] may produce abrupt personality change, confusion, inappropriate behavior for which the individual is partially or completely amnesic, impulsive acts of violence, and, rarely, seemingly well-thought-out crimes against property or persons."[40] It is remarkable that the link between psychomotor (temporal lobe) epilepsy and pathological reaction to alcohol has not been more commonly made. According to Walker, the connection between psychomotor epilepsy and violence was clearly made at least by 1854 in the psychiatric clinical literature.[41]

Monroe summarized his own research and extensive review of the literature:

> We will document evidence for aggressive acts characteristic of instinct dyscontrol and impulse dyscontrol being ictal phenomena and not just postseizural confusional behavior or interictal disturbances of behavior. In fact, it is not hard to identify the postseizural disinhibitions and distinguish them from ictal aggressions. The former disorders do not present a social problem, because such responses are usually poorly coordinated, diffusely directed acts of relatively short duration. They are accompanied by such extreme impairment of consciousness that the acts are ineffectual, in that the primitive homicidal, suicidal, or sexual intentions are not successfully completed. However, it will be our contention that even some of the higher hierarchical levels of episodic dyscontrol, that is, those which are socially effective in terms of their homicidal, suicidal, or sexual intent, are also epileptoid phenomena directly related to undetected excessive neuronal discharges in the central nervous system.[42]

A Soviet writer, Semenov, has also provided a summary of epilepsy and crime:

> Violations of the law committed by epileptics in a state of disturbed consciousness are characterized, as a rule, by the absence of psychologically comprehensible motives, by total disregard of the surrounding situation, and by an absence of any attempt to conceal traces of the violation. Aggressive

---

(1937).

40. M. BLINDER, PSYCHIATRY IN THE EVERYDAY PRACTICE OF LAW § 24(h), at 103 (1973).

41. Walker, *Murder or Epilepsy?*, 133 J. NERV. & MENT. DIS. 430, 431 (1961), citing L. DELASIAUVE, TRAITE DE L'EPILEPSIE (1854).

42. R. MONROE, EPISODIC BEHAVIORAL DISORDERS 113 (1970). *See also* R. MONROE, BRAIN DYSFUNCTION IN AGGRESSIVE CRIMINALS (1978); K. MENNINGER, THE VITAL BALANCE (1963).

> actions against other persons are characterized by extraordinary and senseless cruelty, such as infliction of numerous wounds or dismemberment of the victim's body. However, in certain instances, when the disturbance of consciousness is in the form of ambulatory automatism, the actions of the patient may be outwardly normal. The patient orients himself in space in some measure, recognizes persons he knows, and even answers questions. Nonetheless, his perception of the situation as a whole is distorted; the patient exhibits emotions of fear or spite inappropriate to the situation, and sometimes by his utterances reveals hallucinations or delusions....[Evidence may include] his falling asleep at the place of the violation....[P]atients are deemed not legally responsible.[43]

Electroencephalogram recordings have provided useful techniques in detecting psychomotor epilepsy. Prominent writers in this field have agreed that the epileptogenic foci are located in the anterior temporal and sometimes in the frontal region and the location provides it with distinguishing characteristics from other seizures. There also appears to be a very high degree of functional psychiatric disorder existing between seizures in persons with psychomotor epilepsy.

The patient experiences an impairment, or total loss, of consciousness and resembles a schizophrenic in symptomatology. The attack may last from several minutes to half an hour or so. Amnesia is experienced for the period of the attack. The patient suffers delusions; some experience terror, rage or both, accompanied by outbursts of violence:

> Acts of violence may be committed in these automatisms and may be of a strikingly brutal nature, the patient pursuing his crime to a most revolting extreme.
>
> These furors are characterized by their suddenness, absence of premeditation and of precaution, and amnesia for them. The extraordinary degree of discrimination and judgment displayed in the psychomotor attack often gives the patient's acts a misleading appearance of deliberation. It may be difficult to accept the fact that the author of the crime was not responsible for his acts.[44]

It should be emphasized that this description of the nature of temporal lobe epilepsy attacks is found in a general treatise on clinical

43. Semenov, *Epilepsy*, in FORENSIC PSYCHIATRY 231, 245 (G. Morozov & I. Kalashnik eds. M. Vale trans. 1970).

44. L. KOLB, NOYES' MODERN CLINICAL PSYCHIATRY 267 (7th ed. 1968).

psychiatry. It is, however, noted elsewhere in the same text, under the heading of "Pathological Intoxication" that:

> Occasionally an individual of unstable personality may, on partaking of alcohol, suffer from a transitory mental state much more striking in the nature and severity of the symptoms than ordinary drunkenness, and known as pathological intoxication. The onset is dramatically sudden. Consciousness is impaired, and the patient is confused and disoriented and suffers from illusions, hallucinations of sight, and transitory delusions. Activity is exaggerated, impulsive, and aggressive, even to the point of destructiveness. The emotional disturbances are profound and may consist of rage, anxiety, or depression, perhaps with suicidal attempt. The disorder lasts from a few minutes to a day or more and is usually followed by a prolonged sleep, after which there is an amnesia for the episode.[45]

While this clearly is a typical description of the phenomenon of pathological intoxication, Kolb takes the matter further, writing in 1968:

> There is an increasing tendency to consider that such episodes [of pathological intoxication] with their disturbances of consciousness and perhaps crimes of violence are really instances of psychomotor epilepsy released by alcohol in persons predisposed to such seizures.[46]

Given the identity of the observed behavior and symptoms, including EEG's, the views advanced by Thompson and Marinacci, that a large part of pathological intoxication is attributable to a temporal lobe epileptic attack triggered by alcohol and that many are cases of brain damage in which a reaction is triggered by alcohol, seem compelling.

As to a small subgroup in his study, another researcher, Victor, observed:

> The third and least clearly defined group comprised 21 [of the sample of 241 alcoholic] patients in whom cerebral trauma and alcoholism were associated. This group was distinguished by the fact that the seizures were frequently focal in

45. Kolb at 196.

46. Kolb at 196. *See also* State v. Goza, 317 S.W.2d 609, 612 (Mo. 1958), where testimony indicated: "'In other words, a patient with alcohol may go on and have a seizure or make the seizure more apt to occur, and also if—if there is some—some perhaps emotional distress or psychological stress, this is more apt to cause a patient to have a (psychomotor) seizure also.'"

> character and accompanied by focal EEG abnormalities. In the patients with idiopathic and post-traumatic epilepsy, seizures occurred during periods of sobriety as well as in relation to drinking, but they were far more frequent and severe in the latter circumstance. The period of intoxication which precipitated seizures was not necessarily prolonged; in some cases, a weekend or even a single evening of drinking was sufficient.[47]

As observed upon a review of the literature by Kelley and Reilly, "Thus, the literature does support the concept that certain people with abnormal EEGs, a history of head trauma, or epilepsy may be more susceptible to the effects of alcohol both behaviorally and in terms of EEG changes."[48]

There is possibly an interplay between the environmental and organic functions in the onset of pathological intoxication.[49] Many cases have been described in which it appears that pathological reaction to alcohol and psychomotor epilepsy are the same, the attack involved in the former being triggered by alcohol while the other occurs spontaneously or as the result of environmental factors. For example,

> Charles was a muscular 28-year-old man who was noted for his pugnacious attitude while under the influence of alcohol. After consuming only two or three drinks, he would often fly into rages and become extremely assaultive. He would be amnesic for these episodes. Charles attributed this to alcoholic blackouts, but admitted that his tolerance to alcohol was low. He was a soldier in the Reserve Army and apparently a good one. One day while on maneuvers, a sergeant barked an order at him. Charles suddenly struck the sergeant with his rifle butt and fractured his skull. Before a court martial was ordered, he was examined medically. He could recall the onset of maneuvers, and then "feeling strange, as if in a dream." He was amnesic for all events which followed until his apprehension by the military police. An electroencephalogram showed bilateral spike discharges from the temporal lobes, more pronounced when alcohol was ingested. In fact, a full-blown temporal lobe seizure could be reproduced by

---

47. Victor, *The Pathophysiology of Alcoholic Epilepsy*, 46 RES. NERV. MENT. DIS. 431, 446 (1968). *See also* Victor, *The Role of Alcohol in the Production of Seizures*, 4 MOD. PROB. PHARMACOPSYCHIAT. 185 (1970).

48. Kelley & Reilly, *EEG, Alcohol, and Alcoholism*, in EEG AND EVOKED POTENTIALS IN PSYCHIATRY AND BEHAVIORAL NEUROLOGY 55, 57 (J. Hughes & W. Wilson eds. 1983).

49. J. PINCUS & G. TUCKER, BEHAVIORAL NEUROLOGY (2d ed. 1978).

feeding four ounces of whiskey to him. Charles was discharged from the service as medically unfit, without facing a court martial.[50]

It is important, then, to determine the extent to which psychomotor epilepsy per se is associated with violence apart from any alcohol involvement. One point that needs to be made early is that the association of epilepsy and crime has an unpleasant history which perhaps peaked with Lombroso,[51] who greatly overdid the matter by virtually equating crime and epilepsy. Thus, experts in the field of epilepsy are understandably concerned that such unjustifiably broad equations not be made. The other side of the coin is that a person with a bona fide defense to a criminal charge ought not to loose it because others might feel defamed or disparaged by that outcome. The association of violence and epilepsy has been a popular theme in literature ranging from Euripides[52] at least through Michael Crichton.[53]

Along with the broad question of the biological etiology of crime,[54] the link between temporal lobe (psychomotor) epilepsy and violence is disputed. The disputes tend to center on the question of, given that the actor has a physiological condition which renders him or her liable to psychomotor seizures, whether that condition was a contributing factor in the crime charged. Pincus and Tucker have asserted that "Alcohol is one of the drugs known to precipitate or worsen episodes of violence in individuals with a past history of violent behavior. The state induced by alcohol is known as 'pathological intoxication.'"[55] The connection is similarly assumed in Verdeaux: "In criminal cases, epilepsy determination proves particularly problematic, as experts must be able to ascertain

---

50. McCaldon, *Automatism*, 91 CAN. MED. ASS'N J. 914, 916 (1964).

51. C. LOMBROSO, CRIME, ITS CAUSES AND REMEDIES 371 (1918).

52. "The correlation between epileptic seizures and incontrollably [sic] violent behavior was already known thousands of years ago (e.g., the portrayal of Hercules in a Greek tragedy by Euripides, going on a violent rampage in the throes of a seizure, apparently of the temporal-lobe epilepsy type)." Braga & Filho, *Epilepsia e Dinquencia* (Epilepsy and Delinquency), 19 J. BRASILEIRO PSIQUIATRIA 245 (1970). "An early name for epilepsy was 'the Disease of Hercules'; in a fit of rage, Hercules killed his best friends and his children." H. WEIHOFEN, MENTAL DISORDER AS A CRIMINAL DEFENSE 36 (1954).

53. Epilepsy, specifically psychomotor epilepsy, was an important ingredient in M. CRICHTON, THE TERMINAL MAN (1972). Earlier in THE ANDROMEDA STRAIN (1969), one of Crichton's characters had an attack of epilepsy in response to flashing light; this is now referred to as photogenic epilepsy. TABER'S CYCLOPEDIC MEDICAL DICTIONARY 490 (1981).

54. J. BRANTLEY & M. KRAVITZ, ETIOLOGY OF CRIMINALITY—NONBEHAVIORAL SCIENCE PERSPECTIVES—A DEFINITIVE BIBLIOGRAPHY (NIJ, NCJRS 1979). Some of the literature is restricted to genetic correlates of crime. *See, e.g.*, L. TAYLOR, BORN TO CRIME—THE GENETIC CAUSES OF CRIMINAL BEHAVIOR (1984).

55. Pincus & Tucker, *Violence in Children and Adults—A Neurological View*, 17 J. CHILD PSYCHIAT. 277 (1978). *See also* Loiseau & Henry, *Crime et Epilepsie* (Crime and Epilepsy), 5 BORDEAUX MEDICAL 2609 (1972).

whether the offender was actually under the influence of the illness when he committed a crime."[56]

There is disagreement regarding the frequency of the association of epilepsy and violence, some stressing that it is rare[57] or even possibly nonexistent[58], others questioning that view.[59] In Knox's study, the connection seems rare.[60] This was a study based on a group of 43 patients who had experienced automatisms in the past, selected from 434 patients diagnosed as suffering from epilepsy. Only one patient had acted in an extremely aggressive and violent fashion in the past during epileptic automatisms and was considered potentially homicidal by the hospital staff, based on this and their observations of him. Rarity of the event establishes the connection between epilepsy and violence; it does not refute it, and much of the literature tends to confuse this point because of differing perspectives.[61] Attempts to protect a fairly broad

---

56. Verdeaux, *Etude Neuropsychiatrique et Electroencephalographique des Delinquents* (Neuropsychiatric and Electroencephalographic Study of Delinquents), 10 RIVISTA DI NEUROBIOLOGIA 1180 (1964).

57. Rodin, *Psychomotor Epilepsy and Aggressive Behavior*, 28 ARCH. GEN. PSYCHIAT. 210 (1973).

58. Stevens & Hermann, *Temporal Lobe Epilepsy, Psychopathology, and Violence: The State of the Evidence*, 31 NEUROL. 1127, 1130-31 (1981), suggest that "psychotic behaviors are mediated by systems which differ biochemically from systems responsible for initiating or maintaining epileptic seizures....[P]athologic violence thus seem[s] to be maintained by or depend upon circuitry that differs from and even opposes the mechanisms maintaining or propagating epileptic discharge." The authors conclude that:

> Analysis of the data now at hand indicates that severe psychopathology in individuals with epilepsy requires more than a simple association with TLE [temporal lobe epilepsy]. For more than two decades it has been fashionable to attribute the old pejoratives formerly encompassed in the "epileptic personality" to patients with TLE. This view is supported by anecdote and by an imposing body of research on the limbic system of animals. If, however, well-controlled clinical studies cannot show that TLE is the most significant variable, we must search for more specific and critical factors.

See also Klighman & Goldberg, *Temporal Lobe Epilepsy and Aggression*, 160 J. NERV. MENT. DIS. 324 (1975); Tizard, *The Personality of Epileptics: A Discussion of the Evidence*, 59 PSYCHOL. BULL. 196 (1962) (both reviewing the literature).

59. Falconer, *Clinical, Radiological and EEG Correlations with Pathological Changes in Temporal Lobe Epilepsy and Their Significance in Surgical Treatment*, in TEMPORAL LOBE EPILEPSY 396 (M. Baldwin & P. Bailey eds. 1958); Currie, Heathfield, Henson & Scott, *Clinical Course and Prognosis of Temporal Lobe Epilepsy*, 94 BRAIN 173 (1971); Ounsted, *Aggression and Epilepsy*, 13 J. PSYCHOSOM. RES. 237 (1969); Glaser, *Limbic Epilepsy in Childhood*, 144 J. NERV. MENT. DIS. 391 (1967); Serafetinides, *Aggressiveness in Temporal Lobe Epileptics and Its Relation to Cerebral Dysfunction and Environmental Factors*, 6 EPILEPSIA 33 (1965); Podolsky, *The Epileptic Murderer*, 30 MEDICO-LEGAL J. 176 (1962).

60. Knox, *Epileptic Automatism and Violence*, 8 MED., SCI. & LAW 96 (1968).

61. *See, e.g.*, Desai, *Complex Partial Seizures*, 30 AM. FAM. PHYS. 158, 161 (1984), where it is asserted that "Violent acts occur in less than 0.1 percent of complex partial seizures, and the violent behavior is usually fragmentary, unsustained and short-lived." When violence does

class of persons who have epilepsy is no excuse for denying defendants a legitimate defense in criminal cases. We allow insanity defenses precisely because most people are not insane.

There are a number of discernable reasons for the lack of clarity in the relationship of epilepsy and crime. One is the uncertainty of the original diagnosis of epilepsy. For example, in one study it was found that 14 of 18 juveniles referred by a juvenile court who were clearly identified as having psychomotor epilepsy had engaged in serious acts of violence. Eight had been arrested for acts of extreme personal violence which included two murders.[62] In another study,

> Mark and Ervin[63] found an obvious and known history of epilepsy in 38 [of 400 prisoners studied], an incidence more than 10 times higher than that of the general population. Furthermore, half of the 400 had experienced phenomena resembling epileptic symptoms, including altered states of consciousness and warning stages preceding the violent act, and sleep, drowsiness, or lassitude after the act. EEG abnormalities were seen in 35%.[64]

Pincus asked: "How are we to decide if the incidence of psychomotor seizures in this group is less than 10% or approximately 50%?"[65] In addition, many of the writers refer to "epilepsy" without further differentiation, and others are of the opinion that the various types and manifestations of epilepsy are so diverse that epilepsy can only be used as a generic term.[66] Monroe put the point this way:

> The correlation [between epilepsy and violence] depends to some degree on how one defines epilepsy. For instance, in three of four patients, all homicidal, reported by Winkler[67]...there was no history of typical seizures but in all

---

occur, the author classifies the case as one of complex partial seizures with psychic symptoms. The most common psychic symptom is fear, which can vary from uneasiness to stark terror. "Anger as an ictal event has been discussed extensively, particularly in the lay press, and has been used as a legal defense in some homicide cases. However, anger is a rare ictal phenomenon." It is also noted that complex partial status may be confused with absence status (petit mal seizures) or an organic brain syndrome. Desai at 162. *See also* Gnanamuthu, *Confusional States and Seizures*, 84 POSTGRAD. MED. 149 (1988).

62. Lewis, et al., *Psychotic Symptomatology in a Juvenile Court Clinic Population*, 12 J. AM. ACAD. CHILD PSYCHIAT. 660 (1973).

63. Citing V. MARK & F. ERVIN, VIOLENCE AND THE BRAIN (1970).

64. Pincus, *Can Violence Be a Manifestation of Epilepsy?* 30 NEUROL. 304, 305 (1980).

65. Pincus at 305.

66. Weinberg at 774.

67. Winkler & Train, *Acts of Violence with Electroencephalographic Changes*, 20 J. CLIN. EXP. PSYCHOPATH. 223 (1959).

> instances there was paroxysmal hypersynchrony on EEG examination. The act of violence was out of character for the individual and would be categorized by us [under the new nosology the authors were proposing] as either instinct dyscontrol or impulse dyscontrol. All of the episodes were associated with amnesia and in two of the three there was an aura just before the period of amnesia in which the violent act was committed. Should these patients be considered epileptics? Any statistics comparing epilepsy and acts of violence will depend on how one interprets such data.[68]

As Monroe noted later in his work, "any correlations between EEG abnormality and epilepsy depend on definitions of both the EEG abnormality and the clinical syndrome."[69] Monroe, nevertheless, made the following observation regarding his research undertaking:

> The behavioral disorders we are studying are characterized by precipitous or explosive expressions of primitive impulses of a rageful, fearful, or sexual nature that are recognized by the individual and/or society as being inappropriate, and are often recognized in retrospect by the individual himself as ego-alien. A review of the literature suggests that it is precisely this group of patients who are most likely to have abnormal EEG's, particularly of a paroxysmal nature, usually associated with an altered level of awareness and sometimes (the exact incidence unknown) typical epileptic seizures.[70]

One study by Gunn found no difference in the levels of violence manifested by epileptic and nonepileptic prisoners.[71] In another study by Gunn and Fenton,[72] a high incidence of epilepsy was found among prisoners, but it was estimated that only 2 of 46 males may have committed their crimes during automatic behavior attributable to epilepsy and in another sample of 158 male epileptics that it was probable that no crimes were committed in that state. But others have disputed even this much: "The criminal behavior in both instances, however, went beyond the fragmentary and unsustained character of automatisms; hence, we also question whether their violent behavior occurred during epileptic seizures."[73]

---

68. R. MONROE, EPISODIC BEHAVIORAL DISORDERS 165 (1970).
69. Monroe at 176.
70. Monroe at 165.
71. Gunn, *Social Factors and Epileptics in Prison*, 124 BR. J. PSYCHIAT. 509 (1974); Gunn & Bonn, *Criminality and Violence in Epileptic Prisoners*, 118 BR. J. PSYCHIAT. 337 (1971).
72. Gunn & Fenton, *Epilepsy, Automatism, and Crime*, LANCET 1173 (June 1971).
73. *But see* Delgado-Escueta, *Special Report: The Nature of Aggression During Epileptic*

There is an interesting postscript to these Gunn studies. One subject was excluded as epileptic from the latter sample because of doubt about the diagnosis after he inexplicably beat his wife to death in bed with a claw hammer. He had suffered a seizure when he was two days old which lasted an hour. EEG results conclusively demonstrated that he suffered cerebral damage, but, typically, earlier testimony was to the effect that it was "'not, of course, possible to say how these findings may relate to the crime with which he is charged.'"[74] Also at his trial, a prison doctor "commented that the logical sequence of his actions and the absence of any sign of confusion indicated that he was not suffering from any epileptic condition."[75] Gunn would later argue: "[T]he logical sequence of events is not incompatible with epileptic automatism, for whilst it is true that it is unusual to find a high degree of integrated behavior associated with automatism, behavior which is apparently purposeful, such as searching, drinking, smoking, undressing, are all described" in the literature.[76]

After the subject spent 13 years in prison following his conviction for manslaughter, a series of events led to further investigation.

> [H]e was referred to a neuropsychiatric centre for an opinion about surgical treatment. By arrangement his anticonvulsant drugs were stopped, and four days later he went into *status epilepticus*. His EEG was grossly abnormal with a distinctive slow wave discharge confined to the right fronto-temporal region. At one point during his stay in hospital his speech became slurred, he had only patchy recall from the previous week and he confabulated, though he remained conscious all the time. The neuropsychiatrist reported that the abnormal mental state he witnessed was an unusually severe and prolonged post-ictal effect;[77] yet it might have passed notice without careful questioning. "This, with the finding of a temporal lobe lesion capable of provoking a psychomotor seizure, makes it possible that he might carry out some act during or soon after a fit, and afterwards have no memory or only fragmentary memory of the act." He also added "it is entirely possible that he obscured the typical features of a psychomotor seizure and/or post-ictal confusion, by telling the

---

Seizures, 305 NEW ENG. J. MED. 711, 716 (1981).

74. Gunn, *Epileptic Homicide: A Case Report*, 132 BR. J. PSYCHIAT. 510, 511 (1978).

75. Gunn at 511.

76. Gunn at 512.

77. The post-ictal effect referred to is the period following the seizure.

most convincing and self-protective story he could make up."[78]

Largely because it had been the defendant's "confabulation" following the homicide and the testimony of the prison doctor that contributed to his conviction in the first place despite the evidence of psychomotor epilepsy and the motivelessness of the crime, it was decided that immediate discharge was appropriate. No mention of alcohol is made in the report. Presumably, none was involved. What is unique about the case is that the miscarriage of justice was caught, albeit late in the day for the defendant.

Another reason for muddled results of reported research on the link between epilepsy and violence is the structure of research. In one study, 18 epileptologists reviewed videotapes of 19 patients, 13 of whom had epileptic attacks recorded. Only one showed aggression that could be dangerous to another person, but there were other aggressive acts directed mostly at property or at nothing. The researchers noted that only one of the subjects had an arrest record for assault. This study looks superficially overwhelming since the researchers began with a population of 5,400 patients. But the 13 who were actually observed and reported on were selected from 16 epilepsy programs in the United States and several overseas. The selection was by "officials" who believed that the 13 showed aggressive behavior during seizures. In their discussion, the authors concluded that they had demonstrated "the near impossibility of committing murder or manslaughter during random and unsustained psychomotor automatisms."[79] Having said that, they then observed:

> We did not select patients from a population with known aggressive behavior, violence, and psychosis, and we did not study any patients who were on trial for violent crimes during epileptic attacks. These are important distinctions, because more harmful acts of aggression could characterize the automatisms of *criminals with epilepsy* or *violence-prone patients with psychoses and epilepsy.*[80]

In other words, it would appear that this selected population consisted of epileptics with slight aggressive tendencies during a seizure but did not include those charged with murder or manslaughter from other, broader populations since they were "criminals with epilepsy" or "violence-prone patients with psychoses and epilepsy."

---

78. Gunn at 511.

79. Delgado-Escueta, *Special Report: The Nature of Aggression During Epileptic Seizures,* 305 NEW ENG. J. MED. 711, 715 (1981).

80. Delgado-Escueta at 716 (emphasis added).

The introduction to that article cited the existence of a number of appellate cases in which epilepsy had been, presumably unsuccessfully, used as a defense in cases involving murder, manslaughter or disorderly conduct, and concern was expressed that this was creating the impression of a link between epilepsy and violence. They noted that "In 1979 alone, five cases of murder went to court with epilepsy as the defense."[81] The avowed purpose of this research was to demonstrate that the connection between epilepsy and violence was overdrawn because "some members of the public and the legal and medical professions believe that crimes of violence can be committed during epileptic attacks."[82] Frankly, we would have preferred they studied the population of those who were "criminals with epilepsy"; the research question would, of course, be whether that characterization was true. A retrospective research design would be at least better than one that consciously excluded the most relevant population.

In a similar study, 2 of 19 patients with a history of management problems were observed to engage repeatedly in aggressive conduct but evidently not during a seizure. It is then noted that "we excluded extremely violent or dangerous patients from admission to the hospital."[83] Furthermore, the conclusion that the "rage attacks" were interictal was based on negative surface EEG's. They also said that "The dramatic improvement in the behavior of our patients in a supportive, protected milieu serves to underscore the importance of adverse environmental factors in eliciting aggressive behavior in some epileptics."[84]

To some authors, the affiliation between psychomotor epilepsy and violence is so clear that the issue is defined in other terms:

> We have described the seizures and manifestations of temporal lobe epilepsy in such detail because these symptoms are very similar to the ones that precede episodes of aggression and poor impulse control in some violent individuals. Such violent episodes are like the seizures of temporal lobe epilepsy in many respects. They may be preceded by changes in perception, by depersonalization, forced thinking, or hallucination; they may include a short period of violent muscular activity followed by exhaustion and relief. However, they are not seizures in the usual sense because there is no loss of consciousness, or even loss of memory for the violent behavior.

---

81. Delgado-Escueta at 711.
82. Delgado-Escueta at 711.
83. Ramani & Gumnit, *Intensive Monitoring of Epileptic Patients With a History of Episodic Aggression*, 38 ARC. NEUROL. 570, 571 (1981).
84. Ramani & Gumnit at 571.

> The point here, we believe, is that these similar phenomena of episodic violence reflect a functional abnormality in the temporal lobe. This assumption is supported by the observations of many clinicians that people with a structural disease of the temporal lobe are an unusually disturbed group as compared to the general population, and that those with temporal lobe brain wave abnormalities who may or may not have epileptic seizures often share certain behavioral difficulties, including episodes of dyscontrol and violence. Furthermore, although episodes of violence also occur in people with other symptoms of brain disease—such as memory loss, speech difficulties, loss of sight, and grand or petit mal seizures—the coincidence with seizures of temporal lobe epilespsy [sic] is frequent. Indeed, most of the violent individuals we have seen and treated surgically suffered from both disorders.[85]

Still another reason for apparent variance in the reports of the connection between epilepsy and violence is that much is a matter of perspective. As Pincus remarked: "[W]e might expect to find a high incidence of psychomotor seizures among violent criminals even if violence were uncommon among patients with psychomotor seizures, but we are faced with somewhat confusing reports."[86] Also central is the fact that one can have epilepsy without ever engaging in any violent act; the connection between the condition and behavior is not predictable:

> But even after the diagnosis of epilepsy has been made, it may not always be clear how much of the patient's behavior can be attributed to epilepsy. Even with a patient who is known to have seizures or whose EEG suggests an epileptic tendency, there may be disagreement among competent neurologists about the relation of abnormal behavior, and especially violent behavior, to a seizure state.[87]

In an important report on research regarding the relationship between psychomotor epilepsy and violence, the authors noted that "There is a continuing debate in the literature about whether psychomotor

---

85. V. MARK & F. ERVIN, VIOLENCE AND THE BRAIN 63 (1970).

86. Pincus, *Can Violence Be a Manifestation of Epilepsy?* 30 NEUROL. 304, 305 (1980).

87. Pincus at 305. *See also* Detre & Feldman, *Behavior Disorder Associated with Seizure States: Pharmacological and Psychosocial Management*, in EEG AND BEHAVIOR 366, 371 (G. Glaser ed. 1963): "Many [seizure patients] are admitted [to hospitals] repeatedly and under dramatic circumstances; the medical and nursing personnel engage in heroic interventions to bring the patient 'under control.'"

epilepsy and violence are associated with each other. Although some authors have called attention to an association between the two, others have questioned this relationship."[88]

The population studied consisted of 97 adjudicated delinquents who were "more or less violent." They were categorized by the degree to which their prior records revealed violence. They were also categorized by the degree to which the existence of psychomotor epilepsy was indicated.[89] There was a significant positive correlation between the number of indicators of psychomotor epilepsy present and the degree of violence found. Secondly, of those on whom EEG data were obtained, 29 percent of the subjects who ranked highest on the violence classification showed abnormalities, while none of the subjects in the lowest category of violence showed any abnormality.

The researchers also attempted in this study to determine whether violence tended to occur during an actual attack or between attacks. They isolated by various means 18 who appeared to have had actual psychomotor attacks. Of these, again by various means, it appeared that five had clearly committed acts of violence during an attack and that conclusion appeared probable for another six. The remaining seven had clearly committed their acts of violence other than during a period of actual temporal lobe (psychomotor) seizure. It was also noted that all five of those who clearly had committed acts of violence during an attack had also committed acts of violence while not having a seizure. The conclusion would be that violence can be and is committed during seizure attacks, but the presence of psychomotor epilepsy does not establish that it did.

Glaser, Newman and Schafer have underscored the difficulty of drawing clear lines between ictal and interictal periods: The authors note that "A relatively high incidence of interictal psychological abnormality has been found in patients with psychomotor-temporal lobe seizures....Often, however, it has been difficult to separate an ictal psychic episode from an interictal state, and acute epileptic psychoses actually have been

---

88. Lewis, Pincus, Shanok & Glaser, *Psychomotor Epilepsy and Violence in a Group of Incarcerated Adolescent Boys,* 139 AM. J. PSYCHIAT. 882 (1982) (footnotes omitted). The researchers were from the Department of Psychiatry, New York University School of Medicine, and the Department of Neurology, Yale University School of Medicine, and included a child psychiatrist, a neurologist with special interest in child neurology and a research data analyst. A second neurologist also read the EEG's.

89. In an interview, Delgado-Escueta, in 2 J. Delgado-Escueta, SEIZURE DISORDER UPDATE 1 (1981), discounted an earlier research report by Lewis, Shanok, Pincus, et al., *Violent Juvenile Delinquents: Psychiatric, Neurological, Psychological and Abuse Factors,* 18 J. AM. ACAD. CHILD PSYCHIAT. 307 (1979), largely on the ground that "the authors could not categorically claim which of their patients had a clinical diagnosis of epilepsy. Of the patients they studied, 72% had 'psychomotor symptomatology.' However, the authors stopped short of making a diagnosis of epilepsy." Delgado-Escueta at 21.

recognized as components of the seizure complex since their first description by the French neuropsychiatrists of the mid-nineteenth century."[90] And aggression was found to be present in some patients suffering from psychomotor epilepsy, even during the interictal periods.[91] The line is not so neat.[92] There is obvious spill-over from violence committed in one state or the other. Lewis continued:

> Our past and present studies suggest that psychomotor epilepsy is far more prevalent in the delinquent population than in the general population. The fact that over 18% of these incarcerated delinquent adolescents probably had psychomotor seizures, whereas clinical epilepsy of any kind is thought to exist in approximately 0.5% of the general population, supports this hypothesis.[93]

The authors' estimates put the frequency of all epilepsy at around 1 in 200. Other estimates place the figure closer to 1 in 100.[94] For purposes of estimating the link between epilepsy and crime, the numbers are highly misleading apart from the evident range in their precision, for in most forms of epilepsy, there is simply no reason to suppose there is any connection at all between epilepsy and crime. One must be more discriminate.

It would appear that a good part, if not all, of the dispute regarding the research results studying epilepsy and crime is traceable to what epileptic population is studied: The more inclusive the epileptic population, the less the link.[95] More important for our purposes, however, is that, whether one uses the 0.5 percent or 1 percent figure, those ratios are for comparison of the general population in the United States for all types of epilepsy and not just for psychomotor epilepsy, which is generally considered to be a small part of the general epileptic population but is the type of interest here. The researchers almost certainly understated the frequency of psychomotor epilepsy in this population of delinquents because of the extremely conservative methodology employed. It is also clear that "although the presence of EEG abnormalities, especially in the

---

90. Glaser, Newman & Schafer, *Interictal Psychosis in Psychomotor-Temporal Lobe Epilepsy: An EEG-Psychological Study,* in EEG AND BEHAVIOR 345, 346 (G. Glaser ed. 1963).

91. Glaser, Newman & Schafer at 360.

92. Suspicion has been reported that alcoholism and epilepsy may be linked by more than coincidence. Quirk, *Treatment For Epileptic Alcoholism,* 7 ONTARIO PSYCHOL. 36 (1976). *See also* Chan, *Alcoholism and Epilepsy,* 26 EPILEPSIA 323 (1985).

93. Lewis, Pincus, Shanok & Glaser at 885.

94. B. MILLER & C. KEANE, ENCYCLOPEDIA AND DICTIONARY OF MEDICINE AND NURSING 327 (1972). *See also* Weinberg, *Epilepsy and the Alternatives for a Criminal Defense,* 27 CASE W. RES. L. REV. 771, 780 n.67 (1977).

95. *See also* Stevens, *Psychiatric Aspects of Epilepsy,* 49 J. CLIN. PSYCHIAT. 49, 53 (1988).

clear that "although the presence of EEG abnormalities, especially in the temporal region, may confirm a diagnosis, the absence of such abnormalities does not refute the diagnosis."[96] Thus psychomotor epilepsy is over-represented in this violent delinquent population compared to the general population by a factor ranging into the hundreds. There is no report of the involvement or not of alcohol in any of the pre-incarceration[97] acts of violence. Even the best of the research which approaches from this perspective typically ignores the question of alcohol involvement in either precipitating or aggravating an attack.

Obviously, none of this means that a person who is vulnerable to psychomotor seizures necessarily engaged in the criminal behavior charged because of a mere susceptibility to such a condition or that he or she was necessarily acting in a state of automatism at that particular time. The attacks are intermittent, and the person is more-or-less normal most of the time. We say "more-or-less" because it is not far fetched to assume that persons with psychomotor epilepsy may be very poorly adjusted overall; this affliction is not an isolable issue in their lives. For example, if undiagnosed early, those suffering from epilepsy may be treated as childhood "behavior problems."[98] Still, in this legal context, the task is to help courts to understand that the defendant's proof may actually be relevant to something that he has a right to submit to the jury. Even the researchers who are patently protective of epileptics acknowledge the possibility of violent reactions resulting from epileptic attacks, and the very cases they condemn in the courts are rich sources of examples. The research clearly shows an association between temporal lobe epilepsy and violence, and the question of precise biological causation is for the future. For example, Mark & Ervin[99] suggested the possibility that it is injury to the limbic system which produces both violence and temporal lobe seizures and, as another writer summarized, "The temporal lobe seizures [may] represent *only one* symptom of a malfunctioning limbic system."[100]

Hughes provided the following summary based on a report by Mark and Ervin:[101]

> Perhaps the most convincing evidence of the *possible* relationship of temporal lobe epilepsy to violent behavior is found in the case of Julia, who at one time attacked a girl with a sharp

---

96. Lewis, Pincus, Shanok & Glaser at 886.

97. Or post-incarceration, for that matter. It is generally not safe to assume that alcohol or other drugs are not available in detention facilities.

98. Spirer, *Biochemistry as a Defense*, 4 MIAMI L.Q. 1, 5-6 (1949), (discussing numerous studies in which the EEG was useful in making more discriminate diagnoses).

99. V. MARK & F. IRVIN, VIOLENCE AND THE BRAIN (1970).

100. Hughes, *The Medicolegal EEG*, in EEG AND EVOKED POTENTIALS IN PSYCHIATRY AND BEHAVIORAL NEUROLOGY 361, 372 (J. Hughes & W. Wilson eds. 1983).

101. V. MARK & F. ERVIN, VIOLENCE AND THE BRAIN (1970).

> instrument and actually pierced the heart of that victim. Spikes were found on the temporal lobe during a routine EEG; with implanted electrodes Mark and Ervin recorded epileptic activity from both amygdalae. Stimulation of the amygdala resulted in symptoms similar to those at the beginning of the clinical seizures in this patient. In one instance clear seizure activity was recorded within the amygdala, and at that time the patient got out of bed, ran to the wall, narrowed her eyes, bared her teeth, clenched her fists, and showed all signs of being on the verge of making an attack. Epileptic activity could be elicited as the result of electrical stimulation through these implanted electrodes, and rage behavior was often seen as the patient actually attacked the wall. At another time she smashed a guitar against the wall when seizurelike activity was found within the amygdala. At other times, electrical stimulation of the amygdala initiated rage and violence, and this behavior was preceded by the development of local electrical seizure activity. The authors stated "there could be no doubt that the electrical stimulation of and the abnormal seizure activity from the amygdala preceded and was directly related to Julia's violence." This case represents one of the very few instances in the history of epileptology and criminology in which *suggestive* evidence is brought to bear on the question of a possible direct relationship between temporal lobe epilepsy and violent behavior. However, the legal and medical communities still await a *clear* example of a crime of violence committed during a *definite* seizure.[102]

If the evidence gets much clearer, someone is going to get killed in the laboratory. The focus of many of the studies has been whether the general class of epileptics is more "crime-prone" than the general population. There is no serious question about the affirmative answer to that question. Our perspective is more particularized: The question is whether, in any individual case, the epileptic condition caused the otherwise criminal conduct in question. One persistent problem which has not been solved yet is the problem of false negatives in use of the EEG to detect psychomotor epilepsy. In cases where it is known that the person is an epileptic and it is also clear that attacks may lead to violence, the EEG evidence may be relatively poor. The following description is of such a case. Notice also that while rage attacks or violence in epileptics is generally associated with temporal lobe epilepsy, this case also

102. Hughes at 375-76.

illustrates that grand mal seizures are not inconsistent with violent reactions:

> Patient S228 is a fourteen-year-old boy who has had grand mal epilepsy since the age of eight months, the attacks most often occurring at night. When they do occur during the day usually they are associated with extremely aggressive outbursts. Anticonvulsant medication never completely controlled the attacks, the minimum being one per week. Because of the behavioral problems, he had been followed in the outpatient psychiatric clinic for two years prior to his admission, which was precipitated by the following episode. The father found the patient having a seizure. When his father tried to loosen his belt, the boy suddenly jumped up, threw his father against the wall, began beating him, and indiscriminately breaking up furniture. He desisted only when interrupted by another seizure and had three more grand mal seizures that day....In the hospital, seizures followed by aggressive instinct dyscontrol became so frequent and so frightening to the personnel that it was necessary to transfer the patient to a maximum security ward at the state hospital. Sometimes these episodes were characterized by frantic escape attempts rather than aggressive attacks. Several EEG's were not significant except for moderate amplitude slow waves noted diffusely with some build-up with a rapid return to normal during hyperventilation....Psychological evaluation at the time of his admission to the hospital revealed...definite signs of "organicity" [organic disease]....[103]

What bears emphasis in this chapter, especially in connection with temporal lobe epilepsy, is that we are not just describing temporal lobe epilepsy, but temporal lobe epilepsy triggered by and possibly aggravated by alcohol.

Parallel with the position taken over the years in several versions of the DSM, several psychiatrists have argued that pathological intoxication should not be diagnosed or even recognized unless only an amount of alcohol is involved that is insufficient to render a normal person intoxicated, and a somewhat overlapping number of them have contended that pathological intoxication does not exist; not that the symptoms are feigned, but that there is nothing to simulate. The only conclusion we have been able to derive in trying to reconcile these positions is that what the seemingly unconnected, even contradictory, arguments amount to is

103. R. MONROE, EPISODIC BEHAVIORAL DISORDERS 114-15 (1970).

a claim that pathological intoxication is "really" a manifestation of some other, underlying disease and that alcohol is irrelevant to those other diagnostic categories. In one case, the defense psychiatrist even claimed that the defense witness's "description of defendant's 'glassy-eyed' look during [previous] violent episodes with her was insufficient to support a diagnosis of psychomotor epilepsy, in that in each instance defendant had been drinking, which could account for his behavior, and, moreover, he would become violent, and 'a person who's having these temporal lobe seizures...is not capable of a coordinated, purposeful, directed violent attack because...the nature of the seizure itself would prevent such a thing.'"[104] The position seems to have been taken by this expert witness that drinking was proof of the lack of a seizure.

EPISODIC DYSCONTROL SYNDROME (OR INTERMITTENT EXPLOSIVE DISORDER) AS AN OVERLAPPING OR COMPETING DIAGNOSIS FOR PATHOLOGICAL INTOXICATION

In an excellent forensic case history involving a court-martial for murder, the authors, Ratner and Shapiro, who were the court psychiatric experts in the case, accentuated the fact that "A growing body of literature suggests that violent behavior, especially when it is episodic, explosive, and out of all proportion to the provocation, can be a manifestation of what is currently termed the episodic dyscontrol syndrome."[105] They provided a model of diagnostic skill in the methodology used to establish the insanity defense in that case, even though it was only partially successful.

The DSM-III-R, as had DSM-III, describes another disorder which appears to be similar to pathological intoxication in a number of important respects, and in one important aspect it receives much the same treatment: "This category has been retained in DSM-III-R despite the fact that many doubt the existence of a clinical syndrome characterized by episodic loss of control that is not symptomatic of one of the disorders that must be ruled out before the diagnosis of Intermittent Explosive Disorder can be made." It is labeled "Intermittent Explosive Disorder"[106] and classified under "Impulse Control Disorders Not Elsewhere Classified."[107] It replaces the diagnosis of "explosive personality" found in DSM-II. The description of the symptoms places it under the "irresistible impulse" test of legal insanity, but some of the descriptions of other

---

104. People v. Babbit, 45 Cal. 3d 660, 689-90, 248 Cal. Rptr. 69, 84, 755 P.2d 253, 268 (1988).

105. Ratner & Shapiro, *The Episodic Dyscontrol Syndrome and Criminal Responsibility,* 7 BULL. AM. ACAD. PSYCHIAT. & LAW 422 (1979).

106. DSM-III-R at 321.

107. DSM-III-R at 321.

writers addressed below indicate that it could be encompassed within the general (cognitive only) insanity rules as well.

> The essential features of this disorder are discrete episodes of loss of control of aggressive impulses resulting in serious assaultive acts or destruction of property. The degree of aggressiveness expressed during the episodes is grossly out of proportion to any precipitating psychosocial stressors. There are no signs of generalized impulsivity or aggressiveness between the episodes.
>
> Other disorders that are sometimes associated with loss of control of aggressive impulses must be ruled out before the diagnosis can be made....
>
> The person may describe the episodes as "spells" or "attacks." The symptoms are said to appear within minutes or hours and, regardless of duration, remit almost as quickly. Genuine regret or self-reproach about the consequences of the action and the inability to control the aggressive impulse may follow each episode.[108]

"No information" is listed under "predisposing factors," and it is noted that "the disorder is apparently very rare,"[109] although work is continuing on the frequency of its diagnosis.[110]

Others have been critical of the approach taken by the compilers of the DSM. Yudofsky and Silver stressed the high incidence of head injuries, mostly attributable to automobiles, and the estimates of around 410,000 new head injuries each year from all causes or approximately 180 per 100,000 population.[111] They noted that "Explosive rage and violent behavior have long been associated with focal lesions as well as with diffuse damage to the CNS. Various investigators and nosological systems have labeled and described this condition in different ways. DSM-III calls the condition Intermittent Explosive Disorder and places the category under 'disorders of impulse control not elsewhere classified.'"[112]

> Other names for the syndrome include episodic dyscontrol syndrome, disinhibition syndrome, and explosive personality disorder. It is our feeling that the existing diagnostic labels,

---

108. DSM-III-R at 321.

109. DSM-III-R at 322.

110. Monopolis & Lion, *Problems in the Diagnosis of Intermittent Explosive Disorder*, 140 AM. J. PSYCHIAT. 1200 (1983).

111. Yudofsky & Silver, *Psychiatric Aspects of Brain Injury: Trauma, Stroke and Tumor*, in 4 PSYCHIATRY UPDATE 142 (1985).

112. Yudofsky & Silver at 147.

including that found in DSM-III, can be confusing. Since organic etiologies for the condition are, in our experience, quite common, we do not agree with the statement under "differential diagnosis" in DSM-III that purports "an underlying physical disorder, such as brain tumor or epilepsy, may in rare cases cause this syndrome" (American Psychiatric Association, 1980). Elliott (1982)[113] studied 286 patients with recurrent attacks of intermittent rage, and found 94 percent of this population had evidence of either developmental or acquired brain deficit.[114]

"We agree with DSM-III that 'any toxic agents such as alcohol, that may lower the threshold for violent outbursts, and conditions conducive to brain dysfunctions such as perinatal trauma, infantile seizures, head trauma, and encephalitis may predispose to this disorder.' We therefore submit that the condition should be reclassified as an organic mental disorder and be called organic aggressive syndrome...."[115]

There has been a modicum of litigation involving the diagnosis of intermittent explosive disorder. Much of it is civil litigation involving such diverse matters as whether a home burning fell within an intentional acts exclusion in an insurance policy,[116] worker's compensation,[117] retirement benefits,[118] a will contest,[119] involuntary civil commit-

---

113. Elliott, *Neurological Findings in Adult Minimal Brain Dysfunction and the Dyscontrol Syndrome,* 170 J. NERV. MENT. DIS. 680 (1982).

114. Yudofsky & Silver at 147.

115. Yudofsky & Silver at 147-148. The suggested criteria would be (emphasis in original):

> a). Persistent or recurrent aggressive outbursts, either of a verbal or a physical nature.
>
> b). The outbursts are out of proportion to the precipitating stress or provocation.
>
> c). Evidence from the history, physical examination, or laboratory tests of a specific organic factor that is judged to be etiologically related to the disturbance.
>
> d). The outbursts are *not* primarily related to personality features or disorders such as paranoia, manic disorder, antisocial or narcissistic personality disorder, borderline disorder, or conduct disorder.

116. J. Roth Builders, Inc. v. Aetna Life & Casualty Co., 151 Ill. App. 3d 572, 503 N.E.2d 782 (1987).

117. Miller v. U.S. Fidelity & Guar. Co., 478 So. 2d 200 (La. Ct. App. 1985); Guerra v. Workers' Comp. Appeals Bd., 168 Cal. App. 3d 195, 214 Cal. Rptr. 58 (1985).

118. Dowd v. District of Columbia Police & Firefighters' Retirement & Relief Bd., 485 A.2d 212 (D.C. 1984).

119. Bauer v. Estate of Bauer, 687 S.W.2d 410 (Tex. Ct. App. 1985), (held that testator's belief that family love was missing from his life was not insane delusion, which justified upsetting his will).

ment[120] and a conservatorship action.[121] A number of the cases are involved in various ways with child abuse or neglect and termination of parental rights actions in which the allegation is that the parent, mostly mothers, suffer from intermittent explosive disorder as part of the basis for termination.[122] Most are criminal cases.[123] In some of the criminal cases, alcohol is involved either in the background[124] or the defendant had been drinking prior to the behavior leading to the charges.[125] In other cases, there is a history of drug abuse other than alcohol[126] or use at the time of the offense.[127]

The battle of the experts, whether the case is civil or criminal, is often phrased in the common terminology of whether the defendant suffered from a mental illness, an antisocial personality disorder[128] or an emotional disorder,[129] and in one case the mother was diagnosed as affected by more than one.[130] The summary of the expert testimony does not add much to the DSM description except that some of the experts believe the condition to be organically caused,[131] and in a

---

120. In Interest of Palmer, 363 N.W.2d 401 (N.D. 1985).

121. In re Conservatorship of Torres, 180 Cal. App. 3d 1159, 226 Cal. Rptr. 142 (1986).

122. In Interest of A.M.S., 419 N.W.2d 723 (Iowa 1988); Matter of Welfare of J.A., 417 N.W.2d 696 (Minn. Ct. App. 1988); Matter of Welfare of N.C.K., 411 N.W.2d 577 (Minn. Ct. App. 1987); In re S.P.W., 707 S.W.2d 814 (Mo. Ct. App. 1986).

123. United States v. Kramer, 579 F. Supp. 314 (D. Md. 1984); People v. Williams, 44 Cal. 3d 883, 245 Cal. Rptr. 336, 751 P.2d 395 (1988); People v. Crews, 122 Ill. 2d 266, 522 N.E.2d 1167 (1988); People v. Schultz, 173 Ill. App. 3d 738, 527 N.E.2d 984 (1988); Hancock v. State, 741 P.2d 1210 (Alaska Ct. App. 1987); State v. Thurman, 10 Conn. App. 302, 523 A.2d 891 (1987); Rose v. State, 506 So. 2d 467 (Fla. Dist. Ct. App. 1987); Hicks v. State, 256 Ga. 715, 352 S.E.2d 762 (1987); People v. Snowden, 147 Ill. App. 3d 763, 498 N.E.2d 612 (1986); People v. Parmes, 121 A.D.2d 658, 504 N.Y.S.2d 50 (1986), *aff'g* People v. Parmes, 114 Misc. 2d 503, 451 N.Y.S.2d 1015 (N.Y. Sup. Ct. 1982); State v. Collier, 474 So. 2d 529 (La. Ct. App. 1985); State v. Koon, 285 S.C. 1, 328 S.E.2d 625 (1985); Lautzenheiser v. State, 481 N.E.2d 113 (Ind. 1985); People v. Rodriguez, 103 A.D.2d 121, 479 N.Y.S.2d 25 (N.Y. App. Div. 1984); State v. Pate, 1984 W.L. 7066 (Ohio Ct. App. 1984); Robey v. State, 54 Md. App. 60, 456 A.2d 953 (1983); State v. Shields, 444 So. 2d 287 (La. Ct. App. 1983); Hendershott v. People, 653 P.2d 385 (Colo. 1982).

124. People v. Williams, 44 Cal. 3d 883, 245 Cal. Rptr. 336, 751 P.2d 395 (1988).

125. People v. Parmes, 121 A.D.2d 658, 504 N.Y.S.2d 50 (1986), *aff'g* People v. Parmes, 114 Misc. 2d 503, 451 N.Y.S.2d 1015 (N.Y. Sup. Ct. 1982).

126. Hancock v. State, 741 P.2d 1210 (Alaska Ct. App. 1987), (dependence on both cannabis and alcohol); People v. Snowden, 147 Ill. App. 3d 763, 498 N.E.2d 612 (1986).

127. State v. Shields, 444 So. 2d 287 (La. Ct. App. 1983).

128. People v. Crews, 122 Ill. 2d 266, 522 N.E.2d 1167 (1988); People v. Rodriguez, 103 A.D.2d 121, 479 N.Y.S.2d 25 (N.Y. App. Div. 1984). Some research on the episodic dyscontrol syndrome is directly aimed at improving the clinical distinction between it and "psychopathic personality." *See, e.g.*, Virkkunen, *Reactive Hypoglycemic Tendency Among Habitually Violent Offenders*, 8 NEUROPSYCHOBIOLOGY 35 (1982), which links hypoglycemia and episodic dyscontrol in using the glucose tolerance test to differentiate intermittent explosive disorder and antisocial personalities.

129. People v. Snowden, 147 Ill. App. 3d 763, 498 N.E.2d 612 (1986).

130. Matter of Welfare of J.A., 417 N.W.2d 696 (Minn. Ct. App. 1988).

131. In re S.P.W., 707 S.W.2d 814 (Mo. Ct. App. 1986).

number of the cases, there was presented evidence of a history or subsequent diagnosis of brain injury.[132] In some of the cases, the history of head injury, alcohol and violence are combined, highly suggestive of pathological intoxication, although the expert witnesses did not make that diagnosis.[133] In others, there was testimony that the actor also suffered psychotic episodes including hallucinations.[134]

In most of the criminal cases, the defense is based on insanity, but the defense has also used "extreme emotional disturbance,"[135] the old provocation rule,[136] a plea of guilty but mentally ill;[137] and another was based on diminished capacity.[138] Much appears to turn on whether the state recognizes a control defect (irresistible impulse) test in addition to the tests supporting a claim of cognitive defect,[139] although there is also support for the view that the disorder would qualify under cognitive tests as well.[140] One court even concluded that the defendant was temporarily insane at the time of the child beating, due to intermittent explosive disorder, but found her guilty of child abuse based on the failure to fulfill her legal duty to seek medical treatment when she was quickly returned to sanity.[141]

Pathological intoxication, "adult minimal brain dysfunction," "episodic dyscontrol syndrome," "intermittent explosive disorder," "explosive rage attacks" and "limbic epilepsy" have all been linked to one another by Monroe, who believes that a "limbic ictus" plays a dominant role in all of them.[142] It actually appears that "intermittent explosive disorder" used by the DSM-III-R is synonymous with the term "episodic dyscontrol syndrome" used by some psychiatrists. But the associations may be more extensive than that. Monroe has stated that he believes "that the bouts of [intermittent] aggressiveness, panic, as well as erotomania[143] all have a common underlying mechanism, that of a limbic ictus

132. State v. Thurman, 10 Conn. App. 302, 523 A.2d 891 (1987); Lautzenheiser v. State, 481 N.E.2d 113 (Ind. 1985); State v. Shields, 444 So. 2d 287 (La. Ct. App. 1984).

133. J. Roth Builders, Inc. v. Aetna Life & Casualty Co., 151 Ill. App. 3d 572, 503 N.E.2d 782 (1987).

134. Matter of Welfare of N.C.K., 411 N.W.2d 577 (Minn. Ct. App. 1987); but in Bauer v. Estate of Bauer, 687 S.W.2d 410 (Tex. Ct. App. 1985), it was denied that hallucinations were involved.

135. People v. Parmes, 121 A.D.2d 658, 504 N.Y.S.2d 50 (1986), *aff'g* People v. Parmes, 114 Misc. 2d 503, 451 N.Y.S.2d 1015 (N.Y. Sup. Ct. 1982).

136. State v. Collier, 474 So. 2d 529 (La. Ct. App. 1985).

137. People v. Crews, 122 Ill. 2d 266, 522 N.E.2d 1167 (1988).

138. State v. Thurman, 10 Conn. App. 302, 523 A.2d 891 (1987).

139. Hicks v. State, 256 Ga. 715, 352 S.E.2d 762 (1987); State v. Collier, 474 So. 2d 529 (La. Ct. App. 1985).

140. State v. Shields, 444 So. 2d 287 (La. Ct. App. 1983).

141. Robey v. State, 54 Md. App. 60, 456 A.2d 953 (1983).

142. Monroe, *Episodic Behavioral Disorders and Limbic Ictus*, 26 COMP. PSYCHIAT. 466 (1985).

143. Monroe, *Episodic Sexual Disorders*, 10 MED. ASPECTS OF HUMAN SEXUALITY 50 (1976).

and, in fact, it is not uncommon to see all three in a single patient. It would be preferable then if these were grouped together under a dyscontrol syndrome which would emphasize a possible common therapeutic regimen."[144] It has also been noted that the episodic dyscontrol syndrome "also has included patients who were formerly diagnosed as having pathologic intoxication, implying outbursts of violent behavior in response to a small amount of alcohol, with amnesia and psychotic behavior when out of control."[145]

Monroe acknowledged that his concept of episodic dyscontrol syndrome did not appear in those terms in DSM-III, but that the idea was embedded in the DSM's concept of Intermittent Explosive Disorder. "The term *dyscontrol* was not an official diagnostic label in the DSM-II nor is it utilized in the DSM-III. However, in the latter the concept of the dyscontrol syndrome was incorporated into the diagnostic criteria for "Disorders of Impulse Control Not Elsewhere Classified," particularly 312.34 Intermittent Explosive Disorder."[146]

These concepts are finding their way into significant litigation, as we mentioned. The court reversed an assault conviction in *Hendershott*,[147] on the ground that the trial court erred in refusing to permit the defense to put on evidence of mental impairment in a general intent crime. The defense would have been based on a diagnosis of "adult minimal brain dysfunction" made by an evaluation team consisting of a psychiatrist, a psychiatric nurse and a psychologist.[148] In this instance, adult minimal brain dysfunction was described as resembling "intermittent explosive disorder," which in itself is characterized as involving aggressive behavior "grossly out of proportion to any precipitating psychological stressor."[149] "The symptoms appear within minutes or hours and, regardless of duration, remit almost as quickly."[150] Other language reproduced in the DSM-III-R extract quoted above also was used.[151] The DSM-III (the 1980 version) is also quoted as noting that "features suggesting an organic disturbance may be present, such as non-specific EEG abnormalities or minor, neurological signs and symptoms thought to

---

144. Monroe, *Episodic Behavioral Disorders and Limbic Ictus*, 26 COMP. PSYCHIAT. 466, 472 (1985). *See also* R. MONROE, BRAIN DYSFUNCTION IN AGGRESSIVE CRIMINALS (1978); Monroe, *Brain Dysfunction in Prisoners*, in VIOLENCE AND THE VIOLENT INDIVIDUAL 75, 76 (J. Hays, T. Roberts & K. Solway eds. 1981).

145. Goldstein, *Brain Research and Violent Behavior*, 30 ARCH. NEUROL. 1, 27 (1974).

146. Monroe, *Episodic Behavioral Disorders and Limbic Ictus*, 26 COMP. PSYCHIAT. 466, 471 (1985).

147. Hendershott v. People, 653 P.2d 385 (Colo. 1982).

148. *Hendershott* at 389 n.2.

149. DSM-III at 295.

150. DSM-III at 295.

151. *Hendershott* at 389 n.2.

reflect subcortical or limbic dysfunction."[152] Neither amnesia nor alcohol consumption are mentioned in the testimony of the experts as summarized by the court, although the defendant in this case was drinking. Presumably "limbic dysfunction" is related to "limbic epilepsy" and is associated with "explosive rage" reactions. The court in *Hendershott* describes the phenomenon:

> It has been reported that clinical and experimental evidence indicates that "explosive rage" often results from disorders which affect the limbic system, a phylogenetically ancient portion of the brain which is concerned not only with the expression of emotion but also with neural control of visceral functions and chemical hemostasis. Elliott, *Neurological Factors in Violent Behavior*, 4 Bull. Amer. Acad. Psychiatry and Law 297 (1976); Elliott, *The Neurology of Explosive Rage*, 217 Practitioner 51 (1976). The emotional dyscontrol which characterizes the "explosive rage" bears little resemblance to conventional anger, there being what appears to be a total transformation of the personality during these episodes.[153]

The reference to "explosive rage" attacks seems to be at least partially subsumed under the DSM's label of "Organic Personality Syndrome."[154] These disorders are due to a specific organic factor,[155] and a common manifestation is "recurrent outbursts of aggression or rage."[156] Under "Etiologic factors," it is noted that "A characteristic Organic Personality Syndrome has been described as an interictal phenomenon in some people with temporal lobe epilepsy,"[157] and under "Diagnostic Criteria for Organic Personality Syndrome," it is provided that "This diagnosis is not given to a child or adolescent if the clinical picture is limited to the features that characterize Attention-deficit Hyperactivity Disorder."[158] thus providing the link to the term used in *Hendershott*: "adult minimal brain dysfunction."

Common to many of the cases of pathological intoxication is pre-existing brain damage, and we have already made the link between pathological intoxication and temporal lobe epilepsy. Factually, often the defendant has been drinking, but, as in the case of epilepsy, that fact is not given diagnostic stature even when it should be. Except in cases of

---

152. DSM-III at 296.
153. *Hendershott* at 389 n.2.
154. DSM-III-R at 114.
155. DSM-III-R at 114.
156. DSM-III-R at 114.
157. DSM-III-R at 115.
158. DSM-III-R at 115.

spontaneous attacks of psychomotor epilepsy, the role of alcohol in these syndromes is ignored in much of the "official" psychiatric literature and most of the private research work as well. It is obvious that alcohol is involved with them in a constant or possibly even uniform way, but that does not seem to have been systematically explored even though, at a minimum, alcohol provides part of the link between these disorders. Indeed, it may well be that pathological intoxication ought to be viewed as the legal term for any of these categories of uncontrollable, explosive rage or violence, or even lesser behavior which amounts to a temporary psychotic episode which is triggered by alcohol. The responsibility question is then left to turn on the existence vel non of a fault limiter expressed in terms of the actor's awareness of the possible outcome of drinking, given his or her condition. The existence of alcohol-activated psychomotor epilepsy attacks as subsumed under pathological intoxication has already clearly been established. It also is apparent that these other maladies such as organic personality syndrome, rage attacks, adult minimal brain dysfunction, limbic epilepsy, and episodic dyscontrol syndrome, or intermittent explosive attack, syndrome are also linked at least to some extent to epilepsy or brain damage as well. Psychomotor and limbic epilepsy have also been linked. The difference may be a matter of the detection device used, the EEG, and whether depth probes or only surface probes were used.

In the *Bell* case[159] "episodic discontrol" [sic] in a murder case was also attributed to pre-existing brain damage and described as involving violent behavior followed by amnesia. The court upheld the bench trial conviction over a claim that the defendant had proved insanity by a preponderance. The defendant had shot at the victim's mother three days before his fatal attack on the daughter. Use of alcohol is not mentioned. He recalled details when he confessed, and when he surrendered to a patrol officer shortly after the shooting, he told her the police were looking for him, but he later claimed amnesia for the shooting. The psychiatrist who described the defendant as having "episodic discontrol" also described him as sane. He characterized the condition as "'a syndrome that occurs in people who have had certain damage to certain areas of the brain, in which they are prone to have outbursts of aggressive or violent behavior for which they are amnesic later.'"[160] In this case, the testimony of the state expert indicated that the condition could be detected by EEG's and CAT scanners but that the tests were negative.[161] He also acknowledged that some of his behavior was inconsistent with this diagnosis. Another expert testified that he found no evidence to support the diagnosis. The defense expert, on the other hand,

159. State v. Bell, 471 So. 2d 277 (La. Ct. App. 1985).
160. *Bell* at 279.
161. *Bell* at 279.

testified that he believed the defendant was suffering from episodic dyscontrol but that he had some doubt as to whether the crime resulted from the condition.[162] In another case, *Rose*,[163] the diagnosis was referred to as "episodic dyscontrol syndrome, epileptoid type." The testimony indicated that this diagnosis was consistent with a head injury suffered by the defendant years earlier. The defendant also had a history of alcoholism and drug abuse. The case involved in part a denial of the defense request for further testing since the condition could not be detected by EEG's or the CAT scan, but could be detected with an alphachloralose EEG or by a nuclear magnetic resonance tomography or positron emission tomography. The testimony was to the effect that the alphachloralose EEG examination would involve chemical induction to change the seizure threshold.[164] The appellate court held that the trial court did not abuse its discretion in denying further testing.[165] *Romaine*[166] involved a robbery conviction which was affirmed. The only issue was the sufficiency of the evidence on the defendant's sanity, and the court held that weaknesses in the defense evidence and lay testimony for the state were sufficient to permit the jury to find him sane at the time of the offense. The record of the defendant indicated a "history of sudden outbursts of violence for no apparent reason, which were usually preceded by severe headaches for a period of several hours prior to the episode. After an episode, the defendant would sleep for a long period of time. Sometimes the episodes were preceded by defendant taking a small amount of alcohol."[167] This was diagnosed as "episodic dyscontrol syndrome, which is also known as limbic epilepsy."[168] The defense psychiatrist further testified that:

> episodic discontrol syndrome...is a relatively new discovery, having been noted or discovered in 1970. The usual manifestation of limbic epilepsy involves the appearance that the person is in a state of extreme rage. He will attack by confronting the other individual by both physical and verbal abuse, and by running or tearing apart the room or area in which he is located. His conversation will not appear to be rational or coherent and although the person would be able

---

162. *Bell* at 279.

163. Rose v. State, 506 So. 2d 467 (Fla. Dist. Ct. App. 1987).

164. *Rose* at 469.

165. The trial court had refused to instruct the jury at all on the defense of insanity on the ground that the jury had heard no evidence of insanity. Much of that was attributable to the trial court's refusal to let a master's level psychologist testify as an expert, and on this latter point, the conviction was reversed and remanded for a new trial.

166. People v. Romaine, 79 Ill. App. 3d 1089, 399 N.E.2d 319 (1979).

167. *Romaine* at 1093, 399 N.E.2d at 322-23.

168. *Romaine* at 1093, 399 N.E.2d at 323.

> to understand what was going on, he would not have control over his behavior. A person suffering from an attack of limbic epilepsy is not capable of performing a voluntary act.[169]

The defendant had been drinking on this occasion when he threatened the supervisor of a community correctional center with a baseball bat. The appeal was on the basis of evidence insufficiency, but the court held that the jury was not bound to accept the evidence offered by experts; the state can rely solely on weakness in defense evidence of insanity.

The dyscontrol syndrome and pathological intoxication are closely linked, although the latter has a firmer basis in the literature. But the status of the dyscontrol syndrome is not merely speculative. While some of the writers discussed in this section ignore the role of alcohol in their research, Mark and Ervin provide the conceptual relationship of the dyscontrol syndrome and pathological intoxication:

> Since we do not at present have any way to test directly for the presence of limbic brain disease, we must rely on two indirect methods of diagnosis. The first is to see if the violent person has any signs and symptoms of recognizable brain disease—especially any signs of abnormality in a part of the brain which is close to the limbic brain....
>
> The second indirect way to identify violent persons with limbic brain disease is to compare their behavior with that of people known to have this sort of disease. At the Massachusetts General Hospital, we first reviewed the histories of our patients known to have limbic brain disease and temporal lobe epilepsy, paying close attention to those with implanted electrodes, and especially seeking signs of poor impulse control (which most of these people might have in common). We then checked the symptoms we found such patients did share against the histories of 108 self-referred patients at the Massachusetts General Hospital and 24 patients at the Boston City Hospital, all of whom had a principal complaint of poor impulse control with periods of destructive behavior. We also checked our list against the histories of more than 400 violent prisoners in a large penitentiary.
>
> We found that these violent people usually had four characteristic symptoms, (which were not, however, always present at the same time): (1) a history of physical assault,

---

169. *Romaine* at 1094, 399 N.E.2d at 323.

> especially wife and child beating; (2) the symptom of *pathological intoxication—that is, drinking even a small amount of alcohol triggers acts of senseless brutality*; (3) a history of impusive [sic] sexual behavior, at times including sexual assaults; and (4) a history (in those who drove cars) of many traffic violations and serious automobile accidents. We shall refer to this set of symptoms together as "the dyscontrol syndrome."[170]

We should join the authors in the admonition that "we must repeat that although the three cases we describe here have signs of temporal lobe abnormality, we do not mean to imply either that all people with brain disease are violent, nor that all those people who are violent have brain disease."[171]

What is most appealing about this arrangement suggested by Mark and Ervin on the relationship of pathological intoxication to the dyscontrol syndrome is that it essentially leaves pathological intoxication untouched. The additional criteria which would turn pathological intoxication into the dyscontrol syndrome are sexual and nonsexual assaults and traffic offenses. Yet we know that many of the assault cases which are diagnosed as pathological intoxication are instances of highly unusual behavior for that person, indeed that violence by them is virtually diagnostic itself. Many of these people do not have a history of violence outside the use of alcohol at all, motivated or unmotivated. It appears that Mark and Ervin would then say that when that is not the case, when the actor has a history of violence not explained by alcohol triggering a reaction due to brain damage, the case becomes a candidate for the new episodic dyscontrol syndrome. What is not clear to us is whether, in their scheme of things, the other violence which is not alcohol-related is meant to be "senseless" or "purposeless" violence. If not, the suggestion then must be that spontaneous attacks may appear to be motivated, while alcohol-triggered attacks are not. On the other hand, if the nonalcohol-related acts of violence are unmotivated or poorly motivated, the scheme makes sense in terms of what we already know about pathological intoxication.

---

170. V. MARK & F. ERVIN, VIOLENCE AND THE BRAIN 125-26 (1970) (emphasis added) (footnote omitted). The footnote to point (2) in the quoted text is interesting: "There is some evidence that in pathological intoxication the act of drinking, rather than the alcohol itself, is the stimulus for brutality. Individuals who become violent after taking even a small amount of liquor by mouth may be injected intravenously with enough alcohol to produce clinical drunkenness without any sign of violent behavior."

171. Mark & Ervin at 127.

A good example of the dyscontrol syndrome was Tony D. who suffered from pathological intoxication. He had a history of recurrent brutality, wife beating, and sexual assault, and had been involved in near-fatal car crashes. He was a husky 25-year-old skilled machinist who had been sent to a hospital for the criminally insane after assaulting his mistress and fracturing a number of her facial bones. He had also beaten his wife many times; once he had hit her with a lead pipe, another time he had tried to knife her. His wife also told us that he had tried to smother their infant son with a pillow. He became violent after drinking even a small amount of alcohol. To study alcohol's effect, we gave Tony one drink while recording his brain waves; he promptly grew so violent we had to stop the brain wave examination. Tony's drinking usually started with an auditory hallucination—like the voice of his dead father telling him to kill his brother—and culminated in physical violence, often directed against his wife and child.

Tony had suffered a serious head injury while driving a car. His neurological examination disclosed that although he had normal intelligence, he was quite unable to read and could write his name only with difficulty. It also revealed bilateral temporal lobe brain wave abnormalities. He was treated with Dilantin, an anticonvulsant medication, which produced a marked improvement in his behavior. We were not able to see if the improvement kept up because he refused to return for a follow-up examination and there was no way for us to compel him to continue with treatment.[172]

---

172. Mark & Ervin at 127-28. *See also* Maletzky, *Treatable Violence,* 19 RES. & STAFF PHYS. 40, 44 (1973), (presenting a case history of a violence-prone person diagnosed as suffering from episodic dyscontrol syndrome who was successfully treated with Dilantin (diphenylhydantoin).

> Our patients did not suffer from obvious temporal lobe epilepsy; neither were they schizophrenic, nor grossly brain damaged. In retrospect, it seems that most such patients may be afflicted with a form or variant of temporal lobe epilepsy. There is evidence to suggest that such patients actually have small, nonexpanding lesions of limbic structures, particularly of the amygdalar region—that area of the temporal lobe so exquisitely sensitive to emotional stimuli. Thus, it becomes just as criminal on our part to relegate all such patients to the waste-heap of "sociopathic personality" as it is criminal on their part to perpetrate senseless aggression. It is too easy and quick to judge such patients and believe they must be made to suffer for their crimes; it would be more difficult, yet more profitable and humane to ask what we as physicians can do to discover which among them suffer from a treatable brain dysfunction. Hopefully, in the bargain, we may thus advance our understanding of human violence.

The significance of Tony's inability to read or write is that "difficulty in reading and speaking may be related to an abnormality in the temporal lobe...."[173] Some of Tony's behavior was triggered by alcohol, some was spontaneous. The former is pathological intoxication, and the combined effect, along with the other factors, is the dyscontrol syndrome.

Episodic dyscontrol is also seen by others[174] as a more generic diagnostic category that includes within it the concept of pathological intoxication.[175] Monroe says: "As alcohol suppresses higher cortical function, it ultimately leaves the individual even more susceptible to dyscontrol behavior. Thus, most of the individuals now diagnosed as idiosyncratic intoxication [pathological intoxication] would fit our definition of episodic dyscontrol."[176] Indeed, it is implicit in the study discussed earlier by Bach-y-Rita, Lion, Climent and Ervin.[177] In their report on the need for a multidisciplinary approach to diagnosis in cases of violence, the entire group was labeled as suffering from episodic dyscontrol, yet the sample had within it identified pathological intoxication cases. It has also been described as follows:

More recent research has centered on ethosuximide as an agent of treatment of episodic dyscontrol. In an ongoing, controlled, double-blind, crossover study of a small group of patients, the research concluded that:

> The preliminary data tend to support the hypothesis that ethosuximide, when used in the treatment of patients exhibiting episodic dyscontrol, has the potential for producing an excellent clinical response with few side effects. Many of these patients suffering from episodic dyscontrol form a subcategory of the borderline syndrome. They are differentiated from other borderline states by the presence of dyscontrol episodes, abnormal EEGs, and a history suggestive of organicity. Our present study is being pursued to 1) verify the initial findings, 2) establish operational criteria for the DSM-III classification of intermittent explosive disorder, 3) validate the diagnostic role of the computer analyzed EEG in this syndrome, and 4) develop a medication prediction profile. We are also collecting data to identify the relationships between variables differentiating subcategories of the borderline syndrome, including episodic dyscontrol.

Andrulonis, Donnelly, Glueck, Stroebel & Szarek, *Preliminary Data on Ethosuximide and the Episodic Dyscontrol Syndrome*, 137 AM. J. PSYCHIAT. 11, 12 (1980).

173. Mark & Ervin at 125.

174. This diagnostic term has been used by V. MARK & F. ERVIN, VIOLENCE AND THE BRAIN (1970); R. MONROE, EPISODIC BEHAVIOR DISORDER: A PSYCHODYNAMIC AND NEUROPHYSIOLOGICAL ANALYSIS (1970); K. MENNINGER, THE VITAL BALANCE (1963); Maletzky, *The Episodic Dyscontrol Syndrome*, 34 DIS. NERV. SYST. 178 (1973); Bach-y-Rita, Lion, Climent & Ervin, *Episodic Dyscontrol: A Study of 130 Violent Patients*, 127 AM. J. PSYCHIAT. 11 (1971).

175. Monroe, *Episodic Behavioral Disorders and Limbic Ictus*, 26 COMP. PSYCHIAT. 466 (1985); D. HAMBURG & M. TRUDEAU, BIOBEHAVIORAL ASPECTS OF AGGRESSION 152 (1981).

176. Monroe at 473.

177. Bach-y-Rita, Lion, Climent & Ervin, *Episodic Dyscontrol: A Study of 130 Violent Patients*, 127 AM. J. PSYCHIAT. 11 (1971).

> The syndrome is applied to persons who demonstrate episodes of violence following minimal or no provocation. The violent outbursts last from minutes to hours and are occasionally preceded by an aura, and may be followed by a "postictal" period that may include fatigue, sleep, depression, or elation. The syndrome also includes patients who have violent responses to small amounts of alcohol, the so-called "pathological intoxication"....[178]

Pincus has said that neurologists, "acting as advocates for their patients and not wishing 'to give epileptics a bad name,' have a tendency to discount acts of personal violence as being within the normal range, or to discount the possibility that complex or violent crimes can be ictal events."[179] He forthrightly states that "'Episodic dyscontrol' is a diagnostic phrase used by Mark and Ervin and others as a way of approaching the etiology of violence to avoid the controversy about the diagnosis of epilepsy."[180] He also noted that "small amounts of alcohol aggravate these symptoms."[181] What, then, is "episodic dyscontrol syndrome" but either spontaneous psychomotor epilepsy or psychomotor epilepsy evoked by alcohol? Ervin does not equate episodic dyscontrol syndrome and temporal lobe epilepsy but considers the former to be the broader category:

> Doctor Ervin's conclusion that brain abnormalities may spark violent actions grew from his research with epileptic patients. Working with Dr. Vernon Mark, director of neurosurgical service at Boston City Hospital, and Dr. William Sweet, chief of neurosurgery at Massachusetts General, he studied the fits of destruction and rage exhibited by patients with temporal lobe epilepsy (a disease that affects the limbic structures of the brain—those linked to a person's emotions and instincts).
>
> The investigators found that the violent attacks corresponded with an erratic pattern of electrical activity in the brain, as recorded by electroencephalograph (EEG)....
>
> "Next we probed the question of whether there are individuals who exhibit the same symptoms of violent episodes as the epileptics, but who do not have epilepsy,"

---

178. D. HAMBURG & M. TRUDEAU, BIOBEHAVIORAL ASPECTS OF AGGRESSION 152 (1981). The dyscontrol syndrome is discussed in detail in R. MONROE, BEHAVIORAL DISORDERS (1970).

179. Pincus, *Can Violence Be A Manifestation of Epilepsy?* 30 NEUROL. 304 (1980).

180. Pincus at 305. *See also* Flor-Henry, *Ictal and Interictal Psychiatric Manifestations in Epilepsy: Specific or Non-Specific? A Critical Review of Some of the Evidence*, 13 EPILEPSIA 773 (1972), (dyscontrol syndrome is secondary to subcortical epileptoid activity).

181. Pincus at 305.

> relates Doctor Ervin, a specialist in brain functions. "Our research indicates that the same kind of activity does occur in persons with episodic dyscontrol as goes on in the epileptic."[182]

A further interesting tie between the episodic dyscontrol syndrome and pathological intoxication is found in the observation that "'Unfortunately, when this type of person notices his rising tension and other warning signs, he frequently tries to medicate himself with alcohol,' Doctor Ervin notes. 'This doesn't work. In fact, alcohol makes things worse. It probably affects the limbic system, exacerbating the dyscontrol episodes.'"[183]

A number of researchers give the term much broader meaning. Elliott,[184] for example, discussing "the neurology of explosive rage" (which he subtitles "the dyscontrol syndrome"), includes both organic and functional contributing factors, although he focuses on what he terms organic dyscontrol. He notes that in instances of known temporal lobe epilepsy (complex partial seizures), the incidence is on the order of 20 percent and that it is more frequent among males than females.[185] The condition may be present from birth or can be acquired. Even when it is present at birth, it is Elliott's view that it is often traceable to birth injury. "In the second group explosive rage appears in a previously normal subject after head trauma or other cerebral insults....Clinical, surgical, and electroencephalographic evidence suggests that this delayed effect of closed-head injury is related to contusion of the temporal lobes, which is so often involved by contrecoup lesions....Temporal-lobe epilepsy (synonyms: psychomotor seizures, complex partial seizures) is the most common of the organic conditions associated with explosive rage."[186] Others include encephalitis, brain abscess, hydrocephalus, tumors and head trauma. "Of the metabolic disorders that can cause explosive rage, hypoglycaemia is the most common, whether it be functional, iatrogenic, or due to endogenous hyperinsulinism."[187]

> The fact that rage is not induced by the hypoglycaemia which can occur during a five-hour glucose-tolerance test, even in people who have hypoglycaemic reactions outside the laboratory, emphasizes the role of the social setting. In the

---

182. Rosenthal, *Violence Is Predictable*, 48 TODAY'S HEALTH 56, 57 (1970).
183. Rosenthal at 71.
184. Elliott, *The Neurology of Explosive Rage: The Dyscontrol Syndrome*, 217 NEUROL. & NEUROPSYCHIAT. 51 (1976).
185. Elliott at 53.
186. Elliott at 54.
187. Elliott at 55.

> same way, patients liable to pathological alcoholic intoxication in social life do not develop symptoms from the same amount of alcohol when it is given to them in the laboratory.[188]

However, it will be recalled that many cases of pathological intoxication are reproduced in the laboratory setting, manifested either by EEG abnormalities induced by alcohol or by more manifest clinical observations (such as violence). It does not follow in any event that the instances of failure to trigger a reaction in the laboratory setting are due to the variance in the social milieu, for it may be due to other physiological reasons which do not always exist in the patient.

Elliott discussed the fact that diagnosis is often difficult even in suspected cases. "Electroencephalography is obligatory. A single test, if normal, means little because the abnormalities appear intermittently; repeated tests increase the percentage of positive results, and the yield is further improved by the use of sleep records using nasopharyngeal electrodes. Chemical activation techniques are important. Even then the results may be negative, despite the presence of epileptic discharges as recorded by depth electrodes."[189]

Elliott later reported on a study of 286 patients with a "history of recurrent attacks of uncontrolled rage with little or no provocation,"[190] all involving a change of personality frequently referred to by witnesses as a Jekyll and Hyde transformation.[191] One of his conclusions again stressed the importance of epilepsy. "Epileptologists rightly maintain that few epileptics are violent, but it seems that among people with episodic dyscontrol there is more epilepsy than in the population at large."[192] Elliott considered (in 1982) that the CAT scan was an obligatory procedure,[193] and the CAT scan revealed "unexpected structural abnormalities in 41 per cent of the 148 cases in which it was done,"[194] although in "most cases these abnormalities failed to explain the symptoms on an anatomical basis..."[195]

Sometimes the systematic failure to maintain clear lines between alternative diagnostic categories and the often conflicting perspectives of both psychiatrists and neurologists can lead to almost any of these terms

---

188. Elliott at 55-56.

189. Elliott at 57.

190. Elliott, *Neurological Findings in Adult Minimal Brain Dysfunction and the Dyscontrol Syndrome*, 170 J. NERV. MENT. DIS. 680, 681 (1982).

191. Elliott at 681. *See also* Stone, McDaniel, Hughes & Hermann, *Episodic Dyscontrol Disorder and Paroxysmal EEG Abnormalities: Successful Treatment with Carbamazepine*, 21 BIOL. PSYCHIAT. 208 (1986).

192. Elliott at 684 (footnote omitted).

193. Elliott at 682.

194. Elliott at 685.

195. Elliott at 685.

being applied to the same person. In *Alerte*,[196] the defendant was convicted of murder. Here, in a relatively recent case, one begins to see the impact of a modern "battle of the experts." The court upheld the jury verdict.

> Dr. Fredric A. Gibbs, an expert in the field of epilepsy and electroencephalography, testified that he first met defendant in 1965. At that time, Gibbs administered and read defendant's EEG, which was abnormal, revealing a type of seizure activity in part of the brain. Gibbs stated that this type of abnormality does not produce convulsions, but 2% of the people with this abnormality have rage attacks during which they cannot control their actions or exercise normal judgment. Based on defendant's EEG and history, Gibbs believed defendant suffered from this condition. A 1969 EEG of defendant showed some improvement, but on that day defendant suddenly grabbed Gibbs's necktie and, with a display of unusual strength, started dragging Gibbs toward an open window. A friend of Gibbs's who was present grabbed defendant and helped quiet him down. Gibbs believes that this incident was a rage attack. According to Gibbs, epileptics and people who have rage attacks can have normal EEG'S.-[197] Following a normal EEG of defendant in 1977, Gibbs referred defendant to Dr. Frank Lorimer.
>
> Dr. Lorimer testified that he is a psychiatrist who had examined defendant on three occasions since the occurrence. He concluded, on the basis of those examinations, an interview with defendant's family, and defendant's medical records, that defendant best classifies diagnostically as having organic brain syndrome, non-psychotic with epilepsy. According to Lorimer, defendant's form of epilepsy is limbic epilepsy, a category of epilepsy now gaining medical recognition, which is characterized by rage attacks and blackouts. Normal EEG'S would not be contrary to a diagnosis of epilepsy. Lorimer also testified that on January 12, 1980, defendant's condition of organic brain syndrome was in a psychotic phase because defendant was in a distinct rage attack at that time. Further, Lorimer testified that defendant

---

196. People v. Alerte, 120 Ill. App. 3d 962, 458 N.E.2d 1106 (1983).

197. In People v. Skorka, 147 Ill. App. 3d 976, 498 N.E.2d 607 (1986), Dr. Gibbs testified "that he conducted an alcohol induced EEG on defendant....The results were abnormal, indicating a mild localized depressive reaction to injury in the right frontal temporal area. Dr. Gibbs opined that defendant had a pathological reaction to alcohol...." *Skorka* at 978, 498 N.E.2d at 609. An abnormal EEG distinguishes this case from *Alerte*.

was then unable to appreciate the criminality of his behavior or conform to the requirements of the law.

In rebuttal, Dr. John Hughes, a specialist in electroencephalography and epileptology, testified that he reviewed EEG'S of defendant and found four early EEG'S to be somewhat abnormal and ten subsequent EEG'S, including one considered abnormal by Gibbs, to be normal. According to Hughes, the pattern that Gibbs considered abnormal represented only drowsiness, not an abnormality. Hughes believes that it is impossible for an epileptic to have such a series of EEG'S. Hughes also testified that Lorimer's diagnosis of organic brain syndrome non-psychotic with epilepsy does not appear in the manual containing acceptable diagnoses in the field of psychiatry [a reference to the DSM]. Further, Hughes testified that limbic epilepsy is not a term that is commonly understood and agreed upon by the world neurological community. Psychomotor seizures that fall under the classification of partial seizures with complex symptomatology are the closest things to limbic epilepsy which are medically recognized. In response to a hypothetical question, Hughes testified that activities such as those of defendant on January 12, 1980, could not have been the result of a psychomotor seizure since they were clearly directed and purposive.

Dr. Robert Reifman, a psychiatrist, testified that on the basis of his personal interviews with defendant and his examination of defendant's medical records, he concluded that defendant did not suffer from any mental disease or defect on January 12, 1980, and that defendant could appreciate the criminality of his conduct and was capable of conforming his conduct to the requirements of the law. Reifman diagnosed defendant as having a narcissistic personality, a diagnosis which is consistent with problems in school and violent episodes. Reifman also testified that Gibbs, having read an EEG which Reifman administered to defendant, wrote a letter which stated that the activity manifested in the EEG is not associated with mild or severe behavior....[198]

The court summarized this evidence as follows:

Here, the record reveals that the jury's decision as to defendant's sanity was not improbable, unsatisfactory or palpably erroneous. Both State and defense experts testified that some

198. *Alerte* at 966-67, 458 N.E.2d at 1109-10.

> of defendant's EEG'S were abnormal and some were normal. The experts drew conflicting conclusions from their readings of one of the 1980 EEG'S. Gibbs considered the EEG abnormal, while Hughes considered the pattern to be the result of drowsiness, not abnormality. The experts disagreed with regard to the significance of the normal EEG'S. Lorimer believed that normal EEG'S would not be contrary to a diagnosis of epilepsy, yet Hughes believed it impossible for an epileptic to have such a series of EEG'S. Further, the experts disagreed in their diagnosis of defendant. Lorimer diagnosed defendant as having organic brain syndrome, with limbic epilepsy, which was in a psychotic phase at the time of the victim's death, a diagnosis which is not among the possible diagnoses which appear in the diagnostic and statistical manual of the American Psychiatric Association.[199] Reifman diagnosed defendant as having a narcissistic personality, not a mental disease or defect. Either condition could account for defendant's actions on January 12, 1980, and on the other occasions when he behaved violently. It is within the discretion of the trier of fact to accept one expert's opinion over another's on the question of insanity so as to resolve contradictions.[200]

What is even more interesting (frightening?) about that opinion is that we now understand it.

SOME ADDITIONAL COMMENTS ON MATTERS OF PROOF

The next five chapters deal largely with legal problems generated by the facts established in the first five chapters. We pause in this section to consider briefly some problems of proof that are of obvious importance to the attorney who must litigate one of the cases. There are several levels of problems of proof. We have tried to present what evidence there is that there is a phenomenon of pathological reaction to alcohol. The second and third problems are almost limitless in their possible configurations, but in general terms, they are dealt with in this section. These basically are the need for proof that the defendant is susceptible to pathological intoxication and proof that the defendant was suffering from an attack or was still under its influence at the time of the alleged offense,

---

199. We believe this to be an unjustified statement. Where is it written that the law is incapable of exculpation on the grounds of mental illness unless the group which writes the latest version of the DSM provides prior approval?

200. *Alerte* at 968, 458 N.E.2d at 1111.

that is, that the condition caused or contributed to the crime. In practice, these two questions will not really be separable so that what follows is actually just a matter of emphasis on what has been said in other contexts, or a pulling together of some additional material on a previously identified problem. We had hoped at one point to construct a "logic of proof" chapter that would cover all the possibilities, but the subject matter proved to be too amorphous and complex for anything approaching that level of organization. Hence, these comments are offered.

In gross terms, there will be two kinds of cases: those in which psychomotor epilepsy is present in the background and the task is to prove that the defendant was suffering an attack (a seizure) at the time of the conduct, and those in which such proof is not available. In the first kind of case, it still is not enough to prove that the actor was an epileptic, it additionally must be shown that the epilepsy was responsible for the behavior exhibited that led to the criminal charges. Knox provided this summary:

> In his formulation the medical witness must consider two fundamental questions—first, whether the accused suffers from epileptic fits and then, whether the offence was committed during epileptic automatism. In the first instance he will take into account evidence such as the previous history of fits and a description of these, accounts from witnesses of such fits and related medical investigation and treatment. Detailed physical examination is essential and particular attention is paid to any injuries which might have resulted from seizures, such as laceration of the tongue and scar tissue from burns. Finally, electroencephalographic studies will be required and some activation technique may be indicated.
>
> Following such detailed appraisal it is usually possible to come to a firm conclusion as to whether the accused suffers from epileptic attacks. However, it is likely to be much more difficult deciding whether the offence was committed during epileptic automatism.
>
> In reaching a decision the medical witness may be handicapped in that he has rarely, if ever, witnessed automatism. The senior nurse, skilled in dealing with and supervising patients in a hospital ward for epileptics, may justifiably claim greater clinical expertise than the medical witness himself.[201]

A number of cases are presented by Halleck:

---

201. Knox, *Epileptic Automatism and Violence*, 8 MED., SCI. & LAW 96, 97 (1968).

A forty-three-year-old man who had always been considered a respectable citizen was arrested for exhibiting himself. He had been walking along the lake front of a large city when he suddenly stopped and began to undress publicly. When brought to the police station, he could not remember what he had done and did not know why he had been arrested. He was sent to a mental hospital for a pretrial examination, where an electroencephalogram revealed an abnormal discharge from the left temporal area. Further neurological study suggested the presence of a brain tumor.

A twenty-five-year-old man had a long-standing history of assaultiveness. These actions took place mainly in bars and were associated with heavy drinking. Afterward he could never recall any details of his violence. He eventually became embroiled in an altercation in which he mercilessly assaulted and killed another man. Upon arrest he denied any recollection of the crime. Electroencephalographic study showed a seizure discharge in the temporal area.

A thirty-year-old man, apparently happily married, was arrested for attempting to force sexual attentions upon a ten-year-old boy. There was some indication that this behavior had occurred previously. During the offense his actions seemed carefully designed to avoid apprehension. He had a vague recollection of his behavior, was sure that he had done something illegal but could not give a rational explanation for his actions. An electroencephalographic study was suggestive of psychomotor epilepsy.

Halleck evaluated the cases:

It is not difficult to appreciate the role of epilepsy as a causal factor in the first case. The patient's history plus the purposelessness of his actions supports the relevance of epilepsy as a necessary cause. In the second case, however, there would be some question as to whether assaultiveness always occurred together with the seizures. Even if this could be ascertained, there would still be a question as to the degree to which the organic disorder influenced the disturbed behavior. We would wonder how low this man's threshold for assaultive behavior might have been and if such behavior would have occurred even without seizures. In the third case the apparent goal-directedness of the patient's actions and his partial recall of his behavior would make us skeptical of the importance of epilepsy as a factor. Yet we can never be certain that his behavior, like that of the case of indecent exposure, might have been restrained if there had not been a cerebral abnormality.[202]

Skepticism is expressed in the second case, and in the case of pathological reaction to alcohol as a defense, the involvement of alcohol by definition will always be present. Doubt will, of course, be reinforced in the second kind of case, in which the actor cannot even show psychomotor epilepsy as a pre-existing condition.[203]

The Amount of Alcohol

Two problems will recur throughout the effort to define pathological reaction to alcohol: (1) the inaccurate repetition that the amount of alcohol consumed is of diagnostic value and (2) its confusion with alcohol sensitivity.

This first problem persists even in the modern history of descriptive literature regarding pathological reaction to alcohol: The evident fact that a small amount of alcohol *can* trigger the reaction is often carelessly described not as a sufficient condition, but as a necessary one. In Thompson's early studies, he often stressed the effects of small amounts of alcohol, and he actually achieved laboratory results by using very small amounts. It was clear at that point that small amounts would suffice in some cases, but his method of alcohol activation precluded studying the question whether sometimes larger amounts would be necessary to trigger a response either in behavior or on the EEG.[204] In the later studies by Marinacci and Von Hagen, the authors caution that "The amount of alcohol required to produce such behavior is quite variable and only a very small amount is necessary *in some patients*."[205] Maletzky's studies underscored the fact that his results "confirm the probable existence of a discrete syndrome of pathological reaction to alcohol without reference to the amount of alcohol consumed.[206]

Maletzky was aware that his results were evidently at variance with the observations made by Bach-y-Rita, Lion and Ervin,[207] and he

202. S. HALLECK, PSYCHIATRY AND THE DILEMMAS OF CRIME 164 (1967).

203. Walker, *Murder or Epilepsy?* 133 J. NERV. & MENT. DIS. 430, 436-37 (1961).

204. Thompson, *Acute and Chronic Alcoholic Conditions*, in 2 AMERICAN HANDBOOK OF PSYCHIATRY 1203, 1210 (S. Arieti ed. 1959); Thompson, *The Electroencephalogram in Acute Pathological Alcoholic Intoxication*, 28 BULL. L.A. NEUROL. SOC. 217 (1963).

205. Marinacci & Von Hagen, *Alcohol and Temporal Lobe Dysfunction: Some of Its Psychomotor Equivalents*, 3 BEHAV. NEURO-PSYCHIAT. 2, 11 (1972) (emphasis added).

206. Maletzky, *The Diagnosis of Pathological Intoxication*, 37 QRTLY J. STUD. ALCOH. 1215 (1976).

207. Bach-y-Rita, Lion & Ervin, *Pathological Intoxication; Clinical and Electroencephalographic Studies*, 127 Am. J. Psychiat. 698 (1970).

specifically ascribed the discrepancy to the variation in the amount of alcohol used in the activation procedures. The factor that varied between the two studies was the quantity of alcohol that was used: Maletzky used several times as much as that used by Bach-y-Rita, Lion and Ervin. It was Maletzky who also pointed out that only one author of the 14 Banay had cited thought that the amount of alcohol was significant.

The amount-of-alcohol issue is rarely involved in actual litigation of pathological intoxication, but it may have been important in one case. In *United States v. Walker*,[208] a conviction for assault with intent to rape was affirmed against the argument that the government expert did not have a sufficient basis for his expert opinion. The defense expert, a German national neurologist, made a good case for pathological intoxication.

> Dr. Wolf stated that in his opinion, based upon all the factors in the case and medical records about the accused, which he had examined, the latter was suffering from pathological intoxication...and was not responsible for his actions.
>
> [He testified] that there must be something wrong with an individual other than the fact that he had been drinking, before the condition of "pathological intoxication" will be found. Such condition is observed "almost only in cases of epilepsy heredity and to a large extent they are similar to epileptic seizures or fits." [EEGs were abnormal but he said these are "actually no proof."] The doctor also testified that indulgence in intoxicants will trigger this state and, while it is possible to have the condition without taking of alcohol, that rarely happens and such states are called "episodic."[209]

The army psychiatrist testified:

> What is meant by this term [pathological intoxication] is this: when an individual, after taking *a very minimal amount of alcohol*, behaves inappropriately for him, this is called pathological intoxication.[210] In order to establish this as an

208. United States v. Walker, 12 C.M.A. 658, 31 C.M.R 244 (1962).

209. *Walker* at 245.

210. State v. Holota, 194 A.2d 69 (Conn. Cir. Ct. 1963), involved a conviction by jury for driving under the influence over the defendant's plea of not guilty. He smelled of liquor, failed a sobriety test and later admitted drinking. After he was arrested, he tore up his cell and was sent to a psychiatrist who diagnosed the case as pathological intoxication "which could probably be produced by the ingestion of a 'minute' quantity of alcohol, and that in a state of pathological intoxication the alcohol cannot be considered the causative agent but rather a catalyst, without which the reaction cannot take place." The court said that "Such a finespun distinction is not contemplated by our statute. The test is the effect which alcohol

> entity, one must first establish the *minimal amount of alcohol,* that amount which would not ordinarily affect a normal person to any significant degree, affected the individual involved to a very striking degree. It is common...to talk of people who just can't drink; that one 'wiff' [sic] of alcohol and they aren't themselves. This is what is intended by this term. People who behave in a manner not consonant or not appropriate to their normal behavior following *very minimal amounts of alcohol.* In [defendant's] case, it seems apparent from his description of his behavior, his activities, during the afternoon preceeding [sic] this alleged act, that he had probably had eight to ten beers. This being the case, the possibility of pathological intoxication, namely, an excessive response to a *very minimum amount of alcohol,* is ruled out. Eight to ten beers is not the *minimum kind of alcohol* that is intended by this term.[211]

Also in *State v. Jensen,* relying on standard psychiatric text, experts had testified to the "small amount" criterion of pathological intoxication, and the appellate court used this to refute the claim of evidence insufficiency, citing the evidence of the experts that "pathological intoxication occurs after minimal ingestion of alcohol...."[212]

In *Wright v. State,*[213] the defendant was convicted of murder in the first degree. He had shot a man for no discernable reason. He had been drinking only slightly at the time, estimated as one-quarter of a pint of brandy. The case was evidently tried only on the general plea of not guilty, and his generalized contention on appeal was that he lacked the malice aforethought required of murder of the first degree, and in generalized terms, the court held that this was resolved against him by the jury.

The evidence for the defense was largely by a pediatric neurologist. This expert witness had actually treated the defendant as a child for seizures resulting from ingestion of a foreign substance, and he characterized him as suffering from chronic epilepsy. In addition to the seizures suffered by the defendant during this two- or three-year treatment period, the witness also testified that his EEG's were abnormal at that early time. A second expert for the defense also testified, based on the record, that in his opinion the defendant was suffering an epileptic psychomotor seizure at the time of the shooting. Rebuttal witnesses expressed the opinion that there was no clinical indication that the defendant had any brain damage

---

has upon the individual and not the quantity of alcohol consumed." *Holota* at 71.

211. *Walker* at 251 (emphasis added).

212. State v. Jensen, 282 N.W.2d 55, 63 (N.D. 1979).

213. Wright v. State, 374 A.2d 824 (Del. 1977).

but that he had an "antisocial personality." On this conflicting testimony, the court held that the jury could properly resolve the issue against the defendant.

But the jury got some help from the trial court in reaching this verdict. The defendant raised the contention on appeal that the trial court erred in failing to instruct on the defense of intoxication. To this contention, the appellate court stated that "we conclude that consumption of one fourth of one pint of ginger brandy does not amount to some credible evidence of intoxication."[214] Given the defense evidence of underlying epilepsy, this is an extraordinary ruling, and given the frequently encountered, albeit in our judgment erroneous, statements that pathological intoxication is actually limited to small quantities, this statement would mean that pathological reaction to alcohol as a defense could never be tried on a defense of intoxication, even intoxication relevant only to the existence of a specific intent required by many crimes. It is not possible to tell who created this situation, but it is clear that the mistake made was not linking the alcohol to the epilepsy. In broad terms, neither was viewed as sufficient by themselves, but the jury never got to consider the combined effects because the evidence of drinking was not covered in the instructions to the jury. But there is also no indication in the appellate opinion that defense counsel made any effort to bring out this point through the testimony of either of the two experts called.

If, indeed, the defendant was suffering from brain damage from earlier ingestion of some unidentified substance which actually caused epilepsy, and this in combination with alcohol consumption led to the unexplained violence, the case is a classic one of pathological intoxication and it was just missed. It is imperative in these cases that psychomotor epilepsy not be viewed in isolation when the defendant was drinking alcohol (any amount) at the time of the conduct charged. In effect, the significance of pathological intoxication is that it encompasses the *combined* effects of alcohol and psychomotor epilepsy, and that has been evident in the medical literature for a long time.

History of Automatisms or Seizures

Much of pathological intoxication consists of epileptic seizures triggered by alcohol consumption. There is also considerable evidence that spontaneous attacks may precipitate violence without the involvement of alcohol. Thus, proof problems will overlap. In those cases without alcohol involvement, one author has outlined what, in his view,

214. *Wright* at 831.

it would take to establish that epilepsy alone was responsible for the behavior:

> Walker[215]...outlined certain criteria that are required to establish that a given crime may have been committed as a manifestation of a seizure. These six criteria are (1) that the patient has bona fide epileptic abnormalities, (2) that spontaneous attacks are similar to the one that occurred at the time of the crime, (3) that the period of the loss of awareness is commensurate with the type of epileptic attack usually experienced by the patient or defendant, (4) that the degree of assumed unconsciousness is commensurate with the degree of unconsciousness with previous attacks, (5) that the EEG findings are compatible with a seizure disorder, and (6) that the circumstances are compatible with the assumption of lack of awareness by the individual at the time of the crime.[216]

Of course, the problems of proof of pathological intoxication cannot be reduced to any formula. Individual cases are much too idiosyncratic not only in terms of history and the charged conduct but in variability of the availability of proofs, expert, lay, circumstantial or otherwise.

The most powerful proof available is the defendant's prior record of seizures. Proof of psychomotor epilepsy is not proof of pathological reaction to alcohol. "[E]pilepsy may cause insanity, but does not constitute it, and the two should not be confounded."[217] The defendant had actually requested an instruction that as a matter of law "epilepsy is a mental disease" and that the jury should additionally be informed that "grief, agony or terror is one of the producing causes of epileptic attacks."[218]

> Thus, whether the accused was afflicted with epilepsy, and if so whether it was a mental disease, or whether it had progressed so far as to affect the mind, and if so whether the mind was so affected that the accused was not conscious of the wrongful character of his act at the time of the homicide, were all matters of fact to be established by the evidence."[219]

---

215. SOUTHERN EEG SOCIETY, ELECTROENCEPHALOGRAPHY AND THE LAW (1968) (moot trial proceedings on two cases).

216. Hughes, *The Medicolegal EEG,* in EEG AND EVOKED POTENTIALS IN PSYCHIATRY AND BEHAVIORAL NEUROLOGY 361, 372 (J. Hughes & W. Wilson eds. 1983).

217. Oborn v. State, 143 Wis. 249, 276, 126 N.W. 737, 748 (1910).

218. *Oborn* at 275, 126 N.W. at 747.

219. *Oborn* at 276, 126 N.W. at 748.

"Nor are we decisively informed on the very rare occasion in which neuropathology is proved—it still becomes necessary to judge whether the disease was the cause of the crime."[220] Proof of the connection between an attack of pathological intoxication and the crime is obviously a matter of inference; but a major factor in that assessment is the proof that the actor was susceptible to such a state, and the nature of pathological reaction to alcohol provides much of the inference necessary. As Professor Goldstein put it in reference to psychomotor epileptic attacks:

> There are occasions, however, when the so-called clouded states, epileptic furors and affect epilepsy, lead to sudden changes of mood which may last from a few minutes to a few hours and which may lead to antisocial behavior. In these instances, the task of estimating probabilities will be made easier because most epileptics will have a history of seizures going back many years.[221]

The point here is that even if the jurisdiction does not require specification of the type of mental illness involved in a defense of insanity, certainly it is imperative as a matter of prudence and proof not only to do so, but to stress in detail the exact nature of the disease or defect in question to permit the trier of fact to draw parallels between the general picture and what the evidence shows with respect to this particular defendant. In the case of pathological intoxication, this is particularly important because so much of the proof of the existence of the phenomenon turns on the defendant's actual behavior at the time of the offense charged. As Professor Goldstein put the matter more broadly,

> Only by understanding that illness in detail can one even begin to determine the probability that he was insane at the time of the crime, the part the illness played in the crime, and eventually the man's responsibility for his actions.[222]

The General Crime Scene Conduct

The general picture of the actor's conduct surrounding the commission of the acts serving as the basis of the charge is important in establishing that the defendant had an attack, and although there are discrete components which might be emphasized, such as those discussed

---

220. D. ROBINSON, PSYCHOLOGY AND LAW 61 (1980).

221. A. GOLDSTEIN, THE INSANITY DEFENSE 31 (1967), citing, inter alia, M. SAKEL, EPILEPSY 44-45 (1958).

222. Goldstein at 30.

here, it will no doubt remain true that the totality of the circumstances almost takes on an independent importance.

> The normality or abnormality of the operation of a person's mind, says Professor Wigmore, can only be ascertained by watching the effects through a multifold series of causes. "On the one hand, no single act can be of itself decisive; while on the other hand, any act whatever may be significant to some extent....The first and fundamental rule, then, will be that *any and all conduct* of the person is admissible in evidence.[223]

While there may be minor qualifications as to admissibility, the importance of the conduct is paramount here. In *Hurley v. Commonwealth,*[224] the court affirmed a conviction for murder against a challenge on evidence sufficiency grounds. The evidence of pathological intoxication was only partial. While there was some evidence of strange behavior on the part of the defendant (besides killing the police officer who came to investigate it), there was no history suggesting that the defendant had any organic disease of the brain. Balanced against the general weakness of the defense evidence, it was pointed out that "the jury could consider acts such as the concealment of the gun, the removal of the officer's weapon and night stick, forcing the officer to stand with his hands behind his head, ordering the deputy away from the window on the threat that he would kill the officer and expressions of repentance after the killing."[225]

The defendant's history in *Cook v. State*[226] made it fairly clear that psychomotor epileptic attacks were a possibility, but the evidence was not clear that his condition directly contributed to his commission of the crime charged. He was convicted of armed robbery and convicted by a jury even though his insanity was put in issue. His conviction was affirmed over an appeal based on evidence insufficiency. When he was 15 he was in a car crash and received a head injury in the right frontal area and as a result had a metal plate inserted into his head. A series of blackouts followed that procedure. As a result, he was discharged from the service. He testified that he would become destructive during such periods and would suffer amnesia. His defense psychiatrists administered no tests but concluded anyway that he had psychomotor epilepsy and that at the time of the crime, he might have had an attack. A neurosurgeon administered a test with no results, but it was explained that this proved nothing. Typically, a state-appointed psychiatrist could find nothing wrong with

---

223. H. Weihofen, Mental Disorder as a Criminal Defense 312 (1954).
224. Hurley v. Commonwealth, 451 S.W.2d 838 (Ky. 1970).
225. *Hurley* at 841.
226. Cook v. State, 271 So. 2d 232 (Fla. Dist. Ct. App. 1973).

him. Here is a clear case of it being absolutely certain that the actor is subject to psychomotor seizures, but the evidence did not convince the jury or the appellate court that he had an attack at the time of the crime. Indeed, there was no such evidence. The crime was robbery of a convenience store and was carried out in the usual manner. The opinion turned strongly on the performance of the robbery.

Automatic Behavior

There are numerous cases in which, while it was established that the actor was an epileptic, it was not shown that he had an attack at the time of the offense.[227] Undoubtedly, the best evidence is the automatic behavior characteristic of pathological reaction to alcohol, as well as the absence of signs of normal intoxication; evidence of the senselessness or lack of apparent motive should also assist. Automatic behavior can and often does have an air of purposive conduct, and onlookers, it has been repeatedly pointed out, can easily mistake what they see. Summary findings by Glasgow[228] and Knox,[229] in separate studies, provided a synopsis of their observations regarding epileptic (psychomotor) seizures, although it should be pointed out that neither concerned temporal lobe epileptic seizures which were triggered by alcohol. Some believe that alcohol can not only trigger a seizure, which is obvious enough, but that it can exacerbate it as well. The following is the summary by Glasgow:

> 1. The behaviour, if offensive, will be out of character with the standards of conduct of the past.
>
> 2. The abnormal behaviour will tend to appear suddenly or explosively.
>
> 3. It is likely to be unexpected and inappropriate to the circumstances and where the behaviour is anti-social or criminal there will be no evidence that it is planned or premeditated.
>
> 4. What is done will be senseless or at least poorly motivated. Confused or irrational thinking may be discernible.
>
> 5. No convincing attempt will be made to conceal anti-social or criminal actions.

---

227. These cases are collected in Annotation, *Automatism or Unconsciousness as Defense to Criminal Charge*, 27 A.L.R.4th 1067, 1088-94 (1984).

228. Glasgow, *The Anatomy of Automatism*, 64 N.Z. MED. J. 491 (1965).

229. Knox, *Epileptic Automatism and Violence*, 8 MED., SCI. & LAW 96 (1968). The summary by Knox borrows from and builds on the summary provided by Glasgow.

> 6. The period of abnormal behaviour will be relatively brief, being measured in minutes or at the most an hour or so but certainly not in days or weeks.
>
> 7. Finally, there will be a period of amnesia surrounding the abnormal behaviour. It is possible for "islands" of partial memory to be present during such a period of amnesia but these will be vague memories of important events.[230]

Knox, based on his study, reached these conclusions:

> 1. Acts of violence are unusual in epileptic automatism. They were recorded in only one of the forty-three patients studied.
>
> 2. The abnormal activity tends to appear suddenly and it is probable that should behaviour of a criminal kind occur there will be no evidence of planning or premeditation.
>
> 3. Automatic behaviour is of brief duration and in the majority of cases lasts for only a few minutes.
>
> 4. There will probably be no attempt to conceal any aggressive acts undertaken in automatism.
>
> 5. There will be no amnesia for events occurring prior to loss of consciousness.
>
> 6. There does not necessarily need to be a history of automatism associated with previous epileptic fits.
>
> 7. Whilst an abnormal E.E.G. may support a diagnosis of automatism due to epilepsy a normal E.E.G. does not exclude such a possibility.[231]

In *State v. White*,[232] the defendant carried dynamite into a bar and was convicted by a jury of assault. There was no apparent motive, and his behavior was a bit strange apart from the dynamite. There was evidence by a defense psychiatrist of psychomotor epilepsy, but the court does not report details of the basis of the diagnosis. There is only a reference to the fact that there was abundant evidence of previous mental problems and treatment. The only rebuttal evidence on the insanity issue did not actually contradict anything the defense expert had said. Even so, the jury still convicted him despite the uncontradicted evidence of insanity. The dissenting opinion said that testimony of witnesses to the act was enough to leave it to the jury. In fact, he said the jury could reach this conclusion on only the testimony of the defendant himself. On appeal, the conviction was reversed on evidence insufficiency grounds.

---

230. Glasgow at 492-93.
231. Knox at 104.
232. State v. White, 110 Ariz. 508, 520 P.2d 1132 (1974).

Amnesia

A brief refresher: Amnesia may be due to failure in registration, retention or recall.[233] Anterograde amnesia refers to that period which occurs following the precipitating trauma. Retrograde amnesia refers to loss of memory for events occurring before the precipitating trauma.[234] Organic disorders which produce amnesia include toxic confusional states, head injury epileptic seizures, alcoholic blackouts and hypoglycemic attacks.[235]

> To the neuropsychologist, amnesia is more than simply poor memory. Generally speaking, memory can be conceptualized as involving three stages of information processing: acquisition, retention, and retrieval. In amnesia, there is a profound defect in one or more of these stages. Thus, amnesia is a behavioral syndrome marked by a severe inability to acquire and retain new permanent memories (anterograde amnesia), often coupled with some degree of impairment in the retrieval of previously acquired memories (retrograde amnesia). While this syndrome is most often found in neurologically disordered patients, a variation of it can be seen in persons without evidence of brain dysfunction. This latter condition [is referred to as] psychogenic amnesia....[236]

Every piece of writing or research on pathological intoxication has indicated that amnesia is part of the symptomatology, and this is confirmed by the literature on psychomotor epilepsy as well.

> Epilepsy as a cause of amnesia in criminal defendants has a particularly illustrious history in forensic neuropsychology....In 1964, for example, Jack Ruby, the assassin of Lee Harvey Oswald, based his plea of not guilty by reason of insanity on psychomotor epilepsy. Among other impairments, Ruby claimed to have no memory for the shooting....
>
> Criminal cases involving individuals with epilepsy usually involve those with complex partial ("psychomotor") seizures. Complex seizures are most frequently associated with abnormal electrical discharges from limbic structures

---

233. McCaldon, *Automatism*, 91 CAN. MED. ASS'N J. 914, 915 (1964).
234. TABER'S CYCLOPEDIC MEDICAL DICTIONARY 65 (C. Thomas ed. 14th ed. 1981).
235. Kopelman, *Crime and Amnesia: A Review*, 5 BEHAV. SCI. & LAW 323, 324-25 (1987).
236. Rubinsky & Brandt, *Amnesia and Criminal Law: A Clinical Overview*, 4 BEHAV. SCI. & LAW 27, 33 (1986).

(typically the hippocampus and/or amygdala) underlying the temporal lobes; hence they were once called temporal lobe epilepsy. While experiencing a complex partial seizure, the individual does not have a convulsion, but rather suffers a "clouding" of consciousness and may engage in automatisms. He behaves in quasipurposeful ways, yet is unresponsive to the environment and is not storing new information. When the episode is over, the events which transpired during the ictus are not remembered.[237]

The only dispute here is the degree of the amnesia expected with pathological reaction to alcohol. Recall that Glasgow said that "...[T]here will be a period of amnesia surrounding the abnormal behavior" and that it "is possible for 'islands' of partial memory to be present...."[238] Some courts continue to insist on the significance of total amnesia,[239] although the medical literature often stresses that amnesia may be total[240] or partial[241] and fragmentary.

Amnesia by itself has no effect on criminal liability[242] (except perhaps perjury[243]). "In such cases [as insanity], courts have repeatedly held that it is not amnesia *per se*, but the existence of an underlying

---

237. Rubinsky & Brandt at 38. *See also* PSYCHIATRIC ASPECTS OF EPILEPSY (D. Blumer ed. 1984); Feldman, *Complex Partial Seizures*, in EPILEPSY: DIAGNOSIS AND MANAGEMENT (T. Browne & R. Feldman eds. 1984); Sherwin, *Neurobiological Basis of Psychopathology Associated with Epilepsy*, in EPILEPSY: A HANDBOOK FOR THE MENTAL HEALTH PROFESSIONAL 77 (H. Sands ed. 1982).

238. Glasgow at 492. *See also* J. MACDONALD, PSYCHIATRY AND THE CRIMINAL 221 (1976), (indicating several authorities for the view that amnesia may be partial or complete).

239. "The definition of pathological intoxication given in the doctor's posttrial affidavit states that a person suffering from such a disorder has complete amnesia as to the episode. That element is inconsistent with the defendant's detailed testimony of the circumstances of the stabbings." Commonwealth v. Glass, 401 Mass. 799, 811, 519 N.E.2d 1311, 1319 (1988).

More commonly, evidence of partial amnesia is used by the prosecution in rebuttal. People v. Finkey, 105 Ill. App. 3d 230, 434 N.E.2d 18 (1982), involving affirmance of convictions based on charges of murder and arson tried on an insanity plea, was a case of claimed pathological intoxication, but there was not much evidence. The prosecution stressed the fact of partial rather than complete amnesia as rebuttal evidence.

240. Hobson, *Addiction and Criminal Responsibility*, 30 MEDICO-LEGAL J. 85 (1962), (stressing complete amnesia).

241. "It is noteworthy that the amnesia need not be complete." Thompson, *The Electroencephalogram in Acute Pathological Alcoholic Intoxication*, 28 BULL. L.A. NEUROL. SOC. 217 (1963). Numerous other authors discussed in Chapters 2 and 3 have made the same observation.

242. *See, e.g.*, United States v. Olvera, 4 C.M.A. 134, 15 C.M.R. 134 (1954). *See also* Hermann, *Criminal Defenses and Pleas in Mitigation Based on Amnesia*, 4 BEHAV. SCI. & LAW 5 (1986); Cunnien, *Alcoholic Blackouts: Phenomenology and Legal Relevance*, 4 BEHAV. SCI. & LAW 73 (1986); Annotation, *Amnesia as Affecting Capacity to Commit Crime or Stand Trial*, 46 A.L.R.3d 544 (1972).

243. State v. Molnar, 81 N.J. 475, 410 A.2d 37 (1980).

mental disorder, that enables the plea of insanity."[244] Our task here rather is to explore the problems of proof of the existence of amnesia in order to help establish the defense of pathological intoxication because amnesia, partial to total, is part of the symptomatology of pathological intoxication. Thus, the question of feigning of amnesia looms large.

Amnesia can be faked, of course, and there is no clear way other than the defendant's own story to prove that he in fact suffered amnesia for the period.[245] "Some researchers have suggested that psychophysiological measurements (e.g., galvanic skin response, heart rate, pupil dilation) are useful in detecting feigned memory loss....Recently, however, such measures have been severely criticized for their limited validity and unreliability...."[246] As it stands today, neither experts nor lay persons can detect the difference between genuine and simulated amnesia. "Because experts' opinions are critically important in reaching a decision regarding an individual's status in legal cases, one might expect that objective data exist concerning experts' ability to detect simulated amnesia. Inspection of the literature, however, reveals that such data are lacking."[247]

Memory loss from heavy drinking, often called blackouts, is common and can be taken for amnesia resulting from pathological reaction to alcohol.[248] One author has defined a blackout as a "memory loss, without accompanying loss of consciousness, for events that occur during drinking."[249] Amnesia for the event and prolonged sleep following the attack would not seem to be useful, for they are also often characteristics of the aftermath of getting drunk. The defendant may as well present evidence that he did not have a hangover as in the case of ordinary drunkenness. On the other hand, proof of its existence is critical because without it, there probably was no pathological intoxication. Thus, it is rather the absence of amnesia that proves fatal.[250]

---

244. Rubinsky & Brandt, *Amnesia and Criminal Law: A Clinical Overview*, 4 BEHAV. SCI. & LAW 27, 30 (1986).

245. Gray, *Alcoholic Amnesia*, 1 CRIM. L.Q. 483 (1958-59).

246. Rubinsky & Brandt, *Amnesia and Criminal Law: A Clinical Overview*, 4 BEHAV. SCI. & LAW 27, 42 (1986). The authors are particularly critical of factual statements made in Annotation, *Amnesia as Affecting Capacity to Commit Crime or Stand Trial*, 46 A.L.R. 3d 544 (1972), misdescribing amnesia due to trauma, especially with reference to a person forgetting his or her own identity (they do not). "As we noted earlier, we know of no instance in the literature on organic memory disorders where a patient with a pure amnesic syndrome loses his personal identity. In fact, the loss of personal identity is often considered a pathognomonic [typical] feature of *psychogenic* amnesia...." Rubinsky & Brandt at 43 (emphasis added) (footnote omitted).

247. Schacter, *On the Relation Between Genuine and Simulated Amnesia*, 4 BEHAV. SCI. & LAW 47, 55-56 (1986).

248. Cunnien, *Alcoholic Blackouts: Phenomenology and Legal Relevance*, 4 BEHAV. SCI. & LAW 73 (1986).

249. Lisman, *Alcoholic "Blackout": State-Dependent Learning?* 30 ARCH. GEN. PSYCHIAT. 46 (1974).

250. People v. Knight, 18 A.D.2d 890, 237 N.Y.S.2d 846 (1963). *See also* People v. Codarre,

Weihofen made these remarks regarding feigned amnesia:

> One situation where suspicion of malingering springs to mind is where the defendant says he does not remember the facts of the crime. He remembers the quarrel, "then everything went black," and when he regained consciousness he was standing over his victim's corpse with the smoking revolver in his hand. (Malingering in criminal cases rarely occurs except in homicide cases; feigning insanity, which if successful is likely to mean indefinite commitment to a mental hospital, is not an appealing alternative to conviction for a crime carrying a penalty of only a few years' imprisonment). Feigned amnesia is one of the most difficult forms of malingering to detect, because there are so many disorders in which amnesia may actually occur. These include not only some psychoses, but also epilepsy, head injury, alcoholism, and certain hysterical neuroses. Nevertheless, a differential diagnosis may be able to eliminate all these, and the patient's ignorance may betray him into answers not typical of true amnesia. The electroencephalograph can fairly conclusively eliminate epilepsy by recording a normal brain-wave pattern and can give highly significant information about the possibility of certain other disorders.[251] Skull X-rays, a negative neurological examination, a life history that gives no support to the likelihood of psychosis, hysteria or of alcoholism, suggest the possibility of mere malingering. This suspicion may be strengthened on probing into the character of the alleged amnesia. True amnesia usually affects all areas of memory; but the malingerer is likely to "forget" only the crime. If the amensia [sic] conveniently covers only the incriminating facts, but does not affect colorless data such as the patient's own identity, it is probably feigned.[252]

Certainly, the last part of that needs qualification, for amnesia can be partial. Sodium amytal has been used to try to determine the true extent of amnesia suffered by the actor, but the examination is not generally accepted as proof because it is too subjective.[253] The same

---

20 A.D.2d 98, 245 N.Y.S.2d 81 (1963); People v. Higgins, 5 N.Y.2d 607, 186 N.Y.S.2d 623, 159 N.E.2d 179 (1959); People v. Furlong, 187 N.Y. 198, 79 N.E. 978 (1907); People v. Egnor, 175 N.Y. 419, 67 N.E. 906 (1903).

251. Citing Gibbs, *Medicolegal Aspects of Electroencephalography*, 24 CAN. BAR REV. 359 (1946).

252. H. WEIHOFEN, MENTAL DISORDER AS A CRIMINAL DEFENSE 46-47 (1954).

253. People v. Higgins, 5 N.Y.2d 607, 186 N.Y.S.2d 623, 159 N.E.2d 179 (1959).

criticism can be made of other methods in addition to sodium amytal such as polygraphy and hypnosis. It has been noted that "all these procedures are very sensitive to suggestion and their validity is disputed...."[254]

There have also been attempts to use hypnosis as an aid in recall by the actor in a case of pathological intoxication. In *Breen v. State*,[255] the defendant's conviction of murder in the second degree was affirmed in the beating death of another man who had a fight with him earlier. On a plea of not guilty and not guilty by reason of insanity, the court held that opinion evidence of medical experts regarding psychomotor epilepsy (the defendant was also drinking) was not sufficient to take the question of insanity from the jury. Three experts testified as to psychomotor epilepsy, but some of the testimony was confused and contradictory on the effects of alcohol on an epileptic. The testimony did not indicate any amnesia. He also had a prior record not related to psychomotor epilepsy, like confidence rackets and violence. Basically, there was no evidence that he had an attack at the time of the homicide.

In *People v. Knight*,[256] the crime was manslaughter for a homicide resulting from a stabbing. The case was tried on insanity. The defendant was an epileptic who had been drinking. The court noted that the claim of epilepsy was "amply established" but that "this disease does not render its victims generally incompetent but only during seizures described as episodes of epileptic fury. It is also clear that defendant was not suffering from such a seizure during the day on which his homicidal assault was perpetrated....No impairment of his recollection was asserted...."[257]

Armstead v. State[258] is illustrative of the cases in which the courts will flatly reject a claim that the defendant has a defense of insanity (or diminished capacity or any other defense) based on an assertion that the actor suffered from epilepsy and was drinking at the time of the crime. Here, the defendant did present proof of epilepsy in her history, but absolutely no connection was made between that fact and the attack on the victim. Not a single indicium of pathological intoxication was presented on the facts, and the conviction for murder was affirmed.

Thus, there are no clear-cut patterns of proof of actual amnesia, although some consistency with respect to what is known about amnesia may help persuade; more likely inconsistency will help dissuade. Kopelman[259] does provide the clinician with some guidance in using what is known, but the examination suggested will often lead to

---

254. Kopelman, *Crime and Amnesia: A Review*, 5 BEHAV. SCI. & LAW 323, 334 (1987).
255. Breen v. State, 53 Ala. App. 588, 302 So. 2d 562 (1974).
256. People v. Knight, 18 A.D.2d 890, 237 N.Y.S.2d 846 (1963).
257. *Knight* at 890, 237 N.Y.S.2d at 847.
258. Armstead v. State, 227 Md. 73, 175 A.2d 24 (1961).
259. Kopelman, *Crime and Amnesia: A Review*, 5 BEHAV. SCI. & LAW 323, 337-38 (1987).

inconclusive results. Indeed, not much is even known about the actual mechanics of amnesia.

> In those cases in whom amnesia is not simulated, what is the nature of the underlying deficit? O'Connell (1960)[260] argued that organic amnesia involves a failure of registration and retention, whereas psychogenic amnesia implicates a failure of retrieval, but modern research suggests that such a clear-cut distinction is not very plausible.[261] In the present state of knowledge, any theory about amnesia for crime is bound to be somewhat speculative, and it seems unlikely that any one explanation will cover all cases.[262]

Pupillary Response

Cramer[263] was among those who believe that the absence of pupillary reflexes was corroborative of the diagnosis of pathological reaction to alcohol but that the presence of normal responses does not exclude the diagnosis. Ziehen,[264] Stapel,[265] Binder,[266] Sipkovenski[267] and Schipkowensky[268] all mention retardation of pupillary reflexes or that pupillary reflex abnormalities are more pronounced than in ordinary intoxication.

Bowman & Jellinek[269] also noted that a number of previous writers reported that the existence of reflex rigidity of the pupils was almost universal in pathological intoxication, but other research has cast doubt on the inevitability of this. If pupillary rigidity is, indeed, not necessarily part of the clinical picture, it is unfortunate, for as the authors note, such a change would be "of considerable diagnostic importance, since it lasts much longer than the mental symptoms and is thus, in view of the short duration of the attack, frequently the only sign which the physician can observe."[270] Even as Bowman and Jellinek wrote in 1941, a previous

---

260. O'Connell, *Amnesia and Homicide*, 10 BR. J. DELINQ. 262 (1960).
261. Kopelman, *Amnesia: Organic and Psychogenic*, 150 BR. J. PSYCH. 517 (1987).
262. Kopelman, *Crime and Amnesia: A Review*, 5 BEHAV. SCI. & LAW 323, 336 (1987).
263. Cramer, 13 MSCHR. PSYCHIAT. NEUROL. 56 (1903).
264. G.T. ZIEHEN, PSYCHIATRIE FUR AERZTE UND STUDIERENDE (4th ed. 1911).
265. Stapel, 29 MSCH. PSYCHIAT. NEUROL. 216 (1911).
266. Binder, 35 SCHWEIZ. ARCH. NEUROL. PSYCHIAT. 209 (1935).
267. Sipkovenski, *Nozoloskoj Problematici Patoloskog Pijanstva* (On the Nosological Problems of Pathological Drunkenness), 8 ALKOHOLIZAM, BEOGRAD 5 (1968).
268. Schipkowensky, *Zur Klinik des Pathologischen Rausches* (On Clinical Aspects of Pathological Intoxication), 159 ZBL. GES. NEUROL. PSYCHIAT. 21 (1960). This may be the same author as in the previous note.
269. Bowman & Jellinek, *Alcoholic Mental Disorders*, 2 QRTLY J. STUD. ALCOH. 312 (1941).
270. Bowman & Jellinek at 325.

study[271] noted by them had largely failed to find this clinical change in their sample: The one prior study "[Binswanger] reported observing it in only 6 of 135 patients examined, while 24 showed a sluggish reaction and 105 had normal pupillary reflexes."[272] The samples are not described by Bowman and Jellinek. On the other hand, other clinicians have reported that pupillary rigidity is important in the diagnosis of the condition. For example, Frame has stated:

> A factor often missed but of considerable importance in the diagnosis of this condition, particularly when the condition is used as a defence, is the manifestation of the rigid pupils in response to bright light, as reported by many workers. This is claimed by some to be the only constant neurological sign present and is said to last long after the mental symptoms have passed.[273]

We have found only two cases in which pupillary response was actually involved in the proof of the case, and the two cases span a hundred years. The first was *Choice v. State*,[274] a case of considerable legal importance in this context which is discussed in detail in Chapter 10, and the other was *Higgins*,[275] which was set out in some detail in Chapter 1. In *Choice*, abnormal pupillary response was present right after the killing,[276] and in *Higgins*, the defendant's pupils were dilated and his reaction to light was reported as sluggish.[277]

Speech

Most writers note that one of the signs, not necessarily of pathological intoxication but of the absence of ordinary intoxication, is the absence of the slurred speech associated with drunkenness. But there may be a more positive indication as well. *State v. Welsh*,[278] discussed previously, involved reported changes in speech patterns when the defendant was examined after the crime, and one of the most telling pieces of evidence in *Higgins* involved the speech of the defendant at the time of the

---

271. Binswanger, 152 Z. GES. NEUROL. PSYCHIAT. 703 (1935).
272. Bowman & Jellinek at 325.
273. Frame, *Alcoholism: Some Medico-Legal Aspects*, 2 J. FOR. MED. 151, 160-61 (1955).
274. Choice v. State, 31 Ga. 424 (1860).
275. People v. Higgins, 5 N.Y.2d 607, 186 N.Y.S.2d 623, 159 N.E.2d 179 (1959).
276. *Choice* at 438-39.
277. One expert testified that this condition could not be simulated. *Higgins* at 623, 186 N.Y.S.2d at 635, 159 N.E.2d at 187.
278. State v. Welsh, 508 P.2d 1041 (Wash. Ct. App. 1973).

homicide.[279] It will be recalled that the defense experts conducted a sodium amytal test (truth serum), a test which is not normally considered reliable and is not normally admissible in evidence. It was during this test, however, that the defendant described the speech of his female victim just prior to the attack. Under the influence of the drug, he quoted her as saying "Tommy, why are you shaking? What's wrong with you? Are you sick?" and "You're talking crazy. You're talking nonsense. What's wrong with you?" This recall lends remarkable support that something was wrong with him, but neither the experts nor the court purported to rely upon it much.[280] Indeed, as indicated, it was not admissible evidence. Despite that fact, the appellate court reported it.

Recall Rozhnov's discussion of "pathologic inebriation," which included one unusual aspect of the actor's behavior while in a state of pathological intoxication:

> such persons act in silence; if they speak at all it is very little. The speech of such persons is very characteristic: it is extremely brief. Words are uttered fragmentarily, often in the form of orders; sometimes individual words are repeated several times as commands. These may be either threats or, on the contrary, cries for help. These isolated utterances are so incomprehensible that they give the impression of a foreign language or a nonsensical muttering or repetition of unrelated syllables.[281]

Thus, while there is evidence that speech patterns may be affected, there is little systemic information regarding how prevalent this is. Additionally, there will be instances in which brief utterances of a drunk might fit the description given by Rozhnov. But in *Higgins*, if the evidence is believed, there was obviously a sudden change in his speech just prior to the attack. But, as defense counsel in *Higgins* evidently discerned, strange speech patterns carry more weight if the evidence of intoxication is not present in the case. A defense based on a claim of a spontaneous epileptic attack might fare better than an attack triggered by alcohol, even if the defendant was unaware of the possibility of this occurring.

---

279. People v. Higgins, 5 N.Y.2d 607, 186 N.Y.S.2d 623, 159 N.E.2d 179 (1959).

280. *Higgins* at 622, 186 N.Y.S.2d at 635, 159 N.E.2d at 187.

281. Rozhnov, *Alcoholism and Other Drug Addictions*, in FORENSIC PSYCHIATRY 343, 349 (G. Morozov & I. Kalashnik eds. M. Vale trans. 1970).

Motiveless

One of the most powerful proofs defense counsel have in these cases is "the absence of motive, premeditation, planning, attempt at concealment and memory for the crime," all of which suggest epilepsy.[282] It was noted above that Knox listed among his indications of automatism that typically "there will be no evidence of planning or premeditation."[283] It has been pointed out that the "absence of motive" indicator can cut both ways:

> Absence of motivation is said to be one of the hallmarks of a crime committed during or following an epileptic attack, but there may be a good motive for a crime even though it is not apparent to the police or to the physician. Conversely, there may appear to be a good motive for a crime which was in fact committed in an epileptic automatic state without awareness of the act. The apparent presence or absence of motive for the crime may therefore be misleading.[284]

In *People v. Jones*,[285] the defendant had been having sex with a 12-year-old girl in a home he visited regularly. After a spat with the mother, he grabbed the child to take her away; she tried to escape and he stabbed her six times, killing her. The jury convicted him of murder on his plea of not guilty and not guilty by reason of insanity.

The defense efforts to introduce a "motiveless" factor into the case backfired. A court-appointed doctor had concluded that the defendant probably suffered from psychomotor epilepsy based in part on consistent EEG's. There was a history of head injury and syphilis. He surmised that

---

282. J. MACDONALD, PSYCHIATRY AND THE CRIMINAL: A GUIDE TO PSYCHIATRIC EXAMINATIONS FOR THE CRIMINAL COURTS 107 (1958). But the absence of motive or the "senselessness" of a crime will not often be enough by itself. In People v. Jandelli, 118 A.D.2d 656, 499 N.Y.S.2d 962 (1986), the defendant, a 16-year-old, beat his older sister with a hammer and then slit her throat. Shortly after, he attempted suicide. No one was aware of any motive for the offense, and when the defendant confessed, he did not know why he did it either. But his recall of the attack and the time before and after the attack was sufficient to meet the people's burden on the insanity defense when the defense experts testified that the defendant was suffering from "Penfield's Automatism," which was said to be a species of epileptic attack. No alcohol was involved in the case. Three state experts each testified that they could find no evidence of localized brain damage, which could have caused a seizure. As the court below had noted, the irrationality of a crime does not establish an insanity defense. People v. Jandelli, 116 Misc. 2d 384, 455 N.Y.S.2d 728 (1982).

283. Knox, *Epileptic Automatism and Violence*, 8 MED., SCI. & LAW 96, 104 (1968). *See also* Glasgow, *The Anatomy of Automatism*, 64 N.Z. MED. J. 491, 492 (1965): "where the behaviour is anti-social or criminal there will be no evidence that it is planned or pre-meditated."

284. J. MACDONALD, PSYCHIATRY AND THE CRIMINAL 219 (3d ed. 1976).

285. People v. Jones, 225 Cal. App. 2d 598, 37 Cal. Rptr. 454 (1964).

the defendant may have committed the homicide during an attack, and part of the reason he gave was that the killing was "senseless." This testimony permitted evidence that otherwise might not be admissible to be let in regarding the fact that he was having sexual relations with the girl and broadened the scope of the cross-examination of the expert as well. "'Expert evidence is really an argument of an expert to the court, and is valuable only in regard to the proof of the facts and the validity of the reasons advanced for the conclusions....The weight to be given to the opinion of an expert depends on the reasons he assigns to support that opinion....' (People v. Martin, 87 Cal. App. 2d 581, 584, 197 P.2d 379, 380.)"[286]

Proof by the state of a motive would appear to be very influential. In *People v. Perrotta*,[287] on an appeal essentially based on evidence sufficiency in a conviction for murder in the first degree, the evidence indicated that the defendant beat his former lover to death while he was drinking. While there was some evidence as to pathological intoxication, no details are given by the court. Rebuttal testimony similarly was too truncated in the opinion to make much of it. The central point of the court was that "the evidence discloses previous quarrels of a tempestuous nature and previous threats against the decedent's life. Four days before the beating, defendant threatened to kill [the victim]."[288]

Subsequent Cover-ups

This probably proves nothing in either direction. Knox noted that "There will probably be no attempt to conceal any aggressive acts undertaken in automatism."[289] This opinion was evidently based on observation of the behavior of patients in a hospital setting where seriously punitive responses to violence are not contemplated by the actor. In a true case of psychomotor epilepsy or pathological reaction to alcohol, the actor may nevertheless wish to escape detection. Conversely, many crimes are so stupidly or drunkenly committed that detection and apprehension are inevitable, and this hardly indicates automatic behavior.

---

286. *Jones* at 461.

287. People v. Perrotta, 224 Cal. App. 2d 498, 36 Cal. Rptr. 813 (1964).

288. *Perrotta* at 504, 36 Cal. Rptr. at 817.

289. Knox, *Epileptic Automatism and Violence*, 8 MED., SCI. & LAW 96, 104 (1968). *See also* Glasgow, *The Anatomy of Automatism*, 64 N.Z. MED. J. 491, 492 (1965).

Unplanned

Again the point may best be illustrated by a losing case, perhaps the best of the lot on that score: *Sanders v. State*.[290] The defendant was convicted of robbery with an accomplice. He was only charged with one robbery, and in support of his insanity defense, he put on evidence of psychomotor epilepsy seizure. He actually had committed three robberies and was charged with the middle one, and the state was then allowed to put on evidence of the other two to rebut his claim of a seizure. This type of conduct is obviously planned.

So, too, proof of prior threatening conduct can be damaging. In *United States v. McCracken*,[291] the defendant was convicted of murder in the first degree by a jury. He was a domiciliary patient at a VA hospital where he shot and killed a doctor (and then shot himself). He relied upon the insanity defense based on psychomotor epilepsy without alcohol involvement. His condition was also referred to as automatism and was brought about by a head injury or malaria or both. It manifested itself in frequent seizures, especially at times of stress when he would become violent and would have amnesia associated with the epileptic attack. He had been treated for it for ten years. There was no doubt about psychomotor epilepsy, and there was expert testimony by a defense witness that acts of violence might be committed during the seizures and that amnesia would exist for the period. The only issue factually was whether psychomotor epilepsy caused the crime.

The court held that there was no error in denying the defense motion for directed verdict. The prosecution did have some evidence of sanity at the time of the shooting which consisted largely of the fact that the defendant had threatened the victim beforehand and afterwards said "I told you I would do it." There was also some rather weak testimony by a prosecution psychiatrist. The jury rejected the claim of insanity on that evidence, and that part of the opinion finds no fault in letting them do so.

Having an Accomplice

This factor tends to count more strongly one way because many crimes, particularly crimes of violence, are committed without any planning. But the fact that a crime was planned would strongly indicate that it was not the product of a seizure or pathological reaction to alcohol.[292] One of the features we noticed in reading descriptions of

---

290. Sanders v. State, 449 S.W.2d 262 (Tex. Crim. App. 1969).

291. United States v. McCracken, 488 F.2d 406 (5th Cir. 1974).

292. *See, e.g.*, People v. Skorka, 147 Ill. App. 3d 976, 498 N.E.2d 607 (1986).

pathological reaction to alcohol—some true, some feigned—is that the cases which ring most true are committed alone. If this is actually so, it probably partly reflects the planning factor: A crime committed with an accomplice is more likely to be planned than one committed alone.

State v. Holden[293] illustrates the obvious link between having an accomplice and planning, which is anathema to a defense of either pathological intoxication or psychomotor epilepsy. The defendant pleaded not guilty to a charge of murder in the first degree and was convicted of voluntary manslaughter. His accomplice was convicted of involuntary manslaughter, and both were affirmed on appeal. The victim had hit the defendant's sister, and he set out to beat him up. Eventually he was joined by his accomplice, who was also related to his sister, and when they found him, Holden shot him repeatedly.

Defense expert witnesses testified that the defendant had psychomotor epilepsy, but the court gave no details of the basis for this opinion. The defendant evidently argued that his diminished capacity evidence should take the conviction lower, presumably to involuntary manslaughter, which does not usually require intent to kill as does voluntary manslaughter. The court pointed out, however, that "The jury is free to believe or disbelieve such testimony"[294] and held that the verdict was supported by substantial evidence. This was a premeditated killing which involved searching for the victim over some period of time, and it was accomplished by two people acting in concert. A defense based on temporary insanity will rarely be persuasive under such facts.

General Asininity of the Crime

State v. Helmick[295] upheld a jury verdict of assault and burglary over a claim of pathological intoxication litigated under an insanity plea. The jury had found Helmick insane as to some of the charges, including an assault that took place in a witless attempt to rob a bar using a knife, but found him guilty of an assault that took place some 15 minutes later against the police who came to arrest him. They found him lying on his back on top of a dumpster outside the bar. The court noted that expert testimony had indicated that an attack of pathological intoxication could last "minutes, hours or a whole day," and evidently the jury took this quite literally.

---

293. State v. Holden, 85 N.M. 397, 512 P.2d 970 (1973).

294. *Holden* at 399, 512 P.2d at 972.

295. State v. Helmick, 112 Ariz. 166, 540 P.2d 638 (1975).

Complex Conduct

There is some disagreement whether complex tasks may be performed during a psychomotor attack. Some say yes,[296] some say no, and there is an obvious problem of definition: "'a person who's having these temporal lobe seizures,...is not capable of a coordinated, purposeful, directed violent attack because...the nature of the seizure itself would prevent such a thing.'"[297] Weihofen[298] says, "Automatism, the state in which the patient is deprived of or released from conscious control, may replace or follow the epileptic attack. The patient may automatically carry out very complex acts while in such a state."[299] Part of the problem, of course, is the imprecision of the term "complex."[300]

Type of Crime

No writer has flatly stated that some crimes cannot be committed in a state of pathological intoxication, but obviously some crimes require planning and extensive execution and would seem to be impossible. For example, we would suppose that a complex embezzlement scheme or a scheme to defraud would not appear in the cases, and they have not. There is evidently also no suggestion that relatively complex crimes such as rape and robbery cannot be committed. But robbery and rape cases may carry with them an aura of having been planned and having a motive, and a pathological reaction to alcohol defense in these cases is difficult to establish. But much will depend on the facts of an individual case. Robbery is broadly defined and can include what is essentially assaultive taking of property from another person. That takes little planning and is not complex. But if a gun is carried to the scene in a case of robbery[301] or if the victim is lured or followed to a place of "safety" to commit the crime of rape or robbery, pathological intoxication is not a likely finding. The point is that any crime can be committed in a complex manner, and many crimes can be committed without a

---

296. J. MacDonald, Psychiatry and the Criminal 208-11 (1976).

297. People v. Babbit, 45 Cal. 3d 660, 689-90, 248 Cal. Rptr. 69, 84, 755 P.2d 253, 268 (1988). *See also* People v. Anderson, 63 Cal. 2d 351, 46 Cal. Rptr. 763, 406 P.2d 43 (1965).

298. H. Weihofen, Mental Disorder As a Criminal Defense 36 (1954).

299. Citing Lennox, *Amnesia, Real and Feigned,* 10 U. Chi. L. Rev. 298 (1943).

300. In another sense, complex conduct (or fault) can be shown by repetitive crimes. See Commonwealth v. Sirbaugh, 347 Pa. Super. 154, 500 A.2d 453 (1985), in which the defendant evidently committed 25 burglaries and had an accomplice.

301. *See, e.g.,* State v. Wimer, 168 W. Va. 417, 284 S.E.2d 890 (1981). The defendant had a history of head injury, and an EEG examination indicated the presence of temporal lobe epilepsy. He hired a taxi for a long trip and robbed and killed the driver with a gun he had brought along. He was drinking during the trip.

modicum of planning and foresight and involve little complexity. These are the relevant points, not so much the substantive crime label.

Length and Nature of the Attack

In *State v. Willard*,[302] on a combined plea of not guilty and not guilty by reason of insanity, the defendant was convicted of burglary, kidnapping and assault. He had entered the home of the victim, a 74-year-old woman, and terrorized her all night, including cutting her with a knife numerous times. The entire episode lasted for about eight hours. The defendant was known to the victim, and she had identified him. She testified that during the night, the defendant was calm. She asked him if he was drunk, and he said he was not but that he had smoked some "LSD cigarettes." He later told the examining psychiatrist that he had consumed a fifth of alcohol that day. He also claimed amnesia for the period.[303]

One examining psychiatrist testified that he thought it significant that the episode had lasted for so long and that he thought this made a diagnosis of pathological intoxication less likely. This is a significant point, and *Willard* involves more time than any other case we have found. The literature makes frequent references to how long an episode of pathological reaction to alcohol is likely to last, but there are very few reported cases in which the limits are actually observed or tested.

---

302. State v. Willard, 292 N.C. 567, 234 S.E.2d 587 (1977).

303. A major contention of error on appeal was that a state hospital staff psychiatrist who had examined the defendant was not allowed to testify as to his opinion regarding the exact nature of the mental illness suffered by the defendant: schizophrenia, simple type, and alcohol pathological intoxication, possibly in combination with drug use. The trial court ruled that while he could testify as to psychosis undifferentiated further, he could not testify as to these specific conclusions.

> Thus, it appears the doctor was allowed to state his opinion that the defendant was suffering from some type of psychosis at the time of the crime. The fact that the doctor was not permitted to place a label on the specific type of psychosis would not be reversible error. We also note that no proper foundation for the doctor's opinions as to simple schizophrenia and alcohol pathological intoxication was laid and thus the objections to this testimony were properly sustained.

Willard at 579, 234 S.E.2d at 594. Evidently, the reason for this ruling, and its affirmance, was that the witness also said he could not reach a conclusion as to whether the defendant knew right from wrong at the time of the offense. As such, the testimony did not technically go to the insanity defense in any event. It was in this sense that the court on appeal concluded that no foundation had been laid for expert opinion as to pathological intoxication.

Experts and Admissibility

Most of the cases involve the well publicized battle of experts, and, of course, the defendant lost all of these—that is why there is an appellate case challenging that result. In some of these cases, the issue got to the jury,[304] and in others it did not.[305] And the experts must be available.[306] In some of the cases, there was not much of a battle.[307]

In *State v. Baldwin*,[308] the facts do not, so far as they appear, support a defense of pathological intoxication mostly because the defendant had threatened the victim while he was sober and because prior to the actual killing, he had been drinking on and off for a week. The court affirmed a murder conviction, holding that there was no error in the trial court's denial of a continuance to try to obtain better expert evidence of pathological intoxication. He had been sent to the state hospital on defense request, and his EEG was normal. The defendant then obtained his own psychiatrist, who said an alcohol activated EEG should be done too. Evidently it never was. The state would not pay the $500 for it. The lesson here may be that defense counsel should ask that the state evaluation include alcohol-activation tests as well.

There has been no difficulty in the defense or prosecution presenting expert opinion testimony regarding either insanity in general or in the presentation of ancillary tests[309] such as the EEG under the so-called

---

304. Limp v. State, 228 Ind. 361, 92 N.E.2d 549 (1950). The defense psychiatrist made a diagnosis of pathological intoxication in a burglary case, but one state expert testified that the defendant did not have pathological intoxication, and a second one testified that pathological intoxication was not a psychosis. ("It was within the province of the jury to determine what evidence they would believe."); United States v. Rush, 13 C.M.R. 594 (1953) (a defense expert diagnosed pathological intoxication based on EEG's indicating psychomotor seizures. A prosecution expert also ran EEG's and found no evidence of epilepsy).

305. *See, e.g.*, Rose v. State, 506 So. 2d 467 (Fla. Dist. Ct. App. 1987).

306. The importance of expert testimony on the disposition of the case by the fact-finder seems universally conceded. See the authorities cited in Note, *Expert Services and the Indigent Criminal Defendant: The Constitutional Mandate of Ake v. Oklahoma*, 84 MICH. L. REV. 1326, 1350-51 nn.160-162 (1986) and Note, *The Right to a Partisan Psychiatric Expert: Might Indigency Preclude Insanity?* 61 N.Y.U. L. REV. 703 (1986).

307. In some of the cases, the expert's contribution is minimal. In State v. Bock, 288 N.C. 145, 217 S.E.2d 513 (1975), the court upheld the defendant's conviction of murder in the first degree in the killing of a woman in a dispute over money. The body had 55 stab wounds, and the defendant claimed amnesia for the episode. The defense expert proffered very weak evidence of pathological intoxication and opined that the defendant "could have been unconscious"; so weak, in fact, was the expert testimony that one of the contentions on appeal was that the trial court erred in not letting the defense expert state these findings more conclusively. This testimony was based on a two-hour interview in the sheriff's office. It would appear that the jury did not even believe the intoxication evidence, given their verdict.

308. State v. Baldwin, 276 N.C. 690, 174 S.E.2d 526 (1970).

309. The results of sodium amytal are not generally admissible; A. MOENSSENS, F. INBAU & J. STARRS, SCIENTIFIC EVIDENCE IN CRIMINAL CASES § 15.03 (3d ed. 1986), but we have found

Frye test[310] or under the relevant rules of evidence.[311] Most courts admit EEG recordings under the Uniform Business Records as Evidence Act.[312] The expert's interpretation of an EEG is accepted in all jurisdictions,[313] whether under the *Frye* approach or under a more general relevancy approach.[314]

EEG confirmation of the probable existence of a pathological reaction to alcohol condition would be extremely helpful even though it is established that persons with pathological intoxication susceptibility do not always react violently to any consumption of alcohol. That has been demonstrated clinically, and that is why one cannot just give the defendant a few drinks in his cell and watch him react. But if pre-existing brain damage or disease is the setting for pathological reaction to alcohol, it is likely that the actor will have other, associated problems as well.

The EEG will be most useful in those cases, perhaps even a majority of pathological reaction to alcohol cases in which psychomotor epilepsy

---

one possible pathological intoxication case in which expert opinion was based in part on such a test. In State v. Middleton, 295 Or. 485, 668 P.2d 371 (1983), a felony murder conviction was affirmed.

> This trial turned out to be a battle of the experts. Defendant presented one psychiatrist who testified that defendant suffered from "pathological intoxication" and was unable to form the requisite intent [robbery was the predicate felony] to commit the crime. He based his opinion on interviews, two sodium amytal ("truth serum") tests and an alcohol provocation test.
>
> The testimony of the state's expert witnesses, a psychiatrist and a psychologist, cast doubt on the validity and reliability of the tests that were conducted.

Middleton at 493, 668 P.2d at 375. The jury decided in favor of the prosecution. And in People v. Higgins, 5 N.Y.2d 607, 186 N.Y.S.2d 623, 159 N.E.2d 179 (1959), discussed in detail in Chapter 1, the test was administered but not admitted at trial, yet it was referred to in detail by the court of appeals.

310. Frye v. United States, 293 F. 1013 (D.C. Cir. 1923).

311. A. MOENSSENS & F. INBAU, SCIENTIFIC EVIDENCE IN CRIMINAL CASES (2d ed. 1978); Moenssens, *Admissibility of Scientific Evidence—An Alternative to the Frye Rule*, 25 WM. & MARY L. REV. 545 (1984); Giannelli, *The Admissibility of Novel Scientific Evidence: Frye v. United States, a Half-Century Later*, 80 COLUM. L. REV. 1197 (1980). Narcoanalysis, however, has been consistently excluded. Moenssens & Inbau at 129.

312. *See, e.g.*, Annotation, *Admissibility in Civil Action of Electroencephalogram, Electrocardiogram, or Other Record Made by Instrument Used in Medical Test, or of Report Based Upon Such Test*, 66 A.L.R.2d 536 (1959). *See also* Mayole v. B. Crystal & Son, Inc., 266 A.D. 1008, 44 N.Y.S.2d 411 (143).

313. *See, e.g.*, Conrad, *The Electroencephalograph (EEG) as Evidence of Criminal Responsibility*, 50 J. CRIM. L., CRIMINOLOGY & POLICE SCI. 405 (1959). *See also* A. MOENSSENS & F. INBAU, SCIENTIFIC EVIDENCE IN CRIMINAL CASES § 3.11 (organic neurological disorders) and § 3.14 (bibliography) (2d ed. 1978).

314. *See generally* Giannelli, *The Admissibility of Novel Scientific Evidence: Frye v. United States a Half-Century Later*, 80 COLUM. L. REV. 1197 (1980).

is the underlying cause of the reaction. There are several major difficulties. First, it is not entirely clear as to the extent of false positives and false negatives of EEGs in diagnosing psychomotor epilepsy.[315] Secondly, much depends upon expert interpretation of the multiple, exotic and complex ink tracings on a piece of paper.[316] We have a number of cases in which the battle of experts extended beyond clinical observations to interpretation of this scientific evidence. Another potent method of proof that the defendant suffers from susceptibility to pathological reaction to alcohol is the alcohol-activation test administered after he has been charged.

People v. Williams[317] is illustrative. The defendant walked into an eye clinic in which he had never been a patient and shot to death an optician he did not know. He was found guilty of murder in the first degree. The appeal was taken largely on the ground that as a matter of law, diminished capacity was established by his evidence of an attack of psychomotor epilepsy. The court reversed on this ground in connection with a variety of minor errors.

He had been drinking only the night before the morning of the killing. In fact he may not have been drinking at all. Dr. Thompson conducted an alcohol-activated EEG examination.

> There is absolutely no way, he stated, to produce an abnormal electroencephalogram from an entirely normal brain....when an electroencephalogram shows a brain abnormality, it is 100 percent accurate....Thompson stated that mental illness does not produce an abnormality in the electroencephalogram, unless it is due to organic damage or disease. He also added that the abnormalities he had found in the left and right frontal lobe and the right temporal lobe of defendant could occur with a brain tumor and that would be an excellent cause of psychomotor seizure."[318]

"[T]he condition the defendant was said to be in if he had been suffering a psychomotor epileptic seizure would have made him legally insane as well as unconscious of his actions and diminished in capacity for the requisite specific intents. The instant case was of the type wherein it would have been provident to try the guilt and insanity issues together...."[319]

---

315. Weinberg, *Epilepsy and the Alternatives For a Criminal Defense*, 27 CASE W. RES. L. REV. 771, 784 (1977).

316. Weinberg at 784.

317. People v. Williams, 22 Cal. App. 3d 34, 99 Cal. Rptr. 103 (1971).

318. *Williams* at 52 n.22, 99 Cal. Rptr. at 117 n.22.

319. *Williams* at 53, 99 Cal. Rptr. at 118.

If there is reason to believe that the condition of the defendant's mind that contributed to the reaction to alcohol was a blow to the head, evidence of this should be brought out and will be admissible. If the condition is believed to be epilepsy or some other disease for which there is evidence of a hereditary factor, perhaps this should be brought out if there is not more direct evidence of epilepsy. For example, Professor Weihofen has pointed out that

> Bodily injuries or diseases, such as blows on the head, injuries to the spine, epilepsy, syphilis, etc., may lead to mental disturbances, and it is therefore competent, where the issue of defendant's mental condition has been raised by evidence, to prove that the defendant had suffered such injuries or been afflicted with such diseases. [Citations to a number of cases omitted.] As in the case of other predisposing circumstances, however, there must be some other evidence tending to prove that the defendant was in fact mentally unsound, before proof of such injuries or diseases will be admitted.[320]

United States v. Schlomann[321] provides another example of an attempt to establish EEG confirmation. The defendant was charged with and convicted of unpremeditated murder, and his sanity at the time of the offense was put in question based on claimed pathological intoxication. The issue of evidence sufficiency on that issue was raised on appeal. In the military appellate structure, such claims get virtually de novo review in contrast to the civilian process.

The defendant's condition was characterized as pathological intoxication "as manifested by an epileptic equivalent or 'rage reaction,' triggered by alcohol."[322] An EEG test showed no abnormalities, and an alcohol-activated EEG test was then run and "'showed a moderate buildup of hyperventilation with a burst of slow wave activity, one minute post hyperventilation'" and "'associated with this was a run of what appeared to be 14 per second positive spikes in the right temporal lobe.'"[323] During the test "there was no evidence of behavior suggestive of an episodic epileptic state or psychosis," and the examiners "...concluded that 'pathological intoxication' was not confirmed by psychiatric observation...."[324] Further alcohol activation tests were run by other doctors.

---

320. H. WEIHOFEN, MENTAL DISORDER AS CRIMINAL DEFENSE 321-22 (1954) (citations omitted).

321. United States v. Schlomann, 36 C.M.R. 622 (1966), *aff'd* United States v. Schlomann, 16 C.M.A. 414, 37 C.M.R. 34 (1966). *See also* Schlomann v. Ralston, 691 F.2d 401 (8th Cir. 1982), *cert. denied*, 459 U.S. 1221, 103 S. Ct. 1229, 75 L. Ed. 2d 463 (1983).

322. *Schlomann*, 36 C.M.R. at 630.

323. *Schlomann* at 630.

324. *Schlomann* at 630.

The defendant became belligerent and had to be restrained, but the tests were eventually completed. This expert also said that the prior tests were within normal limits and no focal abnormalities or seizures were elicited. Still other experts testified that the defendant might have been psychotic.[325] Numerous other witnesses testified various ways, both lay and expert. In all, five EEG examinations, two with alcohol activation, could not elicit an abnormal EEG response.

To establish that the defendant was suffering from some psychiatric/psychological/biological defect at the time of the conduct in question is not to establish that the ailment "caused" the behavior. Indeed, if an EEG is part of the proof, the evidence is even more remote: "In general, EEG findings will either be normal, indicate a disturbance of mental function in a known mental patient without establishing whether the anomaly is the cause of the mental disorder, or show anomalies in subjects thought to be normal."[326] Given the symptomatology of pathological reaction to alcohol, especially the fact that the behavior under the circumstances is one of the best indicators of its existence, this may not be as insurmountable a problem as it might be in other cases. The more typical intoxication case is one like *State v. Parker*,[327] in which there was testimony that the defendant "had been drinking for at least 12 hours, that he had been smoking marijuana, that he had not eaten and that he was a diabetic and had not taken his prescribed medicine"[328] before he shot someone. While none of these would be a defense alone or together, how could one possibly separate any of them as "the cause" of the killing? Most pathological reaction to alcohol cases are not so complicated. Usually it is a matter of drinking with a pre-existing brain condition leading to the reaction. But absent the very unusual case in which the amount of alcohol consumed is indeed minimal, how does one establish that pathological reaction to alcohol, not intoxication, "caused" the conduct in question?

The "foundation" for getting to the jury on a claim by the defense of pathological intoxication, when tried as automatism, may face special problems of proof. Here the skepticism of the jury interacts with inadequate proof on the part of the defense and the seemingly easy availability of state expert witnesses who discern no such ailment.[329]

"The heart of the diagnostic problem, of course, is that most mental diseases do not have the confirmatory physical evidence which one

---

325. *Schlomann* at 631-32.

326. Verdeaux, *Etude Neuropsychiatrique et Electroencephalographique des Delinquents* (Neuropsychiatric and Electroencephalographic Study of Delinquents), 10 RIVISTA DI NEUROBIOLOGIA 1180 (1964).

327. State v. Parker, 416 So. 2d 545 (La. 1982).

328. *Parker* at 551.

329. Doepel v. United States, 434 A.2d 449 (D.C. 1981).

expects of physical disease."[330] Cases involving pathological intoxication can fall into that category as well, but in many of them, due to the nature of the cause of the reaction, there will be physical evidence, and thus the opportunity may exist to present evidence of significant impact. A prior history of brain damage, or presently demonstrated brain abnormality fits this pattern, and it can be detected by the administration of an EEG test. The expert may also undertake an alcohol provocation test in appropriate cases.

330. A. GOLDSTEIN, THE INSANITY DEFENSE 35 (1967).

6

Pathological Intoxication and the Mental Disease Requirement in the Law of Insanity

There are issues of special relevance engendered by invocation of the traditional insanity plea in cases of pathological reaction to alcohol. The law of insanity has two features that distinguish it from the law of intoxication, voluntary or involuntary, as well as the law of automatism, or involuntary act. The first is the difference in disposition: Win or lose, the defendant will be subjected to custodial restraint, usually involving automatic commitment.[1] Negotiated acquittals by reason of insanity are more common than jury trials on the issue.[2] Since overall insanity pleas

---

1. Jones v. United States, 463 U.S. 354, 103 S. Ct. 3043, 77 L. Ed. 2d 694 (1983). *See* Wexler, *Redefining the Insanity Problem*, 53 GEO. WASH. L. REV. 528, 547-48 (1985); Slovenko, *Disposition of the Insanity Acquitee*, 11 J. PSYCHIAT. & L. 97, 109 (1983).

2. Most insanity plea dispositions are actually plea bargained. Slobogin, *The Guilty But Mentally Ill Verdict: An Idea Whose Time Should Not Have Come*, 53 GEO. WASH. L. REV. 494, 499 n.26 (1985), collected data from several sources. These data are presented as a percentage of insanity acquittals reached through some form of negotiation and range from 61 percent to 90 percent, although some of these dispositions involved a bench trial as well. Professor Slobogin also provides a survey of release criteria among the several states. Slobogin at 500-04 nn.28-38. *See also* Janofsky, Vandewalle & Rappeport, *Defendants Pleading Insanity: An Analysis of Outcome*, 17 BULL. AM. ACAD. PSYCHIAT. & LAW 203 (1989); Rogers, Bloom & Manson, *Insanity Defenses: Contested or Conceded?* 141 AM. J. PSYCHIAT. 885, 886 (1984), (three year study in Oregon indicated agreed-upon insanity acquittal in 86 percent of all *successful* insanity pleas). This is quite significant because it means that in the large majority of instances in which the defense is prepared to challenge conviction on grounds of insanity, the prosecution experts agree at least with the dispositional conclusion of the defense expert, leaving the "battle of experts" phenomenon to the marginal cases, and those cases are the ones which receive the most attention precisely because they are litigated and often appealed. These data are unavailable specifically for cases of pathological intoxication, but it is suggestive that the defense may be much more successful, at least when they are tried under the insanity defense, than one would infer from reading only reported appellate opinions, which are, of course, initiated by defendants who lost contested cases at trial. Additional data on the general practice of negotiated insanity acquittals are found in NAT'L MENTAL HEALTH ASS'N, MYTHS AND REALITIES: A REPORT OF THE NAT'L COMM'N ON THE INSANITY DEFENSE 5 (1983); Petrila, *The Insanity Defense and Other Mental Health Dispositions in Missouri*, 5 INT'L J. L. & PSYCHIAT. 81 (1982); Fukanaga, Pasewark, Hawkins

succeed with the jury in only about 25 percent to 50 percent of the cases,[3] the task of the defense in this situation is more realistically to persuade a prosecutor that pathological intoxication occurred and that it caused the behavior involved, with a jury trial on the issues relegated to a backup position. Obviously, many prosecutors see the matter the same way.

The other distinctive feature of the insanity plea of central importance here is that the insanity defense is restricted by its terms to cases in which the mental incapacity at the time of the offense charged is attributable to mental disease, and this second qualification is the focus of this chapter. Essentially, the question is whether pathological intoxication satisfies the requirements of insanity law. We will survey those requirements, focus in on two features of special relevance, whether a particular mental disease must be identified and whether the malady must have a more or less permanent status, and, in the final section, we raise the possibility that the "mental disease" requirement of insanity law is not entirely what it seems in any event.

CURRENT INSANITY LAWS

There has been an abundance of recent reconsideration of many aspects of the insanity defense.[4] For the most part, the reevaluation of these tests has been directed only at those which are used on the question of guilt or innocence—insanity at the time of the alleged crime. Different tests are used to determine the procedural matters of capacity to stand trial[5] or to be sentenced or executed.

& Gudeman, *Insanity Plea: Interexaminer Agreement and Concordance of Psychiatric Opinion and Court Verdict*, 5 LAW & HUM. BEHAV. 325 (1981); Singer, *Insanity Acquittal in the Seventies: Observations and Empirical Analysis of One Jurisdiction*, 2 MENT. DISABIL. L. REP. 406 (1978).

3. Slobogin, *The Guilty But Mentally Ill Verdict: An Idea Whose Time Should Not Have Come*, 53 GEO. WASH. L. REV. 494, 500 n.27 (1985).

4. P. LOW, J. JEFFRIES & R. ROWIE, THE TRIAL OF JOHN HINCKLEY, JR.: A CASE STUDY IN THE INSANITY DEFENSE (1986); T. MAEDER, CRIME AND MADNESS: THE ORIGINS AND EVOLUTION OF THE INSANITY DEFENSE (1985); I. KEILITZ & J. FULTON, THE INSANITY DEFENSE AND ITS ALTERNATIVES (1984); D. HERMANN, THE INSANITY DEFENSE: PHILOSOPHICAL, HISTORICAL AND LEGAL PERSPECTIVES (1983); NAT'L MENTAL HEALTH ASS'N, MYTHS AND REALITIES: A REPORT OF THE NATIONAL COMMISSION ON THE INSANITY DEFENSE (1983); Klofas & Yandrasits, *"Guilty But Mentally Ill" and the Jury Trial: A Case Study*, 24 CRIM. L. BULL. 424 (1988); Mickenberg, *A Pleasant Surprise: The GBMI Verdict Has Both Succeeded in Its Own Right and Successfully Preserved the Traditional Role of the Insanity Defense*, 55 U. CIN. L. REV. 943 (1987); George, *The American Bar Association's Mental Health Standards: An Overview*, 53 GEO. WASH. L. REV. 338 (1985); Slobogin, *The Guilty But Mentally Ill Verdict: An Idea Whose Time Should Not Have Come*, 53 GEO. WASH. L. REV. 494 (1985); Wexler, *Redefining the Insanity Problem*, 53 GEO. WASH. L. REV. 528 (1985); Comment, *Recent Changes in Criminal Law: The Federal Insanity Defense*, 46 LA. L. REV. 337 (1985).

5. *See, e.g.*, Miles v. State, 688 S.W.2d 219 (Tex. Ct. App. 1985), which involved both the

The modern law of insanity[6] traces to *M'Naghten*'s case, which requires, inter alia, that the actor had been "labouring under ...a defect of reason, from *disease of the mind*...."[7] The *M'Naghten* ("right/wrong") rule was the clear majority rule in the United States for over one hundred years, but because *M'Naghten* was perceived as limited to cognitive incapacity, many of the jurisdictions which adopted the *M'Naghten* rule supplemented it with the "irresistible impulse" test,[8] which makes impairment of volition, rather than cognition, the criterion of responsibility. It was the function of the additional rule to exonerate if the conduct of the defendant resulted from a significant defect in the actor's ability to control his conduct. Any mental disease of the defendant which makes him unable to control his actions or resist committing an act will be held to have satisfied the volitional test. It is not necessary that the criminal conduct be sudden and unplanned as the name of the test would suggest. Any evidence relevant to the defendant's loss of control because of a mental disease is admissible.[9] *M'Naghten* is essentially cognitive in its orientation, and the additional test was designed to exonerate on the basis of volitional defects as well.

Given the fact that it is an ancient and universally adopted premise of criminal law that "There cannot be, and there is not, in any locality or age, a law punishing men for what they cannot avoid,"[10] it might be surprising to find a majority of states rejecting the irresistible impulse rule, but there is reluctance to recognize a defense which might succeed in a case of unresisted urges. The resulting conflict in the law is clear because while many jurisdictions reject the irresistible impulse test for

---

issue of competency to stand trial and the propriety of a guilty plea acceptance in a case involving claimed epileptic seizures.

6. Historical treatment is found in 3 M. PERLIN, MENTAL DISABILITY LAW § 15.02 (1989); D. HERMANN, THE INSANITY DEFENSE: PHILOSOPHICAL, HISTORICAL AND LEGAL PERSPECTIVES (1983); 2 N. WALKER, CRIME AND INSANITY IN ENGLAND (1968); English, *The Light Between Twilight and Dusk: Federal Criminal Law and the Volitional Insanity Defense*, 40 HASTINGS L.J. 1 (1988) (emphasis is on the volitional prong); Sendor, *Crime as Communication: An Interpretive Theory of the Insanity Defense and the Mental Elements of Crime*, 74 GEO. L.J. 1371 (1986); Crotty, *The History of Insanity as a Defense to Crime in English Criminal Law*, 12 CALIF. L. REV. 105 (1924); Platt & Diamond, *The Origins of the "Right and Wrong" Test of Criminal Responsibility and Its Subsequent Development in the United States: An Historical Survey*, 54 CALIF. L. REV. 1227 (1966).

7. 8 Eng. Rep. 718, 722 (1843) (emphasis added).

8. The leading American case on the irresistible impulse test is Parsons v. State, 81 Ala. 577, 2 So. 854 (1886). H. WEIHOFEN, MENTAL DISORDER AS A CRIMINAL DEFENSE 85 (1954) credits State v. Thompson, Wright's Ohio Rep. 617 (1834), antedating *M'Naghten*, as the original American case. The English version of the irresistible impulse test, probably attributable to Ferrer's Case, 19 How. St. Tr. 886 (1760), is even more ancient. *See also* 1 W. LAFAVE & A. SCOTT, SUBSTANTIVE CRIMINAL LAW § 4.2 n.100 (1986); I. RAY, THE MEDICAL JURISPRUDENCE OF INSANITY 263 (1838).

9. A. GOLDSTEIN, THE INSANITY DEFENSE 71 (1967).

10. Parsons v. State, 81 Ala. 577, 2 So. 854, 859 (1886).

legal insanity, they presumably all accept the basic underpinning of substantive criminal law that no person is to be convicted in the absence of a voluntary act. This conflict will later lead the English courts to draw a distinction between sane and insane automatism, for automatism is but an example of an involuntary act.

Dissatisfaction with these tests led to the adoption of the now-abandoned Durham test[11] and eventually to the formulation of the "substantial capacity" test by the American Law Institute. In the last two decades, the dominant test has been the language proposed by the Model Penal Code:[12] "A person is not responsible for criminal conduct if at the time of such conduct as a result of mental disease or defect he lacked substantial capacity either to appreciate the criminality (wrongfulness) of his conduct or to conform his conduct to the requirements of law."[13]

This "substantial capacity" or "A.L.I." (American Law Institute) test is now the majority rule in the United States, while *M'Naghten* remains a substantial minority rule, sometimes supplemented by the irresistible impulse test. The A.L.I. test is satisfied by either cognitive or volitional impairment and thus reaches results similar to those in jurisdictions which previously had adopted a combination of the *M'Naghten* and the irresistible impulse tests.

There is some movement back to restricting the insanity tests to cognitive impairment to the exclusion of volitional or control-oriented tests.[14] The American Bar Association's proposal[15] has a purely cognitive orientation,[16] as does the new federal statute.[17]

---

11. Durham v. United States, 214 F.2d 862 (D.C. Cir. 1954), overruled by United States v. Brawner, 471 F.2d 969 (D.C. Cir. 1972). Durham held that "[a]n accused is not criminally responsible if his unlawful act was the product of mental disease or defect." *Durham* at 874-75. The "product rule" was pioneered in State v. Pike, 49 N.H. 399, 402 (1870).

12. MODEL PENAL CODE § 4.01 (Proposed Official Draft 1962) (emphasis added).

13. A second section provides: "As used in this Article, the terms 'mental disease or defect' do not include an abnormality manifested only by repeated criminal or otherwise anti-social conduct."

The law does not seem to place any importance on the distinction drawn in *M'Naghten* between disease and defect. The terms are merely descriptive, not prescriptive. As the court said in Durham v. United States, 214 F.2d 862, 875 (D.C. Cir. 1954):

> We use "disease" in the sense of a condition which is considered capable of either improving or deteriorating. We use "defect" in the sense of a condition which is not considered capable of either improving or deteriorating and which may be either congenital, or the result of injury, or the residual effect of a physical or mental disease.

14. "The American Medical Association favored outright abolition [of the insanity test], while both the American Psychiatric Association (APA) and the American Bar Association supported retention of solely a cognitive-based insanity defense." English, *The Light Between Twilight and Dusk: Federal Criminal Law and the Volitional Insanity Defense*, 40 HASTINGS L.J. 1, 5-6 (1988) (citations omitted).

15. AMERICAN BAR ASS'N, CRIMINAL JUSTICE MENTAL HEALTH STANDARDS, Standard 7-6.1 (1984).

16. The American Bar Association's proposal is at least a partial reversion to *M'Naghten*

The basic thrust of the federal Insanity Defense Reform Act of 1984 was to reject the Model Penal Code's formulation and to restrict the test to impairment of the so-called cognitive function, entirely excluding the defense based on impaired volition, although the basic objection to the volitional prong is its application to nonpsychotic volitional impairment.[18] This statute was adopted in the wake of the Hinckley case,[19] and that case has also led to a few state provisions which purport to abolish the insanity defenses entirely[20] by restricting the defense to negation of the mental elements required of the crime. If the *mens rea* is lacking, the defendant is not guilty of the crime and it does not matter what the reason was that the *mens rea* was lacking. Insanity is thus rendered irrelevant by these statutes. In such states, pathological reaction to alcohol would have to be tried on a not guilty plea as a *mens rea*, diminished capacity, involuntary intoxication or automatism defense.[21] There are other variations on these modifications and abolition statutes[22] and proposals which need not be pursued here. They are largely aimed at abolition of the volitional supplement to the *M'Naghten* rules, shifting the burden of proof to the defendant and creation of a new verdict device, designated "guilty but mentally ill," designed to increase convictions.[23]

The complexity of the tasks addressed by these seemingly simple rules is quite impressive.[24] Part of the reason for the great difficulty

---

in the sense that the sole focus is on cognitive impairment to the exclusion of volitional impairment. AMERICAN BAR ASS'N, CRIMINAL JUSTICE MENTAL HEALTH STANDARDS, Standard 7-6.1. (1984), also adopted as American Bar Ass'n, 2 STANDARDS FOR CRIMINAL JUSTICE ch. 7 (2d ed. Supp. 1986) on August 7, 1984, by the ABA House of Delegates.

17. 18 U.S.C. § 17(a) (Supp. V 1987).

18. English, *The Light Between Twilight and Dusk: Federal Criminal Law and the Volitional Insanity Defense*, 40 HASTINGS L.J. 1, 50 n.288 (1988).

19. United States v. Hinckley, 525 F. Supp. 1342 (D.D.C. 1981), *clarified and reconsid. denied*, 529 F. Supp. 520 (D.D.C.)(per curiam), *aff'd*, 672 F.2d 115 (D.C. Cir. 1982)(for the pre-trial rulings); Crim. No. 81-306 (D.D.C. 1981)(for the trial record).

20. IDAHO CODE § 18-207 (1987); MONT. CODE ANN. § 46-14-201 (1987); UTAH CODE ANN. § 76-2-305(1) (Supp. 1989). Abolition or severe restriction of the insanity defense was upheld in State v. Korell, 213 Mont. 316, 690 P.2d 992 (1984) and State v. Watson, 211 Mont. 401, 686 P.2d 879 (1984).

21. Presumably, this would not be true in those states which have now adopted some version of the "guilty but mentally ill" procedure. Slobogin, *The Guilty But Mentally Ill Verdict: An Idea Whose Time Should Not Have Come*, 53 GEO. WASH. L. REV. 494 (1985).

22. Discussion of and citations to abolitionist states may be found in 1 MODEL PENAL CODE AND COMMENTARIES § 4.01, at 180-81 (1985); 1 W. LAFAVE & A. SCOTT, SUBSTANTIVE CRIMINAL LAW § 4.1(d) (1986).

23. Slobogin, *The Guilty But Mentally Ill Verdict: An Idea Whose Time Should Not Have Come*, 53 GEO. WASH. L. REV. 494 (1985).

24. A. GOLDSTEIN, THE INSANITY DEFENSE 20 (1967):

> The insanity defense is caught up in some of the most controversial ideological currents of our time. The direction it takes depends, essentially, upon

encountered with application of the insanity defense derives from the fact that it already is such an accommodation of medical and legal views. On the medical side, there is unhappiness because it does not conform to any nosologically derived mental illness categories and because it is judgmental and not diagnostic at all. On the legal side, it is not viewed with equanimity because it is also a conceptual mess which encompasses four different ideas, only one of which is unique to insanity law.

The insanity defense presently overlaps the traditional defenses of involuntary act, or automatism, (assuming the jurisdiction has the Model Penal Code or that *M'Naghten* has been supplemented with the irresistible impulse rule), lack of the *mens rea* required by the crime and mistaken belief in the existence of facts giving rise to defenses such as self-defense. In addition, it encompasses a judgmental view that the defendant ought not to be held criminally responsible despite the presence of all of the elements of the substantive offense. This legal redundancy is most apparent in bifurcated trials where the defense wants to put on psychiatric or other expert opinion evidence regarding the defendant's legal insanity at the time of the act and subsequently needs to offer indistinguishable evidence in the "guilt" phase to establish that the defendant did not have the *mens rea* required to convict or that he committed no voluntary act. It will be the identical evidence because it is usually the same factual question: the cognitive capacity or volitional faculty of the defendant at the moment of the act.

TWO SPECIAL PROBLEMS OF INSANITY PERTAINING TO PATHOLOGICAL INTOXICATION: PARTICULARITY AND PERMANENCE

Apart from these general problems of insanity law, pathological intoxication invites particular attention to two issues: Does insanity law require identification or specification of a particular, recognized mental disease entity, and is the defense of legal insanity available in cases of so-called "temporary insanity"?

---

the place in social control one assigns to the criminal law as it competes with other methods of regulation by the state, to each of the themes underlying the criminal law, to the confidence one has that the mentally ill offender can be identified and treated, and the importance one attaches to the idea of blame. However difficult it has been in the past to find one's way among considerations of this sort, events are conspiring to make the problem even more complex.

Does Insanity Law Require Proof of a Particular Mental Disease or Defect? Does Pathological Intoxication Qualify as a Mental Disease or Defect?

Whatever the law prescribes as the essential cognitive or volitional incapacity in the actor, the genesis or foundation, perhaps cause, of that impairment has always been restricted to either "disease of the mind" under *M'Naghten* or now "mental disease or defect" under the A.L.I.'s commonly adopted formulation. These terms need definition to determine the extent to which, if at all, pathological intoxication fulfills this independent requisite of the insanity defense. Does the mental condition associated with pathological intoxication comply with the demands implicit in the concept of "disease of the mind" or "mental disease or defect?"

The problem is double-edged. If pathological intoxication qualifies as a "mental disease," then the defendant should be able to raise it on a plea of not guilty by reason of insanity. The converse point is that if it is not a mental disease or defect, presumably the defendant could raise the defense on a general plea of not guilty, even with the use of expert witnesses such as neurologists.[25] There is still a third point: To the extent that the impairment brought about by pathological intoxication impacts the actor's cognitive abilities, abolition of only the volitional prong of the insanity test (as some jurisdictions have recently done) should not affect the answer to the question posed here.

Whether pathological intoxication is a disease concept for these purposes is problematical. In one sense, pathological intoxication is not a primary disease, seen from the perspective of the medical model of mental disease. It can fairly be described as an event and a resulting condition symptomatic of an underlying, physiological abnormality; an analogous phenomenon is the seizure state that is episodically associated with psychomotor or temporal lobe epilepsy, or it may be analogized to the ketoacidosis associated with diabetes. The abnormal reaction is physically controllable to the extent it is caused by alcohol consumption by the actor, but lack of awareness on the part of the actor will forestall that precautionary measure.

The question whether pathological intoxication is a "disease" for purposes of the insanity tests is rarely discussed directly in either the cases or the secondary literature, but given the more generalized discussion above relating to the disease requirement of insanity law, one would have to conclude that pathological intoxication well qualifies. The cases usually assume sub silentio that it does, or that the question is irrelevant, and those courts which are antagonistic to the defense tend to

---

25. United States v. Brawner, 471 F.2d 969 (D.C. Cir. 1972).

treat it as intoxication but on the ground that the pathological reaction was voluntarily induced, not because the condition is not a disease. The question was put by d'Orban: "[I]s Pathological Intoxication (PI) recognized by the courts as a 'disease of the mind'?"[26] While, as discussed in Chapter 7, the concepts of sane automatism versus insane automatism may seem strange to American audiences, the conclusion reached by d'Orban seems even more foreign (though it is correct):

> There are few reports in the literature of homicide committed in a state of alcohol-induced hypoglycaemia,[27] but when the condition could be experimentally reproduced with EEG and blood sugar monitoring, it was successfully used in mitigation. Nowadays, if the person were previously unaware of the possible adverse effects that alcohol may have on him (thus exhonerating him from negligence or recklessness) it may be open to him to plead non-insane automatism and if this were accepted the result would be an acquital [sic]. By contrast, an offence committed as a result of an alcohol-induced seizure would be regarded as insane automatism.... [For this proposition, d'Orban cites *Regina v. Sullivan.*[28]][29]

The idea, it would seem, is that hypoglycemia is not a mental disease and temporal lobe epilepsy is. Both, of course, fall within virtually anyone's definition of pathological intoxication if alcohol triggers the reaction of the actor. A translation to the context of American legal doctrine would be that the pathological intoxication defense should be tried on a not guilty plea when the underlying defect is hypoglycemia (because that is not a mental disease or defect) and should be tried on a plea of not guilty by reason of insanity when it is temporal lobe epilepsy (because that is a mental disease or defect). Surely it would be difficult to justify this distinction either in terms of the dispositional differences which would be occasioned by it or in terms of the "physical disease" versus "mental disease," which must lead to it.

---

26. d'Orban, *Drugs and Alcohol: The Psychiatrist as Expert Witness in Court,* 81 BR. J. ADDICT. 631, 634 (1986).

27. The author cites Gibbens, *The Clinical Phenomena of Mental Disorders, Medico-Legal Aspects,* in HANDBOOK OF PSYCHIATRY, 1 GENERAL PSYCHOPATHOLOGY (M. Shepperd & O. Zangwill eds. 1983); Bovill, *A Case of Functional Hypoglycaemia—A Medico-Legal Problem,* 123 BR. J. PSYCHIAT. 353 (1973); and Hill, Sargant & Heppenstall, *A Case of Matricide,* LANCET 526 (1943).

28. (1984) 1 A.C. 156.

29. d'Orban, *Drugs and Alcohol: The Psychiatrist as Expert Witness in Court,* 81 BR. J. ADDICT. 631, 634 (1986).

In *People v. Freeman*,[30] the court reversed a conviction for negligent homicide by automobile when the defendant claimed the death was due to an epileptic seizure following drinking a couple of highballs. Lederman[31] uses *Freeman* as an example of the differences between the current English style and the approach of some American jurisdictions. In his opinion, the American courts are more prone to adopt a medical definition of disease for purposes of drawing the insane versus non-insane automatism distinction (which most American courts would delineate as involuntary act defenses distinguished from the insanity defense) and are relatively unconcerned in this definitional process with what he refers to as the "social defense" criterion for defining diseases. He also thought that this leads not only to classifying epilepsy as not a disease of the mind, but further to courts greatly restricting the involuntary act defense.

Professor Hermann has identified three competing approaches to defining "mental disease" in the legal context:[32] (1) Mental disease should take as its referent the medical concept of "mental disease"; (2) Szasz's position that if it does not mean physical disease, the term lacks any meaning outside the concept of deviance from social norms, that is, "mental illness" is not literal but metaphorical;[33] and (3) the view that the terms "mental disease" or "mental illness" are merely descriptive of "an abnormal condition of the mind that affects the capacity for conforming behavior."[34] It is obviously the first and third tactics which are critical here and which divide the courts. Professor Hermann states:

> The first approach, which equates mental disease with a medical diagnosis, has been adopted by some courts and is exemplified by the opinion of the Court of Appeals for the District of Columbia in *Carter v. United States*.[35] Here the court made this equation explicit: "Mental 'disease' means mental illness. Mental illnesses are of many sorts and have many characteristics. *They, like physical illnesses, are the subject matter of medical science.*"[36]

---

30. People v. Freeman, 61 Cal. App. 2d 110, 142 P.2d 435 (1943).

31. Lederman, *Non-Insane and Insane Automatism: Reducing the Significance of a Problematic Distinction*, 34 INT'L & COMP. L.Q. 819, 830-31 (1985).

32. D. HERMANN, THE INSANITY DEFENSE: PHILOSOPHICAL, HISTORICAL AND LEGAL PERSPECTIVES 130 (1983). *See also* Fingarette, *The Concept of Mental Disease in Criminal Law Insanity Tests*, 33 U. CHI. L. REV. 229 (1966); Swartz, *"Mental Disease": The Groundwork for Legal Analysis and Legislative Action*, 111 U. PA. L. REV. 389 (1963).

33. T. SZASZ, INSANITY: THE IDEA AND ITS CONSEQUENCES (1987); T. SZASZ, THE MYTH OF MENTAL ILLNESS (1961). *See also* Klofas, Book Review, 16 J. CRIM. JUST. 511 (1988); Miller, Book Review, 15 J. PSYCHIAT. & L. 571 (1987).

34. Hermann at 130 & 135.

35. Carter v. United States, 252 F.2d 608 (D.C. Cir. 1957).

36. Hermann at 130, quoting *Carter* at 617 (emphasis in original). *See also* Weihofen, *The*

The first technique would focus on an independent definition of the term "mental disease" and from that inquiry determine its function in the law of insanity. In fact, the reason it may be useful to try to gain a grasp of the notion of mental disease in the first place and why there is a significant problem is that a smattering of courts will sometimes undertake what appears to be a wholly medical definition of mental disease when they are making a determination whether the defendant is eligible for the insanity defense. One court defined it as "any underdevelopment, pathological condition, lesion or malfunctioning of the brain or any morbid change or deterioration in the organic functions or structure [of the brain.]"[37] Of course, to include terms like "pathological" and "morbid" in a definition of "disease" tends to be a bit question-begging, but it does indicate the considerable extent to which the definition of "disease" is circular in any event. One medical dictionary defines disease as "a pathological condition of the body that presents a group of symptoms peculiar to it and which sets the condition apart as an abnormal entity differing from other normal or pathological body states."[38] Pathology is then defined as a "condition produced by disease."[39] But if one wanted to turn this part of the law entirely over to the medical profession, where or to whom would one look? The story of St. Elizabeth's Hospital in regard to "sociopathic personalities" is well known: First it was not a mental illness and then, following a weekend staff meeting, it was.[40] Many have joined those who have expressed doubts regarding the scientific basis of psychiatry:

> Psychiatry is a "social science," which is to say it is not a science at all, and the same is true of psychology and sociology. The experts drawn from these disciplines do not bring to the trial a body of durable knowledge, a set of scientific laws, or even an assortment of reliable measures and procedures. At most, they tote a loose collection of question-begging diagnoses that are not beyond dispute even within the small clinical population on which they are based.[41]

Definition of Mental Illness, 21 OHIO ST. L.J. 1 (1960), where the same view is taken, while the lack of consensus problem is also acknowledged.

37. Territory v. Alcosiba, 36 Haw. 231, 238 (1942).

38. TABER'S CYCLOPEDIC MEDICAL DICTIONARY 415 (C. Thomas ed. 14th ed. 1981).

39. TABER'S at 1054.

40. In re Rosenfield, 157 F. Supp. 18 (D.D.C. 1957); D. HERMANN, THE INSANITY DEFENSE: PHILOSOPHICAL, HISTORICAL AND LEGAL PERSPECTIVES 131 (1983); Weihofen, *The Definition of Mental Illness*, 21 OHIO ST. L.J. 1, 5 (1960).

41. D. ROBINSON, PSYCHOLOGY AND LAW 61 (1980). Psychoanalysis as a scientific enterprise is defended in M. EDELSON, PSYCHOANALYSIS: A THEORY IN CRISIS (1988).

"The training, orientation and philosophy of the particular psychiatrist is likely to be more of a factor in his diagnosis of such cases than any factual questions that can be settled by observation and examination."[42] Thus, we are forced to the conclusion that "the existence or non-existence of mental illness is not solely a factual question to be determined by objective observation or examination. It is also a question calling for a policy or philosophical judgment concerning what kinds of abnormality should be included in the term 'mental illness.'"[43] Former Chief Justice Burger, while a federal circuit judge, said:

> ...psychiatrists are in disagreement on what is a "mental disease," and even where there exists such a definable and classifiable condition...no rule of law can possibly be sound or workable which is dependent upon the terms of another discipline whose members are in profound disagreement about what these terms mean.[44]

The St. Elizabeth's episode is frequently used to castigate the psychiatrists involved and as justification for not relegating to that profession the task of defining mental illness for purposes of the insanity defense. We agree that delegation would be out of order but mainly because the tasks are so different, treatment versus assignment of responsibility. The fact that the mental disease classifications shift from time to time ought not to be taken as especially unsettling or disqualifying. Scientific theories change too. What is disquieting here is not change or even the frequency of change. The actual basis of rejection is not that there was no convincing objective evidence supporting the view entertained by the medical professionals in advance of the meeting of the staff at St. Elizabeth's, but that there was none after the change was made either.[45] The inconstancy of classificatory or nosological schemes as illustrated, for example, in the modifications between various editions of the DSM merely aggravates this more fundamental objection to viewing psychiatry as science.

> "Mental disease" cannot at present simply be referred to the medical community for determination because there is no authoritative or generally accepted medical definition of mental disease. Even if there were a medical definition that could draw a consensus, it is unlikely that, since it would need to be directed to needs of diagnosis and treatment, it

---

42. Weihofen at 5.
43. Weihofen at 5.
44. United States v. Blocker, 288 F.2d 853, 859-60 (D.C. Cir. 1961).
45. *See also* Eaton, *The Assessment of Mental Health,* 108 AM. J. PSYCHIAT. 81 (1951).

> would necessarily be appropriate to the law in its concern to determine responsibility as a basis for punishment. The focus of medicine is on etiology, dysfunction, and antidote, while the criminal law is concerned exclusively with dysfunction. For instance, medical psychiatry has eliminated from its concept of mental disease conditions for which it cannot provide treatment; the lack of appropriate treatment is not relevant to the criminal law definition of mental disease.[46]

The categorization of diseases is something less than pure science, a point made clear in the example provided by *Granville House*.[47] Granville House operated chemical dependency treatment centers, and it sought a declaratory judgment that chemical dependency be classified as a medical condition rather than a mental condition, thereby making them eligible for medicaid funds. The court demonstrated an excellent grasp of the controversy:

> On one level, the debate appears to take the form of turf skirmishes. The American Medical Association (AMA), since 1957, has classified alcoholism as a physical disease. The American Psychiatric Association (APA), in the Third Edition of its *Diagnostic and Statistical Manual of Mental Disorders* (DSM-III), lists alcoholism as a mental disorder. The World Health Organization, in the Ninth Revision of its *International Classification of Diseases* (ICD-9), also categorizes alcoholism as a mental disorder. However, because the APA has assumed the responsibility, for many years, of providing a revision of the mental disorders section of the ICD, the classification should not be treated as a separate examination of the problem. Basically, the dispute breaks down as one between the physicians and the psychiatrists. Because the federal government chooses to define mental diseases as those listed under the heading of "mental disorders" in the ICD-9, Granville House finds itself before this Court seeking declaratory relief.[48]

The court in *Granville House* also traced the history of the conceptualism of alcoholism in many of its variations, including myriad classifications within the DSM series. It is amply clear that scientific

---

46. Hermann at 131.
47. Granville House, Inc. v. Dept. of Health & Human Services, 550 F. Supp. 628 (D. Minn. 1982).
48. *Granville House* at 632.

evidence is only one of several factors that go into the DSM classification system.[49]

The term "mental disease" and its variants as used in the several insanity tests found in the United States and England is meant to be a legal term which only approximately reflects medical usage. This position has been taken by the House of Lords and, as used in *M'Naghten*, does not correspond exactly with the medical idea of "mental illness." In fact, its existence takes no expert evidence to establish.[50] However, one actually ought not to expect a correspondence between English and American law on what constitutes insanity because, it may be recalled, American courts do not have the procedural latitude of their English counterparts in forcing a plea of not guilty by reason of insanity on the defense. The choice in American courts belongs to the defendant,[51] and this almost certainly has a profound effect on the way courts categorize various illnesses as well as on the seemingly contradictory views among the states as to particular underlying causes. But much is happenstance in both English and American jurisdictions because classification depends in part upon the defensive and prosecutorial choices made. This ought not to be overstated, however, for the courts do control the admissibility of evidence, and it is often their view that the defense evidence, usually expert testimony, will not be admitted except on a plea of not guilty by reason of insanity. In *Salzman v. United States*,[52] J. Skelly Wright, made some nosologically relevant remarks regarding alcoholism and its recognition, generally and in a particular case.

> That there is no clear definition of alcoholism and no complete agreement as to its causes is not a ground for denying it disease status. The same might be said of cancer or epilepsy; certainly the same can be said for mental illness....- The point is not whether the medical profession has come up with an exact label. Rather, the approach is functional—does the medical profession, or a substantial part of it, view alcoholism as a disease, properly the subject of medical treatment?[53]

And, of course, insanity as a legal category does not correspond to even the broadest of medical terms such as psychosis. "To add to the

---

49. *See, e.g.*, Fingarette, *The Perils of Powell: In Search of a Factual Foundation for the "Disease Concept of Alcoholism"*, 83 HARV. L. REV. 793 (1970).

50. Regina v. Sullivan, [1983] 2 All E.R. 673. *See also* J. ARCHBOLD, CRIMINAL PLEADING, EVIDENCE AND PRACTICE § 17.47 (1983).

51. Cohn, *Offensive Use of the Insanity Defense: Imposing the Insanity Defense Over the Defendant's Objection*, 15 HASTINGS CONST. L.Q. 295 (1988).

52. Salzman v. United States, 405 F.2d 358 (D.C. Cir. 1968).

53. *Salzman* at 367.

difficulty, there is a difference of meaning between the legal term 'insanity' and the medical term 'psychosis.' Epilepsy, and the disorder produced by brain damage, are not generally regarded as psychoses, yet they are capable of amounting to insanity in law."[54] In brief, the most important thing to know about the answer to the question "what is a disease" is why the question is being asked.[55]

There is well based concern about the law's insistence on a predicate "disease" that our reasoning regarding responsibility not become inordinately circular so that the existence of mental disease is determined exclusively by reference to the conduct of the actor.[56] Indeed, that concern might be a major reason why the law incorporated the concept of disease into the insanity defense to begin with. In a sense, it is there as a limitation on that circuitous possibility. "[The law] does not punish one whose brain tumor caused a convulsion that led to an accident. Briefly stated, it is recognized that the law must not punish those whose conduct is determined by the laws of nature."[57] "We see, therefore, that *disease* is and always has been a permissible ground of forgiveness so long as it is not willfully imposed on the actor by himself."[58] To insist, however, in all cases, that some underlying mental or physical defect be precisely identified as the "cause" of the aberrant behavior is too blunt an instrument for the setting of day-to-day social policies as meted out in a courtroom. Law based on ignorance is one thing; law based on known ignorance is something else, and when the behavior indicates the existence of pathological intoxication, that information should establish insanity even if the exact cause of the pathological reaction cannot be determined. Such evidence should at least get the defendant's defense to the jury.

---

54. G. WILLIAMS, CRIMINAL LAW: THE GENERAL PART § 146 at 444 (2d ed. 1961) (footnotes omitted).

55. Asking "what is alcoholism" lends itself to similar results. In M. KELLER, M. MCCORMICK & V. EFRON, A DICTIONARY OF WORDS ABOUT ALCOHOL (2d ed. 1982), Mark Keller, in his reprinted Introduction to the First Edition, at xix, says: " *Alcoholism* seems the most critical [of the words in this dictionary], most ubiquitously abused, most ambiguously circumvented, most irrationally combined [e.g.,"chronic alcoholism"], most fatuously misapplied, most cowardly evaded word in the entire list." For a brief discussion of the "the disease concept of alcoholism," *see* Keller, McCormick & Efron at 99. There it is noted that "in the American Medical Association's classification it is categorized among the diseases of the psychobiological unit 'without known cause or structural change.'" It is nevertheless classified as a disease.

The U. S. Supreme Court has recently avoided the question "is alcoholism a disease." Traynor v. Turnage, 485 U.S. 535, 108 S. Ct. 1372, 99 L. Ed. 2d 618 (1988). The dissenting and concurring opinion noted that "despite much comment in the popular press, these cases are not concerned with whether *alcoholism*, simplistically, is or is not a 'disease.'" *Traynor*, 108 S. Ct. at 1384 n.1, 99 L. Ed. 2d at 635 n.1.

56. D. ROBINSON, PSYCHOLOGY AND LAW 58-59 (1980).

57. Robinson at 58.

58. Robinson at 58.

The only generalized judicial or legislative exclusion from the meaning of "mental disease or defect" derives from the America Law Institute proposal. To prevent the "psychopath" from availing himself of an insanity defense, the Model Penal Code provides that "As used in this Article, the terms 'mental disease or defect' do not include an abnormality manifested only by repeated criminal or otherwise antisocial conduct."[59] Even this limited exclusion has been criticized,[60] and two federal circuits previously had adopted this proposal but omitted that part of the test, preferring to leave the issue open.[61] Of course, these are now displaced by recent federal legislation, but the new federal statute also omits any particular exclusion.

The American Law Institute's exclusion of the psychopath from the insanity defense represents the exception to the rule that "[t]he law makes no distinctions between various forms of mental unsoundness as to the test of criminal responsibility."[62] They note that "Most jurisdictions relying on the Model Code formulation have, like the Code, not provided a definition of mental disease or defect."[63] There are others[64] who may believe that only certain psychoses will suffice to satisfy *M'Naghten* (or presumably other, more recently formulated tests), but this is evidently due to the *M'Naghten* requirement of lack of cognition, not because of any categorical restrictions imposed.[65]

---

59. MODEL PENAL CODE § 4.01(2) (Proposed Official Draft 1962).

60. Kuh, *The Insanity Defense—An Effort to Combine Law and Reason,* 110 U. PA. L. REV. 771, 800 (1962); Weihofen, *The Definition of Mental Illness,* 21 OHIO ST. L.J. 1, 6-7 (1960). Weihofen argues:

> Our question in this paper is not whether that conclusion is sound, but the somewhat different, though related, question whether it is wise at this stage of psychiatric development to freeze such a conclusion into a written code. I suggest that it is not. The very concept (and even the name) of psychopathic personality disturbance is a vague and changing one. Research into the nature and etiology of the various conditions that have been lumped together under this label is only beginning. It is entirely possible that we shall see an important break-through in the next few years, which may show that these conditions, or some of them, are properly classifiable as mental illnesses, perhaps even organic illness (some experiments have reported finding among psychopaths certain characteristic brain wave patterns similar to those found in epileptics). It therefore seems premature for the law by its own fiat to say that psychiatry will not, at least in the near future, be able to show that these persons are mentally ill, and that they shall therefore be subjected to punitive and not therapeutic treatment.

61. United States v. Smith, 404 F.2d 720 (6th Cir. 1968); United States v. Currens, 290 F.2d 751 (3d Cir. 1961).

62. H. WEIHOFEN, MENTAL DISORDER AS A CRIMINAL DEFENSE 119 (1954).

63. 1 MODEL PENAL CODE AND COMMENTARIES § 4.01 comment 5 at 176 (1985) (footnote omitted).

64. *See, e.g.,* A. GOLDSTEIN, THE INSANITY DEFENSE 48 (1967).

65. 1 W. LAFAVE & A. SCOTT, SUBSTANTIVE CRIMINAL LAW § 4.2 (1986). *See also* MODEL

The same point was made in *United States v. Lyons*.[66] The courts have for a long time permitted insanity to succeed in cases in which the "disease," such as those caused by constant, long-term drinking, was partly the responsibility of the actor. The Fifth Circuit discussed this matter in *Lyons,* a case in which the defendant relied upon iatrogenic narcotic addiction as the basis of an insanity plea, that he "lacked substantial capacity to conform his conduct to the requirements of the law"[67] on a charge of fraudulent procurement of drugs. The court acknowledged the extensive authority supporting the view that addiction, standing alone, would not satisfy the insanity test then extant.[68] "[T]he panel opinion appears to suggest that 'involuntary' drug addiction can constitute a 'mental disease or defect' bearing on the defendant's criminal responsibility."[69] Probably overruling one of its own cases,[70] the court held that neither voluntary nor involuntary addiction, standing alone, could be a mental disease for purposes of the insanity test, though it might provide evidence of mental illness.[71] The court was obviously not taken with this latter view. However, "if addiction has caused actual physical damage to the structures of a defendant's body, evidence of that addiction has been admitted to show any mental defect resulting from that damage."[72] This position was endorsed:

> We do not doubt that actual physical damage to the brain itself falls within the ambit of "mental disease or defect." To refuse to recognize that a congenital microcephalic, or one who has suffered, say, extensive brain damage from a gunshot wound or other physical trauma, may be thereby rendered unable to appreciate the character of his conduct as wrongful would be presumptuous. Here, within the limits of appropriate legal and policy considerations, the medical model must have its day. The same is true of the question whether such organic brain pathology or psychosis can be caused by drugs.[73]

PENAL CODE § 4.01, Appendix A (1985)(a statement by M. Guttmacher).

66. United States v. Lyons, 731 F.2d 243 (5th Cir. 1984) (reh. en banc).

67. Blake v. United States, 407 F.2d 908, 916 (5th Cir. 1969) (en banc), overruled in part by *Lyons.*

68. *Lyons* at 245.

69. *Lyons* at 246.

70. United States v. Bass, 490 F.2d 846 (5th Cir. 1974).

71. *Lyons* at 246. The court did say that there would be occasions when such addiction would be admissible into evidence to support a finding that the defendant suffered from a mental illness of which narcotic addiction was symptomatic.

72. *Lyons* at 246.

73. *Lyons* at 247.

There is no indication in the opinion that the court meant to limit the application of this rule to those instances in which the defendant was faultless, as he probably was here, in bringing about the modern equivalent of "fixed" or "settled" insanity caused by alcohol abuse over long periods of time. Nor did common law draw any such distinction in terms of fault in inducing a permanent, organic insult to the brain, and it remains something of a puzzle why this is so. The notion developed too early in history for anyone to conclude that the real reason was to cause indefinite commitment, via the insanity plea, of one permanently brain-damaged, while retaining traditional punishment for one who was only temporarily deranged by alcohol or other drugs. The reason for the "settled (albeit self-induced) insanity" rule may be lost in history, but, as *Lyons* indicates, even courts not overly enthusiastic about any insanity defense[74] continue to adhere to it.

Insanity tests are never defined in terms of the pathogenesis of the "disease or defect of the mind" but are expressed in terms of their pathological or abnormal effects on the mental functioning of the actor. Disease is defined in terms of its causes on rare occasions but usually only in terms of its manifestations, its symptomatology. Disease is a collection of symptoms which differentiates it from other diseases and from what is "normal."[75] At the same time, "Lack of knowledge about the nature and causes of particular forms of disorder does not mean that they cannot be recognized and successfully treated in individual patients."[76] To a significant extent, "mental disease" and "insanity" serve to define each other. Professor Goldstein pointed out that

> There has been almost no judicial definition of mental disease in cases concerned with the *M'Naghten* rule. The reason commonly advanced is that the more detailed part of the rule—dealing with knowledge—makes it plain that only a limited number of psychoses and the most extreme forms of mental defect can qualify.[77] In any event, the words are

---

74. *Lyons* also withdrew the volitional aspect of their prior insanity test, based on the Model Penal Code, and restricted the "substantial capacity" part of the cognitive test that remained.

75. TABER'S CYCLOPEDIC MEDICAL DICTIONARY 415 (C. Thomas ed. 14th ed. 1983).

76. ROYAL COMMISSION ON THE LAW RELATING TO MENTAL ILLNESS AND MENTAL DEFICIENCY (1954-1957), REPORT CMND. 169, H.M.S.O., (1957).

77. Citing H. WEIHOFEN, MENTAL DISORDER AS A CRIMINAL DEFENSE 119 (1954); Weihofen, *The Definition of Mental Illness,* 21 OHIO ST. L.J. 1, 6 (1960); Kuh, *The Insanity Defense—An Effort to Combine Law and Reason,* 110 U. PA. L. REV. 771, 785 (1962); Davidson, *The Psychiatrist's Role in the Administration of Criminal Justice,* 4 RUTGERS L. REV. 578, 583 (1950); Wertham, *Psychoauthoritarianism and the Law,* 22 U. CHI. L. REV. 336, 337 (1955); Cleckley, *Psychopathic States,* in 1 AMERICAN HANDBOOK OF PSYCHIATRY 567, 570 (S. Arieti ed. 1959); Krash, *The Durham Rule and Judicial Administration of the Insanity Defense in the District of Columbia,* 70 YALE L.J. 905, 927 (1961).

usually presented, without explanation, as part of the charge to the jury. What little law on the subject does exist is found in cases which reject efforts to assert insanity by persons whose mental conditions are clearly marginal. In this group are cases involving intoxication due to the use of alcohol, narcotics withdrawal, temporary insanity, and borderline mental defects.[78]

We agree with these opinions except for the unqualified inclusion of "temporary insanity" on the list of cases in which it is suggested courts will not submit the insanity issue to the jury. At that point, Professor Goldstein was evidently referring only to the "emotional frenzy" cases.[79] And we certainly would agree with the observation that "The question is not treated as one of law at all, but rather as if the necessary link can be provided by the testimony of expert witnesses."[80] But we simply do not see the evidence for the following observation: "If they are willing to affirm that the frenzy, or the distortion, was attributable to a mental disease *and are willing to name and describe the disease*, then the issue will ordinarily be passed to the jury."[81] The cases cited at this point are cases which let the issue get to the jury. Professor Goldstein says himself that "The cases are relatively silent...on which diseases would qualify."[82] Professor LaFave puts the law this way:

> There has never been a clear and comprehensive determination of what type of mental disease or defect is required to satisfy the *M'Naghten* test. Some believe that only a few types of psychoses will suffice.[83] However, it would seem that any mental abnormality, be it psychosis, neurosis, organic brain disorder, or congenital intellectual deficiency (low IQ or feeblemindedness), will suffice *if* it has caused the consequences described in the second part of the test. Thus, although many psychiatrists apparently believe that only a few psychoses will give rise to a successful insanity defense under the *M'Naghten* rule,[84] this is not because certain illnesses or defects are per se excluded but rather because they do not produce the lack of cognition required under *M'Naghten*.[85]

---

78. A. GOLDSTEIN, THE INSANITY DEFENSE 47-48 (1967).
79. Goldstein at 48.
80. Goldstein at 48.
81. Goldstein at 48 (footnote omitted) (emphasis added).
82. Goldstein at 48.
83. Citing A. GOLDSTEIN, THE INSANITY DEFENSE 23 (1967).
84. Citing A. GOLDSTEIN, THE INSANITY DEFENSE 48 (1967).
85. 1 W. LAFAVE & A. SCOTT, SUBSTANTIVE CRIMINAL LAW 439 (1986) (footnote omitted)

This inexactitude in the meaning of mental disease is not a new device to "let everything in" but is attributable to the unavoidable ambiguity in the concept of disease, especially mental disease, as well as to the deliberate legal policy which tries to recognize that, in the end, insanity is at least, in significant part, a moral or ethical judgment, not just a clinical category. In insanity cases, said Lord Goddard, "it has always been for the jury to find whether or not he is suffering from a disease of the mind....I do not know how abnormality of mind can be defined...."[86]

In a similar vein, Lord Devlin said that the law is "not concerned with the origin of the disease or the cause of it, but simply with the mental condition which has brought about the act."[87] Given what we do know about pathological intoxication and its competing or complementary psychiatric or neurological explanations, that is a critical observation. It has been pointed out that "Diseases are not things in the same sense as rocks, or trees, or rivers. Diseases...are not material."[88] Thus, while there may indeed be something physical associated with a disease, such as low blood-sugar levels (something that is even physically measurable), the symptoms of a disease do not constitute proof of a pathological cause for a criminal act. Indeed, low blood-sugar is not even identical with the disease of hypoglycemia. Nor is temporal lobe epilepsy identical with a lesion in the temporal lobe of the brain.

The principal contemporary legal sentiment was espoused by the court in *McDonald*.[89] The court declared that "a mental disease or defect includes any abnormal condition of the mind which substantially affects mental or emotional processes and substantially impairs behavior controls."[90] This definition seems to us to be admirably question-begging;[91] the determining factor for the existence of a mental disease is its behavioral control consequences. The Model Penal Code drafters noted that the *McDonald* definition is "open-ended in terms of developing medical understanding, [and] is consistent with the underlying theory of the Code."[92] "What psychiatrists may consider a 'mental disease or

---

(emphasis in original). *See also* H. WEIHOFFEN, MENTAL DISORDER AS A CRIMINAL DEFENSE 119 (1954): "The law makes no distinctions between various forms of mental unsoundness, as to the test of responsibility." Rather, a disease of the mind is insufficient reason to establish insanity only if it fails to produce the cognitive or volitional impairment which the formula makes the basis for exculpation.

86. Regina v. Spriggs, [1958] 1 All E.R. 300, 304.

87. Regina v. Kemp, [1956] 3 All E.R. 249, 253.

88. King, *What is Disease?* 21 PHIL. SCI. 193 (1954).

89. McDonald v. United States, 312 F.2d 847 (D.C. Cir. 1962).

90. *McDonald* at 851.

91. Others agree. *See, e.g.*, Nemerson, *Alcoholism, Intoxication, and the Criminal Law*, 10 CARDOZO L. REV. 393, 427 (1988): "Formulated tests have been vague, tautologous, or both." *McDonald* is cited as a principal example.

92. 1 MODEL PENAL CODE AND COMMENTARIES § 4.01, at 177 (1985).

defect' for clinical purposes, where their concern is treatment, may or may not be the same as mental disease or defect for the jury's purpose in determining criminal responsibility."[93] The same perspective is reflected in the Model Penal Code's formulation of the insanity defense.[94]

The specificity problem is likely to come up in the converse fashion: Most frequently, it is the defendant who wants particularization in the instructions, and when the issue arises in this posture, the appellate courts generally do not require it of trial courts. For example, in *Cooley v. Commonwealth*,[95] the defendant was charged with murder and found guilty of manslaughter. He put on evidence of psychomotor epilepsy, and he had been drinking at the time of the killing. He had stabbed his brother to death in a dispute over who would drive the car. He went into a grand mal seizure after the stabbing, and he also claimed amnesia for the time of the homicide. Testimony indicated that he had had psychomotor epilepsy for eight years and was taking medication to control it.

The only issue on appeal was whether the defense was entitled to a particularized instruction regarding the defense of psychomotor epilepsy, and the court held that no special instruction on psychomotor epilepsy is required if the court has already instructed on the defense of insanity. They distinguish two prior cases in which the issue was automatism, which the court held required specific, concrete instructions, because in those cases there was no claimed defect of the mind (somnambulism in *Fain*[96] and prescription drugs in *Burnett*[97]). The distinction

---

93. *McDonald* at 851. *See also* Fingarette, *The Perils of Powell: In Search of a Factual Foundation for the "Disease Concept of Alcoholism,"* 83 HARV. L. REV. 793, 809 (1970), where it is stated:

> it is my conclusion that the widespread (but by no means universal) acceptance in the medical and health professions of the "disease concept of alcoholism" reflects a variety of considerations which are legitimate and important to the *health* professions, but that none of these considerations has any obvious bearing on the legal issue of punishability under the eighth amendment.

94. Brandt, *The Insanity Defense and the Theory of Motivation*, 7 LAW & PHIL. 123 (1988): "We might ask what is a 'disease' or 'defect.' Is this to include a mild neurosis, or any one of the problems listed in the Diagnostic and Statistical Manual (of the Psychiatric Association) edition III, or an I.Q. below 80? The implication of the MPC is that *any* level passes if it is serious enough to cause a 'substantial inability' to identify illegal conduct or to avoid conduct which is illegal." Brandt at 137 (footnotes omitted) (emphasis in original). Brandt also notes that "The American Psychiatric Association, in its 1982 report on 'The Insanity Defense,' proposed that exculpating mental disorders 'must be *serious*. Such disorders should usually be of the severity—if not always of the quality—of conditions that psychiatrists diagnose as psychoses.' This view conflicts with the MPC and is too restrictive...." Brandt at 137 n.26 (emphasis in original).

95. Cooley v. Commonwealth, 459 S.W.2d 89 (Ky. 1970).

96. Fain v. Commonwealth, 78 Ky. 183 (1879).

97. Burnett v. Commonwealth, 284 S.W.2d 654 (Ky. 1955).

seems a trifle slippery; would not a general instruction on automatism, or involuntary act, suffice in *Fain* and *Burnett*? The Connecticut Supreme Court also declined to adjudge a general instruction on insanity insufficient in a case where the defense was insanity by virtue of a pathological reaction to alcohol.[98]

There is only one authority we have found in a pathological intoxication case which even arguably imposes a rule that insanity must be not only attributable to a mental disease, but that it must be a *recognized* mental disease. In *Martinez v. People*,[99] the Colorado Supreme Court said with regard to the trial court's denial of a requested instruction on pathological intoxication: "No authority is cited in support of the proposition that 'pathological intoxication' is a defense which, if proven, will entitle the defendant, who relies upon it, to an absolute acquittal. No authority is cited in support of the definition of 'pathological intoxication' which the tendered instruction contains."[100] The import of that language was softened somewhat when the court also stated that if the condition existed "it certainly would be entitled to consideration only in connection with a plea of not guilty by reason of insanity...."[101] Professor Paulsen has commented in connection with the *Martinez* decision that "[d]efense counsel should, of course, have given the court whatever expert help it required to live comfortably with the word,"[102] Still, questions remain. For example, what expert opinion is needed about what level of "acceptance" by whom, and another is what this means for contested diagnoses. Suppose psychiatrists at trial are in dispute about the "existence" of pathological intoxication? Thought of one way, this is indeed the case, and that is why we spent a good deal of effort to bring out the difference between the meanings of "recognition." Is that a nosological reference, or is it merely phenomenological? For example, a court observed that

> When a well-trained, broad-experienced psychiatrist, reputable in his profession, makes a careful examination and gives persuasive and *scientifically approved reasons* for his conclusions in a given case, the judiciary should give respectful attention and consideration to such deductions and, while they may not be controlling, they should prompt additional thoughtful care in the consideration of surrounding facts.[103]

---

98. State v. Johnson, 40 Conn. 136 (1873).
99. Martinez v. People, 124 Colo. 170, 235 P.2d 810 (1951).
100. 124 Colo. at 179, 235 P.2d at 815 (1951).
101. *Martinez* at 179-80, 235 P.2d at 815.
102. Paulsen, *Intoxication as a Defense to Crime*, 1961 U. ILL. L.F. 1, 17.
103. United States v. Parelius, 83 F. Supp. 617, 622 (D. Haw. 1949).

If the legal concern confronting the attorney is less philosophical and more a desire for citation of authority, one of the most useful documents available to persuade a court that pathological intoxication is an acknowledged mental disease is the Diagnostic and Statistical Manual, published by the American Psychiatric Association and now in its revised, third edition, referred to simply as DSM-III-R. Several points regarding the DSM-III-R need to be addressed.

The DSM is an important, recognized source of classification of mental illnesses. It has been cited in over five hundred appellate cases, is used extensively by clinicians and their staffs and provides the classifications used by the federal government and insurance industry compensation systems. One of the reasons why this latest revision was undertaken was because the American Psychiatric Association was asked to help in revising the International Classification of Diseases for publication of ICD-10 several years hence. ICD-9-CM (for Clinical Modification) is currently the federal government's official basis of classification, and "alcohol idiosyncratic intoxication" (their new term which replaces "pathological intoxication" used in earlier editions) receives the same coding there as in the DSM-III-R. Publication of the series of DSM's began in 1952, and its influence is expected to gain under the approach taken in the latest version. "The impact of DSM-III has been remarkable. Soon after its publication, it became widely accepted in the United States as the common language of mental health clinicians and researchers for communicating about the disorders for which they have professional responsibility."[104] Versions have been translated into over a dozen foreign languages, and its diagnostic criteria and other features have been used in thousands of research efforts. It is for this reason we have been careful to be critical of its treatment of pathological intoxication; we do not find it entirely in line with the existing research. Nevertheless, it does recognize pathological intoxication:

> 291.40. Alcohol Idiosyncratic Intoxication. The essential feature of this disorder is a marked behavioral change—usually to aggressiveness—that is due to the recent ingestion of an amount of alcohol insufficient to induce intoxication in most people. There is usually subsequent amnesia for the period of intoxication. The behavior is atypical of the person when not drinking—for example, a shy, retiring, mild-mannered person may, after one weak alcoholic drink become belligerent and assaultive.

---

104. Spitzer & Williams, *Introduction*, in DSM-III-R.

> This disorder has also been called "pathological intoxication."[105]

Our main criticism is the unwarranted stress placed on the amount of alcohol involved, even to the point of elevating "small amount" to status as a diagnostic criterion (notice the example of "one weak alcoholic drink"), and in our view the first edition expressed the concept better than does thc current version.[106] (Notice also the reference to "the period of intoxication," which conjures up an image of a drunk person.) The Introduction to the DSM-III-R states itself that "It should be understood, however, that for most of the categories the diagnostic criteria are based on clinical judgment, and have not yet been fully validated by data about such important correlates as clinical course, outcome, family history, and treatment response. Undoubtedly, with further study the criteria will be further refined."[107] But the important point here is that pathological intoxication is recognized as a mental disorder. Our quarrel is primarily with one diagnostic criterion. Presently, the disorder is classified under "Organic Mental Disorders," and within that group, it is further classified under "Psychoactive Substance-Induced Organic Mental Disorders." The Manual also notes that

> The approach taken in DSM-III-R is atheoretical with regard to etiology or pathophysiologic process, except with regard to disorders for which this is well established and therefore included in the definition of the disorder. Undoubtedly, over time, some of the disorders of unknown etiology will be found to have specific biological etiologies; others, to have specific psychological causes; and still others, to result mainly from an interplay of psychological, social, and biological factors.[108]

This statement is a fair description of pathological intoxication, or "alcohol idiosyncratic intoxication."

Most courts treat pathological intoxication as qualified for the insanity defense without inquiry. Whether the underlying mental disease or defect can be identified with precision turns in part on reference to its etiology. Pathological reaction to alcohol is not per se a disease or a defect of the mind; it is a symptom of something else. Brain damage has been closely associated with the reaction, and there is strong evidence linking it to psychomotor epilepsy in combination with alcohol. In either

---

105. DSM-III-R at 128-29.
106. DSM-I is discussed in Chapter 4.
107. DSM-III-R at xxiv.
108. DSM-III-R at xxiii.

of these events, at least, a court would classify pathological reaction to alcohol as a defense that could be raised under the insanity plea and, possibly, could not be raised as simply a defense of lack of *mens rea,* or under the automatism approach.

While most authorities assume pathological intoxication is itself a "mental disease or defect" for purposes of insanity law, in our view pathological intoxication actually seems to be a number of mental diseases or defects grouped under one convenient forensic term. While some underlying disease or defect certainly must exist, one may have only the indirect evidence provided by the symptomatology involved in the case to justify the inference that "something is obviously wrong." In some of the cases, it may be difficult to identify that something with precision. The matter is further complicated because of the fuzziness of the medical state-of-the-art with respect to various theories which are not only complimentary to pathological intoxication as the correct diagnosis, but which, in part at least, are in competition in their explanatory power, such as the concept of "intermittent explosive disorder," or episodic dyscontrol syndrome discussed in Chapter 4.

In the end, the answer to the question whether pathological reaction to alcohol should be treated as a disease essentially turns on *why* the question is asked rather than on some objective, external and agreed-upon set of measuring criteria. In mid-1988, a letters-to-the-editor debate erupted in the local press regarding the question whether alcoholism was a disease. We think the most perceptive of these was the one headlined: "Alcoholism is a disease in every sense that counts."[109] The content of the answer depends largely on why an answer is needed. It seems to us that this is precisely why the courts have for the most part not tried to address the issue; the question itself is essentially sterile.

A balance needs to be struck, for we do not want the disease requirement of insanity law to be enforced by a rigid insistence, medically conceived, that an underlying pathology be demonstrated as a prerequisite to submission of the responsibility issue to the jury because we are too often not in any position to do so, given limits on medical and psychiatric knowledge. And that, we believe, is where the law of insanity rests today and properly so: The jury should be instructed that they must find that the defendant had a mental disease or defect and that this condition caused or at least significantly contributed to the conduct charged as a crime, but the matter ought to be left there without further adornments or restrictions which our knowledge will not support.

It appears to us, viewed largely from the perspective of pathological reaction to alcohol as a phenomenon, that the concept of mental disease or defect left indeterminate is both a necessary and sufficient requirement

---

109. ROCKY MOUNTAIN NEWS, June 20, 1988, at 44.

of the insanity defense. If particularization is believed by the defense to be required, surely this can be accomplished in closing argument, since the evidentiary predicate will presumably have been laid by the use of expert witnesses. As one writer argued: "the law should not attempt to be progressive by incorporating psychiatric concepts or analyses into legal standards. Rather, the law should use broad, familiar, psychiatrically naive standards."[110] Perhaps the law is still that propounded by the trial court in *State v. Pike*,[111] where the court said: "whether there is such a mental disease as dipsomania [alcoholism], and whether the defendant had that disease, and whether the killing of Brown was the product of such disease, were questions of fact for the jury."[112] The law frequently embraces ambiguity for its own ends, and perhaps lack of competence to do better serves as warrant. One might go so far as to say that if the enigmatic abstraction of mental disease or defect did not exist, those making legal policy would do well to fabricate it.

Although the meaning of "mental disease or defect" is generally left undefined, the U. S. Court of Appeals for the District of Columbia held in *Brawner* that "mental disease or defect includes *any abnormal condition of the mind* which substantially affects mental or emotional processes and substantially impairs behavior controls."[113] This definition reflects the third approach identified by Professor Hermann.[114] In *Brawner*, the court discarded its 20-year-old *Durham* rule in favor of the substantial capacity test but retained the definition of mental disease or defect it had promulgated in *McDonald v. United States*.[115] While appending the *McDonald* definition to the Model Penal Code test they were adopting in *Brawner*, the court noted that the *McDonald* "standard of mental disease was not without an attribute of circularity"[116] and that the term "mental disease or defect" conveys "various meanings, depending upon how and why it is used, and by whom."[117] Still, more is needed than the *Brawner* definition to exclude even simple drunkenness. The court had readopted and engrafted the *McDonald* definition of mental disease to the A.L.I. test they were adopting because the Model Penal Code did not adequately address the question either.

Brawner, in fact, was quite likely a pathological intoxication case, although like many of them, the term was not used. The defendant had been drinking and had been hit in a fight before the fatal shooting:

---

110. Comment, *Legal and Psychiatric Concepts and the Use of Psychiatric Evidence in Criminal Trials*, 73 CALIF. L. REV. 411 (1985).

111. State v. Pike, 49 N.H. 399 (1870).

112. *Pike* at 407-08.

113. United States v. Brawner, 471 F.2d 969, 983 (1972) (emphasis added).

114. Hermann, *supra*, note 34 and accompanying text.

115. McDonald v. United States, 312 F.2d 847, 851 (D.C. Cir. 1962).

116. *Brawner* at 978.

117. *Brawner* at 978.

> The expert witnesses, called by both defense and prosecution, all agreed that Brawner was suffering from an abnormality of a psychiatric or neurological nature. The medical labels were variously given as "epileptic personality disorder," "psychologic brain syndrome associated with a convulsive disorder," "personality disorder associated with epilepsy," or, more simply, "an explosive personality." *There was no disagreement that the epileptic condition would be exacerbated by alcohol, leading to more frequent episodes and episodes of greater intensity, and would also be exacerbated by a physical blow to the head.* The experts agreed that epilepsy *per se* is not a mental disease or defect, but a neurological disease which is often associated with a mental disease or defect. They further agreed that Brawner had a mental, as well as a neurological, disease.[118]

In summary, pathological intoxication is universally treated as satisfying the mental disease or defect requirement of insanity law largely without discussion and certainly without difficulty, and the necessity for particularization or specification of the underlying mental disease or defect is more a matter of trial tactics than of legal necessity. In fact, identification of the underlying cause of the mental incapacity without labeling it pathological intoxication is more often encountered than the reverse situation. *Brawner* was an example of this.

Is There an Exclusion Doctrine Relating to Temporary Insanity That Might Affect Pathological Intoxication Cases?

There is also a doctrine evidently recognized by some courts which essentially denies the existence of a defense of "temporary insanity," a position which seems wholly out of touch with reality. Nevertheless, there are a number of psychomotor epilepsy cases in which courts have

---

118. *Brawner* at 975 (emphasis added). What was in doubt in the case was whether the defendant was having an attack at the time of the shooting. On that, the experts disagreed. This general problem seemed indeed to be a major reason for shifting from the product test to the substantial capacity test:

> There is often a genuine and difficult question as to the relationship between a particular mental disease and particular offense. What is our concern, however, is that the inherent difficulty of this core problem has been intensified, and the sources of confusion compounded, by a kind of mystique that came to surround the "product" test, and testimony cast in that language.

Brawner at 982 n.10.

denied the defense on these grounds. For example, in *Taylor,*[119] there was considerable evidence that the defendant suffered at the age of twelve from epilepsy of a traumatic origin (a blow to the head), and an instruction to the jury could be interpreted to mean that if the defendant was sane just before the act and just after the act, the jury should find him guilty even if he did have an attack of epilepsy at the time of the crime. But the appellate court actually is more taken with the need to distinguish between true insanity and "emotional insanity" (psychopathy, then sociopathy) than to uphold the notion that there is no defense based on temporary insanity.

> If there is any difference in reason or in principle between the theory of epileptic insanity as here advanced on behalf of the defendant and the theory of emotional insanity that has sometimes been resorted to as a defence of crime, but which has always and uniformly been reprobated and repudiated by the courts, we are unable to perceive it. If epileptic insanity is not different in its actual manifestations from emotional insanity, then, harsh as it may seem, society for its own protection must continue to punish the one as well as the other, as a crime, and cannot permit it to pass with impunity as a shield for criminal action. But we understand that there is a very well defined distinction between epileptic insanity and what is called emotional insanity. While the paroxysms which superinduce the former may come on very suddenly, and while during the continuance of the epileptic condition acts of violence may be committed which the person would not commit in his sane moments, yet it is not apparent that violent action is ever the characteristic of the primary seizure. There are certain well developed symptoms that precede the insane action; and practically there is some considerable lapse of time before the tendency to violent action is developed, if any such tendency does in fact supervene; for that tendency in epilepsy seems to be exceedingly exceptional and of rare occurrence.[120]

The court held that "[t]he theory of emotional insanity is untenable under any circumstances"[121] and affirmed the conviction, noting that epileptic

119. Taylor v. United States, 7 App. D.C. 27 (1895). *See also* authorities cited in Weinberg, *Epilepsy and the Alternatives for a Criminal Defense*, 27 CASE W. RES. L. REV. 771, 789 n.126 (1977).

120. *Taylor* at 41-42.

121. *Taylor* at 44.

insanity as a defense was excluded only if it was the same thing as "emotional insanity."

Weihofen summarizes some of the confusion relating to the notion of "temporary insanity":

> Where a defendant committed the crime under the stress of strong emotion, it is sometimes contended that he was "temporarily insane." This concept of "temporary insanity" has no scientific validity. There are disorders characterized by brief periods of derangement or lack of consciousness—epilepsy, for example. But in such disorders the periods, though transitory, are recurrent. And the electroencephalograph will record the abnormal brain-wave patterns characteristic of the disease even between seizures. What defense attorneys mean by temporary insanity is usually not mental disease at all, but merely a strong emotional agitation which momentarily overwhelmed consciousness in a *sane* person. It is entirely possible for such a condition to occur. A state of dissociation may arise in which the person carries out a series of acts of which he later has little or no recollection. Where this can be proved, it should constitute a defense, on somewhat the same rationale as applies to acts done while sleep-walking. But counsel usually try to defend such cases on a theory of "temporary insanity." Where this is done, the courts apply the conventional insanity test.[122]

While the courts rejected the defense of "emotional insanity," the common law had a well recognized rule that "fixed" insanity, even resulting from long, continued use of alcohol, could be treated by the jury as insanity.[123] This evidently was no more than recognition that long-term alcohol abuse can lead to brain damage sufficient to constitute legal insanity. "Habitual use of alcohol or drugs can result in permanent damage to the brain in the form of an 'organic brain syndrome' or 'organic mental disorder.'"[124] Courts would permit the use of this rule to establish the defense of legal insanity even if the defendant was actually intoxicated at the time of the conduct involved. Undoubtedly, some of the notion that "temporary insanity" is no defense arises in these

---

122. H. WEIHOFEN, MENTAL DISORDER AS A CRIMINAL DEFENSE 122 (1954) (footnotes omitted) (emphasis in original).

123. For example, Perkins and Boyce have pointed out that "The person suffering from delirium tremens is not free from fault, it is true, but the law takes notice only of the *immediate* condition which is a mental disease, and not of the excessive drinking which is *remote*." R. PERKINS & R. BOYCE, CRIMINAL LAW AND PROCEDURE 625 n.1 (6th ed. 1984) (emphasis in original).

124. J. DRESSLER, UNDERSTANDING CRIMINAL LAW 283 (1987), citing DSM-III at 101-62.

cases which need to distinguish "permanent" insanity attributable to alcohol use from simple drunkenness. In the case of alcohol self-induced insanity which is "fixed" or "permanent," the actor is treated as insane even though in a real sense, the condition was voluntarily induced,[125] although it may not have been knowingly induced.

In evaluating mental incapacity caused by or following the consumption of alcohol, these courts have created a confusing and logically unsound distinction between temporary and fixed insanity. The rule as generally stated by the courts is that in order to constitute an excuse, the "affliction must be settled or fixed insanity, not a mere fit of drunkenness",[126] or more elaborately,

> alcoholic insanity, or mental incapacity produced by voluntary intoxication existing only temporarily at the time of the [act] is not justification or excuse therefor. To constitute insanity, caused by intoxication...it must be insanity caused by chronic alcoholism, and not a mere temporary mental condition.[127]

This misleading distinction between temporary and fixed insanity may have originated from Blackstone's use of the words, "an artificial voluntarily contracted madness" to describe the gross intoxication of a normal person.[128]

In *Parker v. State,*[129] the Maryland Court of Appeals put the point in a way more relevant for the present context:

> Regardless of what test is applicable to determining insanity, the majority distinguish between (1) the mental effect of voluntary intoxication which is the immediate result of a particular alcoholic bout; and (2) an alcoholic psychosis resulting from long continued habits of excessive drinking. The first does not excuse responsibility for a criminal act; the second may. In other words, if a person drinks intoxicating liquor and is sane both prior to drinking and after the influence of the intoxicant has worn off, but is insane by the applicable test while under the influence of the intoxicant, he comes under the first category. If he is insane whether or not he is directly under the influence of an intoxicant, even

---

125. H. WEIHOFEN, MENTAL DISORDER AS A CRIMINAL DEFENSE 126-27 (1954).

126. Myers v. State, 174 P.2d 395, 400 (Okla. Crim. App. 1946).

127. *Myers* at 400;; McIntyre v. State, 379 P.2d 615, 616 (Alaska 1963); Jones v. State, 648 P.2d 1251 (Okla. Crim. App. 1982); Collier v. State, 17 Okla. Crim. 139, 151, 186 P. 963, 966 (1920).

128. Hall, *Intoxication and Criminal Responsibility,* 57 HARV. L. REV. 1045, 1058 n.60 (1944).

129. Parker v. State, 7 Md. App. 167, 254 A.2d 381 (1969).

> though that insanity was caused by voluntary drinking, he comes under the second category. The cases usually refer to the first category as a "temporary" insanity and the second category as a "permanent", "fixed" or "settled" insanity. These terms may be an oversimplification. What "permanent", "fixed" or "settled" means within the frame of reference is that the insanity not only existed while a person was under the influence of intoxicating spirits as an immediate result of imbibing, but existed independent of such influence, even though the insanity was caused by past imbibing. So if a person while in the throes of delirium tremens which may meet the test for insanity, commits a crime, he is not responsible for his criminal conduct, although such defect, resulting remotely from excessive drinking is only a temporary toxic state. It would seem that the distinction, notwithstanding the language of the cases, is not so much between temporary and permanent insanity as it is one between the direct results of drinking, which are voluntarily sought after, and its remote and undesired consequences.[130]

The usual reason for not wanting to plead insanity is that the "successful" interposition of this defense will result in incarceration of the defendant if he is perceived as dangerous to himself or others.[131] Indeed, the position seems justified that "the insanity defense is as much a method for restraining those perceived to be dangerously mentally ill as it is a means for determining criminal responsibility."[132] In the case of pathological reaction to alcohol, the insanity is temporary, but that is essentially true of many other insanity cases as well. There is, strictly speaking, no such defense as temporary insanity, or (what is closer to stating the case accurately) all claims of insanity are claims of temporary insanity. The defendant's mental state at the time of the act is all that is ever in question on an insanity plea.[133]

---

130. *Parker* at 178-79, 254 A.2d 388 (1969) (footnote omitted).

131. Confinement of acquittees and the relative length of time spent incarcerated by those convicted and those acquitted are discussed in Slobogin, *The Guilty But Mentally Ill Verdict: An Idea Whose Time Should Not Have Come*, 53 GEO. W. L. REV. 494 (1985).

A few states now provide special commitment procedures that can be brought to bear on defendants who successfully challenge the existence of a *mens rea* requirement by proof of a mental condition short of insanity and are acquitted. 1 P. ROBINSON, CRIMINAL LAW DEFENSES § 64(a) n.9 (J. Robinson 1988 Supp.). *See also* Mandiberg, *Protecting Society and Defendants Too: The Constitutional Dilemma of Mental Abnormality and Intoxication Defenses*, 53 FORDHAM L. REV. 221 (1984).

132. Slobogin at 502, citing Goldstein & Katz, *Abolish the "Insanity Defense"—Why Not?* 72 YALE L.J. 853 (1963).

133. Of course, this excludes those instances in which the issue at question is the competency of the defendant to be placed on trial, but that does not implicate any plea, insanity

Kelly,[134] decided by the California Supreme Court, provides an interesting parallel, for it illustrates a case of "fixed insanity" and intoxication caused by drugs other than alcohol. The defendant pleaded not guilty by reason of insanity and was convicted on a bench trial of assault with a deadly weapon in the motiveless stabbing of her mother. The evidence consisted largely of the testimony and reports of seven psychiatrists. Essentially the case involved insanity caused by drugs (LSD and mescaline) taken over several months. Some of the psychiatrists even called this pathological intoxication despite the fact that no alcohol was involved at all. The view of the experts seems to have been that the defendant "had a pre-existing mental condition [brain damage from longer use of hallucinogens] upon which was superimposed a voluntary [drug] intoxication which brought about a condition of blatant psychosis (pathological intoxication) which was in effect at the time of her crime."[135] Thus, the case was viewed as one of pathological intoxication by a drug other than alcohol, but because the drug was not alcohol and was a powerful hallucinogen, the trial court took the position that "her insanity was no defense because it 'was not of a settled and permanent nature, and, in addition, was produced by the voluntary ingestion of hallucinatory drugs.'"[136]

On the argument that the case fell within the prohibition against convicting a person who was not conscious during the act charged,[137] the court on appeal said that the case was most analogous to voluntary intoxication, not pathological intoxication, and applied the rule reaffirmed in *Conley*[138] that if "the state of unconsciousness is caused by voluntary intoxication...it is not a complete defense." Thus, on this point, the court focused on her recent voluntary ingestion of the hallucinogen to take the defendant's case out of the involuntary act category. Here, unlike the case of true pathological intoxication, it was reasoned that if she knew it was an hallucinogenic drug being taken, there would have been no question of her awareness of the resulting mental state. On the other hand, in the case of pathological intoxication involving only alcohol acting in conjunction with an underlying mental disability, if the defendant is not aware of the problem, he could reasonably expect only intoxication commensurate with the amount consumed, whereas presumably a reaction tantamount to insanity could be expected to be the routine outcome of the use of powerful hallucinogens. Since that is the

---

or otherwise.

134. People v. Kelly, 10 Cal. 3d 565, 111 Cal. Rptr. 171, 516 P.2d 875 (1973).

135. *Kelly* at 570 n.7, 111 Cal. Rptr. 174 n.7, 516 P.2d at 878 n.7.

136. *Kelly* at 571, 111 Cal. Rptr. at 175, 516 P.2d at 879.

137. CAL. PENAL CODE § 26, subd. 4 (West 1988).

138. People v. Conley, 64 Cal. 2d 310, 323, 49 Cal. Rptr. 815, 823, 411 P.2d 911, 919 (1966).

normal reaction of a normal person, such a case should not be classified as pathological intoxication.

But if an actor's condition is taken as psychosis caused by longer-term use of drugs and not just temporary intoxication, then it is a case of legal insanity. The trial court thought that Kelly was insane at the time of the assault as well as before and after it for some considerable period of time[139] but that her insanity would be no defense because the insanity was self-induced. The court held, however, that settled insanity, even if self-induced, placed her within the long-settled rule regarding fixed insanity and reversed. They noted that the evidence indicated that she would have been insane, due to several months' use of the drugs, even if she had not taken drugs the night before the attack.[140]

The court also concluded that the trial court required the insanity not only to be fixed, but permanent. "Such a requirement violates the rule that '[t]emporary insanity, as a defense to crime, is as fully recognized by law as is permanent insanity.'"[141] The court also pointed out that "in the instant case defendant took mescaline the day before the offense. Defendant does not lose the defense of insanity because she may also have been intoxicated at the time of the offense."[142] The trial court was directed to enter a judgment of not guilty by reason of insanity.

Other courts, too, as indicated in Chapter 7, have not ruled out of consideration on insanity pleas brain damage caused by previous and long-standing drug abuse even though the use was voluntary and presumably its effects known.[143] Thus, the common-law category of "fixed" insanity resulting from knowing use of alcohol or other drugs survives.

In the cases in which it has been held that mere "temporary insanity" is no excuse for crime, the courts have seldom had evidence of insanity before them, but rather merely evidence of mental impairment as a result of alcohol intoxication.[144] And writers sometimes deny the existence of a defense of temporary insanity too broadly, having actual reference only to those cases in which there is evidence only of voluntary intoxication.[145] More importantly, in those cases in which there *has*

---

139. *Kelly* at 571 n.11, 111 Cal. Rptr. at 175 n.11, 516 P.2d at 879 n.11.

140. *Kelly* at 570 n.9, 111 Cal. Rptr. at 174 n.9, 516 P.2d at 878 n.9.

141. *Kelly* at 576, 111 Cal. Rptr. at 179, 516 P.2d at 883, citing People v. Ford, 138 Cal. 140, 70 P. 1075 (1902).

142. *Kelly* at 577 n.17, 111 Cal. Rptr. at 179 n.17, 516 P.2d 883 n.17.

143. United States v. Lyons, 731 F.2d 243 (5th Cir. 1984) (en banc). *See also* People v. Conrad, 148 Mich. App. 433, 385 N.W.2d 277 (1986), (expressed in terms of the insanity continuing beyond the period of intoxication; in such case, insanity may be a defense).

144. *See, e.g.,* Jones v. State, 648 P.2d 1251 (Okla. Crim. App. 1982) (a drug/alcohol combination case).

145. *See, e.g.,* J. DRESSLER, UNDERSTANDING CRIMINAL LAW 283 (1987): "The common law does not recognize such a defense [as temporary insanity]. Mental illness is a condition that

been evidence of insanity related to the use of alcohol, the automatic application of the rule that temporary insanity is no excuse has resulted in a failure to inquire into the actual nature of the defendant's mental incapacity.[146]

The courts use the term "temporary insanity" synonymously with "gross intoxication,"[147] but the term certainly does not fit the medical phenomenon of pathological reaction to alcohol. The use of the term arises only in conjunction with cases involving intoxication and is employed by the courts as a means of holding that a given mental condition connected with the use of alcohol is insufficient to relieve the defendant of responsibility. It is an unnecessary device to ensure that those defendants whose mental disability is solely the result of intoxication are not excused from liability.

Thus, it is clear that there should be no per se rule that insanity, to be a defense, must exist entirely apart from ingestion of alcohol.[148] Yet

---

ordinarily is contracted involuntarily. One who voluntarily introduces alcohol or drugs into his body and falls victim to 'artificial voluntarily contracted madness' [citing 4 Blackstone at *25] is not considered entitled to the law's dispensation." (Footnote omitted). What is meant is that the type of "temporary insanity" which has no cause other than voluntary intoxication does not qualify for the insanity defense, and the statement should not be taken as broader than that. The same author also notes that "Intoxication is *involuntary* if the actor is not to blame for becoming intoxicated." Dressler at 284 (emphasis in original). This is recognition that voluntary drinking does not necessarily equate to the legal concept of voluntary intoxication. Awareness on the part of the actor is usually the key factor.

146. *See, e.g.*, State v. Wilson, 104 N.C. 868, 10 S.E. 315 (1889). *See also* J. YEAGER & R. CARLSON, 4 IOWA PRACTICE: CRIMINAL LAW AND PROCEDURE § 6 at 3-4 (1979): "True mental illness is a condition which develops over a period of time, and is not something which is turned on or off in a moment." Even if this statement were true, it ignores the possibility that a person with a constant "mental illness" may not show symptoms of it at all times. Epilepsy is the obvious example. This latter view is also taken in Note, *Mental Illness and the Law*, 36 B.U.L. REV. 254 (1956).

147. For an example of a jury instruction which uses "temporary insanity" and "intoxication" interchangeably, *see* State v. Kavanaugh, 20 Del. 131, 134, 53 A. 335, 336-37 (1902).

148. It is interesting that one country, Norway, classifies pathological intoxication as temporary insanity. J. ANDENAES, THE GENERAL PART OF THE CRIMINAL LAW OF NORWAY § 30 (T. Ogle trans. 1965) provides the following description:

> Intoxication, however, can also lead to *unconsciousness*. As far as alcohol is concerned, one distinguishes between "normal" and pathological alcohol intoxication. In normal alcohool [sic] intoxication, the consciousness is gradually lowered as the amount of alcohol is increased, and the capacity for purposeful movement is at the same time impaired; when the point of complete unconsciousness is reached, the intoxicated person generally has no ability to commit offenses other than those of omission. The picture is different with pathological intoxication. The mental disturbances here often arise suddenly and after consumption of relatively small quantities of alcohol. The general signs of intoxication, such as an uncertain walk and slurred speech, are lacking, but perception is seriously disturbed. Delusions and hallucinations may also appear. The individual usually does not remember anything that

there have been a number of cases in which the court may have held in line with these opinions that the actor must have been insane before he began drinking. As to the "temporary insanity" cases, Professor Goldstein reads the cases as merely holding that an "emotional frenzy" is not sufficient,[149] although he notes the judicial "preference" for a disease of "a fixed or prolonged nature."[150] The courts will, of course, draw a line between a defendant who merely is suffering from alcohol withdrawal symptoms and those with a "fixed" or "settled" insanity.[151]

With respect to this last point, we might interject here a related observation. No where in the DSM's were we able to find a diagnosis of a mental disease or disorder which involved an interactive effect of an external factor with an internal one with the begrudging exception of pathological intoxication. Obviously, various drug/drug combinations can result in temporary mental disability, but they are not dealt with, presumably, because treatment seems uncalled for in such events. But even in the case of a simple, perhaps temporary, reaction, for example, to inhaling a poisonous industrial gas, it will not be found classified as a mental illness although the person's perception of reality was disturbed, albeit not permanently. The law, too, would typically classify such a case as one of involuntary intoxication rather than insanity for want of any mental disease.

Even under the early common law of intoxication and insanity, in cases of insanity which was not self-induced, the idea of temporary insanity was by no means rejected. "In 1668 a married woman being delivered of a child unattended, after having lost sleep for many nights, killed her infant during a temporary frenzy, and the charge to the jury in her trial for murder was 'that if it did appear, that she had any use of her reason when she did it, they were to find her guilty.'"[152] The verdict was not guilty. Temporary insanity has in fact always been recognized under the rules.[153] Indeed, if the law did not assume that insanity could

---

happened while he was intoxicated. Pathological intoxication generally occurs only in those individuals who are predisposed to it (epileptics, neurotics, psychopaths, persons with brain damage); but even persons who otherwise react normally to alcohol may sometimes under the influence of illness, exhaustion or serious mental stress, react abnormally. A person may commit serious crimes, such as rape or murder, while in an unconscious state. It is obvious that not all ideas and sensations cease during pathological intoxication. Perhaps a more accurate picture of the situation is to be found in Swedish forensic psychiatry, which describes it as temporary insanity.

We must also suppose that there are many gradations between the completely normal and the obviously pathological intoxication.

149. A. GOLDSTEIN, THE INSANITY DEFENSE 48 (1967).

150. Citing Barbour v. State, 262 Ala. 297, 78 So. 2d 328, 340 (1955) and other cases.

151. 1 W. LAFAVE & A. SCOTT, SUBSTANTIVE CRIMINAL LAW § 4.10 (1986).

152. R. PERKINS & R. BOYCE, CRIMINAL LAW 951 (3d ed. 1982), citing Anonymous, 1 HALE P.C. 36 (1668).

153. "[I]f his reason and mental powers are either so deficient that he has no will, nor

temporary, a decision that the defendant was capable of standing trial would foreclose the issue of insanity from being litigated again at trial. The difference in the two legal standards does not explain why so many insanity defenses at the time of the crime charged get to the jury, although the defendant has been found capable of standing trial.[154]

The disallowance of an insanity defense on the ground that the insanity was merely temporary certainly has no textual basis in the law found in insanity rules. The *M'Naghten*, irresistible impulse and substantial capacity tests all concern themselves with the mental state of the defendant only at the time the offense was committed. Under the *M'Naghten* test, the relevant inquiry is whether "*at the time of the committing of the act*, the party was laboring under such a defect of reason, from disease of the mind..." as not to know the nature and quality of the act or that what he was doing was wrong.[155] Under the irresistible impulse test, the issue is "Was the defendant *at the time of the commission of the alleged crime*...afflicted with a disease of the mind...by reason of the duress of such mental disease, he had so far lost the power to choose...to avoid doing the act in question, as that his free agency was *at the time* destroyed."[156] The American Law Institute test states that: "A person is not responsible for criminal conduct if *at the time of such conduct* as a result of mental disease or defect he lacks substantial capacity...."[157] There is no requirement under any of the tests that the disorder exist for any period of time; the duration of the disorder is relevant, if at all, only in evidentiary matters concerning proof of the actual existence of the mental disability. While courts do concern themselves with the defendant's mental capacity at the time of trial, a finding of incapacity at this point is not relevant to a determination of criminal responsibility, but only to competency to stand trial. This issue, like competency to stand execution, is an issue totally apart from insanity at the time of the commission of the offense. The text of the new federal test is as follows:

> It is an affirmative defense to a prosecution under any Federal statute that, *at the time of the commission of the acts constituting the offense*, the defendant, as a result of a severe mental disease or defect, was unable to appreciate the nature

---

conscience or controlling mental power, or if through the overwhelming violence of mental disease his intellectual power is for the time obliterated, he is not a responsible moral agent, and is not punishable for the criminal acts." The Trial of Hadfield, 27 How. St. Tr. 1281 (1800).

154. *See also* G. FLETCHER, RETHINKING CRIMINAL LAW 837-43 (1978).

155. M'Naghten's Case, 8 Eng. Rep. 718, 722 (1843) (emphasis added).

156. Parsons v. State, 81 Ala. 577, 596-97, 2 So. 854, 866 (1886) (emphases changed).

157. MODEL PENAL CODE § 4.01 (Proposed Official Draft, 1962) (emphasis added).

> and quality or the wrongfulness of his acts. Mental disease or defect does not otherwise constitute a defense.[158]

The ABA's proposal, which has a purely cognitive orientation, is meant to be restrictive in the wake of the Hinckley affair and yet provides expressly for inclusion of temporary insanity:

> (a) A person is not responsible for criminal conduct if, at the time of such conduct, and *as a result of mental disease or defect,* that person was unable to appreciate the wrongfulness of such conduct.
>
> (b) When used as a legal term in this standard "*mental disease or defect" refers to either:*
>
> (i) *impairments of mind, whether enduring or transitory,* or,
>
> (ii) mental retardation,
>
> which substantially affected the mental or emotional processes of the defendant *at the time of the alleged offense.*[159]

Specifically with reference to epilepsy, which plays such a large role in pathological intoxication, Professor Goldstein has observed:

> A "temporary," even a "recurrent," condition will not suffice. It is not at all clear, however, which forms of insanity will be deemed permanent and which temporary or recurrent. For example, proof of epileptic seizures has been held in a number of states to require that the instruction be given. Yet epileptics have long been considered competent when not in the throes of a seizure and would be among the first instances coming to mind of "recurrent" as opposed to "permanent" insanity.[160]

---

158. 18 U.S.C. § 17(a) (Supp. V 1987) (emphasis added). The new federal rule was initially enacted as part of the Comprehensive Crime Control Act of 1984, Pub. L. No. 98-473, § 20(a), 98 STAT. 1976, 2057 and recodified by Pub. L. No. 99-646, 100 STAT. 3592, 3599 (1986). *See* S. BRAKEL, J. PARRY & B. WEINER, THE MENTALLY DISABLED AND THE LAW (3d ed. 1985). It is also reviewed in English, *The Light Between Twilight and Dusk: Federal Criminal Law and the Volitional Insanity Defense,* 40 HASTINGS L.J. 1 (1988); Comment, *Recent Changes in Criminal Law: The Federal Insanity Defense,* 46 LA. L. REV. 337 (1985). Some of the legislative background is found in United States v. Kowal, 596 F. Supp. 375 (D. Conn. 1984).

159. AMERICAN BAR ASS'N, CRIMINAL JUSTICE MENTAL HEALTH STANDARDS, Standard 7-6.1 (1984) (emphasis added).

160. A. GOLDSTEIN, THE INSANITY DEFENSE 117 (1967) (citations omitted).

In *Sprague v. State,*[161] the court expressly included psychomotor epilepsy within the concept of disease within the insanity rules. The defendant had pleaded both not guilty and not guilty by reason of insanity, and the trial was bifurcated and tried to a jury on the murder charge in the death of his wife. The conviction was affirmed. (He had told someone earlier that "she had it coming.") On the guilt phase, the trial court refused to admit evidence of epilepsy. The court held that such evidence was admissible only on the insanity issue at that phase of the trial. "The testimony was undisputed that the defendant had a history of epilepsy with grand mal seizures. Electroencephalograms of the defendant were abnormal, showing focal lesions in the frontal and temporal lobes of the brain. There was also testimony that focal lesions in the temporal lobe are indicative of psychomotor epilepsy."[162] There was also testimony that "upsets, such as anger, fear or shock, may precipitate a psychomotor seizure...."[163] The defense theory was that seeing her fall down the stairs triggered a reaction, and then he killed her.

> It is also suggested that psychomotor epilepsy, or other pathological conditions of impaired consciousness, should be considered as constituting a defense under the principle requiring that an act be voluntary in order to be criminal.
>
> A psychomotor seizure may also fit the definition of insanity....The term 'mental disease or defect' is not defined in the Model Penal Code. While medically, psychomotor epilepsy may be considered physical rather than mental in origin, the disease is one which, during the period of a seizure, affects the mental processes of the person afflicted. Thus it may be legally classified as a mental disease or defect for the purpose of determining criminal responsibility....The jury...found that the defendant did not suffer a psychomotor seizure at the time of the offense.[164]

Neither Professor Weihofen[165] nor Professor Williams had difficulty in classifying an epileptic attack as within the insanity defense, though Professor Williams here was not speaking of a case of self-inducement:

---

161. Sprague v. State, 52 Wis. 2d 89, 187 N.W.2d 784 (1971).

162. *Sprague* at 98, 187 N.W.2d at 788.

163. *Sprague* at 98, 187 N.W.2d at 788.

164. *Sprague* at 99-100, 187 N.W.2d at 789. Illinois seems to have reached the same conclusion in People v. Grant, 71 Ill. 2d 551, 377 N.E.2d 4 (1978).

165. H. WEIHOFEN, MENTAL DISORDER AS A CRIMINAL DEFENSE 121 (1954), citing a number of cases, and Smith, *Medico-Legal Facets of Epilepsy*, 31 TEX. L. REV. 765, 769 (1953).

> If the medical evidence is that the sleep-walking is a form of nocturnal epilepsy (as may sometimes be shown by EEG evidence), there may be a verdict of insanity under the *McNaughten* rules; yet the defendant may not need incarceration, and may in fact be released after a short period in a general mental hospital; and the problem of inducing him to take precautions for the future remains unsolved.[166]

There is additional confusion on this issue of "temporary insanity" because a number of courts have stressed the existence of a category of "permanent" insanity distinguished by the existence of periods referred to as "lucid intervals."[167] This is obviously subject to much interpretation. The overall point remains the same. The courts have tried to eliminate cases in which they believe that the defense was not based on sufficient evidence of actual lack of cognition, but there are no categorical restrictions expressed in terms of the disease category; the exclusions have been ad hoc on the basis not of the disease type, but failure to satisfy the behavioral demands of *M'Naghten*. The exception may be *Martinez*.

The impermanence of insanity is merely of evidentiary import; insanity does not seem to some to be insanity if it is only temporary. But in the case of pathological intoxication, that observation does not hold because pathological reaction to alcohol is temporary as far as the reaction is concerned, though the underlying mental problem may even be permanent. Thus, once again, pathological intoxication lies across the boundaries of the legal categories, if indeed there is such a legal boundary between permanent and temporary insanity.

What we may conclude here is that all courts will exclude from the insanity defense those instances of mental incapacity such as knowing, self-induced intoxication in which it is apparent that the actor was at fault in bringing about his own incapacity. Legal insanity is the only major affirmative defense which does not have a fault limiter built into it. The "temporary" of the "temporary insanity" term serves as a backup fault limitation in insanity defense cases when the concept of "mental disease or defect" will not accomplish the narrowing design. However, only a minority of courts even use the term "temporary insanity" to accomplish this goal. In effect, these courts use the term "temporary insanity" to designate those cases which they have concluded do not actually involve insanity in the sense of being caused by a mental disease or defect, or, to state the same thing, those in which the actor was at fault in creating the short-term situation. For example, one court said "'Temporary insanity' has a meaning which differentiates it from a condition caused by a

---

166. G. WILLIAMS, CRIMINAL LAW: THE GENERAL PART § 157, at 484 (2d ed. 1961) (footnote omitted).

167. Goldstein at 117.

disease of the brain and confines it to a condition due to causes other than disease, usually intoxication."[168] Thus, temporary insanity means an incapacity that is not insanity; the phrase is an unintended oxymoron, a contradiction. In effect, the doctrine of "temporary insanity" as used by these courts is a doctrine of fault denying access to the insanity defense; it is therefore a legal fault limitation, not an attempt to exclude those instances of clinically temporary insanity due to mental disease or defect. In the original, formative period of development of the insanity defense, the thought may have been that if it was a mental disease that the actor suffered from, then the actor was not at fault. Insanity was an infirmity that one acquired by act of God.

AN ALTERNATIVE VIEW OF THE MENTAL DISEASE REQUIREMENT: ESTABLISHING NON-FAULT ON THE PART OF THE ACTOR

We suggest here that whether the law of insanity requires specification of a particular disease, whether pathological intoxication meets that requirement and whether the condition needs to go beyond the temporary are, in a sense, the wrong questions. They are all different ways to raise the question of the meaning of "mental disease or defect" in various insanity tests, and it is that question that needs to be addressed.

It is less than self-evident why the defense of legal insanity in all its variant forms universally is confined to something called "disease of the mind" or equivalent terminology. If a person substantially lacks cognitive ability, why does the law additionally require that the incapacity be attributable to mental disease? The cases may be better explained with this rule than with deductions beginning with "mental disease": If the defendant lacks some specified level of capacity and is not at fault in bringing it about or if at fault, the condition has become permanent, then in either of these two instances, the defendant is legally insane.

There are, of course, alternative explanations of the function of the mental disease requirement in insanity law.

> Trite as it may sound to some, the law must distinguish between mental disease and character deformity. Critics of the M'Naghten rule of criminal responsibility fail or refuse to realize that its function is not merely to determine which individuals are suffering from mental disorder but also to select those of the mentally disabled whose punishment will

168. Barbour v. State, 78 So. 2d 328, 340 (Ala. 1954).

aid and protect society because they are able to make rational choices between right and wrong.[169]

But the function of the mental disease requirement is not to exclude "mere" character defects; those rarely, if ever, result in impaired cognition, so that the incapacity element of the insanity test would exclude those cases without any additional requirement of mental disease.

Still, one supposes that the term "mental disease or defect" is included in all of the insanity tests, for some purpose, to exclude something. There are two closely connected points here, but identifiably different nevertheless: One question is whether the law concerns itself with the identification of the exact nature of the underlying disease in order to establish per se exclusionary rules. The negative answer to that has been given above. But the other point is that the law of insanity does seem to posit some mental disease or defect even if its isolation and identification, its "differential diagnosis," is lacking in any particular case, and it is in this sense that something is intended to be excluded. Clearly, that something must otherwise satisfy the rest of the extant tests, most notably a significant impairment of the cognitive functions. Evidently what this means, as the English have decided, is that insanity law presupposes, indeed requires, an internal malfunction, while involuntary act (or automatism) exists to deal with externally caused failure of cognition such as purely externally generated trauma.

An alternative approach to that taken by Professor Hermann when he identified the three competing approaches to defining "mental disease"[170] would begin from a different perspective; it would question why mental disease is in the law of insanity as a requirement at all in order, perhaps, to understand its true function as a limitation on the insanity defense. Knowing the purpose of the "mental disease or defect" requirement might help clarify the meaning of the requirement. The view explored, indeed advanced, here is that the function of the "mental disease or defect" requirement of insanity law is to ensure that actors who would use the rule were not at fault in bringing about their own cognitive or volitional incapacity. The condition ousts from its exculpatory protection those cases which entail fault of the defendant in producing the mental incapacity.

The most frequent and obvious effect of the mental disease requirement in the law of insanity is to exclude cases of voluntary intoxication whether by alcohol or other drugs. Originally, the mental disease requirement may primarily have served the function of excluding cases of intoxication, but the law straightaway drew a distinction between

---

169. State v. Sikora, 210 A.2d 193, 202 (N.J. 1965).

170. D. HERMANN, THE INSANITY DEFENSE: PHILOSOPHICAL, HISTORICAL AND LEGAL PERSPECTIVES 130 (1983).

voluntary and involuntary intoxication, and only involuntary intoxication was assimilated into the law of insanity (though without a requirement of mental disease), while voluntary intoxication was largely denied defensive significance.[171] Coercion or unawareness as a requirement of involuntary intoxication accomplished that restriction, so that it was the *lack* of coercion and the *presence* of awareness of the incapacitating effects of alcohol (or other drugs) which served the function of excluding from the law of excuses those cases in which *mens rea* was lacking only due to the fault of the actor. Those cases were relegated to the law of voluntary intoxication, which had very limited defensive utility.[172]

The mental disease requirement is meant to exclude from the defensive protection of the insanity defense those mental disabilities for which the defendant is thought to bear some responsibility. The presence of "disease" is tantamount to the absence of fault on the part of the actor in inducing the mental condition responsible for the crime.[173] This contributes to the idea that mental disease in this context is a legal conclusion, not a medical diagnosis; the latter is relevant to that conclusion, but so is the absence of the ultimate normative conclusion, fault.

If the view developed here is accurate that the primary function of the mental disease requirement of the dominant insanity tests is to exclude from defensive consideration states of mind brought about through the fault of the defendant, it would not be surprising if courts limited the insanity defense by fault principles. What is not justified under this view is denying an insanity defense solely on the ground that the actor's affliction does not satisfy a medical model of mental illness.

---

171. These doctrines are more fully treated in Chapter 8, dealing with involuntary intoxication, and in Chapter 10, which attempts to pull together the various concepts of fault in this context.

172. H. FINGARETTE & A. HASSE, MENTAL DISABILITIES AND CRIMINAL RESPONSIBILITY 106 (1979) (footnote omitted), said:

> Should a person who...voluntarily takes a drug with knowledge of its potentially disabling and disorienting effects on the mind, be completely acquitted of a crime on the ground of insanity because, at the time of the act, he could not distinguish right from wrong? The prospect of complete acquittal for the intoxicated harmdoers, not surprisingly, has met with great resistance. The absence of "mental disease" provides a logical and traditional basis in law for rejecting this defense.

173. The converse does not follow, of course. That is, the absence of fault in causing the aberrant mental condition does not indicate the presence of mental disease. Just because the actor is not at fault in bringing about the abnormal mental condition, it does not follow that anything having the result of a mental state that satisfies the insanity test should do. Many of these cases in which the actor is not at fault and the resulting mental incapacity does not seem fairly attributable to a mental disease are treated as instances of lack of *mens rea* or of automatism rather than insanity. While, for example, the English prevent cases of mental disease from being tried as automatism, they do not, so far as we have seen, prevent cases of automatism from being tried as insanity.

But the courts are divided on this latter point. Some reject that view. For example, in *Commonwealth v. Plank*[174] in which the trial court refused to let evidence of insanity based on chronic alcohol abuse go to the jury, the court said:

> To the extent we focus on the disorder to excuse the act, etiology is irrelevant. *See Commonwealth v. Simms,* 462 Pa. 26, 333 A.2d 477 (1975) (insanity defense allowed where defendant, at the time of the crime, was allegedly acting as a result of a blow or blows to the head); *cf. Commonwealth v. Hicks,* 483 Pa. at 311 n. 5, 396 A.2d at 1186 n. 5 (the Court reserved the question of "the applicability of the defense of insanity where the mental disease is traceable to habitual long term abuse of drugs.").[175]

In *Commonwealth v. Hicks,*[176] the defendant, following a bench trial, was convicted of murder in the third degree. He had been drinking heavily after taking an amphetamine-based diet pill prescribed by his physician. He chased his mother out of the residence, rampaged down the street, finally killing someone. Essentially the court seemed to affirm the conviction on the basis that the trial court found, as the trier of fact, that the alcohol alone was sufficient to account for his mental state.

> It is obvious that an actor should not be insulated from criminal liability for acts which result from a mental state that is voluntarily self-induced. The evidence in this case presents an ample basis for the finding that appellant's behavior was the result of voluntary alcohol ingestion and not mental disease. Even accepting the remote possibility of the existence of a pathological disorder, it was at best a passive condition triggered by the ingestion of alcohol. In either event appellant was not entitled to escape the responsibility for his conduct under the *M'Naghten* Rule.[177]

It is more likely that "mental disease or defect" is meant to be a limitation independent of that found in the law of intoxication and is instead coterminous with the development of an independent fault limitation in the law of insanity to restrict that defense to cases in which

---

174. Commonwealth v. Plank, 329 Pa. Super. 446, 478 A.2d 872 (1984).

175. *Plank* at 450, 478 A.2d at 875.

176. Commonwealth v. Hicks, 483 Pa. 305, 396 A.2d 1183 (1979). *See also* Commonwealth v. Stewart, 377 Pa. Super. 530, 547 A.2d 1189 (1988) *and* Commonwealth v. Sirbaugh, 347 Pa. Super. 154, 500 A.2d 453 (1985), where the court took the same approach, citing *Hicks.*

177. *Hicks* at 311-12, 396 A.2d at 1186 (footnote omitted).

the actor was not at fault for bringing about his own mental incapacity, as opposed to intoxication cases.

We will essentially see this distinction between disease-based insanity and nondisease-based automatism drawn in the English automatism cases where the distinction corresponds to the difference between insane and noninsane automatism. We will try to show in Chapter 7 that their classifications of the cases, however, are strongly disposition-oriented rather than determined by such metaphysical distinctions between different mentally aberrational states the causes of which may be "internal" or "external". Pathological intoxication presents exactly the same problem. Consider the case of an actor who has a pre-existing mental defect such as brain injury or a disease such as temporal lobe epilepsy who consumes alcohol, which triggers a reaction. Are we to say "the cause" was "internal" or "external"? The debate would be fruitless because the important aspect of the answer to the question is why the question was asked in the first place, and the answer to that query is that the disposition of the actor who commits the act in that condition turns in part at least on how it is classified. Distinguishing diseases and defects from other, external causes can have no other point. Indeed, the courts do not even seem to distinguish disease from defect or psychological from neurological causes.[178] We simply do not believe that someone temporarily dazed by a blow to the head who, for example, exposes himself in public ought to be treated as a fit subject for involuntary incarceration in a mental institution for "treatment" when the need for the treatment has long since passed or never arose.

Pathological intoxication has both an internal and an external cause, one controllable by the actor to the extent there is awareness of its effects and the other not within volitional control. The cause is not purely external. How the defendant is to be dealt with when an antisocial act is committed in that condition is the question, and analysis of the concept of "disease or defect" does little to answer that question. The notion of "treatment" infrequently seems suitable, but the fact remains that a pathological reaction to alcohol could recur the next time alcohol is consumed by the same actor, and hence significant danger may be involved. Whether a pathological reaction to alcohol does recur or not is at least within the power of the actor to prevent by the simple expedient of avoiding alcohol.[179] Once it is made clear that this is the case, then

---

178. For example, in Hicks v. State, 256 Ga. 715, 352 S.E.2d 762 (1987), the court rejected an argument that error was committed by the trial court in not allowing additional psychiatric testing of the defendant before trial. The court said "A neurological examination could only have served to assign neurological disease, as opposed to psychological factors, as the cause of the defendant's disorder." *Hicks* at 726, 352 S.E.2d at 775.

179. We have largely avoided questions of treatment, but we might point out here that spontaneous attacks of seizures are largely controllable with medication. One would suppose there will be some linkage between failure to heed advice not to drink and failure to take

the actor's fault in drinking again under the known circumstances of an underlying disease or defect provides the predicate for future handling on the criminal side of the courts. Prior to that point, however, if the actor is not at fault in drinking in the first instance, there is no basis for conviction of a crime. As Lord Denning explained it in *Bratty*:[180]

> The major mental diseases, which the doctors call psychoses, such as schizophrenia, are clearly diseases of the mind. But in *R. v. Charlson*,[181] Barry, J., seems to have assumed that other diseases such as epilepsy or cerebral tumour are not diseases of the mind, even when they are such as to manifest themselves in violence. I do not agree with this. It seems to me that any mental disorder which has manifested itself in violence and is prone to recur is a disease of the mind. At any rate it is the sort of disease for which a person should be detained in hospital rather than be given an unqualified acquittal.[182]

At the same time, a "malfunctioning of the mind of transitory effect caused by the application to the body of some external factor such as violence, drugs (including anaesthetics), alcohol and hypnotic influences cannot fairly be said to be due to disease."[183] The House of Lords then held in *Sullivan*[184] that epilepsy was a disease of the mind for "it matters not whether the aetiology of the impairment is organic, as in epilepsy, or functional, or whether the impairment itself is permanent or is transient and intermittent, provided that it subsisted at the time of the commission of the act."[185] Thus, when the question is whether the defendant has an alternative defense of noninsane automatism which might result in an outright acquittal, it becomes clear that this ailment satisfies the test of insanity. The definition of disease becomes distinctly contextual. We will pursue this English line of cases more fully in the next chapter.

Perhaps the most significant aspect of the proposed new approach by Fingarette and Hasse is that it renders the concept of "mental disease" irrelevant.[186] The proposed doctrine of disability of mind "covers all the legal rubrics mentioned earlier. Indeed, it covers *any* mental pathology whether temporary or chronic, whether self-induced or not, and whether

---

prescribed medication.

180. Bratty v. Attorney-General for Northern Ireland, [1961] 3 All E.R. 523.

181. [1955] 1 All E.R. 859.

182. *Bratty* at 534.

183. Regina v. Quick, 1973 Q.B. 910, 922.

184. Regina v. Sullivan, [1983] 2 All E.R. 673.

185. *Sullivan* at 677.

186. H. FINGARETTE & A. HASSE, MENTAL DISABILITIES AND CRIMINAL RESPONSIBILITY 7 (1979).

it has an identifiable physical origin or not."[187] This is made possible by resting the determination of fault not on "disease," but upon the "context of origin" of the mental condition of the actor at the time of the conduct alleged. This proposal is an ideal treatment for the pathological intoxication problem, and we will specifically take up the matter of fault as a limitation on it in Chapter 10.

187. Fingarette & Hasse at 7.

7

Pathological Intoxication and the Defense of Automatism: The Physical Disease and Trauma Cases

Automatism[1] is a medicolegal term, and the concept is the least familiar of the defenses which might be invoked in a pathological intoxication case, and this may justify a somewhat more detailed treatment of the defense than in the case of other defenses such as insanity which are more familiar to the bench and bar. The defense of automatism, or unconsciousness,[2] is a subpart of the involuntary act defense and has been recognized in this country since 1879.[3] Involuntary acts occur

1. The concept of involuntary act, or automatism, has drawn a great deal of attention. Saunders, *Voluntary Acts and the Criminal Law: Justifying Culpability Based on the Existence of Volition*, 49 U. PITT. L. REV. 443 (1988); Lederman, *Non-Insane and Insane Automatism: Reducing the Significance of a Problematic Distinction*, 34 INT'L & COMP. L.Q. 819 (1985); Holland, *Automatism and Criminal Responsibility*, 25 CRIM. L.Q. 95 (1982); Campbell, *Psychological Blow Automatism: A Narrow Defence*, 23 CRIM. L.Q. 342 (1981); Mackay, *Non-Organic Automatism—Some Recent Developments*, 1980 CRIM. L. REV. 350; Blair, *The Medicolegal Aspects of Automatism*, 17 MED., SCI. & LAW 167 (1977); O'Connor, *The Voluntary Act*, 15 MED., SCI. & LAW 31 (1975); Sullivan, *Self Induced and Recurring Automatism*, 123 NEW L.J. 1093 (1973); Murphy, *Involuntary Acts and Criminal Liability*, 81 ETHICS 332 (1971); Beck, *Voluntary Conduct: Automatism, Insanity and Drunkenness*, 9 CRIM. L.Q. 315 (1967); Elliott, *Automatism and Trial by Jury*, 6 MELBOURNE U.L. Rev. 53 (1967); Edwards, *Automatism and Social Defence*, 8 CRIM. L.Q. 258 (1966); Glasgow, *The Anatomy of Automatism*, 64 N.Z. MED. J. 491 (1965); Fox, *Physical Disorder, Consciousness, and Criminal Liability*, 63 COLUM. L. REV. 645 (1963); Kahn, *Automatism: Sane and Insane*, 1965 N.Z.L.J. 113; Leigh, *Automatism and Insanity*, 5 CRIM. L.Q. 160 (1962); Blackwell, *Automatism and Amnesia*, 79 S. AFR. L.J. 16 (1962); Howard, *Automatism and Insanity*, 4 SYDNEY L. REV. 36 (1962); Jennings, *The Growth and Development of Automatism as a Defence in Criminal Law*, 2 OSGOODE HALL L.J. 370 (1962); Puxon, *The Defence of Automatism*, 106 SOL. J. 163 (1962); Note, *Amnesia, Automatism and Insanity*, 79 S. AFR. L.J. 338 (1962); Prevezer, *Automatism and Involuntary Conduct*, 1958 CRIM. L. REV. 361.

Glasgow, *The Anatomy of Automatism*, 64 N.Z. MED. J. 491, 492 (1965), ascribes the beginnings of the modern use of the automatism defense to Woolmington v. D.P.P., 1935 A.C. 462. Lederman, *Non-Insane and Insane Automatism: Reducing the Significance of a Problematic Distinction*, 34 INT'L & COMP. L.Q. 819, 822 (1985), traces the use of the term on the legal side to Regina v. Harrison-Owen, 35 Crim. App. 108, 111, 112 (1951).

2. 1 W. LAFAVE & A. SCOTT, SUBSTANTIVE CRIMINAL LAW § 4.9(b), at 544 n.17 (1986).

3. Fain v. Commonwealth, 78 Ky. 183 (1879).

whenever the actor's bodily movement, or omission, is "not a product of the effort or determination of the actor, either conscious or habitual."[4] The term "automatism" is usually, though not always, reserved for those situations in which the condition of involuntariness meets that definition but also has a basis in some sort of disability of the actor. Involuntary act is a broader concept than automatism in that it would encompass as well cases such as those in which the actor is dragged to a place it is illegal for him or her to be[5] or cases in which performance of an act is required but impossible for him to accomplish.[6]

It is this customary association with an abnormality that significantly impairs the actor's consciousness that makes the defense so relevant to cases of pathological intoxication because, as we have shown in Chapters 1 through 4, unconsciousness is a common characteristic of pathological intoxication. If one took seriously the insistence by some that the disorder suffered by the actor be one that would not meet the insanity law requirement of a "disease of the mind," as distinct from "brain," then perhaps more cases of pathological intoxication should be tried as cases of automatism than insanity. But the courts are not nearly so rigid and the classification not nearly so simple or neat as that. There is neither agreement on a requirement of mutual exclusivity between the two defenses of insanity and automatism, nor is there significant agreement concerning which maladies belong in which defense if they do not belong in both. The matter becomes more complex when account is taken of the phenomenon of pathological intoxication because of its interactive nature.

In the previous chapter, attention was given to the question whether pathological intoxication is a mental disease or defect for purposes of the laws of insanity; the answer given was rather complex and uncertain, and we will not try to summarize it here. Nevertheless, in any instance in which there is doubt about whether the defense will fit under the insanity rules, automatism may well provide a suitable alternative. Indeed, in many cases, automatism is more suitable than insanity because of the difference in disposition: In many of these cases there simply is no need for continuing incarceration for treatment or other sort of medical intervention. One of the quandaries faced by the "reformers" who are trying to cut back on the scope of the insanity defense is that they may simultaneously but inadvertently increase the scope of the automatism defense because the thrust of the attack on the insanity defense thus far has been elimination of its volitional impairment prong, the domain of the automatism defense.[7] It was also pointed out

---

4. MODEL PENAL CODE § 2.01(2)(d) (Proposed Official Draft 1962).

5. Martin v. State, 31 Ala. App. 334, 17 So. 2d 427 (1944); Larsonneur, 24 Crim. App. 74 (1933).

6. United States v. Spingola, 464 F.2d 909 (7th Cir. 1972).

7. With the appearance of the effort toward abolition, *see, e.g.*, State v. Korell, 213 Mont.

in the previous chapter[8] that most insanity dispositions are actually the result of negotiated agreements. What the defendant gives up in many of those cases is the defense of automatism that would be litigated under a general plea of not guilty in exchange for the state's acquiescence in judicial acceptance of an insanity plea.

THE *ACTUS REUS* ELEMENTS OF A CRIME UNDER MODERN CRIMINAL CODES

The automatism defense is an elemental defense that denies the existence of the requirement of a voluntary act because the actor was unconscious at the time of the behavior complained of. It may be useful to review the element to be negated by the automatism defense.

Actus Reus

An important refinement of the Model Penal Code was to divide the common law concept of *actus reus*,[9] the physical part of a crime, into three distinct components: (1) the physical act; (2) the relevant circumstances and (3) the result.[10] Common law courts and writers

---

316, 690 P.2d 992 (1984); State v. Watson, 211 Mont. 401, 686 P.2d 879 (1984), or severe restriction of the insanity defense, as by elimination of the impaired volition component of the traditional approach to defining this form of exculpation, the law of involuntary act, or automatism, may be asserted in its place. To the extent that the claimed mental incapacity was due to a mental illness or mental disease, the cases have been tried largely as insanity cases. Now, however, defense counsel will no doubt discover what has always been true: The volitional aspect of traditional insanity law overlaps with the defense of automatism and, indeed, that fact is probably the reason for the relative underuse of the automatism defense. More importantly, those cases in which the temporary insanity does not include prospective dangerousness, do not call for incarceration of any sort and the automatism defense serves that end. For the same reasons which underlie the legislative and judicial diminution of volition-impairment defenses, efforts to substitute the use of automatism as a defense will be resisted all the more because of the disposition difference compared to insanity cases.

8. *Supra* Chapter 6, n.2.

9. While the modern code term for *mens rea* is "culpability," there is no comparable contemporary expression for the common law term *actus reus.* Most analysts refer to the collective acts, circumstances and results as "objective elements" to distinguish them from the subjective elements of *mens rea*, Robinson & Grall, *Element Analysis in Defining Criminal Liability: The Model Penal Code and Beyond*, 35 STAN. L. REV. 681, 683 n.9 (1983); Wechsler, *Revision and Codification of Penal Law in the United States*, 7 DALHOUSIE L.J. 219, 226 (1983); it is just as clear to continue to use *actus reus* for this purpose, and here they are used synonymously.

10. "This analysis begins by classifying the material objective elements of crimes as involving either the nature of the actor's conduct (shooting a gun, driving a car, writing a check) or the attendant circumstances (a crowded street, a drunken driver, an empty bank account) or a result of conduct (causing death, injury, deception or financial loss)." Wechsler

unwittingly tended to cloak these distinctions. The major difficulty this caused was in failing to facilitate application of different culpability terms to different elements and to different types of elements. When we speak of "what did the defendant do," we are better served asking what physical acts did he or she perform, under what relevant circumstances and with what results. The important point here is to separate "act" from the other external elements because the law of involuntary act concerns itself only with this first level. The defense of involuntary act is broader than the defense of automatism only in the sense that it denies the existence of the required element of voluntariness of the act alleged for any reason and is not confined to unconsciousness. To understand the defense of involuntary act, it is helpful to have a clear grasp of the meaning of "act" in this context.

The Act

Justice Holmes was an early advocate of the modern code view that "An act is always a voluntary muscular contraction, and nothing else. The chain of physical sequences which it sets in motion or directs to the plaintiff's harm is no part of it...."[11] Austin urged a narrow use in the interest of furthering understanding of the dissimilar significance that the law attaches to the three distinct components of the *actus reus.*[12]

---

at 226. We would, however, classify "gun", "car" and "check" as circumstances. They are external to anything the actor did and are facts existing at the time of the act. *See also* G. WILLIAMS, CRIMINAL LAW: THE GENERAL PART § 11 (2d ed. 1961); J. SALMOND, JURISPRUDENCE 505 (9th ed. 1937).

11. O. W. HOLMES, THE COMMON LAW 54 (1881). THE RESTATEMENT (SECOND) OF TORTS § 2 (1965) provides: "The word 'act' is used throughout the Restatement of this Subject to denote an external manifestation of the actor's will and does not include any of its results, even the most direct, immediate and intended." Note the failure to distinguish between acts and circumstances, or circumstances and results. The focus is only on distinguishing act from mental states, and act from results. Modern criminal codes are more exacting.

12. J. AUSTIN, JURISPRUDENCE 415 (5th ed. 1885). Early promotion of this approach may also be found in Cook, *Act, Intention, and Motive in the Criminal Law*, 26 YALE L.J. 645, 648-53 (1917). He argued:

> Most of the names which seem to be names of acts, are names of acts, coupled with certain of their consequences. For example, If I kill you with a gun or pistol, I shoot you: And the long train of incidents which are denoted by that brief expression, are considered (or spoken of) as if they constituted an *act*, perpetrated by me. In truth, the only parts of the train which are my act or acts, are the muscular motions by which I raise the weapon; point it at your head or body and pull the trigger. These I *will*. The contact of the flint and steel, the ignition of the powder, the flight of the ball towards your body, the wound and subsequent death, with the numberless incidents included in these, are *consequences* of the *act* which I will. I *will* not those consequences, although I may *intend* them.

While both Austin and Holmes distinguish between acts and consequences, they do not further distinguish between circumstances and results (consequences), and modern code drafters recognize that it is necessary to do so. That level of analysis will be pursued later in Chapter 10 on fault; that is where the act/circumstances/results distinctions become more relevant. Both Holmes and Austin also equate "act" with a requirement that it be a voluntary act, or a "willed" act. But these need not be and probably should not be the same idea. It is even more precise to speak of the act independently of whether or not it was a voluntary act.[13] The first question would be whether the defendant shot the gun or spoke the words, and the second question of legal import is whether the acts were done voluntarily rather than, for example, in the throes of an epileptic seizure or while asleep. No advantage derives from combining these two different ideas.[14] More precise analysis calls for distinguishing "act" from "voluntary act" on the one hand and "act" from "circumstances" and "results" as well.[15]

---

13. This is the strategy supported by the MODEL PENAL CODE (Proposed Official Draft 1962). Section 1.13(2) provides: "'act' or 'action' means a bodily movement whether voluntary or involuntary." Voluntary acts are then defined in § 2.02. The matter is also well expressed in 1 NAT'L COMM'N ON REFORM OF THE FED. CRIMINAL LAWS, WORKING PAPERS 110 (1970):

> Argument can be made that inclusion of the word "voluntarily" to modify the phrase "engages in conduct" [in NAT'L COMM'N ON REFORM OF THE FED. CRIMINAL LAWS, STUDY DRAFT § 301, at 24 (1970)] is unnecessary and that it will cause confusion. In ordinary circumstances, we should not describe blinking or twitching, or rolling over in sleep, or stumbling over a rock, or being shoved into someone, as "conduct." At least the strong use of the word "conduct" contains some notion of a person's conducting himself in a certain way, exercising control over himself, some element of volition. To some extent, therefore, the word "voluntarily" is unnecessary and the entire phrase "voluntarily engages in conduct" redundant. There are, however, weak uses of the word "conduct." As the performance in question becomes more like the kinds of performance which ordinarily are voluntary—a highly involved "twitch," sleepwalking, or talking in one's sleep instead of rolling over or snoring—it is not so clear that the word "conduct" is inapplicable; used weakly, the word connotes simply behavior. Partial redundancy seems clearly preferable in this case to incompleteness.

Notice that "behavior" is used in this federal document in the sense of the defendant's entire *actus reus*—act, circumstances and results—but without voluntariness of the act or at least without consideration of the question of the voluntariness of the act.

14. New York, as an example, provides that voluntary act "means a bodily movement performed consciously as a result of effort or determination...." N.Y. PENAL LAW § 15.00(2) (McKinney 1987), while "act" means only "a bodily movement." § 15.00(1).

15. For a more sweeping history of the distinction between voluntary and involuntary acts, *see* Sendor, *Crime as Communication: An Interpretive Theory of the Insanity Defense and the Mental Elements of Crime*, 74 GEO. L.J. 1371 (1986), where it is traced as far back as comments collected in ARISTOTLE, ETHICA NICOMACHEA 1109b (W. Ross trans. 1925). Sendor at 1372 n.6. *See also* Goodman, *Demographic Evidence in Capital Sentencing*, 39 STAN. L. REV.

Another purpose for differentiating clearly between act in the narrow sense and circumstances and results is that it is clear not only that an act must be a voluntary act, it is conversely and equally clear that the voluntariness requirement does not apply to any other element in the definition of a crime. *United States v. Coleman*[16] is illustrative of the point. The defendant was charged with assault (a common law battery)[17] within the territorial jurisdiction of the United States. The defendant had been arrested off federal property and forcibly taken onto federal property, a post office, to permit the arresting person to call for assistance. There, the defendant assaulted the arresting officer. He argued that his conviction should be reversed because he was involuntarily on federal property at the time of the assault.

The defendant hoped to rely upon *Martin v. State,*[18] in which the court had reversed the conviction of a person who had been taken from his home into public and then charged under a statute which made it a crime if a person "appears in any public place...and manifests a drunken condition."

The court, however, affirmed the conviction in *Coleman.* "The assault itself constitutes the necessary voluntary act: the requirement is not that every aspect of wrongful behavior be volitional, but that liability be 'based on conduct which includes a voluntary act.' Model Penal Code § 3.01(1)."[19]

The point perhaps more precisely put is that the defendant's act constituting the assault had to be voluntary, but his location was only a circumstance, and circumstances imply no requirement of voluntariness. In contrast, the statute in *Martin* required the defendant to "appear," and that means voluntarily appear, and he did not do so. In the right case, however, a person could be convicted under that statute even though his intoxication was deemed involuntary, as in the case of an alcoholic if he "appeared" voluntarily, because his intoxicated state would be a circumstance, not an act.[20] In *Martin,* the defendant prevailed because an act required by statute was not voluntarily committed by the defendant ("appear"), and the defendant lost in *Coleman* because the required act, assault, was committed voluntarily. In neither case is there an issue of the voluntariness of the defendant's intoxication or his location on federal property, because those are circumstantial elements, not act elements. Similarly, there is no requirement of "voluntariness"

---

499 (1987).

16. United States v. Coleman, 475 F. Supp. 422 (E.D. Pa. 1979), *aff'd* 620 F.2d 290 (3d Cir. 1980).

17. 18 U.S.C. § 113(d) (1976).

18. Martin v. State, 31 Ala. App. 334, 17 So. 2d 427 (1944).

19. *Coleman* at 424.

20. In effect, this was the holding of the swing vote of Justice White in the case of Powell v. Texas, 392 U.S. 514, 88 S. Ct. 2145, 20 L. Ed. 2d 1254 (1968).

regarding any result which might be required in the definition of an offense.

THE STATUS OF THE VOLUNTARY ACT REQUIREMENT

The requirement of voluntary act is a part of the definition of every crime and is probably of constitutional dimension. Therefore, unconsciousness deriving from pathological intoxication is potentially a defense to any crime, even those of "strict liability" in which there is no *mens rea* requirement with respect to circumstances or result elements.[21] "It is no more rational to hold a person criminally liable for a condition over which he has no control than to hold him liable for some wholly external event."[22] With any crime, the state must prove that the act—narrowly defined—was voluntary, or in the case of omissions,[23] that the defendant had the ability to act and did not. Each crime must include a requirement of a voluntary act,[24] and each act required by the statute must be voluntary if more than one act is required. Those requirements will not vary. The meaning of "voluntary" will sometimes divide the courts, but those two ideas will not: (1) Each crime must include at least one act as one of its elements, and that means a voluntary act (or omission) is a part of each crime; and (2) each act that is actually proscribed by a particular statute must be a voluntary act, whether that particular statute specifically says so or not.

The first proposition is a fundamental principle of criminal and constitutional law.[25] The second is derived both from common law and

---

21. 1 NAT'L COMM'N ON REFORM OF THE FED. CRIMINAL LAWS, WORKING PAPERS 106-17 (1970), discussing Robinson v. California, 370 U.S. 660, 82 S. Ct. 1417, 8 L. Ed. 2d 758 (1962), and Lambert v. California, 355 U.S. 225, 78 S. Ct. 240, 2 L. Ed. 2d 228 (1957). Statutory embodiments of this requirement are found in 2 P. ROBINSON, CRIMINAL LAW DEFENSES § 171(d) n.17 (1984).

22. 1 WORKING PAPERS at 107 (1970).

23. Omissions are sometimes referred to, especially in older literature, as "negative acts." *See, e.g.*, J. SALMOND, JURISPRUDENCE 503 (9th ed. 1937).

24. Ordinarily, the issue is the voluntariness of the act that is an element of the crime, but on rare occasions, a crime is encountered that entirely neglects any act requirement. The best known example was litigated in Robinson v. California, 370 U.S. 660, 82 S. Ct. 1417, 8 L. Ed. 2d 758 (1962), where California had made it a crime to be an addict.

25. The requirement reflected in MODEL PENAL CODE § 2.01(1) (Proposed Official Draft 1962) is constitutionally mandated, based on the Cruel and Unusual Clause of the Eighth Amendment and on the Due Process Clause of the Fourteenth Amendment. Robinson v. California, 370 U.S. 660, 82 S. Ct. 1417, 8 L. Ed. 2d 758 (1962), held that it was unconstitutional for a state to define a status (narcotic addiction) as criminal when the defendant was unable to change that status. While this case is often cited for the proposition that the states cannot make status a crime, it is clearly the present involuntariness of the status that is controlling. *See also* Powell v. Texas, 392 U.S. 514, 88 S. Ct. 2145, 20 L. Ed. 2d 1254 (1968). In *Robinson,* the Supreme Court said:

contemporary code definitions. For instance, the Model Penal Code provides that: "A person is not guilty of an offense unless his liability is based on conduct that includes a voluntary act or the omission to perform an act of which he is physically capable."[26] This statute reiterates those two basic propositions of criminal law and implies a third.

Not everything involved in the defendant's conduct has to be voluntary in order to satisfy this minimal requirement; it is only mandated that his conduct *include* a voluntary act or omission. Thus, an individual could be found to have fulfilled these requirements for the crime of vehicular homicide if he drove while intoxicated and killed someone, and this presumably would be true even if he passed out from intoxication prior to actually causing the death. Although the defendant would not be conscious at the time of the act causing death, and thus not acting voluntarily at the time of the impact, his conduct would have included[27]

> It is unlikely that any State at this moment in history would attempt to make it a criminal offense for a person to be mentally ill, or a leper, or to be afflicted with a venereal disease. A State might determine that the general health and welfare require that the victims of these and other human afflictions be dealt with by compulsory treatment, involving quarantine, confinement, or sequestration. But, in the light of contemporary human knowledge, a law which made a criminal offense of such a disease would doubtless be universally thought to be an infliction of cruel and unusual punishment in violation of the Eighth and Fourteenth Amendments.

Robinson v. California, 370 U.S. 660, 666, 82 S. Ct. 1417, 1420, 8 L. Ed. 2d 758, 763 (1962). *See also* Larsonneur, 24 Crim. App. 74 (1933), which (wrongly) upheld a conviction of the defendant for being an alien "found" in the United Kingdom after she tried to leave the country and was arrested in the Irish Free State and forcibly returned to England, where she was "found." For a satirical account of the trial of a defendant accused of "pulmonary consumption," a case uncommonly comparable to *Robinson*, *see* SAMUEL BUTLER, EREWHON 110-17 (Everyman's Library ed. 1927).

26. MODEL PENAL CODE § 2.01(1) (Proposed Official Draft 1962). MODEL PENAL CODE § 2.01 comment 1 at 119 (Tent. Draft No. 4, 1955) asserts the basic premise: "People whose involuntary movements threaten harm to others may present a public health or safety problem, calling for therapy or even for custodial commitment; they do not present a problem of correction."

27. MODEL PENAL CODE § 2.01(1) (Proposed Official Draft 1962). Regarding that provision, the MODEL PENAL CODE drafters state:

> It will be noted that the formulation does not state that liability must be based on the voluntary act or the omission *simpliciter*, but rather upon conduct which *includes* such action or omission. The distinction has some analytical importance. If the driver of an automobile loses consciousness with the result that he runs over a pedestrian, none of the movements or omissions that accompany or follow this loss of consciousness may in themselves give rise to liability. But a prior voluntary act, such as the act of driving, or a prior omission, such as failing to stop as he felt illness approaching, may, under given circumstances, be regarded as sufficiently negligent for liability to be imposed. In that event, however, liability is based on the entire course of conduct, including the specific conduct that resulted in the injury. It is

a voluntary act, driving. "[T]hus unconsciousness preceded by voluntary action may lead to liability based upon the earlier conduct."[28]

The provision is more or less explicitly aimed at permitting conviction in the situation presented to the courts in *Decina*,[29] where the New York Court of Appeals held that an indictment for criminal negligence in the operation of a motor vehicle which resulted in the death of several persons was sufficient in charging that the defendant drove the vehicle knowing that he was subject to epileptic seizures, even though he may have been unconscious at the exact moment he lost control of the car and killed the victims. However one views the *Decina* approach, it would seem to be applicable to the typical case of pathological intoxication but only to find a precedent voluntary act, the drinking. Even so, it was the defendant's awareness of his condition and the actor's resulting recklessness that cost him the defense of automatism in that case. In other words, the defense of automatism is subject to fault limitations like any other defense; if he was at fault in causing the unconsciousness, liability is still possible. That is a major point and is pursued in Chapter 10.

The voluntary act requirement should not be confused with defenses such as duress, which afford exculpation of a defendant who acts under defined levels of coercion, or choice-of-evils, which enables an actor to attempt to avoid a greater harm even if he has to commit a lesser harm (crime) to do so.[30] In these situations, the defendant has acted voluntarily in the sense that he made a conscious choice as to his conduct. Indeed, it is precisely that point that explains the existence of these special affirmative defenses; they would be unnecessary if the defendant were not considered to have acted voluntarily in the first instance. Conversely, if the defendant's act is not voluntary, there is no crime and an affirmative defense is superfluous. The defense of necessity (choice-of-evils) and duress deal with the desirability of compliance with the criminal law while the voluntary act requirement focuses on the possibility of compliance.

Conduct, then, is "an action or omission and its accompanying state of mind or, where relevant, a series of acts or omissions."[31] It is not clear

---

> enough, in short, that the conduct included action or omission that satisfied the requirements of paragraph (1), and the further requirements for the establishment of culpability....

MODEL PENAL CODE § 2.01 comment 2 at 120-21 (Tent. Draft No. 4, 1955).

28. 1 MODEL PENAL CODE AND COMMENTARIES § 2.01, at 213 (1985).

29. People v. Decina, 2 N.Y.2d 133, 157 N.Y.S.2d 588, 138 N.E.2d 799 (1956). *See also*, Wechsler, *Codification of Criminal Law in the United States: The Model Penal Code*, 68 COLUM. L. REV. 1425, 1436 (1968).

30. MODEL PENAL CODE § 3.02 (Proposed Official Draft 1962).

31. MODEL PENAL CODE § 1.13(5) (Proposed Official Draft 1962).

whether the reference to "its accompanying state of mind" is merely a reference to the consciousness which along with determination must be present to constitute a voluntary act in all cases or whether it contemplates that culpable mental states will be used to modify act requirements in addition to the "consciousness" requirement. If it means the latter, it should more properly have said "a *voluntary* act or omission and its accompanying state of mind." But if it means the former, then "conduct" and "voluntary act" mean the same thing.

THE MEANING OF THE VOLUNTARY ACT REQUIREMENT

For an act to be deemed voluntary in criminal law, it must be willed, or subject to the actor's control. Obviously, acts unconsciously performed are not subject to control. This is underscored in the careful definition found in the decision of the House of Lords in *Bratty v. Attorney-General for Northern Ireland*: "an act which is done by the muscles without any control by the mind such as a spasm, a reflex action, or a convulsion; or an act done by a person who is not conscious of what he is doing such as an act done whilst suffering from concussion or whilst sleepwalking."[32]

There must be conscious control.[33] While these concepts overlap, they are not the same. For example, an intoxicated person dragged into public and then charged with public intoxication cannot be convicted.[34] There is no lack of awareness on his part, but no conviction would be allowed because he committed no voluntary act and was not otherwise responsible for being in public. On the other hand, a person may be physically able to move about and even perform relatively complicated tasks but may be unconscious when doing so. Talking, walking or undertaking even more complex operations in one's sleep are examples. Cases in which the person is not aware of what he is doing in the narrow sense of doing, acting, are referred to as cases of automatism.

What emerges, then, are the relatively straightforward propositions that "act" should be narrowly construed in this analytical structure and that the act element should always be construed to require voluntariness. That is, undoubtedly, a constitutional requirement with respect to at least one of the acts. Voluntariness is quite appropriately defined in some codes to include not only awareness of the act but that the act be determined as well. Thus, consciousness remains a necessary but not sufficient condition to a finding of voluntariness; the "willed" component also remains.

---

32. Bratty v. Attorney-General for Northern Ireland, [1961] 3 All E.R. 523, 532.
33. Gov't of the Virgin Islands v. Smith, 278 F.2d 169 (3d Cir. 1960).
34. Martin v. State, 31 Ala. App. 334, 17 So. 2d 427 (1944).

It is difficult to delineate a clear and comprehensive boundary between acts deemed voluntary and those which are involuntary. Model Penal Code provides a partial, negative definition by example:

> The following are not voluntary acts within the meaning of this Section:
> (a) a reflex or convulsion;
> (b) a bodily movement during unconsciousness or sleep;
> (c) conduct [acts?] during hypnosis[35] or resulting from hypnotic suggestion;
> (d) a bodily movement that otherwise is not a product of the effort or determination of the actor, either conscious or habitual.[36]

The Model Penal Code only obliquely suggests that voluntariness entails awareness of the act.[37] The drafters, however, point out that "The term 'voluntary' involves inquiry into the mental state of the actor, and, indeed, the demand that an act or omission be voluntary can be seen as a preliminary requirement of *culpability*."[38] The New York Code, followed by a number of jurisdictions, is clearer with respect to the requirement that the actor be aware of what he is doing; it provides that a voluntary act is "a bodily movement performed [1] *consciously* [2] as a result of effort or determination...."[39]

In *State v. Utter*,[40] the court summarized the pre-code law that was meant to be codified by the Model Penal Code and others:

> There are two components of every crime. One is objective—the actus reus; the other subjective— the mens rea. The actus reus is the culpable act itself, the mens rea is the criminal intent with which one performs the criminal act. However, the mens rea does not encompass the entire mental process of one accused of crime. There is a certain minimal mental element required in order to establish the actus reus itself. This is the element of volition. *See* Sim, *The Involuntary Actus Reus*, 25 MODERN L. REV. 741 (1962).[41]

---

35. There is disagreement on this point. G. WILLIAMS, CRIMINAL LAW: THE GENERAL PART § 250 (2d ed. 1961); Orne, Book Review, 46 A.B.A. J. 81 (1960) (reviewing P. REITER, ANTISOCIAL OR CRIMINAL ACTS AND HYPNOSIS: A CASE STUDY (1958)).

36. MODEL PENAL CODE § 2.01(2) (Proposed Official Draft 1962).

37. MODEL PENAL CODE § 2.01(2)(d) (Proposed Official Draft 1962).

38. 1 MODEL PENAL CODE AND COMMENTARIES § 2.01, at 215-16 (1985) (emphasis added).

39. N. Y. PENAL LAW § 15.00(2) (McKinney 1987) (numbering and emphasis added).

40. State v. Utter, 479 P.2d 946 (Wash. Ct. App. 1971).

41. *Utter* at 948. Previous military training was blamed in *Utter*, specifically, a conditioned response by the defendant, so the condition was not sufficient to satisfy the disease

Automatism is a special case of involuntary acts which are not consciously controlled because the person is unconscious. If the actor's unconsciousness is due to a mental disease or defect, he will also have the defense of legal insanity, and the two defenses of insanity and automatism will overlap on those facts. The English courts have taken this point a step further by holding that if the unconsciousness is due to mental disease or defect, it cannot be tried as automatism but must be tried as legal insanity, a choice still open to American defense attorneys in most states but now precluded in England. The reason, of course, is the difference in disposition. A case won on automatism results in outright acquittal. A case won on legal insanity merely changes the nature of state control over the individual from criminal to civil. One effect is that under English law, automatism and insanity do not overlap; they are exclusive, based on the judgment whether the underlying cause is a mental disease. We will come back to this problem in more detail later in this chapter.

Another aspect of the relationship of insanity law and automatism was discussed in *State v. Sikora,*[42] where the court held that psychiatric evidence of diminished capacity could not be used to reduce first degree murder to second degree murder, but could only be used on the issue of the death penalty. Speaking of the defense's psychiatric theory sought to be put in evidence by Dr. Galen, the court said: "This automaton concept apparently differs from the 'irresistible impulse' concept in that it proclaims the conscious is subservient to the unconscious in illness or in health, whereas the irresistible-impulse concept attempts to distinguish between impulses which were not resisted and impulses which could not be resisted because of mental illness."[43] Thus, the irresistible impulse or control test posits consciousness, while automatism is based on a claim of unconsciousness. The unconscious state could result from a mental disorder, but need not; it can also be caused, for example, by trauma. The difference in the theory, put forth in the case from the generally accepted view, was that the unconscious is more or less always in control, and that view was rejected by the court in *Sikora.*

It is illusive to think of the conduct requirement exclusively as an objective element. It is actually a blend of objective, external facts, internal mental states and legal evaluation of this complex mix. But fault-finding, obviously, has a large role to play in the decision as to voluntariness, comparable to the law's difficulty with causation, probably

---

requirement of the insanity defense. *But see* Delgado, *Ascription of Criminal States of Mind: Toward a Defense Theory for the Coercively Persuaded ("Brainwashed") Defendant,* 63 MINN. L. REV. 1 (1978). For a reply, *see* Dressler, *Professor Delgado's "Brainwashing" Defense: Courting a Determinist Legal System,* 63 MINN. L. REV. 335 (1979).

42. State v. Sikora, 44 N.J. 453, 210 A.2d 193 (1965).

43. *Sikora* at 477 n.1, 210 A.2d at 206 n.1.

to the point where it is not useful to venture much further than the codes have done in defining either idea. When some type of wholly psychiatric phenomenon is involved without a clear physical attribute, called "functional" as distinct from "organic," this is even more clearly the case.[44]

Most states have not emulated the example of the Model Penal Code in providing a list of involuntary acts,[45] undoubtedly, out of concern that it might be both over-inclusive and under-inclusive, even though it does not purport to be exhaustive. But courts, of course, are aware that the list exists and may use it, given the dearth of any plain guidance from the legislature.

> The possibility of confusion arises from the ambiguity of the word "voluntarily." There are strong uses of that word according to which conduct is not "voluntary" if it is in any substantial sense the product of an identifiable external or nonconscious internal force. In its strongest sense, which stops just short of rejecting the notion of voluntary conduct altogether, a person engages in conduct "voluntarily" only if his conduct is not significantly subject to explanation by any general theory of behaviour [*See, e.g,* the position taken by the psychiatrist, Dr. Galen, in *State v. Sikora,* 44 N.J. 453, 210 A.2d 193 (1965).] The word is *not* intended to have that use here. It is intended to exclude from the kind of conduct which may be criminal that which, in the ordinary sense, occurs beyond the control of the actor; reflexes and twitches are paradigms.[46]

MEDICOLEGAL CONCEPTIONS OF AUTOMATISM

Unconsciousness as a Component of Automatism

Blair, a forensic psychiatrist, has defined automatism in these terms:

---

44. *See, e.g.,* Rose, *Criminal Responsibility and Competency as Influenced by Organic Disease,* 35 Mo. L. Rev. 326 (1970): "It is customary to classify diseases as either organic or functional. Organic diseases are those with demonstrable pathology, that is, with gross microscopic or biochemical abnormalities....In functional diseases there are no demonstrable anatomical, biochemical, or physiological abnormalities." *See also* C. Jeffery, Attacks on the Insanity Defense: Biological Psychiatry and New Perspectives on Criminal Behavior (1985).

45. Model Penal Code § 2.01(2) (Proposed Official Draft 1962).

46. 1 Nat'l Comm'n on Reform of the Fed. Criminal Laws, Working Papers 110 (1970) (emphasis added) (inserted citation in original footnote).

> The word 'automatism' refers in the medicolegal sense exclusively to behaviour and indeed is alternatively frequently called 'automatic behaviour'. It may aptly be defined as 'the existence in any person of behaviour of which he is unaware and over which he has no conscious control'. It entails a concurrent unconsciousness and subsequent amnesia for events which occurred during its existence.[47]

"Unconsciousness" is a critical concept in the medicolegal view of involuntary act in general and more particularly in the phenomenon referred to as automatism. For all the reference to it, the writers usually leave the term undefined. Perhaps it will be useful to try to clarify it somewhat since it is both critical and somewhat counter-intuitive. Anthony Smith has put the matter this way:

> For all our awareness of ourselves the event of being unaware is an easier state to comprehend than consciousness itself. The comatose body exists, functioning in its fashion, but the mind does not, or rather it is not aware of itself doing so....[T]here is neither intentionality, nor perception of reality, nor knowledge of feelings. Instead there is unconsciousness. Or rather there are different forms, and levels, of it....
>
> Medically there is imprecision over the naming of levels of unconsciousness, mainly because a neurological examination of the patient is inevitably limited. Reference is made to semi-coma, semi-consciousness, stupor, coma, and unconsciousness. Coma is deepest, and refers to patients who show no reflex response to any stimulus. The deepest comas of all are tantamount to death....Stupor is shallower, and its patients can be roused by painful stimuli. They make noises, of a kind, and withdrawal movements away from pain. The semi-states are the halfway stages, consciousness is not always either on or off, as victims of concussion ably demonstrate.

---

47. Blair, *The Medicolegal Aspects of Automatism,* 17 MED., SCI. & LAW 167 (1977). Fenwick summarized the medical definition as follows:

> An automatism is an involuntary piece of behavior over which an individual has no control. The behavior is usually inappropriate to the circumstances, and may be out of character for the individual. It can be complex, coordinated, and apparently purposeful and directed, though lacking in judgement. Afterwards the individual may have no recollection or only partial and confused memory for his actions. In organic automatisms there must be some disturbance of brain function sufficient to give rise to the above features.

Fenwick, *Somnambulism and the Law: A Review,* 5 BEHAV. SCI. & LAW 343, 349 (1987).

> First they mumble, then ask where they are, then ask again, and again, and finally comprehend their situation. Only rarely do they remember the accident that led to their concussion, or the time both before and after it.[48]

Disease as a Component of Automatism

What distinguishes automatism from other forms of involuntary act is some sort of disability, in some sense physical, that affects consciousness but which, on the other hand, also serves to differentiate automatism from cases of insanity, for, presumably, the latter are composed of cases of mental disease or defect. Professor Robinson maintains that "Some manifestation other than the conduct constituting the offense is required. But it is a matter of less concern here that the disability causing the excusing condition be of a specified sort that has been previously recognized."[49] There is no indication that a defendant will be barred from a claim of automatism in the face of clear clinical manifestation of automatic behavior solely on the grounds that the experts cannot identify the physical cause of the conduct. While one would certainly want to put in evidence such information if it is available, we have seen no indication that specification of a recognized cause is a requirement here any more than it is in the case of the insanity defense.

A variety of defects suffices for the defense of automatism. If the insanity defense requires a mental disease, presumably automatism defenses might be organized around concepts such as (1) organic; (2) metabolic; (3) traumatic and (4) idiopathic automatisms. One writer has, in fact, suggested such a view. Blair organized his medical material as follows:

- Organic Automatism
  - Alcohol
  - Alcoholic Automatism
  - Pathological Alcoholic Intoxication (note)
  - Drugs
  - Epilepsy (several types)
  - Cerebral Concussion
  - Hypoglycemia
  - Other Causes
    - Anoxia and Carbon Monoxide Poisoning
- Psychogenic Automatisms

---

48. A. SMITH, THE MIND 130-31 (1984).
49. 2 P. ROBINSON, CRIMINAL LAW DEFENSES, § 171(c), at 262 (1984).

Normal Automatism (habitual movements)
Hypnotic
Stress or Strain
Psychopathological dissociations
Somnambulisms
Fugues
Multiple Personalities[50]

Metabolic is, of course, a subpart of organic, so that apart from the instances of unknown cause, there are actually only two types thus far identified: those that are organic and those that are not. This dichotomy is what serves to distinguish the English doctrine of insane automatism (insanity defense) and noninsane automatism (involuntary act defense) and what may serve to distinguish which automatisms are supposed to fall within the ambit of either the automatism defense or the insanity defense. The legal distinction between automatisms that are attributable to mental disease and those that are not is not an arrangement that inspires conviction.[51]

Automatism and Insanity

The issue of the legal status of automatism is best couched in terms not of whether a jurisdiction recognizes the automatism defense, which it must, but to what extent the court recognizes a defense of "automatism" (involuntary act) as one which exists independently of the insanity plea or whether, on the other hand, it requires such cases to be pleaded either as legal insanity or not at all. Automatism is both a medical and legal term. Even as a medical term, it is not meant to describe a disease; it is a symptom of a disease or trauma. Like pathological intoxication, automatism, in the legal sense, is a description of behavior with the

---

50. Blair, *The Medicolegal Aspects of Automatism*, 17 MED., SCI. & LAW 167 (1977).

51. BLACK'S LAW DICTIONARY 122 (5th ed. 1979) also indicates that there is no overlap between automatism and insanity:

> Behavior performed in a state of mental unconsciousness or dissociation without full awareness, i.e., somnambulism, fugues. Term is applied to actions or conduct of an individual apparently occurring without will, purpose, or reasoned intention on his part; a condition sometimes observed in persons who, without being actually insane, suffer from an obscuration of the mental faculties, loss of volition or of memory, or kindred affections. "Ambulatory automatism" describes the pathological impulse to purposeless and irresponsible wanderings from place to place often characteristic of patients suffering from loss of memory with dissociation of personality. Automatism may be asserted as a criminal defense to negate the requisite mental state of voluntariness for commission of a crime....

underlying physiological or psychological cause being relegated to the role of enhancing believability of the claim. In law, but not in medicine, usage may be narrowed by exclusion of cases in which the etiology is linked to something identified as "mental disease."

There is also some question about what it means to "recognize" or not the defense of automatism. No American court has ever permitted conviction for an involuntary act, and in that sense, all courts recognize the defense of involuntary act. On the other hand, if the question is whether expert evidence will be permitted on the defense of automatism without a plea of not guilty by reason of insanity, the answer appears to be that the courts have not significantly discussed the question. It seems to be assumed that it is proper to do so, especially if the position is that the mental maladies triable under the automatism defense are those not triable under the defense of insanity. While the defense of involuntary act must be recognized, it does not follow that the defense of automatism must be recognized procedurally on a plea of not guilty or that the states are precluded from requiring it be raised under a special plea akin to or identical with the insanity plea.

The two insanity defenses under the *M'Naghten rules* and the irresistible impulse test (or under the A.L.I. test, which combines the two) overlap with the voluntariness requirement in criminal law and with the automatism defense, unless the cause of the disability must be different in automatism from what is required in insanity law.[52] The defenses of insanity and automatism overlap, in that insanity may actually, on the facts of different cases, be an attack on the voluntariness of the act, at least in the sense of claiming that the act was unconsciously committed. An insanity defense, factually, may also be a denial of the existence of the required *mens rea,* or a plea of lack of responsibility despite the presence of all of the elements of the crime.

Much of the confusion in the cases and the writings may be obviated if we recognize that there is no doubt that a case of automatism, or unconsciousness, due to physical disease or trauma may be tried as insanity. There are no cases saying otherwise. This is because that approach is actually often detrimental to the defendant's interests. For example, Professor Goldstein said:

> Today, it is probable that most of the conditions which have in the past supported a defense of "involuntary act" would also be able to support the insanity defense. However physical their origins, their impact on the mental state of the affected individual seems clear. That is certainly true in the

52. *See, e.g.,* Lederman, *Non-Insane and Insane Automatism: Reducing the Significance of a Problematic Distinction,* 34 INT'L & COMP. L.Q. 819, 821 n.11 (1985).

> case of epilepsy. And it is probably true in the other instances specifically cited by the ALI [in the Model Penal Code]. Yet, for the moment, the two bodies of doctrine exist alongside one another, offering the defendant the opportunity to prove one or the other, or both.[53]

And where the claim is clearly one of automatism, not insanity, the defendant need not plead insanity in order to introduce appropriate evidence or to secure an appropriate automatism instruction to the jury. One court said "The Attorney General contends that in order for defendant to prove his unconsciousness at the time of the accident it was incumbent upon him to plead insanity. Such is not the law."[54] The uncertainty is the extent of this view.

The cases and some of the writers appear confused on the line between automatism and insanity, and the source of the confusion is directly and importantly relevant to pathological intoxication. Consider, for example, the question whether epilepsy should be dealt with as insanity or automatism. The English and American cases are inconsistent within their respective jurisdictions. But the English upshot is that it must be tried as insanity, and the American position is that it may be tried as either insanity or automatism. But the difference is largely procedural, in that the English courts have more leeway to force the issue than do American courts. It is not so much differing views of epilepsy as it is differing powers to control choice of defenses.[55]

These matters are relatively straightforward. However, there are a multiplicity of mental conditions which may or may not be evaluated as resulting in involuntary acts,[56] and this can vary with the relative severity of the condition in a particular defendant.[57] Other facts can also exist which can cloud the question. Frequently, the inconsequential involvement of alcohol or other drugs diverts attention from the

---

53. A. GOLDSTEIN, THE INSANITY DEFENSE 204 (1967).

54. People v. Freeman, 142 P.2d 435, 439 (Cal. Ct. App. 1943); People v. Cox, 67 Cal. App. 2d 166, 153 P.2d 362 (1944).

55. The English cases will be discussed in detail in a later section. *See also* 1 W. LAFAVE & A. SCOTT, SUBSTANTIVE CRIMINAL LAW § 4.9(c), at 548 n.47 (1986), discussing Regina v. O'Brien, 56 D.L.R.2d 65 [1966], in which the only expert testified that epilepsy was an organic disease of the brain, not a disease of the mind, even though it may affect the mind. On this evidence, the trial court ruled that the defense could only be submitted to the jury as automatism, but the New Brunswick Court of Appeal held, despite this evidence from the expert, that epilepsy was a disease of the mind. Decisions such as this are obviously not medical decisions, but legal decisions based on policy considerations, the major one of which here is the desire to block "outright release for dangerous defendants." LaFave at 548.

56. *See* 2 P. ROBINSON, CRIMINAL LAW DEFENSES, § 171(c), at 262 (1984).

57. Robinson at § 171(c). Such conditions may still be relevant to a defense of diminished capacity even though the disability is not sufficient to lead to a conclusion that the defendant's conduct was not voluntary.

underlying cause of the defendant's condition. For example, is the defendant's mental state triggered by alcohol and resulting automatic behavior during an epileptic seizure to be classified as an involuntary act, or must the defendant rely instead on the defense of legal insanity? Two issues intertwine here. The first is whether epilepsy is considered a mental disease for purposes of insanity law. The second is whether, if the underlying cause of automatism is a mental disease, does the defendant still have the option to plead not guilty and introduce expert testimony of that condition on a defense theory of automatism?

Resolution of the question will have important consequences because a finding of involuntariness of his act on a general plea of not guilty will result in an outright acquittal while a finding in the defendant's favor on a plea of legal insanity may result in further (civil) incarceration. In addition, if the actor's condition is viewed as insanity, the defense may bear at least the burden of coming forward with some evidence on the question and the issue must be specially pleaded before trial with its concomitant de facto discovery on behalf of the state. If the defense is one of involuntariness of the defendant's act, the prosecution might bear the risk of nonpersuasion regarding its voluntariness because that is an element of the crime itself.

The distinction between automatism and insanity is in a substantial state of confusion. Glasgow tendered this description prior to heavy involvement in the area by English courts:

> From the medical point of view the distinction between automatism and insanity is fairly clear. By insanity doctors mean, in general, a major disorder of reasoning, emotion or intellectual powers which extends over a considerable period of time, usually months or years. We do not usually regard as insane, a person suffering from a temporary physical disorder of the brain producing such abnormalities where recovery occurs, say, after a few days. Automatism, on the other hand, in its true form occurs in a person with a background of a normal mental state and consists of a brief period of mental confusion brought about by a few well-defined and recognizable causes such as epilepsy, drug intoxication, head injury or hypoglycaemia. It seems to me that such episodes cannot reasonably be called a "disease of the mind."
>
> They are certainly based on a disease, or disorder of the brain, but there is no exact correlation between disease of the brain and disease of the mind. In most diseases of the mind we are still unable to demonstrate any physical abnormality

of the brain though this may change with increasing knowledge, particularly of biochemistry.[58]

One writer, Morse, has drawn a distinction between psychomotor epilepsy attacks, somnambulism and automatism:

> Taking all into account, a conclusory statement can be made that an automaton is a person, usually ambulatory, who is unconscious mentally but not physically, who is without will (not inner directed), who is not insane, who is not experiencing a seizure (to distinguish him from an epileptic), who is awake (to distinguish him from an somnambulist), and who is not under hypnosis (not outer directed).[59]

No authority is provided for this classification proposal, and it does not reflect the law. Epilepsy has been dealt with by the courts under both automatism and insanity,[60] as has pathological intoxication. The fact is that the legal situation is a good deal more ambiguous and unsettled than Morse reflects and courts are not certain how to deal with pathological intoxication, somnambulism or epileptic seizures, and to a certain extent, counsel determines some of this as a matter of trial tactics, for example, whether a plea of insanity is to be entered at all. Morse's effort seems to be to define automatism as a residual category after excluding cases of insanity and epilepsy. The broader and perhaps more realistic question is not whether pathological intoxication, epilepsy attacks and somnambulism are to be treated as insanity or automatism but whether the answer needs to be the same in all these cases or whether the answer even needs be uniformly given.[61]

Under one scheme of classification, automatism which is a result of organic disease processes (somnambulism is the best example of one which is not[62]) includes within it temporal lobe (psychomotor) epilepsy.[63]

---

58. Glasgow, *The Anatomy of Automatism*, 64 N.Z. MED. J. 491, 494-95 (1965).

59. Morse, *The Aberrational Man—A Tour de Force of Legal Psychiatry*, 13 J. FOR. SCI. 1, 369 (1968).

60. People v. Codarre, 20 A.D.2d 98, 245 N.Y.S.2d 81 (1963).

61. A. GOLDSTEIN, THE INSANITY DEFENSE 203 (1967) suggests that the case may be regarded as one of automatism rather than insanity because of doubt about the "disease" requirement of insanity law.

62. Cases in which somnambulism was successfully interposed as a defense in England are collected in Blair, *The Medicolegal Aspects of Automatism*, 17 MED., SCI. & LAW 167, 180 (1977). *See also* Annotation, *Automatism or Unconsciousness as Defense to Criminal Charge*, 27 A.L.R.4th 1067 (1984). There is some question whether somnambulism, or "sleepwalking" is a manifestation of a disease. *See* Justice Raper, in Fulcher v. State, 633 P.2d 142 (Wyo. 1981); Morse, *The Aberrational Man—A Tour de Force of Legal Psychiatry*, 13 J. FOR. SCI. 1, 12 (1968). Somnambulism is also sometimes referred to as "ambulatory automatism."

It is estimated that of those patients with clear cases of epileptic automatism, 90 percent have temporal lobe epilepsy. In addition, one third of all epileptics have a temporal lobe focus.[64]

According to Fenwick,[65] in Scotland, the courts have held that any automatism that is associated with a pathological condition is an insane automatism.[66] Under this view, pathological reaction to alcohol would be classified as insane automatism, or the equivalent of legal insanity.

Pathological reaction to alcohol usually involves an involuntary act[67] which focuses not so much on the consumption of alcohol, but on the resulting automatic behavior that is part of its symptomatology. The success of the involuntary act defense in criminal law has been rare, whatever the claimed cause of the behavior. Courts disfavor this defense precisely because it could result in a finding of not guilty, not just "not guilty by reason of insanity." And as said before on the latter finding, the defendant can be subjected to incarceration, but if found not guilty on a defense of involuntary act, he is free to go.

> [C]ould he, if he were released, be relied upon never to imbibe alcohol again, and if not, would there be a chance, even a remote one, of his having another bout of pathological intoxication sooner or later during which he would commit another injurious or murderous crime?[68]

Perhaps it is not too far beyond our scope to observe that the difficulty in this issue is the failure to establish either a very comprehensive scheme of defenses on a par with the structure provided for substantive offenses or, unfortunately, to deal with matters of overlap between the two, which is what is involved here. The same factual situation can be described as a lack of an element required of every offense (voluntary act) or in the alternative, as a defense of legal insanity, which is itself also potentially applicable to every offense. Under such a structure, it is understandable that conflicts will arise.

It is reported that a case of sleepwalking resulting in an assault will be appealed from a verdict of insane automatism and a consequent commitment. Fenwick, *Automatism and the Law*, LANCET 754 (Sept. 1989).

63. *See, e.g.*, Rose, *Criminal Responsibility and Competency as Influenced by Organic Disease*, 35 MO. L. REV. 326 (1970).

64. McCaldon, *Automatism*, 91 CAN. MED. ASS'N J. 914, 915 (1964).

65. Fenwick, *Somnambulism and the Law: A Review*, 5 BEHAV. SCI. & LAW 343, 351 (1987).

66. *See also* G. GORDON, THE CRIMINAL LAW OF SCOTLAND (2d ed. 1978).

67. Sim, *The Involuntary Actus Reus*, 25 MOD. L. REV. 741 (1962), which discusses the classic cases of Kilbride v. Lake, 1962 N.Z.L.R. 590, and Larsonneur, 24 Crim. App. 74 (1933). MODEL PENAL CODE § 2.01 (Proposed Official Draft 1962).

68. Blair, *The Medico-Legal Problems of Pathological Alcoholic Intoxication: An Illustrative Case*, 9 MED., SCI. & LAW 94, 97-98 (1969).

Automatism and *Mens Rea*

Mens rea defenses share a common disposition with automatism that distinguishes both from the insanity defense: The defendant is found not guilty of that charge, and automatic commitment procedures do not apply. They are distinguished in terms of disposition, in that *mens rea* defenses can and frequently do result in conviction on a lesser included offense, while charge reductions on a verdict based on an automatism defense are either nonexistent or extremely rare. And the "difference between the two states—of diminished capacity and unconsciousness—is one of degree only: where the former provides a 'partial defense' by negating a specific mental state essential to a particular crime, the latter is a 'complete defense' because it negates capacity to commit any crime at all."[69] They are also distinguished in that the defense of automatism will work as well with an offense based on strict liability whereas that is obviously not the case with a *mens rea* defense.

Culpability defenses and automatism also share the factual quality that either can be disease-based or not and therefore either can overlap with the insanity defense or not. In the simplest case, a mistake can be attributable to a mental disease.[70] In that case, the defense of insanity is available, but so may be the defense of mistake. Both *mens rea* and automatism defenses present the same difficulty to the courts because just as a defendant may wish to put on expert testimony regarding his mental state at the time of the crime in order to establish the fact that he was unconscious at the time, he may want to use the same or similar evidence to establish a lack of *mens rea* for the crime charged. These will obviously overlap[71] because any evidence that will establish automatism, with its requirement of unconsciousness, will by definition establish a *mens rea* defense.[72] Just as clearly, a court that wants to keep out expert testimony in an automatism defense in the absence of a plea of not guilty by reason of insanity will want to keep it out when the defense is lack of *mens rea* but it is less clear that the reverse is true. There are American decisions which let in psychiatric or other expert testimony even in the absence of a plea of not guilty by reason of insanity. Presumably, this issue is the same in the case of *mens rea* defense and automatism defense. It is sensible to suppose that the choice between the two will turn on the

---

69. People v. Newton, 87 Cal. Rptr. 394, 405-06 (Cal. Ct. App. 1970).

70. The cognitive disability involved in automatism was stressed by the Court of Appeal of New Zealand in *Queen v. Cottle*: "action without any knowledge of acting, or action with no consciousness of doing what was being done." 1958 N.Z.L.J. 999.

71. 1 W. LAFAVE & A. SCOTT, SUBSTANTIVE CRIMINAL LAW § 4.9(b), at 544 (1986).

72. 1 W. LAFAVE & A. SCOTT, SUBSTANTIVE CRIMINAL LAW § 4.9(b), at 544 n.19 (1986), discussing State v. Welsh, 508 P.2d 1041 (Wash. Ct. App. 1973), (attack of psychomotor epilepsy relevant to culpability requirements).

strength of the defense proof of mental impairment, so that if it appears extreme, automatism would be the approach and if it is partial, the-lack-of-culpability avenue may be more appropriate. Actually, there is little reason for the defense to choose in advance or at the close of the case because there is no special plea required in advance, and as such, no election should be required because the defenses are not inconsistent.

Though the law of intoxication has several special rules attached to it, the law of voluntary intoxication is essentially a part of the law of mistake, and so it is a culpability defense itself. It is clear that unconsciousness produced through voluntary intoxication (drunkenness) will not excuse through the automatism defense if this is understood to mean that the actor was aware or should have been aware of the likely result of drinking.[73] If the actor, in fact, had a pathological reaction to alcohol, then he is not intoxicated and the defense will be one of insanity or automatism and, as we will discuss later in connection with the Model Penal Code, perhaps a species of involuntary intoxication. There are evidentiary restrictions and limitations on trying insanity cases as culpability defenses, but there has been almost no litigation on the same issue in cases of automatism in which the defense for some reason decides to try the automatism issue as a lack of requisite *mens rea*.

There is an occasional decision in which the court or the defense seems to be of the opinion that lack of *mens rea* is the correct defense category in some pathological intoxication cases. In *Gov't of the Virgin Islands v. Smith*,[74] the court said: "[The insanity rule] is not applicable here. For there was no evidence that the defendant's alleged epileptic seizure was an evidence or result of mental illness. The defendant's claim was merely that he was unconscious at the time of the accident as a result of the alleged seizure and, therefore, did not have the necessary mens rea."[75] To some extent, this characterization of the issue indicates that involuntary act or lack of *mens rea* are both possible defense theories which presumably may be controlled by the defense's own treatment of the question. But what would *Smith* have held if the defendant had pleaded not guilty by reason of insanity?

The issue becomes marvelously confused in the few cases in which the court, or the defense, decides to try the issue of pathological reaction to alcohol as lack of *mens rea* despite evidence of automatism. It is obvious that, in many instances, pathological reaction to alcohol would render the defendant unable to possess the requisite *mens rea* for a wide variety of crimes. It is unlikely that a court would allow lack of *mens rea* due to pathological reaction to alcohol in which the actor was unconscious to be a defense used alone. While this seems at first to be

---

73. Mackay, *Intoxication as a Factor in Automatism*, 1982 CRIM. L. REV. 146.

74. Gov't of the Virgin Islands v. Smith, 278 F.2d 169 (3d Cir. 1960).

75. *Gov't of the Virgin Islands* at 174 (footnote omitted).

a bit illogical—indeed, impossible—the courts have often taken the position that when the defendant wants to rely on a defense of absence of *mens rea* when it is due to "mental disease or defect," the appropriate defense is legal insanity, not the absence of *mens rea*. The conviction is that the responsibility is only one of ascertaining the intent of the legislature in adopting an insanity defense: The legislature has provided a defense, with special procedures that must be followed, in any case in which the defense is essentially predicated on a "mental disease or defect," and the defendant will not be allowed to circumvent those special procedural requirements by entering plainly a plea of not guilty instead of the required plea of not guilty by reason of insanity. But suppose the actor's incapacity was not due to a "mental disease"?

THE ENGLISH TREATMENT OF AUTOMATISM AND INSANITY: THE CONTROLLING IMPORTANCE OF DISPOSITION

The English courts have devised a distinction between insane automatism and noninsane automatism. In cases of insane automatism, the defendant must enter a plea of not guilty by reason of insanity or the evidence of impaired consciousness will not be submitted to the jury. In cases of non-insane automatism, the evidence may be entered under a general plea and the defendant may be acquitted outright if the fact-finder concludes in his favor. The task, of course, is to categorize the cases sensibly.

Morris and Howard have summarized the present English definition of noninsane automatism as follows:

> Automatism may be defined for the present purpose as involuntary action performed in a state of unconsciousness *not amounting to insanity*. As such, it is now clearly established that automatism may constitute an answer to a criminal charge distinct from, and with none of the incidents of, a defence of insanity. The action must be unconscious to distinguish it from irresistible impulse, and involuntary to constitute an answer to the charge. The preponderance of opinion in the common-law jurisdictions is now in favour of the view that it is for the defence to carry the evidentiary burden of producing some evidence in support of a plea of automatism, but for the prosecution to carry the persuasive burden of disproving automatism beyond reasonable doubt.[76]

---

76. N. MORRIS & C. HOWARD, STUDIES IN CRIMINAL LAW 62 (1964) (emphasis added) (citations omitted).

Much of the critical literature regarding the defense of automatism was generated in response to the jury verdict in *Regina v. Charlson*.[77] The defendant attacked his ten-year-old son by striking him on the head with a mallet and throwing him out a window. The attack was unprovoked and otherwise unexplained. The defendant recalled the attack but claimed amnesia for some period following it. The case reports a rather vague background of possible cerebral tumor. He was charged with various levels of assault (battery), including one charge based on an intent to murder, one on intent to cause serious bodily injury and a third one encompassing general intent battery. Presumably, a complete lack of *mens rea* would have been a defense to any of these charges, as would the absence of any voluntary act involved in the assaults. He did not plead insanity, but entered a general plea of not guilty and was acquitted of all the charges based on an instruction which informed the jury that he was not guilty if, due to a brain tumor, he acted without control or knowledge of what he was doing.

The verdict drew attention to the nature of the instructions given in which the court told the jury that no insanity plea had been entered in the case and underscored that the evidence had indicated he was not suffering from a "disease of the mind" at the time of the attack. They were provided this instruction on the defense of automatism:

> [T]here must be a conscious act on the part of the prisoner....A man in the throes of an epileptic fit does not know what he is doing. If a friend bends over to assist him, and in the midst of the fit the epileptic grips his friend by the throat, not knowing what he is doing, and in so doing throttles the friend and causes his death, no offence against the criminal law has been committed, because the actions of an epileptic are automatic and unconscious, and his will or consciousness is not applied to what he is doing. He is not in conscious control of his actions.[78]

Specifically with respect to the third charge, the court instructed: "Was the prisoner knowingly striking his son, or was he acting as an automaton without any control or knowledge of the act which he was committing?"[79]

---

77. Regina v. Charlson, [1955] 1 All E.R. 859.

78. *Charlson* at 860-61.

79. *Charlson* at 862. *Charlson* has been criticized because the trial court did not wait for the prison physician to make a more thorough examination of the "possible" connection between the brain tumor and the attack before submitting the case to the jury. Morse, *The Aberrational Man—A Tour de Force of Legal Psychiatry*, 13 J. FOR. SCI. 368 (1968).

The following year, *Regina v. Kemp*[80] was reported. The defendant's attack on his wife with a hammer could be understood from the evidence to be attributable to the fact that he suffered from arteriosclerosis, which affected his mind. Again, no insanity plea was entered. This time, however, the trial court refused to instruct on automatism and instructed the jury only on the defense of insanity. The medical opinion at the trial was divided on whether the defendant suffered from a "disease of the mind" for purposes of *M'Naghten*. The trial court decided the defendant did, in fact, suffer from a disease of the mind based squarely on the ground that the defendant ought not to be released because he was dangerous.

Thus, the lines were drawn on the issue for the House of Lords to resolve in *Bratty v. Attorney-General for Northern Ireland*.[81] The defendant had strangled the victim, a family friend, with her stocking in his car while they were running an errand. Trial evidence indicated that the defendant was suffering from psychomotor epilepsy at the time of the attack on the victim. No drinking was involved. He described a "terrible feeling" and "blackness" that overcame him but had considerable recall of the actual homicide.

The defense requested submission of three theories: automatism, or involuntary act; lack of *mens rea* (diminished capacity) and insanity. The trial court submitted the case only on the theory of insanity, but the jury found him guilty of murder. The House of Lords affirmed the conviction and upheld the refusal to instruct on automatism despite the evidence of psychomotor epilepsy, thereby upholding the trial court's decision to submit the case to the jury only on grounds of insanity, which left them the options only of convicting the defendant of murder or sending him to confinement in a hospital. The main point of the House of Lords was that the evidence indicated that psychomotor epilepsy was a disease of the mind and, therefore, provided no basis for submission on a general plea. A distinction had now been made which required for an automatism instruction proof that the conduct was not attributable to a disease of the mind.[82] "[I]f the involuntary act proceeds from a disease of the mind, it gives rise to a defence of insanity, but not to a defence of automatism."[83]

In *Bratty*, the Court of Criminal Appeal described automatism as a state in which the person, though capable of moving about and engaging

---

80. Regina v. Kemp, [1956] 3 All E.R. 249.

81. Bratty v. Attorney-General for Northern Ireland, [1961] 3 All E.R. 523.

82. Williams, *Murder—Drunkenness—Insane and Non-Insane Automatism*, 1962 CAMBRIDGE L.J. 3 (1962), (discussing the allocation of the burden of proof to the defendant on the issue of insanity); Leigh, *Automatism and Insanity*, 5 CRIM. L.Q. 160 (1962).

83. *Bratty* at 533. The opinion by Viscount Kilmuir, L.C., acknowledged that in the event of factual dispute as to whether a "disease of the mind" was involved, it might be proper to submit both insanity and automatism to the jury. *Bratty* at 528.

in action, "is not conscious of what he is doing...It means unconscious involuntary action, and it is a defence because the mind does not go with what is being done."[84] The concurring opinion of Lord Denning placed his decision squarely on disposition grounds: "It seems to me that any mental disorder which has manifested itself in violence and is prone to recur is a disease of the mind. At any rate it is the sort of disease for which a person should be detained in hospital rather than be given an unqualified acquittal."[85] In practice then, insanity and automatism became mutually exclusive because a defendant would not let a case of automatism be tried as insanity, given the disposition involved with that plea, and the courts would not let a case of insanity be tried as a defense of automatism for the same reason. Since all of this turned on whether the actor's claim fell within the meaning of "disease of the mind," the putative task for future cases would be to categorize the defense as involving disease of the mind or not.

Though it may have seemed the problem was resolved, *Regina v. Quick*[86] shortly brought out the difficulty which primarily originates in the realization that the theory of "disease of the mind" accommodates more murkiness of meaning than previously assumed. The defendant had attacked a person while under the effects of hypoglycemia. The testimony indicated that hypoglycemia occurs when there is more insulin in the bloodstream than sugar to cope with that insulin and has much the same effect as an excess of alcohol in the body. Sugar is an antidote, but in its absence, the sufferer may become aggressive and violent and may be out of control or not know what he is doing; amnesia may also result for the affected period and following the aggressive and violent periods, he or she will eventually become unconscious.[87] There was testimony that the defendant several times before had become violent when his blood sugar got too low. The evidence also indicated that he had taken the prescribed insulin that morning (although there was also a possibility that too much had been prescribed), but he had also admitted to drinking alcohol, and while not noted by the court, that may have increased the impact of the insulin.[88] He also had not eaten, and that can contribute to hyperinsulinism as well.[89]

---

84. *Bratty* at 527.

85. *Bratty* at 534.

86. Regina v. Quick, 1973 Q.B. 910.

87. *Quick* at 915-16.

88. "The hypoglycemic effect of insulin may also be markedly increased" by combining it with alcohol consumption. Ritchie, *The Aliphatic Alcohols,* in GOODMAN & GILMAN'S, THE PHARMACOLOGICAL BASIS OF THERAPEUTICS 372, 378 (A. Gilman, L. Goodman, T. Rall & F. Murad eds. 7th ed. 1985).

89. Larner, *Insulin and Oral Hypoglycemic Drugs; Glucagon,* in GOODMAN & GILMAN'S, THE PHARMACOLOGICAL BASIS OF THERAPEUTICS 1502 (A. Gilman, L. Goodman, T. Rall & F. Murad eds. 7th ed. 1985).

The court held that the trial court erred in requiring the case to be tried only under the insanity defense (thereby causing the defendant to plead guilty) and the defendant could instead rely on the defense of noninsane automatism. The conviction was quashed. When the behavior is caused by an abnormal bodily condition that affects the mind (psychomotor epilepsy in *Bratty*[90]), the defendant must rely on insanity to raise the defense of automatism. If the condition is externally caused, however, as in *Quick,* then it is not a disease or defect of the mind and the defendant can submit evidence of the defense on a plea of not guilty. The court concluded that Quick's condition "was not caused by his diabetes but by his use of the insulin prescribed by his doctor. Such malfunctioning of his mind as there was, was caused by an external factor and not by a bodily disorder in the nature of a disease which disturbed the working of his mind....Quick was entitled to have his defence of automatism left to the jury."[91]

Quick was as concerned with the disposition question as the court in *Bratty,* and the court discussed the dilemma: Why should Quick be sent to a hospital to receive sugar?[92] At the same time, some of the courts involved in these decisions clearly reflect the view that a person with a dangerous, recurrent condition, by his own claim, should not be permitted to plead the case as one of not guilty alone, which includes the automatism defense, but that such cases should be tried under a plea of not guilty by reason of insanity.

> Our task has been to decide what the law means now by the words "disease of the mind." In our judgment the fundamental concept is of a malfunctioning of the mind caused by disease. A malfunctioning of the mind of transitory effect caused by the application to the body of some external factor such as violence, drugs, including anaesthetics, alcohol and hypnotic influences cannot fairly be said to be due to disease.[93]

This would mean that pathological intoxication should be tried as a case of automatism because it is a "malfunctioning of the mind...caused by the application to the body of some external factor such as...alcohol"[94] and that insanity would not be the appropriate plea. But, of course, there are two causes, one internal and one external (drinking), if one wants to

---

90. *Bratty* at 534.
91. *Quick* at 922-23.
92. Mackay, *Non-Organic Automatism—Some Recent Developments,* 1980 CRIM. L. REV. 350, 357.
93. *Quick* at 922.
94. *Quick* at 922.

use that terminology. The utility of this is limited. Is the failure to maintain a proper diet by a person with diabetes or the failure to take medicine by a person prone to attacks of complex partial seizures to be considered an internal or external cause? The possibility and importance of divergent disposition needs are also implicit in the conclusion of Clements, who wrote the following before *Sullivan*, discussed below, was decided by the House of Lords:

> So the question of whether epilepsy amounts in law to insanity or automatism has been judicially answered both ways. It seems from the case law that the judges take into account the degree of seriousness of the charge against an accused who has committed a prima facie offence whilst suffering from an epileptic attack. In *Bratty's* case, for instance, the killing was done in strange circumstances by a dangerous person who might, if acquitted, repeat his performance; it was not something done purely by accident while in thc throws [sic] of a seizure. But in *Hill v. Baxter* it would have been extraordinary in the extreme to say that epilepsy whilst driving amounted to insanity rather than non-insane automatism, and that was the only defence to a charge on a strict liability offence. In other words, the present policy of the courts is to classify epilepsy according to whether the accused prima facie has committed a serious offence against the person. If this is so, then it is arguable that in *R. v. Sullivan*, since the accused was charged initially with a serious offence (causing grievous bodily harm with intent to do so), the proper course would be to follow *Bratty's* case and to hold that the accused was suffering from a disease of the mind and thus insane within the M'Naghten Rules.[95]

In *Regina v. Sullivan*,[96] the defendant was charged with inflicting grievous bodily harm on the victim, a friend of his, and his defense was based on a well supported and undisputed claim that the attack was the result of an epileptic seizure and that no alcohol was involved in precipitating the attack. The expert evidence was "that the appellant's acts in kicking [the victim] had all the characteristics of epileptic automatism at the third or post-ictal stage of petit mal, and that, in view of his history of psychomotor epilepsy and the hospital records of his behaviour during previous seizures, the strong probability was that the

---

95. Clements, *Epilepsy, Insanity and Automatism*, 133 NEW L.J. 949, 951 (1983).
96. Regina v. Sullivan, [1983] 2 All E.R. 673.

appellant's acts of violence...took place while he was going through that stage."[97]

The trial court ruled, presumably on the basis of *Bratty,* that the defense had to be based on insanity, with its resulting detention in a special hospital if successful, and could not be submitted to the jury as a defense of automatism. As a result of this ruling, the defendant changed his plea to guilty and then appealed that trial court's ruling. The judgment of the House of Lords was that a defense based on psychomotor epilepsy had to be tried as a defense of insanity and could not be tried under the defense of automatism, or noninsane automatism as the defense is known in England, and in a unanimous decision, they reaffirmed *Bratty.* Counsel for the defense argued that while the evidence submitted in *Bratty* indicated that psychomotor epilepsy was a disease of the mind, the expert testimony in this case was that to qualify as a mental disease, the disorder must be prolonged for at least a month. The court rejected that view. "The nomenclature adopted by the medical profession may change from time to time; Bratty was tried in 1961. But the meaning of the expression 'disease of the mind' as the cause of 'a defect of reason' remains unchanged for the purposes of the application of the *M'Naghten* Rules," noting their agreement with the view of Devlin, J., in *Regina v. Kemp.* The court held that "[i]f the effect of a disease is to impair these faculties so severely as to have either of the consequences referred to in the latter part of the rules [that he did not know what he was doing or did not know it was wrong], it matters not whether the aetiology of the impairment is organic, as in epilepsy, or functional, or whether the impairment itself is permanent or is transient and intermittent, provided that it subsisted at the time of commission of the act."[98] The court stressed that the "duration of a temporary suspension of the mental faculties of reason, memory and understanding, particularly if, as in the appellant's case, it is recurrent, cannot on any rational ground be relevant to the application by the courts of the *M'Naghten* Rules, though it may be relevant to the course adopted by the Secretary of State, to whom the responsibility for how the defendant is to be dealt with passes after the return of the special verdict of not guilty by reason of insanity."[99] If a disease renders one insane within the meaning of *M'Naghten,* it is a mental disease within that same rule. One supposes, however, that the cause of the disability still must be a disease of some sort. This would mean, as we believe, that pathological intoxication cases may fall within either automatism or insanity, depending upon the source of the difficulty. But, of course, one will get quite different results if distinction is drawn in terms of disease of the mind being distinct from

---

97. *Sullivan* at 675.
98. *Sullivan* at 677.
99. *Sullivan* at 678.

disease of the brain than if the line is between disease of either sort versus causes such as trauma that are not diseases in either sense. Presumably, for example, one would classify pathological intoxication due to alcohol combined with brain damage from syphilis as fit for the insanity defense whereas pathological intoxication attributable to mixing prescription medicine with alcohol as suitable for the automatism defense. Why one would do so is not clear, however. In general terms, one might wish to use the concept of dangerousness to decide whether incarceration is required and the concept of fault to decide whether to incarcerate in a jail or a hospital, but even these are difficult to gauge. The existence of "disease" is not often a reliable basis of prediction of future dangerousness in general, and it most certainly is not in cases of pathological intoxication, nor is the presence or absence of "disease" a decent measure of fault which is more likely, as the courts have said, to turn on the actor's awareness. Thus, while these cases are highly relevant to the ultimate resolution of some of the questions related to pathological intoxication, it is important to bear in mind that the courts in these specific cases often assume that the class of cases under consideration, and therefore the emerging rule, involves only those in which the reaction was not self-induced with or without fault, although that is a rather dubious classification for the facts in *Quick*.

The court in *Sullivan* said, with respect to the decision in *Kemp*,[100] that "I do not regard that judge as excluding the possibility of non-insane automatism, for which the proper verdict would be a verdict of not guilty, in cases where temporary impairment not being self-induced by consuming drink or drugs, results from some external physical factor such as a blow on the head causing concussion or the administration of an anaesthetic for therapeutic purposes."[101]

It would seem that the arteriosclerosis involved in *Kemp* is now reclassified as noninsane automatism. "I mention this because in [*Quick*] Lawton LJ appears to have regarded the ruling in *R v. Kemp* as going as far as this. If it had done, it would have been inconsistent with the speeches in this House in *Bratty*'s case, where *R v. Kemp* was alluded to without disapproval by Viscount Kilmuir LC and received the express approval of Lord Denning."[102] But the question was not pursued further. "The instant case, however, does not in my view afford an appropriate occasion for exploring possible causes of non-insane automatism."[103]

The court again alluded to the disposition problem as well as the labeling onus when it noted that "it is natural to feel reluctant to attach

---

100. Regina v. Kemp, [1956] 3 All E.R. 249.

101. *Sullivan* at 678.

102. *Sullivan* at 678 (citations omitted).

103. *Sullivan* at 678.

the label of insanity to a sufferer from psychomotor epilepsy of the kind to which the appellant was subject" even though in this context it "includes a purely temporary and intermittent suspension of the mental faculties of reason, memory and understanding resulting from the occurrence of an epileptic fit."[104] The court, however, felt bound by the statute regulating insanity pleas.

The disposition issue is addressed in the English draft code proposal on the new verdict of "not guilty by reason of mental disorder." A distinction is drawn there between "purely transient" disorders of the mind, which would lead to an acquittal, and more permanent conditions, which should lead to a verdict of mental disorder. As applied to pathological intoxication, this would require an assessment of the underlying cause of the condition. It also may not contemplate the situation in which the triggering condition, alcohol or other drug consumption, is entirely within the (nonaddicted) actor's control. Which verdict would be indicated?[105] Presumably, as alluded to in *Sullivan*, the answer would be that if noninsane automatism is applicable, the insanity plea will fail for want of mental disease, and the automatism defense would fail due to the fault of the actor, if there was fault, and otherwise noninsane automatism would succeed. But *Sullivan* did not hold that the insanity plea would fail for want of a mental disease; it held that the automatism defense would fail in its company.

Fenwick summarized his understanding of the English dichotomy between sane and insane automatism as: "The law on automatism in England is muddled and requires revision."[106]

> It is clear that English law relating to sleepwalking is at the moment confused and illogical. A sleepwalker may arise from his bed, murder, plead automatism, and be set free, while an epileptic who arises from his bed in a post-ictal confusional state, murders, and pleads automatism, must be sent to a psychiatric hospital and probably detained there for many years. The Denning [*Bratty*] ruling was that any violent act which is carried out during an automatism and is prone to recur is due to a disease of the mind. If this is applicable to epilepsy, it should be equally applicable to sleepwalking. The difference between sane and insane automatism, although pragmatic, makes little medical sense.[107]

---

104. *Sullivan* at 678.

105. *See* Wasik, *Codification: Mental Disorder and Intoxication Under the Draft Criminal Code*, 50 J. CRIM. L. 393, 398 (1986).

106. Fenwick, *Somnambulism and the Law: A Review*, 5 BEHAV. SCI. & LAW 343 (1987).

107. Fenwick at 355.

But if etiology leads in one direction and disposition needs lead toward another, it is not likely that "pragmatic" law will make much sense, viewed solely from the perspective of medical nosology.

AUTOMATISM IN THE AMERICAN COURTS

The American decisions reflect the difficulty the English courts have had with the disposition issue.[108] However, several things are different in American jurisdictions. First, most jurisdictions will not permit submission of an insanity instruction without a defense request to do so,[109] as is permitted under English law and illustrated in *Kemp*.[110] Indeed, one will not be given without a special plea. Commenting on this procedural point in *Bratty*, Lord Denning said:

> When it is asserted that the accused did an involuntary act in a state of automatism, the defence necessarily puts in issue the state of mind of the accused man: and thereupon it is open to the prosecution to show what his true state of mind was. The old notion that only the defence can raise a defence of insanity is now gone. The prosecution are entitled to raise it, and it is their duty to do so rather than allow a dangerous person to be at large. The Trial of Lunatics Act, 1883, s.2, says that where "it is given in evidence" that the person was insane, the jury shall return a verdict of guilty but insane. It does not say that the defence alone can give such evidence. The prosecution can give it.[111]

While it is true that in American courts the defendant completely controls whether or not to plead not guilty by reason of insanity, it also remains true that courts control the admissibility of evidence. Although American courts cannot, as the English can do, force a plea of not guilty

---

108. Discharge conditions and the existence in some states of conditional discharge authority are discussed in S. BRAKEL, J. PARRY & B. WEINER, THE MENTALLY DISABLED AND THE LAW 731-34 (3d ed. 1985).

109. *But see* Whalem v. United States, 346 F.2d 812 (D.C. Cir. 1965). Constitutional arguments against the "*Whalem* view" are presented in Cohn, *Offensive Use of the Insanity Defense: Imposing the Insanity Defense Over the Defendant's Objection*, 15 HASTINGS CONST. L.Q. 295 (1988).

Even though the courts cannot *sua sponte* interject a plea of not guilty by reason of insanity, it would appear that they can do so on the issue of the defendant's current capacity to stand trial. However, this would seldom be of any utility in a case of pathological intoxication, for it is a temporary, even if recurrent, incapacity which would not ordinarily impair the defendant's ability to assist in his or her defense.

110. Regina v. Kemp, [1956] 3 All E.R. 249.

111. Bratty v. Attorney-General for Northern Ireland, [1961] 3 All E.R. 523, 534.

by reason of insanity, sometimes they can and do deny either alternative defense instructions such as automatism, or more commonly, the admissibility of expert evidence of insanity, when the defendant suffers from mental illness but does not plead insanity. This accomplishes the same procedural effect as the English rule, albeit in a negative and indirect way. But most of these cases where this occurs are actually *mens rea* defense cases.

There is no plea of automatism; this issue is tried under a general plea of not guilty. The practical question, then, will be whether the courts will permit introduction of psychiatric or other expert testimony to prove the existence of an underlying mental disease to establish a noninsanity defense. That is where the battle will be fought as well as at the instruction stage. The issue, writ large, becomes whether a defense factually resting on mental disease or defect disqualifies a defendant from using the defense of automatism or any defense other than insanity. However, we still have no clear picture of the meaning of "mental disease" other than that dictated by the desired disposition, and that is often not clear.

Despite public sentiment, which seems always unfriendly to the insanity defense, the defense of insanity is treated with less hostility by prosecutors and some judges when the defense of automatism is alternatively available to a defendant; then a verdict of not guilty by reason of insanity is seen as a highly desirable outcome.[112] In addition, authorities recognizing the defense of automatism in American jurisdictions are fairly sparse, both in case law and statutes, and they are difficult to classify.[113] The explicit English distinction between noninsane automatism and insane automatism is not used at all. But the basic policy issue (disposition of the defendant) is the same, and so one supposes that the same distinctions are drawn, but that they are drawn covertly. The final point of departure from the English cases is that mutual exclusivity of automatism and insanity is generally not the view held, although there is a great deal of uncertainty about the matter.

Caddell[114] is one of the principal American cases to consider the defense of automatism. The defendant was convicted by a jury of kidnapping and rape of a child. The defendant maintained he had amnesia for the time of the rape and pleaded both not guilty and not guilty by reason of insanity. Although the court affirmed the conviction

---

112. Harding, *Sane and Insane Automatism in Australia: Some Dilemmas, Developments and Suggested Reforms*, 4 INT'L J. L. & PSYCHIAT. 73 (1981).

113. Annotation, *Automatism or Unconsciousness as Defense to Criminal Charge*, 27 A.L.R.4th 1067 (1984), classifies the states as (1) automatism is distinct from insanity and (2) automatism is "includable" in insanity. Annotation at 1076-78. Of course, these are not mutually exclusive categories.

114. State v. Caddell, 287 N.C. 266, 215 S.E.2d 348 (1975).

against a defense contention that the burden of proof should have been on the state, the court did acknowledge that automatism is a defense distinct from insanity. Throughout the cases, these two issues will recur: Can a defendant try a "mental disease" case as automatism, and what is the burden of proof on the automatism defense?

The defendant's evidence (contrary to the advice of his lawyer) was largely provided by a psychiatrist who was the director of the forensic unit at a state hospital to which the defendant had been committed seven times prior to this case. This defense witness testified that the defendant was not insane at the time of the offense. The court recognized that automatism differed from insanity because it need not be due to a disease or defect of the mind, although it did not seem to be of the converse view that the defense of automatism must be due to something other than a "disease of the mind." While the court cites *Bratty* and some of the California cases on the question of the burden of proof, the court is more influenced by *Bratty* where, regarding the burden-of-proof issue, the House of Lords said:

> When the only cause that is assigned for an involuntary act is drunkenness, then it is only necessary to leave drunkenness to the jury, with the consequential directions, and not to leave automatism at all. When the only cause that is assigned for it is a disease of the mind, then it is only necessary to leave insanity to the jury, and not automatism. When the cause assigned is concussion or sleepwalking, there should be some evidence from which it can reasonably be inferred before it should be left to the jury. If it is said to be due to concussion, there should be evidence of a severe blow shortly beforehand. If it is said to be sleepwalking, there should be some credible support for it. His mere assertion that he was asleep will not suffice. Once a proper foundation is thus laid for automatism, the matter becomes at large and must be left to the jury....But at the end of the day the legal burden comes into play and requires that the jury should be satisfied beyond a reasonable doubt that the act was a voluntary act.[115]

It would appear that the burden of going forward with some evidence lies with the defense but that the burden of proof does not shift. What is different about automatism under this view is that the court is to make an initial determination whether more than merely the defendant's claim is presented before submitting the issue to the jury at all. But if it is, the burden remains with the state. There is, however, some question

---

115. *Bratty* at 535-36, per Lord Denning.

whether the ultimate burden shifts to the defendant as well in involuntary act cases.[116]

Indeed, the North Carolina court seemed to go further, saying that they saw no difference in this respect between insanity and intoxication on the one hand and unconsciousness or automatism on the other. The view was that "[i]n all three defenses the contention is the same—the defendant did the act, but should not be convicted because the requisite mental element was not present."[117] It is not clear to what extent they have adopted some variation on the "substantial evidence" rule of the English courts.[118] They do refer to the defense as an "affirmative defense," however. To the extent their previous decision in *Mercer*[119] had held that "[u]nconsciousness is never an affirmative defense," it is overruled.

The concurrence would not overrule *Mercer* because it was not necessary to do so on the evidence in this case. The position is that the state has the burden to prove the existence of a voluntary act under *Winship*.[120] This opinion also quotes from *Bratty* that the burden remains on the state after the defendant has met the burden of going forward. With respect to the "substantial evidence" limitation on getting to the jury on the automatism defense, the opinion is expressed that the court cannot deny the defense just because it is not corroborated by medical testimony; this would allow it to get to the jury solely on the defendant's own testimony.

In *State v. Williams*,[121] decided four years later, in affirming a murder conviction over a contention that an instruction on the defense of unconsciousness should have been given as requested, the court quotes from *Mercer*[122] to the effect that the unconsciousness defense applies only to persons of sound mind such as those who have epilepsy or have received a blow to the head.[123] At any rate, they agree that automatism does not apply to a drunk, which is what the evidence in this case

---

116. 2 P. ROBINSON, CRIMINAL LAW DEFENSES, § 171(d), at 266-67 n.30 (1984).

117. *Caddell* at 289, 215 S.E.2d at 363.

118. Lord Devlin said in Hill v. Baxter, [1958] 1 Q.B. 277, 285, that "I do not doubt that there are genuine cases of automatism and the like, but I do not see how the layman can safely attempt without the help of some medical or scientific evidence to distinguish the genuine from the fraudulent."

119. State v. Mercer, 275 N.C. 108, 165 S.E.2d 328 (1969).

120. In re Winship, 397 U.S. 358, 90 S. Ct. 1068, 25 L. Ed. 2d 368 (1970).

121. State v. Williams, 296 N.C. 693, 252 S.E.2d 739 (1979).

122. *Mercer* in turn was quoting from People v. Wilson, 66 Cal. 2d 749, 59 Cal. Rptr. 156, 427 P.2d 820 (1967).

123. *See, e.g.*, State v. Snyder, 70 N.C. App. 335, 319 S.E.2d 668 (1984), *review denied*, 312 N.C. 89, 321 S.E.2d 907 (1984), holding that the defendant should have been permitted to adduce evidence of a blow to the head and a resulting concussion as proof of unconsciousness even though he had also been drinking heavily.

indicated,[124] although the fact that the defendant has been drinking does not preclude the defense either.[125]

In *State v. Smith,*[126] the court reversed a robbery conviction because the trial court did not instruct on automatism despite the lack of a defense request for such an instruction. The defendant had been drinking heavily and had taken narcotic drugs. She claimed amnesia for the robbery.

Then, in *State v. Jerrett,*[127] the court reversed a conviction for murder and robbery on the failure to instruct on automatism in a case in which the defense rested on post-traumatic syndrome resulting from the Vietnam war.[128] *Caddell* had quoted *Bratty* for the view that "[t]he evidence of the man himself will rarely be sufficient unless it is supported by medical evidence which points to the cause of the mental incapacity."[129] In *Mercer,* the court had said: "Where defendant's evidence, if accepted, discloses facts sufficient in law to constitute a defense to the crime for which he is indicted, the court is required to instruct the jury as to the legal principles applicable thereto. What weight, if any, is to be given such evidence, is for determination by the jury."[130] The court was urged to adopt the view taken in *Bratty* that the defendant's testimony, taken alone, will not support an instruction on automatism, but the North Carolina court said: "We need not determine, however, whether *Mercer* was correctly decided because here there was corroborating evidence tending to support the defense of unconsciousness."[131] In the most recent case, there was expert testimony so that the court did not confront the issue.[132]

The Illinois courts dealt with the automatism defense in *People v. Grant,*[133] where the defendant was convicted of aggravated battery of a police officer. The case was tried solely on the defense of legal insanity, but the point of contention on appeal would become the trial court's failure to instruct on the defense of automatism. The Illinois Court of

---

124. The same is true of one who takes "angel dust"; an instruction on automatism need not be given. State v. Boone, 307 N.C. 198, 297 S.E.2d 585 (1982).

125. State v. Snyder, 70 N.C. App. 335, 319 S.E.2d 668 (1984).

126. State v. Smith, 59 N.C. App. 227, 296 S.E.2d 315 (1982).

127. State v. Jerrett, 309 N.C. 239, 307 S.E.2d 339 (1983).

128. The defendant also claimed that he was exposed to "agent orange" in Vietnam and that a previous examination had revealed symptoms of that exposure.

129. *Caddell* at 362.

130. State v. Mercer, 165 S.E.2d 328, 334 (N.C. 1969).

131. *Jerrett* at 266, 307 S.E.2d at 353.

132. State v. Fields, 324 N.C. 204, 376 S.E.2d 740 (1989). It is also interesting that in *Fields* the court noted for the first time that civil commitment was possible without using the insanity plea to accomplish it. That is an obvious point, but one not often made by courts in criminal cases.

133. People v. Grant, 71 Ill. 2d 551, 377 N.E.2d 4 (1978), *rev'g* People v. Grant, 46 Ill. App. 3d 125, 360 N.E.2d 809 (1977).

Appeals reversed the conviction on the ground that the trial court should have *sua sponte* instructed on the automatism defense in addition to the instructions given on the insanity defense. The dissenting opinion at the intermediate level disagreed with the majority opinion only on that point. The Illinois Supreme Court reversed, holding that the automatism defense was adequately covered by the volitional impairment aspects of the insanity instruction that was given, at least when the defense did not request a separate instruction on automatism.

The defendant was drinking in a bar where he had four drinks over a period of two and one half hours. A dispute involving others in the bar resulted in the police removing another patron. The defendant joined a large crowd outside cheering for the patron when "the defendant burst through the crowd, and, using a parking meter for leverage, he leaped into the air, striking [an officer] twice in the face."[134] The defendant was taken to jail where an hour later he had a grand mal seizure. He claimed amnesia for the episode. Evidence indicated that he had a history of epilepsy and violent attacks on other persons. One such episode in a hospital had been so severe that an officer had shot the defendant to stop his knife attack. He had convictions for voluntary manslaughter and aggravated assault.

The only expert witness to testify, a psychiatrist, was called by the defense, and his diagnosis was that at the time of the offense, the defendant suffered from both alcoholism and epilepsy. He described both grand mal and psychomotor seizures, and his testimony was summarized by the court:

> The psychomotor seizure, he testified, is less obvious to the lay observer. An epileptic lapsing into a psychomotor seizure may be completely mobile and may converse, although with reduced coherence. He noted, however, that a psychomotor seizure is similar to a grand mal seizure in that it is a trance-like state during which the epileptic is unaware of what he is doing or what he has done and is incapable of controlling his actions. Although alcohol, as well as excitement and hyperventilation, may precipitate a psychomotor seizure, the furor of a seizure, once commenced, is independent of the intoxication. A psychomotor seizure can last for seconds or minutes and often precedes a grand mal seizure.[135]

The court also notes that "[a]t the time of the tavern incident, the defendant was taking medication to control both his epileptic condition

---

134. *Grant* at 46 Ill. App. 3d at 127, 360 N.E.2d at 812.
135. *Grant* at 71 Ill. 2d at 555, 377 N.E.2d at 6.

and his nervousness,"[136] although the drug is not identified and that point does not appear to have been pursued. Only very weak lay testimony was presented to rebut the existence of a psychomotor attack at the time of the assault, but the judges were of the opinion that there was enough to justify the jury's verdict. The opinions in the appellate court explore to some extent the nature of the automatism defense and its relation to the insanity defense.

> In the language of section 4-1 of our Criminal Code, it [automatism] is manifested by the performance of involuntary acts that can be of a simple or complex nature. Clinically, automatism has been identified in a wide variety of physical conditions including: epilepsy, organic brain disease, concussional states following head injuries, drug abuse, hypoglycemia[137] and, less commonly, in some types of schizophrenia and acute emotional disturbance.[138]

The court also dealt with the *Bratty* treatment of the relationship between automatism and insanity defenses by quoting from LaFave and Scott:

> If, as just noted, the insanity defense has been utilized as if it "superseded" a no-mental-state defense for those who might pose a continuing danger because of their mental illness, it might logically be asked whether there has developed a comparable relationship between the insanity defense and the no-voluntary-act automatism defense. That is, is there here as well pressure to "make the insanity defense the exclusive avenue for bringing subjective evidence into the trial,"[139] to the end that those who did not act voluntarily might be committed if there is some chance that they are still dangerous?
>
> The few American cases in this area are not particularly helpful in this regard, although they do reflect that what has been described herein as automatism has sometimes been

---

136. *Grant* at 556, 377 N.E.2d at 7.

137. There is even a report that hypoglycemia and psychomotor epilepsy can be related. In Ellenburg v. State, 353 So. 2d 810 (Ala. Crim. App. 1977), which involved a verdict of murder in the second degree on a charge of first degree, on a plea of not guilty and not guilty by reason of insanity, a psychiatrist testified that hypoglycemia could trigger an episode of psychomotor epilepsy resulting in a violent attack. The evidence that this actually occurred, however, was not strong.

138. People v. Grant, 46 Ill. App. 3d 125, 360 N.E.2d 809, 814 (1977).

139. A. GOLDSTEIN, THE INSANITY DEFENSE 207 (1967).

instead labelled insanity, perhaps for the reason suggested above.[140]

The dissenting opinion in *Grant* at the appellate court level addressed the policy issue in more detail. First, they made it clear "that an epileptic striking another person while in a state of automatism not only lacks the volition to perform a voluntary act but is also insane...."[141] Then they addressed the disposition question:

> I share with Lord Denning and the majority of commentators on the subject (LaFave and Scott, 341 [1972 student edition]) a belief in the need for protective custody for persons who repeatedly attack others while in a state of automatism. The situation merits an attempt by the legislature to devise a procedure balancing the rights of the public to be protected against the rights of the person subject to automatism to be at liberty and basing any deprivation of that liberty upon the degree of danger presented by that individual....I do not agree that the Criminal Code is sufficient. Most of the authority cited by the majority discussing automatism is of comparatively recent origin, and the comments of the drafting committee give no indication of any consideration of the problem by that committee.[142]

The opinion of the Illinois Supreme Court agreed with the characterization of the automatism defense as overlapping with the insanity defense to the extent that "[b]oth defenses adhere to the fundamental principle that a person is not criminally responsible for an involuntary act," and that "[t]o that extent, the defense of involuntary conduct and the insanity defense are alternative theories at the disposal of a defendant whose volition to control or prevent his conduct is at issue."[143] They held that "the jury rejected the evidence which would have supported the need for an instruction on the defense of involuntary conduct."[144] The defense argument seems to have been that the jury verdict could have been based on a rejection of psychomotor epileptic attacks as a "mental disease or defect" and hence did not obviate the need for an independent instruction on involuntary act. To this, the court merely said that "[w]hether the defendant's epileptic seizure could be

---

140. W. LAFAVE & A. SCOTT, CRIMINAL LAW 338-39 (1972).

141. *Grant* at 134, 360 N.E.2d at 817.

142. People v. Grant, 46 Ill. App. 3d 125, 136, 360 N.E.2d 809, 818 (1977) (dissenting opinion) (citation omitted).

143. People v. Grant, 71 Ill. 2d 551, 558-59, 377 N.E.2d 4, 8 (1978) (citations omitted).

144. *Grant* at 559, 377 N.E.2d at 8 (1978).

characterized as a mental disease or defect for the purposes of the insanity defense was never at issue,"[145] presumably meaning that the prosecution, not the defense, had conceded the point.

It has been argued that the "reasoning of the court in the Grant case must be rejected because it is neurologically indefensible to place epilepsy and automatism in the category of insanity. The National Association for Epilepsy has been fighting for years to have the labels of insanity and mentally defective removed from this disease."[146] Professor Jeffery is not, of course, arguing for the conviction of Grant by denying to him the defensive label of legal insanity. The argument simply is that if the origin is organic, it is not insanity in the sense meant in *M'Naghten*.

In *People v. Gaines*,[147] a murder conviction following a plea of not guilty and a trial to the court on a defense theory of automatism was affirmed over an appeal contention that the trial court improperly considered the validity of the defense of automatism. It was not disputed that the defendant had stabbed a woman to death, had been drinking (a pint of liquor), and threatened to kill the arresting officers on the street when he was apprehended with the knife in his clothing. Evidence regarding amnesia was in conflict. The defendant claimed it, but an officer testified that he spoke derogatorily to the victim in the emergency room immediately following his arrest.

Both a CAT scan and an EEG were administered at the request of Dr. Anderson for the defense. The pre-activation EEG's, awake and asleep, revealed abnormalities indicative of brain injury.[148] An alcohol activation test was also attempted, but the defendant proved too uncooperative. Dr. Lorimer testified that he had made special studies of "rage attacks," which are clinical manifestations of epilepsy. During an alcohol activation test, he gave the defendant five ounces of liquor and the defendant demanded the whole bottle. He also became verbally abusive and threatened the doctor. This was characterized as a rage attack. Dr. Lorimer "also believed the defendant qualified as a

---

145. *Grant* at 559, 377 N.E.2d at 8. *See also* People v. Dunigan, 96 Ill. App. 3d 799, 421 N.E.2d 1319, 1338 (1981), ("the [trial] court ruled that there was no evidence at trial that defendant's hypoglycemia might or could have caused involuntary criminal behavior"); People v. Wirth, 77 Ill. App. 3d 253, 395 N.E.2d 1106 (1979), ("In *Grant*, the defendant was suffering from a physical disease. In the instant case, the defendant had no disease and his only problem was one of voluntary intoxication. In the instant case, there is no actual evidence of any organic impairment of defendant at any time. The defendant's evidence consists simply of hypothetical speculation by a psychiatrist, clearly different from specific and positive testimony. There is no evidence in this record that hypoglycemia might or could cause involuntary criminal behavior. We accordingly reject defendant's contention." *Wirth* at 258, 395 N.E.2d at 1110).

146. C. JEFFERY, ATTACKS ON THE INSANITY DEFENSE: BIOLOGICAL PSYCHIATRY AND NEW PERSPECTIVES ON CRIMINAL BEHAVIOR 87 (1985).

147. People v. Gaines, 93 Ill. App. 3d 71, 416 N.E.2d 1156 (1981).

148. *Gaines* at 74, 416 N.E.2d at 1158.

pathological intoxicant. According to the doctor, when the defendant drinks whiskey, it complicates his organic brain syndrome and aggravates his epilepsy."[149]

Dr. Gibbs also testified for the defense, but he disputed the EEG interpretation, believing it to be normal. In addition, there was evidence that the defendant had six prior hospitalizations in various mental health facilities but he had not been previously diagnosed as having organic brain syndrome. The court does not say what the prior diagnoses involved. Two doctors testified for the state. At least one of them examined the defendant and all of the records and concluded that the defendant had "an explosive personality with paranoid and anti-social features,"[150] and was sane at the time of the crime.

> The record reveals the trial judge considered the defense of automatism and agreed that the defendant did suffer from organic brain syndrome, but found that this did not preclude the defendant from appreciating the criminality of his actions nor did it preclude the defendant from conforming his actions to those required by law.[151]

Yet the trial transcript actually suggests that the trial court said essentially two things relevant to its findings. One was that the diminished capacity defense applied only to specific intent crimes, and the other was that the defendant was legally sane at the time of the offense. Neither issue was involved in the case since the defense was automatism, not diminished capacity or insanity, yet the appellate court avoided the problem by observing that by finding the defendant sane, the trial court had also precluded a defense of automatism, which was the basis of the defense, presumably on the view that it amounted to a finding of a voluntary act. The logic is questionable: The trial court could have found that the defendant knew right from wrong despite his mental disease, leaving undecided the question of the voluntariness of his act. The point, perhaps, is that a trial court sitting as fact-finder is rarely found in error.

But why did the court convict? That question cuts through every case discussed in this work, and obviously, we cannot answer it with confidence, but we can speculate, for what it is worth. The major point that stands out to us is that even without the evidence of prior "rage attacks," this event alone is enough to persuade the court that the defendant did indeed kill and that he might do it again. The case should have been tried under an insanity plea. While automatism is a "logical"

---

149. *Gaines* at 75, 416 N.E.2d at 1159.
150. *Gaines* at 75, 416 N.E.2d at 1159.
151. *Gaines* at 76-77, 416 N.E.2d at 1160.

defense, according to substantive criminal law theory, it is rarely a satisfactory resolution of the quandary presented by these cases. The court in this case, as a jury would be in jury trials, was confronted with the choice of convicting and perhaps incarcerating the defendant or acquitting and freeing him.

The epilepsy situation is confusing enough, and Harding[152] points out some of the significance of the question:

> The mention of epilepsy gets to the core of the problem which has been of concern throughout this paper: legal ambivalence and unease in dealing with mental conditions. Epilepsy is certainly a disorder of the brain; the judicial impulse is to insist that a "disease of the mind" encompasses at the very least such a disorder. Yet approximately one person in two hundred suffers from some kind of epilepsy; for most of them it is a controllable condition that does not prevent their leading full and normal lives. It is quite unrealistic, therefore, to characterize all epilepsy as insanity for the purposes of the criminal law. Consequently, the decisions and dicta are conflicting, and the matter cannot yet be regarded as settled.[153]

The legal response to the defense of pathological reaction to alcohol is even more complex than the case of epilepsy because many cases of pathological reaction to alcohol are cases of temporal lobe epilepsy in which the seizure is triggered by alcohol. But it is not clear that a person who has manifested violent behavior while in the throes of a seizure triggered by alcohol, which is under his control if he is not an alcoholic, will be similarly afflicted without any external cause. In the pathological reaction to alcohol situation, the defendant is in control: Abstinence from alcohol, in combination with drug therapy, should prevent any future attacks. But the question will remain with the courts whether he will do so. The American situation is exacerbated by the lack of clear authority to maintain control without complete incarceration over defendants found not guilty by reason of insanity, i.e., conditional discharge from mental hospitals is not uniformly available.[154]

---

152. Harding, *Sane and Insane Automatism in Australia: Some Dilemmas, Developments and Suggested Reforms*, 4 INT'L J. L. & PSYCHIAT. 73 (1981).

153. Harding at 80 (footnote omitted).

154. Some states do so provide, and two states have especially well constructed provisions dealing with aftercare of releasees. S. BRAKEL, J. PARRY & B. WEINER, THE MENTALLY DISABLED AND THE LAW 732-34 (3d ed. 1985), discussing special provisions in Maryland and Oregon.

The *Fulcher*[155] decision by the Wyoming Supreme Court dealt with the usual question of evidence sufficiency based on psychiatric evidence and upheld an assault conviction over that objection. More importantly, the court held that such expert opinion evidence could be admitted despite the failure of the defense to plead not guilty by reason of insanity, and in doing so, it gave significant recognition to the defense of automatism as an alternative to the insanity defense, possibly even overlapping with that defense.

The defendant was arrested for public intoxication when he was found lying in an alley, evidently having been beaten up, and placed in a cell with another prisoner, whom he then attacked. He claimed amnesia for the incident. The case was tried on a plea of not guilty. He claimed that a doctor had diagnosed his condition as a concussion from the earlier fight he lost. A forensic psychiatrist also testified that, in his opinion, the defendant had suffered brain injury "and was in a state of traumatic automatism at the time of his attack"[156] on the victim in the jail.[157]

After seemingly reaching out to generate the opportunity to discuss automatism, the majority opinion was careful to delimit the issue:

> Automatism *may* be caused by an abnormal condition of the mind capable of being designated a mental illness or deficiency. Automatism may also be manifest in a person with a perfectly healthy mind. *In this opinion we are only concerned with the defense of automatism occurring in a person with a healthy mind.* To further narrow the issue to be decided in this case, we are concerned with alleged automatism caused by concussion.[158]

The court underscored their awareness that the principle policy reason for making a distinction between automatism and insanity is the issue of disposition of the defendant.

> Unless the plea of automatism, separate and apart from the plea of mental illness or deficiency is allowed, certain anomalies will result. For example, if the court determines that the automatistic defendant is sane, but refuses to rec-

---

155. Fulcher v. State, 633 P.2d 142 (Wyo. 1981).

156. *Fulcher* at 144.

157. Since the evidence was admitted and this was a defense appeal from the ensuing conviction, one assumes that the relevance of the issue of admissibility is related to the prosecution's efforts to rebut the argument by the defense that the state's evidence was not sufficient to convict, the prosecution arguing that the jury even heard evidence favorable to the defense which they should not have heard.

158. *Fulcher* at 145 (emphasis added).

> ognize automatism, the defendant has no defense to the crime with which he is charged. If found guilty, he faces a prison term. The rehabilitative value of imprisonment for the automatistic offender who has committed the offense unconsciously is nonexistent. The cause of the act was an uncontrollable physical disorder that may never recur and is not a moral deficiency.[159]

The converse situation that would arise if the case had to be tried under insanity law is just as anomalous: "[T]reatment is not suited to unconscious behavior resulting from a bump on the head."[160] This is Wyoming's version of the English lump-of-sugar impasse.

The "mental deficiency" statute was further defined to include brain damage, however.[161] To meet this statutory problem, the court said that "'brain damage' contemplated in the statute is some serious and irreversible condition having an impact upon the ability of the person to function. It is undoubtedly something far more significant than a temporary and transitory condition."[162] And this is Wyoming's equivalent case of a malady that may affect mental processes but that is temporary and not recurrent.

As to the burden of proof on the automatism defense, the court chose to follow *Caddell*[163] and held that the defense is an affirmative defense with the burden on the defendant.

While existing Wyoming law had substituted the term "mental illness or deficiency" for the older "insanity" term, the court equated the terms only for purposes of the issue whether such evidence of the defendant's mental condition was admissible though he refused to plead not guilty by reason of "mental illness." The majority held that the trial court had properly received the evidence. The concurring opinion (concurring only because the conviction in the end was affirmed) was of the opinion that this testimony should have been excluded. They would have put the case under a state statute which provided that "[e]vidence that a person is not responsible for criminal conduct by reason of mental illness or deficiency is not admissible at the trial of the defendant unless a plea of 'not guilty by reason of mental illness or deficiency' is made."[164]

---

159. *Fulcher* at 146.
160. *Fulcher* at 146.
161. WYO. STAT. § 7-11-301(a)(iii) (1977).
162. *Fulcher* at 146.
163. State v. Caddell, 287 N.C. 266, 215 S.E.2d 348 (1975).
164. *Fulcher* at 148 (concurring opinion), citing WYO. STAT. § 7-11-304(c) (1977).

Whether or not the evidence was admissible when the restriction on evidence was limited to "insanity," the concurrence believed that "brain damage" clearly fell within its prohibition.[165]

The dissent took a position on the disposition point that underscores its difficulty. That opinion quoted the Model Penal Code provision that "A person is not guilty of an offense unless his liability is based on conduct that includes a voluntary act or the omission to perform an act of which he is physically capable,"[166] and they cited it for the purpose of noting that Wyoming had not adopted the statute. Similarly, the California cases on automatism are dismissed[167] as attributable to the California statute.[168] The opinion carefully avoided taking the position that voluntary acts were not required for criminal liability as a general proposition. The argument was the more limited position that the defense of involuntary act need not be recognized as a defense separately from the defense of insanity. "Wyoming did not adopt that part of the ALI Model Penal Code which would consider automatism as a separate defense...."[169] But this would virtually require the court to be willing to find "mental disease" (or, under the statute involved in *Fulcher*, a "mental illness or deficiency") in any case in which the actor commits an unconscious "act" which would be a crime if he were conscious. So in this case, they are forced to the position that a blow to the head results in "mental illness or deficiency."

Whatever the answer to that question should be, the position taken in this opinion still leaves the consequent query of what the mental hospital staff is supposed to do for the "acquitted" actor. Perhaps the answer is that they are to hold him until it is clear that he is no longer dangerous, if that seems necessary. But the sugar-lump argument for broad recognition of an automatism defense has as its central premise the assumption that a sentencing, now committing, judge has available only the extreme alternative of total commitment to an institution or nothing at all, and that may be a premise with considerable validity in many states today. We take these automatism cases this far in this detail because many of the pathological intoxication cases take us to the same quandary: The problem is the actor needs to not drink, not mix pills, take medication as prescribed, avoid certain chemicals and other situations not manifestly requiring intervention for professional service. Virtually by definition, pathological intoxication situations are controllable once the contributing circumstances are understood.

---

165. *Fulcher* at 149.
166. MODEL PENAL CODE § 2.01 (Proposed Official Draft 1962).
167. *Fulcher* at 155.
168. CAL. PENAL CODE § 26 (West 1988).
169. *Fulcher* at 156.

Clearly, this quandary needs legislative attention in most states. Were the claims made in this case actually believed, something like psychiatric probation would be called for, but few states have any such provision. Indeed, it must be with some irony that the concurring opinion points out that under a Wyoming law applicable to this case:

> If the court finds that the person is no longer affected by mental illness or deficiency, or that he no longer presents a substantial risk of danger to himself or others and is not in need of care, supervision or treatment, the court shall order him discharged from custody.[170]

The statutes provided for traditional commitment,[171] but they also provided for conditions of release, termination and commitment.

> If the court finds that the person is affected by mental illness or deficiency and presents a substantial risk of danger to himself or others, but can be controlled adequately and given proper care, supervision and treatment if released on supervision, the court shall order him released subject to such supervisory orders of the court as are appropriate in the interests of justice and the welfare of the defendant. The court may appoint any person or state, county or local agency which the court considers capable of supervising the person upon release.[172]

Thus, it appears incongruous that one of the prominent cases legitimizing automatism as a defense distinct from and possibly alternative to insanity also emanates from a state that seems to have recognized the need for flexible responses by recent legislative changes.

The issue is whether automatism should exist as a defense in addition to and distinct from the insanity defense. There is the English position on that issue that says, in effect, yes, but only if the actor is not perceived as dangerous (noninsane automatism). There is also the Wyoming legislative approach as interpreted by the dissenting opinion in *Fulcher* that says, in effect, no, automatism must be pleaded and tried as insanity or a modified equivalent, but the hearing court should release from custody those who are not perceived as dangerous and uncontrollable without confinement.

The frequency of the occurrence of pathological intoxication is largely a matter of preference in how broadly the concept is defined. But

---

170. WYO. STAT. § 7-11-306(b) (1977).
171. WYO. STAT. § 7-11-306(d) (1977).
172. WYO. STAT. § 7-11-306(c) (1977).

the broader concept of unconscious or uncontrollable conduct brought about by circumstances beyond the control of the actor is not as uncommon as seems to be thought. The single category of drug-alcohol synergism or potentiation is large by itself, and the device of trying to deal with the problem raised in the myriad fact situations discussed in this volume through the medium of involuntary intoxication has worked for no one's benefit. We would take the Wyoming changes further. Clearly, some disposition label is needed other than "mental deficiency" for those cases or the defendant who wins will lose for a long time with that official determination of his or her mental status. One of the observations contributed by a detailed analysis of the pathological intoxication cases is that it is clear that many defendants lose their claim on grounds which have more to do with the legal structure of decision making than with their guilt.

Polston v. State[173] is *Fulcher* revisited, modified and applied. A mayhem conviction (the defendant bit off the victim's nose) was affirmed. The jury was not instructed on automatism, and the court held that he was not entitled to the instruction. The burden of proof was placed on the defendant to prove automatism and he did not. Thus, based on the facts, this is but a simple case of voluntary and knowing intoxication (he was drunk) and does not warrant an instruction on automatism.

It is interesting to note that the court listed the elements of automatism which the defendant had to prove, and first on the list was the requirement that the "actor must be a person with a healthy mind"; also now included is the requirement that the brain injury be "a simple brain trauma with no permanent aftereffects."[174] The court stated, with respect to the evidence on the second point: "If he suffered a concussion, there was no testimony that it was a simple brain trauma with no permanent aftereffects as required by *Fulcher v. State*...."[175] This seems to modify *Fulcher* so that insanity must be tried as insanity, and insanity is present in cases of permanent brain damage. "We have no difficulty holding that a blow to the head, coupled with a claimed loss of memory and nothing more in the way of evidence, does not require the giving of an instruction on automatism...."[176] The dissent distinguished California authority,[177] relied upon by the majority opinion, on the ground that the instruction was not requested there. While the court does not cite *Bratty* on the threshold evidence issue, the opinion is certainly consistent with the view taken by the English courts. The dissent argued that "evidence of loss of memory in combination with evidence of a blow to the head

173. Polston v. State, 685 P.2d 1 (Wyo. 1984).
174. *Polston* at 6.
175. *Polston* at 8.
176. *Polston* at 9.
177. People v. Ray, 14 Cal. 3d 20, 120 Cal. Rptr. 377, 533 P.2d 1017 (1975).

constitute a sufficient basis to submit the question to the jury."[178] The court also announced that if a future defendant intends to rely on the automatism defense, notice and opportunity to examine must be provided the state. The dissent brings out what it takes to raise the defense to get to the jury. The claim of a blackout and a blow to the head is sufficient for the dissent, not for the majority.

A California statute provides that among those who are not guilty of a crime are those "Persons who committed the act charged without being conscious thereof."[179] The California jury instructions say

> A person who commits an act while unconscious is not guilty of a crime.
>
> This rule of law applies to persons who are not conscious of acting but who perform acts while asleep or while suffering from a delirium of fever, or because of an attack of [psychomotor] epilepsy, a blow on the head, the involuntary taking of drugs or the involuntary consumption of intoxicating liquor, or any similar cause.
>
> Unconsciousness does not require that a person be incapable of movement.
>
> Evidence has been received which may tend to show that the defendant was unconscious at the time and place of the commission of the alleged offense for which he is here on trial. If, after a consideration of all the evidence, you have a reasonable doubt that the defendant was conscious at the time the crime was committed, he must be found not guilty.[180]

---

178. *Polston* at 11.

179. CAL. PENAL CODE § 26, subd. 4 (West 1988). The California cases regarding automatism, or unconsciousness, are collected in Annotation, *Automatism or Unconsciousness as Defense to Criminal Charge*, 27 A.L.R.4th 1067, 1074 (1984). It is noted there, at 1076 n.7, that

> [t]here has been a conflict in California cases as to whether persons of unsound mind or mental condition may use the defense of unconsciousness or whether they must raise the issue only in the sanity hearing phase of the trial. Among the California cases holding or recognizing that an unsound mental condition cannot be the basis of a defense of unconsciousness are People v. Methever (1901) 132 Cal 326, 64 P 481, and People v. Ray (1975) 14 Cal 3d 20, 120 Cal Rptr 377, 533 P2d 1017. Among the California cases which hold or recognize that an unsound mental condition can be the basis of a defense of unconsciousness are People v. Wilson (1967) 66 Cal 2d 749, 59 Cal Rptr 156, 427 P2d 820, People v. Mosher (1969) 1 Cal 3d 379, 82 Cal Rptr 379, 461 P2d 659, and People v. Lisnow (1978) 88 Cal App 3d Supp 21, 151 Cal Rptr 621.

180. CALJIC No. 4.30 (4th ed. 1979). On the burden of proof allocations in cases of claimed unconsciousness, see People v. Babbitt, 45 Cal. 3d 660, 248 Cal. Rptr. 69, 755 P.2d 253 (1988), discussing CALJIC No. 4.31 (4th ed. 1979) and upholding its constitutionality. *See also*

One of the leading California cases on automatism is *People v. Newton*.[181] In *Newton*, the court reversed a manslaughter conviction because the trial court did not, on its own initiative, give an instruction on unconsciousness when there was evidence to support that defense. The evidence was that the defendant had received a bullet wound and was in shock.

> Where not self-induced, as by voluntary intoxication or the equivalent (of which there is no evidence here...), unconsciousness is a complete defense to a charge of criminal homicide...."Unconsciousness," as the term is used in the rule just cited, need not reach the physical dimensions commonly associated with the terms (coma, inertia, incapability of locomotion or manual action, and so on); it can exist—and the above-stated rule can apply—where the subject physically acts in fact but is not, at the time, conscious of acting.[182]

The court had previously held that the instruction on diminished capacity, where supported by evidence, must be given though not specifically requested, and the court held that the same rule should apply to the unconsciousness defense because the "difference between the two states—of diminished capacity and unconsciousness—is one of degree only: Where the former provides a 'partial defense' by negating a specific mental state essential to a particular crime, the latter is a 'complete defense' because it negates capacity to commit any crime at all."[183] The defense appears not to be limited to "persons of sound mind."[184]

As a predicate for even creating any of these problems, the defense of automatism is, first of all, based on the persuasiveness of the view that

---

People v. Hallock, 208 Cal. App. 3d 595, 256 Cal. Rptr. 264 (1989).

181. People v. Newton, 8 Cal. App. 3d 359, 87 Cal. Rptr. 394 (1970).

182. *Newton* at 376, 87 Cal. Rptr. at 404-05.

183. *Newton* at 377, 87 Cal. Rptr. at 405-06.

184. In People v. Kitt, 83 Cal. App. 3d 834, 148 Cal. Rptr. 447 (1978), the court held that it was error, but harmless error, to use an instruction which limited the defense of unconsciousness to persons of sound mind. The error was found not to be prejudicial in this case because the jury had been properly instructed on diminished capacity and had, nevertheless, convicted the defendant of murder in the first degree, thereby rejecting his contention of unconsciousness due to epilepsy. In People v. Caldwell, 102 Cal. App. 3d 461, 162 Cal. Rptr. 397 (1980), which involved a claim of post-traumatic psychomotor epilepsy in a case of robbery and murder, the court affirmed, following *Kitt*, holding that while the giving of an instruction limiting the defense of unconsciousness to persons of sound mind was error, it was not prejudicial because the jury was also instructed on diminished capacity and still found him guilty of murder of the first degree (felony-murder) where the predicate felony was robbery. California modified its jury instruction to eliminate the statement that "[t]his rule of law applies only to cases of the unconsciousness of persons of sound mind," (former CALJIC No. 4.30), and the later version does not limit the unconscious defense to defendants of sound mind. CALJIC No. 4.30 (1979 revision).

the defendant, indeed, was unaware of his conduct, to begin with. Even under the view that an instruction on unconsciousness should be given if supported by "any evidence deserving of any consideration whatsoever,"[185] the defendant lost his appeal on this point in *Heffington.*[186] Winning it would have won him a new trial. The initial charge was assault with intent to commit murder, but this was reduced on appeal to attempted voluntary manslaughter, based either on a "heat of passion" defense or on the theory of diminished capacity.

He pleaded not guilty and not guilty by reason of insanity. There was some evidence of pathological intoxication. He had been drinking about five beers over several hours (according to his wife, who was a state witness) before the fight or attack occurred. He complained of a headache and double vision while driving home from town and asked his wife to drive the truck. His son told him that a "hippie" had "given him the finger" while driving through town. He then drove back into town to start a fight with the victim. He used a knife in the fighting.

He testified that his recollection of the events from the time of his son's remarks was hazy. The defendant had a history of head injuries for which he had sought medical attention, and he testified that he had a decreased tolerance to alcohol following the head injuries. One court-appointed psychiatrist called the defendant's condition "paradoxical intoxication."[187] He had no opinion regarding his condition at the time of the crime. Another psychiatrist stressed he could remember parts of the events and said that his "physical findings" did not support pathological intoxication. Neither psychiatrist said anything about unconsciousness, and it was on this basis that the trial court rejected a request for an instruction on unconsciousness as a defense.

---

185. People v. Sam, 71 Cal. 2d 194, 211, 77 Cal. Rptr. 804, 814, 454 P.2d 700, 710 (1969).

186. People v. Heffington, 32 Cal. App. 3d 1, 107 Cal. Rptr. 859 (1973).

187. In this instance, the expert seems to have interpreted what appears to be a case of pathological intoxication as a related behavioral problem that some writers refer to as "paradoxical rage reactions." Paradoxical rage reaction is used by some researchers to describe what is essentially a toxic reaction to psychotropic medication or even nonprescribed psychoactive illegal drugs. The name evidently derives from the fact that the medication typically is given for its sedative effects or to reduce anxiety but instead may cause aggressive, violent behavior as a "side effect." *See, e.g.*, PSYCHOTROPIC DRUG SIDE EFFECTS (R. Shader & A. DiMascio eds. 1970); Lion, Azcarate & Koepke, *"Paradoxical Rage Reactions" During Psychotropic Medication*, 36 DIS. NERV. SYS. 557 (1975). "The term 'paradoxical rage reaction' has been used in association with reactions to certain pharmacologic agents of the benzodiazepine class, notably chlordiazepoxide and diazepam." An example is Valium. Lion, Azcarate & Koepke do not view the two types of phenomena as unrelated, however. Pathological intoxication seems to be viewed by them as a subcategory of paradoxical rage reaction in which the sedative drug is alcohol. Lion, Azcarate & Koepke at 558. It is, perhaps, in this sense that the term was used in *Heffington.*

The appellate court agreed: "[U]nconsciousness is a complete defense except where it is caused by voluntary intoxication...."[188] The court used the "any evidence" standard for defense instructions but concluded that: "Here,...we find no evidence 'deserving of consideration' that defendant was unaware of his actions. The trial court correctly rejected the unconsciousness instruction."[189] But the court held that sua sponte instruction on voluntary manslaughter based on sudden quarrel, mental disease or intoxication should have been given. The case was remanded for the trial court to reduce or grant a new trial, leaving the disposition up to "the People."[190]

The clear drift is toward restricting the automatism defense in favor of the insanity defense and toward putting the burden of proof on the defense in those remaining cases in which the malady may qualify for automatism rather than insanity. Thus, we have a diverse and complex legal setting and a medical phenomenon which are viewed with great judicial skepticism, and there should be no expectation that the cases will "line up." Not many jurisdictions have confronted the issues in detail, but dispositional concerns predominate here just as they have in England.

Defense counsel are still given little guidance by the law as to how to handle a problematical case, which leads them to handle them in a variety of ways, as did counsel in *Bratty,* where the case was tried on three different theories of nonliability. The fact that *Gaines* was tried on a theory of automatism rather than insanity seems essentially random, but one wonders to what extent the choice of defense theories affects the final outcome of the case, including disposition of the defendant. Some of the judges clearly are influenced by the fact that one may suffer from an underlying condition that can produce an automatism and, nevertheless, have a healthy mind, and therefore, that person should not have to plead insanity to get such evidence to the jury regarding a claim of involuntary act. This is especially true, since automatism does not even necessarily prove insanity because insanity must derive from disease or defect of the mind, and a concussion may not be covered by that language, nor is the case of drug/alcohol combinations.[191] Other judges are more concerned that a "dangerous person" may be acquitted and not confined.

Structuring substantive criminal law to effectuate or facilitate noncriminal coercive "treatment" or confinement responses to dangerous or troublesome behavior undermines the content of criminal law and is probably not the most effective way to deal with mental problems, in any event, even if it is cheaper and often quicker than alternative civil

---

188. *Heffington* at 8, 107 Cal. Rptr. at 864 (citations omitted).

189. *Heffington* at 10, 107 Cal. Rptr. at 866.

190. *Heffington* at 17, 107 Cal. Rptr. at 870.

191. *See, e.g.,* Jones v. State, 648 P.2d 1251 (Okla. Crim. App. 1982); Carter v. State, 376 P.2d 351 (Okla. Crim. App. 1962).

processes. It is plausible to argue that the intolerable confusion regarding the often overlapping defenses of involuntary act and legal insanity is largely, if not entirely, due to the perceived need to have the criminal processes accomplish what the civil, mental health processes are not up to—which is to cause the confinement of people who may be dangerous. But, to state the obvious, the criminal law is designed to identify people believed to be deserving of punishment, while the mental health system is supposed to offer services to those in need of medical treatment. Does the use of one to serve the other pose a significant basis of objection?[192] Legitimate defenses of lack of voluntary act are lost because if the defendant "wins," he is no longer subject to state coercive action and is free to go. But if we think the actor is dangerous, that result is not tolerable, so we scheme to devise a system that forces an involuntary act defense into a legal insanity defense because we know that the insanity defense serves both masters, the defendant can be incarcerated whether he wins or loses.

The simple alternative of acquitting the defendant of the crime and then instituting civil, involuntary commitment proceedings against him never occurs. This existing approach becomes the more tempting when it is realized that it is the defendant himself in a criminal case who must prove that he deserves to be committed only for treatment, not for punishment. All the state has to do is file the charges and prove the *actus reus* of the crime and the decision structure and the defendant will take care of the rest. With such a literal catch-all procedurally available, it is small wonder that prosecutors would like to persuade the courts to try to force involuntary act cases into legal insanity cases.

But this scheme only works when the underlying cause of the involuntary act is such that it overlaps legal insanity by falling within the definition of a "disease or defect of the mind" or equivalent language of the legal insanity defense. That leaves the courts to confront the pure case of involuntary act, that is, when there is an involuntary act, but it is not of the sort that is simultaneously legal insanity. Here, the pressure becomes very strong to deny the clinical existence of such cases and the temptation strong to place the burden of proof on the defendant to make it even more difficult actually to prevail on this defense.

Most cases of pathological reaction to alcohol and psychomotor epilepsy[193] are tried as insanity issues, alone or in conjunction with the

192. The question can be quite broad, for this is a very common use made of criminal law, one not often found in the sterile debates that abound about the "purposes of punishment." Nonsupport and bad check systems are everywhere based on collection of debt through the threat of criminal prosecution. Treatment is enforced in the same way. Restitution is a common goal of the criminal justice systems. One could go on.

193. See the cases and authorities cited in Weinberg, *Epilepsy and the Alternatives For a Criminal Defense*, 27 CASE W. RES. L. REV. 771, 788 nn.112-15 (1977).

general issue, either by entry of the two pleas or because of the automatic operation of local rules. In cases of pathological reaction to alcohol, it is rare to find a court willing to say that a person in the throes of a seizure is, nevertheless, sane. Presumably, the same would be true whether it is a case of pathological reaction to alcohol or psychomotor epilepsy without alcohol involvement. But in the case of psychomotor epilepsy only, it is obviously true that a person with psychomotor epilepsy is, nevertheless, perfectly sane for most of his or her life, or what is referred to as the "interictal" phase. Professor LaFave has summarized this part of the problem:

> While *Kemp* and *Bratty* have received a sympathetic reception on the ground that it is desirable to avoid the result reached in *Charlson*, it has been questioned whether "the broadening of the definition of the phrase 'disease of the mind' may not be a cure worse than the ill it is intended to remedy." By this extention [sic] of the insanity defense into an area which might otherwise be occupied by the defense of automatism, medical experts are "forced into the position of making statements in court they would not make in the clinic," while a defendant who "has acted unconsciously due to a physical or organic disorder [is] faced with a verdict of insanity and committal" to an institution intended only for the treatment of mental illness. It has been suggested that it would be preferable if provision were made whereby one who interposed a successful automatism defense could be detained or conditionally discharged for the purpose of his receiving the surgical or medical treatment which might be necessary to prevent a recurrence of the unconsciousness.[194]

NOTES ON WHAT CONDITIONS MAY QUALIFY FOR THE AUTOMATISM DEFENSE

As we have described the core of pathological intoxication in previous chapters, we should also explore its boundaries, which are associated with the defense of automatism. As usual, pathological intoxication adds an overlay of additional complexity due to the uncertainty of the existing laws such as we have discussed and because pathological intoxication is not yet defined with precise or certain borders.

---

194. 1 W. LAFAVE & A. SCOTT, SUBSTANTIVE CRIMINAL LAW § 4.9(c), at 549 (1986) (footnotes omitted).

> Clinically, automatism has been described in a wide variety of conditions. These include epileptic and post-epileptic states, clouded states of consciousness associated with organic brain disease, concussional states following head injuries and, less commonly, in some types of schizophrenic and acute emotional disturbance. Metabolic disorders such as anoxia and hypoglycemia as well as drug-induced impairment of consciousness can be manifested by automatic behavior. Finally, as is well known, automatic acts can occur during sleepwalking and hypnagogic states.[195]

Other writers have stated:

> At least 14 million people in America are the victims of some form of brain dysfunction involving epilepsy, mental retardation, minimal brain disorders, strokes, brain tumors, head injuries, or malnutrition. Many individuals with cerebral disturbances are detected by such neurological signs as temporal lobe epilepsy as well as electroencephalogram (EEG) abnormalities. Others exhibit irregular EEGs only under special circumstances (for example, after drinking alcohol).[196]

"Abnormal behavior may be determined or modified by genetic, physicochemical, psychologic, and social factors."[197] And so it is with pathological reaction to alcohol or variants on that particular diagnosis. Pathological reaction to alcohol, or pathological intoxication, is clearly a description of a set of symptoms rather than a primary disease. Just as clearly, the defense is in a much better position to make the case for its

---

195. F. WHITLOCK, CRIMINAL RESPONSIBILITY AND MENTAL ILLNESS 120 (1963). *See also* C. JEFFERY, ATTACKS ON THE INSANITY DEFENSE: BIOLOGICAL PSYCHIATRY AND NEW PERSPECTIVES ON CRIMINAL BEHAVIOR (1985); Rose, *Criminal Responsibility and Competency as Influenced by Organic Disease*, 35 MO. L. REV. 326 (1970).

196. J. LEVIN & J. FOX, MASS MURDER 31 (1985). The authors continue:

> Clinical studies suggest that brain disease or injury can result in outbursts of anger and less frequently in episodes of violent behavior. In a Polish study, for example, an organic lesion to the central nervous system was discovered in fourteen of twenty-four killers. Psychiatrist Dr. Mortimer Gross similarly concludes: "There is a large body of evidence pointing to an association between organic brain disease...and violence, particularly of the sudden-impulsive kind."

Gross's article is found in Gross, *The Mind of a Murderer*, MEDICAL WORLD NEWS, Nov. 23, 1973.

197. THE MERCK MANUAL 1455 (15th ed. 1987).

contribution to the crime charged if the underlying cause can be identified. Professor Robinson has pointed out that a

> great variety of disabilities...can cause this excusing condition. Meniere's Syndrome, hyperglycemia and hypoglycemia, concussion, brain tumor, somnambulism, dissociative states, epilepsy, reflex action, and delirium from infection and fever are all examples of the disabilities that can produce the required excusing condition. It would be difficult to compile an exhaustive list.[198]

While it is also clear that some sort of latent mental disorder, in combination with alcohol, is involved, most legal authorities do not seem to further insist on any differentiation among the various sources of the brain damage or mental disease involved in triggering the reaction, although proof of its existence enhances plausibility. For example, in *People v. Jackson (Purnell)*,[199] in an opinion by Froessel, J., a conviction for murder in the first degree (and death penalty) was reversed largely on the basis of the trial court's refusal to let the defendant's expert witness express an opinion as to the defendant's insanity at the time of the homicide, despite the insanity defense. There was evidence of a history of syphilitic infection which had damaged the brain of the defendant. Independently of that, there was a history of head injury at the age of 17, and another one occurred just before the killing. The defendant had been drinking an unknown amount of alcohol (but it may have been more than moderate). Based on this and other evidence, the defense expert said that a hypothetical person in this situation would be suffering from pathological intoxication and would be insane.[200]

In the opinion of some, it makes sense to classify cases of pathological intoxication as under either the legal insanity or the automatism defense, depending upon whether the underlying medical problem which is precipitated by alcohol or other drugs is fairly considered to be a mental disease or defect or not. That is the basic premise of the criminal law as it now stands. How well that holds up is another matter because it is not likely, as we have tried to show previously, that the cases will "line up" well with the interests dictated by differing disposition needs or with abstract definitions of "mental illness."

---

198. 2 P. ROBINSON, CRIMINAL LAW DEFENSES, § 171(c), at 262 (1984) (footnotes omitted). *See also* C. JEFFERY, ATTACKS ON THE INSANITY DEFENSE: BIOLOGICAL PSYCHIATRY AND NEW PERSPECTIVES ON CRIMINAL BEHAVIOR (1985); Rose, *Criminal Responsibility and Competency as Influenced by Organic Disease*, 35 MO. L. REV. 326 (1970).

199. People v. Jackson, 10 N.Y.2d 510, 225 N.Y.S.2d 200, 180 N.E.2d 561 (1962).

200. The defendant was convicted again on remand, but this conviction was also reversed because the trial court failed to instruct on intoxication as a defense. People v. Jackson, 14 N.Y.2d 5, 196 N.E.2d 887, 247 N.Y.S.2d 481 (1964).

What distinguishes the cases discussed in this chapter is that the defendant is suffering from what fairly may be called a malfunctioning of the brain which was caused by external events rather than from "disease of the mind." Legally, the issue is whether such cases are most appropriately assimilated to legal insanity or to the defense of automatism. As Lord Denning for the court put it in *Bratty*, a case involving psychomotor epilepsy,

> The major mental diseases, which the doctors call psychoses, such as schizophrenia, are clearly diseases of the mind. But in R. v. Charlson,[201] Barry, J., seems to have assumed that other diseases such as epilepsy or cerebral tumour are not diseases of the mind, even when they are such as to manifest themselves in violence. I do not agree with this. It seems to me that any mental disorder which has manifested itself in violence and is prone to recur is a disease of the mind. At any rate it is the sort of disease for which a person should be detained in hospital rather than be given an unqualified acquittal.[202]

But there are cases in which, even with this expanded, functional definition of mental disease, the concept of disease as used in insanity law simply will not do service. All conditions which affect the brain and which may precipitate violence (or other criminal conduct) simply will not fit. In another case, *Quick*,[203] the court had to classify an instance of evident overdose of insulin taken by a person suffering from diabetes. In this instance, as we noted earlier in this chapter, the court correctly observed that "Our task has been to decide what the law means now by the words 'disease of the mind.'"[204]

> In our judgment the fundamental concept is of a malfunctioning of the mind caused by disease. A malfunctioning of the mind of transitory effect caused by the application to the body of some external factor such as violence, drugs, including anaesthetics, alcohol and hypnotic influences cannot fairly be said to be due to disease.[205]

In a sense, the question is whether there is a broader category of temporary insanity or automatism which itself encompasses pathological

---

201. [1955] 1 W.L.R. 317.
202. Bratty v. Attorney-General for Northern Ireland, [1961] 3 All E.R. 523, 534.
203. Regina v. Quick, 1973 Q.B. 910.
204. *Quick* at 922.
205. *Quick* at 922.

intoxication. Pathological intoxication in this context can be seen as simply one of the more frequently recurrent instances of temporary insanity induced, at least in part, by external causes, the consumption of alcohol. But in cases like *Quick*, there is no pre-existing body of law like voluntary intoxication and involuntary intoxication to entice the courts away into what we argue are inappropriate analytical approaches to the resulting problem. There is no body of law regarding taking insulin as there is in taking alcohol. Nor is it the fact that one is prescribed and the other is not that makes the critical difference. The difference, if any, is the level of awareness of the actor that the substance may cause dangerous behavior. Normally, this is not true of either insulin or alcohol.[206] The fact that the triggering event was "external" is but one factor in making a determination of fault. Fault in criminal law is largely a function of the concept of *mens rea*, not physical causes. Even in cases of insanity in which the "cause" could fairly be called internal, if the actor was at fault in bringing about that situation, fault could fairly be found. The following are some of the recurrent situations in which a defendant who is without fault may be able to avoid both conviction and the insanity defense and its consequent incarceration for treatment.

Psychomotor (Temporal Lobe) Epilepsy

Psychomotor, or temporal lobe, epilepsy (or complex partial seizures) has been discussed in detail, especially in connection with the English law on automatism, insane and noninsane. It is still problematic under American law whether this is to be viewed as a mental disease or defect and, hence, part of the law of insanity or part of the law of automatism. With respect to epilepsy in particular, the writers have taken various positions. An epileptic attack is an example dwelled upon earlier, and it has been argued that epilepsy does not necessarily result in the defense of automatism but might fall within the reach of the insanity defense or related defensive excuse law. Professor Robinson has pointed out that the literature also supports the idea that behavior involved in an epileptic seizure could be a more-or-less conscious effort to avoid the dangers presented by an hallucination:

> Consider epilepsy, for example, traditionally considered to give rise to an excuse of involuntary act or automatism.

---

206. *See, e.g.*, Sullivan, *Self Induced and Recurring Automatism*, 123 NEW L.J. 1093 (1973): "In the Canadian case of *Hartridge* [57 D.L.R.2d 332 (1966)] it was said by Cullitan CJS that, 'there are factors other than injury and disease of the mind such as self induced drugs and alcohol which may cause a state of automatism and in such cases the verdict will not necessarily be one of complete discharge or freedom from criminal responsibility.'"

> During the "twilight stages" of an epileptic episode, "misinterpretations of events and situations may lead to irrational rages and panics. Hallucinations may be particularly vivid and...general quietude may suddenly be terminated by an explosion of emotional hostility with a concomitant outburst of aggressive behavior." Another stage of such an episode elicits a delirious reaction with "frenzied outbursts of destructive or aggressive behavior often at the behest of hallucinations." These stages of an epileptic episode do not necessarily support the conclusion that the behavior is not a product of the effort or determination of the actor. They may suggest, instead, the presence of different excusing conditions. Hallucination, for example, a defect in perception, may exculpate if, as in insanity, it prevents perception of the nature and quality of the criminal act. The emotional hostility and rage symptomatic of an epileptic episode suggest a defect in control that may exculpate if control is sufficiently impaired, that is, if the responsibility for the impairment of control and the resultant criminal conduct can be attributed to the defect. The manifestations of a temporal lobe epileptic attack, "a dramatic change in mood with extreme irritability, bad temper, ill humor or depression," also suggest control impairment rather than involuntariness.[207]

That, however, assumes that courts are willing to label epilepsy as a mental disease or defect, a point upon which there has been disagreement. Conversely, if the automatism is not due to mental disease or defect, the two defenses will not overlap and automatism will be the appropriate defense based on unconsciousness. Another writer has said:

> The similarity of the "voluntary" aspect of the *actus reus* to the "intentional" element of *mens rea* has created some difficulty in distinguishing the various *actus reus* defenses from the insanity defense. The problem is exacerbated in the case of epilepsy. Although the abnormality is clearly physiological in nature, it also affects the individual's mental condition. Furthermore, most epileptic manifestations will involve sufficient impairment of mental and volitional capacity to adequately support either type of defense. Consequently, epilepsy has at certain times been held to present an insanity defense[208] and, at other times, an autom-

---

207. 2 P. ROBINSON, CRIMINAL LAW DEFENSES § 171(e)(3), at 272-73 (1985) (footnotes omitted). Most of the references regarding the clinical manifestations of epilepsy are to Blair, *The Medicolegal Aspects of Automatism*, 17 MED., SCI. & LAW 167 (1977).

208. Citing, inter alia, People v. Higgins, 5 N.Y.2d 607, 186 N.Y.S.2d 623, 159 N.E.2d 179

atism/unconsciousness defense.[209] Perhaps the best view is that "the two bodies of doctrine exist alongside one another, offering the defendant the opportunity to prove one or the other, or both."[210]....

Although it would appear that total unconsciousness during an epileptic attack will present a complete defense, it is still somewhat unclear whether confused and disoriented conditions short of unconsciousness will provide any relief from criminal liability under an involuntary act defense. The cases often speak in terms of "*absence* of will," but it has been stated that "consciousness has *not* meant what it seems to say; that is, the individual, at least in [cases of somnambulism], need not be 'out cold' in order to claim the defense."[211] Accordingly, the defense will be especially significant to defendants who performed the allegedly criminal acts while suffering from the confusion which often accompanies subjective psychomotor seizures and postconvulsive periods.[212]

Somnambulism

The term "somnambulism" is not always used with precision. Williams expressed the position that "the term 'somnambulism'...[should be] avoided because it is ambiguous, being sometimes used not for sleep-walking but for insane or neurotic automatism otherwise than during sleep."[213] Fenwick provides this "Differential Diagnosis of Epileptic Automatism and Sleepwalking":

> Not all night wanderings are due to sleepwalking. Confusional states resulting from many different organic conditions occur at night. One of the most common is that of epileptic automatism. Here the person, while still asleep, commences either a partial complex seizure or a generalized seizure.

(1959).

209. Citing, inter alia, Gov't of the Virgin Islands v. Smith, 278 F.2d 169 (3d Cir. 1960) and People v. Freeman, 61 Cal. App. 2d 110, 142 P.2d 435 (1943).

210. Citing A. GOLDSTEIN, THE INSANITY DEFENSE 204 (1967).

211. Citing Fox, *Physical Disorder, Consciousness, and Criminal Liability*, 63 COLUM. L. REV. 645, 655 (1963).

212. Weinberg, *Epilepsy and the Alternatives For a Criminal Defense*, 27 CASE W. RES. L. REV. 771, 801-02 (1977).

213. Numerous authorities dealing with somnambulism as a defense are collected in G. WILLIAMS, CRIMINAL LAW: THE GENERAL PART § 157 n.1 (2d ed. 1961).

> Occasionally, these may be accompanied by automatisms. These are usually limited in duration. However, the postictal confusional state may lead to a disorganized and disoriented behavior which at times may closely mimic sleepwalking. Some seizures, usually those that are generalized, may start with a cry which is only rarely confused with that of a night terror. It is important to confirm the diagnosis of nocturnal epilepsy before deciding to treat the patient.[214]

However, that somnambulism is associated with violence is clear enough.[215] How it should be treated defensively has divided the courts and commentators.[216] It is not clear that alcohol plays any triggering role in these cases.

---

214. Fenwick, *Somnambulism and the Law: A Review*, 5 BEHAV. SCI. & LAW 343, 348 (1987).

215. Citations of interest on somnambulism and violence include: ROYAL SOCIETY OF MEDICINE INTERNATIONAL CONGRESS AND SYMPOSIUM SERIES NO. 81, EPILEPSY AND THE LAW—A MEDICAL SYMPOSIUM ON THE CURRENT LAW (P. Fenwick & E. Fenwick eds. 1985); L. WATKINS, THE SLEEPWALK KILLERS (1976); Howard & d'Orban, *Violence in Sleep: Medico-Legal Issues and Two Case Reports*, 1987 PSYCHOL. MED. 17; Fenwick, *Murdering While Asleep*, 293 BR. MED. J. 574 (1986); Schatzman, *To Sleep, Perchance to Kill*, 110 NEW SCIENTIST 60 (1986); Tarsh, *On Serious Violence During Sleepwalking*, Letter, 148 BR. J. PSYCHIAT. 476 (1986); Oswald & Evans, *Serious Violence During Sleepwalking*, 147 BR. J. PSYCHIAT. 688 (1985); Fenwick, *Epilepsy and the Law*, 288 BR. MED. J. 1938 (1984); Raschka, *Sleep and Violence*, 29 CAN. J. PSYCHIAT. 132 (1984); Hartmann, *Two Case Reports: Night Terrors with Sleep Walking—A Potentially Lethal Disorder*, 171 J. NERV. & MENT. DIS. 503 (1983); Bonkalo, *Impulsive Acts and Confusional States During Incomplete Arousal From Sleep: Criminological and Forensic Implications*, 48 PSYCHIAT. Q. 400 (1974), (collecting about 20 cases of murder during sleepwalking between 1791 and 1974. All were males, and alcohol was involved in six of them; two of them may have involved epilepsy); Podolsky, *Somnambulistic Homicide* 1 MED., SCI. & LAW 260 (1961).

American decisions include Lewis v. State, 196 Ga. 755, 27 S.E.2d 659 (1943); Tibbs v. Commonwealth, 138 Ky. 558, 128 S.W. 871 (1910); Fain v. Commonwealth, 78 Ky. 183 (1879); Bradley v. State, 102 Tex. Crim. 41, 277 S.W. 147 (1925).

216. Weinberg, *Epilepsy and the Alternatives For a Criminal Defense*, 27 CASE W. RES. L. REV. 771, 801 n.194 (1977):

> Although the leading case on the subject [of somnambulism], Fain v. Commonwealth, 78 Ky. 183 (1879), totally ignores the defense of insanity, the same court stated in a later case that it could not understand how a showing of somnambulism "would constitute any defense other than that embraced in a plea of insanity." Tibbs v. Commonwealth, 138 Ky. 558, 567, 128 S.W. 871, 879 (1910)....The commentators have also disagreed. Barrow, Fabing, and Weihofen consider somnambulism to be a form of insanity, whereas Glueck classifies it as merely a symptom of mental disorder. R. BARROW & H. FABING, EPILEPSY AND THE LAW 92 (1956); S. GLUECK, MENTAL DISORDER AND THE CRIMINAL LAW 293 (1925); H. WEIHOFEN, MENTAL DISORDER AS A CRIMINAL DEFENSE 122 (1954).

Anoxia

In *Monie*,[217] there was evidence, based on an examination of the actor and a review of standard texts[218] by his treating physician, that an assault which led to the claimant's firing was due to inhalation of tear gas. It was the doctor's opinion that because of the inflammation of his lung tissue, he had limited the supply of oxygen to his brain prior to the incident (hypoxia). The plaintiff said that before he reported to work, he felt like he was on a "cheap drunk," and he also claimed amnesia for the episode. It is also interesting that the specific episode of the assault was triggered by the claimant's being accidentally hit on the head.

Trauma and Concussion

There are a surprisingly large number of cases in which the defendant factually claimed unconsciousness from some traumatic injury, usually a blow to the head. Many of these are disposed of on appeal on such procedural grounds as failure to request the instruction complained of on appeal,[219] other instructions adequately covering the defense,[220] or evidence insufficiency either to justify or require the giving of an instruction[221] or simply jury rejection of the underlying facts presented by the defense.[222] In some of the evidence insufficiency cases, the court simply observes that amnesia is not tantamount to proof of unconsciousness and without more evidence, no special instruction is required.[223] But when the evidence justifies doing so, and the instruction is requested, the courts will reverse for failure to instruct on the unconsciousness defense.[224] Several of these cases are covered in

---

217. Monie v. State Personnel Bd., 229 Neb. 27, 424 N.W.2d 874 (1988).

218. R. GOSSELIN, H. HODGE, S. SMITH & M. GLEASON, CLINICAL TOXICOLOGY OF COMMERCIAL PRODUCTS (5th ed. 1984).

219. People v. Ray, 14 Cal. 3d 20, 120 Cal. Rptr. 377, 533 P.2d 1017 (1975), (instruction not requested and the defendant also tried to rely on self-defense); People v. Sedeno, 10 Cal. 3d 703, 112 Cal. Rptr. 1, 518 P.2d 913 (1974), (instruction on unconsciousness not requested; had it been, it would have been required); People v. Wilburn, 49 Cal. 2d 714, 321 P.2d 452 (1958); People v. Keeling, 152 Cal. App. 2d 4, 312 P.2d 407 (1957).

220. State v. Gish, 87 Idaho 341, 393 P.2d 342 (1964) (no evidence adduced, and other instructions covered it anyway); Gray v. Commonwealth, 247 Ky. 282, 57 S.W.2d 6 (1933), (other instructions covered the matter); State v. Lewis, 136 Mo. 84, 37 S.W. 806 (1896).

221. People v. Jackson, 42 Ill. App. 3d 919, 356 N.E.2d 979 (1976), (turned on burden of proof on insanity defense, and the defendant lost); Watkins v. Commonwealth, 378 S.W.2d 614 (Ky. 1964) (no evidence supported the claim).

222. Reeves v. State, 196 Ga. 604, 27 S.E.2d 375 (1943).

223. People v. Chapman, 261 Cal. App. 2d 149, 67 Cal. Rptr. 601 (1968); Lester v. State, 212 Tenn. 338, 370 S.W.2d 405 (1963), (both held that evidence of amnesia did not require an instruction on insanity).

224. People v. Roerman, 189 Cal. App. 2d 150, 10 Cal. Rptr. 870 (1961); People v. Cox, 67

more detail elsewhere.[225] In *State v. Lorenze*,[226] the court held there was sufficient evidence for the trial court to conclude that the defendant was not insane though the defendant had suffered a head injury.

A cerebral concussion is an injury commonly suffered from a blow to the head. It usually is accompanied by unconsciousness for varying periods of time.[227] Its classification here is problematic only in the sense that what exactly is considered "self-induced" is not clear. Yet it is clear that alcohol combined with a recently suffered concussion can cause abnormal behavior that may well be assaultive. "Automatism is especially liable to occur when persons suffering from epilepsy, subnormality, cortical atrophy or concussion imbibe alcoholic drinks. It must not be forgotten that someone under the influence of alcohol may easily fall and sustain concussion, thereby rendering himself more liable to automatism than he would be from either the alcohol or concussion alone."[228]

> [I]t is seldom that such cases indulge in seriously aggressive crimes unless they develop a state of frenzy or proceed to drink alcohol....[229] In the latter category recovery may entail a passage through stupor, delirium and clouding before consciousness is fully regained. During the stages of delirium or cloudiness the patient, if at large, may commit a really serious criminal act such as assault, violence or homicide.[230]

There are a number of cases involving traumatic automatism or post-concussional behavior. *Fulcher*[231] was discussed earlier. There is evidence that lasting effects of concussional injury can be aggravated by the use of alcohol, resulting in pathological intoxication. In *People v. Washington*,[232] a murder conviction was affirmed where Dr. Marinacci made an electroencephalographic study of the defendant which revealed damage to the left side of the brain resulting from an injury. He testified that the brain damage was aggravated by an intake of alcohol and characterized the defendant's condition as psychomotor epilepsy. The

---

Cal. App. 2d 166, 153 P.2d 362 (1944); Read v. People, 119 Colo. 506, 205 P.2d 233 (1949); Newsome v. Commonwealth, 287 Ky. 649, 154 S.W.2d 737 (1941); State v. Jerrett, 309 N.C. 239, 307 S.E.2d 339 (1983); State v. Olson, 356 N.W.2d 110 (N.D. 1984); Carter v. State, 376 P.2d 351 (Okla. Crim. App. 1962).

225. People v. Newton, 8 Cal. App. 3d 359, 87 Cal. Rptr. 394 (1970); State v. Sikora, 44 N.J. 453, 210 A.2d 193 (1965); Watkins v. People, 158 Colo. 485, 408 P.2d 425 (1965).

226. 596 S.W.2d 762 (Mo. App. 1980).

227. TABER'S CYCLOPEDIC MEDICAL DICTIONARY 323 (C. Thomas ed. 14th ed. 1981). *See also* A. SMITH, THE MIND 130-34 (1984).

228. Blair, *The Medicolegal Aspects of Automatism*, 17 MED., SCI. & LAW 167, 170 (1977).

229. Citing McCaldon, *Automatism*, 91 CAN. MED. ASS'N J. 914 (1964).

230. Blair at 171.

231. Fulcher v. State, 633 P.2d 142 (Wyo. 1981).

232. People v. Washington, 71 Cal. 2d 1061, 80 Cal. Rptr. 567, 458 P.2d 479 (1969).

defendant had been drinking and had received a blow to the head before the killing. Another expert agreed. On rebuttal, the state was allowed to introduce the defendant's long history of prison diagnoses, none showing him insane, and the admission of the rebuttal evidence was upheld.[233] And in *State v. Snyder*,[234] the court held that the trial court erred in not permitting the defendant to introduce evidence of a blow to the head and a resulting concussion as proof of unconsciousness even though he had also been drinking.

Paresis

"General paresis is a form of cerebral syphilis. It usually takes a decade or more after the syphilitic infection is acquired for the symptoms of paresis to manifest themselves."[235] The symptoms "may simulate any psychoneuroses or psychoses."[236] The condition is easily detected by a serologic test for syphilis in the spinal fluid. "Paretics sometimes commit murder, but only rarely."[237] It does appear, however, that alcohol can interact with brain damage caused by syphilis, resulting in pathological intoxication.[238]

Brain Tumors

Brain tumors have been involved in a number of cases and are a rather generic designation for organic brain disease. Still, it hardly fits any view of "mental illness" since, by definition, its origin is organic and it might well serve as a basis for a defense of automatism. More commonly, brain damage of this sort is seen in pathological intoxication cases when bizarre behavior results from the combination of such a medical condition with alcohol or other drug consumption.

---

233. *See also* Read v. People, 119 Colo. 506, 205 P.2d 233 (1949), where the Colorado Supreme Court permitted evidence of involuntary act attributable to a blow to the head, and it permitted this on a general plea after a plea of not guilty by reason of insanity had been withdrawn, although the apparent purpose of the evidence was to reduce a verdict of murder to manslaughter.

234. State v. Snyder, 70 N.C. App. 335, 319 S.E.2d 668 (1984), *review denied*, 312 N.C. 89, 321 S.E.2d 907 (1984).

235. H. Weihofen, Mental Disorder As a Criminal Defense 33 (1954).

236. Taber's Cyclopedic Medical Dictionary 1049 (C. Thomas ed. 14th ed. 1981).

237. Weihofen at 33 (footnote omitted).

238. This is what happened in Chapman v. State, 136 Tex. Crim. 285, 124 S.W.2d 112 (1938).

Diabetes and Hypoglycemia

The medical profession has known for many years that a neat balance exists in the body between glucose level and insulin. Where there is a deficiency of insulin, there is an excess of blood sugar, resulting in the disorder which we know as *diabetes*. On the other hand, an overabundance of insulin produces a sugar deficiency termed *hypoglycemia*.[239]

Seelert,[240] it may be recalled, was evidently the first to have added hypoglycemia to the list of possible causes of pathological reaction to alcohol and was of the view that there were some hypoglycemic conditions which were indistinguishable from pathological reaction to alcohol.[241]

Keller and McCormick described pathological intoxication as associated with hypoglycemia:

> An extraordinarily severe response to alcohol, especially to small amounts, marked by apparently senseless violent behavior, usually followed by exhaustion, sleep and amnesia for the episode. Intoxication is apparently not always involved, and for this reason *pathological reaction to alcohol* is the preferred term. The reaction is thought to be associated with exhaustion, great strain, or *hypoglycemia*, and to occur especially in people poorly defended against their own violent impulses.[242]

Severe cases of hypoglycemia have been described in which the patient becomes aggressive and irritable[243] or even more violent.[244] The condition is sometimes misdiagnosed as of psychiatric origin.[245] Symptoms may appear only briefly and vanish, hence the phenomenon suffers from oversight as in the case of pathological reaction to alcohol,

---

239. Spirer, *Biochemistry as a Defense*, 4 MIAMI L.Q. 1, 7 (1949).

240. Seelert, *Zur Frage der Entwicklungsbedingungen des Pathologischen Rausche*, 86 MSCHR. PSYCHIAT. NEUROL 191 (1933).

241. There is mention of one pathological intoxication patient among 300 treated with subcutaneous insulin in Tomlinson, *Subcutaneous Insulin Therapy: An Analysis of 300 Cases*, 22 PSYCHIAT. Q. 609 (1949).

242. M. KELLER & M. MCCORMICK, A DICTIONARY OF WORDS ABOUT ALCOHOL 150 (1968) (emphasis added).

243. C. TURNER, GENERAL ENDOCRINOLOGY (1948).

244. M. BODANSKY & O. BODANSKY, BIOCHEMISTRY OF DISEASE (1940).

245. Strauss & Wechsler, *Clinical and Electroencephalographic Studies of Changes of Cerebral Function Associated with Variations in the Blood Sugar*, 102 AM. J. PSYCHIAT. 36 (1945).

especially if it has not been diagnosed previously. One writer suggested consideration of the possibility of hypoglycemia "when we hear that the criminal offense does not seem psychologically well motivated, or when there is amnesia for either the whole incident or for single details, or for the time prior to the incident," and he mentions that deep sleep may terminate the episode.[246] The same author adverts to numerous cases which have involved a variety of criminal acts such as theft and assault. Others have attributed violent, unmotivated acts to the same cause.[247]

Coid adverted to the possibility that hypoglycemia may be involved, citing Seelert,[248] and quotes an example from a psychiatric text, which also ties hypoglycemia to temporal lobe epilepsy:

> In most instances the symptoms come on with a rapidity that is reminiscent of an epileptic disturbance and temporal lobe epilepsy is erroneously diagnosed in some cases. In other subjects there is a more gradual buildup of symptoms commencing with weakness, perspiration, ataxia and anxiety combined with an extreme craving hunger for food. This often develops further into a state of disturbed consciousness in which the patient becomes disoriented and confused and may behave in a disinhibited, aggressive, or childish manner that is out of character for him. Some patients...may respond in a dysarthric and incoherent manner which at times suggests drunkenness....Convulsions occur at some stage in about a fifth of the cases.[249]

Coid also notes that hypoglycemia can be accentuated by previous brain damage due to interference with cerebral circulation.[250]

The condition can occur spontaneously, and usually does, but it may be occasioned or more often exacerbated by consumption of alcohol. Podolsky[251] states that "Aggressiveness is an outstanding characteristic of hypoglycemic generated criminality."[252] He described several cases in which the condition led to serious assaultive conduct, including homicide.

---

246. Wilder, *Sugar Metabolism in Its Relation to Criminology,* in HANDBOOK OF CORRECTIONAL PSYCHOLOGY 124 (R. Lindner & R. Seliger eds. 1947).

247. Ziskind & Bayley, *Hyperinsulinism,* 23 J. LAB. & CLIN. MED. 231-40 (1937).

248. Seelert, *Zur Frage der Entwicklungsbedingungen des Pathologischen Rausche,* 86 MSCHR. PSYCHIAT. NEUROL. 191 (1933).

249. E. SLATER & M. ROTH, CLINICAL PSYCHIATRY 369-70 (1969), quoted in Coid, *Mania A Potu: A Critical Review of Pathological Intoxication,* 9 PSYCHOL. MED. 709, 713 (1979).

250. Coid at 713.

251. Podolsky, *The Chemical Brew of Criminal Behavior,* 45 J. CRIM. L., CRIMINOLOGY & POLICE SCI. 675 (1955). At the time of that writing, Podolsky was in the private practice of psychiatry on the staff of Kings County Hospital, Brooklyn, New York.

252. Podolsky at 676.

homicide. In fact, this condition is the only example used by the Model Penal Code in support of their section on pathological intoxication as involuntary intoxication. Podolsky also mentions total or partial amnesia associated with an attack.[253] Our research on psychomotor epilepsy turned up two cases in which psychiatrists testified that, in fact, hypoglycemia could trigger an attack of psychomotor epilepsy.[254] In one of these cases, the defendant had been drinking as well.[255] It is difficult to disagree with Blair, who equates hypoglycemia with pathological intoxication,[256] differentiated only by the precise etiology of the phenomenon.[257]

Hydrocephalus

Hydrocephalus is an increased accumulation of cerebrospinal fluid within the ventricles of the brain.[258] In a report by researchers affiliated with the Gdanske School of Medicine, the authors attribute a case of necrophilia to pathological intoxication.[259] The defendant was found locked in a church by passers-by one night and released. The next morning, it was found that the corpse of a woman laid out in the church had been defiled. The defendant was arrested and ultimately referred for diagnosis. Tests established that he suffered from hydrocephalus, probably of fetal origin, and he had been drinking before the event, for which he had no recollection. He was 33 years of age at the time and had shown no gross psychiatric abnormalities prior to this occurrence. The evaluators believed that the alcohol had intensified the underlying "psychoorganic" condition. "This state of pathologically altered consciousness terminated with him falling asleep at the end of the criminal act....Pathological intoxication was diagnosed."[260] They observed that since necrophilism was a "more or less constant tendency

---

253. Podolsky at 677.

254. Ellenburg v. State, 353 So. 2d 810 (Ala. Crim. App. 1977); People v. Higgins, 5 N.Y.2d 607, 186 N.Y.S.2d 623, 159 N.E.2d 179 (1959).

255. People v. Higgins, 5 N.Y.2d 607, 186 N.Y.S.2d 623, 159 N.E.2d 179 (1959).

256. Blair, *The Medico-Legal Problems of Pathological Alcoholic Intoxication: An Illustrative Case*, 9 MED., SCI. & LAW 94, 96 (1969).

257. Regina v. Quick, 1973 Q.B. 910, involved the defendant over-injecting himself with insulin (and who had also been drinking), a case so important to the English development of sane and insane automatism defenses, which was discussed earlier in this chapter.

258. TABER'S CYCLOPEDIC MEDICAL DICTIONARY 676 (C. Thomas ed. 14th ed. 1981). *See also* A. SMITH, THE MIND 228-33 (1984).

259. Gromska, Smoczynski & Bardzik, *Przypadek aktu Nekrofilii Dokonanego w Upojeniu Pathologicznym* (A Case of Necrophilia Committed in a State of Pathological Intoxication with Alcohol), 3 POLISH J. PSYCH. 207 (1969). We have relied upon a translation we commissioned for this work.

260. Gromska, Smoczynski & Bardzik at 209.

in an individual to satisfy his sexual drive in this particular manner," his behavior on this occasion was grossly inconsistent with his prior normal sexual relations with his wife.

Environmental Poisoning

The difficulty of identifying instances of "temporary insanity" or severe, abnormal behavioral reactions to various environmental poisonings is a result of several factors. A leading contributor is the fact that the medical literature, apart from psychiatrical, focuses so heavily on biological and pharmacological considerations that behavioral ramifications are virtually ignored. Most of the literature dealing with toxicology deals with trauma caused to the body of the affected person and does not deal with behavioral concomitants. The fact that some drug interactions are dangerous is often noted, but what is meant is that it is dangerous to the patient; it is never noted whether it is also dangerous to those around him. When the research strategy is on abnormal behavior backwards to its causes, found largely in psychiatric literature, the focus traditionally of that discipline has been toward psychological and developmental etiology. On the other hand, if one tries to track the literature from serious bodily and mental damage forward to behavioral aspects of that trauma, the literature is seriously deficient (or our research is). While there is literature dealing with drug-induced behavior, the focus there is behavior which is drug-controlled or drug-mediated. For example, there is a good deal on the behavioral impairments associated with alcohol intoxication of the relatively normal type, but that is not what is sought. Still, there is some literature:[261]

> Toluene is widely used for cleaning and degreasing and as a solvent for paints, varnishes, and enamels, and particularly, rubber adhesives. It is a substance of choice among many glue and solvent sniffers. Several reported effects relate to central nervous system damage—eg, euphoria, seizures, optic neuropathy, cerebellar ataxia, and possibly dementia.[262]

---

261. Hawkes, Cavanagh & Fox, *Motoneuron Disease: A Disorder Secondary to Solvent Exposure?* LANCET 73, 74 (Jan. 1989) (citations omitted).

262. Citing for this last point, Hormes, Filley & Rosenberg, *Neurologic Sequelae of Chronic Solvent Vapour Abuse*, 36 NEUROL. 698 (1986). There would appear to be a good deal of inadvertent "glue sniffing" occurring in industrial settings. C. JEFFERY, ATTACKS ON THE INSANITY DEFENSE: BIOLOGICAL PSYCHIATRY AND NEW PERSPECTIVES ON CRIMINAL BEHAVIOR (1985). *See also* Reinl, (Alcohol Hypersensitivity Following Contact with the Fungicide Tetramethylthiuramdisulfide (TMTD)), 22 ARC. TOXIKOL. 12 (1966).

There are reported cases of carbon monoxide poisoning leading to automatistic states.[263] We have no specific information on the possible alcohol interactions in these cases.

Arteriosclerosis

Regina v. Kemp[264] was discussed earlier in connection with the English development of the concept of sane and insane automatism. In that case, the defendant's attack on his wife with a hammer could have been due to the fact that he suffered from arteriosclerosis, which affected his mind. The court treated the case as one of insanity. We have no information on alcohol interaction.

Alcoholic Withdrawal Seizures

A seizure may also be attributable to alcohol withdrawal, sometimes called "alcohol withdrawal delirium" or "DT's"[265] and, when the withdrawal results in seizures, alcoholic grand mal seizures. In these cases, it is only remotely the consumption of alcohol that is the cause of the seizure; the immediate cause is cessation of drinking.[266] Then the legal question becomes whether this should be equated to insanity (akin to the long-standing rule that "settled" insanity resulting from alcohol abuse is, nevertheless, insanity) or to automatism (akin to the cases which classify instances of psychomotor epilepsy with automatism) or whether it should be no defense at all or at least limited to the defensive effects of voluntary intoxication because the defendant brought on the problem himself. *State v. Massey*[267] involved alcoholic grand mal seizures resulting in a homicide, and the court held that an instruction on unconsciousness should be given. Although voluntary intoxication was involved in the background, the court said that the seizures were not the immediate result of voluntary intoxication and that "[s]eizures caused by alcoholism are indistinguishable from the seizures of the many different idiopathic epilepsies."[268] The court held that "the defense of unconsciousness by reason of a seizure is hereby recognized and that it

---

263. Blair, *The Medicolegal Aspects of Automatism*, 17 MED., SCI. & LAW 167, 180 (1977), reporting on H. M. Advocate v. Ritchie (1926) J.C. 45, (1926) S.L.T. 308.

264. Regina v. Kemp, [1956] 3 All E.R. 249.

265. P. LOW, J. JEFFRIES & R. BONNIE, CRIMINAL LAW: CASES AND MATERIALS 726 (2d ed. 1986).

266. Victor, *The Role of Alcohol in the Production of Seizures*, 4 MOD. PROBL. PHARMACOPSYCHIAT. 185 (1970).

267. State v. Massey, 747 P.2d 802 (Kan. 1987).

268. *Massey* at 807.

should be equated with epilepsy [unconsciousness] rather than insanity."[269] Whatever the classification, this is not now recognized as part of pathological intoxication, although some of the early clinical writers confused the two.[270]

CONCLUSION

While the movement begun in the 1950's by those in the field of psychopharmacology to hypothesize biological bases of much mental illness has advanced a great deal, much is still unexplained in these terms.[271] This, at least, is the view from psychiatry, though the effort has, it is said, the result that "psychiatry has drawn closer to the mainstream of modern medicine."[272]

The completion of this remodeling endeavor seems only a matter of time, and it highlights an anomaly in the law. Given the definition of insanity as limited to "mental disease or defect," it would be warranted in criminal law theory to conjecture that as some particular behavioral disorder is reclassified from the diminishing domain of "mental illness" to an identified organic cause (the process evidently does not reconsign in the other direction), presumably, the law would first classify the affliction as fit for the insanity defense and, subsequently, entrust it to the law of automatism when science tells us that "mental disease or defect" is no longer involved. This does not appear to us to operate with any discernable uniformity (epilepsy is a key example), and we suspect that the irregularities of response by the courts are attributable to the fact that it has never been altogether intelligible why mental disease was a limitation on the insanity defense, to begin with. Had the law called it something more patently and overtly conclusory in the first place—like the "disability of mind" defense proposed by Fingarette and

---

269. *Massey* at 807.

270. Two related issues of the burden of proof also arose. The defendant did not ask for an instruction on automatism, and while he did have a seizure which the police observed after the killing, the only proof of a seizure at the time of the killing was the defendant's own testimony. The court partly followed the California view, citing inter alia, People v. Wilson, 66 Cal. 2d 749, 59 Cal. Rptr. 156, 427 P.2d 820 (1967), and one of their own cases, State v. Pettay, 216 Kan. 555, 532 P.2d 1289 (1975), in which the implication was that the defendant's own testimony is sufficient to raise the issue and require an instruction sua sponte. The effect of the defendant's failure to request an instruction on automatism was that on appeal he had to satisfy the court that the failure of the trial court to give the instruction was "clearly erroneous," meaning that it had a possible effect on the jury verdict, and the court held that burden satisfied.

271. Baldessarini, *Drugs and the Treatment of Psychiatric Disorders*, in GOODMAN & GILMAN'S, THE PHARMACOLOGICAL BASIS OF THERAPEUTICS 389 (A. Gilman, L. Goodman, T. Rall & F. Murad eds. 7th ed. 1985).

272. Baldessarini at 390.

Hasse[273]—instead of inventing a mythical source of disability labeled "mental disease," the law might not have the difficulty it has today of making more-or-less irrelevant distinctions between mental incapacity due to "mental illness" or "brain damage" or "metabolic imbalances." Why, after all, does it matter what the source? Once it is clear that the condition is not the fault of the actor and that its origins were not within his or her control, why does the law care if it is "mental illness" or not? The answer is that the "insanity" conclusion now carries with it the possibility of incarceration for treatment of the mental disease. The law of automatism today essentially purports to deal with distinguishing between mental disease and other causes of mental incapacity long after anyone believes there is any reason to distinguish. The law itself, in this context, is not concerned at all with notions of mental disease versus organic etiologies; it is concerned with dangerousness. By its naive former belief that "mental disease" reflected some sort of reality apart from the brain and the body and by ensconcing that belief into the law of insanity, the law now continues to pretend, with lessening credibility, to be on the same search for a disembodied concept of mental disease, while its actual concern centers on the future dangerousness of the actor and no one actually cares whether "mental disease" continues to have any real meaning. The law pretends that the existence of "mental disease" determines whether the offender will be confined to jail or a hospital, while, in fact, the combined influences of fault and dangerousness are the real determinants of whether the actor will be convicted (fault) or acquitted on the basis of insanity (non-fault but dangerous) or acquitted on the basis of automatism (non-fault and not dangerous).

Should pathological intoxication be treated as a "mental disease" and thereby assigned to the law of insanity, or is it a fit subject for the defense of automatism? We have tried to show that this is not a truly productive approach, but the legal answer right now is that sometimes it is mental disease and sometimes it is automatism, and when the actor was at fault in bringing on the disability, it may be no defense at all.

---

273. H. FINGARETTE & A. HASSE, MENTAL DISABILITIES AND CRIMINAL RESPONSIBILITY 201 (1979).

8

Pathological Intoxication and Involuntary Intoxication under the Model Penal Code

ORDINARY INTOXICATION UNDER THE MODEL PENAL CODE

The law has traditionally drawn a distinction between voluntary and involuntary intoxication, although what has actually been meant by the courts when they use the expression "involuntary intoxication" has not been as intelligible as one might assume. Involuntary intoxication is an exception to the law of voluntary intoxication, which is itself, or can be viewed as, an exception to the usual rule that mental aberrations which are the fault of the actor may not completely exculpate. In other words, mistake (the absence of *mens rea*) is not a defense if caused by intoxication unless the intoxication is involuntary. That means involuntary intoxication should be purely a *mens rea* defense, although the Model Penal Code makes it an affirmative defense.[1] The prevailing rule as to involuntary intoxication is that it can be an absolute defense to any type of charge as long as the degree of intoxication established is sufficient to satisfy the test of legal insanity of the jurisdiction even though it is clearly only a temporary mental incapacity.[2] The primary question posed in this chapter is this: Is involuntary intoxication an appropriate defense to encompass pathological intoxication?

Here is how we see the general legal defensive structure. Pathological intoxication should fall under the defense of insanity if the pre-existing, underlying cause precipitated by alcohol consumption is deemed

---

1. MODEL PENAL CODE § 2.08(4) (Proposed Official Draft 1962).

2. This is true at common law and in most states today, but some tampering with those rules can produce a somewhat different conclusion. For example, Missouri has amended its involuntary intoxication statute so that it provides no defense on the basis of impairment of control, MO. ANN. STAT. § 562.076(1) (Vernon Cum. Supp. 1989), whereas the unamended insanity statute does, MO. ANN. STAT. § 562.086(1) (Vernon 1979). Thus, there is no longer a correspondence, found in most states, between the meaning of "insanity" (mental incapacity) based on involuntary intoxication and the insanity defense based on mental disease. However, this is an exceptional situation.

a mental disease or defect. It should fall under the automatism defense if the pathological reaction to alcohol is based on something other than a mental disease, such as a blow to the head or a hypoglycemic condition due to an overdose of insulin. Whether there is any nexus at all between involuntary and pathological intoxication is a point of further definition, but there is no intrinsic necessity to associate coerced drinking, alcohol sensitivity or surprise intoxication with pathological intoxication. That is what the Model Penal Code, evidently based on a limited understanding of the phenomenon of pathological intoxication, may have done. The Code's treatment of the various issues can be discussed with less difficulty if we set out the entire section:

> Section 2.08. Intoxication.
>
> (1) Except as provided in Subsection (4) of this Section, intoxication of the actor is not a defense unless it negatives an element of the offense.
>
> (2) When recklessness establishes an element of the offense, if the actor, due to self-induced intoxication, is unaware of a risk of which he would have been aware had he been sober, such unawareness is immaterial.
>
> (3) Intoxication does not, in itself, constitute mental disease within the meaning of Section 4.01 [the insanity rules].
>
> (4) Intoxication that (a) is not self-induced or (b) pathological is an affirmative defense if by reason of such intoxication the actor at the time of his conduct lacks substantial capacity either to appreciate its criminality [wrongfulness] or to conform his conduct to the requirements of law.
>
> (5) Definitions. In this Section unless a different meaning plainly is required:
>
> (a) "intoxication" means a disturbance of mental or physical capacities resulting from the introduction of substances into the body;
>
> (b) "self-induced intoxication" means intoxication caused by substances that the actor knowingly introduces into his body, the tendency of which to cause intoxication he knows or ought to know, unless he introduces them pursuant to medical advice or under such circumstances as would afford a defense to a charge of crime;
>
> (c) "pathological intoxication" means intoxication grossly excessive in degree, given the amount of the intoxicant, to which the actor does not know he is susceptible.[3]

---

3. MODEL PENAL CODE § 2.08 (Proposed Official Draft 1962).

Section (1) states the usual no-defense rule to the effect that ordinary intoxication is not an affirmative defense, limiting its defensive utility to a negation of the *mens rea* involved in the definition of the crime. It is like the "defense" of mistake, in that intoxication is no more relevant than the charge makes it.

Section (2) adopts what is referred to as the "special rule" of intoxication: Not only is intoxication narrowed to an elemental defense, it will not even be permitted to negate *mens rea* except above the level of "general intent" crimes, which is to say that intoxication can be a defense only to specific intent crimes. The commentaries make it clear that the Model Penal Code meant to include within the compass of specific intent crimes those which require a culpability level of either intent or knowledge.[4] Some states changed this rule to assimilate knowledge-based crimes to "general intent" rather than "specific intent" to further limit the utility of voluntary intoxication as a defense. Thus, while the construct of the Model Penal Code eliminates reliance on the specific-intent/general-intent distinction, functionally it merely assimilates knowledge as an element of the offense charged to intent and permits evidence of intoxication to be adduced when either of them is involved in the charge.[5] Others assimilate knowledge to recklessness.[6]

The Code, following American common law, adopted the rule that intoxication "ought to be accorded a significance that is entirely co-extensive with its relevance to disprove purpose [intent] or knowledge, when they are the requisite mental elements of a specific crime."[7] The drafters noted that the prevailing attitude was toward a special rule of intoxication, a rule which confines its defensive effects to offenses which require a culpability degree greater than recklessness.

> Beyond this, there is the fundamental point that awareness of the potential consequences of excessive drinking on the capacity of human beings to gauge the risks incident to their conduct is by now so dispersed in our culture that we believe it fair to postulate a general equivalence between the risks created by the conduct of the drunken actor and the risks created by his conduct in becoming drunk. Becoming so drunk as to destroy temporarily the actor's powers of perception and of judgment is conduct which plainly has no affirmative social value to counterbalance the potential

---

4. MODEL PENAL CODE § 2.08 comment 2 at 5 (Tent. Draft No. 9, 1959).
5. MODEL PENAL CODE § 2.08 comment at 4-5 & 7-8 (Tent. Draft No. 9, 1959).
6. *See, e.g.*, COLO. REV. STAT. § 18-1-804 (1978).
7. MODEL PENAL CODE § 2.08 comment 3 at 7 (Tent. Draft No. 9, 1959).

> danger. The actor's moral culpability lies in engaging in such conduct.[8]

Based on this rationale, the Code adopted the generally prevailing rule that voluntary, or self-induced, intoxication was sufficient recklessness in itself to warrant denial of its use as a defense in any crime which requires no higher level of culpability.

Section (3) is important to understanding the Code's treatment of pathological intoxication because it makes clear that they adopt the usual rule that ordinary intoxication is not per se a mental disease.

Section (4) recognizes two exceptions to the special rule of intoxication that equates drunkenness[9] with recklessness by providing that two classes of intoxication cases are affirmative defenses and, hence, are available to the defendant even against charges based only on recklessness or even lesser requirements of culpability. These two are cases of intoxication which are not self-induced and pathological intoxication. By this first term, the drafters tried to improve upon the common law habit of referring to intoxication as "voluntary" or "involuntary" with the implication that duress or coercion was all that could be involved.[10] "Self-induced" (voluntary) intoxication is defined in § (5)(b) to require the actor's knowledge that he is ingesting something but only negligence ("ought to know") as to the resulting intoxication. Whether the term "self-induced" in lieu of "voluntary" adequately draws attention to the fact that what is involved is the degree of culpability in getting drunk rather than the actor's ability to avoid that result is open to question; but that was the drafter's intent, and the provision has had substantial effect in state recodification efforts.[11]

PATHOLOGICAL INTOXICATION UNDER THE MODEL PENAL CODE

While pathological intoxication as dealt with in § 2.08 (5)(c) is of principal interest here, although it has been adopted by only a few states,[12] we first need to consider the Code's treatment of involuntary

---

8. Model Penal Code § 2.08 comment 3 at 9 (Tent. Draft No. 9, 1959).

9. We follow the convention of equating drunkenness with alcohol intoxication although we are aware that there are both subjective and physiological determinants of behavior under this condition. *See, e.g.*, Rix, *'Alcohol Intoxication' or 'Drunkenness': Is There a Difference?* 29 Med., Sci. & Law 100 (1989). There is, of course, a large component of subjectivity in experiencing intoxication.

10. 1 Model Penal Code and Commentaries § 2.08, at 363 n.40 (1985).

11. 1 Model Penal Code and Commentaries § 2.08, at 363 (1985), notes that 13 state-revised codes and 7 proposals parallel these proposed provisions relating to "self-induced" intoxication.

12. 1 Model Penal Code and Commentaries § 2.08, at 366 n.49 (1985), mentions Haw.

intoxication. It is the relationship of the two that is crucial to understanding their treatment of pathological intoxication. The Model Penal Code defines pathological intoxication as distinct from traditional understandings of the defense of involuntary intoxication (referred to as intoxication which is "not self-induced"),[13] although both are given the same defensive status: Corresponding to involuntary intoxication, pathological intoxication is made an affirmative defense if the resulting intoxication suffices to meet the insanity test of lack of substantial mental capacity on either its cognitive or volitional divisions, but without, in either defense, a requirement of the mental disease or defect element additionally needed in ordinary insanity cases. Having distinguished involuntary intoxication from pathological intoxication, nonself-induced intoxication is then recognized as consisting of three categories—non-negligent mistake[14] as to the tendency of the ingested substance[15] to intoxicate, consumption pursuant to medical advice[16] and consumption under duress or similar defensive circumstances.[17]

The Code separately treats pathological intoxication so that it means none of those events and defines it as "intoxication grossly excessive in degree, given the amount of the intoxicant, to which the actor does not know he is susceptible." Since Krafft-Ebing first identified it as pathological reaction to alcohol, pathological intoxication has been distinguished from ordinary intoxication on the ground that it is a qualitatively unique psychological phenomenon. The defendant may have a high or low blood alcohol level and, therefore, be intoxicated or not (by that

---

REV. STAT. § 702-230(4)(c) (based on MODEL PENAL CODE § 2.08 (Tent. Draft No. 9, 1959), which in that earlier draft had limited pathological intoxication to those cases "caused by an abnormal bodily condition." The Hawaii version provides "which results from a physical abnormality of the defendant"); N.J. STAT. ANN. § 2C:2-8(e)(3) (West 1982); MICH. S.B. 82 § 715(6) (proposed); and MD. § 15.25(1)(B)(II) (proposed).

13. MODEL PENAL CODE § 2.08(4) (Proposed Official Draft 1962).

14. "Knows or ought to know" is used in MODEL PENAL CODE § 2.08(5)(b) (Proposed Official Draft 1962). Presumably, recklessness would fit between.

15. Alcohol is never mentioned in the intoxication statute.

16. The Model Penal Code provision is not clear whether the doctor's advice cases are examples of non-negligent consumption of intoxicating substances or an independent basis of exculpation. Robinson, *Causing the Conditions of One's Own Defense: A Study in the Limits of Theory in Criminal Law Doctrine*, 71 VA. L. REV. 1 (1985). DEL. CODE ANN. tit. 11 (1979 Repl. Vol. 7A, does not contain a provision on pathological intoxication, but DEL. CRIM. CODE COMMENTARY on § 423, at 90 (proposed 1973), in reference to the section which was adopted on involuntary intoxication, lists as one type of involuntary intoxication "an abnormal reaction to a drug prescribed by a physician." The Delaware commentary lends support to the view that the "doctor's advice" cases are based on lack of negligence, not necessity. On the other hand, if the reaction to a drug is abnormal, is it relevant that it was taken on a doctor's advice?

17. We assume defenses such as duress or necessity are the referents of the phrase "circumstances as would afford a defense to a charge of crime" used in MODEL PENAL CODE § 2.08(5)(b) (Proposed Official Draft 1962).

physiological definition of intoxication), but he clearly is not intoxicated in any behavioral definition of that term. His behavior is atypical for an intoxicated person. As thus conceived, pathological intoxication involves alcohol, but it does not involve intoxication. But the Model Penal Code regards it merely as a form of intoxication, qualitatively indistinguishable or distinguishable only in degree from ordinary involuntary intoxication.

The involuntary intoxication defense presupposes actual intoxication ("a disturbance of mental or physical capacities resulting from the introduction of substances into the body")[18] as a condition of the defense. The only difference between their draft on pathological intoxication and involuntary intoxication is that pathological intoxication covers the situation in which the actor may know that he is consuming alcohol or other drugs but is not aware of the degree of its intoxicating effects on him, whereas involuntary intoxication covers those cases in which the actor is not aware and has no reason to be aware that he is consuming something intoxicating at all. The Model Penal Code's version of pathological intoxication allows for interactive effects of known intoxicants. Cases of drug interaction ought to be classified as pathological intoxication under the Model Penal Code. As a matter of drafting technique, it would appear the Code could as well have merely appended a fourth type of involuntary intoxication by extending the first type of involuntary intoxication so that it would have consisted of non-negligent mistake or lack of awareness as to the tendency of the ingested substance to intoxicate *or to intoxicate to the extent it did.* The federal drafters came to the same conclusion, and it is reflected in their draft:

> Intoxication which (a) is not self-induced, or (b) if self-induced, is grossly excessive in degree, given the amount of the intoxicant, to which the actor does not know he is susceptible, is a defense if by reason of such intoxication the actor at the time of his conduct lacks substantial capacity either to appreciate its criminality or to conform his conduct to the requirements of law.[19]

In reference to the Tentative Draft's inclusion of pathological intoxication, the authors state:

> The draft also treats "pathological" [The Tentative Draft included a separate definition of the term "pathological intoxication." The Study Draft does not use the term, but incorporates the definition thereof in subsection 4(b).]

18. MODEL PENAL CODE § 2.08(5)(a) (Proposed Official Draft 1962).

19. NAT'L COMM'N ON REFORM OF FEDERAL CRIMINAL LAWS, STUDY DRAFT § 502(4) (1970).

> intoxication as not being self induced. This phrase is sometimes used medically to refer to an outburst of irrational, combative, destructive behavior after consumption of small quantities of alcohol. Sometimes it is termed an "acute alcoholic paranoid state." There is dispute among medical authorities as to whether such a syndrome exists. Critical data supporting or disproving pathological intoxication apparently are unavailable. It is a rare occurrence, at the most, and, in spite of reservations of the writer in creating lacunae in the law, it was thought desirable to include its formulation.[20]

The term "paradoxical rage reaction" is used by some writers to describe the behavior associated with what is basically a toxic reaction to psychotropic medication or nonprescribed psychoactive illegal drugs. The name evidently derives from the fact that the medication typically is given for its sedative effects or to reduce anxiety, but instead it may cause aggressive, violent behavior as a "side effect."[21] "The term 'paradoxical rage reaction' has been used in association with reactions to certain pharmacologic agents of the benzodiazepine class, notably chlordiazepoxide and diazepam."[22] An example, as stated earlier, is Valium. Lion, Azcarate & Koepke do not perceive the phenomena as unrelated; to them, pathological intoxication is a subclass of paradoxical rage reaction in which the sedative drug is alcohol.[23] Noting that the literature had discussed rage and violence in connection with the combined use of benzodiazepines other than alprazolam and alcohol, "The following is a report of a patient who developed severe behavioral dyscontrol for the first time after exposure to a combination of alprazolam and alcohol."

---

20. NAT'L COMM'N ON REFORM OF FEDERAL CRIMINAL LAWS, *Consultant's Report on Intoxication Defense; Section 502* [Robinson and Green] (1969), 1 WORKING PAPERS 223, 227 (1970), citing T. HARRISON, PRINCIPLES OF INTERNAL MEDICINE 1390 (5th ed. 1966) and REDLICH & FREEDMAN, THE THEORY AND PRACTICE OF PSYCHIATRY 755 (1966).

The FINAL REPORT § 502(3) (1971) provides that intoxication resulting in satisfaction of the insanity test is a defense when "if self-induced, is grossly excessive in degree, given the amount of the intoxicant, to which the actor does not know he is susceptible...."

Some of the drafters who did not propose adoption of the Model Penal Code's pathological intoxication section have made comments on their decision. Alabama, for example, was influenced by this comment in the WORKING PAPERS. In the commentary to ALA. CODE § 13A-3-2 (1980) it is stated that "While some proposed codes have recognized 'pathological intoxication' as a possible defense, it has been omitted here, as the medical authorities do not agree whether such a syndrome exists. See New Federal Criminal Code, Working Papers, p. 227."

21. *See, e.g.,* PSYCHOTROPIC DRUG SIDE EFFECTS (R. Shader & A. DiMascio eds. 1970).

22. Lion, Azcarate & Koepke, *"Paradoxical Rage Reactions" During Psychotropic Medication*, 36 DIS. NERV. SYS. 557 (1975).

23. Lion, Azcarate & Koepke at 558.

> Ms. A experienced an episode of severe behavioral dyscontrol and amnesia. An hour after drinking approximately 3 oz. of 80-proof whiskey (her usual daily consumption over the past several years), she broke into a neighbor's house and "smashed everything in sight," destroying approximately $50,000 worth of property and inadvertently sustaining lacerations of both wrists from broken glass. Afterward, she returned to her house, fell asleep, and upon awakening had an incomplete recollection of the event, recalling only vague images and sounds of breaking glass. She then surrendered herself to the police and was admitted to a psychiatric unit....Ms. A had not evinced clinically significant behavioral dyscontrol after exposure to either alcohol or alprazolam alone and developed her destructive rage only while taking a combination of the two.[24]

Is this a case of pathological intoxication or involuntary intoxication? A case such as this goes beyond mere intoxication, even though the matter could sensibly be dealt with as involuntary intoxication under existing classification schemes as well as the one proposed by the Model Penal Code. However, the case seems more appropriately labeled temporary insanity through no fault of the actor.

The Model Penal Code is the only source of any significance that understands pathological intoxication largely as a problem of simple intoxication aggravated beyond what the actor expected. The medical concepts of pathological intoxication have postulated that there was some underlying cause of the behavioral reaction to the alcohol, that the drinking triggered some underlying condition; and we have noted that some authorities divide the underlying causes into either those considered "mental disease" (befitting a defense of legal insanity) or those underlying conditions such as brain damage, which are more accurately assimilated to automatism. In what may be the quintessential case assumed by the Model Penal Code, a drug might potentiate the effects of alcohol and make the actor surprisingly intoxicated, given the amount consumed. The precision of the trichotomy dissipates, but only to a slight extent, when it is realized that a drug can cause a temporary aberrational condition of the mind and then cause a reaction to alcohol or other drug. Such a case can be seen as either involuntary intoxication or pathological intoxication, as was the earlier case involving Ms. A.

What mainly divides the Model Penal Code's pathological intoxication view from others, then, is that it includes merely transient irregular

---

24. Terrell, Letter: *Behavioral Dyscontrol Associated With Combined Use of Alprazolam and Ethanol*, 145 AM. J. PSYCHIAT. 1313 (1988).

conditions of the brain which can cause an abnormal reaction to alcohol or other drugs. Classical pathological intoxication posited a more permanent underlying cause of the reaction, and that is why we tend to view the Model Penal Code version as merely involuntary intoxication; it includes cases in which there is absolutely nothing wrong with the actor and encompasses the pure drug/drug cases as well as the LSD-in-the-punch-bowl cases. It is a *transient* reaction to a *transient* condition. This is significant because in these cases there will be no serious questions regarding disposition because there is no argument that there is anything medically wrong with the defendant. Whether conviction follows, presumably, will be based on the level of fault involved, if any, in becoming intoxicated, but that is the only issue. In cases of classical pathological intoxication, where the added dimension is present, the need for an additional appraisal arises because the underlying condition is still there. Yet, so is the opportunity to mix drugs "still there." Should Ms. A be in a hospital?

Because the Model Penal Code's sense of pathological intoxication as only quantitatively distinguishable from ordinary intoxication is fundamentally at variance with virtually all of the legal and medical literature on the subject, conceivably, the most felicitous way to deal with their approach would be to classify it as a third, distinct view of pathological intoxication in terms of etiology, symptomatology and legal consequences. It would be viewed as an augmentation of the established categories of disease-based pathological intoxication, which is best suited to the insanity defense, and nondisease-based pathological intoxication, which is within the purview of the traditional involuntary act defense, automatism in particular.

The pathological intoxication defense which the American Law Institute drafted is more akin to what is usually called alcohol sensitivity, which describes a situation in which a person becomes more intoxicated (not psychotic or unconscious, but drunker) than the amount of alcohol or other substance consumed normally would betoken.[25] At a relatively inconsequential level, for example, liver function impairment from a variety of causes can result in a person becoming more intoxicated on less alcohol as compared to a healthy person, whose reaction will be relatively predictable and constant. In addition, the degree of intoxication, measured by the behavioral impact of the alcohol, may vary within the same person with respect to such factors as food in the stomach, fatigue, ambient temperature and emotional state. The important point is that these differences relate to relatively narrow quantitative variations in the rapidity of onset or the degree of resulting intoxication. But there is no question in such cases that we are talking about drunkenness, all within

25. Bowman & Jellinek, *Alcoholic Mental Disorders,* 2 QRTLY J. STUD. ALCOH. 312 (1941).

relatively narrow limits of variance. An example of more consequence for the individual arises in those cases in which alcohol and other drugs or two prescriptions drugs (or more) interact with each other in such a way that their effect upon each other is greatly intensified or their combined power is more than additive. In these cases, the reaction could be variable with that person in the sense that his reaction to drinking six beers will be vastly different from his reaction to the same amount after taking certain controlled or uncontrolled drugs.[26] Even if the reaction is extreme and even if the actor unquestionably should be exculpated for resulting conduct, the situation still is one of involuntary intoxication, not pathological intoxication as that concept has historically been developed, because the reaction was entirely attributable to external causes and not to any underlying condition of the actor.

It has been repeatedly emphasized in the literature that pathological intoxication, or pathological reaction to alcohol, is a qualitatively different phenomenon from ordinary intoxication, even exaggerated intoxication.[27] "This warning is especially important since some textbooks, in the endeavor to make concise statements, have defined [pathological reaction to alcohol] as intoxication following the ingestion of small quantities of alcohol."[28] Alcohol sensitivity, meaning an abnormally strong influence on a person of a given amount of alcohol, may be either permanent or temporary. Permanent alcohol sensitivity can be hereditary[29] or acquired, as, for example, it can even result from brain injury, as can pathological intoxication. Temporary intolerance, or potentiation, may result from very short-term effects of drug-alcohol combinations[30] or

---

26. Multiple drug cases show up with some frequency in the case law. Most of them involve illegal "street" drugs, but some are prescription. For example, State v. Davis, 653 S.W.2d 167 (Mo. 1983), involved affirmance of a murder conviction attacked on evidence sufficiency grounds under an insanity plea. The defendant shot and killed a police officer with a shotgun. He had been a chronic alcoholic for over 20 years, had been taking prescription drugs, including Valium, Librium, Dilantin, and "Antibuse" [sic], probably had been drinking, displayed evidence of prior head injuries and had been under psychiatric care. "Experts testified that appellant suffered from a vascular malformation or scar tissue in his brain." *Davis* at 170.

27. Bowman and Jellinek at 323.

28. Bowman and Jellinek at 322.

29. *See, e.g.*, Agarwal & Goedde, *Human Aldehyde Dehydrogenase Isozymes and Alcohol Sensitivity*, 16 ISOZYMES CURR. TOP. BIOL. MED. RES. 21 (1987) ("flushing response" among some oriental families—Japanese, Chinese & Korean—may contribute to relatively low incidence of alcoholism); Mizoi, Tatsuno, Adachi, Kogame & Fukunaga, *Alcohol Sensitivity Related to Polymorphism of Alcohol-Metabolizing Enzymes in Japanese*, 18 PHARMACOL. BIOCHEM. BEHAV. 127 (Supp. I 1983); Yoshida, *Differences in the Isozymes Involved in Alcohol Metabolism Between Caucasians and Orientals*, 8 ISOZYMES CURR. TOP. BIOL. MED. RES. 245 (1983); Ewing, Rouse & Aderhold, *Studies of the Mechanism of Oriental Hypersensitivity to Alcohol*, 5 CURR. ALCOH. 45 (1979).

30. One explanation may be the variability of the permeability of the blood-brain barrier which may be affected by drugs. *See, e.g.*, Bloom, *Neurohumoral Transmission and the*

even just from hunger or physical exhaustion. It can be of more lengthy duration; for example, when moving to a higher altitude, the oxygen deprivation (hypoxia) experienced, it is thought, will increase the degree of intoxication in the same person for the same amount of alcohol.[31] In still other cases its etiology is never diagnosed.[32] As another potentially important instance, it has been said that "In practical terms...a woman will be less likely than a man to predict accurately the effect of a given amount of alcohol consumed."[33] A major reason for this is the hypoglycemia associated with PMS. In many of these alcohol sensitivity cases, the usual symptoms of intoxication—motor incoordination and slurred speech—are present, and that distinguishes these cases from pathological intoxication in the sense we have used it, but we are in no position to say that some of these cases have not resulted in temporary insanity rather than merely exaggerated intoxication.[34] That has been one of the

---

Central Nervous System in GOODMAN & GILMAN'S, THE PHARMACOLOGICAL BASIS OF THERAPEUTICS 236, 245 (A. Gilman, L. Goodman, T. Rall & F. Murad eds. 7th ed. 1985).

31. *But see* Collins & Mertens, *Age, Alcohol, and Simulated Altitude: Effects on Performance and Breathalyzer Scores*, 59 AV. SPACE ENV'T MED. 1026 (1988), suggesting a need for redefinition of performance effects of altitude and alcohol.

32. J. ANDENAES, THE GENERAL PART OF THE CRIMINAL LAW OF NORWAY § 30 (T. Ogle trans. 1965), citing G. Rylander & E. Bendz, RATTSPSYKIATRI 67 (1947), relates a Swedish case which provides an example of an offense committed during pathological intoxication which had no known origin but which, presumably, would fall within the loose category of "alcohol intolerance."

> A twenty-five-year-old man had been with his wife and small son at a Christmas dinner with relatives and had taken a few drinks. He became brutal and unpleasant to his wife on the way home. Weeping, she begged him to desist until after they had come home and put the boy to bed. When they arrived at home, the man grabbed his wife by the throat with one hand and seized a big butcher knife with the other. The wife tore herself free and ran out of the house, screaming for help. Before the neighbors could come to her aid, the man had killed his son with the knife, and had jumped out of the window, inflicting serious injuries on himself.
>
> It was later learned that when the man was about eighteen, he drank a few glasses of wine at a family party and suddenly became rebellious and acted indecently. After that, he abstained from alcohol until the fatal day when he made this one exception. He had then been married for a few years. The marriage was a happy one, the husband enjoyed his home life, and the little boy was the apple of his eye. Afterwards, he became deeply depressed over his conduct, which he could not explain, and he contemplated suicide. On the way home that fatal night an enormous rage had overcome him. "It was as if everything became red in front of my eyes." He could not remember what had happened from that moment on until he jumped out of the window. He hazily recalled the sound of the broken glass and the stinging pains from the glass splinters.

33. Blume, *Women and Alcohol*, 256 J. A.M.A. 1467, 1468 (1986).

34. We mean to be cautious on the subject of PMS as well as the other conditions so as not to be understood as suggesting that alcohol sensitivity is the limit of the role played by alcohol in these cases, especially in cases of PMS; we do not know whether it plays more of

principal objections to the term "pathological intoxication." It does not result in drunkenness at all; it results in a temporary psychosis. This is one of the reasons we said in the introduction that the term "pathological intoxication" was misleading and that the better term, used originally by Krafft-Ebing, is "pathological reaction to alcohol." Banay's article, relied upon in the commentary to this Model Penal Code section, is entitled "Pathologic Reaction to Alcohol." It is doubtful that the latter term could be used exclusively to designate cases of insanity and automatism while reserving the term "pathological intoxication" for the event described by the Model Penal Code as exaggerated and surprise intoxication. Besides, the term "pathological intoxication" is needed to cover "pathological reaction to alcohol" when the triggering agent is not alcohol. It would serve as well to acknowledge that the term "pathological intoxication" is used in three, somewhat overlapping, ways: (1) a psychotic reaction to an ingested substance based on an underlying mental disease; (2) a psychotic reaction to an ingested substance due to an abnormal bodily condition not considered a mental disease or defect; and (3) an unanticipated, high level of intoxication due to some interaction between the substance and some transient condition of the actor or between another substance taken by the actor.

It is evident that the Code is referring to alcohol sensitivity, which results in common intoxication; the actor may be ignorant of his susceptibility or not. The referent case is one of alcohol potentiation, such as when alcohol is mixed with certain other drugs and the person very quickly becomes extraordinarily drunk on ordinary amounts of alcohol, or when pre-existing bodily conditions such as fatigue or hypoglycemia cause the same effect. Given this limited notion of pathological intoxication found in the Code, it would have served as well to include it within the scope of involuntary intoxication and omit a separate section on it entirely. Historically, these cases have usually been treated as instances of involuntary intoxication because most of the courts have always understood that the term "involuntary" in this context includes lack of awareness of the fact or degree of intoxicating effects as well as instances of duress.

What, then, distinguishes the Code's definitions of involuntary intoxication and pathological intoxication? If this is their proposal—that if the actor did not know someone put LSD in the punch, it is a case of involuntary intoxication because he did not know the punch was intoxicating at all; whereas if he did not know that his prescription drug would cause an adverse reaction if combined with another drug like alcohol, it is a case of pathological intoxication because he did know the

---

a role than has as yet come to our attention. Our assertion in the text is that alcohol may cause a magnified level of ordinary intoxication in these instances. Whether it is capable of causing a psychotic reaction in some of these instances is not known to us.

drugs were intoxicating but not how intoxicating—then its rejection by most of the states leaving the issue of unexpected intoxication to the involuntary intoxication defense and other pathological cases to the law of insanity or automatism seems well considered.[35]

That is not what pathological intoxication meant prior to this draft. Without the Model Penal Code, the case of drug/drug combination reaction would be treated as involuntary intoxication and if the effects were so severe that the actor was unconscious as a result, the matter would be dealt with as one of automatism. If, instead, the reaction was caused by an underlying mental condition such as psychomotor epilepsy, some courts would treat it as insanity and others as automatism, and the difference would often be explained in terms of whether psychomotor epilepsy was thought to be a mental disease, although the actual ground of decision would probably be the disposition of the actor. In effect, we now have three kinds of pathological intoxication, both factually and legally, but it is not at all clear what the Model Penal Code provisions add or detract from this present situation. At best, it is probably redundant with the defense of involuntary intoxication. Several states see it this way.[36] At worst, it undermines recognition of pathological

---

35. There is also some indication that some other countries also classify this type of pathological intoxication as involuntary intoxication. The Scandinavian Countries of Denmark, Norway and Sweden "recognize that so-called pathologic intoxication is an involuntary intoxication. Cases where a relatively small amount of alcohol or drugs have a completely abnormal effect are examples of pathological intoxication." Hearings on Reform of the Federal Criminal Laws, Before the Subcomm. on Criminal Laws & Procedures of the Senate Judiciary Comm., 92nd Cong., 2d Sess., pt. 3, subpt. C, at 2551 (1972).

36. Some drafts contain language substantially comparable to the Model Penal Code but do not label it pathological intoxication, classifying it instead as another instance of involuntary intoxication. For example, STATE OF MD., COMM'N ON CRIM. LAW, 1 PROPOSED CRIM. CODE § 15.25 (1972), provided that one species of involuntary intoxication "means intoxication caused without the negligence or fault of the defendant by...substances introduced in quantities which produce intoxication grossly excessive in degree, considering the amount of the intoxicant, to which the defendant does not know that he is unusually susceptible." It is noted that Model Penal Code § 2.08 was "redrafted to avoid use of the new concepts of 'self-induced intoxication' and 'pathological intoxication' in favor of the traditional 'involuntary intoxication.'"

Similarly, LEGIS. SERV. COMM'N, PROPOSED OHIO CRIM. CODE § 2901.35, at 55 (1971), defined involuntary intoxication to include intoxication "which is grossly excessive considering the nature and amount of the intoxicating substance involved, and which is caused either by an abnormal bodily condition, or by an unexpected reaction with other substances in the body." The statutes do not use the term "pathological intoxication" and so are often omitted when states are listed as having recognized the concept by statute. Indeed, the commentaries to the Ohio code make reference to Leggett v. State, 21 Tex. App. 382, 17 S.W. 159 (1886), as within the purview of this provision, a case in which "the defendant was held to be involuntarily intoxicated when his condition was caused in part by a blow on the head after his having taken an amount of liquor insufficient to make him drink [sic, "drunk"?] under normal circumstances." PROPOSED OHIO CRIM. CODE at 56.

While the present Arizona statutes use the term voluntary intoxication, they do not attempt to define involuntary intoxication. ARIZ. REV. STAT. ANN. § 13-503 (Supp. 1988).

intoxication based on insanity and automatism defenses. Perhaps no harm is done if this species of pathological intoxication is subsumed under the heading of involuntary intoxication and if it continues to be recognized that the definition used by the Model Penal Code is not exclusive of the other two forms of pathological intoxication, which are insanity and automatism.

The Model Penal Code still is directed only to the actor who suffers no more than surprise drunkenness, and although that surely should be a defense in the proper circumstances, it is not the quintessence of pathological intoxication and is already embraced by traditional common law and Code formulations of the involuntary intoxication defense. In the cases contemplated by the Model Penal Code, the dominant agent of causation of the dangerous behavior is alcohol intoxication, and that is not the case in pathological intoxication in which the actor is not intoxicated at all in the sense of drunkenness. To the Model Penal Code, intoxication which is not self-induced is merely accidental intoxication, and pathological intoxication is getting drunker than might have been expected under the known circumstances. We cannot say that is wrong, but we can say it is largely inconsistent with everything that preceded this draft over the past century in defining the concept of pathological intoxication. We should point out again that their main work on this part of the Model Penal Code was published in 1959.

The Code misdescribed the clinical phenomenon in a way that is likely to lead to serious misinterpretation if it is taken to be exclusive, and the provision has gained some acceptance in the new criminal codes, although some recognize it for what it is. The drafter of one version of the proposed California Penal Code, for example, says the section seems "akin to accidental intoxication."[37] But accidental intoxication would

---

However, the ARIZ. CRIM. CODE COMM'N, ARIZ. REV'D CRIM. CODE § 502, at 73 (1975), had included a section on involuntary intoxication which was not adopted, and its commentary noted that involuntary intoxication "applies in four situations: first, intoxicants taken under duress; second, intoxication caused by a genuine mistake as to the characters of the substance taken; third, intoxication unexpectedly occurring from prescribed medication; and, fourth, intoxication from a weakness unknown to the defendant and grossly excessive to [sic] the amount of stimulant taken." ARIZ. CRIM. CODE COMM'N at 74. This fourth category reflects the Model Penal Code's view of pathological intoxication. The Arizona statute acknowledges Kentucky as the source of its language, and substantially identical language is found in KY. CRIM. COMM'N, KY. PENAL CODE, § 235, commentary at 24-25 (Final Draft 1971). Kentucky's provision appears in turn to be based on *State v. Altimus*, 306 Minn. 462, 238 N.W.2d 851 (1976), and *Altimus* seems to have gotten the fourth provision from the Model Penal Code's provision on pathological intoxication.

37. CAL. PENAL CODE, § 510, Tent. Draft No. 1, at 37 (1967): "The Model Penal Code's further proviso that intoxication is not a mental disease is a self-evident proposition. Its concept of 'pathological intoxication' seems akin to accidental intoxication and is also unnecessary if evidence of intoxication is made generally admissible with respect to any culpable mental state." This proposal would also render irrelevant any distinction drawn in terms of whether the actor was culpable in contributing to his own mental condition caused

have been covered by the previous section, dealing with intoxication which is not knowingly or negligently self-induced, had that section included mistake as to resulting intoxication as well as the circumstance of what was consumed. Confusion will continue for three reasons. First, by drafting a separate section on pathological intoxication, there is still an indication that they were trying to enunciate an additional rule. Secondly, the statute itself, nevertheless, appears to be largely redundant with the defense of involuntary intoxication. Third, the content of the commentaries which accompanied the draft go well beyond their statute and tie into the medically more accurate comprehension of pathological intoxication.

The most important clinical criticism is that the Code's statutory characterization of pathological intoxication is framed in quantitative rather than qualitative terms. The reference is to the "degree" of "intoxication," which must be "gross," "given the amount of the intoxicant..." This strongly denotes two points, both of which are wrong or misleading. It strongly suggests a requirement of a relatively small amount of intoxicant; and, secondly, it is almost certainly going to be taken as a reference to drunkenness because of the repetitive use of the term "intoxication." The defense of pathological intoxication is, after all, described in § 2.08, which is entitled "Intoxication." Thus, a strictly textual analysis will indicate to the reader that there is little doubt that the Model Penal Code is talking about drunkenness which happens to result because of alcohol sensitivity, caused by drug potentiation of the alcohol or otherwise, not pathological reaction to alcohol in the sense of alcohol aggravating a pre-existing affliction of the actor.[38]

This equation has already been made by some courts[39] and by

---

by the intoxication unless additional provision was adopted, as the drafter recognized, that "explicitly provides that whenever recklessness or negligence suffices to establish the offense, an exculpation based upon intoxication is precluded by law," as the Model Penal Code has provided. Cal. Tent. Draft at 36.

38. In P. LOW, J. JEFFRIES & R. BONNIE, CRIMINAL LAW: CASES AND MATERIALS 731 (2d ed. 1986), the authors, some of whom were also involved in the updating and rewriting of the American Law Institute's commentaries to the Model Penal Code, appear to believe that pathological intoxication as formulated by the Model Penal Code addresses both brain pathology and alcohol sensitivity. They state: "This response, which may appear to involve loss of contact with reality, is a direct effect of the intoxication itself; the person will return to normal as the blood alcohol level falls. The disorder is thought to be associated with predisposing brain pathology as a result of which the individual may lose 'tolerance' for alcohol." They also make the observation that the condition "has arisen in litigation only a handful of times."

39. In United States v. Gertson, 15 M.J. 990 (1983), a conviction for assault was affirmed. The defendant claimed the defense of pathological intoxication as formulated by the Model Penal Code, but there was no evidence to support it other than the fact that he had been drinking. Despite the lack of evidence for the claim, the court then went on broadly to deny that military law (Marine Corps) recognized pathological intoxication. After citing the relevant portions of the Model Penal Code and DSM-III, the court characterized the problem

prominent writers. For example, Professor LaFave in the principal criminal law treatise used by the courts relies upon this Model Penal Code taxonomy and discusses pathological intoxication in the context of the intoxication defense but not in the context of the defenses of insanity or automatism, and there he says "the intoxication is involuntary only if the defendant was unaware that he is susceptible to an atypical reaction to the substance taken."[40] One could hardly argue with his interpretation of the Model Penal Code because that is what the statute, unfortunately, says. And while he includes in his treatise a section which discusses the relationship between automatism (including epilepsy) and insanity,[41] pathological intoxication is not discussed in connection with either insanity or automatism, at least not in those terms.[42]

Because of the Model Penal Code's handling of the subject, Professor Robinson, like Professor LaFave, understandably makes the assumption that pathological intoxication refers to getting unusually drunk on small amounts of alcohol. "An actor who becomes grossly intoxicated upon drinking two cans of beer after a three day fast and who does not know that he will be susceptible to such gross intoxication under such circumstances may be pathologically intoxicated."[43] That image and that understanding will be the legacy of the Model Penal Code. That excerpt does not describe a pre-Model Penal Code pathological reaction to alcohol.

Another reason for supposing that the Model Penal Code meant only alcohol sensitivity or potentiation is the fact that there is no justification for selecting one particular psychopathological mental condition known to afflict humans and to single it out in the code without mentioning all or even any of the rest, e.g., schizophrenia, particularly in the middle of a statute on intoxication as a defense.

The Code is all the more surprising because a reading of the comments to the original draft published in 1959 suggests that they meant to describe pre-code pathological intoxication or something akin to it. The failure appears to be in the language of the draft. What they describe in the statute is involuntary intoxication; what they describe in the commentary to that statute is pathological intoxication as it has been known in the medical literature. The commentary describes the pathological intoxication section as:

---

as "low tolerance for alcohol."

40. 1 W. LAFAVE & A. SCOTT, SUBSTANTIVE CRIMINAL LAW § 4.10(f) (1978).

41. LaFave & Scott at § 4.9(c).

42. LaFave & Scott at §§ 4.1-4.6, 4.9.

43. Robinson, *Causing the Conditions of One's Own Defense: A Study in the Limits of Theory in Criminal Law Doctrine*, 71 VA. L. REV. 1, 46 n.153 (1985).

> designed to provide a defense in a few, extremely rare, cases in which an intoxicating substance is knowingly taken into the body and, because of a bodily abnormality, intoxication of an extreme and unusual degree results. Such cases involve a short, atypical reaction to alcohol. It may be violent and may occur after small amounts of alcohol.[44]

There is, however, no known link between surprise intoxication and violence. Why would the subject of violence even be brought up unless they were talking about a qualitatively different reaction to alcohol? We think these qualifications were in the comments but not in the statute they proposed. People who get very drunk and are surprised or otherwise caught off guard by their intoxication do not turn violent just because of this surprise intoxication. There has to be more than that involved.

At that point, the commentary cites the Banay article discussed earlier in Chapter 2[45] describing it as "a review of the literature and case reports on pathological intoxication," and the language just quoted is undoubtedly based on it. It is important to remember that while this draft was developed after Banay had written his summary of the older clinical psychiatric literature to that time, the subsequent EEG-based studies and the clear link to pre-existing conditions such as temporal lobe lesions and brain damage had not yet been reported. Those became evident in the early 1960's. However, even at the time of Banay's article—and in that article, the phenomenon is referred to by him as a psychotic condition, not drunkenness—and Banay was unquestionably of the opinion that "pathologic reaction to alcohol is clearly differentiated from acute alcoholic intoxication."[46]

Next, however, the comments quote another case report by Podolsky[47] of a homicide committed while the actor was suffering from hypoglycemia,[48] and that is followed by still another reported instance involving hypoglycemia.[49] Selection of these illustrations indicates

---

44. MODEL PENAL CODE § 2.08 comment 7 at 11 (Tent. Draft No. 9, 1959).

45. Banay, *Pathologic Reaction to Alcohol,* 4 QRTLY J. STUD. ALCOH. 580 (1944).

46. Banay at 580.

47. Podolsky, *The Chemical Brew of Criminal Behavior,* 45 J. CRIM. L., CRIMINOLOGY & POLICE SCI. 675, 676 (1955) (cited there as Podalsky).

48. The blood sugar level is reported there as "below 100 mgm." It would have to be a good deal lower than that to be hypoglycemic.

49. Reported in a "London Letter," 122 J. A.M.A. 190 (1943). MODEL PENAL CODE § 2.08 comment at 12 n.29 (Tent. Draft No. 9, 1959). In the latter instance, it was reported that alcohol lowered the blood sugar level of the actor. The problem is that alcohol will usually increase the blood sugar level until well after drinking stops and then it may lower it dramatically; but the time delay would make alcohol consumption and hypoglycemia antithetical. There evidently are instances in which reactive hypoglycemia may occur under the facts given, but there are insufficient details given to determine if that is what was

confusion over what they are trying to describe because in the article by Podolsky, the emphasis is on hypoglycemia per se, not on hypoglycemia aggravated by alcohol. Most of the cases he discusses do not involve alcohol at all but are cited as instances of spontaneous hypoglycemia. Hypoglycemia is a candidate for traditional notions of pathological intoxication because it is an underlying condition which can be aggravated by alcohol. But where does the Model Penal Code intend for those cases to be handled in which the attack is spontaneous? If they are to be treated as cases of insanity when alcohol is not involved, then why would not the same insanity triggered by alcohol qualify as well if the actor was unaware of the potential, as, indeed, he must be for their pathological intoxication defense? And if insanity covers these situations, then why a statute on it, and why in the intoxication defense section? In our view, the hypoglycemia cases belong under either insanity or automatism, depending upon one's view of the mental-disease issue, and that remains true whether the attack was triggered by alcohol or was spontaneous. Instead, the Model Penal Code creates the appearance of wanting it treated as drunkenness in which the actor was taken by surprise.

Banay did include one 1933 summary which associated pathological intoxication and hypoglycemia,[50] but the Banay article is essentially a description of many of the previously reported discussions of pathological intoxication and the one article summarized was the first one to discover a link between pathological intoxication and hypoglycemic conditions. Seelert certainly did not think that he was describing surprise intoxication. Our point here is not to dispute that hypoglycemia belongs on the list of underlying conditions which when combined with alcohol can cause pathological intoxication, for clearly it does. What we dispute is that when it does, the resulting condition belongs in the category of involuntary intoxication or anything comparable to it.

In *Regina v. Quick*,[51] which we discussed in connection with the English position on automatism in Chapter 7, the court confronted the question whether hypoglycemia in combination with alcohol could be raised under a defense of automatism or must be raised in connection with the insanity defense only. Whatever the view, *Quick* was most certainly not taken by the English court as being a case of involuntary intoxication: Quick was not drunk—or surprised, or foresaw or should have foreseen complications due to abnormal bodily condition, or otherwise. What was at issue was whether the defendant should be required to plead the case as one of insanity or permitted to go to the jury on the automatism defense alone. Obviously, we agree with that

---

diagnosed. *See also* Regina v. Quick, 1973 Q.B. 910.

50. Seelert, *Zur Frage der Entwicklungsbedingungen des Pathologischen Rausche*, 86 MSCHR. PSYCHIAT. NEUROL. 191 (1933).

51. Regina v. Quick, 1973 Q.B. 910.

characterization of the issue in contrast to that implicit in the Model Penal Code draft, which introduces a third possibility.

Because of some of the language, partly because of the citation to Banay and use of the term "pathological intoxication," the impression remains that the drafters meant to recognize a more medically sanctioned concept of pathological intoxication and to assimilate one unusual kind of "intoxication" to the exculpatory law of insanity. We rhetorically asked earlier why they included this statute at all. Here is their answer:

> [A] provision is required because of a concern that bizarre behavior, caused in part by an abnormal bodily condition (in some cases, in others the atypical intoxication can be related to mental disturbance), would not seem to result from "mental disease" and thus would not fall under Section 4.01 [the insanity defense]. There is substantial dispute among physicians whether "pathological intoxication" is a distinct clinical entity. Yet the term seems the best to employ for legal purposes in describing a grossly abnormal reaction to alcohol, without respect to the medical reason for the reaction.[52]

If the insanity defense would be appropriate when the reaction was due to a "mental disturbance," what would prevent the case from being tried under the insanity defense and if not that, then as automatism? They also approvingly cite *Martinez v. People*,[53] where the court denied an instruction on pathological intoxication because the defendant had failed to plead insanity.[54] But under their draft, that would not be the correct ruling because they have suggested by its placement and language that the term "pathological intoxication" is not aimed at mental disease but targets only unusual and unexpected intoxication so that the defendant there should, under the position of the Code drafters, have gotten his instruction on pathological intoxication without a special plea.

Pathological intoxication was not a "distinct clinical entity" prior to this draft, although it most certainly was a recognized "clinical entity" and as a result of this draft is even less distinct now. But it was not a distinct entity before because the resulting unconsciousness or insanity could have a variety of causes, some of which were mental diseases, some of which were mental defects, some of which were arguably either (such as temporal lobe epilepsy) and some of which were brain damage as from trauma or temporary malfunctioning of the brain due to biochemical imbalances. Still others, despite manifest clinical signs of pathological intoxication, would never be known.

---

52. MODEL PENAL CODE § 2.08 comment 7 at 12 (Tent. Draft. No. 9, 1959).
53. Martinez v. People, 124 Colo. 170, 235 P.2d 810 (1951).
54. MODEL PENAL CODE § 2.08 comment at 12 n.30 (Tent. Draft No. 9, 1959).

As originally drafted, pathological intoxication meant "intoxication grossly excessive in degree, given the amount of the intoxicant, which is caused by an abnormal bodily condition not known to the actor."[55] Two changes were made in the final version. The first dropped the restriction of "bodily condition,"[56] and the second was to include the language to the effect "that the actor must not know of his susceptibility to the excessive reaction. With this change, there seems no reason to require that the reaction be 'caused by an abnormal bodily condition,' as provided by the former draft."[57] With the bodily-condition limitation, the defenses of pathological intoxication and automatism would overlap if the condition was extreme enough to result in unconsciousness. But when the bodily-condition element was removed, it is not clear how pathological intoxication differs from automatism or insanity, since the cause of the reaction can now be a mental condition as well as a bodily condition.

In *State v. Holzman*,[58] the conviction of the defendant for simple assault was upheld by the Superior Court of New Jersey on a de novo appeal on the lower court record. The defense was that she had mixed a small amount of alcohol and prescribed medication, a sedative. The court reasoned that simple assault could be predicated on a *mens rea* of recklessness. The New Jersey criminal code provides that "When recklessness establishes an element of the offense, if the actor, due to self-induced intoxication, is unaware of a risk of which he would have been aware had he been sober, such unawareness is immaterial."[59] This is the "special rule of intoxication" which applies only to voluntary, or self-induced, intoxication. The court defined the meaning of self-induced as

> Intoxication caused by substances which the actor knowingly introduces into his body, the tendency of which to cause intoxication he knows *or ought to know*, unless he introduces them pursuant to medical advice or under such circumstances as would afford a defense to the charge of crime.[60]

---

55. MODEL PENAL CODE § 2.08(5)(c) (Tent. Draft No. 9, 1959).

56. Some states retain the 1959 Model Penal Code draft language referring to "which results from physical abnormality." Hawaii provides "which results from a physical abnormality of the defendant." HAW. REV. STAT. § 702-230(5)(c) (Supp. 1988). The New Jersey provision on pathological intoxication, N.J. STAT. ANN. § 2C:2-8(e)(3) (West Supp. 1989), is based on MODEL PENAL CODE § 2.08, but the 1971 commentaries, which contain the same provision, are based on MODEL PENAL CODE § 2.08 (Tent. Draft No. 9 1959) and still refer to a limitation in terms of the intoxication having to be due to "bodily abnormality."

57. MODEL PENAL CODE, § 2.08, Status of Section at 40 (Proposed Official Draft 1962).

58. State v. Holzman, 424 A.2d 454 (N.J. Super. 1980).

59. N.J. STAT. ANN. § 2C:2-8(b) (West Supp. 1989).

60. N.J. STAT. ANN. § 2C:2-8(e)(2) (West Supp. 1989) (emphasis added).

The court concluded that the intoxication of the defendant was self-induced under this standard. Notice that the statutes, patterned on the Model Penal Code, when taken together, permit a finding of recklessness under the first section quoted, based on a negligence standard set out in the second section with respect to the likely effect of alcohol consumption. In combined effect, "self-induced" intoxication can be found on the basis of negligence as to the effect of the substance consumed despite the fact that the first statute quoted seems, on the contrary, to require recklessness as to the intoxication. In addition, the court does not discuss the language of the second section quoted regarding the meaning of the "unless" clause relating to prescribed medicine.

This interpretation then left open the question of pathological intoxication. The state code had also adopted the Model Penal Code language defining pathological intoxication as "intoxication grossly excessive in degree, given the amount of the intoxicant, to which the actor does not know he is susceptible."[61] To the contention that she fell within the purview of this affirmative defense, the court said that pathological intoxication applied only to instances "which happened because of some underlying organic condition."[62] The statute, of course, says no such thing, and while the first draft of the Model Penal Code on pathological intoxication had included the requirement that the reaction be "caused by an abnormal bodily condition,"[63] this was dropped in the Proposed Official Draft[64] which New Jersey actually adopted. Alluding to the nosological dispute about whether pathological intoxication is a distinct clinical entity, the commentaries to the Model Penal Code draft took the position that "the term seems the best to employ for legal purposes in describing a grossly abnormal reaction to alcohol, without respect to the medical reason for the reaction."[65]

Deletion of the "bodily condition" limitation[66] in the final version was designed to reflect the view just quoted that the abnormal reaction could as well be due to abnormal mental conditions as to bodily conditions. It is also interesting to note the insistence on a legal nosology that is free to disregard psychiatric nosological considerations: "without respect to the medical reason for the reaction." Nevertheless, the revised commentaries on the Model Penal Code describe the defense as though the qualification were still present,[67] and the later commentaries do not

61. N.J. STAT. ANN. § 2C:2-8(e)(3) (West Supp. 1989).

62. *Holzman* at 456. The court also said that the "word 'pathological' itself means diseased or due to a disease." Does this exclude drug-alcohol combinations?

63. MODEL PENAL CODE § 2.08(5)(c) (Tent. Draft No. 9, 1959).

64. MODEL PENAL CODE § 2.08(5)(c) (Proposed Official Draft 1962).

65. MODEL PENAL CODE § 2.08 comment at 12 (Tent. Draft No. 9, 1959).

66. MODEL PENAL CODE § 2.08 (Proposed Official Draft 1962).

67. 1 MODEL PENAL CODE AND COMMENTARIES § 2.08, at 364 (1985).

otherwise clarify the sense of their conception of pathological intoxication; the original commentary is essentially repeated.

Recall that section (3) provides that intoxication is not a disease. Since the insanity defense will require proof of a mental disease or defect, cases of pathological intoxication are not eligible if they are perceived to be only special cases of intoxication. Since that is exactly the way the Model Penal Code sees the situation, or at least drafted on the situation, they have not just singled out a special case of insanity and described it as involuntary intoxication, they have created the impression that they excluded it from the insanity defense and have forced it to be tried as involuntary intoxication even when an underlying abnormal mental condition is involved. This, of course, means that if the defendant wins under the pathological intoxication section, he is free to walk from the courtroom, whereas treatment would have been an alternative had this section not been included and the matter more clearly have been left to the law of insanity. If, to use their primary example, a person suffers from a spontaneous attack of hypoglycemia, he may be committed for treatment (or at least education regarding medical means of prevention or management) if he wins on the insanity defense, which he surely could do in some courts, but if the defendant by drinking triggered the reaction himself, albeit inadvertently, and therefore falls within the ambit of their version of pathological intoxication, he will not be subject to any further state action, for his disposition will be an outright acquittal, as it would also be if he had defended on the ground of automatism. The same will be true of underlying conditions which are more clearly in the category of "mental disease."

The Model Penal Code seems to have made a special case of pathological intoxication in order to take it out of the law of insanity and deliberately to put it under intoxication, where it could be called involuntary or voluntary depending upon the actor's state of mind at the time of drinking. Pathological intoxication would be recognized as part of the law of insanity or automatism without this section, as the case law overwhelmingly shows. Why the drafters selected one medical category of mental disease and turned it alone into a singular legal defense is something of a mystery, but we can at least explore it a bit. There are two ways to state the "mystery": (1) Why did they not leave their formulation of pathological intoxication to the law relating to involuntary acts, i.e., put it under automatism? (2) Why did they not leave pathological intoxication to the law of insanity?

Pathological intoxication might be handled as the defense of automatism, or involuntary act, under the Model Penal Code. Section 2.01 restates the normal rules that require each crime be based on conduct which includes a voluntary act. Reflexes, convulsions, movements while unconscious or asleep, hypnotically suggested movements, and any other act not the product of effort or determination are listed and excluded from the ambit of the concept of voluntary act.[68] "People whose involuntary movements threaten harm to others may present a public health or safety problem, calling for therapy or even for custodial commitment; they do not present a problem of correction."[69]

The revised commentaries do suggest that there is no reason that even ordinary intoxication cases could not be so extreme as to fall under the defense of involuntary act. "So long as liability can be premised on culpable voluntary behavior prior to unconsciousness, there appears no sound reason to preclude the possibility that intoxication may be so extreme that one is unconscious and incapable of voluntary action."[70] One assumes this would be equally true of pathological intoxication, and in those cases, there is a real possibility that liability could not "be premised on culpable voluntary behavior prior to unconsciousness." The following passage exhausts what the Model Penal Code has to say about automatism:

> Any definition must exclude a reflex or convulsion. The case of unconsciousness is equally clear when unconsciousness implies collapse or coma, as perhaps it does in ordinary usage of the term. There are, however, states of physical activity where self-awareness is grossly impaired or even absent, as in epileptic fugue, amnesia, extreme confusion and equivalent conditions.[71] How far these active states of automatism should be assimilated to coma for this legal purpose presents a difficult issue.
>
> There is judicial authority supporting the assimilation. An alternative approach, however, is to view these cases as appropriate for exculpation on the ground of mental disease or defect excluding responsibility. This view has also had support in the decisions. It offers the advantage that it may facilitate commitment when the individual is dangerous to the community because the condition is recurrent. By the same token, however, it bears harshly on the individual whose condition is nonrecurrent, as in the case where an extraordinary reaction follows the administration of a therapeutic drug.

---

68. MODEL PENAL CODE § 2.01(1) & (2) (Proposed Official Draft 1962).

69. 1 MODEL PENAL CODE AND COMMENTARIES § 2.01, at 215 (1985) (citations omitted).

70. 1 MODEL PENAL CODE AND COMMENTARIES § 2.08, at 353 (1985).

71. Citing N. MORRIS & C. HOWARD, STUDIES IN CRIMINAL LAW (1964); H. WILY & K. STALLWORTHY, MENTAL ABNORMALITY AND THE LAW 138-41, 151-85 (1962); Clapham, *An Interesting Case of Hypoglycaemia*, 33 MEDICO-LEGAL J. 72 (1965); Rapaport, *Consciousness: A Psychopathological and Psychodynamic View*, in PROBLEMS OF CONSCIOUSNESS: TRANSACTIONS OF THE SECOND CONFERENCE 18, 21-25 (H. Abramson ed. 1951); Wright, *Variations in States of Awareness in Schizophrenic Patients*, in PROBLEMS OF CONSCIOUSNESS: TRANSACTIONS OF THE SECOND CONFERENCE 100 (H. Abramson ed. 1951).

> And there may be difficulty in regarding some of these conditions as a "mental disease or defect" within the meaning of Section 4.01 or other tests, although cognition is sufficiently impaired to satisfy that aspect of the test.
>
> The provision does not define "unconsciousness" and thus does not attempt a legislative resolution of the issue. It employs the term that has had standing in the statutory law of many states, leaving the problem of interpretation, as it has previously rested, with the courts.[72]

There are two possibilities as to why pathological intoxication was not left to the law of insanity. The first, which also applies to automatism, is that it was felt that pathological intoxication required special treatment because the drafters wanted to place a fault limitation on the use of the pathological intoxication defense and restrict its use to non-fault situations. They did not want to place a similarly explicit fault limiter on the insanity defense or on the involuntary act defense, although it is not clear why either of these would be so. It would, of course, be novel in both cases. In the case of involuntary act, they have already created a fault limitation by approval of the decision in *Decina*,[73] which labeled as a culpable voluntary act a person's getting into an automobile to drive while aware of a possible blackout.

The idea of placing a fault limitation on defenses is certainly not novel, but the idea of doing so is not ordinarily associated with the defense of insanity, whereas fault has long been the distinguishing feature between voluntary and involuntary intoxication. The thought might have been that because the reaction could be triggered by the actor through his or her own conduct, a form of self-inflicted insanity, there was believed to be a need for an explicit fault limitation to be built into

---

72. 1 MODEL PENAL CODE AND COMMENTARIES § 2.01, at 219-20 (1985) (citations omitted).

Evidently only one legislative body has accepted the invitation to resolve the last question: Hawaii required that an involuntary act defense which "is based on a physical or mental disease, disorder, or defect which precludes or impairs a voluntary act or a voluntary omission, the defense shall be treated exclusively according to the provisions...." of the insanity defense. HAW. REV. STAT. § 702-200(2) (1985). The commentary to § 702-201 explains that "The Code attempts to provide 'therapy or...custodial commitment' for those dangerous individuals who are unable to conform their conduct to the requirements of the law because of some condition which would be difficult to regard as a 'mental disease or defect' under orthodox treatment of penal irresponsibility. At the same time, because treatment is flexible and tailored to the condition in question, it does not bear 'harshly on the individual whose condition is nonrecurrent.'" However, in 1986, this statute was amended to provide in addition that "a defense based on intoxication which is pathological or not self-induced which precludes or impairs a voluntary act or a voluntary omission shall be treated exclusively according to this chapter," i.e., the chapter which includes the provision relating to involuntary acts. HAW. REV. STAT. § 702-200(2) (Supp. 1988).

73. Discussed *supra*, Chapter 7, text accompanying note 29.

such a defense, so the decision was made to move the defense to the involuntary intoxication section where such a limitation would not be unusual. No other psychiatric phenomenon is singled out for special treatment other than psychopathy, which is denied any status. Pathological intoxication is the only temporary psychosis which is explicitly recognized, and the reason for doing so may only have been to place a fault limitation on its invocation.

The Model Penal Code's views of involuntary intoxication, pathological intoxication and involuntary act are actually all examples of mental incapacity that are not disease-based, and it is unfortunate that the fault idea was executed in such a circumscribed fashion. The concept of fault as a limitation on defenses is more fundamental than their treatment of it: The relevant category is nondisease-based nonculpability. It is difficult to believe that they thought an exculpatory mental condition could only be brought about by either (1) mental disease or defect; or (2) ingested substances. All such conditions, including simple mistake, could have been treated comparably, and in that unitary approach, they could also have included standards for determination of when fault on the part of the actor would limit the availability of the defense.

One reason the Model Penal Code had to build a fault limitation into their version of the pathological intoxication defense is that it does not provide for any requirement of "mental disease or defect" which might otherwise have provided the necessary functional analogue to a fault limitation. Conversely, the fact that they had to put in an explicit fault limitation expressed in terms of the actor's awareness of the likely outcome of drinking while having no explicit fault limitation at all in the insanity defense indicates that they believe the concept of disease serves that purpose under insanity law. Here the defense is written as applicable when the condition occurs "by reason of intoxication," while under the insanity defense it must arise "by reason of disease or defect."

This structure also indicates that the drafters did not believe that pathological intoxication was a mental disease or defect, and that suggests the second, related possible explanation. The drafters assumed that pathological intoxication might otherwise not be recognized as appropriately treated under insanity law because they believed that mental disease or defect was not involved. In fact, that is the reservation they expressed in the quoted material above. Yet, their own citation of medical authority, as we discussed, partially contradicts that conclusion. The comments say that intoxication which is not self-induced may provide an excuse "only if the resulting incapacitation is as extreme as that which would establish irresponsibility had it resulted from mental disease." Thus, mental-disease cases are clearly meant to be excluded from their concept of pathological intoxication. Yet, historically, mental-disease cases were at the core of the concept of pathological intoxication, and unless they mean to undo or ignore all that, then they must mean for those cases of pathological intoxication to be tried as insanity cases.

Another problem presented by the definition of pathological intoxication used by the Model Penal Code is that by writing a notice provision into the definition, they confuse responsibility questions in terms of the medical definition of the condition. The error was not inadvertent, however; it seems to be exactly what they meant to do. Professor Paulsen was a special consultant to the Model Penal Code's provision on intoxication (§ 2.08), and he subsequently described pathological intoxication in these terms:

> In situations of pathological intoxication, the violent and abnormal effects of drinking are completely surprising to the drinker, without warning in experience or education. In these rare cases the consequences of even a single drink may, in reality, be more lurid than the fertile imagination of the most dedicated prohibitionist.[74]

The Model Penal Code would permit negation of the existence of the condition by proof of the defendant's awareness of the condition. That is nonsensical if they are indeed attempting to describe a medical reality, although it is not if they mean to describe only involuntary intoxication. The medical reality is that the actor is or is not susceptible to pathological reaction to alcohol and the person's awareness is irrelevant to that fact. The actor's awareness is relevant only to criminal liability, and the two points ought to be kept separate, for they are quite distinct matters.

The fact that pathological intoxication is defined as nonexistent if the actor was aware that his condition[75] might lead to such a reaction is of small moment; that is only a matter of aesthetics. The Model Penal Code can define pathological intoxication in terms of the actor's lack of awareness of the condition precisely because they are not defining a medical condition, they are defining a legal condition of exculpation. Were pathological intoxication given its medical interpretation, the draft

74. Paulsen, *Intoxication as a Defense to Crime*, 1961 U. ILL. L.F. 1, 17.

75. When MODEL PENAL CODE § 2.08(5)(c) (Tent. Draft No. 9, 1959) contained the provision limiting the defense to reactions caused by an abnormal bodily condition, the phrase being never defined. Does it include fatigue, drugs in the body or latent psychosis? Does this include mental conditions as well? Does it include brain damage that contributes to mental illness? These, of course, are the same problems courts have in trying to distinguish automatism from insanity in pathological intoxication cases and otherwise. The English distinction between sane and insane automatism may turn on the same distinction, although it would seem that those courts are beginning to take a more pragmatic view influenced heavily by the differing dispositions involved. These matters have been addressed in Chapter 7.

would be patently absurd. It would say then that the defendant did not have psychomotor epilepsy if he knew he had it. What is meant there is that the *defense* of pathological intoxication does not exist when culpable awareness existed. But handling the fault issue in this manner leaves the obvious problem that pathological intoxication is not intoxication in the ordinary sense at all.

The effect of this draft, given the influence it has had and will continue to have, is that we must now recognize still a third category of pathological intoxication. The first two consisted of a temporary psychotic condition brought on by a triggering effect of alcohol on an underlying mental disease or defect that legally assimilates to temporary insanity. The second type, which was also stressed by the early clinicians, was closely related, but the underlying cause could not fairly be said to be attributable to a condition that would fall within the legal idea of mental disease or defect under insanity laws, though the effect of the alcohol on the actor was the same as if it were. These are the automatism cases. The third type now introduced by the Model Penal Code, despite the best efforts of everyone else to distinguish it, is surprise intoxication, where the unforeseen aspect is the resulting degree of intoxication, but it is intoxication nevertheless. It is distinguishable from involuntary intoxication only in that the mistake by the actor is with respect to the resulting intoxication rather than the existing circumstance of the nature of the intoxicant consumed. This is basically pathological intoxication as a species of involuntary intoxication, to be distinguished from the legal insanity type and the automatism, or involuntary-act, type.

Most jurisdictions do not have the Model Penal Code provision on pathological intoxication. More states have adopted their provision regarding involuntary intoxication than have adopted their section on pathological intoxication. Presumably in those states, it is a matter of choice of defense counsel how the case is to be tried, or the courts will have to give some indication as to when and why one defense category is more appropriate, or required. We have tried to show that whether the defense of pathological intoxication is more germane to insanity, involuntary act or involuntary intoxication depends largely on the type of pathological intoxication involved, but there will still be the possibility of overlapping defenses in a case of pathological intoxication in which the defendant acted in an unconscious state due to mental disease or defect. In that case, the facts will fit both insanity and automatism. But while only a few states adopted the provision on pathological intoxication, it is not at all uncommon for the Model Penal Code to have influence in the courts, including the federal courts,[76] well beyond the sway they may have in the legislative branch. It may be important, then, to understand

76. Kane v. United States, 399 F.2d 730 (9th Cir. 1968).

just how badly drafted that pathological intoxication section actually is, and that is the reason we took time with it.

CONCLUSION

As the law continues to struggle with pathological intoxication, an aesthetically appealing trichotomy emerges in light of the Model Penal Code's proposal. Pathological intoxication would be conceived of as stemming from (1) mental disease, ideally dealt with under insanity law; (2) physical disease or trauma, presumably belonging to the defense of involuntary act or automatism; and (3) exaggerated and surprise intoxication, to be handled as the defense of involuntary intoxication.

There are enough problems with this view that it is difficult to endorse it enthusiastically. First, the concept of mental disease is all that practically separates insanity and automatism, and that is a thin reed to build upon. All that separates involuntary intoxication from insanity is the same concept, and it is largely a legal conclusion, not an objective, identifiable fact. And if the actor is rendered unconscious, there may be no difference between involuntary intoxication and automatism or involuntary act. If one could count on a reliable factual distinction between the categories of defenses, it would be important to make those distinctions, but the important matters are the nature of the disposition of the defendant when the case is resolved, fault on the part of the actor and the legal notions of what constitutes "mental disease or defect," and this distinction between mental disease and other causes is not a distinction we would expect to endure. Still, such a trichotomy is probably better than the level of understanding presently exhibited in a variety of contexts.

9

Diminished Capacity and "Extreme Mental and Emotional Disturbance" as Defense Theories for Pathological Intoxication

DIMINISHED CAPACITY AND DIMINISHED RESPONSIBILITY DISTINGUISHED

When account is taken of the fact that the diminished capacity doctrine does somewhat less for defendants who are mentally disturbed but sane than voluntary intoxication law has done for drunks for a century longer, a desire for doctrinal consistency should have dictated its creation. The status[1] and meaning[2] of diminished capacity are equivocal and fluid and we will not try to provide a summary.[3] There is little agreement on the subjects raised in this section, but to provide some points of reference, this brief review is offered.[4]

Under the doctrine of diminished capacity, testimony, usually expert testimony, is allowed into evidence to show an abnormal mental condition of the defendant at the time of the act charged, a condition less incapacitating than legal insanity, for the purpose of negating a *mens rea* requirement, and such evidence is permitted without a plea of not guilty by reason of insanity.[5] The diminished capacity defense is also a label

---

1. 2 MODEL PENAL CODE AND COMMENTARIES § 210.3, at 70-71 nn.75-77 (1980).

2. 2 MODEL PENAL CODE AND COMMENTARIES § 210.3, at 65-73 (1980).

3. *But see* Weinberg, *Epilepsy and the Alternatives for a Criminal Defense*, 27 CASE W. RES. L. REV. 771, 798 n.179 (1977).

4. *See* United States v. Gold, 661 F. Supp. 1127 (D.D.C. 1987), which discusses diminished capacity versus diminished responsibility involving the new federal insanity rules.

5. Arenella, *The Diminished Capacity and Diminished Responsibility Defenses: Two Children of a Doomed Marriage*, 77 COLUM. L. REV. 827 (1977). The general theoretical underpinnings of the defense of diminished capacity have been stated by Professor Robinson:

> Mental illness commonly negates an element without amounting to insanity. As a failure of proof defense, at least in cases where the defendant is still guilty of a lesser included offense, it is often called "partial responsibility" or "diminished capacity." Its name highlights the fact that it is something short of insanity; but it is nonetheless an unfortunate choice of terms because there

attached to expert testimony that the defendant could not, and therefore did not, form the requisite mental state at the time of the commission of the charged offense.[6] It can be admitted into evidence to show the defendant lacked the capacity to form a mental state required by the crime, although, like intoxication, it is often limited to defeating a showing of specific intent[7] and in many of the states which recognize it, it is essentially limited to attempts to reduce murder in the first degree, which requires premeditation and deliberation in addition to an intent to kill, to second degree, usually to avoid the death penalty. Thus, it simply allows evidence to be admitted that is relevant to the *mens rea* question,[8] although it often applies, because of the nature of the evidence, to the ability to form the *mens rea* rather than consisting of more direct evidence of whether the defendant actually had the requisite mental state.[9] Like intoxication and mistake in general, the defense may only reduce the level of the crime to one for which the defendant did have the requisite *mens rea.* Many states recognize this defense in some configurations either by case law[10] or by statute.[11]

With varying degrees of clarity, the law distinguishes between diminished capacity and diminished responsibility.[12] The diminished

---

> is nothing *partial* about the defense. The mental illness either negates a required element of an offense or it does not, thereby providing a complete defense *to that offense* or providing no defense. It is true that many offenses, especially homicide offenses, have lesser included offenses with less demanding culpability elements. Thus mental illness may negate the culpability element of the greater offense but not the lesser offense. When this occurs, the net effect of the mental illness is to reduce the defendant's liability from the greater to the lesser.

Robinson, *Criminal Law Defenses: A Systematic Analysis,* 82 COLUM. L. REV. 199, 206 (1982) (footnotes omitted) (emphasis in original).

6. Comment, *The Relevance of Innocence: Proposition 8 and the Diminished Capacity Defense,* 71 CALIF. L. REV. 1197, 1198 (1983).

7. *See, e.g.,* State v. McVey, 376 N.W.2d 585 (Iowa 1985).

8. *See, e.g.,* MODEL PENAL CODE § 4.02(1) (Proposed Official Draft 1962).

9. Under the (former) California diminished capacity doctrine, one probably could further differentiate the cases in their treatment of the "malice" requirement of murder, but we will not pursue the matter further here. *See* H. FINGARETTE & A. HASSE, MENTAL DISABILITIES AND CRIMINAL RESPONSIBILITY 119-20 (1979).

10. California was one of the leading jurisdictions to develop the defense of diminished capacity without the aid of legislation. *See, e.g.,* G. FLETCHER, RETHINKING CRIMINAL LAW § 4.2 (1978). Proposition 8 has changed the California law underlying a number of the California cases discussed here. Comment, *The Relevance of Innocence: Proposition 8 and the Diminished Capacity Defense,* 71 CALIF. L. REV. 1197 (1983).

11. 1 P. ROBINSON, CRIMINAL LAW DEFENSES § 64 (1984).

12. United States v. Frisbee, 623 F. Supp. 1217 (N.D. Cal. 1985); Morse, *Undiminished Confusion in Diminished Capacity,* 75 J. CRIM. L. & CRIMINOLOGY 1, 7-9 (1984). *See also* Dressler, *Reaffirming the Moral Legitimacy of the Doctrine of Diminished Capacity: A Brief Reply to Professor Morse,* 75 J. CRIM. L. & CRIMINOLOGY 953 (1984); Hermann, *Criminal Defenses and Pleas in Mitigation Based on Amnesia,* 4 BEHAV. SCI. & LAW 5, 10 (1986).

responsibility defense is rare in the United States[13] but is found more commonly in England. The defendant may be declared guilty of a lesser offense but is not acquitted even when a greater offense was actually committed because of some mental impairment which is deemed to justify such treatment. It is a mitigation of punishment despite the presence of all of the elements of the crime, including the mental state required. When a defendant successfully invokes diminished capacity, it means he did not commit the offense, although a lesser offense may be found. When a defendant qualifies under diminished responsibility, the offense was committed but leniency is provided in the form of reducing the grade or degree of the offense committed. For example, under the old English Infanticide Act of 1914, murder of a newborn child by the mother would be reduced from murder to manslaughter because it was thought that the special stress of the particular situation called for such a result even though the killing might have been quite intentional. Common law's reduction of murder to manslaughter under the provocation ("heat of passion") rule could be thought of as such a rule because it allowed reduction by the jury of an intentional killing when the actor was adequately provoked and was in the "heat of passion" at the time of the killing without having had time to cool down. A current English example is found in the English Homicide Act of 1957, which reduces murder to manslaughter when a person's "abnormality of mind...substantially impaired his mental responsibility."[14] The distinguishing factor from diminished capacity is that here the defense is available despite the

---

13. An example of a limited version of diminished responsibility is provided by the Model Penal Code:

> Whenever the jury or the Court is authorized to determine or to recommend whether or not the defendant shall be sentenced to death or imprisonment upon conviction, evidence that the capacity of the defendant to appreciate the criminality [wrongfulness] of his conduct or to conform his conduct to the requirements of law was impaired as a result of mental disease or defect is admissible in favor of sentence of imprisonment.

MODEL PENAL CODE § 4.02(2) (Proposed Official Draft 1962).

This is essentially a statement of the insanity test affecting liability in which the phrase "substantial capacity" used in that test is reduced to "capacity" on what is solely a question of sentencing unrelated to liability for the underlying crime. Since virtually anything is relevant in an attempt to reduce a death penalty possibility to a lesser penalty, this does not actually constitute diminished responsibility in the sense of a rule which reduces the level of the crime. That is the reason the code states that "The Model Code does not recognize diminished responsibility as a distinct category of mitigation." 2 MODEL PENAL CODE AND COMMENTARIES 72 (1980).

14. Homicide Act, 5 & 6 Eliz. 2, ch. 11, § 2(1) (1957). The provision was commented on in Hughes, *The English Homicide Act of 1957,* 49 J. CRIM. L., CRIMINOLOGY & POLICE SCI. 521, 526 (1959): "The doctrine is professedly borrowed from Scottish law which has applied it since the middle of the nineteenth century."

existence of the *mens rea,* whereas diminished capacity permits evidence needed to negate the *mens rea.*[15] Used in the sense of mitigation only, "No American jurisdiction has adopted a diminished capacity defense [diminished responsibility, as we use the terms] comparable with that which has been developed in Europe."[16]

It remains true that diminished capacity needs to be distinguished from pure *mens rea* issues because there are significant procedural differences, most importantly whether expert witnesses will be heard without a special plea of not guilty by reason of insanity with its attendant risks of civil incarceration in a hospital. There also usually are crime limitations imposed on the defense of diminished capacity, while no such limitations exist on ordinary *mens rea* defenses. Insanity can be a defense even if the mental condition does not negate the existence of *mens rea,* and insanity is not limited to certain crimes. On the other hand, the defense of insanity may be relied upon only if the special plea is entered, while this is not generally required of the diminished capacity defense.[17] The Model Penal Code provides a straightforward example of a statutory statement of a very broad version of the diminished capacity defense: "Evidence that the defendant suffered from a mental disease or defect is admissible whenever it is relevant to prove that the defendant did or did not have a state of mind that is an element of the offense."[18]

Most states have not adopted a provision this broad, and many do not recognize the doctrine at all. Those which do recognize it restrict it to murder charges to reduce the degree of murder, often solely for the purpose of restricting application of the death penalty,[19] while others limit it to specific intent crimes. Thus, when the sole function of the rule is to reduce the grade of an offense, it differs little in practical effect from a rule of diminished responsibility. Still, the critical difference is that, technically, the evidence is admitted to negate *mens rea* either by proving

---

15. Lewin, *Psychiatric Evidence in Criminal Cases for Purposes Other Than the Defense of Insanity,* 26 SYRACUSE L. REV. 1051, 1054-65 (1975). Another example is found in the Italian Penal Code: "Anyone who, at the time he committed the act, was by reason of infirmity, in such state of mind as to greatly diminish, without precluding his capacity to understand and to will, shall be liable for the offense committed; but the punishment shall be reduced." The Italian Penal Code art. 89, at 32-33 (E. Wise trans. 1978).

16. Hermann, *Criminal Defenses and Pleas in Mitigation Based on Amnesia,* 4 BEHAV. SCI. & LAW 5, 10 (1986).

17. Colorado permits the defense of diminished capacity in all cases but requires a special plea for such evidence to be deemed admissible. *See, e.g.,* People v. Low, 732 P.2d 622 (Colo. 1987). In *Low,* unlike the view expressed by many courts and writers, the defense is characterized as an affirmative defense. *Low* at 632.

18. MODEL PENAL CODE § 4.02(1) (Proposed Official Draft 1962).

19. *See, e.g.,* State v. Sikora, 44 N.J. 453, 210 A.2d 193 (1965), where the court held that psychiatric evidence of diminished capacity could not be used to reduce first degree murder to second degree murder, but could be used to mitigate on the issue of the death penalty.

directly that the actor did not have the requisite culpability or, less directly, that he lacked the capacity to entertain it, to prove that the higher offense was not in fact committed. As the Model Penal Code now explains:

> Courts complicate the matter by using the phrase [diminished responsibility] for two entirely different concepts. The first is essentially a rule of evidence. It posits that evidence of mental incapacity or abnormality is admissible whenever relevant to prove that the defendant did not have a state of mind required for commission of the offense. This use of mental defect is quite different from the insanity defense. Insanity is a defense in the sense that it exculpates the defendant even if it does not negate any element of the offense with which he is charged. Furthermore, insanity is defined without reference to particular crimes and provides a general bar to criminal liability. In its evidentiary aspect, diminished responsibility is not an independent defense in this sense; it exculpates the defendant only if it negates the state of mind required for the commission of the offense charged. In that way, it functions as does mistake—that is, it is simply one way of showing that the defendant did not satisfy every element of the crime charged.[20]

The status of the defense has been in flux since introduced in California in 1949 in *People v. Wells,*[21] as has recently been summarized as follows:

> Although some form of the concept has been used over time by 15 states, it has failed to capture major support and has even lost the support it previously enjoyed. Criticism from the legal community and growing use of the American Law Institute test in jurisdictions that had previously embraced the diminished capacity concept have resulted in calls for its abandonment.[22]

---

20. 2 MODEL PENAL CODE AND COMMENTARIES § 210.3 comment 5 at 65 (1980).

21. People v. Wells, 33 Cal. 2d 330, 202 P.2d 53 (1949). *See* Louisell & Hazard, *Insanity as a Defense: The Bifurcated Trial,* 49 CALIF. L. REV. 805 (1961).

22. S. BRAKEL, J. PARRY & B. WEINER, THE MENTALLY DISABLED AND THE LAW 711 (3d ed. 1985) (footnotes omitted). *See also* H. FINGARETTE & A. HASSE, MENTAL DISABILITIES AND CRIMINAL RESPONSIBILITY 119-20 (1979).

DIMINISHED CAPACITY AND PATHOLOGICAL INTOXICATION

There might be two kinds of cases in which diminished capacity may be invoked to reduce the level of the degree of the charge committed by the actor. The first would be where the degree of derangement suffered under pathological intoxication was not as thoroughly disabling as other cases; it is unlikely that the cases will always be absolute. The other type of case might be where the law otherwise is not refined enough to reflect different degrees of fault as a limitation on defenses such as insanity even in those jurisdictions which would have no difficulty in applying insanity rules to pathological intoxication in a clearer case.

No doubt the strongest legal argument for the existence of diminished capacity is the fact that such an ameliorative effect has been recognized for some time in the case of intoxication which is voluntary in every sense of the word. In those cases, the courts by a large majority will permit such a knowingly self-induced condition to, for example, reduce murder of the first degree to murder of the second degree, a degree not requiring specific intent or premeditation and deliberation.[23] If we are to allow such a reduction in a case of simple drunkenness, it hardly seems consistent to reject any ameliorative rule in cases in which the actor was partly or even entirely without blame in occasioning the situation. Indeed, that argument has been viewed as persuasive by a number of the courts which have accepted the defense of diminished capacity without the aid of a statute. Other states restrict the admissibility of evidence of mental illness to those cases in which the defendant has entered a special plea of not guilty by reason of insanity.

The admissibility of psychiatric evidence in the absence of a plea of not guilty by reason of insanity is the battleground. It is not difficult to understand the defense perspective. The defendant is often advantaged by a rule which permits reduction, and certainly by exculpation entirely, in lieu of the possible indeterminate commitment authorized or required to follow an acquittal on the basis of legal insanity. "Many courts have refused, however, to allow psychiatric testimony unless it was offered to establish a mental disease or defect that would support an insanity defense."[24] Nor is it difficult to understand the prosecution's viewpoint that such a rule of unfettered admissibility of psychiatric testimony would undercut one of the most fundamental reasons for the existence of the insanity plea in the first instance: to cause the commitment of the defendant believed to be dangerous no matter what the outcome of the criminal charges. Indeed, it was the admissibility of such evidence in the

---

23. Keedy, *A Problem of First Degree Murder: Fisher v. United States*, 99 U. PA. L. REV. 267 (1950).

24. 2 MODEL PENAL CODE AND COMMENTARIES § 210.3 comment 5 at 66 (1980).

absence of a plea of not guilty by reason of insanity that was in issue in *Wells.*[25] The U. S. Supreme Court has said:

> ...when a statute establishing different degrees of murder requires deliberate premeditation in order to constitute murder in the first degree, the question whether the accused is in such condition of mind, by reason of drunkenness or otherwise, as to be incapable of deliberate premeditation, necessarily becomes a material subject of consideration by the jury.[26]

While the logic seems compelling, our focus here is not to rehash the desirability of the recognition of a diminished capacity defense but to treat the question of pathological intoxication as a suitable situation for its invocation where it is recognized. The American version of diminished capacity is often the compromise doctrine invoked by defense counsel in uncertain situations, and one would not be surprised to see it used in the context of pathological reaction to alcohol.

The California courts have had some experience with pathological intoxication in the context of diminished capacity prior to its abolition. In *People v. Anderson,*[27] the court held that the trial court erred in not giving an instruction on diminished capacity in a prosecution for murder in the first degree after the defendant had attempted to prove that he was unconscious at the time of the attack by reason of a psychomotor epileptic seizure. *People v. Castillo*[28] reversed a murder conviction on the ground that the evidence was sufficient to justify an instruction on diminished capacity based on pathological intoxication, which might have the effect of reducing murder to manslaughter under the California theory that the jury could find an absence of malice required of the crime of murder. The defendant got into a bar fight after drinking only a modest amount of beer. He went home and got a shotgun, then came back and shot the man with whom he had been fighting. Dr. Minard was one of the expert witnesses for the defense:

> He concluded that defendant had an unusual reaction to alcohol, a condition he described as alcoholic pathological intoxication. A person suffering from this condition may react exceptionally following the consumption of a small amount of alcohol and perform acts of violence without apparent motivation. The subject will almost always undergo a

---

25. People v. Wells, 33 Cal. 2d 330, 202 P.2d 53 (1949).
26. Hopt v. Utah, 104 U.S. 631, 634, 26 L. Ed. 873, 874 (1882).
27. People v. Anderson, 63 Cal. 2d 351, 46 Cal. Rptr. 763, 406 P.2d 43 (1965).
28. People v. Castillo, 70 Cal. 2d 264, 74 Cal. Rptr. 385, 449 P.2d 449 (1969).

> complete amnesia. The condition is quite similar to psychomotor epilepsy, which is caused by an electrical disturbance in the temporal lobe of the brain....Dr. Minard stated that his observation of defendant and study of his history indicated that defendant was suffering from a psychomotor seizure during the commission of the homicide and that no person so afflicted could premeditate or deliberate [or harbor malice aforethought].[29]

However, *Castillo,* which is based on the leading California case, *Conley,*[30] may hold no special support for pathological intoxication because ordinary intoxication may fall within the same doctrine. The court applied their usual rubric that "the court should instruct the jury upon every material question upon which there is any evidence deserving of any consideration whatever."[31] More significant use was made of pathological intoxication as diminished capacity in *People v. Austin.*[32]

> Dr. George M. Thompson, a specialist in neurology, psychology and electroencephalography, testified that: he performed electroencephalographic tests on defendant. First, a standard encephalogram was conducted; next an "alcohol activated" examination was performed; this test consisted of defendant drinking two ounces of 80 proof alcohol and then being examined 15 minutes later; during the third of such tests the doctor detected "spiking" on the recorded tracings of defendant's brain waves; "spiking" does not occur in a normal brain pattern. As a result of the clear "spiking" pattern, Dr. Thompson concluded that the defendant was abnormally sensitive and susceptible to the effects of alcohol in relatively small doses. It was the doctor's opinion that the abnormality, indicating brain scar tissue, was probably "moderately severe" on a scale of "slight to very severe." Because of such possible brain change a small amount of alcohol taken on an empty

---

29. *Castillo* at 268, 74 Cal. Rptr. at 386-87, 449 P.2d at 450-51.

30. People v. Conley, 64 Cal. 2d 310, 49 Cal. Rptr. 815, 411 P.2d 911 (1966). *Conley* is criticized for, among other things, being "nearly impenetrable" in Johnson, *The Supreme Court of California 1975-1976—Forward: The Accidental Decision and How It Happens,* 65 CALIF. L. REV. 231 (1977). Some have read it not as diminished capacity, but as diminished responsibility. 2 MODEL PENAL CODE AND COMMENTARIES § 210.3, at 67-69 (1980).

See also People v. Wolff, 61 Cal. 2d 795, 40 Cal. Rptr. 271, 394 P.2d 959 (1964). Comment, *Keeping Wolff From the Door: California's Diminished Capacity Concept,* 60 CALIF. L. REV. 1641 (1972) (authored by Ann Fingarette Hasse); Comment, *Diminished Capacity: Its Potential Effect in California,* 3 LOY. L.A.L. REV. 153 (1970).

31. People v. Cram, 12 Cal. App. 3d 37, 90 Cal. Rptr. 393 (1970), reviews these rules.

32. People v. Austin, 270 Cal. App. 2d 845, 76 Cal. Rptr. 154 (1969).

> stomach could set off an attack of psychomotor epilepsy which would cause a loss of memory and very likely assaultive behavior. If such an attack had occurred, defendant might still have amnesia or might simply show a greater degree of confusion and muddled thinking than an average person who had consumed the same amount of alcohol. Dr. Thompson thought that it was unlikely [sic, likely?][33] that defendant suffered from acute pathological alcoholic intoxication.
>
> Dr. Thompson testified that psychomotor epilepsy precipitated by alcohol becomes known under the term acute pathological alcoholic intoxication. Such is a condition in which a person has brain abnormality due to brain injury, scar tissue on the brain or some other brain damage. The doctor stated that sometimes a person who is abnormally susceptible to small amounts of alcohol may have a psychomotor seizure and attack precipitated by alcohol. At such times the person may walk around and carry out formulated behavior but he may have a loss of memory, either total or partial, for the time period of the attack, and often carries out abnormal behavior, frequently assaultive in nature.[34]

The court reversed the conviction for murder in the second degree on the basis of *Castillo* because of failure to instruct on the theory of diminished capacity, which might have reduced the verdict to manslaughter. It should be noted that this doctrine applies quite independently of the insanity plea; here the defendant had only pleaded not guilty.

In *People v. Drew,* decided in 1978, the California Supreme Court adopted the Model Penal Code's "substantial capacity" test to replace their *M'Naghten* rule.[35] That did not, however, affect their view of the diminished capacity defense. Indeed, the same day as their adoption of the A.L.I. test, they also held that the diminished capacity test was not limited to murder cases but applied as well to other specific intent crimes.[36]

The diminished capacity test (as well as *Drew's* adoption of the Model Penal Code test of insanity) was abolished by the California legislature[37] following its invocation in the trial of Dan White for murder of the mayor and a supervisor of San Francisco. The defense is reported

---

33. The quoted passage makes sense only if "unlikely" means "likely."

34. *Austin* at 850-51, 76 Cal. Rptr. at 157.

35. People v. Drew, 22 Cal. 3d 333, 149 Cal. Rptr. 275, 583 P.2d 1318 (1978).

36. People v. Wetmore, 22 Cal. 3d 318, 149 Cal. Rptr. 265, 583 P.2d 1308 (1978).

37. For the history and abolition of the rule, *see* Comment, *The Relevance of Innocence: Proposition 8 and the Diminished Capacity Defense,* 71 CALIF. L. REV. 1197 (1983).

to have been based on "biochemical change" in the defendant's brain caused by high levels of blood sugar from eating "junk food" which evidently exacerbated his diagnosed "manic depression."[38] The jury apparently agreed with the defense experts and found the defendant guilty of voluntary manslaughter on the charge of murder. The facetious label of "Twinkie defense" was immediately placed on the defense.

One of the most important federal decisions dealing with diminished capacity is found in *United States v. Brawner,*[39] where the Court of Appeals for the District of Columbia gave the rule considerable support. They overturned their previous rule[40] and permitted psychiatric and other expert testimony to be admitted to negate specific intent although there had been no plea of not guilty by reason of insanity entered by the defense. Lower federal courts have held that while Federal Rule of Evidence 704(b) may have affected the scope of the conclusions of experts, it did not change the fundamental holding of *Brawner,* which permits psychiatric testimony regarding the existence of the mental state required by the crime charged, at least when the issue is one of specific intent.

In *United States v. Gold,*[41] the government, in response to a defense statement of intention to use psychiatric testimony regarding the defendant's mental state at the time of the crime charged but without entering a plea of insanity, made a motion *in limine* to exclude such testimony as in contravention of the Insanity Defense Reform Act of 1984[42] and Federal Evidence Rule 704(b). Rule 704(b) provides that "No expert witness testifying with respect to the mental state or condition of a defendant in a criminal case may state an opinion or inference as to whether the defendant did or did not have the mental state or condition constituting an element of the crime charged or of a defense thereto. Such ultimate issues are matters for the trier of fact alone." Subsection (b) of Rule 704 was added by amendment under the Insanity Defense Reform Act of 1984.[43] The court held that the evidence was admissible "on the factual issue of the defendant's mental state or condition during the relevant time, but defendant shall not be allowed to introduce testimony or evidence that proposes an opinion or inference as to whether

---

38. THE NEW YORK TIMES, May 22, 1979, at D17, col. 3.

39. United States v. Brawner, 471 F.2d 969 (D.C. Cir. 1972).

40. Fisher v. United States, 80 U.S. App. D.C. 96, 149 F.2d 28 (D.C. Cir. 1945). *See also* Taylor, *Partial Insanity as Affecting the Degree of Crime—A Commentary on Fisher v. United States,* 34 CALIF. L. REV. 625 (1946). The diminished capacity defense of *Brawner* was rejected by the court in Bethea v. United States, 365 A.2d 64 (D.C. 1976). *See also* Doepel v. United States, 434 A.2d 449 (D.C. 1981), reaffirming that rejection in a case of claimed pathological intoxication, *and* Doepel v. United States, 510 A.2d 1044 (D.C. 1986).

41. United States v. Gold, 661 F. Supp. 1127 (D.D.C. 1987).

42. 18 U.S.C. § 17 (Supp. IV 1986).

43. 18 U.S.C. § 20 (Supp. II 1984).

defendant did or did not have the mental state or condition necessary to constitute an element of the crime."[44]

In reaching this conclusion, the court relied heavily on *United States v. Frisbee*.[45] In that case, the defense announced their intention to introduce expert testimony that "due to some combination of pathological intoxication, organic brain damage, and an alcoholic blackout or seizure, he did not possess the requisite specific intent during the relevant time period to have committed first degree murder."[46] That court held that the new rules did not overturn *Brawner* but limited the scope of the expert testimony that could be offered. The limitation, as understood by the *Frisbee* court and adopted by the *Gold* court, was that "the Court will only allow the experts to testify concerning their diagnoses, the facts upon which those diagnoses are based, and the characteristics of any mental diseases or defects the experts believe the defendant possessed during the relevant time period. No testimony directly or indirectly opining on the issue of specific intent will be allowed."[47]

While some jurisdictions simply will not recognize pathological intoxication in this context because they do not recognize the defense of diminished capacity,[48] the degree to which pathological reaction to alcohol is viewed as appropriately assimilated to the defense of diminished capacity is almost certainly directly correlated to the degree of skepticism entertained regarding the evidence supporting the concept of pathological reaction to alcohol in the first instance. Diminished capacity is a compromise defense, lying between no defense and the complete defense of legal insanity. In many states, diminished capacity is limited to homicide crimes. If pathological reaction to alcohol is recognized as having occurred in a particular case, there is no reason for the defense to be available only in homicide-based crimes.

It undoubtedly remains true that in those instances in which the defense will operate to acquit outright, that is, there is no lesser included offense to serve as a "net", the courts will certainly not favor the defense when the choice of a plea of not guilty by reason of insanity was open

---

44. *Gold* at 1132.

45. United States v. Frisbee, 623 F. Supp. 1217 (N.D. Cal. 1985).

46. *Frisbee* at 1219.

47. *Frisbee* at 1224. *See also* G. WEISSENBERGER, FEDERAL RULES OF EVIDENCE ch. 704 at 310 (1987), "For example, an expert may testify as to the diagnosis of the accused's mental condition but may not state an opinion on whether the defendant was legally insane," citing United States v. Prickett, 604 F. Supp. 407, 409 (S.D. Ohio 1985).

48. *See, e.g.*, State v. Croscup, 604 S.W.2d 69 (Tenn. Crim. App. 1980). In an appeal of a conviction for murder, the appellate court indicates there was some opinion evidence that the defendant suffered from pathological intoxication, but no details are provided. The conviction was affirmed on an evidence sufficiency appeal, and the court upheld a refusal to give an instruction on diminished capacity because Tennessee law did not require it. The defendant had been confined to a mental hospital from age 7 until he escaped at age 19.

to the defense. Perhaps the principal reason to invoke the diminished capacity defense over the insanity defense is tactical in the sense of avoiding the indeterminate commitment that may follow a successful interposition of the plea of not guilty by reason of insanity.[49] Yet, in many of these cases for which specific intent is required (larceny, for example) the defendant conceivably could win outright merely on a defense of voluntary intoxication.

The American courts, and an occasional statute, have shown a strong preference for the defense of insanity in any instance where the defendant claims innocence because of some mental aberration[50] or where, viewed more technically, the defense might challenge the voluntariness of the defendant's act[51] or the culpability required for the commission of the crime. In *People v. Low*,[52] for example, the state supreme court disapproved a trial court's acquittal of the defendant of first degree assault on the ground of lack of *mens rea* due to the effects of "toxic psychosis" (dextromethorphan hydrobromide, from cough drops), which the prosecution referred to as "chemically induced insanity" even though the defendant had failed to plead not guilty by reason of insanity or the affirmative defense of impaired mental condition as provided by statute.[53] The court noted that "Had the trial court found as a factual matter that Low was involuntarily intoxicated, assuming the finding was supported by sufficient competent evidence, its judgment of acquittal would have been proper."[54] But because it did not, the court erred in even admitting the expert testimony since it was relevant only to a plea of insanity or impaired mental condition, and the defendant pleaded neither of these as required by statute.

There are cases of evident pathological intoxication which are tried under the defense of diminished capacity outside California and the

---

49. Weinberg at 799 (1977).

50. Some states provide for commitment procedures to apply when defendants successfully challenge the existence of a *mens rea* based on a mental condition less than insanity and are acquitted. 1 P. ROBINSON, CRIMINAL LAW DEFENSES § 64(a) n.9 (J. Robinson 1988 Supp.). *See also* Mandiberg, *Protecting Society and Defendants Too: The Constitutional Dilemma of Mental Abnormality and Intoxication Defenses*, 53 FORDHAM L. REV. 221 (1984).

51. The California Supreme Court has also commented that the "difference between the two states—of diminished capacity and unconsciousness—is one of degree only: where the former provides a 'partial defense' by negating a specific mental state essential to a particular crime, the latter is a 'complete defense' because it negates capacity to commit any crime at all." People v. Newton, 87 Cal. Rptr. 394, 405-06 (Cal. Ct. App. 1970).

52. People v. Low, 732 P.2d 622 (Colo. 1987).

53. COLO. REV. STAT. § 16-8-103.5(1) (1986). As previously enacted, the defense was limited to specific intent crimes. It was later amended as a result of the court's decision in Hendershott v. People, 653 P.2d 385 (Colo. 1982), to include general intent crimes as well. The amendment also added the special, mandatory pleading rules litigated in People v. Low, 732 P.2d 622, 631-32 (Colo. 1987), which provides the legislative background. *Hendershott* is more fully discussed in Chapter 10.

54. *Low* at 628.

federal courts.[55] For example, in *State v. Poulsen*,[56] the "judge was informed that Poulsen had sustained numerous head injuries, suffered from severe headaches and exhibited irrational behavioral changes, including fits of uncontrollable rage, particularly when he had ingested alcohol. The State did not seriously dispute these facts."[57] On this occasion, the defendant was charged with beating and kicking his mother after drinking.[58] He had requested appointment of a medical expert to help him establish his defense of diminished capacity. The court both recognized the defense and reversed for failure to appoint a defense expert.

In *State v. Welsh*,[59] the defendant pleaded not guilty to a charge of assault. He had attacked his former wife with a razor, but the attack was not premeditated. Evidence indicated that the defendant suffered from psychomotor epilepsy, but it also indicated that attacks were usually precipitated by alcohol, which suggests it was a case of pathological intoxication. A number of prior incidents had occurred after his drinking and were followed by amnesia. He had been drinking on this occasion, but he was not drunk. The defendant was well aware of his susceptibility and, in fact, had been getting treatment. His doctor saw him after the attack and testified that his speech appeared to be different from his normal pattern. The jury was told by the trial court to ignore this evidence because the defendant had elected not to plead the insanity defense. The court on appeal, however, held that it was relevant to the question of intent required by the charge, even on a general plea. "Evidence of mental disease or defect which falls short of criminal insanity is admissible if relevant to prove lack of specific intent."[60]

PATHOLOGICAL INTOXICATION AND "EXTREME MENTAL OR EMOTIONAL DISTURBANCE" AS DIMINISHED RESPONSIBILITY: MODEL PENAL CODE § 210.3(1)(B)

From early times,[61] common law developed a rule variously

---

55. Cases involving pathological intoxication tried as diminished capacity, in addition to the cases cited elsewhere in this chapter, include State v. Thurman, 10 Conn. App. 302, 523 A.2d 891 (1987); State v. Holden, 85 N.M. 397, 512 P.2d 970 (1973); People v. Williams, 22 Cal. App. 3d 34, 99 Cal. Rptr. 103 (1971).

56. State v. Poulsen, 726 P.2d 1036 (Wash. Ct. App. 1986).

57. *Poulsen* at 1039.

58. On a charge such as assault, it may be that the successful invocation of the diminished capacity defense would have the effect only of reducing the crime to a lower level but might also exculpate entirely, depending upon the facts and the structure of lesser included offenses of the jurisdiction on the particular charge.

59. State v. Welsh, 508 P.2d 1041 (Wash. Ct. App. 1973).

60. *Welsh* at 1043.

61. The provocation rule existed at least from 1628, according to Coke, and perhaps even

referred to as the rule of provocation or "heat of passion" by which a jury could reduce the level of the offense, but like most diminished capacity doctrines, it was limited in its effects to reducing murder to manslaughter[62] for an intentional homicide.[63] Briefly, the common law elements were these. There had to be adequate (also called sufficient) provocation. This is an objective element[64] and a question of law for the court in most jurisdictions. In more recent years, there has been disagreement over how objective the test ought to be, that is, whether or to what extent the jury should take account of the physical or mental peculiarities of the particular defendant.[65] The typical case involves sexual misconduct with a relative (spouse or child) or an assault or battery against the defendant as the provocation. It is often said that words were never adequate provocation, but this was meant to exclude insulting words, not informational words.

The second element at common law, heat of passion, was subjective; the defendant actually had to be extremely upset by the provocation, not just coldly waiting for the chance to kill. The third element of common law required the killing to be "sudden." By this it was meant that there had to be an absence of a sufficient cooling-off period, "a sufficient time for the voice of reason to be heard." This was an objective limitation, and the defendant lost this mitigation defense after a time even if he was still subjectively "in the heat of passion" or even if the "heat of passion" was regenerated by later recollection of the original provocation.[66] There was a fourth common law element that some referred to as a causation requirement. All that is meant is that the defendant must vent his or her "heat of passion" specifically on the provocateur and not just take it out on the first person encountered.[67]

---

antedated the Norman conquest. Donovan & Wildman, *Is the Reasonable Man Obsolete? A Critical Perspective on Self-Defense and Provocation*, 14 LOY. L.A.L. REV. 435, 446-50 (1981).

62. It could also be used in cases in which the defendant was charged with attempted murder or assault with intent to murder. Maher v. People, 10 Mich. 212 (1862).

63. The American statutes in effect at the time of the original draft of the Model Penal Code proposal are found at MODEL PENAL CODE § 201.3, comment at 41-44 (Tent. Draft No. 9, 1959).

64. H. WEIHOFEN, MENTAL DISORDER AS A CRIMINAL DEFENSE 190 (1954).

65. *See, e.g.*, State v. Lee, 108 Wis. 2d 1, 321 N.W.2d 108 (1982); Weston v. State, 28 Wis. 2d 136, 135 N.W.2d 820 (1965); State v. Hoyt, 21 Wis. 2d 284, 128 N.W.2d 645 (1964). *See also* Dressler, *Rethinking Heat of Passion: A Defense in Search of a Rationale*, 73 J. CRIM. L. & CRIMINOLOGY 421 (1982); Donovan & Wildman, *Is the Reasonable Man Obsolete? A Critical Perspective on Self-Defense and Provocation*, 14 LOY. L.A.L. REV. 435 (1981); Ingber, *A Dialectic: The Fulfillment and Decrease of Passion in Criminal Law*, 28 RUTGERS L. REV. 861 (1975); Williams, *Provocation and the Reasonable Man*, 1954 CRIM. L. REV. 740.

66. *See, e.g.*, State v. Yarborough, 39 Kan. 581 (1888).

67. Death of third parties is discussed in People v. Spurlin, 156 Cal. App. 3d 119, 202 Cal. Rptr. 663 (1984).

There is no question in these cases that the actor possessed the mental culpability required by the definition of the crime of murder; the assault is usually quite clearly undertaken with a specific intent to kill. The rule is one of mitigation for an acknowledged crime, mitigation designed roughly to reflect the view that provocation ought to be taken into account because "the law, out of indulgence to the frailty of human nature, or rather, in recognition of the laws upon which human nature is constituted, very properly regards the offense as of a less heinous character than murder, and gives it the designation of manslaughter."[68] In a case of diminished capacity or other excuses, by contrast, the defense is permitted to attack the existence of an element required by the definition of the crime itself. This justification defense of provocation admits the elements of the offense and offers mitigation.

As outlined above, the important parts of the test have historically been viewed as objective, in that, for example, the effects of the provocation have been tested against the likely reaction of the reasonable person, not the actor, and individual variations are not taken into account.[69] There has, not surprisingly, been much dissatisfaction with any rule in criminal law that is couched solely in terms of objective standard. The criticism is even more apt here precisely because this defense is a matter of mitigation in an instance in which the offense has clearly occurred and matters of mitigation seem to call for individual evaluation. It was not until the advent of the Model Penal Code that much headway was made to relax the requirements and allow the jury to be instructed to take account of the actor's particular "situation," a word to which we will return.

This rule occupies a rather unique place in criminal law because it takes more from the essence of diminished responsibility than of diminished capacity, in that it is not a denial of the existence of *mens rea* but rather a partially excusing explanation for it, mitigating the higher offense but not exculpating the actor. Voluntary intoxication, by comparison, typically is permitted to reduce a higher degree of any offense which requires specific intent to either a lower-level offense based on general intent or to no offense at all if there is no lower applicable offense.

The Model Penal Code § 210.3 proposed this version of the original common law provocation rule:

> (1) Criminal homicide constitutes manslaughter when....
> (b) a homicide which would otherwise be murder is committed under the influence of extreme

---

68. Maher v. People, 10 Mich. 212, 219 (1862).
69. A. GOLDSTEIN, THE INSANITY DEFENSE 196-97 (1967).

> mental or emotional disturbance for which there is reasonable explanation or excuse. The reasonableness of such explanation or excuse shall be determined from the viewpoint of a person in the actor's situation under the circumstances as he believes them to be.[70]

Judged by their accompanying commentaries, modern code versions of this defense[71] seem designed mainly to modernize the language used in describing the defense and to eliminate categorical restrictions on the nature of the provocation required to make the defense available. But it is likely that the new statutes may be very broadly interpreted in comparison to the common law scope of the defense. There has also been more latitude permitted in more recent cases to allow something akin to "cumulative provocation" so that a single event may not be required.[72] The modern codes based on the Model Penal Code also do not contain a specific reference to "suddenness"; it is apparently only one factor to be taken into account in determining the reasonableness of the defendant's reaction. "Brooding may intensify"[73] feelings is the way the Model Penal Code puts the matter. But the texts of the modern codes go well beyond these points. In the effort to remove judge-created limitations on the defense, the drafts now contain no requirement at all that there be a provoking event. So it would seem that provocation is no longer a necessary condition to the defense, even though it was the crux of the original idea.

The comments to the Model Penal Code draft state that "We thus treat on a parity with provocation cases in the classic sense, situations where the provocative circumstance is something other than an injury inflicted by the deceased on the actor but nonetheless, is an event calculated to arouse extreme mental or emotional disturbance."[74] The only additional language that could be taken as suggesting the need for an external provoking event is the reference to the subjective requirement with respect to "circumstances" which are to be taken "as [the actor] believes them to be." If the drafting intent were only to broaden out which provocations are adequate and not to eliminate the requirement entirely, surely the drafting could be clearer. The way we read the statute, it was designed to encompass those situations in which the

---

70. MODEL PENAL CODE § 210.3(1)(b) (Proposed Official Draft 1962).

71. According to 2 MODEL PENAL CODE AND COMMENTARIES § 210.3, at 51 (1980), these provisions "have become the basis for statutory revision in the recent enactments of at least 15 states and in recent proposals in at least eight additional jurisdictions" (footnotes omitted).

72. *See, e.g.*, People v. Casassa, 49 N.Y.2d 668, 427 N.Y.S.2d 769, 404 N.E.2d 1310 (1980).

73. MODEL PENAL CODE § 201.3 comment (Tent. Draft No. 9, 1959).

74. MODEL PENAL CODE § 201.3 comment at 41 (Tent. Draft No. 9, 1959).

"extreme mental or emotional disturbance" has a wholly internal origin such as an abnormal reaction to alcohol or to symptoms of diseases such as epileptic attacks. Some courts read the language in such a way that perhaps an external event (one causing "emotional stress" to which the actor "reacts,"[75] such as the recent death of a spouse) is still required; and some cases can be interpreted to involve a sort of "emotional provocation," so the question may not have been fully tested as of yet.[76] Those events may instead have only been relevant to the "actor's situation" element. Professor Wechsler referred to the defense as involving "mitigation based upon a mental or emotional trauma of significant dimensions."[77] The original commentaries noted that "mitigation may be appropriate where the actor...strikes out in a blinding rage and kills an innocent bystander."[78] Ambiguity remains in these comments, however, because they can be said to only have eliminated the need for the provocation to come from the person killed.

One opinion has specifically rejected the idea that their modified version of the Model Penal Code revision of the provocation rule permits reliance on purely internal stimulus, although it is not clear that this position commanded the adherence of a majority of the court. In addition, the state version of the Model Penal Code had been revised deliberately to make it more "objective." Finally, the court was strongly influenced by the fact that this broader interpretation was not necessary because in that state, mental disturbance short of insanity could be tried instead as diminished capacity under existing state law whereas "the Model Penal Code does not recognize the diminished capacity defense."[79]

---

75. People v. Shelton, 88 Misc. 2d 136, 385 N.Y.S.2d 708 (1976).

76. *See, e.g.*, State v. Ott, 297 Or. 375, 686 P.2d 1001 (1984).

77. Wechsler, *Codification of Criminal Law in the United States: The Model Penal Code*, 68 COLUM. L. REV. 1425, 1446 (1968).

78. 2 MODEL PENAL CODE AND COMMENTARIES § 210.3 comment 5 at 61 (1980).

79. State v. Bishop, 753 P.2d 439, 470 (Utah 1988). But it does. *See* MODEL PENAL CODE § 4.02(1) (Proposed Official Draft 1962) set out *supra* in the text. The commentaries note that "If states of mind are accorded legal significance, psychiatric evidence should be admissible when relevant to prove or disprove their existence to the same extent as any other relevant evidence." 1 MODEL PENAL CODE AND COMMENTARIES § 4.02, at 219 (1985). That is the essence of diminished capacity, and the commentaries also note that this defense under § 4.02(1) "differs importantly from certain notions of diminished, or partial, responsibility." COMMENTARIES at 219.

Even if the court in *Bishop* meant to say that the Model Penal Code did not recognize diminished responsibility, that too would seem to be wrong. That is exactly what the revised version of the old "provocation rule" does; it reduces murder to manslaughter despite the presence of the requisite culpability for murder. MODEL PENAL CODE § 210.3(1)(b) (Proposed Official Draft 1962) provides in part that murder may be reduced to manslaughter when it "is committed under the influence of extreme mental or emotional disturbance for which there is reasonable explanation or excuse." Section 210.3(1)(b), as a species of diminished responsibility, is limited to charges of murder, while MODEL PENAL CODE § 4.02(1) (Proposed Official Draft 1962) is unrestricted in its application. Section 210.3(1)(b), in fact, seems based

The opinion's approach on this point was to distinguish the Model Penal Code—presumably an unnecessary tactic unless the court believed that under the Model Penal Code, an external event is not required. New York appears to require no external event,[80] and Connecticut has flatly stated that the "defense does not require a provoking or triggering event...."[81]

Would mental illness short of legal insanity suffice to make out the diminished responsibility defense of extreme mental or emotional disturbance quite apart from any specific provoking event? If the exclusive focus is on the actor's resulting mental or emotional state, then the answer would be that under the Model Penal Code version of the provocation rule, pathological intoxication may be triable under the rule of § 210.3 on extreme mental or emotional disturbance as well as the rule of § 4.02(1) involving diminished capacity. The one additional question under this approach involves another dimension of the question whether there was a reasonable excuse for his disturbed emotional condition.

There is another aspect of the new "provocation" rules that is particularly of interest in the context of pathological reaction to alcohol as a possible defense. Many of the new statutes, in describing the standard of conduct required to be observed, make reference to "the actor's situation." This is designed to foster a compromise between a totally subjective and a totally objective standard which might force a jury to ignore the fact, for example, that the actor just lost his or her spouse and was in the grip of extreme grief at the time of the killing. The drafters wanted to take into account some facts such as the defendant is married, blind, etc. "Other states adopt a middle position [between those purely objective and those mostly subjective] which ostensibly retains the 'reasonable man' standard but then undercuts it by instructing the jury to place the 'reasonable man' in the situation of the defendant."[82] It was clear under the pre-Model Penal Code cases that the courts took into

---

on the English Homicide Act of 1957, 5 & 6 Eliz. 2, ch. 11, § 2(1) (1957), which also reduces murder to manslaughter if "abnormality of mind...substantially impaired his mental responsibility."

The provisions of § 210.3(1)(b) do not negate a culpability requirement of a crime definition, but surely evidence of mental disease or defect, such as pathological intoxication, is admissible to prove that the defendant acted under extreme mental or emotional disturbance, to show that the disturbance had a reasonable explanation. In this event, is the doctrine one of diminished capacity or diminished responsibility? It would seem to be the latter in the sense that the defense is not designed to negate an element of a crime. "The focus on mental elements distinguishes diminished capacity from 'diminished responsibility.'" Comment, *Legal and Psychiatric Concepts and the Use of Psychiatric Evidence in Criminal Trials*, 73 CALIF. L. REV. 411, 429 n.59 (1985).

80. *See, e.g.*, People v. Casassa, 49 N.Y.2d 668, 427 N.Y.S.2d 769, 404 N.E.2d 1310 (1980).

81. State v. Elliot, 411 A.2d 3, 7 (Conn. 1979). *See also* State v. Zdanis, 182 Conn. 388, 438 A.2d 696 (1980).

82. A. GOLDSTEIN, THE INSANITY DEFENSE 197 (1967).

account neither temporary susceptibility to insult or provocation such as by ordinary alcohol intoxication[83] nor those of a permanent nature,[84] although none of the cases present a situation like that posed by pathological reaction to alcohol.

The meaning of the provoking event required by common law is an issue quite distinct from the question of the meaning of the actor's "situation" under the Model Penal Code. Our view of the provocation rule has been stated: It appears to us that it has been eliminated entirely and that no provoking event is required. But the meaning of "the actor's situation" could reduce the expansiveness provided by this new approach if "in the actor's situation" is given too narrow an interpretation.

The Model Penal Code did not discuss the meaning of "situation" in great detail, but they did say this much about it:

> There is an inevitable ambiguity in "situation." If the actor were blind or if he had just suffered a blow or experienced a heart attack, these would certainly be facts to be considered, as they would be under present law. But the heredity, intelligence or temperament of the actor would not now be held material in judging negligence; and could not be without depriving the criterion of all its objectivity....The draft is not intended to displace discriminations of this kind; it is designed to leave the issue to the courts[.][85]

They also acknowledged in general terms that they "introduce a larger element of subjectivity in the appraisal, though it is only the actor's 'situation' and 'the circumstances as he believes them to be,' not his scheme of moral value, that are thus to be considered. The ultimate test, however, is objective; there must be a 'reasonable' explanation or excuse for the actor's disturbance."[86] Nevertheless, they say that the term "situation" is "designedly ambiguous and is plainly flexible enough to allow the law to grow in the direction of taking account of mental abnormalities that have been recognized in the developing law of diminished responsibility."[87] Whether this defense can encompass as well those "mental abnormalities" exacerbated or triggered by alcohol consumption, or whether those cases are meant to be exclusively dealt with under the involuntary intoxication provisions, is not clear because, as discussed in Chapter 8, the Model Penal Code seems to have a limited view of pathological intoxication, at least in their intoxication statutes. To

---

83. Keenan v. Commonwealth, 44 Pa. 55 (1863).
84. Commonwealth v. Webb, 252 Pa. 187, 97 A. 189 (1916).
85. MODEL PENAL CODE § 2.02 comment 3 at 126 (Tent. Draft No. 4, 1955).
86. MODEL PENAL CODE § 201.3 comment 1 at 41 (Tent. Draft No. 9, 1959).
87. 2 MODEL PENAL CODE AND COMMENTARIES § 210.3 comment 5 at 72 (1980).

the extent this approach only reduces murder to manslaughter, the defendant will, of course, view the involuntary intoxication or the automatism defense as preferable, and perhaps the same would be true of the insanity defense in some cases.

Professor Goldstein has taken the view, evidently based on his reading of the Model Penal Code commentaries, that "Apparently, the only subjective elements to be considered are physical disabilities or emotional disturbances caused by dramatic external events."[88] We do not believe that such a narrow reading is justified. What is the evidence, for example, that the "extreme emotional disturbance" cannot have an internal (for instance, metabolic) origin? Indeed, as the drafters of the Model Penal Code themselves later stated in their comments, "if he were experiencing an unanticipated reaction to a therapeutic drug, it would be deemed atrocious to appraise his crime for purposes of sentence without reference to any of these matters."[89] We believe the drafters correctly recognized that the source of the mental or emotional disturbance was irrelevant so long as it was not the fault of the actor. Perhaps it is possible that this passage refers only to the subjective mental state of the actor who has also received external provocation; but that seems too limited, given the language of the statute and the fact that another example in the same sentence is the person who "just suffered a traumatic injury,"[90] unless here the traumatic injury was meant to serve both the function of the arguably required provocation and, simultaneously, is taken to be a factor affecting the actor's subjective state of mind, or situation. But why would one differentiate between the two cases?

The question is particularly apt here because of the large amount of evidence in the literature already presented that a person in the throes of a pathological reaction to alcohol often shows a paranoid-like response. Indeed, in many of the reports, it appears the actor could claim self-defense. It has been argued in one case that "where insane delusions enter into a case through the evidence, those delusions are in fact realities with the person affected, and may, if sufficient, constitute adequate cause equally so as if the delusions had a real existence; that under the law the accused is to be charged upon the same basis as if the insane delusions entertained by him existed in fact."[91] The argument seems to have been largely rejected by the court on the assumption that the provocation had to be real, but that is not required by all courts. In some jurisdictions, it is a matter of actual subjective perception of the actor that controls whether there was any provocation at all. Indeed, that was the situation

---

88. A. GOLDSTEIN, THE INSANITY DEFENSE 198 (1967).
89. MODEL PENAL CODE § 201.3 comment 5 at 48 (Tent. Draft No. 9, 1959).
90. MODEL PENAL CODE § 201.3 comment 5 at 48 (Tent. Draft No. 9, 1959).
91. Witty v. State, 75 Tex. Crim. 440, 454, 171 S.W. 229, 237 (1914).

in *Maher v. People*,[92] perhaps the leading pre-Model Penal Code case on the subject of the provocation rule. Adultery was the provocation there, but adultery was never shown to have actually occurred.[93]

Two other points need to be made. The "heat of passion" defense will be narrower than other defenses such as insanity and perhaps even diminished capacity because it is limited to homicide cases. On the other hand, in those jurisdictions in which diminished capacity is not a defense at all, it might be possible to use this defense in homicide cases if, at least, the court is willing to interpret the provocation rule as either not requiring any external provocation or viewing the external provocation which exists solely in the defendant's perception as sufficient. Indeed, later commentaries note that this defense "may allow an inquiry into areas which have been treated as part of the law of diminished responsibility or the insanity defense,"[94] and it should be noted that external provocations are not relevant to either of the other two defenses.

Finally, in the revised commentaries to this section, it is noted that

> This formulation effects substantial changes in the traditional notion of provocation. For one thing, the Code does not require that the actor's emotional distress arise from some injury, affront, or other provocative act perpetrated upon him by the deceased. Under the Code, mitigation may be appropriate where the actor believes that the deceased is responsible for some injustice to another or even where he strikes out in a blinding rage and kills an innocent bystander. In some such cases, the cause and intensity of the actor's emotion may be less indicative of moral depravity than would be a homicidal response to a blow to one's person. By eliminating any reference to provocation in the ordinary sense of improper conduct by the deceased, the Model Code avoids arbitrary exclusion of some circumstances that may justify reducing murder to manslaughter.[95]

In other words, it would appear that the Code makes the two changes argued for here. With respect to the adequacy of provocation, they both modified the "adequacy" question by broadening out the actor's "situation" and with respect to the "provocation" part of that common law formulation, they eliminated it.[96]

---

92. Maher v. People, 10 Mich. 212 (1862).

93. *See also* Davis v. State, 161 Tenn. 23, 28 S.W.2d 993 (1930), where the argument was given more credence.

94. 2 MODEL PENAL CODE AND COMMENTARIES § 210.3 comment 5 at 54 (1980).

95. 2 MODEL PENAL CODE AND COMMENTARIES § 210.3 comment 5 at 60-61 (1980).

96. We might also raise an additional question here, even though it is probably academic.

To what extent has pathological intoxication been litigated as manslaughter under the provocation rules? One case, *Leggett v. State*,[97] arguably falls within this category. The defendant had a history of brain injury suffered in a fall from a horse, and he also had a history of typhoid fever "which, at the time at least, affected the brain."[98] At the time just prior to the killing, the defendant had consumed perhaps one drink of whiskey and then received a blow to the head. He pursued his assailant but killed the wrong man. His conviction for murder was reversed, largely on the ground that the trial court should have, *sua sponte*, instructed on voluntary manslaughter based upon the provocation rule (and this, despite the fact that he killed the wrong person, evidently, as the result of mistaken identity.) Witnesses believed him to be insane at the time of the attack, and several who knew him testified that he had acted like a wild man and, when apprehended, manifested "exceptional and extraordinary strength,"[99] after which he had fallen asleep.

In addition to the failure to instruct on provocation, the court indicated that the trial court, as requested, should have instructed on the insanity defense as well, based on the evidence of the possible effects of the blow to the head combined with drinking, or the combination of the blow, the alcohol, and the "predisposing cause" (the prior head injury and typhoid). Inferentially, this may be classified as an instance of pathological reaction to alcohol, even though there was also testimony that the reaction may have occurred solely from the blow to the head, and as an instance of involuntary intoxication being treated by the court as insanity, there having been no fault on the part of the actor in bringing about any aspect of the case except having taken a drink. There was no evidence that the defendant had previously suffered such a reaction to alcohol alone.

In another case perhaps of some value by analogy, the defendant was involuntarily intoxicated from a drug that had been added to a bowl of punch. As a result, he took another person's car, which would have been justified had the facts been as he (erroneously) supposed, given his delusional state. The court held that this was a defense.[100]

Why is the crime of murder reduced to manslaughter under these circumstances, but other crimes are not reduced? Why, for example, would not the same rationale provide for reduction of property destruction crimes?

97. Leggett v. State, 21 Tex. App. 382, 17 S.W. 159 (1886).

98. *Leggett* at 395, 17 S.W. at 160.

99. Leggett at 396, 17 S.W. at 160.

100. People v. Scott, 146 Cal. App. 3d 823, 194 Cal. Rptr. 633 (1983).

PATHOLOGICAL INTOXICATION AS A SENTENCING CONSIDERATION

We include, perhaps for no reason other than a sense of aesthetic completion, the observation that if the jurisdiction recognizes no level or type of defense that applies to pathological intoxication, certainly, the trial court may view the evidence differently than its appellate courts regarding the general question of the existence of pathological intoxication as a real phenomenon and that it may have been involved in the defendant's actions. One case even involved invocation of executive clemency at the request of the trial court.[101] Probation and parole conditions[102] that the person not drink alcohol are common and are just as commonly ignored by officials.[103] Yet this might be an alternative because the only known response that will prevent the onset of pathological reaction to alcohol is not treatment, but avoidance of alcohol. Perhaps the past occurrence of the event in combination with the threat of future incarceration would be sufficient to accomplish this end.

It is clear that mental illness is and should be taken into account in sentencing even if the defendant was capable of committing a crime and

---

101. People v. McNerlin, 11 N.Y.2d 738, 226 N.Y.S.2d 443, 181 N.E.2d 456 (1962), without opinion upheld murder in the first degree on a plea of not guilty by reason of insanity based on pathological reaction to alcohol. The court then sent a letter recommending executive clemency, noted in People v. McNerlin, 44 Misc. 2d 340 n.1, 253 N.Y.S.2d 912 n.1 (1964). The defendant's original conviction was reversed on the ground announced in Jackson v. Denno, 378 U.S. 368, 84 S. Ct. 1774, 12 L. Ed. 2d 908 (1964).

102. Hicklin v. State, 535 P.2d 743 (Wyo. 1975). The defendant pleaded nolo contendere to assault, and the conviction was affirmed. The defendant had been drinking and ended up in a shootout with local deputies. After acceptance of the plea, the court gave the defendant 19 years' probation. Hospital staff personnel had called it pathological intoxication. Elaborate probation conditions aimed at preventing his drinking were established for that period of time. A $50,000 performance bond was also required, the court noting that the defendant had a net worth of $400,000. The court on appeal reduced the period of probation and remanded for other considerations or reconsideration by the trial judge who had imposed the conditions.

103. The psychomotor epilepsy/alcohol issue has also been involved in parole revocation hearings. In Mozingo v. Craven, 341 F. Supp. 296 (C.D. Cal. 1972), psychomotor epilepsy was a prominent issue in a parole revocation hearing challenged under 28 U.S.C. § 2254 (1970) (statutory habeas corpus). There was also proof that the petitioner had been drinking. The petitioner had been in a bar fight and drinking. Evidently, parole was revoked only on the drinking question. He won a new state board hearing on procedural grounds.

Van Ermen v. Percy, 489 F. Supp. 791 (E.D. Wis. 1980) also involved parole revocation and a habeas challenge. Revocation was upheld. Drinking in combination with evidence of pathological intoxication was sufficient for revocation. The violation of parole conditions was clear, and the only question was whether revocation was warranted.

standing trial or entering a guilty plea,[104] although the state's ability to put on evidence of future dangerousness is not without constitutional limitations.[105]

---

104. *See, e.g.*, AMERICAN BAR ASS'N, CRIMINAL JUSTICE MENTAL HEALTH STANDARDS, Standard 7-9.4. *See also* Dershowitz, *The Role of Psychiatry in the Sentencing Process*, 1 INT'L J. L. & PSYCHIAT. 63 (1978).

105. Barefoot v. Estelle, 463 U.S. 880, 103 S. Ct. 3383, 77 L. Ed. 2d 1090 (1983); Estelle v. Smith, 451 U.S. 454, 101 S. Ct. 1866, 68 L. Ed. 2d 359 (1981).

10

Fault as a Limitation on the Defense of Pathological Intoxication

Lord Bacon interpreted the law to be that "If a madman commit a felony he shall not lose his life for it, because his infirmity came by act of God; but if a drunken man commit a felony, he shall not be excused, because the imperfection came by his own default."[1] No one disagrees with the sentiment that underlies this Baconian distinction. Not surprisingly, the task lies in its application. Approaching the problem of pathological intoxication with a semblance of analytical rigor in the context of existing structures of criminal law defenses is difficult because neither the cases, statutes nor existing writings on those defenses provides a suitable foundation from which one can infer with certainty the defensive effects of pathological intoxication or explore systematically the existence of various limitations on that defense. Not only do the answers vary greatly among the state and federal courts, there is also no congruity even with respect to the questions to be put, and most statutes, as well as writers, are silent on most issues. It is not all unsatisfactory tidings to attorneys that there is extraordinary license in the realm of issue identification.

In determining the meaning of "fault" as a limitation on defenses in general, we would assume distinctions would be drawn in several areas. For example, one might suppose that fault as a limitation on well recognized defenses would reveal a body of law that distinguished between the meaning of fault as to different defenses and indicated whether fault defeats the defense entirely or under some circumstances only reduces the efficacy of the defense. One might further expect these questions to receive differing responses according to whether the defense is considered to be an "affirmative defense" (justification) or an excuse (usually a *mens rea* type of defense) or a hybrid such as insanity law. But these simple points lie at the outer boundaries of the law today even on well established defenses on commonly encountered fact situations.

---

1. M. BACON, ELEMENTS OF THE COMMON LAWS OF ENGLAND 29 (1636).

When the concept of pathological intoxication is made to overlay this disarray of criminal defense law and is compounded by the fact that we are interested here not in the defenses per se but in limitations on those defenses expressed in terms of fault, the task becomes somewhat overwhelming and the results nearly chaotic.

At the same time, if the task is only descriptive, much of the relevant law could more easily be viewed not as overwhelmingly complex but as rather embryonic. In the quest for finding fault on the part of the defendant, some courts do not distinguish between the act of drinking, awareness of the intoxicating nature of what is being ingested, awareness of the incapacitating results of that conduct, and the question of the probability of engaging in harmful conduct as a result of self-incapacitation. Nor, indeed, does one find much difference between the various defenses in these terms, even though they would appear to be radically different defenses. Finally, the courts tend to chose between negligence and something slightly higher or slightly lower in defining the nature of the fault they seek.

That is the state of the law of fault as a limitation on the defense of pathological intoxication in a nutshell. The theoretical construct of defenses in criminal law is not well developed, the status of pathological intoxication as a defense is not well understood, fault as a limitation on defenses in general is not developed and is even more obscure in pathological intoxication cases.

None of this should lead to the conclusion that fault is not important in the law of pathological intoxication. The contrary is devastatingly true in a few jurisdictions and is the norm in all jurisdictions. It largely depends on how fault is viewed by the courts and what is treated as fault on the part of the actor in bringing about his mental condition at the time of the offense charged.[2]

The discussion of these issues is not facilitated by the fact that the term "pathological intoxication" now seems to be used in three different conventions. It might be restricted to those instances in which the actor has what we could agree is an underlying mental disease or defect in which alcohol precipitates a reaction amounting to legal insanity. The

---

2. An equivalent situation exists in the law of the choice-of-evils or necessity defense. There, fault as a limitation on the defense is dealt with in the Model Penal Code by linking, roughly, the level of fault in bringing about the situation and the crime of which the actor may be convicted so that, for example, if he were negligent in bringing about a situation in which he committed homicide, he could be convicted for negligent homicide, whereas if he were reckless in doing so, he could be convicted of manslaughter. MODEL PENAL CODE, § 3.02 comment (Tent. Draft No. 8, 1958). At the opposite extreme lies Colorado with its provision that to prevail, the situation must be "occasioned or developed through *no conduct* of the actor...." COLO. REV. STAT. § 18-1-702 (1986) (emphasis added). The fault limitations found in American necessity statutes are discussed in more detail in Tiffany & Anderson, *Legislating the Necessity Defense in Criminal Law*, 52 DEN. L.J. 839, 865-69 (1975).

principal example we have used is the case of a person with temporal lobe epilepsy who drinks and thereby triggers an attack. But pathological intoxication also encompasses those cases in which there is no mental disease or defect, hypoglycemia, for example, but essentially the same temporary reaction is brought about. Many of those cases are treated as automatism by some English and American judges. Some would put psychomotor epilepsy in the second category. We do not particularly acquiesce to the idea, but a third use of the term "pathological intoxication" was brought about by the Model Penal Code, treating what amounts to surprise intoxication as being within its purview, such as by consuming drugs or a combination of drugs while unaware of their combined effects, a situation that the Model Penal Code drafters placed within the involuntary intoxication defense but gave it somewhat special treatment. A description and critique of these diverse issues are the subject of this chapter.

THE EARLY DEVELOPMENT OF INTOXICATION AND INSANITY LAW AND THE CONCEPT OF FAULT

Fault and Intoxication

In the leading reported case involving intoxication in early English law, the fault of the actor in becoming inebriated was stressed. Singh reports:

> *Reniger v. Feogossa,*[3] argued in the Exchequer Chamber in the time of Edward VI in 1551, is the first reported case containing an early statement of the law. There it was said:—
>
> > 'If a person that is drunk kills another this shall be felony, and he shall be hanged for it, and yet he did it through ignorance, for when he was drunk he had no understanding nor memory; but inasmuch as that ignorance was occasioned by his own act and folly, he shall not be privileged thereby.'[4]

"Lord Bacon, writing in the seventeenth century, said substantially the same thing when he declared that if a drunken man commit a felony he shall not be excused because his imperfection came by his own

3. Reniger v. Feogossa, 1 Plowd. 1, 75 Eng. Rep. 1 (1551).

4. Singh, *History of the Defence of Drunkenness in English Criminal Law,* 49 L.Q. REV. 528, 530 (1933) (citation omitted).

default."[5] Hale summarized these opinions in his statement that a drunken person "shall have no privilege by his voluntarily contracted madness, but shall have the same judgment as if he were in his right senses."[6] Thus, the very early conception was that a severely intoxicated person is mad but guilty nevertheless. Hale also added two qualifications to that generally accepted statement of the rules regarding intoxication as a defense:

> 1. That if a person by the unskilfulness of his physician, or by the contrivance of his enemies, eat or drink such a thing as causeth such a temporary or permanent phrenzy, as *aconitum* or *nux vomica*, this puts him into the same condition in reference to crimes as any other phrenzy and equally excuseth him.
>
> 2. That although the *simple* phrenzy occasioned *immediately* by drunkenness excuse not in criminals, yet if by one or more such practices an *habitual or fixed* phrenzy be caused though this madness was contracted by the vice and will of the party, yet this habitual and fixed phrenzy thereby caused puts the man into the same condition in relation to crimes, as if the same were contracted involuntarily at first.[7]

While Singh viewed the first of these qualifying rules as reflective of the previously existing law, he thought the latter might have been in advance of its time, though it is now universally recognized as substantially accurate.[8]

As Blackstone expressed it, intoxication was an instance of "deficiency of will,"[9] and he refers to drunkenness as "artificial, voluntarily contracted madness or intoxication, which, depriving men of their reason, puts them in a temporary phrenzy...."[10] And, although it is sometimes stated that drunkenness actually aggravated the actor's liability,[11] that appears to be untrue, except perhaps in the sense of sentencing discretion, despite the claims of Coke and Blackstone.[12]

---

5. Singh at 530, citing M. BACON, ELEMENTS OF THE COMMON LAWS OF ENGLAND 29 (1636).
6. 1 M. HALE, HISTORY OF THE PLEAS OF THE CROWN 32 (1778).
7. Hale at 32 (emphasis added).
8. *See, e.g.*, People v. Guillett, 342 Mich. 1, 69 N.W.2d 140 (1955); Myers v. State, 174 P.2d 395 (Okla. Crim. App. 1946).
9. 4 W. BLACKSTONE, COMMENTARIES ON THE LAWS OF ENGLAND 26 (1769).
10. Blackstone at 25.
11. Blackstone at 25-26, citing E. COKE, 1 INSTITUTES 247.
12. Singh, *History of the Defence of Drunkenness in English Criminal Law*, 49 L.Q. REV. 528, 531 (1933). *See also* R. PERKINS & R. BOYCE, CRIMINAL LAW 1000 (3d ed. 1982).

Involuntary intoxication and insanity share the ancient characterization that neither is a "voluntarily contracted madness,"[13] but voluntary intoxication is. There appears to be no corollary observation that includes the possibility of a category of voluntary insanity; insanity is assumed to be an "involuntarily contracted madness," either because insanity is limited to mental disease (God-given) or because insanity law is made to serve that function of designating the mental state in question as one not voluntarily assumed. Thus, involuntary intoxication is allowed as a complete *mens rea* defense or excuse, but if the mental impairment is "voluntarily contracted madness," it is not permitted to be given its full logical relevance. Involuntary in this includes both coercion and mistake, at least as long as neither involved culpability. For reasons less clear, even a "voluntarily contracted madness" will be recognized by the courts as insanity if it has become permanent as in the case of "fixed" or "settled" insanity, which has its origins in alcohol or other drug abuse.[14] Perkins and Boyce have expressed the opinion that:

> Since the refusal to place intoxication and insanity on the same basis (insofar as criminal incapacity is concerned) is due to the fact that the former is usually a "voluntarily contracted madness," it follows that they should be dealt with alike when the intoxication is involuntary, and such is the law....[15]

The defense of involuntary intoxication in the sense of force or fraud has infrequent but unanimous recognition in the cases, and it receives lip service in the writings. At least since the dictum of Baron Parke in *Pearson's Case*, reflecting Hale's view, that "If a party be made drunk by stratagem, or the fraud of another, he is not responsible,"[16] the idea has existed that involuntary intoxication in the sense of inadvertent intoxication could be a complete defense. Professor Hall's skeptical view of the early English and American cases is frequently cited:

> The amazing thing about the factual situations met in the decisions on intoxication, which, because of the usual judicial stress on fraud and coercion as exculpatory, becomes apparent only after close study of the cases, is that *involuntary intoxica-*

---

13. Reniger v. Feogossa, 1 Plowd. 1, 75 Eng. Rep. 1 (1551).

14. Perhaps it had to do not so much with fault finding in the definition of crimes and defenses as with the futility of punishment, since the defective mental state was permanent.

15. R. PERKINS & R. BOYCE, CRIMINAL LAW 1001 (3d ed. 1982), citing, inter alia, Pearson's Case, 2 Lew. C.C. 144, 168 Eng. Rep. 1108 (1835); People v. Robinson, 2 Park. Crim. R. 235, 304 (N.Y. 1855); Burrows v. State, 38 Ariz. 99, 297 P. 1029 (1931); Strickland v. State, 137 Ga. 115, 72 S.E. 922 (1911); Hanks v. State, 542 S.W.2d 413 (Tex. Crim. App. 1976); State v. Gilcrist, 25 Wash. App. 327, 606 P.2d 716, 717 (1980).

16. Pearson's Case, 2 Lew. C.C. 144, 145, 168 Eng. Rep. 1108 (1835).

> *tion is simply and completely nonexistent*....The opinions invariably hold that the intoxication was "voluntary," but with equal uniformity they reiterate that fraud or coercion is a perfect defense....As regards "coercion," the caselaw implies that a person would need to be bound hand and foot, and the liquor literally poured down his throat, or that he would have to be threatened with immediate serious injury, before the exception, so universally voiced, would have any effect on judicial decision. So far as the extant law is concerned, there would be no difference in the actual rule if it were announced flatly that no intoxicated person could ever claim that his condition was effected by fraud or coercion.[17]

While cases of involuntary intoxication are rarely reported,[18] they do exist.[19] But the major point we would make about the first observation—the important point, we think—is that Professor Hall's observation was made with reference to reported appellate cases and that defendants who win on the factual issue of involuntary intoxication at the trial level obviously do not appeal and the state cannot. Professor Hall was describing cases which, by definition, the defendant has already lost on the factual question of voluntariness of the intoxication. If one judged only by appellate cases, the conclusion would be both obvious and wrong that defendants almost never win on any criminal defense. When defendants do lose on the involuntary intoxication defense at the trial level and appeal on questions of the appropriateness of jury instructions, they do sometimes win those appeals, but more often the appellate court essentially agrees with the fact finder. Most reported cases hold only that the evidence was sufficient to permit the jury to find that the intoxication was voluntary. None hold that involuntary intoxication instructions need not be given when there was evidence to support that theory, at least in the absence of fault on the part of the actor in bringing about the involuntary intoxication. Like cases of pathological intoxication, only cases in which the defendant lost at the trial court level are reported because the state cannot appeal acquittals.

While the hypothetical literature and an occasional case[20] usually

---

17. Hall, *Intoxication and Criminal Responsibility*, 57 HARV. L. REV. 1045, 1056 (1944).

18. In 1960, Jerome Hall again maintained there were no real cases of involuntary intoxication. J. HALL, GENERAL PRINCIPLES OF CRIMINAL LAW 539 (2d ed. 1960).

19. *See, e.g.*, State v. Alie, 82 W. Va. 601, 96 S.E. 1011 (1918); People v. Penman, 271 Ill. 82, 110 N.E. 894 (1915); State v. Brown, 38 Kan. 390, 16 P. 259 (1888). *See* Annotation, *When Intoxication Deemed Involuntary So As To Constitute a Defense to Criminal Charge*, 73 A.L.R.3d 195 (1976).

20. Burrows v. State, 38 Ariz. 99, 297 P. 1029 (1931), involved a case of duress in which the jury was instructed in those terms but rejected the defense. The court did not instruct on inadvertent intoxication, presumably because that was not involved in the case, only duress

posit an instance of involuntary consumption, as by duress or fraud, the courts almost universally assume the defense actually has to do with the defendant who unknowingly consumed alcohol or other drugs.[21] Indeed, it has been suggested that the term "voluntary intoxication" be defined to include the phrase "or other foreseeable incapacity."[22] This would have the effect of clearly including within the definition of involuntary intoxication those instances in which the intoxication was not foreseeable even if the actor was aware of the factual circumstance that it was alcohol and voluntarily drank.

It would be well if we could sum up the law by stating that involuntary intoxication "is to be dealt with the same as if it were the result of mental disease or defect," as Perkins and Boyce put it,[23] and precisely pointed out that:

> One who is aware of a peculiar susceptibility may be found to be reckless in even slight indulgence, but both argument and authority, says Wharton,[24] lead to the conclusion that if by temporary debility or disease a man is maddened by a quantity of wine which on former occasions he wisely and soberly took as a tonic, the intoxication is involuntary.[25]

However, it remains true, as we will show, that some courts are reluctant to apply the law of involuntary intoxication under any circumstances, and it appears that their reason for doing so is because of a great concern that drinking might become an excuse for crime. That is a fair concern, but it ought to be applied with some discrimination. In cases of pathological reaction to alcohol, the claim of lack of responsibility usually rests on the defendant's claim that he did not know of the resulting pathological reaction, not that he did not know he was consuming alcohol or that he did not know that alcohol may make one drunk.

The law of voluntary intoxication consists of placing limitations on the defense of lack of *mens rea*, and it results from a generalized conclusion that the actor was at fault in creating a high-risk situation of

---

was involved. It would not seem that one could take this case as holding that mistake would not do as well as duress to find "involuntary" intoxication.

21. 1 W. LAFAVE & A. SCOTT, SUBSTANTIVE CRIMINAL LAW § 4.10(f) n.51 (1986), collects cases of involuntary intoxication and state statutes which codify the defense.

22. Mackay, *Intoxication as a Factor in Automatism*, 1982 CRIM. L. REV. 146, 156.

23. R. PERKINS & R. BOYCE, CRIMINAL LAW 1005 (3d ed. 1982), citing People v. Penman, 271 Ill. 82, 110 N.E. 894 (1915); Choate v. State, 19 Okla. Crim. 169, 197 P. 1060 (1921); Hanks v. State, 542 S.W.2d 413 (Tex. Crim. App. 1976); United States v. Jewett, 438 F.2d 495 (8th Cir. 1971).

24. 2 WHARTON'S CRIMINAL LAW § 110 (14th ed. 1979).

25. Perkins & Boyce at 1005.

temporary insanity by gross intoxication which caused the lack of *mens rea*. As the courts have long said of voluntary intoxication, as distinct from pathological intoxication, "A man who voluntarily puts himself in condition to have no control of his actions, must be held to intend the consequences."[26] Thus the ancient common law rule was that "voluntary drunkenness is no excuse for crime."[27] It is thought that the very early common law refused to take any account of voluntary intoxication in determining criminal liability.[28] Factors underlying this no-defense rule may have included moralistic judgments regarding drunkenness,[29] although this is disputed,[30] and concern that drunkenness, if allowed to reduce criminal responsibility, would either be feigned[31] or would be resorted to as a shield by one planning the commission of a crime.[32] Concern that drunkenness could be feigned or simulated for the purpose of the commission of a particular offense appears repeatedly in American case law.[33] Even this broad statement would soon be modified to exclude its application to so-called specific intent crimes.[34]

Addressing the risk-creation justification, the drafters of the Model Penal Code stated the position which underlies their treatment of the intoxication defense and probably captures the common law position as well:

> [T]here is the fundamental point that awareness of the potential consequences of excessive drinking on the capacity of human beings to gauge the risks incident to their conduct is by now so dispersed in our culture that we believe it fair to postulate a general equivalence between the risks created by the conduct of the drunken actor and the risks created by his conduct in becoming drunk.[35]

The inapposite nature of this rationale to a pathological intoxication defense is readily apparent. First, there is often no excessive drinking involved, the knowledge of the consequences of which may be attributed

---

26. People v. Garbutt, 17 Mich. 9, 19 (1868).

27. Pearson's Case, 2 Lew. C.C. 144, 168 Eng. Rep. 1108 (1835).

28. Singh, *History of the Defense of Drunkenness in English Common Law*, 49 L.Q. REV. 528, 530 (1933).

29. United States v. Drew, 25 F. Cas. 913 (C.C.D. Mass. 1828) (No. 14,993): "the law not permitting a man to avail himself of the excuse of his own gross vice and misconduct...."

30. Singh at 536-37.

31. Hale at 32.

32. For a discussion of the development of common law principles regarding intoxication see J. HALL, GENERAL PRINCIPLES OF CRIMINAL LAW 529-38 (2d ed. 1960).

33. *See, e.g.*, State v. Kavanaugh, 20 Del. 131, 53 A. 335 (1902).

34. Roberts v. People, 19 Mich. 401 (1870).

35. MODEL PENAL CODE, § 2.08 comment 3 at 9 (Tent. Draft No. 9, 1959).

to the defendant by virtue of wide dissemination of this knowledge within the society.[36] Secondly, even in cases involving what many would classify as excessive drinking, the result may be out of all proportion to the risk actually assumed by or fairly assignable to the actor. Most of us do not commit homicide when we have had too much to drink.

> Common experience teaches that consumption of too much alcohol causes the consumer to do foolish things, but it does not teach that the consumption of any alcohol, in however small a quantity, will have this effect. If, therefore, a man becomes wildly aggressive after consuming half a glass of beer...we cannot rely on the factor of common experience to fasten the blame upon him.[37]

Indeed, under most instances of codification of the defense of pathological intoxication, the defense is unavailable if the defendant knew he was susceptible to such a reaction to alcohol.[38]

The law of voluntary intoxication, then, did not so much develop a fault limitation as most defenses did, as it was itself a fault limiter on a claim of absence of *mens rea* for the commission of a crime; the law of voluntary intoxication *is* a fault limiter on another defense. The difference between voluntary intoxication and involuntary intoxication is not the actor's mental state, it is the existence of fault. In the case of voluntary intoxication, the actor was at fault in bringing his own claim of lack of *mens rea*, and in the case of involuntary intoxication, the actor was not at fault in doing so. Indeed, in the event of involuntary intoxication, the defense may range beyond a mere negation of *mens rea* and encompass a lack of responsibility coterminous with the insanity defense, albeit without the special disposition mandated there. In some jurisdictions, that could even encompass volitional impairment, depending on the insanity test used, and would encompass even strict liability crimes.

Although pathological intoxication is not ordinary intoxication at all, the "involuntary intoxication" cases do provide an analogy, albeit one to be dealt with cautiously. Those cases are analogous because they are an example of an actor himself inducing "insanity." Indeed, what differenti-

---

36. The builders of the pyramids were warned: "You speak stupidly and cannot remember the words that come out of your mouth. You fall and break your limbs, and no one reaches out a hand to you. Your drinking friends stand up and say 'Away with the drunk.' And if someone comes asking after you, they find you lying on the ground like a child." HIGH TIMES ENCYCLOPEDIA OF RECREATIONAL DRUGS 91-93 (1978).

37. P. BRETT, AN INQUIRY INTO CRIMINAL GUILT 202 (1963).

38. MODEL PENAL CODE §§ 2.08(4), (5)(c) (Proposed Official Draft 1962).

ates the involuntary intoxication doctrine from legal insanity per se is the cause of the insanity. In the case of involuntary intoxication, it must be due to an intoxicated state of mind; and in the case of insanity, it is due to a "disease or defect of the mind."

Voluntary intoxication is differentiated from both of these not on the basis of whether the defendant knew right from wrong, or whatever the insanity test may be, but due to the fault involved in the source of the disability to reason, in this case, the "voluntary" action of the defendant. It is this notion of voluntariness in its various meanings in bringing about the condition that divides the disabilities which will excuse from those which will not, and it is not the nature of the disability which determines that. The nature of the disability only affects the fate of the actor after exoneration. In essence, this concept of voluntariness is a matter of fault on the part of the actor.

There is another factor that is irrelevant to the meaning of fault. It is remarkable that, with rare exception, neither the common law cases nor the modern statutes make any distinction between whether the intoxicant was legal or illegal to possess or use. Thus, LSD is accorded the same significance as alcohol, and illegal drinking by a minor is treated the same as legal drinking by an adult. While the Model Penal Code does not make it explicit that "legal" drugs are to be equated with "illegal" drugs, it does make clear the equation of alcohol and other drugs: "The definition [of intoxication]...does not confine the term to alcoholic intoxication. The use of drugs is to be treated in the same way as the use of alcohol if the drugs similarly excite the passions or impede mental powers in connection with allegedly criminal acts."[39] "The great majority of states with revised codes addressing the issue have included drugs within the intoxication provision."[40] The contemporary courts are of the same opinion.[41]

While the American courts continued to deny that voluntary intoxication was a general excuse for any crime, a narrow exception began to appear as in the case of murder in the first degree based on a requirement of premeditation. But the general rule usually prevailed. For example, in *People v. Robinson*,[42] the court upheld an instruction which informed the jury that "though the prisoner may have been excited by strong drink at the time of the alleged offence, even to such an extent as not to know what she was doing, she must answer for the consequences; her self-inflicted insanity must not be allowed to avail her for her

---

39. MODEL PENAL CODE § 2.08 comment 8 at 12 (Tent. Draft No. 9, 1959).

40. 1 MODEL PENAL CODE AND COMMENTARIES § 2.08 comment 4 at 366 (1985). *But see* COMMENTARIES at 366 n.51, which lists seven states which do not mention drugs other than alcohol in their intoxication statutes.

41. 1 W. LAFAVE & A. SCOTT, SUBSTANTIVE CRIMINAL LAW § 4.10 n.2 (1986).

42. People v. Robinson, 2 Park. Crim. R. 235 (N.Y. 1855).

defence"[43] and which stated that "if [the actor's] derangement be voluntary—if his madness be self-invited—the law will not hear him when he makes his intoxication his plea to excuse him from punishment."[44]

The rule of voluntary intoxication based on fault finds fruition in cases such as *Hanks v. State*,[45] where the defendant claimed that his drinking companion and victim had put something in his drink and that he drank it anyway, knowing this. The court held that

> this evidence was not sufficient to raise the issue of involuntary intoxication. If appellant was aware that a suspected drug had been placed in his drink, as he testified, and in spite of such knowledge he drank the beverage, any intoxication resulting therefrom could not be classified as *involuntary*. To constitute involuntary intoxication, there must be an absence of an exercise of independent judgment and volition on the part of the accused in taking the intoxicant.[46]

Certainly clear knowledge that consumption of alcohol may lead to unusual reactions will cause the case to be classified as one of voluntary intoxication despite some underlying mental illness.[47]

Intoxication and Specific Intent: The Limits of Fault

Under the exculpatory rule of voluntary intoxication, the fact of voluntary intoxication may be admitted into evidence but only to disprove the *mens rea* of specific intent crimes. In 1923, Bishop summarized the rule: "Evidence of intoxication therefore is admissible for the purpose of ascertaining...whether he was incapable of entertaining the specific intent charged, where such intent, under the law, is an essential ingredient of the particular crime alleged to have been committed."[48] "Specific intent"

---

43. *Robinson* at 301.

44. *Robinson* at 287, 303. The murder charge in this case, however, was based on a statute which, like those in states following the early Pennsylvania model, made murder by poisoning a distinct basis for conviction apart from premeditation, or perhaps as an example of it, but this particular statute, unlike those other state statutes, did not divide murder into degrees. The court acknowledged that the states which did require premeditation for murder of the first degree would allow evidence of intoxication to be introduced as relevant to whether the actor entertained premeditation as well as an intent to kill, but distinguished the case on these grounds. *Robinson* at 305-07.

45. Hanks v. State, 542 S.W.2d 413 (Tex. Crim. App. 1976).

46. *Hanks* at 416.

47. Pauling v. State, 276 S.C. 92, 275 S.E.2d 881, 882 (1981).

48. 1 J. BISHOP, CRIMINAL LAW 299 (9th ed. 1923).

refers to a mental state in which the actor desires a particular result. A "general intent" crime is any other crime. The same rule has also been codified in terms which agree with our definition of "specific intent." Alaska provides "...evidence that the defendant was intoxicated may be offered whenever it is relevant to negate an element of the offense that requires that the defendant intentionally cause a result."[49] While the Model Penal Code does not use the term in their statutes, the meaning there seems to be in accord. Their definition of intent includes what common law called "specific intent." An actor acts intentionally when "if the element involves...a result [of the actor's conduct], it is his conscious object...to cause such a result...."[50] The distinction derives from common law when the principal types of *mens rea* were intent and recklessness. Thus, in the majority of jurisdictions which have adopted the exculpatory rule, evidence of intoxication may be introduced to disprove "specific intent" where such intent is an element of the crime charged, but not to disprove the *mens rea* of "general intent" crimes.[51] In general intent crimes, "voluntary intoxication cannot be a legitimate subject of inquiry."[52]

The rule that voluntary intoxication may be permitted to defeat a showing of specific intent, but not general intent, supports the perspective that the nature of the fault limiter in intoxication is the recklessness as to the harmful result, not the "immorality" involved in drinking, because recklessness is precisely what general intent meant at common law. Thus, one who is intoxicated is, in the law's consciously imprecise reckoning, also reckless, and so this mental state could be substituted for the requirement of recklessness inherent in any general intent crime. In this way, common law limited the defendant's liability to the level of fault: recklessness.

This is the rule widely followed today. Voluntary intoxication (meaning drunkenness) is not per se a defense. The rule simply is that evidence of intoxication is admissible to negate a finding of the requisite *mens rea*[53] involved in the charge. It may be of defensive import if it is extreme enough,[54] but it is not given its full "logical relevance." Its

---

49. ALASKA STAT. § 11.81.630 (1983).

50. MODEL PENAL CODE § 2.02(2)(a)(i) (Proposed Official Draft 1962).

51. *See, e.g.*, State v. Murphy, 185 N.J. Super. 72, 447 A.2d 219 (1982).

52. Wilson v. State, 60 N.J.L. 171, 184, 37 A. 954, 958 (1897). *See also* Mitchell, *The Intoxicated Offender—Refuting the Legal and Medical Myths*, 11 INT'L J. LAW & PSYCHIAT. 77, 88-90 (1988).

53. Commonwealth v. Rumsey, 309 Pa. Super. 137, 454 A.2d 1121 (1983), upheld a statute which limits the use of evidence of voluntary intoxication to reducing murder to a lower degree. *See also* Commonwealth v. Laing, 310 Pa. Super. 105, 456 A.2d 204 (1983).

54. *See* State v. Martin, 213 N.J. Super. 426, 517 A.2d 513 (1986), requiring the jury be instructed that the defense of intoxication applies only "where the alcohol has so prostrated the person's faculties as to make him incapable of performing such mental acts." *Martin* at 438,

relevance is usually limited to "specific intent" crimes.[55] Although this rule developed in the middle of the nineteenth century,[56] the concept of a "specific intent" crime has not received uniform treatment ("methods of defining specific intent are highly manipulable").[57] Used realistically, it seems dictated by logic. For example, the court instructed in *State v. Kavanaugh*:[58] "To regard the fact of intoxication as meriting consideration in such a case [as larceny, a specific intent crime] is not to hold that drunkenness will excuse crime, but to inquire whether the very crime which the law defines has been in point of fact committed."[59]

The rule has also varied in England from the question of the actor's capacity to form a specific intent to the question, today, whether the actor did, in fact, have such an intent.[60] There is still a division of American rules as to whether the ordinary intoxication rules relate to the actual *mens rea* held by the defendant or whether they go to the question of capacity to entertain the required *mens rea*.[61] Despite a good deal of criticism among Commonwealth writers,[62] the same dichotomy has been

---

517 A.2d at 520.

55. Hall, *Intoxication and Criminal Responsibility*, 57 HARV. L. REV. 1045, 1050-51 (1944).

56. Singh at 538-39.

57. People v. Kelley, 21 Mich. App. 612, 176 N.W.2d 435 (1970) (Levin, J.). "Twelve years after *Kelly* [sic], Levin was now a member of the supreme court, which, in *People v. Langworth*, continued to struggle with the general/specific issue recognizing 'the illogic and incongruity of the general intent-specific intent dichotomy.' While acknowledging its power to abolish this common-law rule, the court declined to do so claiming such a move 'would do nothing to help solve the problem of the intoxicated offender, both from the standpoint of the offender and...of society which suffers from the acts of the intoxicated offender.'" Boettcher, *Voluntary Intoxication: A Defense to Specific Intent Crimes*, 65 U. DET. L. REV. 33, 43-44 (1987) (footnote omitted).

58. State v. Kavanaugh, 20 Del. 131, 53 A. 335 (1902).

59. *Kavanaugh* at 136, 53 A. at 337.

> [F]or although...voluntary intoxication constitutes neither excuse for nor palliation of crime, yet in cases in which a specific or particular intent or purpose is an essential or constituent element of the offense, as in the case of larceny, intoxication, even though voluntary, becomes a matter for consideration, and is competent evidence on the question whether the defendant was capable of forming such an intent or purpose at the time the act was perpetrated.

Kavanaugh at 135, 53 A. at 337.

60. d'Orban, *Drugs and Alcohol: The Psychiatrist as Expert Witness in Court*, 81 BR. J. ADDICT. 631, 636 (1986), contrasting the view expressed on inability to form an intent with actual formation of specific intent.

61. Boettcher at 34 (1987). *Compare* People v. Crittle, 390 Mich. 367, 212 N.W.2d 196 (1973) (whether the defendant in fact has the requisite *mens rea*), *with* People v. Savoie, 419 Mich. 118, 349 N.W.2d 139 (1984), overruling *Crittle* (capacity standard).

62. J. SMITH & B. HOGAN, CRIMINAL LAW 190-201 (5th ed. 1983); G. WILLIAMS, TEXTBOOK OF CRIMINAL LAW 464-83 (2d ed. 1983); Quigley, *Specific and General Nonsense*, 11 DALHOUSIE L.J. 75 (1987); Schabas, *Intoxication and Culpability: Towards an Offence of Criminal*

applied under English[63] and Canadian law[64] but has been rejected in Australia.[65] Reform proposals[66] have not been enacted. A few states have now even abolished the specific intent rule so that intoxication is not even admissible to disprove intent.[67]

The Model Penal Code also adopts the so-called "special rule" of intoxication. In cases where recklessness suffices for liability, intoxication that is self-induced will provide no defense. Self-induced intoxication can only be a defense for crimes which require a *mens rea* level higher than recklessness. "When recklessness establishes an element of the offense, if the actor, due to self-induced intoxication, is unaware of a risk of which he would have been aware had he been sober, such unawareness is immaterial."[68] The idea was codified by the Model Penal Code but traces at least to Austin's work on jurisprudence.[69]

That formulation, of course, leaves somewhat unclear the status of the defense in crimes requiring knowledge but not intent, and, indeed, the states are either divided or undecided on the question whether knowledge falls within the rules relating to specific intent crimes or general intent crimes. The modern codes use "knowledge" extensively in addition to intent and recklessness, and courts and legislatures early on had to confront the question whether new definitions of a crime like murder which required only knowledge as to the result was a specific or general intent crime; the common law provided no answer to the question.[70] Reactions have varied.[71] For example, Colorado, because of the confusion generated in appellate cases, had to amend its statutes to make clear that "knowledge," as a term of culpability, fell within the ambit of "recklessness" for these purposes and was not assimilated to

---

Intoxication, 42 U. TORONTO FAC. L. REV. 147 (1984); Orchard, *Drunkenness as a "Defence" to Crime*, 1 CRIM. L.J. 59, 132 (1977); Comment, *Criminal Law—Mens Rea—General Principles—Intoxication as a Defence*, 55 CAN. BAR REV. 691 (1977); Gold, *An Untrimmed 'Beard': The Law of Intoxication as a Defence to a Criminal Charge*, 19 CRIM. L.Q. 34 (1976); Smith, *Case Comment on D.P.P. v. Majewski*, 1976 CRIM. L.R. 374; Williams, *Intoxication and Specific Intent*, 126 NEW L.J. 658 (1976).

63. D.P.P. v. Majewski, [1976] 2 All E.R. 142.

64. Leary v. Regina, [1978] 1 S.C.R. 29, 74 D.L.R.3d 103.

65. Regina v. O'Connor, 29 A.L.R. 449 (1980).

66. *See, e.g.,* Quigley, *Reform of the Intoxication Defence*, 33 MCGILL L.J. 2 (1987).

67. Note, 9 U. Ark. Little Rock L.J. 657 (1986-87). *See also* Commonwealth v. Sirbaugh, 347 Pa. Super. 154, 500 A.2d 453 (1985); Commonwealth v. Laing, 310 Pa. Super. 105, 456 A.2d 204 (1983). Pennsylvania has a statute, 18 PA. C.S. § 308 (Supp. 1974 to 1981), which limits the effects of drug or alcohol intoxication to reducing "murder from a higher degree to a lower degree of murder."

68. MODEL PENAL CODE § 2.08(2) (Proposed Official Draft 1962).

69. J. AUSTIN, LECTURES ON JURISPRUDENCE 512-13 (1879).

70. Singh, *History of the Defence of Drunkenness in English Criminal Law*, 49 L.Q. REV. 528, 545 n.80 (1933).

71. *See, e.g.,* Burke, *The Defense of Voluntary Intoxication: Now You See It, Now You Don't*, 19 IND. L. REV. 147, 150 (1986).

"intent." The legislature made it clear that the definition of "knowledge" crimes fell under general intent.[72] The purpose of the amendment was to make the voluntary intoxication defense unavailable to such crime and to confine it to the more limited classification of crimes which require intent to achieve a result.[73]

This rule, that voluntary (self-induced[74]) intoxication cannot be considered to disprove the *mens rea* of any general intent crime, has been the subject of criticism on the basis that it precludes inquiry into whether or not the defendant, in fact, entertained the *mens rea* necessary to be guilty of the crime charged.[75]

It bears emphasis, however, that the specific-intent/general-intent distinction which bars defensive evidence of intoxication to defeat a showing of general intent applies only to voluntary intoxication and not to uncontrollable mental conditions.

State v. Seely[76] illustrates a number of these points. The defendant was charged with aggravated battery and appealed his conviction on that charge. After a day-long bout of drinking, he evidently participated in a gang beating of the victims. One point on appeal was that he should have received a jury instruction on the insanity defense. The court held that if the evidence merely shows a loss of control due to drinking, the intoxication is voluntary and even temporary insanity due to intoxication does not entitle the defendant to an insanity defense instruction. The rule would be otherwise if the intoxication had been involuntary.

The court drew a distinction proffered by Jellinek and evidently endorsed by the United States Supreme Court in *Powell v. Texas*.[77] "Jellinek insists that conceptual clarity can only be achieved by distinguishing carefully between 'loss of control' once an individual has commenced to drink and 'inability to abstain' from drinking in the first place."[78] There is still another meaning of "loss of control" in this context. The evidence in this case indicated no loss of control with

---

72. COLO. REV. STAT. § 18-1-501(6) (1986).

73. Other states have reached the same conclusion and have eliminated "knowledge crimes" from the scope of the exculpatory rule. *See, e.g.*, State v. Cameron, 104 N.J. 42, 514 A.2d 1302 (1986).

74. MODEL PENAL CODE § 2.08(2) (Proposed Official Draft 1962). "Self-induced intoxication" is further defined in the Code as "intoxication caused by substances which the actor knowingly introduces into his body, the tendency of which to cause intoxication he knows or ought to know, unless he introduces them pursuant to medical advice or under such circumstances as would afford a defense to a charge of crime...." MODEL PENAL CODE § 2.08(5)(b) (Proposed Official Draft 1962).

75. *See, e.g.*, Hall, *Intoxication and Criminal Responsibility*, 57 HARV. L. REV. 1045, 1061-84 (1944); Note, *Volitional Fault and the Intoxicated Criminal Offender*, 36 U. CIN. L. REV. 258, 285-87 (1967).

76. State v. Seely, 212 Kan. 195, 510 P.2d 115 (1973).

77. Powell v. Texas, 392 U.S. 514, 88 S. Ct. 2145, 20 L. Ed. 2d 1254 (1968).

78. *Powell* at 524-25, 88 S. Ct. at 2150, 20 L. Ed. 2d at 1263.

respect to drinking, but there was evidence that the defendant had a tendency to become violent when drinking, to abnormally lose control *from* drinking and that he was fully aware of that tendency. Thus, even the suggestion in the evidence by a medical witness that there was a possibility of psychomotor epilepsy that contributed to the defendant's violence would not justify an insanity defense because his intoxication was voluntary in the sense that he was aware of the possible extreme effects of alcohol on him, whatever its medical or psychological cause might be. Still, one might suppose that the better practice would be to submit such issues to the jury when they are factual rather than, as this trial court did, to deny the insanity defense instruction because the trial court believed the actor was aware of the probable effects of alcohol on the defendant.[79] This is an example of a court using voluntary intoxication as a fault limiter because the insanity defense does not have one.

The defendant's second contention on this appeal was that he should have been permitted an instruction to the jury on the lesser offense of unaggravated battery, which, unlike aggravated battery, did not require a specific intent to injure. On this point, the court ruled that the defendant was correct and entitled to a new trial and this was because of the generally, though not universally, accepted view that even voluntary intoxication is a defense to a specific intent charge. Voluntary intoxication continues to bear only on specific intent crimes in some jurisdictions. Involuntary intoxication may be a defense to any charge if it rises to the level of insanity under the state rule.[80] The central point is this: The defense is defeated only to the extent of the fault which limits it. The defense of lack of *mens rea* is lost only to the extent that it cannot be used on a general intent crime but can be used for any offense of which the *mens rea* is higher than the level of fault.

Fault and Insanity Law

The one affirmative defense which has not developed a fault limitation on its invocation or scope is the insanity defense. Such limitations are made explicit in modern codes with respect to defenses such as necessity,[81] self-defense[82] and duress[83] and to the excuse of

---

79. *See, e.g.,* State v. De Moss, 244 Kan. 387, 770 P.2d 441 (1989).

80. Heyward v. State, 470 N.E.2d 63 (Ind. 1984); State v. Mriglot, 88 Wash. 2d 573, 564 P.2d 784 (1977).

81. MODEL PENAL CODE § 3.02(2) (Proposed Official Draft 1062).

82. MODEL PENAL CODE § 3.04(2)(b)(i) (Proposed Official Draft 1062).

83. MODEL PENAL CODE § 2.09(2) (Proposed Official Draft 1962). *See also* Regina v. Fitzpatrick, [1977] No. Irel. 20 (Ct. Crim. App.), involving fault in creating the duress defense by joining the I.R.A.

"mistake" (lack of *mens rea*).[84] But as we have pointed out above, there is no explicit fault category in the law that we could call something like "self-induced insanity" or "voluntary insanity." The evident view is that "Mental illness...has never...been viewed as a condition which a person can choose either to impose upon himself or to forego."[85]

It is a central thesis of this work that some courts, albeit a minority of them, tend to categorize the pathological intoxication defense in the camp of voluntary intoxication when they believe the defendant was "at fault" and that they do so specifically to invoke the fact that voluntary intoxication is a fault limitation and hence no defense at all, except, as we discussed in some detail, perhaps to specific intent crimes. In doing so, the courts sometimes compound the error by treating the actor's fault as drinking rather than limiting fault to the culpability, if any, of the actor that was involved as to the resultant risks created in knowingly drinking.

"The starting point from an historical point of view is the ancient position which did not regard mental disorder, or insanity, as having any bearing upon the matter of criminal guilt. Principles of criminal liability dating prior to the Norman Conquest persisted into the thirteenth century and 'a man who has killed another by misadventure, though he may deserve a pardon, is guilty of a crime; and the same rule applies...to a lunatic...'"[86] Thus, as one might expect, insanity law did not antedate development of the concept of *mens rea*. Still,

> By the time of Henry III (1216-1272) it was not uncommon for the king to grant a pardon as a special act of grace for one who had committed homicide while of unsound mind,[87] and in the reign of Edward I (1272-1307) although there was no change in the theory of guilt as a strict matter of law, such a homicide was regarded as pardonable to the extent that it entitled the defendant to a special verdict saying he committed the crime while mad and this practically insured the issuance of a pardon, which in time came to be granted as a matter of course.[88] During the reign of Edward II (1307-1327) insanity was beginning to be recognized as a defense to crime, and life was spared although chattels were still

---

84. MODEL PENAL CODE § 2.04(2) (Proposed Official Draft 1962).

85. English, *The Light Between Twilight and Dusk: Federal Criminal Law and the Volitional Insanity Defense*, 40 Hastings L.J. 1, 21 (1988). *But see* Mitchell, *Culpable Mental Disorder and Criminal Liability*, 8 INT'L J. LAW & PSYCHIAT. 273 (1988).

86. R. PERKINS & R. BOYCE, CRIMINAL LAW 950 (3d ed. 1982), citing 3 W. HOLDSWORTH, HISTORY OF ENGLISH LAW 371 (5th ed. 1942).

87. F. POLLOCK & F. MAITLAND, HISTORY OF ENGLISH LAW 480 (2d ed. 1899).

88. Citing 2 J. STEPHEN, HISTORY OF THE CRIMINAL LAW OF ENGLAND 151 (1883); 1 F. WHARTON & M. STILLE, MEDICAL JURISPRUDENCE ch. 26 (5th ed. 1905).

forfeited, while in the time of Edward III (1327-1377) absolute "madness" became a complete defense to a criminal charge.[89]

There is language in documents surviving from 1278 which may be a reference to the release to sureties of a defendant when "the King learns by inquisition taken by the justices to deliver Noting gaol [Nothingham jail] that Hugh hanged his daughter whilst suffering from madness, and not by felony or of malice aforethought."[90]

Fingarette and Hasse, as others before, have made the point that intoxication, when severe enough and when viewed solely in terms of the actor's mental state, is a form of insanity. "[I]nsanity and gross intoxication are alike in being conditions of irrationality at the time of the offending act;...the two cases differ significantly as to ultimate culpability because of the differences in the *origin* of that irrationality."[91] To complete the picture, what distinguishes insanity from both voluntary and involuntary intoxication is the concept of "mental disease or defect" which must be the reason for the actor's inability to reason, his "irrationality." One court even instructed the jury: "If the defendant had a mental disease...he is innocent—as innocent as if the act had been produced by involuntary intoxication..."[92]

Despite the close link, there is little in the early literature that explicitly links the development of insanity and intoxication law. It is speculative, of course, but it would seem that a definition of insanity

---

89. R. PERKINS & R. BOYCE, CRIMINAL LAW 950 (3d ed. 1982), citing, *inter alia*, S. GLUECK, MENTAL DISORDER AND THE CRIMINAL LAW 125 (1925) (some citations omitted).

90. Calendar of Close Rolls, Edward I, 7 Edw. I 518 (1278). More extensive and critical material may be found in S. GLUECK, MENTAL DISORDER AND THE CRIMINAL LAW (1925) and F. WHARTON & M. STILLE, MEDICAL JURISPRUDENCE (5th ed. 1905). H. WEIHOFEN, MENTAL DISORDER AS A CRIMINAL DEFENSE 53 (1954) (footnote omitted):

> Insanity did not become a defense to crime in England until the beginning of the fourteenth century, and the authorities on the subject prior to the seventeenth century are so general in their terms that they can be regarded as little more than "antiquarian curiosities." The early institutional writers, Bracton, Littleton, and Fitzherbert, did not treat of insanity as a defense to crime at all, and their discussion of it as an excuse to civil liability is fragmentary. Coke, writing in the seventeenth century, discussed the criminal liability of persons *non compos mentis,* but only in a casual manner.

What we now commonly refer to in describing the history of the insanity defense as the "wild beast" test was evidently developed in *Arnold's Case,* 16 How. St. Tr. 695, 765 (1724), where reference is made to a defendant who "doth not know what he is doing, no more than an infant, than a brute, or a wild beast...." *See generally* Platt & Diamond, *The Origins and Development of the "Wild Beast" Concept of Mental Illness and Its Relations to Theories of Criminal Responsibility,* 1 J. HIST. BEHAV. SCI. 355 (1965).

91. H. FINGARETTE & A. HASSE, MENTAL DISABILITIES AND CRIMINAL RESPONSIBILITY 10 (1979) (emphasis in original).

92. State v. Jones, 50 N.H. 369, 373 (1871).

which contained no fault limitation (other than "mental disease") would force recognition that intoxication was an exception and that involuntary intoxication was an exception to normal intoxication. The fault rationale appears at the very outset of intoxication law because it is so obvious.

Hawkins referred to insanity law in terms of a limitation expressed as a "natural disability,"[93] and this would seem to exclude self-induced insanity, unless, of course, an underlying "natural disability" triggered by self-administered alcohol would serve. While there is nothing explicit in the writings of the early authorities, it is, nevertheless, clear that what they had in mind was something of a permanent nature such as "fixed" or "settled" insanity from alcohol abuse, but not temporary derangement. But they, undoubtedly, were aware of no other kind, and if that is so, one hardly would expect them to discuss the subject of temporary insanity triggered by alcohol. It would be another hundred years or more before it was known that alcohol could also trigger a temporary mental derangement equivalent to a psychotic state and the link could not earlier be made to cases of temporary, self-induced insanity. They could not arise without that knowledge.

Development of insanity law seems to have always been motivated by recognition that the actor was not at fault for either his condition or acts in that condition.[94] As we have shown, the development of the law of voluntary intoxication was based on the contrary assumption that the actor was at fault. Involuntary intoxication, as Perkins and Boyce have observed, "does not necessarily establish criminal incapacity on his part; it establishes only that his derangement [if the intoxication amounted to that] is without culpability and hence is to be dealt with the same as if it were the result of mental disease or defect."[95]

What will be important on the legal side is how discerning the courts of that jurisdiction are in the treatment of the fault limiter. Whether a jurisdiction adopts the control test or restricts the scope of the insanity test to the cognitive test of *M'Naghten* or its progeny is relatively unimportant in the case of pathological reaction to alcohol, for it is clear that either test can be met in a true case. Some are of the opinion that merely drinking is fault enough. Most, fortunately, will couch the limiter in terms of some level of recklessness, that is, some level of awareness by the actor that a violent reaction or other criminal behavior is likely to follow ingestion of alcohol. Almost all of the appellate cases, of course,

---

93. 1 W. HAWKINS, PLEAS OF THE CROWN (1824).

94. *See, e.g.*, Brandt, *The Insanity Defense and the Theory of Motivation*, 7 LAW & PHIL. 123, 136 (1988): "The thesis I suggest about the insanity defense is that it is essentially the claim that the state of mind of the agent at the time of his unlawful act prevents conclusive inference from his act to a defective level of moral/legal motivation (as being its necessary condition), hence it provides a release from culpability."

95. R. PERKINS & R. BOYCE, CRIMINAL LAW 1005 (3d ed. 1982) (citations omitted).

demonstrate a defense approach which has not succeeded because only the defendant may ordinarily appeal the verdict. When the defense has been successful in eliciting a not guilty verdict, there is only rarely a report of the case at the appellate level. Still, we have found no appellate case in which the success or failure of the defense of pathological intoxication turned on the exact test of insanity used in that court. What is important is the fault limiter.

Fault and the Law of Automatism

The idea of a fault limiter on the automatism defense introduces the possible concept of culpable automatism versus nonculpable automatism (including nonculpable insane automatism?), which will further divide itself into what level of culpability would be required to defeat the defense. As to the main point here, one English writer has stated the point this way: "[T]he idea of 'fault,' although fundamental in the development of the intoxication plea, is also equally applicable to the defence of automatism."[96] Thus, much, perhaps all, of the material we developed with respect to the fault limiter in self-induced intoxication or insanity cases would be fully applicable in the case tried as one of automatism when the automatism is also self-induced.

AN ANALYTICAL STRUCTURE OF FAULT AS A LIMITATION ON DEFENSES

There will be three general questions regarding a fault limiter: (1) To what exactly must the fault culpability relate, that is, fault with respect to what? (2) must the actor actually be aware, or will fault be an objective standard? and (3) will the culpability level that denotes fault be unitary or variable depending upon the substantive offense involved or the defense theory invoked?

The general position taken here is that the structure of the definition of crimes themselves serves as well to provide a basis of analysis of the elements of fault limitations on defenses. As crimes must have acts, circumstances and results, so must defenses have acts, circumstances and results parallel to the crime in cases of excuses and somewhat more independent of the crimes in cases of justifications. Fault limitations in turn must relate to one or the other of these. As inclusion and exclusion decisions, and decisions regarding the level or degree are made as to crimes on the basis of the level of culpability with respect to

---

96. Mackay, *Intoxication as a Factor in Automatism*, 1982 CRIM. L. REV. 146.

the *actus reus* elements of the crime, so levels of fault can be described. The obvious limitation on this approach is that the clarity and precision with which crimes have been defined are not matched by our definition practices in the realm of defenses. Many defenses would be of questionable constitutionality if the notions of legality (vagueness) that are applied to state crime definitions were applied by the courts with equal vigor to their definitions of defenses.

The *Actus Reus* Elements of Crimes and Fault Limitations on Defenses

The Act. We discussed in Chapter 7 in connection with the defense of automatism, the relationship between the structure of crimes under modern codes as well as common law in terms of the narrow definition of act and its concomitant requirement that the act must be voluntary. The parallel to the defense of pathological intoxication is that the "involuntary act" of drinking should place the resulting incapacitation in the category of defenses which will excuse the resulting state of mind as innocently induced. To be voluntary, the drinking (or whatever other act that created the incapacity) must be both voluntary and done knowingly, both "willed" and "conscious," as we said in that context with respect to the act requirement in defining crime. Absent these, the act cannot be considered a basis for finding fault. Defensive claims based on an involuntary act of drinking are claims of involuntary intoxication, not pathological intoxication.

The Circumstances. Manifest in the older views of the basic structure of the substantive criminal law is the failure to go any further than to distinguish act from the consequences of the act.[97] The modern approach is to further separate those physical realities (age of the victim, for example) or even mental realities (nonconsent of the victim, for example) outside a defendant's act, into circumstances and results. A circumstance is essentially an existing condition under which the defendant acts. A circumstantial element exists at the time of the defendant's act whereas a result is then subsequently caused by the act of the defendant under those circumstances.

The law may wish to and frequently does differentiate the criminal from the noncriminal and the more seriously criminal in both these terms, and that differentiation is aided by drawing the further distinction between circumstances and results, either in terms of what the law may

97. J. AUSTIN, JURISPRUDENCE 415 (5th ed. 1885).

require as circumstances or results, or what *mens rea* those circumstances or results require.

To label someone's conduct a crime almost invariably requires that the defendant's act shall have been done under certain criminal circumstances. Taking property is not a crime; it may be a crime if done without consent of the person entitled to possession of the property. Driving is not a crime; driving while intoxicated is a crime. Driving without a license is a crime, and so on. Thus, circumstances are used to distinguish the criminal from the noncriminal.

One could also differentiate the level of criminality of a defendant's conduct by whether he was armed with a gun when he attempted murder, or one might wish to distinguish by whether the victim died or not, or both. That is, in different crimes, one might wish to emphasize the existence of particular circumstances or the achievement *vel non* of a specified result. Circumstantial elements are used extensively for grading purposes, along with result elements and varying levels of culpability with respect to either circumstances or results.

Another important consideration in support of a clear distinction between circumstances and results as objective elements in crime definitions is the fact that not all *mens rea* terms will apply to all levels of analysis. It is common, for example, to limit "intent" to results, while knowledge, recklessness and criminal negligence potentially will apply to both circumstances and results.

The parallel under discussion here is that it may make a difference—for example, regarding a claim of mental incapacity which is arguably self-induced through fault—whether the fault is found with respect to the circumstances causing the condition or to the resulting condition itself; hence the distinction between circumstances and results may be important to the courts. While we will try to categorize the cases in this manner, most courts are essentially ignorant of the distinction because defenses and limitations on defenses are not as precisely defined as are crimes. Yet it would seem to matter a great deal if the defendant had reason to know the probable results of drinking alcohol compared to a defendant who knew it was alcohol but did not have reason to know the probable results of drinking it. These, in fact, are mingled together in many cases. This is not a failure to distinguish negligence from recklessness, but rather acts from circumstances, and circumstances from results. Here, again, most disputes which will arise surrounding the question whether the actor did or did not have sufficient awareness at the circumstance level will be cases that probably are tried as involuntary intoxication cases, such as drug potentiation cases. These are the cases that the Model Penal Code treats as involuntary intoxication claims.

The Result. One of the principal characteristics of modern criminal codes is the extent to which they have enlarged upon common law crimes or earlier code crimes. The view increasingly taken is that what is important is the defendant's state of mind in relation to his or her conduct under specified circumstances. While results expressed as actual injury are still important, they increasingly are important as aggravating elements rather than necessary for criminal liability. The judgment seems to be that if it is properly made criminal for a person recklessly to cause injury to another person (or property), it should not be entirely determinative of his guilt that the injury actually occur. The defendant is thought deserving of criminal condemnation for having engaged in conduct under circumstances which created a risk from which harm might ensue if this is done with a specified *mens rea*. Thus, new crimes are created to encompass such situations. An example is the new crime of reckless endangerment,[98] which only requires the creation of a risk of harm. It is something of a curiosity that these are actually result-oriented crimes in which the harm is viewed as more inchoate in nature. It is somewhat removed from the actual injury of anyone in that the victim need not be aware that anything even occurred. In such a crime, the result is endangerment, and the culpability requirement at that level is recklessness. This increasingly inchoate nature of crime under modern criminal codes would itself be worth more in-depth exploration as perhaps being a new generational view of the harm principle in criminal law. The observation is made here only to make explicit that a result may now be rather intangible in nature but that such intangible "harm" may still be a result requirement that is independent of the *mens rea* which the offense may require with respect to it.

The relevance of this observation here is that fault as a limitation on existing defenses may be voiced in terms of risk creation as well as known results, and precision is lacking on the question. For example, must the actor be aware not only of the likelihood of a resulting reaction, or of the further results of intoxication itself on his behavior? Is it enough that he is aware that there is some effect on his behavior, or is the requirement more precise? Again, we will try to discuss the cases with these questions in mind, but the general answer is that it is the exceptional opinion that is careful enough to make these discriminations. The extent to which this is due to a failure of counsel to formulate the trial issue with sufficient clarity is not known, but it is obvious that requested instructions that are tailored to the case could help.

Modern Fault Terminology: Culpability and Fault

A list of *actus reus* elements in criminal law, both at common law and today, would be unlimited, but *mens rea* requirements are now quite

98. MODEL PENAL CODE § 211.2 (Proposed Official Draft 1962).

restricted. The problems associated with common law *mens rea* terms were their multiplicity and concomitant vagueness. While perhaps not always a shared perspective,[99] one of the most important accomplishments of the drafters of the Model Penal Code was to address both of these problems of culpability simultaneously.[100]

Numerous writers have concluded that there was no coherence in the cases in reference to common law terms of culpability.[101] In background research for the unsuccessful attempt to adopt a modern criminal code in the federal system, one consultant found 78 then-extant *mens rea* terms,[102] and this situation remains largely unchanged.[103]

---

99. The value of legislative precision is not universally enshrined:

> [Sections] 16, 17 and 18 of the 1962 Draft [of the German Penal Code] contained attempts to define the concepts "intention," "motive" and "knowledge," "negligence" and "wantonness." The revised Code rejects these attempts, in my view rightly so. Subjective elements of offenses cannot be the object of precise legislative definition; any such definition curtails the dynamic quality of codification, principally the opportunity for continuing rediscovery and adjustment by both courts and scholarship. The evil that can flow from legislative definition of such concepts can be seen clearly from judicial attempts to avoid the undesirable consequences of imperfect definitions by distinctions that border on the ludicrous.

Binavince, *The Structure and Theory of the German Penal Code*, 24 AM. J. COMP. L. 594, 600 (1976).

It would be easier to pass this off as a "cultural difference" were it not for the now-sharp demarcation between the modern state codes and the present condition of our federal criminal law. There is no doubt that despite its more limited substantive coverage, the present federal law is notoriously "dynamic" in its amenability to application to situations not before even remotely assumed to be within its ambit. Is there a perceived need for the courts of a central government to engage in more "continuing rediscovery" of the bounds of the criminal law than is thought necessary in the application of the criminal laws of lesser sovereignties? Are these questions related to the view that the principle of legality in American criminal cases finds expression almost entirely in federal cases which review state legislation, not federal cases which review federal legislation? *See* Amsterdam, *The Void-for-Vagueness Doctrine in the Supreme Court*, 109 U. PA. L. REV. 67 (1960).

Where the states show the same federal preference for vagueness is in their definition of and limitations on defenses.

100. *See, e.g.*, Packer, *The Model Penal Code and Beyond*, 63 COLUM. L. REV. 594, 601 (1963). Even the extensively proposed revisions of federal law going back to the Brown Commission Report in 1970 have largely tracked the work of the American Law Institute in the Model Penal Code. Robinson, *Some Thoughts on the Culpability Provisions of the Proposed Federal Criminal Code*, 72 J. CRIM. L. & CRIMINOLOGY 488 (1981).

101. 1 W. LAFAVE & A. SCOTT, SUBSTANTIVE CRIMINAL LAW, § 3.4 (1986).

102. Present federal criminal law is composed of a bewildering array of terms used to describe the mental element of an offense. The National Commission's consultant on this subject identified 78 different terms used in present law. They range from the traditional 'knowingly,' 'willfully,' and 'maliciously,' to the redundant 'willful, deliberate, malicious, and premeditated,' and 'knowingly and willfully,' to the conclusive 'unlawfully,' 'improperly,' and 'feloniously,' to the self-contradictory 'willfully neglects.' No federal statute attempts a comprehensive and precise definition of the terms used to describe the requisite states of

The general culpability structure established by the Model Penal Code provisions, in contrast, is largely limited to four terms, and they are carefully defined though obviously still not without residual ambiguity. One sometimes finds nonconforming terms of culpability in the Model Penal Code and some of the codes patterned on it as well,[104] but by and large, the nomenclature is adhered to. This structure has, in general terms, achieved virtually unanimous adherence across the country although, of course, still not including the federal system[105] or other states which have not adopted modern criminal codes.

The "act," such as drinking, must be "voluntary," and that does not vary, but one of the areas of continuing confusion in criminal law is whether "act" ever requires anything more than a finding of voluntariness with its necessarily associated dual requirements of consciousness and determination, in which case, knowledge may be a necessary requirement in any case.

Determining the correct *mens rea* requirement of each circumstance and result required by the crime has historically, undoubtedly, been the most perplexing part of criminal law. This is not so much attributable to inherent theoretical difficulty as it is to pervasive ambiguity in the law itself both in terms of what possibilities existed and what choices previously had been made. It is that task that the Model Penal Code was designed to facilitate by refinement of the nomenclature involved.

Under the impetus provided by the Model Penal Code, there are now four categories of culpable mental states which are designed to be the exclusive terminology[106] for the vast majority of crimes: purpose (or intent), knowledge,[107] recklessness and negligence.[108]

---

mind. Nor are the terms defined in the statutes in which they are used. Instead, the task of giving substance to the 'mental element' used in a particular statute has been left to the courts. S. Rep. No. 605, 95th Cong., 1st Sess. pt. 1, at 55 (1977). *See also,* 1 NAT'L COMM'N ON REFORM OF THE FEDERAL CRIMINAL LAWS, WORKING PAPERS 148-151 (1970), which describes the plethora of meanings given to the single *mens rea* concept of "willfulness."

103. *See* N. ABRAMS, FEDERAL CRIMINAL LAW AND ITS ENFORCEMENT (1986).

104. The Model Penal Code has its occasional wayward term. MODEL PENAL CODE § 213.3(1)(d), Corruption of Minors and Seduction (Proposed Official Draft 1962) includes "by a promise of marriage which the actor *does not mean to perform*."

105. The only exception has been an early and aborted criminal code draft in California which used only three culpability categories. CALIFORNIA JOINT LEGISLATIVE COMMITTEE FOR REVISION OF THE PENAL CODE, THE PENAL CODE 29-31 (undated, *circa* 1972).

106. For a broader discussion of the categories of *mens rea*, including several continental and Soviet structures, *see* G. FLETCHER, RETHINKING CRIMINAL LAW § 6.5 (1978).

107. The term "willfully" is eschewed in the MODEL PENAL CODE § 2.02(8) (Proposed Official Draft 1962). The point of defining it as a synonym for "knowledge" is primarily to indicate its interpretation outside the code defining it. "Willfully" has, of course, achieved a reputation as a badly used and abused term because of its "flexibility" of meaning. Judge Hand seemed to express the views of the American Law Institute when the matter was discussed on the floor: "It is a dreadful word." 1955 AMERICAN LAW INSTITUTE, PROCEEDINGS 160.

108. Several states use "criminal negligence" in lieu of the Model Penal Code's

Only two of these terms are in serious contention as conveying the meaning of fault in the cases to be discussed on pathological intoxication. Any higher culpability proven to have been held by the defendant will satisfy a lower statutory requirement.[109] Essentially, liability will be predicated on strict liability (for drinking at all), or the courts will limit liability by requiring either recklessness or negligence. It may be helpful to define and discuss the terms in advance.

Recklessness. Recklessness had two subtly different and contending connotations at common law. Most courts defined it the way it is defined today by the Model Penal Code:

> A person acts recklessly with respect to a material element of an offense when he consciously disregards a substantial and unjustifiable risk that the material element exists or will result from his conduct. The risk must be of such a nature and degree that, considering the nature and purpose of the actor's conduct and the circumstances known to him, its disregard involves a gross deviation from the standard of conduct that a law-abiding person would observe in the actor's situation.[110]

Less commonly, one found the term defined in some earlier cases to require actual awareness only of the underlying facts (the circumstances in today's nomenclature) but imposed an objective (reasonable person) standard as to the risk of results that such facts augured. The dominant definition required awareness of both the facts and risks of results on the part of the defendant, and whether a reasonable person would appreciate the risks of results suggested by the known facts was not relevant.

Recklessness at an extreme level is probably all that was meant by more colorful common law language such as "man-endangering state of mind," "black and malignant heart, devoid of social duty and fatally bent on mischief," and so on. These characterizations then and today simply

---

"negligence", probably to emphasize the distinction between tort and criminal liability. That distinction lies largely in the criminal law requirement of a *gross* deviation from the standard of care imposed. *See, e.g.*, N.Y. PENAL LAW § 15.05(4) (McKinney 1987).

The Model Penal Code made clear that each objective element in the definition of the crime (each act, each circumstance and each result) had to have an associated culpability requirement except in a narrow class of strict liability offenses for which only a fine could be imposed. MODEL PENAL CODE § 2.02(1) (Proposed Official Draft 1962) provides: "*Minimum Requirements of Culpability.* Except as provided in Section 2.05, a person is not guilty of an offense unless he acted purposely, knowingly, recklessly or negligently, as the law may require, with respect to each material element of the offense."

109. MODEL PENAL CODE § 2.02(5) (Proposed Official Draft 1962).

110. MODEL PENAL CODE § 2.02 (2)(c) (Proposed Official Draft 1962).

denote an extremely high degree of recklessness, the kind of recklessness that distinguishes murder from involuntary manslaughter at common law, for example.

Lower degrees of recklessness, not negligence, were frequently at common law referred to as "negligence" but with a modifier. Typical examples were "criminal negligence," "wanton negligence," and "culpable negligence"—language which today would be in some of these instances a contradiction. In these cases, the court almost always seems to mean what we today would call recklessness, sufficient, for example, to find involuntary manslaughter but not murder.

Both at common law and today, the concept of recklessness comprises a balancing of three ideas: (1) what is at risk (for example, risk of slight property damage versus death of another human being); (2) the level of risk or its probability (for example, quite likely versus a one-in-a--thousand chance); and (3) the actor's justification for creating and disregarding that risk (for example, was he rushing a person he believed very ill to the hospital or was he speeding in a drag race?). It is a balancing of these considerations that determines whether a conscious disregard of a risk was substantial and unjustifiable, the first two going to substantiality and the third element going to its justifiability. Conscious disregard of many risks of everyday living is deemed justifiable; our mere driving a car involves justified risks. The amount of discretion accorded the trier of fact under these definitions should be obvious and is attributable not only to the inexactitude of the terms involved, but also the fact that "unjustifiability" is explicitly built into the definition of the crime or defense any time recklessness is a culpability element. In other contexts such as affirmative defenses (for example, self-defense), the terms of justifiability are spelled out in some detail, which is quite unlike the more abstract and general technique taken to defining recklessness.

Recklessness is often distinguished from criminal negligence in that it is considered a subjective state of mind, whereas negligence is considered an objective standard under which the defendant's actual state of mind is irrelevant. However, while it is true that the concept of recklessness is predominately subjective, there is still an objective component of recklessness because, in the end, the defendant's evaluation of the relevant factors will be held up to a reasonable person ("law--abiding person") standard in determining whether he was justified in disregarding the risk of which he was aware. The test is subjective to determine whether the defendant was reckless. But the definition requires a high degree of recklessness as well, and the degree is measured in terms of a reasonable person.

Negligence. Historically, negligence was used infrequently in criminal law. Its principle common law use was in screening the availability of affirmative defenses. This was accomplished by requiring that they be reasonable under the circumstances so that if the defendant was negligent in relying on the affirmative defense, he would lose that defense. Common law even limited the elemental defense of mistake in the same way, despite the illogic of the position, and some state codes continue that position. But most criminal codes now rely on criminal negligence as to either circumstances or results to establish liability in some instances. The new crime of negligent homicide is the leading example.[111] The Model Penal Code defines negligence as follows:

> A person acts negligently with respect to a material element of an offense when he should be aware of a substantial and unjustifiable risk that the material element exists or will result from his conduct. The risk must be of such a nature and degree that the actor's failure to perceive it, considering the nature and purpose of his conduct and the circumstances known to him, involves a gross deviation from the standard of care that a reasonable person would observe in the actor's situation.[112]

Criminal negligence differs markedly from the other three culpability terms used in the code, for it rests almost entirely on an objective standard of guilt. The person's actual state of mind is essentially irrelevant. The inclusion, however, of the language "gross deviation" is deliberate and is intended to forestall mass inclusion of tort law into criminal law. While tort negligence and criminal negligence share objectivity of evaluation, the criminal standard of evaluation is higher. It is the same "reasonable person" who serves as the benchmark, but the deviation from that standard must be greater than for civil liability only. The considerations which go into the balance are the same as those delineated in the previous section on recklessness, but in this instance, awareness of the relevant circumstances and attendant risks is not required, although there must still be a "substantial and unjustifiable risk" that the result will occur or that a circumstance exists.

The definition is largely objective; however, the Model Penal Code interjected a subjective component by taking into account "circumstances known to" the defendant and by referring to the "care that a reasonable person would observe in the actor's situation."[113] The commentaries note that

---

111. MODEL PENAL CODE § 210.4 (Proposed Official Draft 1962).
112. MODEL PENAL CODE § 2.02(2)(d) (Proposed Official Draft 1962).
113. MODEL PENAL CODE § 2.02(2)(d) (Proposed Official Draft 1962).

> There is an inevitable ambiguity in 'situation.' If the actor were blind or if he had just suffered a blow or experienced a heart attack, these would certainly be facts to be considered, as they would be under present law. But the heredity, intelligence or temperament of the actor would not now be held material in judging negligence; and could not be without depriving the criterion of all its objectivity....The draft is not intended to displace discriminations of this kind; it is designed to leave the issue to the courts[.][114]

As applied to resulting incapacity on the part of the actor in cases of pathological intoxication, the standard becomes extremely subjective (on the jury's part), particularly when the "result" is not identified with clarity any more than is the concept of negligence to which it applies. In many of the pathological intoxication cases, the "actor's situation" will be extremely critical.

In summary, we will try to determine what fault means by reference to the circumstances of what is consumed. We will then look at the additional circumstance, if any, of any underlying mental or physical condition of the actor (the actor's situation) and the resulting incapacitation or tendency to violence. Finally, the question will be whether, with respect to each of these, the courts require actual awareness (recklessness), objective fault (negligence) or no fault at all ("strict liability").

At least three factors will obscure the clarity of the results of the analysis. First, there now appear to be three kinds of pathological intoxication recognized by the courts, and there may be some unarticulated differences in the way the fault limitation is treated in the varying context. Secondly, the persistence of careless wording in court opinions will not go unnoticed. Third, in many of the cases, the courts will be content to rest their decision, as they should, on the observation that the defendant was aware without their then being called upon to determine whether anything less would suffice to defeat the defense. Because of these factors, classification is often problematical in the terms we have established, but perhaps it is a beginning.

THE ANALYSIS APPLIED: THE VARIOUS MEANINGS OF FAULT IN THE CONTEXT OF INVOLUNTARY AND PATHOLOGICAL INTOXICATION

The suggestion here is that the courts should not just refer to the defendant as having been "at fault" but should ascribe a precise term of

114. MODEL PENAL CODE, comment 3 at 126 (Tent. Draft No. 4, 1955).

culpability associated in the case with that element of the defense. Thus, a defense is provided to the extent that the fault thus assigned is commensurate with the level of fault required by the commission of the offense charged. For example, if the actor was negligent with respect to the existence of pathological reaction to alcohol, he would be liable for negligent homicide if he killed, manslaughter if he was reckless, and murder in the event of extreme recklessness. But if insanity is a justification, it would be probable that mere negligence in claiming it would defeat it, as it does with negligence in the claim of self-defense. Even there, however, many states (and the Model Penal Code) would reduce the homicide claimed in self-defense to the level of homicide which reflected the fault culpability. Common law sometimes recognized this under the rubric of "imperfect self-defense." This, of course, is a jury function, guided by instructions. In the context of pathological intoxication, the choices will essentially reduce to recklessness and criminal negligence with respect to the result of an abnormal reaction and perhaps its nature, but the existence of the relevant circumstances will come into play as well.

The "fault" associated with alcohol consumption should be limited to either the normal or known concomitants of intoxication and not include the unexpected. The American authority, like the English, is not clear whether the standard of fault is objective (negligence) or subjective, and if the latter, whether it means recklessness or knowledge. It is also not clear whether the answers to these questions might vary with respect to what substantive culpability requirements exist as part of the crime charged against the actor or what defense theory is utilized by the defense. That is the first set of problems.

There are three distinct kinds of situations or factors operating here with respect to the question of the exact culpability required for the fault limitation to operate, and we have outlined the general analytical structure of the act, circumstances and results. The first focuses on the defendant's act in causing his or her own incapacity, that the actor voluntarily ingested or consumed something. The court would clearly exclude from liability anyone whose drinking was deemed involuntary, such as either under sufficient duress or merely unknowing (as by breathing a noxious gas accidentally released into the environment). Nothing more needs to be sustained in those situations. Presumably, the articulated rules of fault governing defenses such as duress will prevail. These are cases of involuntary intoxication in the almost hypothetical sense of "involuntary."

A second factor deals with the actor's awareness of relevant circumstances. In the case of alcohol consumption, there generally will be two relevant circumstances. One is an awareness that it is alcohol or some other drug that is being consumed. The other is that some other circumstantial fact such as pre-existing brain injury, permanent or temporary, causes the temporary psychosis.

The third factor deals with the actor's awareness of the results on him, which may be viewed either as the resulting automatism or mental incapacity or impairment in the case of pathological intoxication, or simple, but perhaps, surprise intoxication otherwise. For example, in cases which involve mixing drugs and alcohol, some cases involve an unawareness on the part of the actor that his drink had been altered. Presumably, those are the easy cases.[115] In still other cases, the actor knows that he is mixing drugs but claims unawareness of the effects on him of doing so. Finally, as to results, the defendant may be aware of some prior abnormal effect on him but not know that the condition could cause him to commit a crime. If this defensive situation is treated the same as one of simple intoxication, lack of actual awareness of resulting crimes will usually be irrelevant, at least unless a specific intent crime is charged. But the law with respect to normal intoxication is based on known, relatively narrow ranges of responses to alcohol consumption. Pathological intoxication may require more individual inquiry, precisely because it is abnormal and variable.

Pathological intoxication typically involves the situation in which the actor is well aware that he is drinking alcohol and knows its normal effect, both on himself and on others. Thus, the novel, and difficult, cases are those in which the actor is not aware of the second circumstance that makes the difference between his reaction and normal intoxication, or even when he is aware of that fact, he is not aware that this combination will have this effect on his mental condition, when the impact of the alcohol is extraordinary and unexpected.

In each of these cases, what needs deciding is the culpable mental state at each level, circumstances or results, that establishes "fault" on the actor's part. It is not surprising that the courts seem adrift somewhat on the question,[116] given the fact that the various situations have been

---

115. *See, e.g.*, Burns, 58 Crim. App. 364 (1974).

116. In an analogous situation, the U. S. Supreme Court recently dealt with the question whether the Veterans Administration had properly developed and applied regulations which excluded veterans from obtaining an extension on the period of benefit eligibility beyond the normal ten-year limit. Traynor v. Turnage, 485 U.S. 535, 108 S. Ct. 1372, 99 L. Ed. 2d 618 (1988). Such an extension was allowable when non-use was attributable to "a physical or mental disability which was not the result of [their] own willful misconduct." 38 U.S.C. § 1662(a)(1) (1982). Plaintiffs maintained they were alcoholics who fell within this exception, but the Court in a 4-3 decision upheld the VA's determination that their alcoholism was due to their own "willful misconduct," although it seems to be conceded that alcoholism is a "mental disorder."

The dissenters delved a bit more into the question of the "fault limiter" expressed in the term "willful misconduct." The Veterans Administration had defined the term to mean "an act involving conscious wrongdoing or known prohibited action" (38 CFR § 3.1(n) (1987)) and "the intentional doing of something either with the knowledge that it is likely to result in

somewhat homogenized by the courts and that no single answer may be sufficient for all the situations. Even for the same personal situation, an actor may be charged with a variety of crimes which have different constituent elements. The suggestion is that we use the analysis now familiar in the context of defining crime and apply the same concepts and the same level of precision to the analysis of defenses as well as to the requirements to defeat the defense in question in the context of various charges.

As something of an oversimplification, it can be said that there are two judicial views extant. The majority subscribes to Weihofen's

---

serious injury or with wanton and reckless disregard of its probable consequences," (VA Manual M21-1, § 14.04). And in a later Administrator's Decision, No. 988, with respect to resulting organic damage from alcohol consumption, as distinguished from alcoholism itself, the decision opined that "While it is proper to hold a person responsible for the direct and immediate results of indulgence in alcohol, it cannot be reasonably said that he expects and *wills* the disease and disabilities which sometimes appear as secondary effects."

The dissenters, in an opinion by Justice Blackmun, noted that

> All of this surely can be said of some primary alcoholics [as the VA had classified the plaintiffs], whose drinking begins innocently enough and who feel only much later the effects of a dependency so disabling that it requires repeated hospitalization.
>
> Individuals suffering from a wide range of disabilities, including heart and lung disease and diabetes, usually bear some responsibility for their conditions. And the conduct that can lead to this array of disabilities, particularly dietary and smoking habits, is certainly no less voluntary than the consumption of alcohol. Nevertheless, the VA has expressed an unwillingness to extend the definition of willful misconduct to all voluntary conduct having some relation to the development of a disability. In justifying the exclusion of secondary organic effects of alcoholism, such as cirrhosis of the liver, from the reach of the willful misconduct presumption, the VA has explained: "[H]istorically, the question of willful misconduct has never been raised in other related situations where personal habits or neglect are possible factors in the incurrence of disability. For example, the harmful effects of tobacco smoking on circulation and respiration were known long before tobacco was incriminated as a causative factor in the high incidence of cancer, emphysema and heart disease. Yet smoking has not been considered misconduct. It is unreasonable and illogical to apply one set of rules with respect to alcohol and a different one in a situation closely analogous."
> Decision No. 988, p. 2.

Traynor, 108 S. Ct. at 1391, 99 L. Ed. 2d at 643-44 (concurring and dissenting opinion).

In the case of pathological intoxication, in addition to the awareness of the circumstances which give rise to an abnormal reaction to alcohol, we are confronted with the additional factor of the actor's resulting behavior which further complicates the analysis. It is interesting, as the dissenters noted, that the VA distinguished between resulting alcoholism and resulting physical illnesses even though the regulations made no such distinction. As we read the regulations, the minimum "culpable mental state" required to find "willful misconduct" is recklessness with respect to either result. Perhaps it is thought that recklessness was to be found in the case of resulting alcoholism but not in the case, say, of cirrhosis of the liver. That would appear to be difficult to justify.

summary that "Where the defense relies on the consequential effect of intoxication on a mind already mentally disordered, the defendant is entitled to have this clearly presented in the charge...."[117] However, these courts will test the liability of the actor by his awareness of the probable effects of the combination of alcohol and pre-existing mental disorder. In a few jurisdictions, however, a crime committed as a result of pathological reaction to alcohol in combination with a pre-existing mental condition will be treated solely as a case of intoxication, with its built-in fault limiter automatically applicable so that there will be no defense at all except perhaps under the usual rules relating to voluntary intoxication; that is, such a situation might reduce the verdict of guilty for a specific intent crime to one involving only general intent.

The Fault Lies in Negligence or Recklessness as to the Circumstances of What Is Consumed

Many of the cases stress that the fault lies in the circumstances of either what is being consumed or the defendant's own condition, the combination of which causes the pathological reaction to alcohol. Montana has amended its statutes to provide that intoxication is not a defense "unless the defendant proves that he did not know that it was an intoxicating substance when he consumed, smoked, sniffed, injected, or otherwise ingested the substance causing the condition."[118] Whether this statute is meant to apply to pathological intoxication in addition to ordinary intoxication is not clear, but it is clear that even pathological intoxication seen as an unexpected degree of intoxication, as under the Model Penal Code, is excluded by it, though other forms may not be. The uncertainty regarding pathological intoxication is that the statutory restriction imposed by this statute is aimed, by its terms, at "intoxication" and presumably means the defense of voluntary intoxication and not the defenses of automatism or insanity. Perhaps it is no more than an unusual way of rejecting voluntary intoxication even in specific intent crimes. Its significance here is not its subtlety or complexity, but only the unusual clarity with which fault is defined, and that clarity is achieved at some cost.

Most writers conceive of pathological intoxication as those situations in which the actor experiences an unusual effect of ingestion of known substances. Instances which deal with the actor's awareness of relevant circumstances are most commonly relegated to the law of involuntary intoxication as an adjunct to the duress cases in which the involuntariness

---

117. H. WEIHOFEN, MENTAL DISORDER AS A CRIMINAL DEFENSE 125 (1954).
118. MONT. CODE ANN. § 45-2-203 (1987).

derives from ignorance rather than force. In *State v. Brown*,[119] the charge was being drunk in a public place; thus, intoxication was the charge rather than a defense issue. The trial court had instructed the jury that mistake as to the intoxicating nature of the substance consumed would be no defense and, on this point was reversed. No limitation was expressed in terms of "fraud or artifice" or of duress, as had been the practice of courts, although those facts are often present in the case.[120] "What prevents the intoxication from being voluntary in these cases of fraud is not the trickery of the other person but the innocent mistake of fact by the one made drunk, and an actual ignorance of the intoxicating character of the liquor or drug has the same effect whether the mistake is induced by the artifice of another or not."[121]

In the case of alcohol consumption, two kinds of relevant circumstances will recur. The first is that it is a drug being consumed, and the second is that some other condition exists (such as pre-existing brain injury, permanent or temporary) that causes the resulting temporary psychosis. We think it is best to treat those cases as problems at the result level for purposes of fault analysis because it would not even matter if the actor was aware, for example, that he had suffered traumatic brain injury if it had never before affected his drinking. It is awareness or unawareness of the resulting incapacity that is the essence of pathological intoxication.

This thought would indicate that there is a significant difference between a case in which the actor did not know that his marijuana had been spiked with a stronger drug and a case in which a person takes alcohol while on prescription drugs and suffers an unanticipated reaction. One actor may be said to be unaware at the circumstance level and the other is unaware at the result level. Should such a difference matter so that one of these is classified within the legal category of involuntary intoxication while the other is grouped under pathological intoxication? The Model Penal Code draws this distinction and then provides that the fault limiter differs between them. The fault associated with the actor's susceptibility to ordinary involuntary intoxication is negligence, while it is knowledge in cases of pathological intoxication as they define that term.[122] But even here it seems that the thinking is that one is held to understand the ordinary effects of alcohol. Pathological intoxication is actually defined to mean those extraordinary cases in which that understanding is not present because of an abnormal condition of the actor's mind or body; this can only be measured by the consequence of

---

119. State v. Brown, 38 Kan. 390, 16 P. 259 (1888).

120. *See, e.g.*, Choate v. State, 19 Okla. Crim. 169, 197 P. 1060 (1921); State v. Alie, 82 W.Va. 601, 96 S.E. 1011 (1918); People v. Penman, 271 Ill. 82, 110 N.E. 894 (1915).

121. R. PERKINS & R. BOYCE, CRIMINAL LAW 1002 (3d ed. 1982) (citation omitted).

122. MODEL PENAL CODE § 2.08(4) & (5)(b)(c) (Proposed Official Draft 1962).

consumption, and so again the fault is at the result level. There is nothing under this approach which prevents the abnormality from being temporary or being caused by medicine that altered the actor's body chemistry in some important way.

What may explain some of the apparent anomaly is that if the person is not aware of what he is consuming, there may or may not be fault found. If no fault is found, then presumably there will be no liability. If, however, the actor should have been aware of what was being consumed, the issue is then passed to the result level; the question becomes the hypothetical question of "if the actor did know it was LSD in the punch," would fault be found as to the resulting state of mind, and the answer would be affirmative. What happens is that, given the awareness we just assigned to him ("he should have been aware the punch contained LSD"), there is nothing unusual in the reaction to the LSD; it is the normal reaction to that drug that the actor experienced. What will turn on these distinctions is that, under the Model Penal Code, there would appear to be a different fault limiter as to pathological intoxication, where the actor must "not know" that he is susceptible. As to circumstances in ordinary "involuntary intoxication," negligence will convict, but as to pathological intoxication and the result level, only knowledge will convict. It will not be surprising to note in advance of a more detailed discussion that the courts in cases of pathological intoxication often permit less than knowledge of the resulting incapacity to defeat the defense of pathological intoxication.

In *City of Minneapolis v. Altimus*,[123] a case known to many criminal law experts, the defendant was convicted of careless driving and hit-and-run of another car. The events arose out of an unexpected effect of a prescribed drug. The conviction was reversed, the court holding that it was error to refuse to instruct the jury on involuntary intoxication and temporary insanity. The court quoted the familiar passage from Hale:[124] "That if a person by the unskilfulness of his physician, or by the contrivance of his enemies, eat or drink such a thing as causeth such a temporary or permanent phrenzy...this puts him into the same condition, in reference to crimes, as any other phrenzy, and equally excuseth him." The trial court did, however, instruct on the effect of intoxication on the specific intent required of assault, and upon this additional charge, the jury acquitted him. Thus, the trial court's opinion was that involuntary intoxication was unavailable and that only voluntary intoxication could be used as a partial defense. The appellate court disagreed with the first point and said that "Four different kinds of involuntary intoxication have been recognized: Coerced intoxication, pathological intoxication,

---

123. City of Minneapolis v. Altimus, 306 Minn. 462, 238 N.W.2d 851 (1976).

124. 1 M. HALE, HISTORY OF THE PLEAS OF THE CROWN 32 (1778).

intoxication by innocent mistake,[125] and unexpected intoxication resulting from the ingestion of a medically prescribed drug."[126]

As to this last classification, the court required the actor to be non-negligent as to the intoxicating character of the drug prescribed. "The first requirement is that the defendant must not know, or have reason to know, that the prescribed drug is likely to have an intoxicating effect. If the defendant knows, or has reason to know, that the prescribed drug will have an intoxicating effect, then he is voluntarily intoxicated."[127] "[W]e today hold that the defendant in the instant case bears the burden of establishing by the preponderance of the evidence that he was temporarily insane due to involuntary intoxication."[128] Notice how the issue of fault, here meaning negligence as to circumstances (the nature or quality of the drug taken), determines whether the court would classify the situation as temporary insanity due to involuntary intoxication or voluntary intoxication and how insanity and involuntary intoxication are equated by the court.

This last point led to the objection raised by the concurring opinion in *Altimus*:

> In my view [the insanity defense statute] has no application to the defense asserted because involuntary intoxication due to the ingestion of a medically prescribed drug is simply not a form of mental "illness" or "deficiency" as those terms are commonly used. To describe the asserted mental state of defendant in this case as one of insanity stretches that word far beyond its ordinary meaning....In my opinion, the defense of involuntary intoxication does not rest upon so tenuous a statutory basis. Involuntary intoxication is a defense anchored firmly in the theory of mens rea, which has long been a part of Anglo-American common law.[129]

Two Colorado cases, *Hendershott v. People,*[130] decided by the Supreme Court and *People v. Matthews,*[131] decided by the Court of Appeals, both deal significantly with issues of diminished capacity and

---

125. The court later cited People v. Penman, 271 Ill. 82, 110 N.E. 894 (1915), as an example. "In *Penman*, the defendant killed his victim after apparently taking cocaine tablets which, due to the deception of another, he believed to be breath purifiers. The Illinois Supreme Court held that this would constitute involuntary intoxication and a full defense to criminal liability if it caused the defendant to become temporarily insane." *Altimus* at 469, 238 N.W.2d at 856.

126. *Altimus* at 468, 238 N.W.2d at 856 (citations omitted).

127. *Altimus* at 470, 238 N.W.2d at 857 (citations omitted).

128. *Altimus* at 472, 238 N.W.2d at 858.

129. *Altimus* at 474, 238 N.W.2d at 859 (concurring opinion).

130. Hendershott v. People, 653 P.2d 385 (Colo. 1982).

131. People v. Matthews, 717 P.2d 970, 971 (Colo. App. 1985).

the permissible range of state-imposed limitations on defenses negating *mens rea*. They also confront the question of fault, which, in both of these cases, relates to the actors' awareness of the circumstance or result of their own mental condition. In *Hendershott*, it was the existence of an underlying mental condition (adult minimal brain dysfunction, similar to intermittent explosive disorder), and in *Matthews*, it was that alcohol could interact with and trigger an attack of psychomotor epilepsy.[132] In both cases, the defendant had been drinking. Here we want to stress the fault issues in these two cases even though they are intertwined with then-existing state statutory measures related to diminished capacity.

In *Hendershott*, the defendant was charged with assault in the third degree, which can be committed knowingly or recklessly. He offered psychiatric and psychological evidence to show he suffered from "adult minimal brain dysfunction" in order to negate the requisite culpability elements of the charge. The trial court held that such evidence was not admissible because a state statute established an affirmative defense of "impaired mental condition" for specific intent crimes and the trial court construed the statute to preclude use of similar mental impairment evidence in other cases such as this involving only general intent crimes. That ruling was reversed. The court applied the usual rule on voluntary intoxication as quoted from their earlier decision in *People v. DelGuidice*:[133]

> [W]e held that self-induced intoxication was not an affirmative defense to second degree murder and, therefore, evidence of voluntary intoxication was not admissible to negate the culpability element of "knowingly" for that offense. Our decision echoed the legislative policy [of the intoxication defense statute] which provides that the voluntary intoxication of an accused is not a defense to a criminal charge, except to negate a specific intent when that intent is an element of the charge.[134]

But the court went on in *Hendershott* to draw a distinction that is one of the most problematic involved with pathological reaction to alcohol, voluntary intoxication versus pathological intoxication:

> The concept of self-induced intoxication, by definition, requires that the defendant be aware at the outset that the

---

132. *Matthews* probably is more accurately characterized as involving the issue of fault relating to results rather than circumstances. It is discussed here because there are benefits from discussion in connection with *Hendershott*.

133. People v. DelGuidice, 199 Colo. 41, 606 P.2d 840 (1979).

134. *Hendershott* at 396.

> substance he is about to ingest may affect his mental faculties. It is a matter of common knowledge that the excessive use of liquor or drugs impairs the perceptual, judgmental and volitional faculties of the user. Also, because the intoxication must be "self-induced," the defendant necessarily must have had the conscious ability to prevent this temporary incapacity from coming into being at all. Self-induced intoxication, therefore, by its very nature involves a degree of moral culpability. The moral blameworthiness lies in the voluntary impairment of one's mental faculties with knowledge that the resulting condition is a source of potential danger to others. *See generally* Model Penal Code § 2.08, Comment 3 (Tent. Draft No. 9, 1959). It is this blameworthiness that serves as the basis for *DelGuidice's* rule of exclusion [of evidence of intoxication in general intent crimes]. Thus, when a defendant chooses to knowingly introduce intoxicants into his body to the point of becoming temporarily impaired in his powers of perception, judgment and control, the policy enunciated in *DelGuidice* prohibits him from utilizing his intoxication as a defense to crimes requiring the *mens rea* of "knowingly," "willfully," "recklessly" or "with criminal negligence." There is nothing in *DelGuidice,* however, that is inconsistent with permitting a defendant to contest these culpability elements by evidence of a mental impairment caused by a known mental disease or defect, or by other evidence of an incapacity not directly caused by self-induced intoxication. Nor does *DelGuidice* prohibit evidence of voluntary intoxication to disprove the defendant's commission of the proscribed act by showing, for example, that he was comatose and hence incapable of any physical activity.[135]

Three years later in *Matthews,*[136] the Colorado Court of Appeals, in a one-page decision by Judge Kelly, upheld the trial court's pre-trial decision not to permit the defense to put on evidence of pathological intoxication (by now called alcohol idiosyncratic intoxication, after the DSM-III-R) on a not guilty plea to a charge of arson, a general intent crime under Colorado law. Of course, if the actor is unconscious, pathological intoxication would be a *mens rea* defense even to a general intent crime. The opinion shows remarkable ignorance of the concept. "The fact that the result of the ingestion of alcohol may be more severe

---

135. *Hendershott* at 396-97 (emphasis added). *See also* State v. Burge, 195 Conn. 232, 487 A.2d 532 (1985) (following *Hendershott*).

136. *Matthews* at 971.

in one person that [sic] in another because of an idiosyncratic pathology does not make the ingestion involuntary."[137]

The facts are not reported in the opinion, which makes the quoted language even more misleading, but they are available in the appellate briefs. The arson charges arose from an incident in which the defendant was found in an apartment building laundry room with a disconnected gas pipe and burned matches in the area. He had been drinking earlier. He was an epileptic and claimed that he had forgotten to take his medicine that day. He also claimed amnesia for the episode. Witnesses at the scene did not think he was drunk, but not entirely "crazy" either. The defense psychiatrist, whose testimony was excluded from trial, expressed the opinion that the defendant's conduct was consistent with alcohol idiosyncratic intoxication and described it in usual terms, stressing that it was not the same as ordinary drunkenness. It appeared that the defendant was unaware of his vulnerability to alcohol because, while he was aware of his epilepsy, the evidence indicated that his prior attacks had not been triggered by alcohol consumption, but were spontaneous. The psychiatrist also was of the opinion that "He would not have had reason to believe that the amount of alcohol which he drank over that period of time would result in such bizarre behavior and such an unfortunate outcome."[138]

Obviously, the defense argued that *Hendershott*[139] controlled the case, as indeed it did in having upheld the admissibility of evidence of minimal brain dysfunction, even on a not guilty plea, for the purpose of disproving the existence of a *mens rea* element of the charge. Even the state's brief conceded that *Hendershott* had held that "a defendant may introduce evidence of a mental impairment to negate the *mens rea* of general intent, as well as specific intent, crimes,"[140] but it was argued that the distinction drawn in *Hendershott* permitted exclusion of such evidence in cases of voluntary intoxication, which indeed it does. The state then argued that

> pathological intoxication involves the same element of moral culpability as does voluntary intoxication. The voluntariness of the ingestion of alcohol is no different for voluntary intoxication then for pathological intoxication. Nothing in the record suggests that the defendant did not drink the six-pack of beer and quarter pint of vodka voluntarily.[141]

---

137. *Matthews* at 971.
138. *Matthews*, Opening Brief of Defendant-Appellant at 6.
139. Hendershott v. People, 653 P.2d 385 (Colo. 1982).
140. Answer Brief at 8.
141. Answer Brief at 9.

The state argument insinuates that the rule is that drinking per se provides the necessary culpability, for there is certainly nothing in the record to indicate that the defendant was aware of the possible combined effects of his epilepsy and alcohol consumption. In response to this point, the state merely observed: "[T]he knowledge that excessive use of alcohol impairs the faculties of the user is similar for both voluntary and pathological intoxication."[142] What can this mean? Was the amount of drinking that was described by the state's own brief "excessive"? If this drinking provides the "fault" necessary to defeat a case of temporary insanity based on pathological intoxication without even letting the issue go before the jury, then the appellate court was right in their cryptic observation that "Pathological intoxication is nonetheless voluntary, and does not constitute a defense to a general intent crime."[143] Notwithstanding the minor dispute over the diagnostic importance of the amount of alcohol, there will certainly always be some alcohol (or other drug) involved because that is a matter of definition, and this court appears prepared to say that drinking will always be enough to defeat the defense of pathological reaction to alcohol. It is remarkable that certiorari was not granted by the higher court in this case because the lower court's incredible opinion will almost certainly be disowned even if it is not coherent enough to overrule. While this opinion could be classified below as one in which drinking per se rather than fault serves as the fault limitation on the defense of pathological intoxication, it does not actually appear to be the law of Colorado but only an isolated and inadequate handling of the issue at the state's intermediate court level.

Thus, this may be the only opinion in the history of the United States that has flatly denied that pathological intoxication can ever be a defense to any crime regardless of the amount of alcohol consumed and regardless as well of any awareness on the part of the defendant that he ought not to drink at all. Not even a negligence standard was applied to limit the defense, even though the state's prior cases called for that view to be followed. *Matthews* purports to define pathological intoxication off the books, even though the defendant legally consumed alcohol with no awareness or reasonable basis for awareness proved with respect to possible adverse consequences either to the actor or to anyone else. That is quite an accomplishment in a single page opinion. Given the depth of the treatment in the briefs of the parties, which was adequate for the procedural posture of this appeal, the court was made aware of the concept of pathological intoxication, unlike the earlier case of *Martinez*.[144] What appears to be misunderstood is criminal law, not psychiatry.

---

142. Answer Brief at 9.
143. *Matthews* at 971.
144. Martinez v. People, 124 Colo. 170, 235 P.2d 810 (1951).

People v. Velez[145] is an illustration of a court treating the case as one of voluntary intoxication because of the actor's fault, characterized as negligence based on using street drugs. The defendant was convicted for assault with a deadly weapon, and the appellate court upheld the conviction, challenged largely on the ground that the defendant was entitled to an instruction on involuntary intoxication. The defendant had taken what he knew to be marijuana from people he did not know, and it turned out to be laced with PCP, a fact of which the defendant was unaware. It was conceded that his subsequent conduct amounted to unconscious behavior. In traditional terminology, the question essentially can be represented in terms of whether this constituted voluntary intoxication, which would not be a defense to this "general intent" crime,[146] or involuntary intoxication with concomitant unconsciousness, which would be a complete defense. The court held it was voluntary intoxication.

The court first noted that liability in the event of voluntary intoxication was essentially liability predicated on negligence:

> Clearly, then, one who becomes voluntarily intoxicated to the point of unconsciousness can have no actual intent to commit a crime; rather, criminal responsibility is justified on the theory that having chosen to breach one's duty to others of acting with reason and conscience, one may not entirely avoid criminal harm caused by one's breach of duty. It is therefore apparent the imposition of criminal responsibility for acts committed while voluntarily intoxicated is predicated on a theory of criminal negligence.[147]

The court then noted that, unlike most cases of alcohol intoxication, the intoxication in this case resulted from consumption of an illegal drug, but it eschewed reliance on that in making its decision, even though it seems to have done so indirectly. The court observed that in their judgment,

> it is common knowledge that unlawful street drugs do not come with warranties of purity or quality associated with lawfully acquired drugs such as alcohol. Thus, unlike alcohol, unlawful street drugs are frequently not the substance they purport to be or are contaminated with other substances not apparent to the naked eye.[148]

---

145. People v. Velez, 175 Cal. App. 3d 785, 221 Cal. Rptr. 631 (1985).
146. People v. Conley, 64 Cal. 2d 310, 49 Cal. Rptr. 815, 411 P.2d 911 (1966).
147. *Velez* at 794-95, 221 Cal. Rptr. at 637.
148. *Velez* at 795, 221 Cal. Rptr. at 637.

The court then provided a review of cases it evidently would regard as not involving "negligence" and those that did constitute negligence:

> In accordance with this view, courts have allowed the defense of involuntary intoxication based on the ingestion of an unlawful drug where the defendant reasonably believed he was consuming a lawful substance or where the unlawful drug was placed without defendant's knowledge *in a lawful substance.* (See *People v. Scott*,...146 Cal.App.3d at pp. 826-827, 194 Cal.Rptr. 633 [PCP...surreptitiously placed in punch at family reunion party]; *People v. Carlo* (1974), 46 A.D.2d 764, 361 N.Y.S.2d 168 [defendant took hallucigenic [sic] pill in reasonable belief it was aspirin or lawful tranquilizer]; *Commonwealth v. McAlister* (1974), 365 Mass. 454, 313 N.E.2d 113,...[coffee spiked with drug that produced reaction consistent with LSD]; *People v. White* (1970), 131 Ill.App.2d 652, 264 N.E.2d 228 [Drug put in defendant's beer without his knowledge]; *People v. Penman* (1915) 271 Ill. 82, 110 N.E. 894 [intoxicating pills reasonably believed to be breath perfume].
>
> Conversely, in *State v. Hall* (Iowa 1974) 214 N.W.2d 205, 73 A.L.R.3d 85, defendant voluntarily took a pill that casual acquaintances had given him, telling him it was a "little sunshine" and would make him feel "groovy."...Holding instructions on involuntary intoxication were properly refused.[149]

The issue of negligence was not given to the jury but used by the appellate court as an excuse why an arguably incorrect instruction on burden of proof need not have been given at all and was therefore harmless error. Ignoring the issue generated by the burden of proof allocation in the following instruction, the jury had answered "no" to the query put them: "Do you find...that the defendant consumed a powerful and unpredictable drug involuntarily?"[150] The court did not provide in the opinion the full range of trial court instructions given, but if the jury was left with the question phrased not in terms of awareness or even negligence but merely "was the taking of the drug involuntary," it surely would be a misleading way in which to pose the issue.

There are a variety of questions regarding the meaning of negligence in this context. One is: negligence with respect to what? Two primary types of cases arise: those in which the actor does not know the intoxicating effects of what he is consuming, as when PCP is put into his

149. *Velez* at 796-97, 221 Cal. Rptr. at 638-39 (emphasis in original).
150. *Velez* at 788 n.2, 221 Cal. Rptr. at 633 n.2.

marijuana cigarette without his knowledge or when he inhales toxic industrial fumes, and those in which the effect derives from a combination of drugs, including alcohol, i.e, cases of drug potentiation and synergism.[151] The only difference between the cases is that it is more believable that a defendant was unaware when a combination of drugs is involved, but that is a matter of purely evidentiary import; it seems doubtful that the law should vary on account of it. *Velez* appears to be closer to an outlaw rule akin to the felony-murder rule or the old "unlawful act doctrine," reflecting an amorphous judicial attitude that is often reflected elsewhere in the criminal law that mistake is not a defense if, taking the facts as the actor believed them to be, he would be doing something "wrong" (or illegal in most modern versions) in any event. We have assumed, as usually seems to be the case, that fault that defeats a defense means fault defined in terms of mental culpability. Historically, and to some slightly lesser extent today, that has not always been the case. For example, it is still not uncommon for a court to follow the *Prince* type of thinking and deny the existence of a defense of mistake (absence of *mens rea*) because what the actor was doing was morally wrong in any event.[152] Even as restricted by some courts, it may still mean that absence of *mens rea* may not be a defense if his conduct was otherwise illegal. Such a holding could impact cases of pathological intoxication in which, for example, underlying mental disease interacts with illegal drugs and leads to temporary insanity. It is a fascinating topic, but we can leave it with the observation made earlier that courts have not, by and large, distinguished between legal and illegal drugs in this context, and perhaps that is the short answer to this problem.

---

151. "Synergism" refers to the joint action of two separate entities, such as drugs, resulting in a total effect greater than the aggregate effects of both. This is to be distinguished from "additive effect." "Potentiation" refers to a process by which the action of one drug is enhanced by combination with another. M. KELLER, M. MCCORMICK & V. EFRON, A DICTIONARY OF WORDS ABOUT ALCOHOL (2d ed. 1982).

A more complete description is provided by Klaassen, *Toxicology*, in GOODMAN & GILMAN'S, THE PHARMACOLOGICAL BASIS OF THERAPEUTICS 1592, 1596-97 (A. Gilman, L. Goodman, T. Rall & F. Murad eds. 7th ed. 1985).

> *Interactions between Chemicals*....Numerous terms describe pharmacological and toxicological interactions. An *additive* effect describes the combined effect of two chemicals that is equal to the sum of the effect of each agent given alone; the additive effect is the most common. A *synergistic* effect is one in which the combined effect of two chemicals is greater than the sum of the effect of each agent given alone....*Potentiation* is the increased effect of a toxic agent acting simultaneously with a nontoxic one....*Antagonism* is the interference of one chemical with the action of another....*Functional or physiological antagonism* occurs when two chemicals produce opposite effects on the same physiological function....*Chemical antagonism or inactivation* is a reaction between two chemicals to neutralize their effects....

152. Regina v. Prince, L.R. 2 Cr. Cas. Res. 154 (1875).

Whether instances of drug potentiation or synergism are to be classified as pathological intoxication is not agreed upon, but it is our view that they are more accurately seen as cases of involuntary intoxication, not as pathological intoxication, because there is not ordinarily any mental disease or brain damage involved even if the term is taken broadly. Glasgow provides a classic example, and he refers to it as pathological intoxication:

> [One case] was that of a man in his early thirties, who, one Saturday night, when his wife was at the pictures, went next door to his mother-in-law's house where she was alone and raped her. He then left the house. His mother-in-law promptly rang the police who arrived shortly afterwards and found him in his own house next door sitting at this kitchen table with a glass of beer beside him and a cigarette in his mouth. He said that he had no memory of any events since shortly after tea that night until shortly before the arrival of the police. He was duly charged with rape and was remanded to a hospital where I saw him. The circumstances were that he was happily married, that he was on good terms with his mother-in-law, that he was a good worker and that he had never before been in trouble of any kind. He was utterly astonished at what was alleged to have happened, his astonishment being equalled only, apparently, by that of his mother-in-law. No one could shake him on his period of amnesia surrounding the assault. From childhood he had been subject to asthma which had gradually decreased in severity and for which, from time to time, he took a tablet called isoprenaline. On this particular night he had not gone to the pictures with his wife because he had an attack of asthma and after tea he took two of his tablets. He then took a bottle of beer from the refrigerator and sat down with the evening paper. He had no further memory of what happened until shortly before the police arrived. He had never before taken alcohol in any form together with his tablets.
>
> Isoprenaline is related to benzidrine [sic] or amphetamine sulphate and although I was unable to find any reference in the medical literature to the effects of alcohol and isoprenaline taken together, there is quite a considerable amount of information on the effects of the closely related substance benzidrine [sic] and alcohol. These two together may produce a state of pathological intoxication with abnormal, possibly violent behaviour associated with amnesia. I had little doubt in my mind that this was the explanation of

> this extraordinary and stupid behaviour, which was quite out of character for this man.[153]

Numerous instances are reported of drug interactions or potentiation in which the actor is fully aware of what he is taking but is not aware of the effects which might occur. Many of these cases are drug and alcohol cases, but presumably alcohol is treated as simply another drug for these purposes.[154] A drug-alcohol case, or perhaps just a drug case like *Altimus,* was recently reported in Florida in which the claim was made that the homicide which provided the basis of a murder charge resulted from the use of anabolic steroids, although the article also notes that the defendant had been drinking in combination with them.[155] It has also been reported that the use of steroids creates a risk of addiction to them, and a man was quoted as saying that his attempts to stop using them created withdrawal symptoms which included the fact that he "sometimes felt uncontrollably violent, paranoid and suicidal."[156] Other psychiatrists have reported that some people experience extreme mental disturbances while still taking the drug. "Psychiatrists Harrison Pope, Jr., at McLean Hospital in Belmont, Massachusetts, and David Katz of Harvard Medical School, report that steroid use can lead to major psychiatric disturbances."[157] Several of their interviewees had experienced extreme mental disturbances including paranoia, hallucinations and temporary psychoses. "Another respondent, convinced of his own immortality, deliberately drove a car into a tree at 40 miles per hour while a friend videotaped him."[158] The article does not report on effects of steroids in combination with alcohol or other drugs. One now even sees warnings about combinations of certain foods and some drugs.[159]

---

153. Glasgow, *The Anatomy of Automatism,* 64 N.Z. MED. J. 491, 493 (1965).

154. *See, e.g.,* Baldessarini, *Drugs and the Treatment of Psychiatric Disorders,* in GOODMAN & GILMAN'S, THE PHARMACOLOGICAL BASIS OF THERAPEUTICS 387, 408 (A. Gilman, L. Goodman, T. Rall & F. Murad eds. 7th ed. 1985), where in discussing antipsychotic drug administrations, the author notes that "such drugs can strongly potentiate sedatives and analgesics prescribed for medical purposes, as well as nonprescription sedatives and hypnotics, antihistamines, and cold remedies. Patients should also be warned to expect enhancement of the effects of alcohol." There is discussion of potentiation of antidepressants by alcohol, Baldessarini at 422, and monoamine oxidase (MOA) inhibitors at 425-26. *See also* Harvey, *Hypnotics and Sedatives,* in GOODMAN & GILMAN'S, THE PHARMACOLOGICAL BASIS OF THERAPEUTICS 339, 358 (A. Gilman, L. Goodman, T. Rall & F. Murad eds. 7th ed. 1985), regarding barbiturates.

155. THE DENVER POST, June 26, 1988, at 10A.

156. ROCKY MT. NEWS, Sept. 1, 1988, at 96. The Associated Press story was based on a letter in the New England Journal of Medicine.

157. DISCOVER, Sept. 1988, at 8.

158. DISCOVER at 8. D'Orban, THE LANCET 694 (Sept. 1989).

159. FAMILY CIRCLE, Apr. 26, 1988 at 77.

Traditional notions of involuntary intoxication are simply irrelevant to a claimed defense of pathological reaction to alcohol because in the latter cases, the defendant essentially concedes the elements constituting voluntary intoxication, that he knew he had been drinking. Pathological intoxication, as we have been describing the term, expressed in the analytical structure used by the Model Penal Code posits awareness of all of these facts: the voluntary act of consumption, the circumstantial facts of alcohol or other drug and how much is being consumed and the resulting probable or usual level of intoxication. The defense of pathological intoxication lies not in a claim that the actor was intoxicated at all, but rather that alcohol as a chemical agent triggered a psychotic reaction attributable to some underlying physiological or other cause and to complete the defense, that he was unaware that such a result was likely or that he had no reason to believe that such a reaction was probable or even possible.

One problem with the use of negligence as a fault limiter on defenses is the extraordinarily high subjective content of a term like "negligence." Secondly, while the Model Penal Code (as do others) sometimes takes the approach of defeating defenses on the basis of negligence of the actor so that negligence is a limit on many affirmative defenses, this may be true with respect only to those defenses which are considered justifications, such as self-defense, necessity and duress. The matter is not so clear as to excuses, and to compound the uncertainty, it is not clear whether insanity is a justification or an excuse. The law simply has little experience clearly relating fault to the insanity defense. If insanity is considered an excuse rather than a justification, i.e., the defense, like mistake, goes to a claimed absence of *mens rea* for the offense charged, then it obviously calls for a fault culpability that is related to the *mens rea* required of the offense charged.

That is roughly the situation with respect to the insanity defense, but as we have seen, pathological intoxication may also be tried as automatism, diminished capacity, lack of *mens rea* (mistake), "extreme emotional mental or emotional disturbance," involuntary intoxication, or it may be classified as voluntary intoxication. As to the latter, since its excusing properties are limited in most instances to reducing specific intent crimes to general intent crimes and, in fact, represent a rejection of pathological intoxication in the particular case, we may leave it aside. As to lack of *mens rea*, other than a few jurisdictions which require mistakes to be reasonable, the level of the *mens rea* required by the offense would dictate which culpability states would defeat the defense of pathological intoxication which created the mistake on the part of the actor. Diminished capacity presumably would be treated the same way as insanity by that jurisdiction, although it, more clearly than insanity, is a *mens rea* defense in the sense of lack of capacity to form the *mens rea* rather than, as in mistake, a claim simply that it did not exist.

Involuntary intoxication, which is where the Model Penal Code classifies at least some cases of pathological intoxication, is defined as limited to those actors who do not "know" they are susceptible, a seemingly very high fault culpability. Less clear is whether the Model Penal Code drafters intended to include on the exculpatory side not only force or medical advice as to the act, and mistake as to the relevant circumstances (alcohol or other drugs), but also mistake as to the probable result of intoxication. The intoxication is self-induced if he "knows or ought to know" its "tendency to cause intoxication." In that event, he will be classified as merely drunk.

The Fault Lies in Knowingly Drinking Alcohol: Strict Liability as to the Consequent Mental Incapacity

In the 1860 Georgia case of *Choice v. State,*[160] the defendant was convicted of murder of a constable who had previously tried to serve papers on him. Testimony suggested the possibility of a pathological reaction to alcohol, although, of course, that term was not yet in use. Several doctors testified that the defendant had suffered a serious head injury eight years earlier while being dragged behind a horse buggy, and other testimony established that he had been drinking prior to the homicide. However, his motor response was not the uncoordinated response of an intoxicated individual, but the purposeful motor behavior characteristic of pathological reaction to alcohol.[161] In addition, abnormal pupillary response was present right after the killing,[162] and the defendant "after being carried to the calaboose, went to sleep, while a mob was clamoring for his life" some fifteen feet away.[163] In addition to this evidence, the defendant was prepared to offer evidence of amnesia for the episode. Medical diagnoses differed at trial.[164] There was no disagreement regarding the fact that friends had repeatedly observed the defendant engage in violent behavior when he drank, all subsequent to sustaining the head injury.

The defendant appealed on a number of grounds, but most centered on the trial court's instructions regarding the defense of insanity[165] and whether his conviction was against the weight of medical evidence. There was, in fact, considerable medical testimony that a lesion of the

---

160. Choice v. State, 31 Ga. 424 (1860).
161. *Choice* at 430.
162. *Choice* at 438-39.
163. *Choice* at 436.
164. *See, e.g.,* the discussion of oniomania and mania-a-potu, *Choice* at 428.
165. *Choice* at 471.

brain combined with the use of alcohol could result in insanity. One doctor testified that he

> would draw a difference in an act caused by mania, produced by intoxicating drinks, and by drunkenness. A blow upon the head, so as to fracture the brain or produce a severe contusion, may produce "elision" in the brain, so as to act as a predisposing cause to insanity....When this madness and raving [are] produced by the use of liquor, the liquor is merely an exciting cause....A man in this state of insanity, though produced by liquor, is unconscious of right and wrong. Stupor is apt to follow an act of excitement, and when aroused from that state, [he] is unconscious of what has taken place.[166]

The critical instruction objected to by defense counsel but upheld by the court is as follows:

> But, though it is the general rule, that insanity is an excuse, yet, there is an exception to this rule, and that is, when the crime is committed by a party in a fit of intoxication, though the party may be as effectually bereft of his reason by drunkenness as by insanity produced by any other cause. For drunkenness shall not be an excuse for any crime or misdemeanor, unless such drunkenness was occasioned by the fraud, artifice or contrivance of another. *Nor does it make any difference, that a man by constitutional infirmity, or by accidental injury to the head or brain, is more likely to be maddened by liquor than another man. If he has legal memory and discretion when sober, and voluntarily deprives himself of reason, he is responsible for his acts in that condition.*[167]

Choice is an important case, and it seems to us that *Choice* is badly misunderstood by a subsequent line of cases. The misunderstanding focuses on the use of the phrase "voluntarily deprives himself of reason." While the court does not dwell on the matter, it is not an unfair reading of the opinion to suppose by "voluntarily" the court meant to include "knowingly." Viewed in this light, the court was merely holding that if the defendant was aware of the underlying condition and the likely

---

166. *Choice* at 427-28.

167. *Choice* at 472, and substantially the same form at 455 (emphasis added). *See also* Thomas v. State, 105 Ga. App. 754, 125 S.E.2d 679 (1962), which cited and applied the same language.

effects on him of drinking alcohol, then his resulting insanity was not a defense.[168]

What is the evidence of this view of *Choice*? First, the reference of the court to the rule that "drunkenness shall not be an excuse for any crime or misdemeanor, unless such drunkenness was occasioned by the fraud, artifice or contrivance of another" is a rule of ancient origin, but even it encompasses the notion that intoxication can be considered involuntary intoxication if it is unknowingly induced. Secondly, the court quotes Story, J., on this point: "'There are men,' says Mr. Justice Story, 'soldiers who have been severely wounded in the head especially, who well know that excess makes them mad; but if such persons willfully deprive themselves of reason, they ought not to be excused for one crime, by the voluntary perpetration of another.' *United States vs. Drew, 5 Mason's U.S. Rep., 28.*" [25 F. Cas. 28 (C.C.D. Mass. 1828) (No. 14,993)][169] "Willfully" and "who well knows" are terms of subjective fault and are not terms of strict liability.

Third, there was ample evidence in this case that the defendant's reaction to alcohol after his head injury was consistently and extremely abnormal and that the defendant well knew this. One assignment of error on behalf of the defendant was that the court had not allowed evidence that the family of the defendant had long refused to allow him to possess deadly weapons.[170] The appellate court essentially treated the evidence exclusion as harmless in the sense of unnecessary or redundant evidence based upon the other testimony of the dangerousness of the defendant when he was drinking: "For what prudent family would not have dreaded to see deadly weapons in the hands, or about the person, of William A. Choice—one who, while in his cups, as all the proof demonstrates, was so dangerous, both to friend and foe?"[171] It is amply clear that the defendant knew that he reacted abnormally and violently when drinking, and the court stresses the existence of that evidence.

The term "voluntary intoxication" to this day is made to carry too many meanings, and it ought not to be surprising to find it carrying a broad meaning in 1860. But even Justice Story's quoted language regarding an actor "who well knows that excess makes them mad"

---

168. While juries are no longer instructed in terms of presumptions based on "natural and probable consequences" as they once were, Sandstrom v. Montana, 442 U.S. 510, 99 S. Ct. 2450, 61 L. Ed. 2d 39 (1979), the idea of requiring notice before fault is assigned is captured in the statement: "Massachusetts has never recognized voluntary intoxication as a complete defense to any crime because a person is presumed to intend the natural, probable, and usual consequences of his voluntary acts." 32 J. NOLAN, MASSACHUSETTS PRACTICE: CRIMINAL LAW § 645, at 465 (1976).

169. *Choice* at 481. For reasons unknown to us, this quote, attributed to Justice Story, is not in the opinion version of *Drew* we have located.

170. *Choice* at 464.

171. *Choice* at 464.

underscores the fact that it is the defendant's awareness of the likely outcome that renders his drunkenness to be voluntary intoxication or, more accurately in pathological intoxication cases, renders the insanity defense unavailable.

In *Choice*, the defendant's claim that his drinking, not his reaction to drinking, was involuntary was soundly rejected on grounds entirely apart from lack of knowledge,[172] so that it was not at all in the sense of involuntary consumption of alcohol that the court discussed this issue. We read the opinion as dealing with neither the question of the

---

172. While it was never put forth as a direct request to charge the jury, there was a suggestion on the part of the defense that the defendant was involuntarily intoxicated in the sense that we would say today that an alcoholic cannot refrain from drinking. To this, the court was quite clear:

> Upon this proposition, however, I plant myself immovably; and from it, nothing can dislodge me but an Act of the Legislature, namely: that neither moral nor legal responsibility can be avoided in this way.

Choice at 473. The court was even more adamant later:

> On the trial of Kleim, before Judge Edmonds, of spiritual rapping notoriety, in 1845, we find the first clear legal recognition of this *moral* insanity doctrine—a doctrine which destroys all responsibility to humane and divine law; and one originating, as I verily believe, in an utter misconception of man's moral and physical nature; an off-shoot from that Bohon Upas of *humanism*, which has so pervaded and poisoned the northern mind of this country, and which, I fear, will cause the glorious sun of our Union to sink soon in the sea of fratricidal blood!

Choice at 475. In Karpman, *On Reducing Tensions and Bridging Gaps Between Psychiatry and the Law*, 48 J. CRIM. L., CRIMINOLOGY & POLICE SCI. 164 (1957), "moral insanity" is described as what was later called psychopathy.

> Sometimes, especially in older cases, courts have spoken of "moral" insanity, consisting of a morbid propensity to commit homicide or other crime, coupled with mental sanity. This conception stems from studies by James Cowles Pritchard in England and Dr. Benjamin Rush and Isaac Ray in America, more than a century ago, postulating the existence of a congenital defect of the moral sense in conjunction with normal or even superior intellectual powers. The term "moral insanity" was first used by Pritchard in 1835, to denote a peculiar morbid condition in which the emotional sphere is overthrown and the moral sense is benumbed or lost, but the intellectual faculties are supposedly not affected....[T]his notion of a "moral" insanity pervaded the whole field of psychiatry during the nineteenth century. Today, many in this group would be classified as psychopaths—itself still a vague category, although it is gradually being delimited.

H. WEIHOFEN, MENTAL DISORDER AS A CRIMINAL DEFENSE 92 (1954) (footnote omitted). Some courts, however, have equated "moral insanity" and the so-called "irresistible impulse" test for legal insanity, and have rejected both of them. Weihofen at 94. *See also* R. PERKINS & R. BOYCE, CRIMINAL LAW 969-71 (3d ed. 1982).

defendant's ability to abstain from drinking, which was rejected, nor with the "contrivance" of third-parties issue.[173] That leaves the rejection of his defense to rest on the fault involved in his awareness of his condition based on repeated prior episodes. The court did not say that the defendant's awareness or unawareness of the condition was not relevant and that he had no defense of insanity[174] if liquor was at all involved. That interpretation may have some following, nevertheless.[175]

The principle focus of the courts in developing the contours of the no-defense rule of intoxication was the fact that the actor was at fault in bringing about his own disability. And it appears that fault was not the "immorality" of drinking, but the actor's awareness of the effects of alcohol on the normal person. And it is exactly for this reason that the law developed a special rule of intoxication which held that if the actor was at fault in getting drunk, that act itself was tantamount to extreme recklessness which, under common law, rendered the actor guilty of general intent crimes, but (in later law) not specific intent crimes.

The reluctance of courts to relieve from responsibility a defendant who drank while knowing of his infirmity and the use of the doctrine of voluntary intoxication to achieve that result are also illustrated by *State v. Wilson.*[176] In a trial for murder, one of the defenses presented was

---

173. Even Professor Hall seems to have read the case as holding that the defendant was liable even though the prior head injury led to a lack of control over drinking. Hall, *Intoxication and Criminal Responsibility,* 57 HARV. L. REV. 1045, 1057-58 (1944). We view it not as a matter of voluntariness of the act, but as a matter of awareness of the consequences.

174. "For the law, acting upon the assumption, perhaps, that all men are more or less insane, and that it is a question of degree only, has established a standard or test by which Courts are to be governed in the trial of criminal cases." *Choice* at 475.

175. *See* Annotation, *When Intoxication Deemed Involuntary So As To Constitute a Defense to Criminal Charge,* 73 A.L.R.3d 195, 234-36 (1976), which seems to read *Choice* as ignoring the issue of knowledge on the part of the accused of the existence of the underlying condition, and the discussion *infra* in connection with Evilsizer v. State, 487 S.W.2d 113 (Tex. Crim. App. 1972).

At about the same time that *Choice* was decided, Stephen, J., directed a jury in an English case that

> if a man by drunkenness brings on a state of *disease* which causes such a degree of madness, even for a time, which would have relieved him from responsibility if it had been caused in any other way, then he would not be criminally responsible. In my opinion, in such a case, the man is a madman, and is to be treated as such, although his madness is only temporary.

R. v. Davis, 14 Cox C.C. 563 (1881) (emphasis added). *See also* 2 J. STEPHEN, A HISTORY OF THE CRIMINAL LAW OF ENGLAND 168 (1883): "If it is not, it ought to be the law of England that no act is a crime if the person who does it is at the time...prevented either by defective mental power or by any disease affecting his mind from controlling his own conduct, unless the absence of the power of control has been produced by his own default."

Of course, this language needs qualification in the other direction, for it is not limited to one who is unaware.

176. State v. Wilson, 104 N.C. 868, 10 S.E. 315 (1889).

that the defendant "was insane and mentally irresponsible at the time of the killing, from the effect of a blow he had formerly received on the head, which either alone, or joined with the effect of the spirituous liquor he had drank [sic], would make the homicide excusable."[177] The judge instructed the jury that drunkenness was no excuse for crime and stated:

> [I]f the prisoner was so mentally or physically constituted by nature, or because so constituted by a blow received on the head several years before, that when he drank liquor he lost his reason, and became furious, and unable to control himself, *and the prisoner, knowing this, voluntarily drank liquor at the time of the homicide,* and by the immediate effect of the liquor became frantic even to the extent that for the time being he did not know right from wrong, and in his condition slew the deceased without justification or excuse, he would be guilty of murder.[178]

We believe this is all *Choice* meant to say.

The courts of Texas, on the other hand, may have taken *Choice* further than it was intended to go and arguably have adopted a line of cases consistent with their extraordinarily negative view of alcohol in any context.[179] The defendant in *Evilsizer*[180] complained of the trial court's refusal to give an instruction that insanity could be found by the jury to be based on a combination of pre-existing Korsakoff's syndrome[181] and alcohol consumption. The requested instruction would have informed the jury that:

---

177. *Wilson,* 10 S.E. at 316 (the material quoted was omitted from the North Carolina report).

178. *Wilson* at 872, 10 S.E. at 316 (emphasis added).

179. *See* Tiffany & Anderson, *Legislating the Necessity Defense in Criminal Law,* 52 DEN. L.J. 839, 866-67 (1975), discussing the Texas court view of alcohol consumption as a contributing factor giving rise to a situation in which the defendant claimed the necessity or choice-of-evils defense. In one case, the defendant injured himself after drinking and was denied the defense on a charge of driving under the influence of alcohol when, because he did not have access to a telephone, he tried to get himself to the hospital for treatment of the wound. Butterfield v. State, 317 S.W.2d 943 (Tex. Crim. App. 1958).

180. Evilsizer v. State, 487 S.W.2d 113 (Tex. Crim. App. 1972).

181. Korsakoff's syndrome, named after a Russian neurologist, 1854-1900, has been defined as "Personality characterized by a psychosis with polyneuritis, disorientation, muttering delirium, insomnia, illusions, and hallucinations....Occurs as a sequel to chronic alcoholism but may be due to other intracranial pathology." TABER'S CYCLOPEDIC MEDICAL DICTIONARY 780 (C. Thomas ed. 14th ed. 1981). Further definition and sources of information are provided in M. KELLER, M. MCCORMICK & V. EFRON, A DICTIONARY OF WORDS ABOUT ALCOHOL 154 (2d ed. 1982).

> [I]f the accused is in any degree mentally impaired or infirm, and such impairment or infirm condition of his mind was stimulated or aggravated by the use of intoxicants to such an extent as to cause the accused to become temporarily insane,...then such temporary insanity if found by the jury by a preponderance of evidence, to have existed at the time of the commission of the offense or offenses, will excuse or justify the act or acts alleged to have been committed by the accused.[182]

This instruction request is, of course, wrong in not requiring the self-induced insanity to be without fault in its origin. But instead of upholding the rejection of the request on that ground, the court seems to have held that pathological intoxication cannot be a defense even when the actor is not aware of the condition, a position that goes well beyond *Choice.*

> [I]f the pre-existing condition of mind of the accused is not such as would render him legally insane in and of itself, then the recent use of intoxicants causing stimulation or aggravation of the pre-existing condition to the point of insanity cannot be relied upon as a defense to the commission of the crime itself.[183]

A Texas statute provided:

> Neither intoxication nor temporary insanity of mind produced by the voluntary recent use of ardent spirits, intoxicating liquor, or narcotics, or a combination thereof, shall constitute any excuse for the commission of crime. Evidence of temporary insanity produced, however, by such use of ardent spirits, intoxicating liquor or narcotics, or a combination thereof, may be introduced by the defendant in mitigation of the penalty attached to the offense for which he is being tried.[184]

This statute was adopted in 1881, evidently, in response to a case in which there was an acquittal on the basis of "temporary insanity."[185] It merely states the usual rule of intoxication, that voluntary (knowing) intoxication is not a defense even if it reaches the level of (temporary)

182. *Evilsizer* at 115.
183. *Evilsizer* at 116.
184. TEX. PENAL CODE ANN., art. 36 (1881).
185. *See* Evers v. State, 31 Tex. Crim. 318, 20 S.W. 744 (1892).

legal insanity. This provides no support for *Evilsizer*. "The question presented by appellant is whether temporary insanity produced by the combined effect of a pre-existing, weakened condition of the mind and the recent consumption of intoxicants constitutes a defense to murder with malice,"[186] and the court held that it did not; also there is no discussion of any fault limitation, either in general or on the facts of this case. The fault would seem to lie in drinking. How, in 1972, did such a view suddenly emerge? Part of the answer may lie in *Chapman v. State*,[187] cited as precedence in *Evilsizer*, in which the defendant tried to rely on alcohol in combination with a pre-existing condition, syphilis, which it was argued had caused brain damage, the court held, in an opinion by Krueger, J., upholding his murder conviction:

> Appellant complains because the court declined to instruct the jury that if they believed from the evidence that appellant was affected with syphilis and that said disease, together with the recent use of ardent spirits, produced a state of temporary insanity to acquit him. We are of the opinion that appellant was not entitled to such an instruction. Although it may be conceded that he had syphilis, if this alone did not produce temporary insanity, but the voluntary recent use of ardent spirits in addition thereto caused him to become temporarily insane, then the recent use of ardent spirits would be the direct and immediate cause of the claimed insanity, but for which he would not have been temporarily insane.
>
> Consequently it follows that although he may have had syphilis or may have been in a weakened physical condition due to some other cause, yet if the recent use of ardent spirits was the primary cause which produced the temporary insanity, he would be in the same condition, in the eyes of the law, as a healthy, robust man who indulged in the use of ardent spirits and as a result became temporarily insane. It may be true that a person affected with syphilis is more susceptible to intoxication. This, however, would not constitute any defense, but under the law might be considered by the jury in mitigation of the punishment to be assessed.[188]

While this opinion, upon which *Evilsizer* relied, makes no mention of any facts well known to the defendant, as in *Choice*, regarding known, dangerous susceptibility to alcohol by the defendant (which could be understood to temper the language used), in the subsequent opinion in

---

186. *Evilsizer* at 115.

187. Chapman v. State, 136 Tex. Crim. 285, 124 S.W.2d 112 (1938).

188. *Chapman* at 290-91, 124 S.W.2d at 115-16.

Chapman by Graves, J., on a motion for rehearing, the court additionally observed germane to the facts of that case that

> The State's theory was that appellant was drunk from the use of ardent spirits, and that *his usual habit and custom when drunk was to pull his pistol and attempt to kill some one against whom he had a real or fancied grudge*....[T]estimony was persuasive in showing that appellant was not insane but only drunk, and *doing the same thing that he usually did when he was drunk.*[189]

While it would be better procedure to have submitted these questions to the jury more plainly, it is apparent that the court did not lay down a general rule regarding temporary insanity. The proposed instruction was, the court held, properly denied in a case in which the defendant was well aware that his violent conduct was highly predictable, based on what appears to have been numerous occasions. *Chapman* was clearly a case of fault on the part of the defendant in bringing about his mental state just as *Choice* was. This is an important point that is sometimes overlooked in later selective quotations in some cases. Even in this opinion, had it not been for the motion for rehearing, these facts would not have appeared in the appellate opinion at all, and it seems highly likely that later opinions are based on a lack of awareness of the actual facts of *Chapman*. Thus, the limitation is not in terms of self-induced insanity, or in terms of temporary insanity, or due to the Texas statute quoted above, but rather the fault lies in repeatedly dangerous insanity knowingly or recklessly self-induced.

It appears that the language in the Texas cases regarding the supposed rule setting forth the nonexistence of temporary insanity as a defense is confined to the effects of the Texas statute which equates intoxication and temporary insanity and is therefore just another way to say that voluntary intoxication is not a defense, an equation sometimes made not only by Texas courts[190] but by all the other courts as well.[191] As another court put it:

> In addition to being at times stricken with madness through the agency of accident and disease, man's mind is sometimes clouded by his own deliberate folly, thus inducing a form of artificial temporary insanity. The most frequent example, as

---

189. *Chapman* at 295, 124 S.W.2d at 118 (emphasis added).

190. *See, e.g.,* Cruse v. State, 125 Tex. Crim. 123, 66 S.W.2d 324 (1933); Evers v. State, 31 Tex. Crim. 318, 20 S.W. 744 (1892).

191. *See, e.g.,* Barbour v. State, 262 Ala. 297, 78 So. 2d 328 (1954); Grant v. State, 250 Ala. 164, 33 So. 2d 466 (1948).

> well as the most ancient one, is that of intoxication through the intemperate use of alcoholic beverage.[192]

Thus, when "temporary insanity" is synonymous with voluntary intoxication, it is no more of a defense than is voluntary intoxication, but that hardly means that the definition of legal insanity requires long-term mental disability. It denotes no more than a special use of the term "temporary insanity" to equate voluntary drunkenness and insanity and then to hold that this form of insanity is not a defense. Under the revised version of the former statute, the comments note that "Like [former] Article 36, Section 8.04 speaks only of *voluntary* intoxication and ignores the defensive or mitigating effect of intoxication when it is induced involuntarily (*e.g.*, by force, fraud, or mistake).[193]

There are two major points here. Intoxication and insanity ("phrenzy") were factually related, but intoxication either had to come about through no fault of the actor or, even if it was in some sense the actor's, it had to be "fixed or settled" insanity (as later courts were to call it[194]) in order to be a complete defense. The resulting mental incapacity had to be either faultless or fixed. Clearly, in the vast number of cases, what distinguished voluntary intoxication from involuntary intoxication or insanity is that it normally had to be found to have been "occasioned by his own act and folly." This is marvelously phrased because it recognizes that it must not only be self-induced, but must have been through his folly as well as through his own act. Unless there are facts relevant to *Evilsizer* and comparable to those in *Chapman* and *Choice* of which we are unaware, *Evilsizer* missed this point, for there the court arguably found that it was enough to lose the defense that the actor brought about the situation through his own conduct rather than through his own fault.[195] It was those twin ideas which later were reduced to the term now used, "voluntary intoxication."[196]

The interpretation that the Texas court required no "act of folly" upon which to base a finding of fault is supported in another case. In

---

192. Fendler v. Roy, 331 Mo. 1083, 58 S.W.2d 459, 465 (1932).

193. TEX. PENAL CODE ANN. § 8.04 comment at 224 (Vernon 1974).

194. In addition, one court has said that the rule of "fixed or settled insanity" due to alcohol abuse "must contemplate a mental disease or disorder which manifests itself intermittently or permanently irrespective of consumption of alcohol. Otherwise any individual diagnosed as an alcoholic would be able to assert the defense of insanity on that basis alone." State v. McNally, 336 So. 2d 713, 715 (Fla. Dist. Ct. App. 1976).

195. For a parallel problem in the case of the necessity defense, *see* COLO. REV. STAT. § 18-1-702 (1986), where it is provided that the defense is available only if the situation is brought about "through no *conduct* of the actor..." (emphasis added). Nothing is said of fault at all.

196. Singh, *History of the Defence of Drunkenness in English Criminal Law*, 49 L.Q. REV. 528, 534 (1933).

Watts v. State,[197] in which the conviction for attempted murder was upheld over a claim of insufficient evidence and improper jury instruction, the jury was told that "Temporary insanity caused by voluntary intoxication does not constitute a defense to the commission of crime,"[198] and the court conceded that "The instruction in effect told the jury to ignore his insanity defense based on temporal lobe epilepsy and dementia if they felt the use of alcohol was a cause of that insanity."[199] "According to one of appellant's own medical experts, epileptic seizures can be triggered by the use of alcohol. The jury could find that appellant was temporarily insane because of his use of alcohol, and so the trial court was correct to include the instruction on temporary insanity caused by voluntary intoxication."[200] There is no mention of awareness of a possible reaction on the part of the defendant or any other fault, apart from the fact of drinking.

The judicial carelessness illustrated by cases such as *Choice* and *Chapman,* regarding the element of knowledge of his own condition as bearing on the availability of pathological reaction to alcohol as a defense, has had its effect in Texas courts in *Evilsizer* and *Watts* and was exhibited once again in *Kane v. United States.*[201] The defendant was charged with murder in the shooting of his wife and found guilty of voluntary manslaughter. The defendant had three prior head injuries; one was so severe that he was unconscious for a couple of months according to court records. He had consumed a considerable amount of beer before the shooting and had only a spotty recollection of the events. Witnesses testified that he appeared in shock after the shooting and that he was incoherent. No particular motive was ever raised.

Three of the four psychiatrists who testified, two of them court-appointed, concluded that the defendant had "a mental disease known as 'pathological intoxication.'"[202]

> They described pathological reaction to alcohol as a latent mental condition caused by head injuries or brain damage. This condition lowers the tolerance level to alcohol so that not only does intoxication occur more readily but the results of intoxication are far more drastic than would normally be the case. Among such drastic reactions which may result from consumption of a relatively small amount of alcohol are

---

197. Watts v. State, 680 S.W.2d 667 (Tex. Ct. App. 1984).
198. *Watts* at 672.
199. *Watts* at 672.
200. *Watts* at 672.
201. Kane v. United States, 399 F.2d 730 (9th Cir. 1968).
202. *Kane* at 735.

> confusion, amnesia, loss of perception to reality, and violent conduct.[203]

The psychiatrists testified that at the time of the shooting the defendant was unaware of what he was doing, did not know the nature and quality of his action and was in an uncontrolled state. In ruling on the defendant's insanity defense, the Ninth Circuit accorded great significance to the fact that "none of [the psychiatrists]...associated their opinion in any way with any mental disorder other than pathological intoxication."[204] Why the court seemed to place this artificial restriction on the meaning of mental disease is not made clear. Evidently, the court was concerned with the relatively unknown nature of the condition. It noted the American Law Institute's definition of pathological intoxication in the Model Penal Code but stated:

> There is no present judicial recognition of an affirmative defense based on "pathological intoxication" as [defined by the Model Penal Code], and we do not intend anything said in this opinion as an intimation that such a defense should be recognized. We need not reach that question because it was not raised in the trial court [independently of the insanity defense]. Counsel for Kane did not ask for an instruction submitting such a defense, and no such instruction was given.[205]

The court held that they need not reach the question of whether such a defense should be recognized because the defendant had failed to satisfy "the M'Naghten concept that the mental condition which produced such disability must have been brought about by circumstances beyond the control of the actor."[206]

Kane had made it clear in his own testimony that he was aware that consumption of alcohol was causing loss of consciousness, although none of the previous incidents had involved any violence. Still, the language in places is gratuitously restrictive enough to be misleading, like those earlier cases of *Choice* and Evilsizer; and *Kane* is often cited with those cases. For example, the court stated that pathological intoxication

> presumably comprehends not only the idea that a person so afflicted knows that he has a lower tolerance to alcohol than in the case of one not so afflicted, but that he knows that,

---

203. *Kane* at 735.
204. *Kane* at 735.
205. *Kane* at 736-37.
206. *Kane* at 735.

> once the tolerance level has been reached, the conduct induced thereby is usually more radical than would otherwise be the case.[207]

This sounds curiously like pathological intoxication does not exist if the actor knows he is susceptible, which is exactly what the Model Penal Code says, and we have tried to show in Chapter 8 that this is a major problem with that draft. On point here is the fact that the drafters were not describing insanity due to pathological intoxication, but surprise intoxication. One writer similarly viewed the *Kane* decision as a misinterpretation of the Model Penal Code.[208] Nevertheless, the court held that the "disability which he does acquire from drinking liquor was within his own control and cannot be classified as a mental illness excusing criminal responsibility."[209] This blends the issues of the "disease" requirement and the fault limitation.

The court thought that because of the defendant's awareness of his condition, the instruction would have been rightly refused if it had been requested because it lacked an evidentiary basis. It should be stressed, however, that the defendant's awareness was limited to the fact that he sometimes had amnesia when drinking. It should also be underscored that the court's statement that pathological intoxication is not recognized is, of course, not accurate.

---

207. *Kane* at 737.

208. Note, *Pathological Intoxication and the Voluntarily Intoxicated Criminal Offender,* 1969 UTAH L. REV. 419, 426.

> The court in *Kane* recognized that an essential element of the defense of pathological intoxication under the Model Penal Code would be the requirement that an actor "does not know he is susceptible" to intoxication "grossly excessive in degree." That appellant had such knowledge is unclear from the court's opinion, since his prior reactions to alcohol had been different not only in degree, but also in kind, from that which he experienced prior to shooting his wife. [Footnote by the author: The Court's reference to knowledge of a reaction "grossly excessive in degree" must have been viewed as defendant's tendency to lose consciousness and experience amnesia. However, the court's opinion does not mention any kind of violent reaction by defendant such as that which occurred in the shooting of his wife. It seems a harsh interpretation of defendant's knowledge of his affliction to attribute to him an expectation which would exceed the type of reaction he had suffered earlier.] Since evidence reviewed proved a history of reaction that could not be termed "grossly excessive in degree," to hold appellant to a subjective foresight of violent behavior was inconsistent with his past reactions. Such a conclusion suggests that the court viewed too narrowly the term of the Model Penal Code definition which requires the defendant *not to know* he is susceptible to an atypical reaction.

209. *Kane* at 736.

In *United States v. Burnim*,[210] a later Ninth Circuit decision, the defendant was convicted of unarmed bank robbery. His defense was insanity, and the case was tried without a jury. The trial court found that he did have organic brain damage. "The Court finds, however, that the government has proved beyond a reasonable doubt that the absence of capacity did not stem solely from the organic brain defect alone, but that the absence of capacity stemmed from a combination of the brain defect and alcohol which the defendant had voluntarily ingested prior to the robbery."[211] The trial court also found that the defendant would have been sane but for the alcohol. "'I have to take the alcohol out of the formula because that was voluntary, and if I take it out...it leaves only this organic brain defect,'"[212] and that alone did not establish insanity.

The court cites *Kane*, their own opinion, on the fault limiter:

> Kane was charged with murder. His defense was insanity. The evidence showed that, like Burnim, he suffered from brain damage. Psychiatrists described him as "sane but vulnerable"..., making him subject to "pathological intoxication," which meant that, if he drank, he could become "insane"....Kane knew that his drinking could cause blackouts and violent behavior, and his drinking was voluntary.[213]

The *Burnim* court stressed that the defendant in *Kane* was aware of abnormal effects of alcohol on him, and the court belatedly even said that alcohol caused prior violent behavior by him, a fact not reported in *Kane* at all. The court, subsequent to *Kane*, had changed from the *M'Naghten* rules to the American Law Institute's rules in *Wade*,[214] but the court pointed out that "nothing in *Wade* purports to change the rule that the mental disability required by the new insanity rules, however defined, must have been brought about by circumstances beyond the control of the actor."[215] Presumably, lack of control here includes lack of awareness.[216]

Thus, we are still left with a line of cases in which the actor was aware of the probable adverse reaction to alcohol but the courts continue to refer to the fault limitation only in terms of drinking, rather than

---

210. United States v. Burnim, 576 F.2d 236 (9th Cir. 1978).

211. *Burnim* at 237.

212. *Burnim* at 237.

213. *Burnim* at 237.

214. Wade v. United States, 426 F.2d 64 (9th Cir. 1970).

215. *Burnim* at 238. *See also* United States v. Henderson, 680 F.2d 659, 661-62 (9th Cir. 1982) (insanity caused by voluntary intoxication is not a defense); United States v. Knott, 1990 W.L. 4631 (9th Cir. 1990).

216. *See also* United States v. Cooper, 465 F.2d 451 (9th Cir. 1972), involving Valium, a case which the court describes as not having reached the issue of voluntary intoxication.

awareness on the part of the actor. Another case of this ilk is *State v. Wicks*,[217] in which an assault conviction was affirmed. The trial court refused to submit an insanity instruction to the jury on the ground of insufficient evidence to support it and was upheld in doing so. The case was dealt with only as psychomotor epilepsy even though, apart from the insanity defense, which did not go to the jury, the defense also relied on the voluntary intoxication defense which did go to the jury. The defendant had been drinking very heavily. Brain damage was also involved; the defendant had a history of severe head injury, bullet fragments remained in his head from another incident, and he had a history of seizures and blackouts. He also said he was taking "pain pills."

The majority of the court held that "evidence of voluntary intoxication, by itself, is insufficient to justify an insanity instruction. This is so even if defendant although sane suffers from a preexisting mental illness. The voluntary use of intoxicants is the direct and immediate cause of insanity, not the preexisting mental illness...*Evilsizer v. State*."[218] Consonant with *Evilsizer* itself, the statement is needlessly broad. The record was replete with evidence from which the jury could make a fair determination that the defendant was well aware that alcohol alone or with other drugs triggered a violent reaction and had caused his repeated hospitalizations in the past, although one of the dissents pointed out that not all of the prior admissions for treatment followed alcohol use and it is possible that the defendant had not made the connection. As the court understated the matter, "the evidence demonstrates defendant suffers from some form of mental illness which is aggravated by the abuse of alcohol and other drugs."[219] Thus, the broad statement that the insanity defense is not available when alcohol in combination with an underlying illness together produces legal insanity is simply not called for on these facts and is highly misleading. It seems, in fact, to be dragged out to cover the error committed when the trial court improperly took the issue of fault away from the jury through ignorance or oversight.

The majority opinion repeatedly only refers to the condition as voluntary intoxication until, toward the end of the opinion, it is expressed in another, albeit equally misleading, way when the court concluded that the defendant "may not avail himself of the insanity defense since his alleged insanity was voluntarily achieved through the abuse of intoxicants such as alcohol and drugs."[220] If "voluntarily" as used here by this court means or includes "knowingly," then no harm is done. But that is not at all clear. In fact, the dissent thought the majority did not mean to use the actor's awareness of the likely effects as the basis of the fault limiter but

217. State v. Wicks, 98 Wash. 2d 620, 657 P.2d 781 (1983).

218. *Wicks* at 622, 657 P.2d at 782 (footnote omitted).

219. *Wicks* at 625, 657 P.2d at 783.

220. *Wicks* at 625-26, 657 P.2d at 783-84 (footnote omitted).

used the fact of drinking as sufficient by itself. One of the dissents is notable:

> There was also evidence produced that the defendant was not aware of the atypical effect which alcohol would have on him. Underlying insanity triggered by alcohol consumption is a defense if the defendant was unaware that alcohol would trigger his mental condition and in the present case the jury should have been so instructed.
>
> The crucial distinction which must be made is between voluntary and involuntary action....
>
> The central reason for prohibiting the assertion of mental conditions brought on by voluntary intoxication as a complete defense is that one who consumes alcohol or drugs should realize the possibility of potentially dangerous effects. Hasse, *Drug Intoxication and Criminal Responsibility: Old Dilemmas and a New Proposal*, 16 Santa Clara L. Rev. 249, 259 (1976). Thus, one whose consumption is not voluntary should not be denied the right to claim the defense of insanity. State v. Mriglot, *supra* at 575, 564 P.2d 784. Similarly, one whose consumption of alcohol or drugs is voluntary but who is unaware of some atypical effect which such consumption may have upon him or her should be permitted to claim the defense. *See, e.g., People v. Murray*, 247 Cal. App. 2d 730, 732, 56 Cal. Rptr. 21 (1967) (dictum) (intoxication involuntary if defendant was unaware of combined effects of drugs and alcohol); Comment, *Pathological Intoxication and the Voluntarily Intoxicated Criminal Offender*, 1969 Utah L. Rev. 419, 426-28 (complete defense should be allowed for person having "grossly excessive" reaction of which he or she was previously unaware). In particular, one whose underlying insanity is triggered by consumption of alcohol or drugs and who is previously unaware of the triggering effect may claim that he or she is legally insane.[221]

Does the majority in *Wicks* actually disagree with anything said in this dissenting opinion? Or did the majority opinion rest on the assumption that the defendant was on notice even though the issue was improperly withheld from the jury?

The tendency of some courts to treat cases of pathological intoxication as if they were cases of voluntary intoxication seems to have stemmed from an unfamiliarity with the medical entity of pathological

---

221. *Wicks* at 626-27, 657 P.2d at 784 (dissenting opinion).

reaction to alcohol. In some cases, the defense was not even phrased in terms of pathological reaction to alcohol or pathological intoxication; what was presented to the court was evidence of an abnormal reaction to alcohol but with varying attempts to present the reaction as a recognizable medical syndrome.[222] Even today, as *Wicks* demonstrates, there is sometimes a concomitant failure to recognize that no intoxication is involved in such cases. This may well be attributable to the way they were tried.

Evilsizer has also been cited even by courts which may require awareness on the part of the actor before he loses his insanity defense, based on pathological intoxication. In *McKinney v. State*,[223] the defense relied upon the insanity defense at an assault trial and the jury heard conflicting psychiatric evidence. The defendant was drinking heavily and for unexplained reasons (perhaps jealousy) attacked another person with a knife. He had just been released after three months in jail for another assault. Following this attack, he prevented others from calling for help, saying "let that son of a bitch die."[224]

The court quoted the passage from *Evilsizer* that "'if the pre-existing condition of mind of the accused is not such as would render him legally insane in and of itself, then the recent use of intoxicants causing stimulation or aggravation of the pre-existing condition to the point of insanity cannot be relied upon as a defense to the commission of the crime itself.'"[225] Some of the prior cases discussed were written in an extremely careless fashion,[226] and the Alaska Supreme Court recognized this: "[W]here an individual *has knowledge* of the adverse effects of his drinking and can choose whether or not to drink, society can legitimately expect him to conform his conduct to its demands."[227]

Evans v. State[228] reaffirms the rule that insanity brought on by alcohol can be a defense under the insanity rules unless the actor was aware of the condition or otherwise had knowledge of the adverse effects, and it clarified some prior equivocal statements that were subject to misinterpretation. The case involved an affirmance of a jury conviction when the defendant's expert was not allowed to testify to a condition of organic brain syndrome. The defendant had been drinking heavily, and his "testimony reflects that he [was] aware of his blackouts and his

---

222. State v. Kavanaugh, 20 Del. 131, 53 A. 335 (1902); State v. Wilson, 104 N.C. 868, 10 S.E. 315 (1889).

223. McKinney v. State, 566 P.2d 653 (Alaska 1977).

224. *McKinney* at 657.

225. *McKinney* at 665.

226. Even when the defendant won on this issue, the opinion is not a model of clarity in Terrill v. State, 74 Wis. 278, 42 N.W. 243 (1889).

227. *McKinney* at 665 (emphasis added). *See also* O'Leary v. State, 604 P.2d 1099 (Alaska 1979).

228. Evans v. State, 645 P.2d 155, 158 (Alaska 1982).

tendency toward violent behavior when intoxicated."[229] The court, however, appears to have simultaneously adopted *Evilsizer*[230] and the rule of *McKinney*.[231] The only way to do so and yet be consistent with the language they used is to read *Evilsizer* as requiring knowledge of the underlying condition before the insanity defense is lost. But the court said that "If a pre-existing recognized mental disease or defect is severe enough to render the intoxication involuntary, then, according to the state, it must be severe enough to constitute an insanity defense by itself without regard to the intoxicated state of the accused."[232]

Evilsizer was cited for that strange proposition. But that is not what *Evilsizer* said in the first place. The Alaska court may have meant that since they do not recognize alcoholism as a disease (the defendant was an alcoholic), then intoxication resulting from his alcoholism would not be available under the insanity defense. *Evilsizer*, on the other hand, was addressing the problem of a combination of some underlying condition aggravated by alcohol. Where *Evilsizer* went wrong was only in not making it clear that their position stemmed from the assumption that the actor was aware of the potential reaction, based on prior experience or medical advice or otherwise. These are simply not the same issues. Alaska here, in effect, may have held no more than that intoxication resulting from alcoholism will not be treated as involuntary intoxication. On the other hand, this passage may use "involuntary" in the sense of unexpected rather than uncontrollable.

The issue was not clarified when the court also said that "all intoxication is to be regarded as voluntary unless it is unknowingly or externally compelled"[233] and that "the better rule is one which views the accused's voluntary state of intoxication as irrelevant to the issue of insanity,"[234] and "we specifically disavow and overrule any indications to the contrary in...*McKinney*...and *McIntyre*."[235] And finally, "involuntary intoxication does constitute a defense."[236] What it comes down to is what *Choice* should have said in the first place: It is a matter of the actor's culpability in bringing about the condition, and the term "voluntary intoxication" is being used in several different ways.

According to one writer,[237] even the English courts have what appear to be counterparts to the *Choice/Evilsizer* type of opinions. In

---

229. *Evans* at 157.
230. *Evans* at 160 n.7.
231. *Evans* at 158.
232. *Evans* at 160.
233. *Evans* at 160.
234. *Evans* at 160.
235. *Evans* at 160 n.11.
236. *Evans* at 159.
237. d'Orban, *Drugs and Alcohol: The Psychiatrist as Expert Witness in Court*, 81 BR. J. ADDICT. 631, 633-34 (1986).

Fenton,[238] the facts and legal issues were somewhat removed from our concern here, but there was one aspect of the case which seems parallel. The main issue was the question whether intoxication combined with a personality characterized as "aggressive psychopath" fell within the definitional limitation of the diminished responsibility defense under the Homicide Act of 1957, which required the actor be suffering from an abnormality of mind arising, inter alia, from any inherent cause or induced by disease or injury. No injury or underlying mental disease was shown in the case, so the case was not one of pathological intoxication. Nevertheless, it is interesting because the trial court had instructed the jury that they should convict if satisfied with the evidence—that the combined effect of mental factors other than alcohol was insufficient to amount to irresponsibility—standing alone, without their taking the alcohol into account. This instruction was upheld on appeal. "The [trial] judge...ruled that the effect of the alcohol consumed by the appellant was to be ignored since the effect of the alcohol did not amount to an abnormality of mind due to inherent causes."[239] "[W]e do not see how self-induced intoxication can of itself produce an abnormality of mind due to inherent causes. Accordingly the judge was not in error when he told the jury to ignore the effect of the alcohol."[240] There was no mention made by the court of any fault limitation in terms of the defendant's being aware of the possible reaction to alcohol, but it does not appear on the evidence that the four homicides were committed in a state other than that of a drunken fury. Thus, while the statement of the court is broad, it seemed to convey adequately the law of voluntary intoxication to the diminished responsibility section of the Homicide Act on the facts of that particular case. The jury undoubtedly read the instruction to mean they were to ignore the fact that the defendant was drunk, not to ignore the fact that he had consumed alcohol. But we have already argued that it is wrong to give such a broad instruction that alcohol is not relevant to an abnormal mental state when the evidence indicates a pathological reaction to alcohol.

The courts remain divided over the meaning of "involuntary" intoxication. In general terms, does "involuntary" in the law of involuntary intoxication mean only unwilling consumption, or does it also include lack of awareness as to what or how much is being consumed and the probable level of intoxication? As late as 1982, the Superior Court of Pennsylvania, without reliance on a statute, held that the defendant's awareness of the effects of a combination of prescribed medicine and alcohol was not relevant on a charge of involuntary manslaughter because "Appellant does not contend that he was coerced into taking

238. Regina v. Fenton, 61 Crim. App. 261 (1975).

239. *Fenton* at 263.

240. *Fenton* at 263-64.

either medication...or alcohol. If he was mistaken in his belief that he could withstand the effects of the combination, that hardly makes his having consumed them involuntary. An instruction on involuntary intoxication was not called for in this case."[241] While this may mean that the actor's awareness that he is combining alcohol and drugs defeats a finding of involuntary intoxication and that the prosecution does not have to show an awareness of a probable reaction, it may also mean that the court took a literal approach to the rule and held that absent coercion, intoxication, however inadvertent, is nevertheless voluntary. It is difficult to divine a rationale for this view.

In another case involving a defense of involuntary act, tried to the court, *State v. Venegas*,[242] a conviction for negligent homicide was affirmed. Two experts testified that the defendant was suffering from pathological intoxication at the time of the offense, and there was no rebuttal evidence on the part of the prosecution. The opinion does not give the basis of the expert opinion, and the only evidence cited by the court indicates a case of ordinary intoxication, at least during the time before he drove the car.

The offenses occurred after several miles of high-speed chase, and the court made it clear that it did not believe that the defendant had a pathological reaction to alcohol but crafted the opinion on the assumption that he did. Arizona's code contained the usual provision found in modern codes that the "minimum requirement for criminal liability is the performance by a person of conduct which includes a voluntary act"[243] and another which defined voluntary act to mean "a 'bodily movement performed consciously and as a result of effort and determination.'"[244] The court on appeal held that voluntary intoxication would still not be a defense because "unconsciousness caused by voluntary intoxication is no defense to a general intent crime."[245]

The opinion is not a model of clarity, but there was evidence the defendant knew he was too drunk to drive before he drove. In addition, there was evidence that the defendant knew he became intoxicated on two beers and that he drank more than that before driving. As the court said, "the disability which appellant acquired from drinking liquor was within his own control and he knew the consequences of his drinking."[246] While the court stresses that the defendant must have been conscious to drive the way he did, the legal points are actually twofold. First, if the defendant was unconscious, it was through his own fault

---

241. Commonwealth v. Todaro, 446 A.2d 1305, 1308 (Pa. Super. 1982) (citation omitted).
242. State v. Venegas, 137 Ariz. 171, 669 P.2d 604 (1983).
243. *Venegas* at 173, 669 P.2d at 606.
244. *Venegas* at 173, 669 P.2d at 606.
245. *Venegas* at 174, 669 P.2d at 607.
246. *Venegas* at 174, 669 P.2d at 607.

(knowledge) that he became so drunk. The second point was that he voluntarily undertook to drive the car before any pathological reaction to alcohol so that his conduct, in the words of the statute, did include a voluntary act. Perhaps even the drinking itself would satisfy this minimal demand of the law.

Sooner or later, it was bound to happen again after *Evilsizer* that a major decision would actually apply the position that the fault that will defeat the pathological intoxication defenses lies solely in drinking, where there was in fact no fault shown in terms of the actor's awareness of the effects of alcohol on him. In *State v. Hudson* (decided by the Arizona Supreme Court in 1986, in an en banc decision[247]) despite the fact that the defendant had an extraordinary history of head injuries and was drinking at the time of the aggravated assault, the two court-appointed experts did not classify the case as pathological intoxication and actually did not even believe he was legally insane. They provided no background information for the jury and testified only in conclusory terms regarding the insanity test. In fact, the defendant had prior head injuries, one resulting from a fall out of a barn at age three or four; he had once been shot in the head, resulting in insertion of a metal plate into his skull; he had split his scalp open once in a car crash; and, finally, he had once been hit in the head, resulting in unconsciousness and hospitalization for five or six days. The jury, however, never heard that testimony. What is of interest here is the trial court's instruction to the jury: "The defense of insanity is not available to a defendant who, because of his voluntary use of alcohol, has a temporary episode of mental incapacity so as to be unable to know right from wrong or to not know the nature and quality of his acts."[248]

The state Supreme Court concluded that this instruction was correct despite the total absence of any reference in the opinion as to any evidence of the actor's awareness of any link at all between drinking and violence on his part. "[T]he insanity defense is not available to a defendant whose voluntary use of intoxicating alcohol and/or drugs aggravates a pre-existing mental disorder or creates a temporary episode of mental incapacity."[249] For this, the court cited only their own lower state court's opinion in another case.[250] In that case, the appellate court had interpreted a previous decision of the Arizona Supreme Court, *State v. Cooper*,[251] as having held (as the Maryland Appellate Court had said in *Parker v. State*[252]) that "where a person drinks intoxicating liquor and

247. State v. Hudson, 152 Ariz. 121, 730 P.2d 830 (1986).
248. *Hudson* at 125, 730 P.2d at 834.
249. *Hudson* at 126, 730 P.2d at 835.
250. State v. Curry, 127 Ariz. 1, 617 P.2d 785 (1980).
251. State v. Cooper, 111 Ariz. 332, 529 P.2d 231 (1974).
252. Parker v. State, 7 Md. App. 167, 254 A.2d 381 (1969).

is sane both prior to drinking and after the influences of the intoxicant have worn off, but is insane by the applicable test while under its influence, he is not excused from the responsibility of the criminal act because his insanity is only temporary."[253] Perhaps the court only meant to suggest that the appropriate defense is involuntary act or automatism. At least under the automatism defense, the defendant might get a true picture of his mental condition put before the jury.

The Fault Lies in Negligence or Recklessness as to the Consequent Mental Incapacity

Negligence: The Roberts Line of Cases. In *Roberts v. People*[254] in 1870, the Michigan Supreme Court reversed an assault conviction because the trial court did not draw the now familiar distinction between intoxication as a defense to a general intent crime and a specific intent crime, holding that intoxication was, or could be, a defense to the latter so that while intoxication may be no defense to a charge of murder based on a culpability standard of knowledge or extreme recklessness, it could be a defense to a charge of assault with intent to murder (equivalent to today's attempted murder), which is based on the higher culpability standard of intent to achieve a particular result, a homicide in this instance.

Following a quarrel earlier in the day, the defendant inexplicably shot a man with whom he had been on friendly terms previously. Immediately after his arrest, he was taken to jail and fell into a deep sleep from which he could not be aroused for several hours. He experienced amnesia regarding all events subsequent to the drinking. Testimony was offered to prove that on one previous occasion, the defendant, after two ordinary doses of whiskey administered for neuralgia, had been "deprived of the use of his mental faculties."[255] The defendant's mother and grandmother were insane.

Having determined that a new trial was required in any event, the court went on to consider the second major issue raised by the defense. Counsel argued that the trial court also erred in refusing to grant an insanity instruction which told the jury that the offense was excusable if caused by insanity "aroused and called into action by the stimulus he drank."[256] Despite evidence of pathological reaction to alcohol, the trial court gave a general insanity instruction and an instruction that voluntary intoxication was no defense (even to a general intent crime). On what

---

253. State v. Curry, 127 Ariz. 1, 617 P.2d 785 (1980).
254. Roberts v. People, 19 Mich. 401 (1870).
255. *Roberts* at 405-06.
256. *Roberts* at 407.

first seems like similar grounds to those who misconceive the *Choice* decision, the court opined that the defendant may have proved no more than alcohol sensitivity (the court did not use that term but described this possibility under the evidence as not "tending to show anything more than the effects of intoxication upon a sane mind somewhat easily affected, in one, among the almost infinite varieties, of form in which those effects exhibit themselves in men of different mental and physical organizations, whose minds are otherwise sane...."[257]) or perhaps that a "dormant tendency to insanity had been aroused into action,"[258] in which case it would prove

> not the effect of insanity *alone*, as *independent* of or *contradistinguished* from intoxication, but the effect of some unknown degree of insanity, *combined with* and *produced by the intoxication* and disappearing with it, and which, *but for that intoxication would not have occurred.*[259]

The court said that insanity thus caused by intoxication would be no defense[260] and that: "If, therefore, the intoxication was voluntary...any degree of insanity thus produced would be a part of the consequences of such voluntary intoxication"[261] and would be treated as voluntary intoxication and its defensive effects limited as explained in the first holding.

Roberts is sometimes cited for this proposition, but the court next took up the important point overlooked or ignored in *Evilsizer* and a few other later cases.

> And if, from his past experience or information, he had, while sane and before drinking, on that day, *good reason to believe* that, owing to a dormant tendency to insanity, *intoxication would be likely to produce an extraordinary degree of mental derangement* beyond the effects likely to be produced upon persons clear of any such tendency, he must be held to have intended this extraordinary derangement as well as the intoxication and the other results produced by it.[262]

The court indicated that in such an event, the matter would be treated as voluntary intoxication with the effects already noted; it could

257. *Roberts* at 421.
258. *Roberts* at 421.
259. *Roberts* at 422 (emphasis in original).
260. *Roberts* at 422.
261. *Roberts* at 422.
262. *Roberts* at 422 (emphasis added).

defeat a showing of specific intent, but not general intent. The converse, and important, proposition is put as follows:

> *But if he was ignorant that he had any such tendency to insanity, and had no reason from his past experience, or from information derived from others, to believe that such extraordinary effects were likely to result from the intoxication; then he ought not to be held responsible for such extraordinary effects*....[T]he same degree of competency should be required to render him capable of entertaining, or responsible for, the intent, as when the question is one of insanity alone....[263]

The *Roberts* rule is that the actor must not be culpable with respect to the possible or probable abnormal reaction from ingesting alcohol. It is not enough to defeat the defense of pathological intoxication to "cause the condition of one's own defense";[264] to lose the exculpatory effects of insanity, the self-inflicted insanity must be unleashed with some level of culpability (fault) on the part of the actor. A later Illinois decision, *Upstone*,[265] affirmed the principle even more precisely. The defendant was charged with murder and asserted insanity as a defense, but the prosecution maintained that he was intoxicated at the time of the homicide, having established that the defendant was drinking with the deceased. The defendant adduced considerable evidence that "if he let liquor alone he was all right, and that when he drank liquor it made him 'crazy wild.'"[266] "The manifestations of conduct on the part of the defendant at the time were of a very strange, wild and irrational character."[267] Thus, based on the defendant's own evidence, the trial court informed the jury in the following terms:

> The court further instructs you, that if you believe, from the evidence, beyond a reasonable doubt, each of the following propositions, to-wit: that at about two hours before the commission of the alleged homicide defendant was sane, and had the power to abstain from drinking alcohol; that defendant then knew that the drinking of alcohol by him would have the effect to render him insane or crazy; that defendant, so knowing the effect of alcohol upon him, and being sane, and having the power to abstain from taking alcohol, did

---

263. *Roberts* at 422-23 (emphasis added).

264. Robinson, *Causing the Conditions of One's Own Defense: A Study in the Limits of Theory in Criminal Law Doctrine*, 71 VA. L. REV. 1 (1985).

265. Upstone v. People, 109 Ill. 169 (1883).

266. *Upstone* at 174.

267. *Upstone* at 174.

> then and there voluntarily drink alcohol; that the alcohol so drank by the defendant then and there made him insane or crazy; that while insane or crazy from the effects of such alcohol defendant committed the act charged in the indictment, at the time and place, and in the manner and form, therein charged,—then you should find defendant guilty.[268]

And in *People v. Toner*,[269] the Michigan court again said:

> If the respondent...had good reason to believe that, owing to a dormant tendency to insanity, intoxication would be likely to produce an extraordinary degree of mental derangement, beyond the effects likely to be produced upon persons clear of any such tendency, he must be held to have intended this extraordinary derangement, as well as the intoxication and other results produced by it....[270]

Thus, a conventional recounting of the law that "voluntary intoxication is not a defense even if it results in insanity at the time of the act", can have diverse meanings, depending upon the facts to which it is applied. Voluntary drinking in the sense of knowingly consuming what is known to be an alcoholic beverage can be confused with awareness of the results of drinking, whether that is normal intoxication or pathological reaction to alcohol. When a person has an underlying, pre-existing condition which may trigger an atypical reaction, they are not the same thing. *Upstone*, in 1883, drew the line more clearly than some courts do today. Most courts do realize that fault is required, but few do not or may not, depending upon how one reads the cases.

It would seem at this point that the type of opinion authored in *Choice* and *Chapman* could be dismissed as no more than a familiar example to lawyers of an appellate court allowing a sloppy trial court's instruction to pass muster on review on the unarticulated ground that the error committed by omission of a specification to find facts not underscored or seemingly even required at all by that charge might equitably be ignored in the case at hand because those facts, relating to the actor's condition and the possible effects of drinking, were well known to him and to everyone else who knew him, and all this was obvious to judge and jury and eventual readers of the opinion. The doctrine of "harmless error" and the rule that all of the instructions taken together govern review of the adequacy of jury instructions, while neither fits tidily here, provide the best explanation of the outcome of the appeal. To this day,

---

268. *Upstone* at 177.
269. People v. Toner, 217 Mich. 640, 187 N.W. 386 (1922).
270. *Toner* at 645, 187 N.W. at 388.

some writers do not appear to understand that the court was holding in *Choice*, as virtually every subsequent authority has construed it, that the defense of insanity was lost if the defendant not only voluntarily brought it on, but triggered it culpably or caused the condition to be manifested through his own fault, that is, while aware of his susceptibility. But some writers, as well as some courts, continue to misstate the rule by omitting any reference to fault:

> Nor, it seems, is there any exemption from responsibility merely because a man, by reason of previous injury to his head or brain, or other constitutional infirmity, is more liable to be maddened by liquor than another man.[271]

Choice was the origin of that unfortunate statement of the law. We have tried to show that it is wrong in failing to limit its application to situations in which the actor is aware of his condition and the likely result of drinking. A century later, it is the dictum in *Roberts* that stands out as important. In *People v. Kelley*,[272] the court reversed a robbery conviction due to failure to instruct correctly on voluntary intoxication in relation to a specific intent crime. "The Supreme Court ruled [in *Roberts*] that if the jury found that Roberts knew that intoxication would trigger a dormant tendency to insanity, then insanity would be a defense only if the defendant was insane without regard to his intoxication."[273] They quote much of the same language set out earlier from *Roberts*.[274] "The *Roberts* opinion states only that intoxication may not be relied upon to establish a defense *other* than intoxication when the actor knows before he begins to drink that drinking may cause a condition which would create a factual basis for that defense. This did not create an exception to the intoxication defense itself."[275]

Further research on this matter of the *Choice* decision unearthed something interesting. In *State v. Kavanaugh*,[276] a Delaware decision in 1902, a prosecution for larceny, the court held:

> It is also settled that it makes no difference in the degree of responsibility for crime that a man, by a constitutional infirmity or by accidental injury to the head or brain, is more liable to be maddened by liquor than another man. If he has

---

271. W. CLARK & W. MARSHALL, A TREATISE ON THE LAW OF CRIMES § 6.10, at 440 (M. Barnes ed. 7th ed. 1976).

272. People v. Kelley, 21 Mich. App. 612, 176 N.W.2d 435 (1970).

273. *Kelley* at 625, 176 N.W.2d at 441.

274. Roberts v. People, 19 Mich. 401, 422 (1870); *Kelley* at 425, n.19, 176 N.W.2d at 441 n.19.

275. *Kelley* at 625, 176 N.W.2d at 441.

276. State v. Kavanaugh, 20 Del. 131, 53 A. 335 (1902).

> legal memory and discretion when sober, and voluntarily deprives himself of reason, *knowing of his infirmity,* he is responsible for his acts whilst in that condition.[277]

It is not clear whether this language, virtually identical to *Choice* except for the italicized portion, was taken without citation from *Choice* or whether both *Choice* and *Kavanaugh* took it from some earlier, common source; neither cited another source. But the underlined portion of the *Kavanaugh* statement does not appear in the earlier statement quoted above from *Choice.* Was it added to *Choice* by *Kavanaugh* or deleted by *Choice* from a common source? We have been unable to find the language in any case or writing prior to *Choice,* and it would appear that *Choice* itself was the source and that later decisions such as *Wilson*[278] (more in a moment) and *Kavanaugh* which added a notice requirement were direct modifications of the language of *Choice.* The unmodified *Choice* language was repeated in two later cases in Georgia. In *Massey,*[279] there was only some rather vague testimony by the defendant that he suffered losses of memory sometimes from a blow to the head received earlier and his chief contention was that he had taken too much "dope" the day of the rape, and in *Thomas,*[280] it is not apparent from the opinion exactly how the issue was submitted to the jury; neither case adds anything to clarify *Choice.*

While we believe *Kavanaugh* to be the correct statement, it, nevertheless, appears to have both adopted the language of *Choice* and modified it significantly—modified it, we believe, to what the *Choice* court should have said on those facts in the first place, as explained earlier. Part of the difficulty is that the trial court's instruction in *Choice* was used by that court as a headnote and lends itself readily to repetition without a sufficient view of the facts actually involved in the case.[281] That is exactly what the Georgia Supreme Court did in one of the later Georgia cases[282] as the Georgia Court of Appeals had done earlier.[283]

Kavanaugh, as we said, did not even cite *Choice.* *Kavanaugh* is difficult to categorize because it refers both to actors who are ignorant of their infirmity and those who know of their infirmity. The *Kavanaugh* opinion did, however, cite the AMERICAN & ENGLISH ENCYCLOPEDIA OF LAW,[284] which had appeared two years earlier in 1900. It used the

---

277. *Kavanaugh* at 131, 53 A. 335 at 336 (emphasis added).
278. State v. Wilson, 104 N.C. 868, 10 S.E. 315 (1889).
279. Massey v. State, 222 Ga. 143, 149 S.E.2d 118 (1966).
280. Thomas v. State, 105 Ga. App. 754, 125 S.E.2d 679 (1962).
281. *Massey* at 148-49, 149 S.E.2d at 123.
282. Massey v. State, 222 Ga. 143, 149 S.E.2d 118 (1966).
283. Thomas v. State, 105 Ga. App. 754, 125 S.E.2d 679 (1962).
284. 17 THE AMERICAN & ENGLISH ENCYCLOPEDIA OF LAW (D. Garland & L. McGehee eds. 2d ed. 1900).

almost identical language (with the knowledge requirement) used by both *Choice* (without the knowledge requirement) and *Kavanaugh,* and the ENCYCLOPEDIA had the knowledge requirement in its version.[285]

In *State v. Wilson,*[286] a North Carolina case decided in 1889, the court approved an instruction that said in substance:

> if the prisoner was so mentally or physically constituted by nature, or because so constituted by a blow received on the head several years before, that when he drank liquor he lost his reason, and became furious, and unable to control himself, and the prisoner, *knowing this,* voluntarily drank liquor at the time of the homicide, and by the immediate effects of the liquor became frantic even to the extent that for the time being he did not know right from wrong, and in this condition slew the deceased without justification or excuse, he would be guilty of murder.[287]

The passage in the ENCYCLOPEDIA was obviously taken from *Choice,* and just as obviously, the modification "knowing of his infirmity" was added to it as the North Carolina court had done in *Wilson* the year before publication of the ENCYCLOPEDIA; it was that version of the law that was used by the *Kavanaugh* court. To compound the mystery, the editors of the ENCYCLOPEDIA cited *Choice* and *Wilson* both for the proposition that knowledge is required ("knowing of his infirmity") to defeat the defense, although *Choice* had omitted it. The contradiction of citing both *Choice* and *Wilson* for the knowledge requirement was further compounded in the ENCYCLOPEDIA by this passage:

> *Rule Not Applicable Where Party Ignorant of Infirmity.*—If a person be subject to a tendency to insanity which is liable to be excited by intoxication, of which he is ignorant, having no reason from his past experience or from information derived from others to believe that extraordinary effects are likely to result from his intoxication, he ought not to be held responsible for such extraordinary effects; and so far as the jury believes that his actions resulted from these, and not from the natural effects of drunkenness or from previously formed intentions, the same degree of competency should be required to render him capable of entertaining the intent, or responsi-

285. 17 ENCYCLOPEDIA at 405.

286. State v. Wilson, 104 N.C. 868, 10 S.E. 315 (1889).

287. *Wilson,* 10 S.E. at 316 (emphasis added).

> ble for it, as when the question is one of insanity alone. Roberts v. People, 19 Mich. 401.[288]

It would seem that two cases, often taken as representing opposing views, *Choice* and *Roberts*, are cited for the same proposition and, indeed, most courts, such as *Wilson* and *Kavanaugh*, took that to be the law despite the careless instruction which was approved in *Choice*.

The same point regarding fault made in *Roberts* is made in another case of pathological reaction to alcohol. In *United States v. Cockerell*,[289] the trial court set aside the defendant's guilty plea and conducted a court-martial on multiple counts of attempted murder. The conviction was affirmed on appeal. The defendant, who said he was quite intoxicated at the time, went berserk, shot up a room full of people and claimed some amnesia for the episode. Two army psychiatrists testified he had pathological intoxication and that pathological intoxication established his insanity.

> All psychiatrists were of the opinion that appellant's acts took place within a period of pathological intoxication. The clinical symptoms which characterize pathological intoxication were described as a sudden onset of irrational behavior, usually violent and indiscriminate, following ingestion of minimal amounts of alcohol. After an episode, the individual usually goes into a deep, protracted sleep, and has total amnesia for the period involved. The defense psychiatrists indicated that a majority of the psychiatric community accepted the entity of "pathologic intoxication" but a substantial number of psychiatrists refused to recognize it.[290]

One of the psychiatrists testified further:

> It is not known whether this is a neurologic problem....The literature talks of two primary diagnostic categories that might explain pathologic intoxication. One is psychomotor seizures; these are bursts of neurologic activity in the brain that causes

---

288. 17 ENCYCLOPEDIA at 405 n.2.

289. United States v. Cockerell, 49 C.M.R. 567 (1974).

290. *Cockerell* at 575. This reference to "a substantial number of psychiatrists refused to recognize" pathological intoxication is a good example of statements sometimes encountered in the opinions when judges are evaluating the status of pathological intoxication, and such statements are the reason for inclusion of Chapter 4. It is important to understand the distinction between professional doubts about the nosological utility of the concept of pathological intoxication on the one hand, as opposed to doubts about whether it actually occurs and whether it did in the case under consideration on the other hand. Statements such as the one quoted leave a suspicion that the court is not clear as to which is involved.

> patients to do things and they usually are amnistic [sic] for the event, they have absolutely no control over it....The other thing...is that he might have this neurotic propensity under the influence of alcohol which would be called a dissociative reaction...multiple personality. Multiple personality patients behave as if they're entirely separate, they also have amnesia for the event.[291]

The court declared: "Where the possible mental defect, disease or derangement, would not have surfaced except for the use of intoxicants, the voluntary ingestion of alcohol which activates such condition will not serve to negate criminal responsibility when the individual is aware, from prior experience, that such ingestion of alcohol will create the condition."[292]

The court traced the history of the recognition of pathological reaction to alcohol in military courts[293] and dealt with the defendant's knowledge of his condition as follows:

> Any voluntary choice carries with it responsibility and if the person is aware of prior episodes of irrational behavior after consumption of alcohol then he is aware that his choice to drink alcohol increases the risk of harm to others. Jurisprudence will not recognize a criminal defense to exist on the basis that alcohol causes a condition of temporary insanity, when that individual has prior knowledge that consumption of alcohol activates the condition, because one obviously cannot escape accountability for his voluntary acts which eventually results in criminal acts upon others. It is the

---

291. *Cockerell* at 579.

292. *Cockerell* at 579.

293. "Early decisions by military courts have held that pathologic intoxication is not a mental derangement within the meaning of the *Manual* definition of insanity.... [The 1953 issue of] the military service's joint technical manual, 'Psychiatry In Military Law,' TM 8-240" seemed to reject pathological intoxication as a defense, but the court noted that the 1968 issue of TM 8-240 "represents a retreat from the earlier position in 1953. Our 'technical manual' now admits that 'pathologic intoxication' *may* amount to insanity, providing it amounts to 'a psychosis.'" *Cockerell* at 575-76 (citations omitted).

They also cite the DSM (edition not given) and the MODEL PENAL CODE § 2.08 (Proposed Official Draft 1962) and even the skepticism of J. MACDONALD, PSYCHIATRY AND THE CRIMINAL 178 (2d ed. 1969), where he says "The association of amnesia, violence and alcohol does not justify diagnosis of the dubious hypothetical syndrome, pathological intoxication." They pointed out, however, that the civilian psychiatrists in the case had classified pathological intoxication as a psychosis. The court also indicates, *Cockerell* at 576, that psychosis is not necessarily equivalent to insanity.

option of choice to consume intoxicants that is the basis for this criminal responsibility.[294]

They quote from the ubiquitous *Roberts*: "He must be held to have purposely blinded his moral perceptions, and set his will free from the control of reason—to have suppressed the guards and invited the mutiny; and should therefore be held responsible as well for the vicious excesses of the will, thus set free, as for the acts done by its prompting."[295]

The *Cockerell* court held: "It is evident from the record that appellant had ample prior notice of his propensity for violent conduct following minimal ingestion of alcohol."[296] "Such prior notice of the effect of alcohol upon his actions is sufficient to deny to him the use of pathological intoxication as a defense even though a psychiatrist may classify him as temporarily 'psychotic' for that period of time."[297] "'It is the capacity for choice and control that determines responsibility.'"[298]

If, in fact, a given disorder is the result of *no more than* the introduction of alcohol or other drugs into the body, it should be treated as intoxication, which, under most existing law, would serve only to negate specific intent. If, on the other hand, the mental disorder is proved to be the result not merely of the introduction of such substances into the body, but of the combined effect of alcohol on a pre-existing mental or bodily condition,[299] it does not fall within the definition of intoxication and should be entitled to the same consideration as any other mental disorder under a plea of not guilty by reason of insanity, provided the actor was not aware of the combined effects.[300]

We have tried to show that the language of *Roberts* quoted earlier must be qualified by the court's perception that the defendant was well aware of the fact that he had previously and repeatedly engaged in violent behavior when drinking, and twelve years later, the same court

---

294. *Cockerell* at 577.

295. Roberts v. People, 19 Mich. 401, 419 (1870).

296. *Cockerell* at 577. He had told one of the doctors this was so.

297. *Cockerell* at 578.

298. *Cockerell* at 579, quoting from United States v. Hernandez, 20 C.M.A. 219, 43 C.M.R 59 (1970).

299. Several proposed codes contain a provision which facilitates making this distinction. For example, PROPOSED DEL. CRIM. CODE § 422 (1973) provides: "Intoxication does not, *in itself*, constitute mental illness or mental defect...." (emphasis added); MICH. H.B. 4004 § 715(2) (1971). Such provisions derive from MODEL PENAL CODE § 2.08(3) (Proposed Official Draft 1962).

300. This is not the same point made by the Model Penal Code when they recognized, despite their off-the-mark view of pathological intoxication, that: "Certainly one who lacks the capacity described in the [section defining insanity] because of mental disease ought not to be limited in the presentation of his defense simply because he is intoxicated as well as insane at the time of acting. The draft makes it clear that such evidence is admissible." MODEL PENAL CODE § 2.08 comment 4 at 9 (Tent. Draft No. 9, 1959).

not only held that the jury should be instructed on insanity in a case of pathological reaction to alcohol, but held that the insanity instruction should specifically address the issue of the joint effect of liquor and a brain injury.[301] The court criticized the trial judge's instruction on the grounds that

> the jury were led to suppose that the question of criminal responsibility was to be solved by looking at the question of mental unsoundness and brain injury, and the question of the effect of liquor and intoxication as separate and unconnected factors. But it was not the theory of the defence that either the injury and the mental infirmity on the one hand or the drinking and intoxication on the other, distinctly and separately considered, brought about the alleged incapacity. The position of the defence was that the alleged state of insanity and incapacity was superinduced through the conjoint but consequential operation of the liquor and the brain disorder. And the defendant was entitled to have this theory clearly recognized in the charge.[302]

The requirement imposed by some courts that a mental disease must be unrelated to the use of alcohol to be entitled to consideration under a plea of not guilty by reason of insanity probably resulted from an unfamiliarity with alcohol psychoses other than delirium tremens and a consequent assumption that whatever mental disorder was present was a state of intoxication. More importantly, the holding probably represents an attempt to adhere to the common law doctrine that intoxication is not a defense to crime.

Commonwealth v. Brennan[303] is another case that deals with the combination of an underlying mental disease and alcohol consumption in what we believe to be the proper manner. The defendant was convicted of first degree murder for the killing of his wife. He was an alcoholic who had abstained from alcohol for 11 years, but the victim's affair with another left him depressed, and he drank heavily and took both Valium and marijuana the day of the killing. On the issue of criminal responsibility, the defense expert testified that

> in his opinion, the defendant was an alcoholic who probably had a genetic predisposition for alcoholism, but also that he had a mental disease or defect apart from the alcoholism. He diagnosed this condition, often seen in alcoholics, as organic

---

301. People v. Cummins, 47 Mich. 334, 336-37, 11 N.W. 184, 185-86 (1882).
302. *Cummins* at 337, 11 N.W. at 186.
303. Commonwealth v. Brennan, 399 Mass. 358, 504 N.E.2d 612 (1987).

> brain syndrome, which he described as damage to the limbic system. He stated that the limbic system is the more primitive part of the brain which is related to emotions and reactions and which can become irreversibly affected by the consumption of alcohol. He characterized organic brain syndrome as an "irreversible condition which cannot recover unless the individual stops drinking. Drinking will trigger off these reactions characteristic of a chronic brain syndrome. And it is my opinion that when Mr. Brennan was drinking, he showed all these reaction characteristics of this organic, physiological brain syndrome."[304]

He also testified that "when Brennan drank he displayed aberrant, unpredictable behavior, emotional reactions, and violence, none of which occurred when Brennan was not drinking."[305] The trial court ruled inadmissible the expert's opinion regarding the defendant's criminal responsibility. The court on appeal reversed on this point.

> The expert's testimony would have warranted a finding that the defendant's mental disease or defect, organic brain syndrome, was the cause of his lack of criminal responsibility. Although Dr. Weisman was of the opinion that the defendant had the capacity to understand the nature of his conduct when he did not consume alcohol, and that his conduct when alcohol-free is unaffected by the mental condition or defect, he was nevertheless of the opinion that the defendant suffered from an underlying disease or defect, apart from the alcoholism, which was the cause of his lack of criminal responsibility. The jury should have been permitted to hear this testimony....[L]ack of criminal responsibility is established even if voluntary consumption of alcohol activated the illness, unless he knew or had reason to know that the alcohol would activate the illness....This rule does not eliminate the requirement that the lack of substantial capacity must arise from the underlying disease or defect rather than the voluntary consumption of alcohol.[306]

---

304. *Brennan* at 359-60, 504 N.E.2d at 613-14. The expert witness also testified that he did not have the benefit of a CAT scan or EEG tests but indicated that they would not necessarily show evidence of organic brain syndrome. *Brennan* at 360 n.2, 504 N.E.2d at 614 n.2.

305. *Brennan* at 360, 504 N.E.2d at 614.

306. *Brennan* at 362-63, 504 N.E.2d at 615-16.

The court also noted that the same issue had arisen before. "In *Commonwealth v. Shelley*,[307]...the court observed that the instruction given 'did not treat adequately the situation in which voluntary alcohol consumption unforeseeably activates a latent mental disease or defect unrelated to alcohol use.'"[308] These holdings are the exact antithesis of the *Hudson*[309] line of decisions by the Arizona Supreme Court discussed earlier. Of course, the jury, on his own evidence, would be warranted in finding the defendant guilty despite his temporary mental condition because of his awareness of his reaction to alcohol. It is, nevertheless, the jury's function to do so under proper instructions which the trial court did not give in this case. The general issue on the defense is fault, not drinking per se as the Arizona court dealt with it.

In a large number of these cases, it is not possible to determine what minimum level of fault is required to defeat the defense theory because the state has ample evidence that the defendant actually knew of the likely result of drinking or drug taking, and this serves to obscure the answer to the question whether some lesser level of fault would also have defeated the pathological intoxication defense theory. For example, in *United States v. Santiago-Vargas*,[310] the defendant was convicted of assault with intent to murder. He had been consuming alcohol in combination with Valium,[311] and his contention was that this placed him within the Model Penal Code's concept of pathological intoxication. Without deciding whether they recognized such a defense or what it would take to defeat it, the court held that "appellant does not come within its scope because he knew that, when intoxicated, he behaved in a violent manner."[312]

Recklessness; More on Roberts. It is clear that self-induced insanity will not exculpate unless the actor was without fault in bringing about

---

307. Commonwealth v. Shelley, 381 Mass. 340, 350, 409 N.E.2d 732, 738 (1980).

308. *Brennan* at 363, 504 N.E.2d at 615-16.

309. State v. Hudson, 152 Ariz. 121, 730 P.2d 830 (1986).

310. United States v. Santiago-Vargas, 5 M.J. 41 (C.M.A. 1978).

311. Alcohol/drug cases are collected and summarized in Annotation, *Automatism or Unconsciousness as Defense to Criminal Charge*, 27 A.L.R.4th 1067, 1113-16 (1984).

312. *Santiago-Vargas* at 42-43. For another case involving simultaneous consumption of Valium and alcohol, see State v. Jensen, 282 N.W.2d 55 (N.D. 1979). The defendant killed two hitchhikers and was convicted of murder in the second degree, and the conviction was affirmed. The appeal was essentially on evidence sufficiency on this point, and there does not appear to be evidence of pathological intoxication apart from the drug-alcohol combination. However, the court seized on the fact that in rebuttal to the pathological intoxication evidence offered by defense experts, one psychiatrist testified that the same person cannot at times have a pathological reaction to alcohol and at other times drink normally while another testified that pathological intoxication may occur with small amounts of alcohol. The first is blatantly wrong, and while the second is correct, the court chose to read the testimony as saying that it can *only* occur with small amounts, which is also wrong.

the situation. What remains to be determined is the precise meaning of fault in this context. While we separate the cases into whether culpability appears to be based on negligence or on a higher requirement of recklessness, the cases, in fact, are quite problematical and much of that ambiguity is due to the fact that recklessness or knowledge will, of course, suffice for any court that actually only requires only negligence as the level of fault.

In 1888 in *Yarborough*,[313] the fact that the defendant had twice attacked other persons after drinking "even to a slight extent"[314] was urged by counsel to call for leniency. Reflecting the thought underlying the rules relating to voluntary intoxication, the court was of another view:

> a wicked and depraved disposition was developed or produced by the voluntary act of the party. If the indulgence in a slight degree in intoxicating liquor awoke in the defendant the spirit of hell, he should have refrained from touching the intoxicating draught; he should have chosen the better part, and not found wanting in strength to keep it.[315]

The court compared the defendant, Yarborough, to Jekyll and Hyde and to Cassio in Othello: "He voluntarily stripped himself of all those balancing instincts by which even the worst of us continues to walk with some degree of steadiness among temptations; and in his case to be tempted, however slightly, was to fall."[316]

A Note on Fault in Automatism Cases. The discussions of fault limiters are found most often when the defendant attempts to defend on the basis of insanity, and less often are these cases tried as automatism defenses. Do American courts recognize a doctrine of negligently or recklessly self-induced automatism[317] that will defeat a defense of involuntary act, and will the answer vary with respect to what crime is charged, that is, whether the substantive offense requires merely negligence or something greater? The English and Canadian courts have had more experience with the issue, and a brief discussion of them might help clarify the questions involved.

In *Majewski*,[318] the court (Lord Edmund-Davies) stated:

---

313. State v. Yarborough, 39 Kan. 581 (1888).
314. *Yarborough* at 597.
315. *Yarborough* at 598.
316. *Yarborough* at 598-99.
317. Harding, *Sane and Insane Automatism in Australia: Some Dilemmas, Developments and Suggested Reforms*, 4 INT'L J. OF LAW & PSYCHIAT. 73, 78 n.32 (1981).
318. D.P.P. v. Majewski, [1976] 2 All E.R. 142.

> Then is it the case that a man is always to be absolved by the criminal law from the consequences of acts performed when in a state of automatism, *regardless* of how that state was brought about? The law is certainly clear and commendable in relation to cases where the actor is wholly free from fault in relation to the onset of such a mental state....But a markedly different attitude has long been taken in respect of a state of automatism brought about by the *voluntary* act of the person charged with a crime.[319]

Glanville Williams later argued that "If evidence of automatism negatives the requisite mental state,...the fact that the automatism was caused by the accused's fault cannot supply the missing ingredient of the offence,"[320] but the English law is clear that the fault limitation will operate in the case of automatism just as it does in a case in which intoxication is claimed: "[A]utomatism not resulting from disease of the mind leads to an absolute acquittal, unless induced by voluntary intoxication due to the consumption of alcohol or drugs, or unless foreseeability or foresight with respect to its occurrence supplies the necessary element of fault, or *mens rea,* where negligence or recklessness constitutes a basis of liability."[321]

Cases which involve alcohol as a precipitating factor causing or contributing to the actor's automatism fall under the "external factor doctrine" so that the case will be treated as one of noninsane automatism under the English distinction between insane and noninsane automatism. The rationale derives from the opinion expressed in *Quick* that in the case at least of a diabetic, "in most cases the disordered mental condition can be rectified quickly by pushing a lump of sugar or a teaspoonful of glucose into the patient's mouth"[322] so confinement is not essential. Abstention from alcohol in the case of a person vulnerable to pathological reaction to alcohol will also rectify the condition. Under this view, if the actor is without fault in bringing on the automatism, then the defendant will be acquitted outright, for the case will not be viewed as one of insanity or insane automatism.

There is also some English authority for the view that if alcohol operated in conjunction with a recently experienced concussion to cause unconsciousness, or noninsane automatism, the defense of automatism

319. *Majewski* at 162.
320. G. WILLIAMS, TEXTBOOK OF CRIMINAL LAW 621 (1978).
321. Regina v. Rabey, 79 D.L.R.3d 414, 425 (1978).
322. Regina v. Quick, 1973 Q.B. 910, 918.

should not be lost[323] merely because the actor was aware that he was drinking.[324]

Self-inducement of the automatism, of course, is not the entire question in these cases; this is made clear in the opinion of the Supreme Court of Canada in *King*.[325] The defendant was acquitted of impaired driving which was occasioned by an anesthetic administered by his dentist without a caution as to its effects. The court said that he would not be guilty, though driving while impaired, if he was "through no fault of his own, disabled when he undertook to drive and drove, from being able to appreciate and know that he was or might become impaired,"[326] and when the defense is based on a condition resulting from voluntary ingestion of alcohol, the Canadian courts have reached the same results. For example, in *Bray*,[327] the defendant was acquitted of the same charge upon proof that the impairment resulted from the combined effect of alcohol and prescribed drugs. The court held that the prescribing physician had been vague in his instructions to the defendant regarding "the very serious effect that the consumption of alcohol on the medication would have upon his physical reaction."[328] Thus, the opinion does not turn only on the "voluntariness" of the conduct of the defendant in bringing about his own condition, but in the fault associated with doing so.[329]

Under the English cases, except in the case of simple intoxication,[330] it has been pointed out that "Although 'fault' is inherent in those cases where voluntary intoxication alone is the cause of automatism, this is not necessarily true of those few cases where additional factors combine with the intoxication to produce such a condition."[331] Another Canadian opinion deals with alcohol consumption combined with an underlying condition.

---

323. For cases which had recognized concussion *simpliciter* as a basis for a finding of automatism, *see* N. MORRIS & C. HOWARD, STUDIES IN CRIMINAL LAW 69 n.2 (1964).

324. Stripp, 69 Crim. App. 318 (1978).

325. Regina v. King, 35 D.L.R.2d 386 (1962). *See also* Edwards, *Automatism and Social Defence*, 8 CRIM. L.Q. 258 (1966); Edwards, *Automatism and Criminal Responsibility*, 21 MOD. L. REV. 375 (1958).

326. *King* at 400.

327. Regina v. Bray, 24 C.C.C.2d 366 (1976).

328. *Bray* at 369.

329. For similar cases, *see* A. MEWETT & M. MANNING, CRIMINAL LAW 251-60 (1978); M. SCHIFFER, MENTAL DISORDER AND THE CRIMINAL TRIAL PROCESS 95-99 (1978).

330. D.P.P. v. Majewski, [1976] 2 All E.R. 142. The House of Lords treated the case as one of simple intoxication; however, the evidence indicated that the defendant had ingested both alcohol and other drugs. This was, nevertheless, treated as the recklessness sufficient to satisfy the *mens rea* requirements of the crime of assault, under this particular statute, with which he was charged.

331. Mackay, *Intoxication as a Factor in Automatism*, 1982 CRIM. L. REV. 146, 153.

> What about the consumption of alcohol by the accused? He had never had memory lapses prior to this occasion. He never drank excessively. He never had any previous contact with a psychologist or a psychiatrist nor any reason to believe that drinking might bring on such a state. There is no evidence that he drank to intoxication that night or that he was impaired by alcohol before going into the dissociative state. In my view, he could not reasonably foresee that such a state might be triggered off by the moderate consumption of alcohol.[332]

Mackay summarizes part of the issue and believes that actual awareness is required:

> It is submitted therefore that before the fault element can be used to remove the automatism defence from the jury's consideration in this type of case, there must be some evidence adduced by the prosecution that the accused was aware that such a condition might be triggered off by consumption of the intoxicant.[333]

It cannot, of course, be only the fact of drinking which serves as the fault limiter: "If intoxication through drink or drugs is correctly regarded as an 'external factor' which may produce automatism, and it is difficult to see how this cannot be so, then surely it must be treated on an equal footing with all other external factors."[334] It is the actor's culpability with respect to his susceptibility which must supply the necessary fault.

Assuming this to be the correct view, the additional issue is what it means to limit the automatism defense by "fault." The English rule may be that a reasonable person, or "objective" standard, is to be used.[335] That approach is objectionable for two reasons: First, it essentially predicates criminal liability on an objective standard; secondly, it takes no account of the nature of the offense charged.

It is not uncommon for liability to be based on objective standards, but apart from the relatively recently invented crime of negligent homicide, such liability has been rare in our history. It is true that defenses denominated "affirmative defenses" may be lost customarily on the grounds that the actor was not reasonable in his actions. Self-defense is an example. But in these cases, where automatism is sought to be relied upon as the defense, the defense is not in the nature of an affirma-

332. Regina v. Cullum, 14 C.C.C.2d 294 (1973).
333. Mackay at 153 (footnote omitted).
334. Mackay at 152.
335. Regina v. Caldwell, [1981] 1 All E.R. 961.

tive defense. An affirmative defense, as used here, means the defendant admits the elements of a crime but enters a defense in the nature of a confession and avoidance, a justification for engaging in the conduct charged. That is not the case with the defense of automatism. The automatism defense is essentially a denial of the existence of a voluntary act, which is an element in all crimes. A more appropriate approach would be to permit fault involving only negligence to satisfy a charge based on negligence, recklessness to defeat a charge predicated on recklessness, and so on. In the words of Lord Edmund-Davis:

> I have long regarded as a convincing theory in support of penal liability for harms committed by voluntary inebriates, the view of Austin (*Lectures on Jurisprudence*, 1879, pp. 512-513), who argued that a person who voluntarily became intoxicated is to be regarded as acting recklessly, for he made himself dangerous in disregard of public safety.[336]

The use of the terms "recklessly" and "disregard," in fact, suggests the court did not mean to apply an objective standard; instead, both terms imply a subjective awareness of risk. But even this approach lacks a sophisticated accounting for the fact that not all crimes involve a unitary culpability requirement and so has inherent in it some ambiguity regarding the allowable level of conviction in the face of fault on the part of the actor. Notwithstanding this qualification, the Butler report[337] proposed to provide a defense to a defendant "who suffers from hypoglycaemia, for example, who does not know that in that condition the ingestion of a small amount of alcohol can produce a state of altered consciousness, as well as to a person who has been prescribed a drug on medical grounds without warning of the effect it may produce."[338] Indeed, this more refined approach is taken under the English Draft Criminal Code,[339] which conditions the automatism defense on the fact that the "act or condition is the result neither of anything done or omitted with the fault required for the offence nor of voluntary intoxication."[340] The current English (and American) law on the point is obscure,[341] and "the draft would clarify the position so that the only kind of fault relevant

---

336. *Majewski* at 169.

337. REPORT OF THE COMMITTEE ON MENTALLY ABNORMAL OFFENDERS, CMND. 6244 (1975).

338. REPORT at para. 18.56.

339. Wasik, *Codification: Mental Disorder and Intoxication Under the Draft Criminal Code*, 50 J. CRIM. L. 393, 399 (1986).

340. Draft Criminal Code, Clause 43(1)(b).

341. Mackay, *Intoxication as a Factor in Automatism*, 1982 CRIM. L. REV. 146; Ashworth, *Reason, Logic and Criminal Liability*, 91 L.Q. REV. 102 (1975).

for liability would be the degree of fault appropriate for the offence with which the defendant was charged."[342]

It is apparent in a number of cases that the defendant was at least reckless by consuming alcohol in the first place because in fact, he knew of the consequences. For example, in *West v. State*,[343] the defendant's rape conviction was affirmed. A defense expert identified the defendant as suffering from pathological intoxication (there was also some evidence of brain damage)[344] which the court referred to as being "drunk."[345] There was also lay testimony which tended to confirm the existence of previous pathological intoxication episodes but also tended to indicate that the defendant was well aware of this. "The appellant also stated that he continued to drink even after he heard stories of his behavior while he was drinking."[346] While there was ample proof of awareness of the consequences of drinking at all, the case was tried entirely on the question whether the defendant actually had suffered an attack of pathological intoxication and it appears both the jury and the appellate court believed he had not.[347]

Other courts have reached the same conclusion when the condition was known to the defendant. In *United States v. Jewett*,[348] which affirmed a conviction for murder, the defendant had suffered a previous severe head injury when he had been struck on the head with an axe which penetrated his brain and had spent considerable time in a mental institution as a result.[349] The evidence indicated that the defendant was normal when he did not drink but became violent when he did and that he was aware of the connection. His own defense expert testified that "defendant is not insane except when he has a psychotic episode induced by drinking alcoholic beverages."[350] It was his opinion that the defendant suffered epileptic seizures which were controllable with medication but that "When he did drink, he not infrequently became quite violent, and sometimes had psychotic episodes."[351] On the basis

---

342. Wasik at 400.

343. West v. State, 511 So. 2d 258 (Ala. Crim. App. 1987).

344. *West* at 264.

345. *West* at 261.

346. *West* at 261. *See also* Pauling v. State, 276 S.C. 92, 275 S.E.2d 881 (1981): "Appellant admitted that he knew, when he drank alcohol, he had unusual reactions. His testimony shows that he voluntarily consumed alcohol knowing the unusual reaction that it would have on him." *Pauling* at 94, 275 S.E.2d at 882.

347. A prosecution expert testified that he was merely drunk at the time of the offense. The court held that the instructions given were proper, but it is not clear exactly what they were. The court also held that amnesia did not affect the ability of the defendant to stand trial. *West* at 265.

348. United States v. Jewett, 438 F.2d 495 (8th Cir. 1971).

349. *Jewett* at 498.

350. *Jewett* at 498.

351. *Jewett* at 498.

of this evidence, the trial court instruction was upheld which informed the jury that:

> If you find that the defendant was legally insane at the time of the criminal act he is charged with occurred, but you find beyond a reasonable doubt that his mental disability was the result of his voluntarily drinking alcoholic beverages, and if you further find beyond a reasonable doubt that he was aware of the effects of his drinking alcoholic beverages, then the defendant's mental disability does not relieve him of criminal responsibility.[352]

The Driving Cases. In *People v. Decina,*[353] the defendant lost consciousness while driving and his car jumped a curb, killing four people. His conviction for negligent homicide (defined as requiring recklessness) was overturned on an evidence issue, but the opinion paved the way for a possible ensuing conviction.

The defendant had a history of brain damage which led to increasingly severe seizures. In the year preceding the homicides, he had four or five seizures which resulted in loss of consciousness. The last seizure was a few months prior to the homicides. A medical expert witness diagnosed him as having epilepsy. The defense demurred to the indictment on the issue of temporal concurrence, that is, that the defendant had no *mens rea* at the time of the homicides because at that time he was unconscious. The defendant was well aware of his condition at the time he undertook to drive.

> [D]efendant knew he was subject to epileptic attacks and seizures that might strike *at any time*....With this *knowledge*, and without anyone accompanying him, he deliberately took a chance by making a conscious choice of a course of action, in disregard of the consequences which he knew might follow from his conscious act, and which in this case did ensue. How can we say as a matter of law that this did not amount to culpable negligence within the meaning of section 1053-a?....To have a sudden sleeping spell, an unexpected heart or other disabling attack, without any prior knowledge or warning thereof, is an altogether different situation....[354]

---

352. *Jewett* at 497.

353. People v. Decina, 2 N.Y.2d 133, 157 N.Y.S.2d 558, 138 N.E.2d 799 (1956).

354. *Decina* at 140, 157 N.Y.S.2d at 565, 138 N.E.2d at 803-04 (emphasis in original). *See also* State v. Olsen, 108 Utah 377, 160 P.2d 427 (1945), upholding a conviction for involuntary manslaughter when the defendant fell asleep at the wheel of a truck and struck a child.

The court held that the demurrer was properly overruled by the trial court.[355] In effect, his fault, his awareness of possible consequences, deprived him of his defense of temporal concurrence, or involuntary act.

The Model Penal Code deals with *Decina* as involving a defense of involuntary act, presumably because no alcohol was involved which could have precipitated the attack. Thus, the conduct which might serve as the basis of a finding of fault on the part of the actor did not consist of drinking while aware of the underlying condition, but driving while aware of it.[356] Their basic provision is that "A person is not guilty of an offense unless his liability is based on conduct that includes a voluntary act or the omission to perform an act which he is physically capable."[357] *Decina* is used to illustrate the operation of the provision that the actor's conduct need only include a voluntary act, so that "unconsciousness preceded by voluntary action may lead to liability based upon the earlier conduct."[358] It should be emphasized that the language refers only to a necessary basis of liability, not a sufficient one, and the code would insist as well on culpability, though that was amply clear in *Decina*.

In *People v. Freeman*,[359] the defendant also claimed that the automobile crash resulting in the death of another person was caused by the fact that he was an epileptic and that he was unconscious due to a seizure at the time of the crash as well as from the time that he entered the automobile. This claim goes beyond *Decina,* where the defendant only claimed unconsciousness at the time of the crash. He had consumed two highballs prior to driving, and testimony indicated that he was going home from a friend's house because he felt ill: "I think I can make it home & that is where I belong."[360] On a charge of negligent homicide, the jury was instructed to convict if they found that the defendant knew he was subject to attacks of unconsciousness or if he was criminally negligent with respect to the probability of causing substantial harm.[361]

---

355. One judge dissented: "To say that one drove a car in a reckless manner in that his unconscious condition caused the car to travel recklessly is to make two mutually contradictory assertions. One cannot be 'reckless' while unconscious. One cannot while unconscious 'operate' a car in a culpably negligent manner or in any other 'manner.'" *Decina* at 146-47, 157 N.Y.S.2d at 571, 138 N.E.2d at 808 (dissenting and concurring opinion).

356. *See also* State v. Gooze, 14 N.J. Super. 277, 81 A.2d 811 (1951). The defendant became unconscious while driving after being diagnosed as having Meniere's syndrome and warned that he should not drive because he was susceptible to recurrent episodes. His conviction for vehicular homicide based on recklessness was upheld. The court relied upon Bushnell v. Bushnell, 103 Conn. 583, 131 A. 432 (1925) and State v. Olsen, 108 Utah 377, 160 P.2d 427 (1945), which had also relied upon *Bushnell.*

357. MODEL PENAL CODE § 2.01(1) (Proposed Official Draft 1962).

358. 1 MODEL PENAL CODE AND COMMENTARIES § 2.01, at 213 (1985).

359. People v. Freeman, 142 P.2d 435 (Cal. Ct. App. 1943).

360. *Freeman* at 114, 142 P.2d at 437.

361. *Freeman* at 114-15, 142 P.2d at 438.

The court interpreted the instructions as informing the jury the defendant did know of his susceptibility; he was not yet having an attack at the time of his decision to drive, and because of this, the court reversed his conviction. As read, the instructions assumed the existence of a fault limiter because of the defendant's making a decision to drive knowing of the possible seizure. "No principle of criminal jurisprudence was ever more zealously guarded than that a person is guiltless if at the time of his commission of an act defined as criminal he has no knowledge of his deed,"[362] the court said.

In *People v. Spragney*,[363] the defendant was convicted of vehicular manslaughter after his car ran a red light, hit another vehicle and killed a passenger in it. Witnesses said he did not smell of alcohol after the crash but that his coordination was strange, his speech slow, slurred and not understandable, and that he had a fixed stare.

> The first important defense witness was Doctor George N. Thompson. He had performed two electroencephalograms on defendant about three and one-half months after the accident. One of them proved something wrong with defendant's right frontal brain lobe. The abnormality was consistent with either grand mal or psychomotor epilepsy. The latter results in seizures in which a person acts like a robot out of touch with reality. He appears conscious but, in fact, is not. He may appear to be going through an acute psychosis. This type of seizure is not recognizable by most doctors, except neurologists. During a seizure a person is unconscious in the sense that he is unaware of his surroundings, although to the unknowing he would give the impression of being conscious.[364]

Two other doctors also testified that the defendant had organic brain damage and suffered from frontal lobe epilepsy. While there had been one prior incident involving running a red light, the court thought that this alone did not establish that the defendant should have been aware of the underlying reason for either event, although the reversal was based at least in part on the admission of unexplained evidence of post-crash license suspension (for failure to post security after the accident).

The California cases do not actually turn on the existence of the California unconsciousness statute.[365] The requirement of a voluntary,

---

362. *Freeman* at 117, 142 P.2d at 439.
363. People v. Spragney, 24 Cal. App. 3d 333, 100 Cal. Rptr. 902 (1972).
364. *Spragney* at 336-37, 100 Cal. Rptr. at 904.
365. CAL. PENAL CODE § 26, subd. 4 (West 1988).

conscious act as a predicate for liability transcends statutory law, as other cases make clear. For example, *Freeman* was followed in the Kentucky case of *Smith v. Commonwealth*,[366] where the defendant was convicted on his first trial of voluntary (reckless) homicide in the killing of a roadside pedestrian. The defense was that he was unconscious at the time of the homicide, and defense experts testified that he was an epileptic. Other evidence indicated that while he evidently was not aware of his specific medical malady, he was well aware that he was subject to blackouts which were due to mild seizures. He had frequent blackouts prior to the homicide. Even the defense introduced evidence to bolster the impression that the defendant had blacked out previously while driving on two occasions. The prosecution then provided evidence of three other instances. In all, he had six such episodes over the previous nine months during which in two of them a passenger in his car had to stop the vehicle, and in another, he injured his mother as well as himself. Nevertheless, the court reversed his conviction on the instructions. The instructions told the jury that he would be guilty if he drove knowing that he was likely to have such blackouts and that it was dangerous to the lives of others for him to drive. The court's opinion was that the instructions should have stated that he was not guilty unless they found that he failed to take reasonable precautions in the operation of his vehicle. Presumably, on his second trial, this instruction was given, but on the same evidence, the second jury convicted and the court later upheld the conviction for voluntary manslaughter.[367]

Despite this disagreement with the precise trial court instructions, in the first appeal, the court gave an affirmative answer to the issue it posed: "whether a person who is unaware of the fact that he is an epileptic but does know that he is subject to frequent blackouts, even while driving an automobile, is guilty of voluntary manslaughter if he strikes and kills another person with an automobile while in an epileptic blackout."[368] Thus, *Smith* also illustrates the fault principle. While the actor was unconscious at the time of the homicide, he was aware that this might occur—which was not the situation in *Charlson*,[369] the famous English automatism case in which the epileptic attack on the defendant's son was unexpected but was the situation in the equally prominent American decision in *People v. Decina*[370] which included the better

366. Smith v. Commonwealth, 268 S.W.2d 937 (Ky. 1954).

367. Smith v. Commonwealth, 282 S.W.2d 840 (Ky. 1955). *See also* Corder v. Commonwealth, 278 S.W.2d 77 (Ky. 1955), (insufficient evidence of diabetic coma at the time of the alleged offense).

368. Smith v. Commonwealth, 268 S.W.2d 937, 938 (Ky. 1954).

369. Regina v. Charlson, [1955] 1 All E.R. 859.

370. People v. Decina, 2 N.Y.2d 133, 157 N.Y.S.2d 558, 138 N.E.2d 799 (1956).

known holding involving a blackout where the defendant, too, was well aware of the danger.[371]

The Doctor's Advice Cases. The law on the point was intelligible neither before nor after Lord Hale proffered his confident dictum that "...if a person by the unskilfulness of his physician..., eat or drink such a thing as causeth such a temporary or permanent phrenzy, as *aconitum*[372] or *nux vomica*,[373] this puts him into the same condition in reference to crimes as any other phrenzy and equally excuseth him."[374] Essentially, the ambiguity can be framed in terms of whether the doctor's advice cases are intended to describe either an excuse or a justification; that is, whether a person reacting to a prescribed drug is not negligent or whether he was justified in risk taking.[375] Most of the cases assume the former position, placing these cases in the category of surprise intoxication. In *Commonwealth v. Wallace*, the court said:

> Although the circumstances of a person who drives after taking a prescription drug unaware of its possible effects differ significantly from those of a person forced to drive after having a potion rammed down his throat or after being tricked, such circumstances also differ substantially from those of a person who drives after voluntarily consuming alcohol or drugs whose effects are or should be known.[376] The law recognizes the differences, and authorities have characterized as "involuntary intoxication by medicine" the condition of a defendant who has taken prescribed drugs with severe unanticipated effects. See LaFave & Scott, Criminal Law § 45,

371. 1 MODEL PENAL CODE AND COMMENTARIES 212-13 (1985) notes that the defense of pathological intoxication, tried under a theory of involuntary act or automatism, can be defeated if the defendant acted voluntarily (knowingly) in drinking to bring on the incapacity as in *Decina*. *See especially* pp. 215-16 regarding "voluntary" being equivalent to *mens rea*.

372. A poisonous herb.

373. A poisonous seed.

374. 1 M. HALE, HISTORY OF THE PLEAS OF THE CROWN 32 (1778).

375. It is not made clear in the Model Penal Code proposal whether the exculpation in doctor's advice cases is due to non-negligent consumption of intoxicating substances or whether it is meant to be a justification in the nature of the choice-of-evils defense. Robinson, *Causing the Conditions of One's Own Defense: A Study in the Limits of Theory in Criminal Law Doctrine*, 71 VA. L. REV. 1 (1985).

376. "In the case of alcohol, our cases posit that 'the effects of liquor upon the mind and actions of men are well known to everybody.' *Commonwealth v. Taylor*, 263 Mass. 356, 362, 161 N.E. 245 (1928). See also *Commonwealth v. Hawkins*, 3 Gray 463, 466 (1855). The same assumption applies where there is a voluntary consumption (usually illicit) of statutorily defined drugs obtained other than through a physician's prescription. See *Commonwealth v. Sheehan*, 376 Mass. 765, 771, 383 N.E.2d 1115 (1978); *Commonwealth v. Loretta*, 386 Mass. 794, 799-800, 438 N.E.2d 56 (1982)." Commonwealth v. Wallace, 439 N.E.2d 848, 850 n.7 (Mass. App. Ct. 1982).

> at 348 (1972); Perkins, Criminal Law 897 (2d ed. 1969) ("such intoxication is involuntary, because the patient is entitled to assume that an intoxicating dose would not be prescribed"). See also *Commonwealth v. Sheehan*, 376 Mass. 765, 771 n.6, 383 N.E.2d 1115 (1978), where the court noted that no evidence had been offered that the consumption in that case was involuntary, and pointed out that "[d]ifferent considerations may well be appropriate in determining criminal responsibility where a defendant's conduct is affected by a forced, an unknowing, or a lawful consumption of drugs."
>
> Although there are few cases involving unanticipated effects of prescription drugs on a defendant's driving ability, and although each case depends on the specific statutory provision involved, the concept of "involuntary intoxication" has been applied to motor vehicle violations of the type under consideration in the present case. Authorities elsewhere indicate that such a nonvoluntary taking of a drug excuses certain motor vehicle offenses....
>
> [W]e hold that it was error to preclude the defendant from introducing evidence that he did not know of the possible effects of the medication on his driving ability, that he did not receive warnings as to its use, and that he had no reason to anticipate the effects which the drug induced.[377] His failure to receive warnings from his physician and pharmacist, if there is evidence of such failure, is relevant both to the charge of driving under the influence of drugs...and to the charge of negligence....[378]

Many courts share this tenet.[379] Other courts are of the opinion that even though the actor was alert to the intoxicating potency of the medicine, the prescription justifies the danger which may be involved.[380]

---

377. "We do not imply that a jury could not in some instances find that a defendant had information sufficient to place on him a duty of inquiring of his doctor as to the possible effects of a prescription drug. In such circumstances, a conviction [for driving under the influence] would be proper if it is found that the defendant was negligent in not asking, and hence not knowing, of such possible effects on his driving." *Wallace* at 853 n.15.

378. Commonwealth v. Wallace, 439 N.E.2d 848, 850-53 (Mass. App. Ct. 1982) (some citations omitted).

379. Perkins v. United States, 228 F. 408, 415-16 (4th Cir. 1915); Jones v. State, 648 P.2d 1251, 1258 (Okla. Crim. App. 1982), (ignorance of the effects of prescribed medication may result in involuntary intoxication); Crutchfield v. State, 627 P.2d 196 (Alaska 1980), (not guilty of driving under the influence when his doctor did not warn him that use of the medicine while driving was prohibited); City of Minneapolis v. Altimus, 306 Minn. 462, 469-71, 238 N.W.2d 851, 856-57 (1976); Burnett v. Commonwealth, 284 S.W.2d 654, 658-59 (Ky. 1955).

380. Johnson v. Commonwealth, 135 Va. 524, 534-35, 115 S.E. 673, 677 (1923), (dictum involving taking whiskey to relieve pain).

Most of the cases are as ambiguous as Hale's original formulation of the rule,[381] and there can be significant variation in the situations in any event.[382] If the medicine induces drowsiness in the patient, this would not necessarily indicate any danger at all if driving avoidance and other precautions were taken. The problem with the dominant view is that it suggests a certain amount of unreality. Certainly one soon becomes aware of the effects of prescribed drugs, in which case the fact that they are prescribed can have no effect on the actor's level of awareness. Professor Robinson has observed that "there is apparently no coherent view as to whether medical advice acts as proof of nonnegligence as to the substance's effects or as proof of a justification for taking an acknowledged risk."[383] Perhaps, too, the dichotomy is a false one. The definition of negligence used by the Model Penal Code presumably reflects common law as well, and it provides that:

> A person acts negligently with respect to a material element of an offense when he should be aware of a substantial and unjustifiable risk that the material element exists or will result from his conduct. The risk must be of such a nature and degree that the actor's failure to perceive it, considering the nature and purpose of his conduct and the circumstances known to him, involves a gross deviation from the standard of care that a reasonable person would observe in the actor's situation.[384]

It is clear that balancing is already built into the very definition of negligence, so that if the conduct and its attendant risk creation is justified, it is not negligent to begin with and requires no further justification. In this sense, it is not necessary at all to choose between theories for the doctor's advice cases, for they amount to the same thing. The common law approach, then, would be to weigh the justification for the self-induced incapacity or impairment against the risk of which the actor should have been aware. Certainly this is true with respect to

---

381. State v. Plummer, 117 N.H. 320, 326, 374 A.2d 431, 435 (1977), (may be involuntary intoxication); Saldiveri v. State, 217 Md. 412, 425, 143 A.2d 70, 77 (1958), (intoxication from unskillful administration of a drug provides a defense); Choate v. State, 19 Okla. Crim. 169, 197 P. 1060 (1921). And, of course, recall that this was one view of the evidence that could have been taken in Regina v. Quick, 1973 Q.B. 910, discussed in connection with the defense of automatism in Chapter 7, a case which may have involved a prescribed overdose of insulin.

382. State v. Gilcrist, 552 P.2d 690 (Wash. Ct. App. 1976), (intoxication resulting from a physician's prescription is involuntary, even if an overdose was inadvertently taken).

383. Robinson, *Causing the Conditions of One's Own Defense: A Study in the Limits of Theory in Criminal Law Doctrine*, 71 VA. L. REV. 1, 45 n.150 (1985).

384. MODEL PENAL CODE § 2.02(2)(d) (Proposed Official Draft 1962). What is said here applies equally well to the concept of recklessness.

defining crime in the first instance and presumably remains true in the context of our present concern, which is the related question of what it takes to defeat defenses.

In the Model Penal Code, while it is explicit that negligence or higher levels of culpability will result in a finding of self-induced intoxication, there are two exceptions: the doctor's advice cases and those cases which involve "such circumstances as would afford a defense to a charge of crime,..."[385] presumably, a reference to both duress and necessity as defenses. The doctor's advice cases are put under ordinary nonself-induced intoxication rather than under pathological intoxication, and the negligence limitation does not apply directly to them. The resulting intoxication is self-induced if the actor "ought to know" the substance is intoxicating "unless he introduces them pursuant to medical advice...." As a result, it remains unclear from this provision whether the doctor's advice cases are meant to be examples of non-negligent consumption of intoxicating substances or an independent basis of exculpation. The original comments stated that "intoxication which may follow from obeying medical advice is not considered self-induced under the draft."[386] The more recent version of the comments, if anything, strengthens the statement: "[I]ntoxication that may follow from obeying medical advice is not to be considered self-induced."[387] This dictum seems not only to render irrelevant any fault that might have been found with respect to the circumstance of the nature of the thing consumed, but also to render his action faultless even if the actor is cognizant of the impairment resulting from consumption. That is why these cases have always stood out as an exception in the law of intoxication.

There will rarely be a case in which drinking alcohol is medically necessary or prescribed, but there are cases in which a patient is taking more than one drug under medical supervision, and there are medications which have much the same effect as alcohol intoxication. In these instances, one would be hard pressed empirically to justify a distinction between those who mix alcohol and prescription drugs and those who mix two prescription drugs or nonprescription drugs which might have the same effect. For that matter, why would there be any difference between an unknown drug reaction to a single drug as distinct from an unknown drug interaction? If immunity from fault finding in the doctor's advice cases is granted at the level of the resulting incapacity, however, it will remain ambiguous whether the same rule would apply in the cases of mixing drugs.

---

385. MODEL PENAL CODE § 2.08(5)(b) (Proposed Official Draft 1962).

386. MODEL PENAL CODE § 2.08 comment 6 at 11 (Tent. Draft No. 9, 1959), citing dictum in Saldiveri v. State, 217 Md. 412, 425, 143 A.2d 70, 77 (1958).

387. 1 MODEL PENAL CODE AND COMMENTARIES § 2.08, at 364 (1985), citing *Saldiveri*.

The Fault Lies in Anticipated Harm

There are two probable or possible relevant outcomes of ingesting alcohol: the effect on the actor's mental state and the external results to which that mental state might lead. We have tried to show that the question is not solely whether the actor caused the automatistic condition by his own actions, but additionally whether he did so through some fault. And we have discussed cases in which the requirement ranged from no fault at all, or in which fault lies in alcohol ingestion alone, through to the view that fault lies in the actor's actual knowledge of the resulting mental incapacity. We raise here the further consideration whether the awareness, or any other culpability level, must as well pertain to the actual result or threat of harm to others.

The court addressed the question of a fault limiter applicable to automatism in *Quick*.[388] The court made the statement that "a self-induced incapacity will not excuse"[389] and noted that "Quick's own conduct that day might well have caused a severe fall in blood sugar," primarily by not eating right that day or in not taking sugar if he was aware that he was becoming hypoglycemic. The court said:

> Such malfunctioning [transitory ones, for example, caused by alcohol], unlike that caused by a defect of reason from disease of the mind, will not always relieve an accused from criminal responsibility. A self-induced incapacity will not excuse..., nor will one which could have been reasonably foreseen as a result of either doing, or omitting to do something, as, for example, taking alcohol against medical advice after using certain prescribed drugs, or failing to have regular meals while taking insulin.[390]

This language also indicates, as Mackay has pointed out, that "the question of foreseeability will be restricted to the facts surrounding the cause of the incapacity rather than to the question of whether or not the actual harm caused should have been foreseen."[391] But that is not the universal interpretation of the decision in *Quick*. What is uncommon here is not so much the disagreement over the level of fault, but to what facts the fault or culpability (*mens rea*) must apply and that it might actually concern the harm caused or threatened. While there is much logic to the view, it is not common to encounter the view that the fault lies in anticipation of the harm caused, rather than the more common and

---

388. Regina v. Quick, 1973 Q.B. 910.
389. *Quick* at 922.
390. *Quick* at 922 (citation omitted).
391. Mackay, *Intoxication as a Factor in Automatism*, 1982 CRIM. L. REV. 146, 147.

restricted view that the fault lies in the actor's level of awareness in his conduct causing his condition. Sullivan, for example, has argued:

> Yet, even though [the defendant] may have been clearly responsible for his condition the defence of automatism may still have succeeded at trial....*[A]t the very least*, the prosecution would have had to prove that [the defendant] foresaw he would attack someone....But an accused charged with assault who merely foresaw that his conduct would lead to a loss of consciousness but who had not foreseen that he would be violent must be acquitted. Assault cannot be committed negligently.[392]

Nevertheless, the interpretation has also been placed on *Quick* that the actor's resulting mental state is what is relevant, not the conduct to which it might lead, and the language is suggestive of negligence as the appropriate level of fault. The same observation could be made with higher fault requirements such as recklessness or knowledge.[393]

The rule that automatism may be a defense whatever fault was involved in causing the condition was, at least as of several years ago, according to Harding,[394] adopted by the High Court of Australia. In an earlier Australian case (in Victoria) in which the condition was brought about by a fifteen-year-old boy mixing Valium and scotch, the court held that he was entitled to have his defense of sane automatism put to the jury. Then in 1980, the High Court itself may have taken the same view, suggesting that it was not the source of the incapacity that was relevant, but the voluntariness of the act at the time of the alleged offense. Dean Harding opined that the law will not be left to stand that way:

> [T]he doctrine of culpable automatism appears to be in shreds in Australia. Whether involuntariness arises from intoxication or failure to take a drug to control an epileptic condition or from negligently induced hypoglycaemia or from concussion consequent upon negligent driving would seem to be immaterial; it is enough that the prosecution for whatever reason cannot show beyond reasonable doubt that the act of the accused was voluntary. Glanville Williams's logic [that the actor's fault in causing the absence of an element of the crime still cannot supply that missing element] is for the moment in

---

392. Sullivan, *Self Induced and Recurring Automatism*, 123 NEW L.J. 1093, 1094-95 (1973) (emphasis in original).

393. G. WILLIAMS, TEXTBOOK OF CRIMINAL LAW 621 (1978).

394. Harding, *Sane and Insane Automatism in Australia: Some Dilemmas, Developments and Suggested Reforms*, 4 INT'L J. L. & PSYCHIAT. 73 (1981).

> the ascendant. However, once the full implications begin to emerge, it is likely that judicial policy in this area of law will change direction again.[395]

One need not track down the law of Australia to find the same rule. The defendant in *Fain v. Commonwealth*,[396] perhaps the best known American case in point, relied upon the automatism defense where he claimed that a sleep disorder (somnambulism) caused him to react with violence upon being awakened. The court said:

> If the prisoner is and has been afflicted in the manner claimed, and knew, as he no doubt did, his propensity to do acts of violence when aroused from sleep, he was guilty of a grave breach of social duty in going to sleep in the public room of a hotel with a deadly weapon on his person, and merits, for that reckless disregard of the safety of others, some degree of punishment, but we know of no law under which he can be punished. Our law only punishes for overt acts done by responsible moral agents. If the prisoner was unconscious when he killed the deceased, he cannot be punished for that act, and as the mere fact that he had the weapon on his person and went to sleep with it there did no injury to any one, he cannot be punished for that.[397]

The issue discussed here is not confined to automatism cases; the litigation simply has centered there. The general question remains: If the fault limiter is identified even in terms of whether it means negligence, knowledge or something else, does it relate to the actor's resulting state of mind or resulting conduct? The question will be the same, and presumably, so will the answer, whatever defense theory is used, automatism or insanity.

TWO FURTHER PROBLEMS OF FAULT: SPECIFICITY AND VARIABILITY

There are two additional problems regarding the fault limitation on the pathological intoxication defense: (1) How similar must the prior experience or other basis of knowledge be to the present experience; and (2) will the actor's culpability that will defeat the defense be determined by the *mens rea* required of the offense charged? These will in practice

395. Harding at 79.
396. Fain v. Commonwealth, 78 Ky. 183 (1879).
397. *Fain* at 192-93.

interrelate rather closely, even though they are theoretically quite different concerns.

How Specific Must the Warning Signs Be?

It will be recalled that the Model Penal Code includes within their definition of pathological intoxication the requirement that "the actor does not know that he is susceptible."[398] It is curious that the Code in this instance defeats the defense on no less a requirement than knowledge,[399] whereas many defenses under the Code are lost on less—normally negligence, as we have seen. But here the question is more subtle: knowledge of what? By its terms, this statute makes knowledge of susceptibility the test. Susceptibility to what? "Intoxication grossly excessive in degree, given the amount of the intoxicant...."[400] Thus, while the culpability requirement is high, it relates only to intoxication, not harm to others.

What standard of warning or notice the court was using in *Kane*[401] is not apparent. The court was content to observe that there "is no evidence in this record that Kane did not know that he is susceptible...."[402] Recall also that in *Kane* the defendant had been aware that he suffered from previous blackouts when he drank but had not before experienced violence as part of the reaction and had not engaged in any prior conduct of this seriousness before while drinking, but this time he killed his wife.

State v. Hall[403] brings out some of the refinement sought under modern criminal codes with respect to the exact nature of the fault involved that will serve, inter alia, to distinguish voluntary from involuntary intoxication. The defendant was convicted of killing his companion while having hallucinations that he was killing a rabid dog.

---

398. MODEL PENAL CODE § 2.08(5)(c) (Proposed Official Draft 1962).

399. The MODEL PENAL CODE § 2.02(2)(b) (Proposed Official Draft 1962) defines knowledge:

> A person acts knowingly with respect to a material element of an offense when:
>
> (i) if the element involves the nature of his conduct or the attendant circumstances, he is aware that his conduct is of that nature or that such circumstances exist; and
>
> (ii) if the element involves a result of his conduct, he is aware that it is practically certain that his conduct will cause such a result.

400. MODEL PENAL CODE § 2.08(5)(c) (Proposed Official Draft 1062).

401. Kane v. United States, 399 F.2d 730 (9th Cir. 1968).

402. *Kane* at 730.

403. State v. Hall, 214 N.W.2d 205 (Iowa 1974). *See also* Note, *The Voluntary Intoxication Defense in Iowa,* 73 IOWA L. REV. 935 (1988).

The hallucinations resulted from ingestion of LSD. The defendant had obtained the pill from friends who said it would make him feel "groovy." The majority concluded that the resulting drug intoxication was voluntary on the ground that there was no evidence that anyone tricked him or forced him into taking the drug. The dissenters maintained:

> The testimony shows defendant took a pill which he knew to be a drug but which he did not know to be LSD and which he testified he thought to be harmless, although he had been told it would make him feel groovy. There is nothing to indicate he knew it could induce hallucinations or lead to the frightening debilitating effects of mind and body to which the doctors testified. The majority nevertheless holds the defendant's resulting drug intoxication was voluntary. I disagree.[404]

To this point the division of positions is no more precise than one would have expected of a common law court. However, the dissent took the matter further: "In other words, does voluntary in this context refer to the *mechanical* act of ingesting the pill or does it refer to a willing and intelligent assumption of the possible harmful consequences of that act?"[405] Translated to the context of pathological reaction to alcohol, does the fault lie in knowing one is drinking, or knowing the "possible harmful consequences" of drinking? More abstractly, the question becomes whether the actor must be aware of the relevant circumstances and advert to the possible risk of the result, or, suffice to say, can the defendant's act, in the narrow sense of voluntary bodily conduct, be called knowing even if he is totally unaware of the circumstances that will make his act dangerous or of the danger itself?[406] The majority evidently believed that the actor must only satisfy what is otherwise the bare, minimal basis for criminal liability: a voluntary act. However, the answer given by the dissent was that "I am convinced voluntary as here used should relate to a knowledgeable acceptance of the danger and risk involved. Applied to the instant case, that rule would demand submission of the issue to a jury."[407]

One of the cases reported by Marinacci, discussed in Chapter 3, illustrates the point that fault has a lot of gradations and is at least as

---

404. *Hall* at 214 (dissenting opinion).

405. *Hall* at 214 (dissenting opinion).

406. *See, e.g.*, State v. Coyle, 86 S.C. 81, 67 S.E. 24 (1910) (insanity instruction was given but limited by "fault in bringing about" the fight).

407. *Hall* at 214 (dissenting opinion). *See also* People v. Walker, 33 Ill. App. 3d 681, 338 N.E.2d 449 (1975), where the intoxication resulted from mixing beer and wine with medicine that the defendant had been given by another person. He was not aware that the medicine contained a drug that would have a potentiating effect on the alcohol.

complex as the *mens rea* used in defining crimes. It was there reported that "History revealed that this patient had had a head injury three years previously and was unconscious for seven days. Subsequently, he had episodes of confusion following the ingestion of alcohol. Previously such ingestion had resulted only in minor confusional behavior."[408] Is this sufficient warning to justify rejection of an insanity defense on the subsequent charge of murder?

Like the English, there has been an American case of fault in the context of the automatism defense. In *Watkins v. People*,[409] the intoxicated defendant was threatening a bar employee with a gun when the bartender hit him over the head with a blackjack. The defendant shot and killed the bartender. He relied upon the defense of traumatic amnesia, which an expert witness said could be caused by a blow to the head and, especially in connection with being already intoxicated, could have rendered the actor incapable of entertaining criminal intent. However, the trial court, while instructing on this defense, limited its effect to reducing murder in the first degree to murder in the second degree, to which the defense took exception, claiming that it should either render the actor not guilty at all or that it should at least reduce the crime to manslaughter. But the court held that the instruction was properly limited to first degree murder because that crime required "express malice," i.e., a deliberate and premeditated murder. Murder in the second degree, however, required only "implied malice," which was typically defined in terms of recklessness. The court believed that the defendant's conduct placed him at fault. "We hold that what occurred here after the blow falls well within the orbit of what might have been expected to happen under the circumstances."[410] A prior decision of their court[411] was distinguished on the ground that "the alleged amnesia with which the defendant Read claimed to be afflicted was not brought on by her own misconduct...."[412] The court also cited with approval a decision rendered in South Carolina[413] where an instruction was upheld which included language that the actor was liable "because he would have been in the wrong in bringing himself into that condition...."[414]

---

408. Marinacci, *A Special Type of Temporal Lobe (Psychomotor) Seizures Following Ingestion of Alcohol*, 28 BULL. L.A. NEUROL. SOC. 241, 245 (1963). *See also* Marinacci, *The Electroencephalogram in Forensic Alcoholism*, 20 BULL. L.A. NEURO. SOC. 177, 185 (1955).

409. Watkins v. People, 158 Colo. 485, 408 P.2d 425 (1965).

410. *Watkins* at 491, 408 P.2d at 428.

411. Read v. People, 119 Colo. 506, 205 P.2d 233 (1949).

412. *Watkins* at 494, 408 P.2d at 429 (1065).

413. State v. Coyle, 86 S.C. 81, 67 S.E. 24 (1910).

414. *Coyle* at 87, 67 S.E. at 27. The court there said: "'Insanity' arising during the progress of a difficulty voluntarily brought on by defendant and as the result of a blow rightfully inflicted by his adversary, should not constitute excuse for his after conduct in such difficulty."

The Appellate Court in *People v. Grant*[415] also addressed the notion of fault as a limitation on the automatism defense, noting, consistent with the approach taken by other courts and by the Model Penal Code, that

> there is no requirement that every act preceding the actual commission of the offense be voluntary. Thus, the jury may, on remand, determine that the defendant attacked Officer Vonderahe while in a state of automatism, but that he nevertheless committed an offense for which he is criminally responsible if he had prior notice of his susceptibility to engage in violent involuntary conduct brought on by drinking alcoholic beverages or by some other conscious causal behavior.[416]

They later noted that

> On remand, the defendant will again run the risk of being convicted for the offense of aggravated battery or obstructing a police officer if the jury finds that he was not insane when he attacked Officer Vonderahe and that he either consciously committed the offense or recklessly brought about his alleged psychomotor epileptic seizure and its accompanying state of automatism.[417]

The language is important because it is uncommon to find an opinion that unquestionably puts a modern label on the meaning of "fault" in this context.

And the court expressed the same view of the relevance of the actor's awareness of dangerous antecedent circumstances in *Government of the Virgin Islands v. Smith*:[418]

---

415. People v. Grant, 46 Ill. App. 3d 125, 360 N.E.2d 809 (1977), *rev'd on other grounds,* 71 Ill. 2d 551, 377 N.E.2d 4 (1978). The Supreme Court held that the instructions on insanity, which had dealt with volitional incapacity, had adequately covered the defense of automatism, especially where the defendant did not request a separate instruction. In the higher court, the defendant argued that the jury may have been confused because it was not clear whether the claimed epileptic seizure was the "mental disease or mental defect" covered by the insanity instructions. The main point of difference in the two appellate opinions was over the scope of a trial court's obligation here to instruct sua sponte on the defense of involuntary act when the case had been tried as one of insanity only.

416. People v. Grant, 46 Ill. App. 3d 125, 131-32, 360 N.E.2d 809, 815 (1977).

417. People v. Grant, 46 Ill. App. 3d 125, 133, 360 N.E.2d 809, 816 (1977).

418. Gov't of the Virgin Islands v. Smith, 278 F.2d 169 (3d Cir. 1960).

> ...[T]he defendant is wrong in his contention that the mere fact of unconsciousness from an epileptic seizure entitled him, without more, to an acquittal. It is only fair to point out in this connection, however, that the inference could be drawn from the evidence that the defendant did not know at the time of the accident that he suffered from epilepsy. It also appears from the evidence that an epileptic may lawfully operate a motor vehicle in the Virgin Islands.[419]

By reference to the fact that the defendant was not precluded from driving by the mere fact of being epileptic, the court focused the question of fault on a particularized awareness of impending danger at the time of driving.[420] Indeed, the court even suggested that the evidence might support the view that the defendant did not even know he was an epileptic. Perhaps a distinction needs to be drawn between the fault limiter operating in cases in which the fault lies in driving as opposed to where the fault lies in drinking, but it is not indisputable what that distinction might be.

Is the Fault Standard Unitary or Variable?

Offenses were often used to be defined at common law with a unitary *mens rea*,[421] but now they are more subtle and complex in that regard. Defenses also are frequently now "lost" because of limitations expressed as a single unitary, usually culpability terms such as "reckless" or broader terms such as "at fault." The American Law Institute made it clear that a basic tenant of their draft was that the *mens rea* requirement for each material element required by an offense definition can vary among different elements. As the Model Penal Code put it, "[T]he problem of the kind of culpability that is required for conviction must be faced separately with respect to each material element of the offense, although the answer may in many cases be the same with respect to each such element."[422]

If we were to speak of fault in the commission of modern offenses, it is clear that the concept can be, and often is, quite variable as to different elements, assuming that the meaning of fault varies with the culpability required to define the crime. The complexity of defining crime today can be contrasted with the fairly unsophisticated techniques used

---

419. *Smith* at 175 (citation omitted).

420. *See also* People v. Freeman, 142 P.2d 435 (Cal. Ct. App. 1943).

421. *See, e.g.*, Robinson & Grall, *Element Analysis in Defining Criminal Liability: The Model Penal Code and Beyond*, 35 STAN. L. REV. 681 (1983).

422. MODEL PENAL CODE § 2.02 comment 1 at 124 (Tent. Draft No. 4, 1955).

by courts when the defining involves defenses rather than crimes. The fact is that they have received little assistance from the legislative branch in defining defenses, or their limitations, compared to what modern legislation has provided in the case of defining crimes. Robinson has pointed out that in those instances in which a code provides a single fault limitation on the defense, "[i]t appears to presume a culpability system in which every offense has a single culpability requirement."[423]

A parallel question is whether there should be variability not by the crime charged, but by the defensive element involved. The answer need not, as we have already indicated, be the same for the result of committing a crime as for the resulting condition of the actor. As to the former, we alluded to the law of voluntary intoxication, which we may view as sufficiently entrenched and appropriately applicable to set it aside. Recall that our critical cases resolve to two—the existence of the underlying or pre-existing condition which renders the actor susceptible and the effect that drinking alcohol under those conditions will have on the actor. One rule of thumb might be that the fault limitation applies if either of these is accompanied by a defendant's mental state which is as high as the culpability level of the crime of which he is to be convicted. These fault levels and culpability requirements can both vary. For example, a defendant can know that he often, even always, goes "crazy" when he drinks, although he has no notion of why this is the case. Another person may be aware that he is an epileptic and has been advised that this renders it dangerous for him to drink, but his experience indicates otherwise and he continues to drink. If he knows either of these facts, he could be convicted of any resulting crime up to and including murder, though perhaps not premeditated murder.

Furthermore, despite this unexplained distinction between a defendant who gets drunk unexpectedly and one who has a genuine pathological reaction to alcohol, the problems are compounded by the Model Penal Code's total failure to make any connection between the culpability elements required by the crime and the culpability of the defendant in defeating the defense. At a minimum, confusion will arise because crimes can and do vary in the culpability requirements for different objective elements, whereas these defenses turn on a single, invariable culpability.

Presumably, we could continue to rely on numerous and confusing ad hoc determinations, or we can try to develop some principles of decision which would go somewhat beyond simply trying to find something called "fault" on the part of the actor. Another question regarding the fault limiter on defenses that we have been trying to

---

423. Robinson, *Causing the Conditions of One's Own Defense: A Study in the Limits of Theory in Criminal Law Doctrine*, 71 VA. L. REV. 1, 19 (1985).

identity is whether the fault limitation is the same for each of the defenses of insanity, involuntary act (automatism) and involuntary intoxication or lack of *mens rea*, even assuming that we are considering the same charge as a constant.

Fingarette and Hasse have proposed a unified defense labeled the "Disability of Mind" doctrine that would encompass a variety of presently existing mental defect defense categories, and each would be subject to a fault limitation so that there would be culpable disabilities as well as nonculpable disabilities.[424] Automatism presumably would be subject to the same fault limitation as the insanity defense.

In their development of the "Disability of Mind" defense, Fingarette and Hasse recognize that gross intoxication (not pathological intoxication) should be equated with insanity for the initial purpose of identifying a state of mind that might excuse,[425] and they then turn to the question of fault in bringing about that condition.[426] It is their view that, while it is possible for the actor to have been even more at fault in the "context of origin" of the irrational state of mind, nevertheless, a minimal floor should be created so that such a state of mind would not be a defense to crimes based on recklessness,[427] a result reached by the Model Penal Code in their voluntary intoxication section.[428] This would suffice in its precision in crimes which require only one *mens rea* or culpability element but might not be sufficiently precise to clarify the result in more complex crime definitions such as child abuse. More importantly, this construct, too, overlooks the most significant point. This limitation would apply when the irrational state of mind, and hence the lack of *mens rea*, was "culpably induced."[429] But it would appear that "culpably induced" can include negligence,[430] so that a defense to a crime based on recklessness can be lost by negligence in bringing about the situation. But should negligence as the highest level of culpability on the part of the actor suffice to convict for murder? Or even manslaughter? In addition, the authors make it clear they mean to encompass a broader category of cases such as taking medication. Negligent self-administration of a drug is hardly a fit basis for conviction for murder or manslaughter. They do concede the major point, however, that if there is no culpability involved at all in bringing about the "irrational state of mind," then the actor should not be liable at all. Perhaps the most significant aspect of the

---

424. H. FINGARETTE & A. HASSE, MENTAL DISABILITIES AND CRIMINAL RESPONSIBILITY (1979).
425. Fingarette & Hasse at 201.
426. Fingarette & Hasse at 211-16.
427. Fingarette & Hasse at 215.
428. MODEL PENAL CODE § 2.08 (Proposed Official Draft 1962).
429. Fingarette & Hasse at 215.
430. Fingarette & Hasse at 214-15.

proposed new approach is that it renders the concept of "mental disease" irrelevant.[431]

FAULT AND THE PATHOLOGICAL INTOXICATION DEFENSE UNDER THE MODEL PENAL CODE

Pathological intoxication, like automatism, was initially a purely medical term originating in psychiatry or clinical psychology but perhaps now is in transition to being both a forensic and medical term. Only the Model Penal Code and the few states which follow it on this point metamorphose pathological intoxication into a forensic term by recognizing it as a distinct category of legal defense. The fact that they define the existence of the concept of pathological intoxication in terms which exclude its existence if the actor is aware of the probable reaction clearly establishes that this cannot be an unadulterated medical view; the condition and the reaction will exist or not, although legal responsibility may well turn on awareness. But unlike automatism, where the medical concept can at least be entirely subsumed under an existing legal defense category, involuntary act, pathological intoxication has not been recognized as exclusively pertaining to any one traditionally recognized defense. Thus, most codes, which are largely silent on the matter, and all of the cases will recognize pathological intoxication only as a medical description of symptoms to be tested against a variety of legal defense categories such as insanity, involuntary intoxication, automatism, "extreme mental or emotional disturbance," and diminished capacity or other *mens rea* type of defenses. Only the few codes which follow the Model Penal Code may be interpreted to limit the pathological intoxication defense to one defense category, involuntary intoxication, and if they do so, it will be based on a misconception regarding the nature of pathological intoxication.

Recall that the Model Penal Code has a very limited conception of pathological intoxication. They described the defense in a way seemingly limited to cases of surprise intoxication, but intoxication nevertheless. In their view, voluntary intoxication and involuntary intoxication are defenses which relate only to the general defense of lack of *mens rea*; they are special cases of mistake, but like other cases of involuntary intoxication, the defense may be used to negate even crimes based on culpability levels of recklessness and less. Thus, discussion of fault limiters in the Model Penal Code calls for exploration of the problem in several different contexts.

---

431. Fingarette & Hasse at 7.

Variability to enhance the possibilities of refinement, and careful definition to increase precision, are two features which characterize modern code drafting in substantive crime definitions, but these efforts are not matched by the Model Penal Code or other modern codes in drafting defenses, and pathological intoxication cases bring this out. The complexity of modern fault limiters, as well as their transformation from what some understood as originally being moral fault limitations on defenses, can be illustrated through the Model Penal Code's treatment of the intoxication defense.

Fault in Insanity Cases Under the Model Penal Code

In our view, pathological intoxication is more often and more properly treated as a defense of insanity if the underlying cause is considered mental disease and as automatism otherwise. We have pointed out earlier that the drafters of the Model Penal Code either reject, or more likely only ignore, the insanity definition of pathological intoxication. They appear to leave that part of it to the law of insanity without further elaboration. There is no direct fault limitation on the insanity defense in the Model Penal Code except that which is implicit in the requirement of mental disease or defect. This point has been discussed in Chapter 6.

Fault in Automatism Cases Under the Model Penal Code

Whether the Model Penal Code drafters understand that pathological intoxication overlaps with the defense of automatism has been discussed in Chapter 7. While common law did not admit evidence of intoxication on the issue of the voluntariness of the actor's conduct, as distinct from its relevance to the existence of the requisite *mens rea*,[432] the Model Penal Code evidently means to admit intoxication for these purposes.[433] The main point made by the Code in this context is brought out in their view of *Decina* and similar situations in which the actor culpably brings about the unconscious state. These were discussed in connection with the driving cases earlier in this chapter.

---

432. MODEL PENAL CODE § 2.08 comment at 4 n.4 (Tent. Draft No. 9, 1959).
433. *See also* 1 MODEL PENAL CODE AND COMMENTARIES § 2.08, at 353 (1985).

Fault in Surprise Intoxication (Pathological Intoxication) Cases Under the Model Penal Code

The overriding significance of the contribution of the Model Penal Code in this area of defenses is their recognition and, indeed, insistence upon a distinction between "involuntary" in the sense of coercion or fraud, and "involuntary" in the sense of being unaware either of the circumstances or the results. Not only have courts commonly missed this point, even the best of the early jurisprudential writers missed it, too.[434] But it is a distinction that may prove to be as critical to the law of defenses as it already is to the law of defining crimes.

The main departure of the Code from existing law was to provide a definition of the fault limiter and non-fault cases used at common law and expressed only in the otherwise undefined term "involuntary intoxication." This is done in their definition of intoxication which is not self-induced where the actor has a complete defense, an affirmative defense, if the intoxication was both not self-induced and caused the actor to be legally insane. To fall within that category, however, the actor must have been without fault in getting that drunk, and the affirmative defense will not be available if the intoxication is considered to be self-induced. The intoxication will not be self-induced if either (a) the actor did not knowingly consume the intoxicant; or (b) he did not know, nor should he have known, that the substance has a tendency to cause intoxication. "Intoxication that (a) is not self-induced...is an affirmative defense if by reason of such intoxication the actor at the time of his conduct [is insane]...."[435]

By intoxication which is not self-induced, the Model Penal Code means to capture the traditional category of almost entirely hypothetical cases[436] in which the actor was forced to drink or was unaware he was consuming alcohol or other drugs. While it has been said that the Model Penal Code "has taken a similarly tough stand"[437] to that described by Hall, this is unlikely as to the awareness factor, given their clear requirement that the normal intoxication described is not self-induced, and therefore can be a defense, unless the actor "knows or ought to know" of its "tendency...to cause intoxication."[438] On the other hand, this may be a fair characterization of their approach as to the coercion factor because there the drinking must be "under such circumstances as would afford a defense to a charge of crime,"[439] which is in reference to

---

434. STROUD, MENS REA 115 (1914); J. AUSTIN LECTURES ON JURISPRUDENCE 512-13 (1879).
435. MODEL PENAL CODE § 2.08(4) (Proposed Official Draft 1962).
436. MODEL PENAL CODE § 2.08 comment 9 at 10 n.25 (Tent. Draft No. 9, 1959).
437. Paulsen, *Intoxication as a Defense to Crime*, 1961 U. ILL. L.F. 1, 19.
438. MODEL PENAL CODE § 2.08(5)(b) (Proposed Official Draft 1962).
439. MODEL PENAL CODE § 2.08(5)(b) (Proposed Official Draft 1962).

the duress defense. This, in turn, is limited in its scope to those situations in which a person has made a threat of unlawful force against another and the threat is of such a nature that "a person of reasonable firmness in his situation would have been unable to resist."[440]

An anomaly exists in the Model Penal Code's treatment of fault limiters for ordinary and pathological intoxication, and that is the extent to which the actor's mental state limits the availability of the defense in the two different contexts, intoxication which is self-induced and intoxication which is not self-induced or pathological. Essentially, the problem is that in the case of the defense which they define as "not self-induced" intoxication, the actor loses the defense if he is negligent in his assessment of the intoxicating effect of the substance consumed. The code provides

> (5)...(b) "self-induced intoxication" means intoxication caused by substances that the actor knowingly introduces into his body, the tendency of which to cause intoxication he knows or ought to know, unless he introduces them pursuant to medical advice or under such circumstances as would afford a defense to a charge of crime....[441]

The draft makes it clear, however, that mere negligence as to the "tendency of [the substance] to cause intoxication" defeats the defense of involuntary intoxication.[442] This is true regardless of the charge involved, a position seemingly at odds with positions taken elsewhere in the code that liability in the case of a failed defense ought to turn on the degree of culpability inherent in the failure.[443] Presumably, the difference is thought justifiable because the effect of losing the defense here makes the appropriate defense voluntary intoxication, so that it will still constitute a defense under the Model Penal Code for crimes which require intent or knowledge on any element.

On the other hand, in the case of their version of the pathological intoxication defense, it is not lost unless the defendant "knows" he is

---

440. MODEL PENAL CODE § 2.09(1) (Proposed Official Draft 1962).

441. The Model Penal Code's "ought to know" in § 2.08 (5)(b) (Proposed Official Draft 1962) is equivalent to negligence.

442. IND. CODE ANN. § 35-41-3-5 (a)(2) (Burns 1985) provides that it is a defense based on intoxication "[w]hen he did not know that the substance might cause intoxication." Thus, it is defined solely in terms of results and culpability as to results. That is typical of crimes such as homicide which are defined solely in terms of results, the *mens rea* as to whatever circumstances become relevant are only implicit: Both *actus reus* and *mens rea* elements at the circumstances level are whatever it takes to support the conclusions as to the result element. In effect, this is their definition of involuntary intoxication.

443. For example, see their treatment of the defense of "extreme emotional disturbance" in MODEL PENAL CODE § 210.3 (Proposed Official Draft 1962).

susceptible. Here, the fault limitation is identified as knowledge, and it is related to the circumstance of the actor's pre-existing condition and the grossly excessive intoxication that may result. In the case of nonself-induced intoxication, ordinary involuntary intoxication, the fault limitation is negligence and relates to the result level of intoxication. There is no explanation for the difference in standards.[444] Thus, in the case of voluntary intoxication, the Model Penal Code does not permit the condition to defeat the showing of recklessness for the commission of a crime even though, as we just pointed out, it can be incurred on the basis of merely negligence.[445] In rough terms, the jury is permitted to equate the conscious risk creation necessary to commit a crime based on recklessness by equating "voluntary intoxication" with that recklessness requirement and the jury can find voluntary intoxication on the basis of negligence. However, in the case of pathological intoxication under this code's treatment, the limit is knowledge of an actor's susceptibility to the abnormal reaction.

The distinction between the Code's letting the defense be defeated by a showing of negligence in the case of nonself-induced intoxication, but only knowledge in the case of pathological intoxication, has been criticized on the ground that the former may be too harsh and the latter too lenient. The criticism is at least partly justifiable if we are to assume that the Model Penal Code was actually drafting on pathological reaction to alcohol in the latter provision because, in that case, the actor is suddenly thrown into a state that most authorities would characterize as automatistic and there is no control beyond that point. By contrast, a person who simply becomes unexpectedly intoxicated still might be expected to exercise some control over, for example, whether to drive after he becomes aware that he is intoxicated.[446] Still, under the code, neither is a defense unless the defendant also becomes legally insane, and since that involves a substantial impairment of either cognitive functions or volitional control, then indeed the two defenses probably ought to receive more similar treatment.[447]

---

444. Professor Robinson also agrees with the interpretation that the Model Penal Code's comparable provision on "self-induced" intoxication contemplates limiters cast in terms of "knowledge" with respect to consumption and only "negligence" with respect to the resulting intoxication. Robinson, *Causing the Conditions of One's Own Defense: A Study in the Limits of Theory in Criminal Law Doctrine*, 71 VA. L. REV. 1, 43-44 (1985).

445. MODEL PENAL CODE § 2.08(2) (Proposed Official Draft 1962).

446. *See, e.g.*, State v. Brown, 38 Kan. 390, 16 P. 259 (1888), where, on a charge of public intoxication, the court noted that "If, after becoming drunk, he was still sufficiently in the possession of his faculties to know what he was doing, and to know the character of his acts, and went voluntarily into a public place, he would be guilty." *Brown* at 397, 16 P. at 262.

447. Professor Robinson has suggested that the pathological intoxication section might be read as limited by the "ought to know" language of the nonself-induced section. Robinson at 47 n.153. The obvious difficulty is that the Code is simply not constructed that way. Two distinct defenses are provided, and they each have their own definitions drafted at the same

As to the fault limit on the defense of involuntary intoxication, this is not fault in committing the crime, it is fault in getting drunk; and to be without fault in getting drunk, the actor must know he is drinking something and must be at least negligent with respect to the intoxicating tendencies of the thing consumed. Advertence as to the actual resulting intoxication is not made relevant. Fault is knowingly drinking what he should have known was an intoxicating substance. If both of these are present, the situation, apart from coercion, was what common law courts referred to a voluntary intoxication and what the Model Penal Code calls self-induced intoxication. As a practical matter, it will be the intoxicating nature of the thing consumed that will be at stake, and on this, negligence suffices to take the case out of the category of intoxication that is not self-induced.

Thus, fault is given a very broad meaning. In effect, negligent intoxication is equated to voluntary or self-induced intoxication, and such intoxication is not a defense to a crime predicated on a minimum requirement of recklessness or higher. This is another reason to believe that the Code's section on pathological intoxication was meant to cover the situation in which a drug/alcohol combination, for example, results in a quantitatively higher level of intoxication than would be expected solely from the alcohol. That situation does not fit comfortably in this section because it is the result of which the actor is unaware even though he knows he is consuming a drug and alcohol. Even though negligence might be thought to be an appropriate limiter here, it should limit at the result level, not as to the circumstance of its being alcohol that he consumed.

The medical advice cases seem to be an exception to these fault limiters which otherwise apply. If the problem is a typical drug-alcohol combination with a prescribed drug and an unexpected effect, which provision applies?

Fault in Justification Defenses and the Mitigating Defense of "Extreme Emotional Disturbance" under the Model Penal Code

Consistent with their overall use of the fault limitation in cases of claimed justified use of force and other affirmative defenses, the Model Penal Code provides in broad coverage that:

> The justification provisions of Article 3 [General Principles of Justification] of the code have been so framed that when the actor believes the force that he employs is necessary for any

---

level of generality.

> of the purposes which may establish a justification, his belief affords him a defense although it is erroneous, subject to the qualification of Section 3.09(2) that when "the actor is reckless or negligent in having such belief or in acquiring or failing to acquire any knowledge or belief which is material to the justifiability of his use of force," he may be convicted of "an offense for which recklessness or negligence, as the case may be, suffices to establish culpability."[448] See Tentative Draft No. 8, p. 76.[449] These provisions assure that homicides in self-defense, defense of others, defense of property, effectuation of arrest or crime prevention, where the actor's belief in the necessity rests on unreasonable grounds, must be approached as crimes of recklessness or negligence, if they are crimes at all. Such homicides, accordingly, are manslaughter at most under the draft—whether or not there was intent to kill.[450]

Thus, the situation that's clearly covered, as an example, is where the defendant intentionally killed in self-defense but was reckless in his assessment of the need to do so. In that event, he would be guilty of reckless manslaughter. It is not clear under the Model Penal Code whether or how that provision or some other would apply a fault limitation to the defense of extreme mental or emotional disturbance as a partial justification. By comparison, a provision in the federal Brown Commission Report,[451] a provision adopted by some states,[452] provides as part of their proposal, which otherwise parallels the Model Penal Code, that "An emotional disturbance is excusable, within the meaning of this paragraph, if it is occasioned by any provocation, event or situation for which the offender was not culpably responsible." This, presumably, would track the case law developments regarding self-induced insanity discussed earlier. The difference would seem to be that under the Model Penal Code, if the principle of § 3.09 applied (by its terms, § 3.09 covers only §§ 3.04 to 3.07), the offense would be determined by the culpability level in acting on the mitigating defense, whereas it seems the defense is lost completely under the federal proposal if there was any fault at all, so that the crime would usually be murder if an intent to kill was involved, for example. In addition, the federal proposal is deficient in not defining

---

448. MODEL PENAL CODE comment 4 at 45 (Tent. Draft No. 9, 1959).

449. For example, other defenses such as self-defense are lost when based on negligence of the person who had intentionally killed someone under circumstances which, to a reasonable person, would not pose immediate threat of serious bodily injury or death.

450. MODEL PENAL CODE § 201.3 comment 4 at 45 (Tent. Draft No. 9, 1959).

451. Brown Comm'n, Final Report § 1602(b) (1971).

452. 2 MODEL PENAL CODE AND COMMENTARIES § 210.3, at 65 n.62 (1980).

the meaning of "culpably responsible" used in that provision. Would it include, for example, negligence in bringing about the situation? The revised Model Penal Code commentaries then conclude that:

> Perhaps some additional clarification was achieved by the National Commission on Reform of Federal Criminal Laws. Its proposal provides for mitigation of punishment where the actor causes the death of another "under the influence of extreme emotional disturbance for which there is a reasonable excuse."[453] After specifying that reasonableness shall be determined in a manner parallel to that of the Model Code, the National Commission further states that an emotional disturbance is excusable "if it is occasioned by any provocation, event or situation *for which the offender was not culpably responsible.*"[454] Under this formulation, extreme emotional disturbance will not reduce murder to manslaughter if the actor has intentionally, knowingly, recklessly, or negligently brought about his own mental disturbance, such as by involving himself in a crime. This idea is implicit in the Model Code formulation, but some revision efforts have followed the National Commission and included such language in the statute itself.[455]

The approach, then, becomes the familiar one under the Model Penal Code. As we have discussed previously, the critical component of the defense is the emphasis on the actor's "situation." Any fault at all by the actor in placing himself in that situation, including negligence, will cost him the defense entirely. How that result is "implicit in the Model Penal Code formulation" is less than clear. Perhaps the thinking is that while it may be somewhat inconsistent to permit fault based on mere negligence to take the offense of manslaughter back up to murder (which requires extreme recklessness to commit), just as surely, negligence cannot reduce the offense to negligent homicide because the intentional homicide was already reduced from murder to manslaughter when the actor was not at fault at all.

---

453. Citing BROWN COMM'N, FINAL REPORT § 1602(b) (1971).

454. 2 MODEL PENAL CODE AND COMMENTARIES § 210.3, at 63-65 (1980) (emphasis in the original).

455. 2 MODEL PENAL CODE AND COMMENTARIES § 210.3, at 63-65 (1980) (footnote omitted).

PROOF OF FAULT: BURDENS AND WEIGHTS

With possibly one exception, there is no reason that evidence of pathological reaction to alcohol should be treated by the courts any differently than other evidence of insanity (or automatism or other type of defense). Basically, if the case is tried on a general plea under a theory of involuntary act or lack of *mens rea* for the crime, while it is not universal,[456] the general view will be that the state bears the burden of nonpersuasion because each is an element of the offense charged. As an example of an elemental defense case, *mens rea*, in *Government of the Virgin Islands v. Smith*,[457] the defendant was convicted of involuntary manslaughter in a bench trial. The defendant claimed that he had a seizure while driving. He had experienced a previous seizure and had another one two months after the accident. While the other seizures sounded like grand mal seizures, the defense expert thought the incident involved in this case was one of psychomotor epilepsy. The defendant won reversal and remand for a new trial despite the fact that the trial court made an express factual finding that the court did not believe the defendant had a seizure of any kind even though the evidence of an EEG test suggested an epileptic disorder. No drinking was involved in the accident. The circuit court said that this was a possible finding but thought the trial court had placed the burden on the defendant to prove the involvement of psychomotor epilepsy.[458] The defendant's burden was merely to go forward. The court said: "[T]he defendant was not required to *convince* the trial judge of this fact but merely to raise a doubt in his mind which was a reasonable one on all the evidence."[459] The court had also characterized this as not an insanity case but a *mens rea* case because "there was no evidence that the defendant's alleged epileptic seizure was an evidence or result of mental illness."[460] It did not, however, discuss the involuntary act (automatism) defense.

At the other extreme, if the case is tried as "emotional disturbance," the matter will be treated as an affirmative defense and the defense will bear the burden. Finally, if the case is tried as one of legal insanity, the courts will be in one of two camps, those which put the risk of nonpersuasion on the state (the burden to prove insanity once the issue is raised by the defense) and those which require the defense not only to raise the

---

456. Annotation, *Automatism or Unconsciousness as Defense to Criminal Charge*, 27 A.L.R.4th 1067 (1984).

457. Gov't of the Virgin Islands v. Smith, 278 F.2d 169 (3d Cir. 1960).

458. The trial court had stated that "'the question is whether or not the evidence as adduced by the defense convinces the Court as a factual situation that he had an epileptic seizure of some kind on the night in question.'" *Smith* at 173.

459. *Smith* at 174 (emphasis in original).

460. *Smith* at 174.

issue of insanity but to prove it, usually by a preponderance of the evidence.[461]

The one exception is the point that has been made earlier. There is need to develop a fault limitation in insanity, automatism and diminished capacity cases as it has developed somewhat in cases of intoxication defenses, serving there to differentiate voluntary intoxication from involuntary intoxication. The absence of such a rule may in part explain cases such as *Choice, Evilsizer* and *Hudson*; in the latter of these at least, the court simply refuses to permit any defense involving alcohol which results in temporary insanity. While this may just be blind ignorance resulting from anti-crime, anti-insanity, and anti-alcohol attitudes, it is also possible that the courts, or some of them, may feel trapped by the current structure of the law in this area. What is missing is the clear and explicit ability to tell the jury to differentiate between those who were aware of their abnormal reaction to alcohol and those otherwise situated. And on this point, burdens of proof are rarely litigated.

The question raised here is, who has what burden on fault limitations on the insanity defense? Everywhere the defense will have the burden of going forward with some evidence to raise the insanity issue, usually both by special plea and by some evidence. The majority rule now even puts the burden of persuasion on the defense.[462] But is non-fault an element in that requirement? Perhaps it should be in the context of pathological intoxication. And in those jurisdictions in which the defense also has the burden of proof (or risk of nonpersuasion), the defense should take the lead in not only establishing pathological intoxication, but of adducing what proof is possible that the defendant was not aware of any special susceptibility or proclivity toward violence or other relevant conduct.

A BRIEF CRITIQUE OF THE ANALYSIS OF FAULT IN PATHOLOGICAL INTOXICATION CASES

We postulated at the outset of this analysis the existence of a series of important variables (such as what act, circumstances or results to which the fault might relate) as well as two general levels of culpability—negligence and recklessness—in addition to the possibilities that, to defeat the defense of pathological intoxication, the fault might have to be both rather particular and relevant in terms of the actor's awareness of his susceptibility and that the fault limiter might be variable in its application

461. *See generally,* 2 P. Robinson, Criminal Law Defenses § 173 (1984).
462. 2 P. Robinson, Criminal Law Defenses § 173(a) (1984) (J. Robinson 1988 Supp.).

(varying, that is, with the different levels of culpability required by the crime charged).

To some extent, the variables do operate, but the ambiguity in the cases prevents truly reliable generalizations. Courts talk about the law one way on facts that support another view of the holdings. There is evident a tendency on the part of the judges, more pronounced than among the writers, to want to simplify and then dichotomize the issues into "voluntary intoxication" and "involuntary intoxication", much of this fed by a lack of an explicitly recognized fault limitation on the insanity defense. Whether this obscures a desire to treat the matter of pathological intoxication differently, depending upon the nature of the facts and the defense theory chosen by defense counsel, is not entirely clear, but the appearance is that the defense theory matters even less than the facts. What is important is the jurisdiction and the court's generalized attitude toward defendants involved with alcohol and resulting harmful conduct. While the Texas courts tend to explain their decisions by reference to a statute which they chose to read as abolishing the defense of temporary insanity, we doubt it actually has any influence at all on their decisions, anymore than the California unconsciousness statute actually dictated the related decisions in that state. The mystery of what was held in the leading decision in *Choice* remains unsolved. Essentially, outside of Texas and Arizona (and the Colorado Court of Appeals), the courts show no particular bias against the defense of pathological intoxication. In many of the cases, the facts were just not developed well enough to prevail and in others, the defendant was merely drunk and everyone, including the jury, knew it. The important cases, where there was clear and substantial evidence of pathological intoxication, almost certainly turn in large measure on the issue of fault.

We do not see any appreciable increase in trends one way or another in case outcomes or refinements of analytic approach over time, despite the advent of a majority of states which have now adopted modern criminal codes based, directly or indirectly, on the Model Penal Code. Older cases such as *Roberts* and *Higgins* handled the issues better than relatively modern Ninth Circuit decisions. Much of that can be laid at the door of the Model Penal Code in their poor treatment of defenses and fault limitations in general and their botching the concept of pathological intoxication into nothing more than a species of surprise intoxication, surprise in terms of the degree of ordinary intoxication.

What is clear is that today the bulk of pathological intoxication cases will be fought on the battleground of fault, not on whether pathological intoxication "exists."

To the extent we can tell how matters stand in the cases today, it would appear that the most frequently invoked fault standard is negligence. It is more frequent than either strict liability or actual awareness or disregard of risks. Negligence is such an amorphous concept that it serves to obscure an otherwise clear distinction between circumstances (existing facts) and results (things the actor caused). In effect, courts (and statutes)[463] which let a defense be defeated on the basis of negligence alone, as distinct from actual awareness, do not require, indeed, do not permit, more refined analysis. Negligence as to circumstances is negligence as to results, and the reverse is true as well. When the fault limiter is reduced from some level of awareness of facts or effects to unparticularized negligence alone, obviating any necessity for inquiry into the actor's actual state of mind to measure against the fault standard, any attempt at analysis is doomed, for there is little pattern to detect. The criminal law is reduced to a level of vagueness and indeterminacy that would be an embarrassment were the definition of a crime involved. It is not even clear that the legality requirements apply to criminal law defenses, much less to limitations on them such as we are dealing with here. Like the definitions of crimes themselves, judicial notions of fault, fatal to defenses, ought to be used with some precision and some discrimination, for the latter is not possible without the former.

---

463. Robinson, *Causing the Conditions of One's Own Defense: A Study in the Limits of Theory in Criminal Law Doctrine*, 71 VA. L. REV. 1, 24 (1985): "At least two jurisdictions consider it [causing the conditions of one's own defense] in the context of insanity...." citing P.R. LAWS ANN. tit. 33, § 3154 (1983) ("Transitory mental unsoundness caused purposely does not excuse criminal liability"); WASH. REV. CODE ANN. § 10.77.010(7) (Supp. 1984-1985) ("No condition of mind proximately induced by the voluntary act of a person charged with a crime shall constitute 'insanity'"). This, of course, is another way to view the Texas cases discussed above.

11

Conclusion

Perhaps it is the perception of anomalies in the law, no less than in science,[1] that compels clarification or even modification of the normal. So it seems, at least, with pathological intoxication and some of the related diagnostic classifications of mental abnormalities we have discussed. Because those classifications involve the areas of convergence of the diverse rules of insanity, intoxication and automatism, and try their strengths and weaknesses by pitting one legal defense category against the other, they often require reassessment of those ordinary defenses as they are used in the routine case.

Pathological intoxication describes a temporary but possibly recurrent set of recognizable symptoms confirming a psychotic state sufficient for a finding of legal insanity or automatism caused by a pre-existing disease or defect of the mind or physical injury or disease such as temporal lobe epilepsy or brain injury, or other bodily abnormality such as hypoglycemia of the actor functioning in combination with the consumption of any amount of alcohol or other drug. As used by the Model Penal Code, the term includes extreme intoxication resulting from any cause of which the actor had no reason to be aware. In our view, the actor should be liable for any crime committed while in such a condition which requires as its level of culpability whatever culpability the actor demonstrated in precipitating his or her own aberrant mental condition. For example, negligence in not knowing the probable reaction to drinking would support a conviction for negligent homicide but not murder. In many contexts, however, courts and legislative bodies have said, as they have with other defenses, that the defense is lost entirely in the face of negligence on the part of the actor in bringing about the situation. Still other courts treat the case as outright drunkenness without attention to the fact that the actor may not have been at fault at all.

---

1. T. KUHN, THE STRUCTURE OF SCIENTIFIC REVOLUTIONS (1962).

While discussion of pathological intoxication is not known for its uniformity of definition or precision of content, it would be compatible with present usage to distinguish between pathological reaction to alcohol and pathological intoxication. The latter would be the broader term; while pathological reaction to alcohol would be confined to cases of consumption of alcohol, pathological intoxication would encompass as well instances of self-induced intoxication unrelated to alcohol, as in drug/brain injury or drug combination cases or perhaps even simple cases of adverse reaction to drugs. The narrower usage was the idea as the term was first used by clinical psychiatrists, but the legal facts of significance are the temporary, abnormal condition of the mind that results and the fault with which it was induced, rather than either the chemical agent involved or the exact nature of the underlying cause, so no advantage seems to inhere in staying with the original sense. In fact, from a legal vantage point, the subject is not even self-inflicted insanity; it is mental disability, intoxication, insanity or automatism, for which the actor may or may not have been responsible. It is not drunkenness, and if it is insanity, it is temporary insanity.

It would have been tidy had we been able to conclude that there were "three faces of pathological intoxication" which consisted of temporary insanity attributable to an underlying mental disease triggered by alcohol consumption, a second type imputable not to mental disease, but to brain injury or trauma and related "external" causes which correspond to the definition of automatism; and a third type which corresponds to the Model Penal Code's treatment of the issue as essentially alcohol intolerance and so fits agreeably within the category of voluntary intoxication. In this scheme, we would have pathological intoxication of three sorts, ordered both by their causes and legal consequences which correspond to each other: insanity, automatism and intoxication. There might even be something to this strategy if we were less skeptical that "mental disease" had any real meaning. But it is the concept of mental disease which supposedly separates insanity law from involuntary intoxication and from automatism, and it is the concept of "unconsciousness" which separates some automatism from involuntary intoxication. Either person could otherwise meet the insanity test if the intoxication or loss of consciousness is extreme. But we do not think the concept of mental disease is useful as a basis of differentiating causes of mental disability. It is manipulated to assist the courts in the fault determination and the disposition question, and the reason it is so susceptible to manipulation is that it has no meaning of its own which is independent of describing irresponsibility.

We have expressed the opinion that the gist of the problem is that mental disease has no meaning other than that it serves as a verbal standard for a surreptitious or at least oblique method to designate the case as one of non-fault on the part of the actor, and in a few cases, it may be used to differentiate insanity from automatism. In the most common of the cases involving temporal lobe epilepsy, there is no agreement on whether that itself constitutes a mental disease or defect or whether the person with that condition who reacts to alcohol is "insane." The Model Penal Code's formulation of the pathological intoxication defense simultaneously requires non-fault and excludes "mental disease or defect" as elements. We believe these putatively dual requirements are essentially redundant. Even if one could separate the cases of insanity from both involuntary intoxication and automatism, separating those two defenses is not easy either. Automatism requires unconsciousness, while involuntary intoxication requires only insanity without mental disease. Some say the cause of the automatism must be external, but of course that fits involuntary intoxication as well. Also in the simplest of the cases, drug combinations, a case can be made for each of the two defenses if, for example, the drugs in combination cause a temporary mental derangement or malfunctioning of the mental processes that could be characterized as "unconscious."

The correctional quandary, the resolution of which sustained the decision of the House of Lords in *Bratty*,[2] is actually three dimensional: (1) There usually is nothing a hospital can do for a person who has committed violence during a period of pathological intoxication; (2) penal incarceration will be unwarranted in those cases in which the actor was unaware of the likelihood of such a reaction; and (3) few will want to release defendants on their assurance that they will avoid alcohol or will take prescribed medicine to control the seizures or otherwise manage the underlying causes. The same point put another way is that the system must first decide responsibility then disposition, and responsibility will be guided by principles of fault, disposition by perceptions of dangerousness. There is, in addition, the problem of standards of release if the defendant is found not guilty by reason of insanity and incarcerated in a mental institution.[3] And this, of course, underscores another problem with the law of insanity, and that is that its procedures are drafted on the assumption that long-term mental incapacity is always involved. In the typical case of temporal lobe epileptic attack triggered by alcohol, the person often should be eligible for release at the time of commitment.

To deny recognition of pathological reaction to alcohol as a criminal defense for want of "fit" with existing legal categories is more obdurate than denial of it as a diagnostic category on the psychiatric side. The concept of pathological intoxication mediates between the way problems in this context are viewed in the medical and legal realms. For most medical practitioners, the term is too broad because numerous etiologies

---

2. Bratty v. Attorney-General for Northern Ireland, [1961] 3 All E.R. 523.

3. *See generally*, S. BRAKEL, J. PARRY & B. WEINER, THE MENTALLY DISABLED AND THE LAW 725-26 (3d ed. 1985); A. GOLDSTEIN, THE INSANITY DEFENSE 147-51 (1967).

are possible. Some psychiatrists reject the concept because they are of the view that there may be other diagnostic categories they think more appropriate or that there may be physical causes of the abnormal reaction. It seems only a matter of time until a physical basis is found for all seriously incapacitating "mental illnesses." Medical practitioners will not, initially at least, be content solely with symptomatic treatment or relief, and there is a need to discover more concrete physiological or psychological causes. Those are nosologic problems of psychiatry and ought not to affect the utility of the concept in law. After all, psychiatrists only use the term "insanity" in a courtroom.

Law, on the other hand, will concern itself with three aspects of the case: the resulting mental condition of the actor gauged against jurisdictional rules of responsibility, the fault or absence of fault involved in bringing it about, and what is to be done to protect both the public and the rights of the defendant. Absent culpability on the part of the actor in bringing about the condition, why do some courts also appear to reject the concept as a legally useful description of a phenomenon when its existence is not seriously in dispute? We can only speculate why the minority of courts do so. To expand (or to be perceived as expanding) defenses today, especially those involving alcohol and insanity, is politically dangerous, and the sentiment in this country is clearly turning against alcohol and other drugs. Thus, a defense which ought to be recognized may go by the wayside in a few jurisdictions. They will continue to convict and imprison people who manifest not "immorality," but a pernicious medical malady, a susceptibility, sufficiently singular as to be almost certainly unfamiliar to many judges. Since alcohol is involved as a precipitating factor, the reluctance of courts to give the defense any credence or status is even greater lest it appear that one favors "letting drunks get away with murder," figuratively or literally, with predictable adverse political consequences for those judges. There are ad hoc explanations for other cases here and there, but that, we think, is the gist of the problem. All of the Texas pathological intoxication cases cannot have been poorly tried.

The opinions which reflect some reluctance to recognize pathological intoxication also might be explained on the ground that some courts are not comfortable with a largely behavioral definition of insanity and feel that it is not a "mental disease or defect" in the absence of anything more than behavioral evidence of "its" existence. But this only militates toward use of the legal defense of automatism where the American authorities do not limit the scope of an otherwise relevant negation of the elements of an offense. We suspect that this explanation assumes a higher level of sophistication than was actually displayed in those opinions. In any event, much of that could be offset with better trial of the cases. We have tried to show that most of them, especially the early cases, seemed to involve no more than careless use of language on facts that supported much less. But some of the later ones appear to invite explanation no less disingenuous than occasional judicial antipathy toward drinkers who get into trouble "because of their drinking." Other explanations would include incredulity that the person was not aware of the possible reaction or the feeling that "temporary insanity" was too accessible and advantageous as an exculpatory classification for someone who committed a "senseless" homicide. Perhaps all of these are involved. Despite the existence of these minority decisions, we should not lose sight of the fact that most courts give pathological intoxication appropriate recognition. We might also contribute to the body of literature devoted to expressing concern regarding the tensions between law and psychiatry. Based on the literature from both sides that we have consumed for this study, it seems overstated. Most lawyers, including judges, and most psychiatrists, and those from other medical specialties who have written directly or indirectly on the subject of pathological intoxication understood its content, utility and limitations.

What of the opponents? We do not want to make too much of the recurrent amount-of-alcohol issue, but the impression is sometimes conveyed that it is of broader significance. It is actually only urged as a sine qua non of pathological intoxication in two places: psychiatric texts which appear merely to repeat it as a requirement, and those who place their objection on grander nosological reservations. In effect, the DSM, though not all psychiatrists who have actually researched the question, has recognized no alcohol-induced psychosis unless intoxication is flatly excluded by limiting the phenomenon to those cases in which only nonintoxicating amounts were consumed. One could posit a continuum of responses to pathological intoxication from (1) denying a defense if any alcohol is involved, ranging through (2) recognition of a pathological intoxication only if no more than small amounts of alcohol are involved, to (3) the view that the amount of alcohol is irrelevant. There are several things interesting about the posited continuum. The first is that it does, indeed, reflect the views demonstrated in the literature. But the second is that it does not follow any preconceived notions about psychiatry versus the law. The first view reflects the law of a few jurisdictions, jurisdictions which probably for other reasons want to deny any defense based on the consumption of alcohol. The second reflects the general view of some psychiatrists and the DSM, is not a medical position at all and is not based on any evidence at all, but it is an attitude espoused only by those few psychiatrists who have been vocal about not wanting to recognize pathological intoxication for other reasons, reasons not always easy to determine. The third reflects the view of most psychiatrists and neurologists and most courts.

Thus, especially when it is seen that the first two views are as a practical matter the same, the camps break down into those who are antagonistic toward the defense because it is predicated on drinking, and those who understand that it is the underlying condition that actually is operating and that liability should turn on the actor's awareness of the likelihood of a reaction. It comes to this: The first camp finds fault in drinking, and the second finds fault in knowing risk creation of harm to others. The first camp would abolish the defense.

One could also posit a dichotomous response to pathological intoxication in terms of whether there was a demonstrable, underlying and recognized disease, supposing that law would insist that the experts in mental diseases be able to diagnose one or would deny the defense, while psychiatrists, being more experienced and sophisticated in the realm of mental illness would be the comfortable ones in recognizing that all aberrant behavior does not have a known, clear explanation. But here again, this does not reflect the views expressed in the literature. It is the law that seems more content to say "we don't know why he was crazy, but he was." The oft-asserted conflict between "psychiatry and law" is actually a good deal more internecine than that model would have it.

As we read the cases, what controls the outcome of most of the litigation is the court's concept of fault as applied in the case at hand, whatever the defense strategy may be; and when the court finds fault, there is a tendency to push the case into the category of voluntary intoxication, which is a fault limiter itself on *mens rea* defenses. They do this by approving of strict instructions defining fault as "voluntary intoxication," by affirming convictions against attacks based on evidence insufficiency and less frequently by denying the "existence" of pathological intoxication. The real issue in all these cases, and many courts will say so, is fault in combination with the question of disposition of the defendant. If he was at fault, he should be punished under the criminal law. If he was not a fault, he should not be convicted of a crime, but he may be dangerous nevertheless, and if so he should be dealt with by commitment under the law of insanity. That is the overall judicial perspective, and it is not an unreasonable one at all. The distinctions between the defenses described in their usual terms matter little by comparison. It is in this sense that we think "mental disease" and "non-fault" are the same totem. If a person is legally insane, why would it matter how he got that way? Why insist that it be because of "mental disease"? We think it is just a way to eliminate fault as the alternative view of the actor's behavior. The issue could be addressed more directly by elimination of the mental disease or defect requirement and putting to the jury the question of fault couched in just those terms, rather as we now do in the defense of mistake and the *mens rea* requirements in substantive offenses. But we have no explicit fault limitation on the insanity defense other than the category of voluntary intoxication. Pathological intoxication brings out this anomaly.

These factors can be said about any insanity or automatism case. There are several unique things about pathological intoxication that justify separate legal recognition of it. The law already has developed a well recognized, special body of law that treats cases of mental aberration attributable to the use of intoxicants differently from all other criminal cases. Pathological intoxication has been viewed by some (including the Model Penal Code) as an exception to that body of exceptional law, as virtually coexistent with a claim of non-fault for the mental condition involved. It is more in line with traditional use of the term to view the case as one of temporary insanity. The purpose served here is the opposite, for pathological intoxication opens the explicit possibility that fault was involved, unlike the ordinary case of insanity. The same is true of automatism cases.

Were we ever to come around to taking a position similar to what has been urged by Fingarette and Hasse in which we would drop the existing labels in favor of two questions (the actor's mental condition and the fault vel non involved in its onset), then it might not be necessary to have a legal label of pathological intoxication. As things are now, however, pathological intoxication signals a unique event, an abnormal reaction to alcohol (or other drugs) that calls for unique handling. Intoxication is equated with fault and insanity is equated with nonfault in the usual case, but pathological intoxication cautions that either can be involved. That is what is singular about it. Fault is a variable in these cases, not a foregone conclusion. In a sense, pathological intoxication mediates not only between medicine and law, it also signals the bifurcation into the standard categories of voluntary intoxication on the one hand, and insanity or automatism on the other.

Bibliography

BOOKS

ABRAMS, N. FEDERAL CRIMINAL LAW AND ITS ENFORCEMENT (1986).

ALCOHOL AND ALCOHOLISM (R. Popham ed. 1970).

ALCOHOL-RELATED DISABILITIES (G. Edwards, M. Gross, M. Keller, J. Moser & R. Room eds. 1977).

ALPERS, B. CLINICAL NEUROLOGY (5th ed. 1963).

THE ALPHA SYLLABUS (B. Brown & J. Klug eds. 1974).

THE AMERICAN AND ENGLISH ENCYCLOPEDIA OF LAW (D. Garland & L. McGehee eds. 2d ed. 1900).

AMERICAN BAR ASS'N, CRIMINAL JUSTICE MENTAL HEALTH STANDARDS (1984), also adopted as AMERICAN BAR ASS'N, 2 STANDARDS FOR CRIMINAL JUSTICE ch. 7 (2d ed. 1986 Supp.).

AMERICAN HANDBOOK OF PSYCHIATRY (S. Arieti ed. 1959).

AMERICAN PSYCHIATRIC ASS'N, DIAGNOSTIC AND STATISTICAL MANUAL OF MENTAL DISORDERS (1952) (DSM-I).

AMERICAN PSYCHIATRIC ASS'N, DIAGNOSTIC AND STATISTICAL MANUAL OF MENTAL DISORDERS (2d ed. 1968) (DSM-II).

AMERICAN PSYCHIATRIC ASS'N, DIAGNOSTIC AND STATISTICAL MANUAL OF MENTAL DISORDERS (3d ed. 1980) (DSM-III).

AMERICAN PSYCHIATRIC ASS'N, DIAGNOSTIC AND STATISTICAL MANUAL OF MENTAL DISORDERS (3d ed. rev. 1987) (DSM-III-R).

ANDENAES, J. THE GENERAL PART OF THE CRIMINAL LAW OF NORWAY (T. Ogle trans. 1965).

ANNUAL REPORT FOR 1909 OF THE INSPECTOR UNDER THE INEBRIATES ACT (1911).

ARCHBOLD, J. CRIMINAL PLEADING, EVIDENCE AND PRACTICE (1983).

ARISTOTLE, ETHICA NICOMACHEA (W. Ross trans. 1925).

AUSTIN, J. LECTURES ON JURISPRUDENCE (1879).

AUSTIN, J. JURISPRUDENCE (5th ed. 1885).

BACON, M. ELEMENTS OF THE COMMON LAWS OF ENGLAND (1636).
BARROW, R. & H. FABING. EPILEPSY AND THE LAW (1956).
BATCHELOR, I. HENDERSON AND GILLESPIE'S TEXTBOOK OF PSYCHIATRY (10th ed. 1969).
BENNETT, A. ALCOHOLISM AND THE BRAIN (1977).
BISHOP, J. CRIMINAL LAW (9th ed. 1923).
BLACKSTONE, W. COMMENTARIES ON THE LAWS OF ENGLAND (1769).
BLACK'S LAW DICTIONARY (5th ed. 1979).
BLEULER, E. LEHRBUCH DER PSYCHIATRIE (6th ed. 1937).
BLINDER, M. PSYCHIATRY IN THE EVERYDAY PRACTICE OF LAW (1973).
BODANSKY, M. & O. BODANSKY. BIOCHEMISTRY OF DISEASE (1940).
BONHOEFFER, K. DIE AKUTEN GEISTESKRANKHEITEN DER GEWOHNHEITSTRINKER (1901).
BRAIN ISCHEMIA: QUANTITATIVE EEG AND IMAGING TECHNIQUES (G. Pfurtscheller, E. Jonkman, & F. Lopes da Silva eds. 1984) (based on the International Symposium on Quantitative EEG and Imaging Techniques in Brain Ischemia, Austria, 1983).
BRAKEL, S., J. PARRY & B. WEINER. THE MENTALLY DISABLED AND THE LAW (3d ed. 1985).
BRANTLEY, J. & M. KRAVITZ. ETIOLOGY OF CRIMINALITY—NONBEHAVIORAL SCIENCE PERSPECTIVES—A DEFINITIVE BIBLIOGRAPHY (NIJ, NCJRS 1979).
BRETT, P. AN INQUIRY INTO CRIMINAL GUILT (1963).
BUTLER, S. EREWHON (Everyman's Library ed. 1927).
BUTLER, W. SOVIET LAW (1983).

CATANZARO, R. ALCOHOLISM: THE TOTAL TREATMENT APPROACH (1968).
CAVANAGH, J. & J. MCGOLDRICK. FUNDAMENTAL PSYCHIATRY (1958).
CLARK, W. & W. MARSHALL. A TREATISE ON THE LAW OF CRIMES (M. Barnes 7th rev. ed. 1976).
COHEN, S. THE ALCOHOLISM PROBLEMS: SELECTED ISSUES (1983).
COKE, E. INSTITUTES.
COLEMAN, L. THE REIGN OF ERROR (1984).
COMPREHENSIVE TEXTBOOK OF PSYCHIATRY (A. Freedman, H. Kaplan & B. Sadeck eds. 1975).
CRICHTON, M. THE ANDROMEDA STRAIN (1969).
CRICHTON, M. THE TERMINAL MAN (1972).

DAVIDSON, H. FORENSIC PSYCHIATRY (1952).
DELASIAUVE, L. TRAITE DE L'EPILEPSIE (1854).
DELGADO-ESCUETA, J. SEIZURE DISORDER UPDATE (1981).
DORLAND, W. THE AMERICAN ILLUSTRATED MEDICAL DICTIONARY (22d ed. 1951).

DRESSLER, J. UNDERSTANDING CRIMINAL LAW (1987).

EAST, W. AN INTRODUCTION TO FORENSIC PSYCHIATRY IN THE CRIMINAL COURTS (1927).

EDELSON, M. PSYCHOANALYSIS: A THEORY IN CRISIS (1988).

EEG AND BEHAVIOR (G. Glaser ed. 1963).

EEG AND EVOKED POTENTIALS IN PSYCHIATRY AND BEHAVIORAL NEUROLOGY (J. Hughes & W. Wilson eds. 1983).

EMERSON, H. ALCOHOL AND MAN (1935).

ENGLISH, O. & S. FINCH. INTRODUCTION TO PSYCHIATRY (3d ed. 1964).

EPILEPSY: A HANDBOOK FOR THE MENTAL HEALTH PROFESSIONAL (H. Sands ed. 1982).

EPILEPSY: DIAGNOSIS AND MANAGEMENT (T. Browne & R. Feldman eds. 1984).

FINGARETTE, H. & A. HASSE. MENTAL DISABILITIES AND CRIMINAL RESPONSIBILITY (1979).

FLETCHER, G. RETHINKING CRIMINAL LAW (1978).

FORENSIC PSYCHIATRY (G. Morozov & I. Kalashnik eds. M. Vale trans. 1970) (Originally published as SUDEBNAIA PSIKHIATRIIA in 1967 by a research group at the Serbskii Central Scientific Research Institute of Forensic Psychiatry).

GIBBS, F. ATLAS OF ELECTROENCEPHALOGRAPHY (1952).

GIBBS, F. & E. GIBBS. ATLAS OF ELECTROENCEPHALOGRAPHY (1941).

Gleick, J. CHAOS (1987).

GLUECK, S. MENTAL DISORDER AND THE CRIMINAL LAW (1925).

GOLDSTEIN, A. THE INSANITY DEFENSE (1967).

GOODMAN & GILMAN'S, THE PHARMACOLOGICAL BASIS OF THERAPEUTICS (A. Gilman, L. Goodman, T. Rall & F. Murad eds. 7th ed. 1985).

GORDON, G. THE CRIMINAL LAW OF SCOTLAND (2d ed. 1978).

GOSSELIN, R., H. HODGE, S. SMITH & M. GLEASON. CLINICAL TOXICOLOGY OF COMMERCIAL PRODUCTS (5th ed. 1984).

GREEN & STEELMAN, EPILEPTIC SEIZURES (1956).

HAGGARD, H. & E. JELLINEK. ALCOHOL EXPLORED (1946).

HALE, M. HISTORY OF THE PLEAS OF THE CROWN (1778).

HALL, J. GENERAL PRINCIPLES OF CRIMINAL LAW (2d ed. 1960).

HALLECK, S. PSYCHIATRY AND THE DILEMMAS OF CRIME (1967).

HAMBURG, D. & M. TRUDEAU. BIOBEHAVIORAL ASPECTS OF AGGRESSION (1981).

HANDBOOK OF CORRECTIONAL PSYCHOLOGY (R. Lindner & R. Seliger ed. 1947).

HANDBOOK OF PSYCHIATRY (P. Solomon & V. Patch eds. 1974).

HANDBUCH DER GEISTESKRANKHEITEN (O. Bumke ed. 1928).

HANDBUCH DER PSYCHIATRIE (G. Aschaffenburg ed. 1912).
HARRISON, T. PRINCIPLES OF INTERNAL MEDICINE (5th ed. 1966).
HAWKINS, W. PLEAS OF THE CROWN (1824).
HENDERSON, D. & R. GILLESPIE. TEXTBOOK OF PSYCHIATRY (1969).
HERMANN, D. THE INSANITY DEFENSE: PHILOSOPHICAL, HISTORICAL AND LEGAL PERSPECTIVES (1983).
HIGH TIMES ENCYCLOPEDIA OF RECREATIONAL DRUGS (1978).
HINSIE, L. & R. CAMPBELL. PSYCHIATRIC DICTIONARY (3d ed. 1960).
HINSIE, L. & R. CAMPBELL. PSYCHIATRIC DICTIONARY (4th ed. 1970).
HOLDSWORTH, W. HISTORY OF ENGLISH LAW (5th ed. 1942).
HOLMES, O. W. THE COMMON LAW (1881).

IMRIE. ACUTE ALCOHOL POISONING IN EMERGENCIES IN GENERAL PRACTICE (1957).

JEFFERY, C. ATTACKS ON THE INSANITY DEFENSE: BIOLOGICAL PSYCHIATRY AND NEW PERSPECTIVES ON CRIMINAL BEHAVIOR (1985).

KEILITZ, I. & J. FULTON. THE INSANITY DEFENSE AND ITS ALTERNATIVES (1984).
KELLER, M. & M. MCCORMICK. A DICTIONARY OF WORDS ABOUT ALCOHOL (1968).
KELLER, M., M. MCCORMICK & V. EFRON. A DICTIONARY OF WORDS ABOUT ALCOHOL (2d ed. 1982).
KOLB, L. NOYES' MODERN CLINICAL PSYCHIATRY (7th ed. 1968).
KOLB, L. NOYES' MODERN CLINICAL PSYCHIATRY (9th ed. 1977).
KOMMENTARII K UGOLOVNOMU KODEKSU RSFSR (I. Severin ed. 1980) (COMMENTARIES TO THE CRIMINAL CODE OF THE RSFSR).
KONNER, M. THE TANGLED WING: BIOLOGICAL CONSTRAINTS ON THE HUMAN SPIRIT (1982).
KRAFFT-EBING, R. LEHRBUCH DER PSYCHIATRIE (1897).

LAFAVE, W. & A. SCOTT. SUBSTANTIVE CRIMINAL LAW (1986).
LAWYERS' MEDICAL CYCLOPEDIA (1970).
LEVIN, J. & J. FOX. MASS MURDER (1985).
LOMBROSO, C. CRIME, ITS CAUSES AND REMEDIES (1918).
LOW, P., J. JEFFRIES & R. BONNIE. CRIMINAL LAW: CASES AND MATERIALS (2d ed. 1986).
LOW, P., J. JEFFRIES & R. ROWIE. THE TRIAL OF JOHN HINKLEY, JR.: A CASE STUDY IN THE INSANITY DEFENSE (1986).

MACDONALD, J. PSYCHIATRY AND THE CRIMINAL: A GUIDE TO PSYCHIATRIC EXAMINATIONS FOR THE CRIMINAL COURTS (1958).
MACDONALD, J. PSYCHIATRY AND THE CRIMINAL (2d ed. 1969).
MACDONALD, J. PSYCHIATRY AND THE CRIMINAL (3d ed. 1976).

MAEDER, T. CRIME AND MADNESS: THE ORIGINS AND EVOLUTION OF THE INSANITY DEFENSE (1985).
MALOY, B. NERVOUS AND MENTAL DISEASES (1935).
MARK, V. & F. ERVIN. VIOLENCE AND THE BRAIN (1970).
MAUDSLEY, H. RESPONSIBILITY IN MENTAL DISEASE (1906).
MCNICHOL, R. THE TREATMENT OF DELIRIUM TREMENS AND RELATED STATES (1970).
MENNINGER, K. THE VITAL BALANCE (1963).
THE MERCK MANUAL (15th ed. 1987).
MERRITT, H. A TEXTBOOK OF NEUROLOGY (4th ed. 1967).
MEWETT, A. & M. MANNING. CRIMINAL LAW (1978).
MILLER, B. & C. KEANE. ENCYCLOPEDIA AND DICTIONARY OF MEDICINE AND NURSING (1972).
MOENSSENS, A., F. INBAU & J. STARRS. SCIENTIFIC EVIDENCE IN CRIMINAL CASES (3d ed. 1986).
MOENSSENS, A. & F. INBAU. SCIENTIFIC EVIDENCE IN CRIMINAL CASES (2d ed. 1978).
MONROE, R. BRAIN DYSFUNCTION IN AGGRESSIVE CRIMINALS (1978).
MONROE, R. EPISODIC BEHAVIORAL DISORDERS (1970).
MORRIS, N. & C. HOWARD. STUDIES IN CRIMINAL LAW (1964).

NOLAN, J. MASSACHUSETTS PRACTICE: CRIMINAL LAW (1976).
NOYES, A. MODERN CLINICAL PSYCHIATRY (2d ed. 1939).
NOYES, A. & L. KOLB. MODERN CLINICAL PSYCHIATRY (5th ed. 1960).

PERKINS, R. & R. BOYCE. CRIMINAL LAW AND PROCEDURE (6th ed. 1984).
PERLIN, M. MENTAL DISABILITY LAW (1989).
PINCUS, J. & G. TUCKER. BEHAVIORAL NEUROLOGY (2d ed. 1978).
PITTMAN, D. & C. GORDON. THE REVOLVING DOOR (1958).
POLLOCK, F. & F. MAITLAND. HISTORY OF ENGLISH LAW (2d ed. 1899).
PRICE'S TEXTBOOK OF THE PRACTICE OF MEDICINE (1966).
PROBLEMS OF CONSCIOUSNESS: TRANSACTIONS OF THE SECOND CONFERENCE (H. Abramson ed. 1951).
PSYCHIATRIC ASPECTS OF EPILEPSY (D. Blumer ed. 1984).
PSYCHIATRY UPDATE (1985).
PSYCHOTROPIC DRUG SIDE EFFECTS (R. Shader & A. DiMascio eds. 1970).

RAY, I. THE MEDICAL JURISPRUDENCE OF INSANITY (1838).
RECENT ADVANCES IN CLINICAL NEUROPHYSIOLOGY (L. Widen ed. 1967).
REDLICH & FREEDMAN, THE THEORY AND PRACTICE OF PSYCHIATRY (1966).
REITER, P. ANTISOCIAL OR CRIMINAL ACTS AND HYPNOSIS: A CASE STUDY (1958).
RESTAK, R. THE BRAIN (1984).
THE RESTATEMENT (SECOND) OF TORTS (1965).

RHYTHMIC EEG ACTIVITIES AND CORTICAL FUNCTIONING (Proceedings of the International Symposium on Event-Related Changes in Cortical Rhythmic Activities. Behavioural Correlates. Austria, 1979) (G. Pfurtscheller, P. Buser & F. Lopes da Silva eds. 1980).

ROBINSON, D. PSYCHOLOGY AND LAW (1980).

ROBINSON, P. CRIMINAL LAW DEFENSES (1984).

ROYAL SOCIETY OF MEDICINE INTERNATIONAL CONGRESS AND SYMPOSIUM SERIES NO. 81, EPILEPSY AND THE LAW—A MEDICAL SYMPOSIUM ON THE CURRENT LAW (P. Fenwick & E. Fenwick eds. 1985).

SAKEL, M. EPILEPSY (1958).

SALMOND, J. JURISPRUDENCE (9th ed. 1937).

SCHIFFER, M. MENTAL DISORDER AND THE CRIMINAL TRIAL PROCESS (1978).

SLATER, E. & M. ROTH. CLINICAL PSYCHIATRY (1969).

SMITH, A. THE MIND (1984).

SMITH, J. & B. HOGAN. CRIMINAL LAW (5th ed. 1983).

SOUTHERN EEG SOCIETY, ELECTROENCEPHALOGRAPHY AND THE LAW (1968).

STEPHEN, J. HISTORY OF THE CRIMINAL LAW OF ENGLAND (1883).

STODDART, W. MIND AND ITS DISORDERS (1921).

STROUD. MENS REA (1914).

SZASZ, T. LAW, LIBERTY AND PSYCHIATRY: AN INQUIRY INTO THE SOCIAL USES OF MENTAL HEALTH PRACTICES (1963).

SZASZ, T. THE MYTH OF MENTAL ILLNESS (1961).

SZASZ, T. INSANITY: THE IDEA AND ITS CONSEQUENCES (1987).

TABER'S CYCLOPEDIC MEDICAL DICTIONARY (C. Thomas ed. 14th ed. 1981)

TANULMANYOK AS ALKOHOLIZMUS PSZICHIATRIAI KOVETKEZMENYCIROL (Results of Psychiatric Studies on Alcoholism) (I. Tariska, G. Gereby & G. Kardos eds. 1969).

TAYLOR, L. BORN TO CRIME—THE GENETIC CAUSES OF CRIMINAL BEHAVIOR (1984).

TEMPORAL LOBE EPILEPSY (M. Baldwin & P. Bailey eds. 1958).

THOMPSON, G. ALCOHOLISM (1956).

THOMPSON, G. THE PSYCHOPATHIC DELINQUENT AND CRIMINAL (1953).

TURNER, C. GENERAL ENDOCRINOLOGY (1948).

VIOLENCE AND THE VIOLENT INDIVIDUAL (J. Hays, T. Roberts & K. Solway eds. 1981).

WALKER, N. CRIME AND INSANITY IN ENGLAND (1968).

WATKINS, L. THE SLEEPWALK KILLERS (1976).

WEISSENBERGER, G. FEDERAL RULES OF EVIDENCE (1987).

WEIHOFEN, H. MENTAL DISORDER AS A CRIMINAL DEFENSE (1954).

WHARTON, F. WHARTON'S CRIMINAL LAW (14th ed. 1979).

WHARTON, F. & M. STILLE. MEDICAL JURISPRUDENCE (5th ed. 1905).

WHITLOCK, F. CRIMINAL RESPONSIBILITY AND MENTAL ILLNESS (1963).
WILLIAMS, G. CRIMINAL LAW: THE GENERAL PART (2d ed. 1961).
WILLIAMS, G. TEXTBOOK OF CRIMINAL LAW (1978).
WILLIAMS, G. TEXTBOOK OF CRIMINAL LAW (2d ed. 1983).
WILY, H. & K. STALLWORTHY. MENTAL ABNORMALITY AND THE LAW (1962).
WINSLADE, W. THE INSANITY PLEA: THE USES AND ABUSES OF THE INSANITY DEFENSE (1983).
WORLD HEALTH ORGANIZATION. ALCOHOL-RELATED DISABILITIES (G. Edwards, M. Gross, M. Keller, J. Moser & R. Room eds. 1977).
WORLD HEALTH ORGANIZATION. INTERNATIONAL CLASSIFICATION OF DISEASES (9th rev. 1977).
WORLD HEALTH ORGANIZATION. INTERNATIONAL CLASSIFICATION OF DISEASES—CLINICAL MODIFICATION (9th rev. 1977).
WORLD HEALTH ORGANIZATION. MANUAL OF THE INTERNATIONAL STATISTICAL CLASSIFICATION OF DISEASES, INJURIES, AND CAUSES OF DEATH (1977).

YEAGER, J. & R. CARLSON. IOWA PRACTICE: CRIMINAL LAW AND PROCEDURE (1979).

ZIEHEN, G. PSYCHIATRIE FUR AERZTE UND STUDIERENDE (4th ed. 1911).

ARTICLES

Adrian & Matthews, 57 BRAIN 355 (1934).
Agarwal & Goedde, *Human Aldehyde Dehydrogenase Isozymes and Alcohol Sensitivity*, 16 ISOZYMES CURR. TOP. BIOL. MED. RES. 21 (1987).
Alpers, *Relation of the Hypothalamus to Disorders of Personality: Report of a Case*, 38 ARC. NEUROL. PSYCHIAT. 291 (1937).
American College of Nuclear Physicians & Society of Nuclear Medicine, *Positron Emission Tomography: Clinical Status in the United States in 1987*, 29 J. NUCL. MED. 1136 (1988).
Amsterdam, *The Void-for-Vagueness Doctrine in the Supreme Court*, 109 U. PA. L. REV. 67 (1960).
Anchersen, *Rettspsykiatriske Problemer i Forbindelse Med Sovn og Vissthetsforstyrreiser* (Legal Psychiatric Problems Related to Sleep and Modifications of Consciousness), 87 TIDSSKR. NORSKE LAEGEFOREN 1796 (1967).
Andrulonis, Donnelly, Glueck, Stroebel & Szarek, *Preliminary Data on Ethosuximide and the Episodic Dyscontrol Syndrome*, 137 AM. J. PSYCHIAT. 11 (1980).

Annotation, *Admissibility in Civil Action of Electroencephalogram, Electrocardiogram, or Other Record Made by Instrument Used in Medical Test, or of Report Based Upon Such Test,* 66 A.L.R.2D 536 (1959).

Annotation, *Amnesia as Affecting Capacity to Commit Crime or Stand Trial,* 46 A.L.R.3D 544 (1972).

Annotation, *Automatism or Unconsciousness as Defense to Criminal Charge,* 27 A.L.R.4TH 1067 (1984).

Annotation, *When Intoxication Deemed Involuntary So As To Constitute a Defense to Criminal Charge,* 73 A.L.R.3D 195 (1976).

Arenella, *The Diminished Capacity and Diminished Responsibility Defenses: Two Children of a Doomed Marriage,* 77 COLUM. L. REV. 827 (1977).

Ashworth, *Reason, Logic and Criminal Liability,* 91 L.Q. REV. 102 (1975).

Bach-y-Rita, Letter, 128 AM. J. PSYCHIAT. 660 (1971).

Bach-y-Rita, Lion, Climent & Ervin, *Episodic Dyscontrol: A Study of 130 Violent Patients,* 127 AM. J. PSYCHIAT. 11 (1971).

Bach-y-Rita, Lion & Ervin, *Pathological Intoxication: Clinical and Electroencephalographic Studies,* 127 AM. J. PSYCHIAT. 698 (1970).

Baldessarini, *Drugs and the Treatment of Psychiatric Disorders,* in GOODMAN & GILMAN'S, THE PHARMACOLOGICAL BASIS OF THERAPEUTICS (A. Gilman, L. Goodman, T. Rall & F. Murad eds. 7th ed. 1985).

Banay, *Pathologic Reaction to Alcohol,* 4 QRTLY J. STUD. ALCOH. (1944).

Bazelon, *Introduction,* in FORENSIC PSYCHIATRY (G. Morozov & I. Kalashnik eds. M. Vale trans. 1970).

Beck, *Voluntary Conduct: Automatism, Insanity and Drunkenness,* 9 CRIM. L.Q. 315 (1967).

Bennett, *Mental Disorders with Temporal Lobe Epilepsy,* 26 DIS. NERV. SYST. 275 (1965).

Berger, *Uber das Elektrenkephalogramm den Menschen,* 87 ARCHIVES FOR. PSYCH. 527 (1929).

Binavince, *The Structure and Theory of the German Penal Code,* 24 AM. J. COMP. L. 594 (1976).

Binder, 35 SCHWEIZ. ARCH. NEUROL. PSYCHIAT. 209 (1935).

Bing & Schonberg, 55 SCHWEIZ. MED. WSCHR. 157 (1925).

Binswanger, 152 Z. GES. NEUROL. PSYCHIAT. 703 (1935).

Blackwell, *Automatism and Amnesia,* 79 S. AFR. L.J. 16 (1962).

Blair, *The Medico-Legal Problems of Pathological Alcoholic Intoxication: An Illustrative Case,* 9 MED., SCI. & LAW 94 (1969).

Blair, *The Medicolegal Aspects of Automatism,* 17 MED., SCI. & LAW 167 (1977).

Bloom, *Neurohumoral Transmission and the Central Nervous System,* in GOODMAN & GILMAN'S, THE PHARMACOLOGICAL BASIS OF THERAPEUTICS (A. Gilman, L. Goodman, T. Rall & F. Murad eds. 7th ed. 1985).

Blume, *Women and Alcohol,* 256 J. A.M.A. 1467 (1986).

Boettcher, *Voluntary Intoxication: A Defense to Specific Intent Crimes,* 65 U. DET. L. REV. 33 (1987).

Bonhoeffer, 6 DEUTSCHE KLINIK 540 (1906).

Bonkalo, *Impulsive Acts and Confusional States During Incomplete Arousal From Sleep: Criminological and Forensic Implications,* 48 PSYCHIAT. Q. 400 (1974).

Bowman & Jellinek, *Alcoholic Mental Disorders,* 2 QRTLY J. STUD. ALCOH. 312 (1941).

Braga & Filho, *Epilepsia e Dinquencia* (Epilepsy and Delinquency), 19 J. BRASILEIRO PSIQUIATRIA 245 (1970).

Brandt, *The Insanity Defense and the Theory of Motivation,* 7 LAW & PHIL. 123 (1988).

Branthwaite, in ANNUAL REPORT FOR 1909 OF THE INSPECTOR UNDER THE INEBRIATES ACT (1911).

Burke, *The Defense of Voluntary Intoxication: Now You See It, Now You Don't,* 19 IND. L. REV. 147 (1986).

Busch, 24 J. PSYCHOL. NEUROL. 101 (1918).

Campbell, *Psychological Blow Automatism: A Narrow Defence,* 23 CRIM. L.Q. 342 (1981).

Chafetz, in COMPREHENSIVE TEXTBOOK OF PSYCHIATRY 1341 (A. Freedman, H. Kaplan & B. Sadeck eds. 1975).

Chan, *Alcoholism and Epilepsy,* 26 EPILEPSIA 323 (1985).

Ciafardo, *Delito en Estado de Inconsciencia por Embriaguez Pathologica en un Degenerado* (Crime in the State of Unconsciousness From Pathological Intoxication in a Degenerate), 2 R. PSIQT. CRIMINOL. 625 (1937).

Clapham, *An Interesting Case of Hypoglycaemia,* 33 MEDICO-LEGAL J. 72 (1965).

Claude, *Sur le Diagnostic des Formes Larvees de l'Epilepsie Alcoolique at des Crises Psycho-Motrices de l'Ivresse Pathologigue; son Importance Medico-Legale* (On the Diagnostics of the Early Forms of the Epileptic Alcoholic and of the Psychomotor Seizure of Pathological Intoxication; Its Medical-Legal Importance), 40 PROGR. M. PAR. 497 (1912).

Cleckley, *Psychopathic States,* in 1 AMERICAN HANDBOOK OF PSYCHIATRY 567 (S. Arieti ed. 1959).

Clements, *Epilepsy, Insanity and Automatism,* 133 NEW L.J. 949 (1983).

Cohen, *Pathological Intoxication,* 10 DRUG ABUSE & ALCOHOLISM NEWSLETTER 1 (June 1981).

Cohn, *Offensive Use of the Insanity Defense: Imposing the Insanity Defense over the Defendant's Objection,* 15 HASTINGS CONST. L.Q. 295 (1988).

Coid, *Mania A Potu: A Critical Review of Pathological Intoxication*, 9 PSYCHOL. MED. 709 (1979).

Collins & Mertens, *Age, Alcohol, and Simulated Altitude: Effects on Performance and Breathalyzer Scores*, 59 AV. SPACE ENV'T MED. 1026 (1988).

Comm'n on Classification of Terminology of the Int'l League Against Epilepsy, *Proposal for Revised Clinical and Electroencephalographic Classification of Epileptic Seizures*, 22 EPILEPSIA 489 (1981).

Comment, *Artificial Nutrition and the Terminally Ill: How Should Washington Decide?* 61 WASH. L. REV. 419 (1986).

Comment, *Criminal Law—Mens Rea—General Principles—Intoxication as a Defence*, 55 CAN. BAR REV. 691 (1977).

Comment, *Diminished Capacity: Its Potential Effect in California*, 3 LOY. L.A.L. REV. 153 (1970).

Comment, *Keeping Wolff From the Door: California's Diminished Capacity Concept*, 60 CALIF. L. REV. 1641 (1972) (authored by Ann Fingarette Hasse).

Comment, *Legal and Psychiatric Concepts and the Use of Psychiatric Evidence in Criminal Trials*, 73 CALIF. L. REV. 411 (1985) (authored by Peter R. Dahl).

Comment, *Recent Changes in Criminal Law: The Federal Insanity Defense*, 46 LA. L. REV. 337 (1985).

Comment, *The Relevance of Innocence: Proposition 8 and the Diminished Capacity Defense*, 71 CALIF. L. REV. 1197 (1983).

Conlon & Trimble, *Magnetic Resonance Imaging in Psychiatry*, CAN. J. PSYCHIAT. 702 (1987).

Conlon, Trimble, Rogers & Callicott, *Magnetic Resonance Imaging in Epilepsy: A Controlled Study*, 2 EPILEP. RES. 37 (1988).

Conrad, *The Electroencephalograph (EEG) as Evidence of Criminal Responsibility*, 50 J. CRIM. L., CRIMINOLOGY & POLICE SCI. 405 (1959).

Cook, *Act, Intention, and Motive in the Criminal Law*, 26 YALE L.J. 645 (1917).

Courjon, *Apport de l'Exploration Fonctionelle du System Nerveux dans le Diagnostic et le Pronostic des Traumatismes Craiens Recents*, 70 ACTA NEUROL. BELG. (1970).

Courville, *Traumatic Lesions of the Temporal Lobe as the Essential Cause of Psychomotor Epilepsy*, in TEMPORAL LOBE EPILEPSY (M. Baldwin & P. Bailey eds. 1958).

Cozzo, *Considerazioni Sulle Psicosi da Intossicazione Alcoolica Acuta e Sulle Psicosi da Intolleranza All'alcool* (Remarks on Psychosis Due to Acute Alcohol Intoxication and on Psychosis Due to Alcohol Intolerance), 39 LAV. NEUROPSICHIAT. 451 (1966).

Cramer, 13 MSCHR. PSYCHIAT. NEUROL. 56 (1903).

Crotty, *The History of Insanity as a Defense to Crime in English Criminal Law*, 12 CALIF. L. REV. 105 (1924).

Csiky & Ander, *Reszegseg, Koros Reszegseg es Beszamithatosag orvosi Szempontbol* (Intoxication, Pathological Intoxication and Responsibility From the Medical Point of View), 6 ORV. SZLE 415 (1960).

Cuffin & Cohen, *Comparison of the Magnetoencephalogram and Electroencephalogram*, 47 ELECTROENCEPH. CLIN. NEUROPHYSIOL. 132 (1979).

Cunnien, *Alcoholic Blackouts: Phenomenology and Legal Relevance*, 4 BEHAV. SCI. & LAW 73 (1986).

Currie, Heathfield, Henson & Scott, *Clinical Course and Prognosis of Temporal Lobe Epilepsy*, 94 BRAIN 173 (1971).

d'Orban, *Drugs and Alcohol: The Psychiatrist as Expert Witness in Court*, 81 BR. J. ADDICT. 631 (1986).

Davidson, *The Psychiatrist's Role in the Administration of Criminal Justice*, 4 RUTGERS L. REV. 578 (1950).

Decsi, *Beitrag aur Forensischen Bedeutung der Pathologischen Rauschzustande* (Contribution to the Forensic Significance of the State of Pathological Intoxication), 29 PSYCHT. NEUR. WSCHR. 37 (1927).

Delgado, *Ascription of Criminal States of Mind: Toward a Defense Theory for the Coercively Persuaded ("Brainwashed") Defendant*, 63 MINN. L. REV. 1 (1978).

Delgado-Escueta, *Special Report: The Nature of Aggression During Epileptic Seizures*, 305 NEW ENG. J. MED. 711 (1981).

Denno, *Human Biology and Criminal Responsibility: Free Will or Free Ride?* 137 U. PA. L. REV. 615 (1988).

Dershowitz, *The Role of Psychiatry in the Sentencing Process*, 1 INT'L J. LAW & PSYCHIAT. 63 (1978).

Desai, *Complex Partial Seizures*, 30 AM. FAM. PHYS. 158 (1984).

Detre & Feldman, *Behavior Disorder Associated with Seizure States: Pharmacological and Psychosocial Management*, in EEG AND BEHAVIOR 366 (G. Glaser ed. 1963).

Donovan & Wildman, *Is the Reasonable Man Obsolete? A Critical Perspective on Self-Defense and Provocation*, 14 LOY. L.A.L. REV. 435 (1981).

Dressler, *Professor Delgado's "Brainwashing" Defense: Courting a Determinist Legal System*, 63 MINN. L. REV. 335 (1979).

Dressler, *Reaffirming the Moral Legitimacy of the Doctrine of Diminished Capacity: A Brief Reply to Professor Morse*, 75 J. CRIM. L. & CRIMINOLOGY 953 (1984).

Dressler, *Rethinking Heat of Passion: A Defense in Search of a Rationale*, 73 J. CRIM. L. & CRIMINOLOGY 421 (1982).

Eaton, *The Assessment of Mental Health*, 108 AM. J. PSYCHIAT. 81 (1951).

Edwards, *Automatism and Criminal Responsibility*, 21 MOD. L. REV. 375 (1958).

Edwards, *Automatism and Social Defence*, 8 CRIM. L.Q. 258 (1966).

Ellington, *The Electroencephalogram and Criminal Responsibility*, 3 J. FOR. MED. 115 (1956).

Elliott, *Automatism and Trial by Jury*, 6 MELBOURNE U.L. REV. 53 (1967).

Elliott, *Neurological Findings in Adult Minimal Brain Dysfunction and the Dyscontrol Syndrome*, 170 J. NERV. MENT. DIS. 680 (1982).

Elliott, *The Neurology of Explosive Rage: The Dyscontrol Syndrome*, 217 NEUROL. & NEUROPSYCHIAT. 51 (1976).

English, *The Light Between Twilight and Dusk: Federal Criminal Law and the Volitional Insanity Defense*, 40 HASTINGS L.J. 1 (1988).

Ewing, Rouse & Aderhold, *Studies of the Mechanism of Oriental Hypersensitivity to Alcohol*, 5 CURR. ALCOHOL 45 (1979).

Falconer, *Clinical, Radiological and EEG Correlations with Pathological Changes in Temporal Lobe Epilepsy and Their Significance in Surgical Treatment*, in TEMPORAL LOBE EPILEPSY 396 (M. Baldwin & P. Bailey eds. 1958).

Feldman, *Complex Partial Seizures*, in EPILEPSY: DIAGNOSIS AND MANAGEMENT (T. Browne & R. Feldman eds. 1984).

Fenwick, *Epilepsy and the Law*, 288 BR. MED. J. 1938 (1984).

Fenwick, *Murdering While Asleep*, 293 BR. MED. J. 574 (1986).

Fenwick, *Somnambulism and the Law: A Review*, 5 BEHAV. SCI. & LAW 343 (1987).

Fenwick, *The Inverse Problem: A Medical Perspective*, 32 PHYS. MED. BIOL. 5 (1987).

Fingarette, *The Concept of Mental Disease in Criminal Law Insanity Tests*, 33 U. CHI. L. REV. 229 (1966).

Fingarette, *The Perils of Powell: In Search of a Factual Foundation for the "Disease Concept of Alcoholism"*, 83 HARV. L. REV. 793 (1970).

Fleming, *A Psychiatric Concept of Acute Alcoholic Intoxication*, 92 AM. J. PSYCHIAT. 89 (1935).

Fleszar-Szumigajowa, 13 PSYCHIATRIA SAD I KRYMINAT (ARCHIVES OF COURT [FORENSIC] MEDICINE) 23 (1961).

Flor-Henry, *Ictal and Interictal Psychiatric Manifestations in Epilepsy: Specific or Non-Specific? A Critical Review of Some of the Evidence*, 13 EPILEPSIA 773 (1972).

Fox, *Physical Disorder, Consciousness, and Criminal Liability*, 63 COLUM. L. REV. 645 (1963).

Framc, *Alcoholism: Some Medico-Legal Aspects*, 2 J. FOR. MED. 151 (1955).

Fukanaga, Pasewark, Hawkins & Gudeman, *Insanity Plea: Interexaminer Agreement and Concordance of Psychiatric Opinion and Court Verdict*, 5 LAW & HUM. BEHAV. 325 (1981).

George, *The American Bar Association's Mental Health Standards: An Overview*, 53 GEO. WASH. L. REV. 338 (1985).

Giannelli, *The Admissibility of Novel Scientific Evidence: Frye v. United States a Half-Century Later*, 80 COLUM. L. REV. 1197 (1980).

Gibbs, *Medicolegal Aspects of Electroencephalography*, 24 CAN. BAR REV. 359 (1946).

Gibbs & Gibbs, *Electroencephalographic Evidence of Thalamic and Hypothalamic Epilepsy*, 1 NEUROL. 136 (1951).

Gibbs & Gibbs, *Thalamic and Hypothalamic Epilepsy*, in 2 ATLAS OF ELECTROENCEPHALOGRAPHY 329 (1952).

Gibbs, Gibbs & Lennox, *Cerebral Dysrhythmias of Epilepsy*, 39 ARC. NEUROL. PSYCH. 298 (1938).

Gibbs, Gibbs & Lennox, *Electroencephalographic Classification of Epileptic Patients and Control Subjects*, 50 ARC. NEUROL. PSYCH. 111 (1943).

Gibbs, Gibbs & Lennox, *Epilepsy: A Paroxysmal Cerebral Dysrhythmia*, 60 BRAIN 377 (1937).

Glaser, *Limbic Epilepsy in Childhood*, 144 J. NERV. MENT. DIS. 391 (1967).

Glaser, Newman & Schafer, *Interictal Psychosis in Psychomotor-Temporal Lobe Epilepsy: An EEG-Psychological Study*, in EEG AND BEHAVIOR 345 (G. Glaser ed. 1963).

Glasgow, *The Anatomy of Automatism*, 64 N.Z. MED. J. 491 (1965).

Gnanamuthu, *Confusional States and Seizures*, 84 POSTGRAD. MED. 149 (1988).

Gold, *An Untrimmed 'Beard': The Law of Intoxication as a Defence to a Criminal Charge*, 19 CRIM. L.Q. 34 (1976).

Goldstein, *Brain Research and Violent Behavior*, 30 ARC. NEUROL. 1 (1974).

Goldstein & Katz, *Abolish the "Insanity Defense"—Why Not?* 72 YALE L.J. 853 (1963).

Goodman, *Demographic Evidence in Capital Sentencing*, 39 STAN. L. REV. 499 (1987).

Gordon, Sloggett, Harvey, Kraiuhin, Rennie, Yiannikas & Meares, *Magnetoencephalography: Locating the Source of P300 via Magnetic Field Recording*, 23 CLIN. EXP. NEUROL. 101 (1987).

Gray, *Alcoholic Amnesia*, 1 CRIM. L.Q. 483 (1958-59).

Greenblatt, Levin & DiCori, *The Electroencephalogram Associated with Chronic Alcoholism, Alcoholic Psychosis and Alcoholic Convulsions*, 52 ARCH. NEUROL. PSYCHIAT. 290 (1944).

Gromska, Smoczynski & Bardzik, *Przypadek aktu Nekrofilii Dokonanego w Upojeniu Pathologicznym (A Case of Necrophilia Committed in a State of Pathological Intoxication with Alcohol)*, 3 POLISH J. PSYCH. 207 (1969).

Gross, *The Mind of a Murderer*, Medical World News, Nov. 23, 1973.

Gunn & Bonn, *Criminality and Violence in Epileptic Prisoners,* 118 BR. J. PSYCHIAT. 337 (1971).

Gunn & Fenton, *Epilepsy, Automatism, and Crime,* LANCET 1173 (June 1971).

Gunn, *Epileptic Homicide: A Case Report,* 132 BR. J. PSYCHIAT. 510 (1978).

Gunn, *Social Factors and Epileptics in Prison,* 124 BR. J. PSYCHIAT. 509 (1974).

Hall, *Intoxication and Criminal Responsibility,* 57 HARV. L. REV. 1045 (1944).

Harding, *Sane and Insane Automatism in Australia: Some Dilemmas, Developments and Suggested Reforms,* 4 INT'L J. LAW & PSYCHIAT. 73 (1981).

Hari & Antervo, *Comparison of Magneto- and Electroencephalographic Techniques in Event-Related Response Research—A Brief Survey,* in *Behavioral Neuroscience in Scandinavia,* SCAND. J. PSYCHOL. 170 (Supp. 1, 1982).

Hartmann, *Two Case Reports: Night Terrors with Sleep Walking—A Potentially Lethal Disorder,* 171 J. NERV. & MENT. DIS. 503 (1983).

Harvey, *Hypnotics and Sedatives,* in GOODMAN & GILMAN'S, THE PHARMACOLOGICAL BASIS OF THERAPEUTICS 339 (A. Gilman, L. Goodman, T. Rall & F. Murad eds. 7th ed. 1985).

Hauser, *Epidemiology of Epilepsy,* 19 ADV. NEUROL. 313 (1978).

Hawkes, Cavanagh & Fox, *Motoneuron Disease: A Disorder Secondary to Solvent Exposure?* LANCET 73 (Jan. 1989).

Heilbronner, 48 MUNCH. MED. WSCHR. 962 (1901).

Hemmingsen, Vorstrup, Clemmesen, Holm, Tfelt-Hansen, Sorensen, Hansen, Sommer & Bolwig, *Cerebral Blood Flow During Delirium Tremens and Related Clinical States Studied With Xenon-133 Inhalation Tomography,* 145 AM. J. PSYCHIAT. 1384 (1988).

Henriksen, Mogelvang & Thomsen, *Magnetic Resonance in Clinical Physiology,* 8 CLIN. PHYSIOL. 541 (1988).

Henry, *Positive Spike Discharges in the EEG and Behavior Abnormality,* in EEG AND BEHAVIOR 315 (G. Glaser ed. 1963).

Hermann, *Criminal Defenses and Pleas in Mitigation Based on Amnesia,* 4 BEHAV. SCI. & LAW 5 (1986).

Hermann, Wyler & Richey, *Epilepsy, Frontal Lobe, and Personality,* 22 BIOL. PSYCHIAT. 1055 (1987).

Herschmann, *Totschlag im Pathologischen Rausch* (Manslaughter in Pathological Intoxication), 69 ARCH. KRIMINOL. 115 (1917).

Hill, Sargant & Heppenstall, *A Case of Matricide,* LANCET 526 (1943).

Hirschmann, *Zur Kriminologic der akuten Alcoholpsychosen* (The Criminology of Acute Alcoholic Psychoses), 6 KRIMINALBIOL. GEGENWARTSFR. 55 (1964).

Hobson, *Addiction and Criminal Responsibility*, 30 MEDICO-LEGAL J. 85 (1962).

Hoff, 36 MEDIZIMISCHES KLINIK 1425 (1954).

Holland, *Automatism and Criminal Responsibility*, 25 CRIM. L.Q. 95 (1982).

Hollender & Hirsch, *Hysterical Psychosis*, 120 AM. J. PSYCHIAT. 1066 (1964).

Hollender, *Pathological Intoxication—Is There Such an Entity?* 32 J. CLIN. PSYCHIAT. 424 (1979).

Holmes, *How to Evaluate the Patient After a First Seizure*, 83 POSTGRAD. MED. 199 (1988).

Hormes, Filley & Rosenberg, *Neurologic Sequelae of Chronic Solvent Vapour Abuse*, 36 NEUROL. 698 (1986).

Howard & d'Orban, *Violence in Sleep: Medico-Legal Issues and Two Case Reports*, 1987 PSYCHOL. MED. 17.

Howard, *Automatism and Insanity*, 4 SYDNEY L. REV. 36 (1962).

Hudolin, *Complicaciones Agudas del Alcoholismo* (Acute Complications of Alcoholism), ARCH. BIOL. MED. EXP. (Supp. 3, 1969), substantially reprinted in ALCOHOL AND ALCOHOLISM (R. Popham ed. 1970).

Hughes, Cohen, Mayman, Scholl & Hendrix, *Relationship of the Magnetoencephalogram to Abnormal Activity in the Electroencephalogram*, 217 J. NEUROL. 79 (1977).

Hughes, Gianturco & Stein, *Electro-Clinical Correlations in the Positive Spike Phenomenon*, 13 ELECTROENCEPH. CLIN. NEUROPHYSIOL. 599 (1961).

Hughes, *The English Homicide Act of 1957*, 49 J. CRIM. L., CRIMINOLOGY & POLICE SCI. 521 (1959).

Hughes, *The Medicolegal EEG*, in EEG AND EVOKED POTENTIAL IN PSYCHIATRY AND BEHAVIORAL NEUROLOGY 361 (J. Hughes & W. Wilson eds. 1983).

Huszar & Ir'anyi, *Typusos es Atypusos Reszegsegi Allapotok Elkulonitesenek Elmeszakertoi Problemai* (The Differentiation of Typical and Atypical States of Intoxication According to Expert Opinion), 20 IDEGGYOGY. SZLE BP. 202 (1967).

Ingber, *A Dialectic: The Fulfillment and Decrease of Passion in Criminal Law*, 28 RUTGERS L. REV. 861 (1975).

Ir'anyi, *Die Gerichtsarztliche Beurteilung des Pathologischen Rausches* (Medicolegal Evaluation of Pathological Intoxication), 18 PSYCHIAT. NEUROL. MED. PSYCHOL. LEIPZ. 267 (1966).

Janofsky, Vandewalle & Rappeport, *Defendants Pleading Insanity: An Analysis of Outcome*, 17 BULL. AM. ACAD. PSYCHIAT. & LAW 203 (1989).

Jennings, *The Growth and Development of Automatism as a Defence in Criminal Law*, 2 OSGOODE HALL L.J. 370 (1962).

Johnson, Adinoff, Bisserbe, Martin, Rio, Rohrbaugh, Zubovic & Eckardt, *Assessment of Alcoholism-Related Organic Brain Syndromes with Positron Emission Tomography,* 10 ALCOH. CLIN. EXPER. RES. 237 (1986).

Johnson, *The Supreme Court of California 1975-1976—Forward: The Accidental Decision and How It Happens,* 65 CALIF. L. REV. 231 (1977).

Jones, *Medical Aspects of Chemical Tests for Intoxication,* 8 CLEV.-MARSHALL L. REV. 228 (1959).

Julius & Bohacek, (*The Alcoholic Psychoses in Forensic Psychiatry*), 1 NEUROPSIHIJATRIJA, ZAGREB 21 (1953).

Kadish, *The Decline of Innocence,* 26 CAMBRIDGE L.J. 273 (1968).

Kahn, *Automatism: Sane and Insane,* 1965 N.Z.L.J. 113.

Kantorovich & Constantinovich, *Effect of Alcohol in Catatonic Syndromes: Preliminary Report,* 92 AM. J. PSYCHIAT. 651 (1935).

Karpman, *On Reducing Tensions and Bridging Gaps Between Psychiatry and the Law,* 48 J. CRIM. L., CRIMINOLOGY & POLICE SCI. 164 (1957).

Kaufman, Marshall & Walker, *Activated Electroencephalography,* 58 ARCH. NEUROL. & PSYCHIAT. 533 (1947).

Kaufman, Marshall & Walker, *Metrazol Activated Electroencephalography,* 26 J. NERV. & MENT. DIS. 476 (1947).

Keedy, *A Problem of First Degree Murder: Fisher v. United States,* 99 U. PA. L. REV. 267 (1950).

Keller, *A Lexicon of Disablements Related to Alcohol Consumption,* in WORLD HEALTH ORGANIZATION, ALCOHOL-RELATED DISABILITIES (No. 32, 1966).

Keller, *A Lexicon of Disablements Related to Alcohol Consumption,* in ALCOHOL-RELATED DISABILITIES 23 (G. Edwards, M. Gross, M. Keller, J. Moser & R. Room eds. 1977).

Kelley, Solomon & Emmanuel, in HANDBOOK OF PSYCHIATRY 415 (P. Solomon & V. Patch eds. 1974).

Kelley & Reilly, *EEG, Alcohol, and Alcoholism,* in EEG AND EVOKED POTENTIALS IN PSYCHIATRY AND BEHAVIORAL NEUROLOGY 55 (J. Hughes & W. Wilson eds. 1983).

Kershman, *Syncope and Seizures,* 12 J. NEUROL., NEUROSURG. & PSYCHIAT. 25 (1949).

Kessler, Partain, Price & James, *Positron Emission Tomography: Prospects for Clinical Utility,* 22 INVEST. RADIOL. 529 (1987).

Killefer & Stern, *Chronic Effects of Hypothalamic Injury: Report of a Case of Near Total Hypothalamic Destruction Resulting from Removal of a Craniopharyngioma,* 22 ARC. NEUROL. 419 (1970).

King, *What is Disease?* 21 PHIL. SCI. 193 (1954).

Kitaguchi, Kobayashi, Tobimatsu, Goto & Kuroiwa, *Computed Tomography and Magnetic Resonance Imaging in a Young Patient with Wernicke's Encephalopathy*, 234 J. NEUROL. 449 (1987).

Klaassen, *Toxicology*, in GOODMAN & GILMAN'S, THE PHARMACOLOGICAL BASIS OF THERAPEUTICS 1592 (A. Gilman, L. Goodman, T. Rall & F. Murad eds. 7th ed. 1985).

Klighman & Goldberg, *Temporal Lobe Epilepsy and Aggression*, 160 J. NERV. MENT. DIS. 324 (1975).

Klofas & Yandrasits, *"Guilty But Mentally Ill" and the Jury Trial: A Case Study*, 24 CRIM. L. BULL. 424 (1988).

Klofas, Book Review, 16 J. CRIM. JUST. 511 (1988).

Knox, *Epileptic Automatism and Violence*, 8 MED., SCI. & LAW 96 (1968).

Konuma, *Some Topics in Forensic Psychiatric Studies on Offences During Drunkenness*, 4 JAP. J. STUD. ALCOH. 6 (1969).

Kopelman, *Amnesia: Organic and Psychogenic*, 150 BR. J. PSYCH. 517 (1987).

Kopelman, *Crime and Amnesia: A Review*, 5 BEHAV. SCI. & LAW 323 (1987).

Kosbab & Kuhnley, *Pathological Intoxication*, 15 PSYCHIAT. OP. 35 (1978).

Kotani, *EEG Studies on Endogenous Psychoses and Alcohol Intoxication*, 12 BULL. OSAKA MED. SCH. 303 (Supp. 1967).

Krafft-Ebing, 27 DTSCH. Z. STARZNEIK. 444 (1869).

Krash, *The Durham Rule and Judicial Administration of the Insanity Defense in the District of Columbia*, 70 YALE L.J. 905 (1961).

Kuh, *The Insanity Defense—An Effort to Combine Law and Reason*, 110 U. PA. L. REV. 771 (1962).

Kuten, *Der Pathologische Rausch* (Pathological Intoxication), 4 M. KLIN. 1369 (1908).

Lange, *Die "Dammerige" Form des krankhaften Alkoholrausches, ihre Kennzeichnenden Besonderheiten und ihre Abweichungen von den "klassischen" pathologischen Rauschformen* (The "Semiconscious" Form of Pathological Innebriatation [sic], Its Characteristics, and How It Differs from "Classical" Pathological Forms of Inebriation), 39 PSYCHIAT. NEUROL. MED. PSYCHOL. 193 (1987).

Langness, *Hysterical Psychosis in the New Guinea Highlands: A Bena Bena Example*, 28 PSYCH. 258 (1965).

Larner, *Insulin and Oral Hypoglycemic Drugs; Glucagon*, in GOODMAN & GILMAN'S, THE PHARMACOLOGICAL BASIS OF THERAPEUTICS 1502 (A. Gilman, L. Goodman, T. Rall & F. Murad eds. 7th ed. 1985).

Lederman, *Non-Insane and Insane Automatism: Reducing the Significance of a Problematic Distinction*, 34 INT'L & COMP. L.Q. 819 (1985).

Leenders, Gibbs, Frackowiak, Lammertsma & Jones, *Positron Emission Tomography of the Brain: New Possibilities for the Investigation of Human Cerebral Pathophysiology,* 23 PROG. NEUROBIOL. 1 (1984).

Leigh, *Automatism and Insanity,* 5 CRIM. L.Q. 160 (1962).
Lennox, *Alcohol and Epilepsy,* 2 QRTLY J. STUD. ALCOH. 1 (1941).
Lennox, *Amnesia, Real and Feigned,* 10 U. CHI. L. REV. 298 (1943).
Lennox, *Phenomena and Correlates of the Psychomotor Triad,* 1 NEUROL. 357 (1951).
Lewin, *Psychiatric Evidence in Criminal Cases for Purposes Other Than the Defense of Insanity,* 26 SYRACUSE L. REV. 1051 (1975).
Lewis, *Psychological Medicine,* in PRICE'S TEXTBOOK OF THE PRACTICE OF MEDICINE 1172 (1966).
Lewis, *Personality Factors in Alcoholic Addiction,* 1 QRTLY J. STUD. ALCOH. 21 (1940).
Lewis, et al., *Psychotic Symptomatology in a Juvenile Court Clinic Population,* 12 J. AM. ACAD. CHILD PSYCHIAT. 660 (1973).
Lewis, Pincus, Shanok & Glaser, *Psychomotor Epilepsy and Violence in a Group of Incarcerated Adolescent Boys,* 139 AM. J. PSYCHIAT. 882 (1982).
Lewis, *Psychiatric Resultants of Alcoholism: Alcoholism and Mental Disease,* 2 QRTLY J. STUD. ALCOH. 293 (1941).
Lewis, Shanok, Pincus, et al., *Violent Juvenile Delinquents: Psychiatric, Neurological, Psychological and Abuse Factors,* 18 J. AM. ACAD. CHILD PSYCHIAT. 307 (1979).
Lion, Azcarate & Koepke, *"Paradoxical Rage Reactions" During Psychotropic Medication,* 36 DIS. NERV. SYS. 557 (1975).
Lion, *Medical Treatment of Violent Individuals,* in VIOLENCE AND THE VIOLENT INDIVIDUAL 343 (J. Hays, T. Roberts & K. Solway eds. 1981).
Lisman, *Alcoholic "Blackout": State-Dependent Learning?* 30 ARCH. GEN. PSYCHIAT. 46 (1974).
Loiseau & Henry, *Crime et Epilepsie* (Crime and Epilepsy), 5 BORDEAUX MEDICAL 2609 (1972).
Louisell & Hazard, *Insanity as a Defense: The Bifurcated Trial,* 49 CALIF. L. REV. 805 (1961).
Lustig, *Uber Alkoholismusprobleme in Sowjetischer und europaischer Sicht* (Problems of Alcoholism in Soviet and European Views), 115 WIEN. MED. WSCHR. 400 (1965).

MacDonald, *Alcoholism and Drug Addiction,* 21 OHIO ST. L.J. 96 (1960).
MacDonald, *Alcoholism as a Medicolegal Problem,* 11 CLEV.-MARSHALL L. REV. 1 (1962).
Mackay, *Intoxication as a Factor in Automatism,* 1982 CRIM. L. REV. 146.
Mackay, *Non-Organic Automatism—Some Recent Developments,* 1980 CRIM. L. REV. 350.

Malamud, *Psychiatric Disorder with Intracranial Tumors of Limbic System*, 17 ARC. NEUROL. 113 (1967).

Malamud, *Psychiatric Symptoms and the Limbic Lobe*, 22 BULL. L.A. SOC. NEUROL. PSYCHIAT. 131 (1957).

Maletzky, *The Alcohol Provocation Test*, 39 J. CLIN. PSYCHIAT. 403 (1978).

Maletzky, *The Diagnosis of Pathological Intoxication*, 37 QRTLY J. STUD. ALCOH. 1215 (1976).

Maletzky, *The Episodic Dyscontrol Syndrome*, 34 DIS. NERV. SYST. 178 (1973).

Maletzky, *Treatable Violence*, 19 RES. & STAFF PHYS. 40 (1973).

Mandelzys & Marceau, *Relationship of Violence to Alpha Levels in a Biofeedback Training Paradigm*, 37 J. CLIN. PSYCHOL. 202 (1981).

Mander, Weppner, Chick, Morton & Best, *An NMR Study of Cerebral Oedema and Its Biological Correlates During Withdrawal From Alcohol*, 23 ALCOH. & ALCOHOLISM 97 (1988).

Mandiberg, *Protecting Society and Defendants Too: The Constitutional Dilemma of Mental Abnormality and Intoxication Defenses*, 53 FORDHAM L. REV. 221 (1984).

Marcus & Coulston, *Water-Soluble Vitamins: The Vitamin B Complex and Ascorbic Acid*, in GOODMAN & GILMAN'S, THE PHARMACOLOGICAL BASIS OF THERAPEUTICS 1551 (A. Gilman, L. Goodman, T. Rall & F. Murad eds. 7th ed. 1985).

Marinacci, *A Special Type of Temporal Lobe (Psychomotor) Seizures Following Ingestion of Alcohol*, 28 BULL. L.A. NEUROL. SOC. 241 (1963).

Marinacci & Von Hagen, *Alcohol and Temporal Lobe Dysfunction: Some of Its Psychomotor Equivalents*, 3 BEHAV. NEURO-PSYCHIAT. 2 (1972).

Marinacci, *The Electroencephalogram in Forensic Alcoholism*, 20 BULL. L.A. NEUROL. SOC. 177 (1955).

Marshall & Walker, *The Value of Electroencephalography in the Prognostication and Prognosis of Post-Traumatic Epilepsy*, 2 EPILEPSIA 138 (1961).

Martin, Adinoff, Weingartner, Mukherjee & Eckardt, *Alcoholic Organic Brain Disease: Nosology and Pathophysiologic Mechanisms*, 10 PROG. NEURO-PSYCHOPHARMACOL. & BIOL. PSYCHIAT. 147 (1986).

May & Ebaugh, *Pathological Intoxication, Alcoholic Hallucinosis, and Other Reactions to Alcohol: A Clinical Study*, 14 QRTLY J. STUD. ALCOH. 200 (1953).

Mayet, *Les Differentes Formes Anentales de l'Ivresses Alcoolique; Ivress Normale; Ivresses Abnormales; Peudo-Ivresses Pathologigues*, 16 PROV. M. 74 (1902).

McCaldon, *Automatism*, 91 CAN. MED. ASS'N J. 914 (1964).

Mednick, Volavka, Gabrielli & Itil, *EEG (Electroencephalogram) as a Predictor of Antisocial Behavior*, 19 CRIMINOLOGY 219 (1981).

Meggendorfer, *Intoxikationspsychosen*, in 7 HANDBUCH DER GEISTESKRANKHEITEN (O. Bumke ed. 1928).

Meyer, *Alcohol as a Psychiatric Problem*, in ALCOHOL AND MAN 293 (H. Emerson ed. 1935).

Michel, *Le Probleme de la Responsabilite Penale dans les Differentes Formes de L'Ivress Ethylique* (The Problem of Penal Responsibility in Different Forms of Alcohol Intoxication), 4 REV. ALCSME 181 (1957).

Mickenberg, *A Pleasant Surprise: The GBMI Verdict Has Both Succeeded in Its Own Right and Successfully Preserved the Traditional Role of the Insanity Defense*, 55 U. CIN. L. REV. 943 (1987).

Miller, Book Review, 15 J. PSYCHIAT. & L. 571 (1987).

Mitchell, *Culpable Mental Disorder and Criminal Liability*, 8 INT'L J. LAW & PSYCHIAT. 273 (1986).

Mitchell, *The Intoxicated Offender—Refuting the Legal and Medical Myths*, 11 INT'L J. LAW & PSYCHIAT. 77 (1988).

Mizoi, Tatsuno, Adachi, Kogame & Fukunaga, *Alcohol Sensitivity Related to Polymorphism of Alcohol-Metabolizing Enzymes in Japanese*, 18 PHARMACOL. BIOCHEM. BEHAV. 127 (Supp. 1, 1983).

Moenssens, *Admissibility of Scientific Evidence—An Alternative to the Frye Rule*, 25 WM. & MARY L. REV. 545 (1984).

Monkemoller, *Der Pathologische Rauschzustand und Seine Forensische Bedeutung* (The Pathological Intoxication State and Its Forensic Significance), 59 ARCH. KUMANTHROP. 120 (1914).

Monopolis & Lion, *Problems in the Diagnosis of Intermittent Explosive Disorder*, 140 AM. J. PSYCHIAT. 1200 (1983).

Monroe, *Brain Dysfunction in Prisoners*, in VIOLENCE AND THE VIOLENT INDIVIDUAL 75 (J. Harp, T. Roberts & K. Solway eds. 1981).

Monroe, *Episodic Behavioral Disorders and Limbic Ictus*, 26 COMP. PSYCHIAT. 466 (1985).

Monroe, *Episodic Sexual Disorders*, 10 MED. ASPECTS OF HUMAN SEXUALITY 50 (1976).

Morozov, Kachayev & Lukacher, *Characteristics of Forensic Psychiatric Examination of Pathological and Simple Alcohol Intoxication*, 17 SUDEBNO-MEDITSINSKAIA EKSPERTIZA 51 (April-June 1974).

Morozov, Kachayev & Lukacher, *On the Pathogenesis of Pathological Intoxication*, 73 ZHURNAL NEUROPATHOLOGII PSITHIATRII 1196 (1973).

Morse, *The Aberrational Man—A Tour de Force of Legal Psychiatry*, 13 J. FOR. SCI. 1 (1968).

Morse, *Undiminished Confusion in Diminished Capacity*, 75 J. CRIM. L. & CRIMINOLOGY 1 (1984).

Murphy, *Involuntary Acts and Criminal Liability*, 81 ETHICS 332 (1971).

National Council on Alcoholism, Criteria Committee, *Criteria for the Diagnosis of Alcoholism*, 129 AM. J. PSYCHIAT. 127 (1972).

Nemerson, *Alcoholism, Intoxication, and the Criminal Law,* 10 CARDOZO L. REV. 393 (1988).

Newman, *Alcohol Injected Intravenously: Some Psychological and Psychopathological Effects in Man,* 91 AM. J. PSYCHIAT. 1343 (1935).

Note, 9 U. ARK. LITTLE ROCK L.J. 657 (1986-87).

Note, *Amnesia, Automatism and Insanity,* 79 S. AFR. L.J. 338 (1962).

Note, *Alcohol Abuse and the Law,* 94 HARV. L. REV. 1660 (1981).

Note, *Expert Services and the Indigent Criminal Defendant: The Constitutional Mandate of Ake v. Oklahoma,* 84 MICH. L. REV. 1326 (1986).

Note, *Mental Illness and the Law,* 36 B.U.L. REV. 254 (1956).

Note, *Pathological Intoxication and the Voluntarily Intoxicated Criminal Offender,* 1969 UTAH L. REV. 419.

Note, *The Legal Problems of Epilepsy,* 29 TEMP. L.Q. 364 (1956).

Note, *The Right to a Partisan Psychiatric Expert: Might Indigency Preclude Insanity?* 61 N.Y.U. L. REV. 703 (1986).

Note, *The Voluntary Intoxication Defense in Iowa,* 73 IOWA L. REV. 935 (1988).

Note, *Toward an Ohio Natural Death Act: The Need for Living Will Legislation,* 46 OHIO ST. L.J. 1019 (1985).

Note, *Volitional Fault and the Intoxicated Criminal Offender,* 36 U. CIN. L. REV. 258 (1967).

O'Connell, *Amnesia and Homicide,* 10 BR. J. DELINQ. 262 (1960).

O'Connor, *The Voluntary Act,* 15 MED., SCI. & LAW 31 (1975).

Ochernal & Szewczyk, *On the Problem of Abnormal Alcoholic Intoxication in Forensic and Psychiatric Judgments,* 30 PSYCHIAT. NEUROL. MED. PSYCHOL. 365 (1978).

Orchard, *Drunkenness as a "Defence" to Crime,* 1 CRIM. L.J. 59 (1977).

Orne, Book Review, 46 A.B.A. J. 81 (1960).

Osakwe, Book Review, 59 TUL. L. REV. 858 (1985).

Oswald, *Gutachten uber einen Fall von Pathologischen Rauschzustand* (Expert Opinion on a Case of Pathological Intoxication Condition), 10 ARZTE. SACHVERST ZTG. 223 (1904).

Oswald & Evans, *Serious Violence During Sleepwalking,* 147 BR. J. PSYCHIAT. 688 (1985).

Ounsted, *Aggression and Epilepsy,* 13 J. PSYCHOSOM. RES. 237 (1969).

Packer, *The Model Penal Code and Beyond,* 63 COLUM. L. REV. 594 (1963).

Paraire, Juillet, Delivre & Lefevbre, *Problems de Toxicophilie Chez les Jeunes Adultes au Stade des Obligations Militaires (Problems of Drug Addiction in Young Adults at the Time of Military Duty),* 128 ANN. MED.-PSYCHOL. 93 (1970).

Paulsen, *Intoxication as a Defense to Crime,* 1961 U. ILL. L.F. 1.

Perr, *Pathological Intoxication and Alcohol Idiosyncratic Intoxication—Part I: Diagnostic and Clinical Aspects,* 31 J. FOR. SCI. 806 (1986).

Perr, *Pathological Intoxication and Alcohol Idiosyncratic Intoxication—Part II: Legal Aspects,* 31 J. FOR. SCI. 812 (1986).

Petrila, *The Insanity Defense and Other Mental Health Dispositions in Missouri,* 5 INT'L J. LAW & PSYCHIAT. 81 (1982).

Pincus & Tucker, *Violence in Children and Adults: A Neurological View,* 17 J. AM. ACAD. CHILD PSYCHIAT. 277 (1978).

Pincus, *Can Violence Be A Manifestation of Epilepsy?,* 30 NEUROL. 304 (1980).

Pionkowski, Wojdyslawska & Patura, *Upojenie Alkoholowe na Podlozu Patologicznym* (*Pathological Intoxication with Alcohol*), 9 PSYCHIAT. POL. 161 (1975).

Platt & Diamond, *The Origins and Development of the "Wild Beast" Concept of Mental Illness and Its Relation to Theories of Criminal Responsibility,* 1 J. HIST. BEHAV. SCI. 355 (1965).

Platt & Diamond, *The Origins of the "Right and Wrong" Test of Criminal Responsibility and Its Subsequent Development in the United States: An Historical Survey,* 54 CALIF. L. REV. 1227 (1966).

Podolsky, *Somnambulistic Homicide,* 1 MED., SCI. & LAW 260 (1961).

Podolsky, *The Chemical Brew of Criminal Behavior,* 45 J. CRIM. L., CRIMINOLOGY & POLICE SCI. 675 (1955).

Podolsky, *The Epileptic Murderer,* 30 MEDICO-LEGAL J. 176 (1962).

Pollner, *A Koros Reszegseg Fogalma es a Hazai Gyakorlat* (The Concept of Pathological Intoxication and Its Application in Our Country), in TANULMANYOK AS ALKOHOLIZMUS PSZICHIATRIAI KOVETKEZMENYCIROL (Results of Psychiatric Studies on Alcoholism) 65 (I. Tariska, G. Gereby & G. Kardos eds. 1969).

Pollock, *The Prevalence of Mental Disease Due to Alcoholism,* in H. EMERSON, ALCOHOL AND MAN 345 (1935).

Prevezer, *Automatism and Involuntary Conduct,* 1958 CRIM. L. REV. 361.

Profous, *Problems of Pathological Drunkenness and Pathological Effects in Tipsyness in Forensic Psychiatric Practice,* 70 CESK. PSYCHIATR. 29 (1974).

Puxon, *The Defence of Automatism,* 106 SOL. J. 163 (1962).

Quigley, *Reform of the Intoxication Defence,* 33 MCGILL L.J. (REVUE DE DROIT DE MCGILL) 2 (1987).

Quigley, *Specific and General Nonsense,* 11 DALHOUSIE L.J. 75 (1987).

Quirk, *Treatment For Epileptic Alcoholism,* 7 ONTARIO PSYCHOL. 36 (1976).

Racz, *Legfelsobb Birosag Elvi Allasfoglalasa az Abortiv Pathologias Reszegsegrol* (The Position of the Supreme Court on Abortive Pathological Alcoholism), 1 ALKOHOLOGIA, BP. 36 (1970).

Raecke, *Zur Lehre vom Pathologischen Rausche* (Toward a Theory of Pathological Intoxication, 53 VJSCHR. GER. M. 49 (1917).

Rakhal'skii, *O Svoyeobraznykh Pskhoticheskikh Sostoyaniyakh pre Alkogol'noi Intoksikatsii* (On Atypical Psychotic States in Alcohol Intoxication), 57 ZH. NEVROPAT. 1299 (1957).

Rall & Schleifer, *Drugs Effective in the Therapy of the Epilepsies,* in GOODMAN & GILMAN'S, THE PHARMACOLOGICAL BASIS OF THERAPEUTICS 446 (A. Gilman, L. Goodman, T. Rall & F. Murad eds. 7th ed. 1985).

Ramani & Gumnit, *Intensive Monitoring of Epileptic Patients With a History of Episodic Aggression,* 38 ARC. NEUROL. 570 (1981).

Rapaport, *Consciousness: A Psychopathological and Psychodynamic View,* in PROBLEMS OF CONSCIOUSNESS: TRANSACTIONS OF THE SECOND CONFERENCE 18 (H. Abramson ed. 1951).

Raschka, *Sleep and Violence,* 29 CAN. J. PSYCHIAT. 132 (1984).

Ratner & Shapiro, *The Episodic Dyscontrol Syndrome and Criminal Responsibility,* 7 BULL. AM. ACAD. PSYCHIAT. & LAW 422 (1979).

Rauch, *Zur Behandlung der akuten Alkoholvergiftung* (The Treatment of Acute Alcohol Poisoning) 45 MED. KLINIK 1348 (1950).

Reckel, *Pathological Intoxication in Forensic-Psychiatric Evaluations of Alcoholic Intoxication,* 151 ARCH. KRIMINOL. 65 (1973).

Reeves & Plum, *Hyperphagia, Rage, and Dementia Accompanying a Ventromedialhypothalamic Neoplasm,* 20 ARC. NEUROL. 616 (1969).

Reinl, *Alcohol Hypersensitivity Following Contact with the Fungicide Tetramethylthiuramdisulfide (TMTD),* 22 ARCH. TOXIKOL. 12 (1966).

Ritchie, *The Aliphatic Alcohols,* in GOODMAN & GILMAN'S, THE PHARMACOLOGICAL BASIS OF THERAPEUTICS 372 (A. Gilman, L. Goodman, T. Rall & F. Murad eds. 7th ed. 1985).

Ritter, *Ueber die Forensische Bedeutung des Normalen und Pathologischen Rausches* (On the Forensic Significance of Normal and Pathological Intoxication), 13 MSCHR. PSYCHT. NEUR. 36 (1903).

Rix, *'Alcohol Intoxication' or 'Drunkenness': Is There a Difference?* 29 MED., SCI. & LAW 100 (1989).

Robinson, *Causing the Conditions of One's Own Defense: A Study in the Limits of Theory in Criminal Law Doctrine,* 71 VA. L. REV. 1 (1985).

Robinson & Grall, *Element Analysis in Defining Criminal Liability: The Model Penal Code and Beyond,* 35 STAN. L. REV. 681 (1983).

Robinson, *Criminal Law Defenses: A Systematic Analysis,* 82 COLUM. L. REV. 199 (1982).

Robinson, *Some Thoughts on the Culpability Provisions of the Proposed Federal Criminal Code,* 72 J. CRIM. L. & CRIMINOLOGY 488 (1981).

ROCKY MOUNTAIN NEWS, June 20, 1988, at 44.

Rodin, *Psychomotor Epilepsy and Aggressive Behavior,* 28 ARCH. GEN. PSYCHIAT. 210 (1973).

Rogers, Bloom & Manson, *Insanity Defenses: Contested or Conceded?* 141 AM. J. PSYCHIAT. 885 (1984).

Rommeney, *Ungewohnliche Formen des Alkoholrausches* (Unusual Forms of Alcohol Intoxication), 41 DTSCH. Z. GES. GERICHTL. MED. 277 (1952).

Rose, *Criminal Responsibility and Competency as Influenced by Organic Disease*, 35 MO. L. REV. 326 (1970).

Rose, Sato, Smith, Porter, Theodore, Friauf, Bonner & Jabbari, *Localization of Magnetic Interictal Discharges in Temporal Lobe Epilepsy*, 22 ANN. NEUROL. 348 (1987).

Rose, Smith & Sato, *Magnetoencephalography and Epilepsy Research*, 238 SCIENCE 329 (1987).

Rosenthal, *Violence Is Predictable*, 48 TODAY'S HEALTH 56 (1970).

Rozhnov, *Alcoholism and Other Drug Addictions*, in FORENSIC PSYCHIATRY 343 (G. Morozov & I. Kalashnik eds. M. Vale trans. 1970).

Rubinsky & Brandt, *Amnesia and Criminal Law: A Clinical Overview*, 4 BEHAV. SCI. & LAW 27 (1986).

Sato & Smith, *Magnetoencephalography*, 2 J. CLIN. NEUROPHYSIOL. 173 (1985).

Saunders, *Voluntary Acts and the Criminal Law: Justifying Culpability Based on the Existence of Volition*, 49 U. PITT. L. REV. 443 (1988).

Schabas, *Intoxication and Culpability: Towards an Offence of Criminal Intoxication*, 42 U. TORONTO FAC. L. REV. 147 (1984).

Schacter, *On the Relation Between Genuine and Simulated Amnesia*, 4 BEHAV. SCI. & LAW 47 (1986).

Schatzman, *To Sleep, Perchance to Kill*, 110 NEW SCIENTIST 60 (1986).

Schenk, *Der Pathologische Rausch* (Pathological Intoxication), 26 D. MED. ZTG. 657 (1905).

Schipkowensky, *Zur Klinik des Pathologischen Rausches* (On Clinical Aspects of Pathological Intoxication), 159 ZBL. GES. NEUROL. PSYCHIAT. 21 (1960).

Schroeder, *Intoxikationspsychosen*, in HANDBUCH DER PSYCHIATRIE 180 (G. Aschaffenburg ed. 1912).

Schultze, 20 MEDIZINISCHERS KLINIK 581 (1921).

Schwade & Geiger, *Abnormal Electroencephalographic Findings in Severe Behavior Disorders*, 17 DIS. NERV. SYST. 307 (1956).

Schwade & Geiger, *Behavior Disorders of the Impulsive-Compulsive Type with Consistent Abnormal EEG Findings*, 7 ELECTRO-ENCEPH. CLIN. NEUROPHYSIOL. 473 (1955).

Schwade & Geiger, *Matricide with Electroencephalographic Evidence of Thalamic or Hypothalamic Disorder*, 14 DIS. NERV. SYST. 18 (1953).

Schwade & Geiger, *Severe Behavior Disorders with Abnormal Electroencephalograms*, 21 DIS. NERV. SYST. 616 (1960).

Schwade & Otto, *Homicide as a Manifestation of Thalamic or Hypothalamic Disorder with Abnormal Electroencephalographic Findings,* 52 WIS. MED. J. 171 (1953).

SCIENTIFIC AMERICAN (Oct. 1938).

Seelert, *Zur Frage der Entwicklungsbedingungen des Pathologischen Rausche,* 86 MSCHR. PSYCHIAT. NEUROL. 191 (1933).

Semenov, *Epilepsy,* in FORENSIC PSYCHIATRY 231 (G. Morozov & I. Kalashnik eds. M. Vale trans. 1970).

Sendor, *Crime as Communication: An Interpretive Theory of the Insanity Defense and the Mental Elements of Crime,* 74 GEO. L.J. 1371 (1986).

Serafetinides, *Aggressiveness in Temporal Lobe Epileptics and Its Relation to Cerebral Dysfunction and Environmental Factors,* 6 EPILEPSIA 33 (1965).

Sherwin, *Neurobiological Basis of Psychopathology Associated with Epilepsy,* in EPILEPSY: A HANDBOOK FOR THE MENTAL HEALTH PROFESSIONAL 77 (H. Sands ed. 1982).

Siebert, 38 NEUROL. ZBL. 610 (1919).

Sim, *The Involuntary Actus Reus,* 25 MOD. L. REV. 741 (1962).

Singer, *Insanity Acquittal in the Seventies: Observations and Empirical Analysis of One Jurisdiction,* 2 MENT. DIS. L. REP. 406 (1978).

Singh, *History of the Defence of Drunkenness in English Criminal Law,* 49 L.Q. REV. 528 (1933).

Sipkovenski, *Nozoloskoj Problematici Patoloskog Pijanstva* (On the Nosological Problems of Pathological Drunkenness), 8 ALKOHOLIZAM, BEOGRAD 5 (1968).

Skelton, *Alcohol, Violent Behavior, and the Electroencephalogram,* 63 S. MED. J. 465 (1970).

Slobogin, *The Guilty But Mentally Ill Verdict: An Idea Whose Time Should Not Have Come,* 53 GEO. WASH. L. REV. 494 (1985).

Slovenko, *Disposition of the Insanity Acquitee,* 11 J. PSYCHIAT. & L. 97, 109 (1983).

Smith, *Case Comment on D.P.P. v. Majewski,* 1976 CRIM. L.R. 374.

Smith, *Legal Recognition of Neocortical Death,* 71 CORNELL L. REV. 850 (1986).

Smith, *Medico-Legal Facets of Epilepsy,* 31 TEX. L. REV. 765 (1953).

Spirer, *Biochemistry as a Defense,* 4 MIAMI L.Q. 1 (1949).

Spitzer & Williams, *Introduction,* in DSM-III-R.

Stafford-Clark & Taylor, *Clinical and EEG Studies of Prisoners Charged with Murder,* 12 J. NEUROL., NEUROSURG. & PSYCHIAT. 325 (1949).

Stapel, 29 MSCH. PSYCHIAT. NEUROL. 216 (1911).

Stehle, *Thalamic Dysfunction Involved in Destructive-Aggressive Behavior Directed Against Persons and Property,* 12 ELECTROENCEPH. CLIN. NEUROPHYSIOL. 264 (1960).

Stevens & Hermann, *Temporal Lobe Epilepsy, Psychopathology, and Violence: The State of the Evidence,* 31 NEUROL. 1127 (1981).

Stevens, *Psychiatric Aspects of Epilepsy*, 49 J. CLIN. PSYCHIAT. 49 (1988).

Stone, McDaniel, Hughes & Hermann, *Episodic Dyscontrol Disorder and Paroxysmal EEG Abnormalities: Successful Treatment with Carbamazepine*, 21 BIOL. PSYCHIAT. 208 (1986).

Strauss & Wechsler, *Clinical and Electroencephalographic Studies of Changes of Cerebral Function Associated with Variations in the Blood Sugar*, 102 AM. J. PSYCHIAT. 36 (1945).

Strauss, *Las Tosicofrenias Alcoholicas en la Republica de Panama* (Alcoholic Psychoses in the Republic of Panama), 13 BOL. ASS'N MED. NAC. PANAMA 65 (1950).

Stuchlik, *Soudne Psychiatricky Vyznam Paticke Opilosti* (Significance of Pathological Intoxication in Forensic Psychiatry), 66 CSL. PSYCHIAT. 289 (1970).

Sullivan, *Self Induced and Recurring Automatism*, 123 NEW L.J. 1093 (1973).

Sutherling, Crandall, Darcey, Becker, Levesque & Barth, *The Magnetic and Electric Fields Agree with Intracranial Localizations of Somatosensory Cortex*, 38 NEUROL. 1705 (1988).

Swartz, *"Mental Disease": The Groundwork for Legal Analysis and Legislative Action*, 111 U. PA. L. REV. 389 (1963).

Tarsh, Letter, *On Serious Violence During Sleepwalking*, 148 BR. J. PSYCHIAT. 476 (1986).

Taylor, *Partial Insanity as Affecting the Degree of Crime—A Commentary on Fisher v. United States*, 34 CALIF. L. REV. 625 (1946).

Teixeira, 19 REV. MED. PARANA 194 (1950).

Terrell, Letter, *Behavioral Dyscontrol Associated With Combined Use of Alprazolam and Ethanol*, 145 AM. J. PSYCHIAT. 1313 (1988).

Thompson, *Acute and Chronic Alcoholic Conditions*, in 2 AMERICAN HANDBOOK OF PSYCHIATRY 1203 (S. Arieti ed. 1959).

Thompson, *Legal Aspects of Pathological Intoxication (Alcoholic Insanity)*, 2 J. SOCIAL THEORY 182 (1956).

Thompson, *Relationship of Sexual Psychopathy to Psychomotor Epilepsy and Its Variants*, 121 J. NERV. & MENT. DIS. 374 (1955).

Thompson, *The Electroencephalogram in Acute Pathological Alcoholic Intoxication*, 28 BULL. L.A. NEUROL. SOC. 217 (1963).

Thompson, *The General Practitioner and the Dangerous Patient*, 11 G.P. (KANSAS CITY) 59 (1955).

Tiffany & Anderson, *Legislating the Necessity Defense in Criminal Law*, 52 DEN. L.J. 839 (1975).

Tizard, *The Personality of Epileptics: A Discussion of the Evidence*, 59 PSYCHOL. BULL. 196 (1962).

Tobben, *Ein Beitrag zur Forensischen Bedeutung des Pathologischen Rausches* (A Contribution to the Forensic Significance of Pathological Intoxication), 33 D.Z. GES-GER M. 103 (1940).

Tomlinson, *Subcutaneous Insulin Therapy: An Analysis of 300 Cases,* 22 PSYCHIAT. Q. 609 (1949).

Turunen, *Acute Alcohol-Induced Psychic Disturbances,* 88 DUODECIM 310 (1972).

Venzlaff, *Die "Pathologischen" Alkoholreaktionen-Atiologie, Klinik and Forensisch-Psychiatrische Beurtelung* (The "Pathological" Alcohol Reactions; Etiology, Clinical Diagnosis and Forensic-Psychiatric Assessment), 47 MED. WELT 2623 (1965).

Verdeaux, *Etude Neuropsychiatrique et Electroencephalographique des Delinquents* (Neuropsychiatric and Electroencephalographic Study of Delinquents), 10 RIVISTA DI NEUROBIOLOGIA 1180 (1964).

Victor, *The Pathophysiology of Alcoholic Epilepsy,* 46 RES. NERV. MENT. DIS. 431 (1968).

Victor, *The Role of Alcohol in the Production of Seizures,* 4 MOD. PROBL. PHARMACOPSYCHIAT. 185 (1970).

Virkkunen, *Reactive Hypoglycemic Tendency Among Habitually Violent Offenders,* 8 NEUROPSYCHOBIOL. 35 (1982).

Volkow, Mullani, Gould, Adler, Guynn, Overall & Dewey, *Effects of Acute Alcohol Intoxication on Cerebral Blood Flow Measured with PET,* 24 PSYCHIAT. RES. 201 (1988).

Voss, 31 ZBL. NERVENHEILK 678 (1908).

Wachkoly, *Zur Kasuistik des Pathologischen Alkoholrausches* (Toward a Formal Ethical Theory of Pathological Alcohol Intoxication), 11 BEITR. GER. M. (1931).

Walker, *Murder or Epilepsy?* 133 J. NERV. & MENT. DIS. 430 (1961).

Walter, Colbert, Goegler, Palmer & Bond, *A Controlled Study of the Fourteen- and Six-per-Second EEG Pattern,* 2 ARCH. GEN. PSYCHIAT. 559 (1960).

Walton, *Some Observations on the Value of Electroencephalography in Medico-Legal Practice,* 31 MEDICO-LEGAL J. 15 (1963).

Wasik, *Codification: Mental Disorder and Intoxication Under the Draft Criminal Code,* 50 J. CRIM. L. 393 (1986).

Wechsler, *Codification of Criminal Law in the United States: The Model Penal Code,* 68 COLUM. L. REV. 1425 (1968).

Wechsler, *Revision and Codification of Penal Law in the United States,* 7 DALHOUSIE L.J. 219 (1983).

Weihofen, *The Definition of Mental Illness,* 21 OHIO ST. L.J. 1 (1960).

Weinberg, *Epilepsy and the Alternatives for a Criminal Defense,* 27 CASE W. RES. L. REV. 771 (1977).

Weinberg, Brickett, Robertson, Harrop, Cheyne, Crisp, Baff & Dykstra, *The Magnetoencephalographic Localisation of Source-Systems in the Brain: Early and Late Components of Event Related Potentials,* 4 ALCOHOL 339 (1987).

Wertham, *Psychoauthoritarianism and the Law,* 22 U. CHI. L. REV. 336 (1955).

Wexler, *Redefining the Insanity Problem,* 53 GEO. WASH. L. REV. 528 (1985).

Wilder, *Sugar Metabolism in Its Relation to Criminology,* in HANDBOOK OF CORRECTIONAL PSYCHOLOGY 124 (R. Lindner & R. Seliger eds. 1947).

Williams, *Intoxication and Specific Intent,* 126 NEW L.J. 658 (1976).

Williams, *Murder—Drunkenness—Insane and Non-Insane Automatism,* 1962 CAMBRIDGE L.J. 3 (1962).

Williams, *Provocation and the Reasonable Man,* 1954 CRIM. L. REV. 740.

Winkler & Train, *Acts of Violence with Electroencephalographic Changes,* 20 J. CLIN. EXP. PSYCHOPATH. 223 (1959).

Wright, *Variations in States of Awareness in Schizophrenic Patients,* in PROBLEMS OF CONSCIOUSNESS: TRANSACTIONS OF THE SECOND CONFERENCE (H. Abramson ed. 1951).

Yoshida, *Differences in the Isozymes Involved in Alcohol Metabolism Between Caucasians and Orientals,* 8 ISOZYMES CURR. TOP. BIOL. MED. RES. 245 (1983).

Yudofsky & Silver, *Psychiatric Aspects of Brain Injury: Trauma, Stroke and Tumor,* in 4 PSYCHIATRY UPDATE 142 (1985).

Zakowska-Dabrowska & Strzyzewski, *Value of Experimental Administration of Alcohol in the Diagnosis of So-Called Pathological Intoxication,* 3 PSYCHIAT. POLSK. 565 (1969).

Ziskind & Bayley, *Hyperinsulinism,* 23 J. LAB. & CLIN. MED. 231 (1937).

MISCELLANEOUS (REPORTS)

AMERICAN LAW INSTITUTE, 1984 ANNUAL REPORT 20.

AMERICAN LAW INSTITUTE, MODEL PENAL CODE (Proposed Official Draft 1962).

AMERICAN LAW INSTITUTE, 1 MODEL PENAL CODE AND COMMENTARIES (1985).

AMERICAN LAW INSTITUTE, 2 MODEL PENAL CODE AND COMMENTARIES (1980).

AMERICAN LAW INSTITUTE, MODEL PENAL CODE (Tent. Draft No. 4, 1955).

AMERICAN LAW INSTITUTE, MODEL PENAL CODE (Tent. Draft No. 9, 1959).

1955 AMERICAN LAW INSTITUTE, PROCEEDINGS.

HEARINGS ON REFORM OF THE FEDERAL CRIMINAL LAWS, BEFORE THE SUBCOMM. ON CRIMINAL LAWS & PROCEDURES OF THE SENATE JUDICIARY COMM., 92nd Cong., 2d Sess., pt. 3, subpt. C, (1972).

KY. CRIM. COMM'N, KY. PENAL CODE, § 235, commentary (Final Draft 1971).

LEGIS. SERV. COMM'N, PROPOSED OHIO CRIM. CODE (1971).

NAT'L COMM'N ON REFORM OF FED. CRIMINAL LAWS, WORKING PAPERS (1970).

NAT'L COMM'N ON REFORM OF FED. CRIMINAL LAWS, *Consultant's Report on Intoxication Defense; Section 502* [Robinson and Green] (1969), 1 WORKING PAPERS 223 (1970).

NAT'L COMM'N ON REFORM OF THE FED. CRIMINAL LAWS, STUDY DRAFT (1970).

NAT'L MENTAL HEALTH ASS'N, MYTHS AND REALITIES: A REPORT OF THE NAT'L COMM'N ON THE INSANITY DEFENSE (1983).

REPORT OF THE COMMITTEE ON MENTALLY ABNORMAL OFFENDERS, CMND. 6244 (1975).

ROYAL COMMISSION ON THE LAW RELATING TO MENTAL ILLNESS AND MENTAL DEFICIENCY (1954-1957), REPORT CMND. 169, H.M.S.O. (1957).

STATE OF MD., COMM'N ON CRIM. LAW, 1 PROPOSED CRIM. CODE (1972).

CASES

Alcosiba, Territory v., 36 Haw. 231 (1942).
Alerte, People v., 120 Ill. App. 3d 962, 458 N.E.2d 1106 (1983).
Alie, State v., 82 W. Va. 601, 96 S.E. 1011 (1918).
Anderson, People v., 63 Cal. 2d 351, 46 Cal. Rptr. 763, 406 P.2d 43 (1965).
Armstead v. State, 227 Md. 73, 175 A.2d 24 (1961).
Arnold's Case 16, How. St. Tr. 695 (1724).
Austin, People v., 270 Cal. App. 2d 845, 76 Cal. Rptr. 154 (1969).

Babbit, People v., 45 Cal. 3d 660, 248 Cal. Rptr. 69, 755 P.2d 253 (1988).
Baldwin, State v., 276 N.C. 690, 174 S.E.2d 526 (1970).
Barber, People v., 115 N.Y. 475, 22 N.E. 182 (1889).
Barbour v. State, 262 Ala. 297, 78 So. 2d 328 (1954).
Barefoot v. Estelle, 463 U.S. 880, 103 S. Ct. 3383, 77 L. Ed. 2d 1090 (1983).
Bass, United States v., 490 F.2d 846 (5th Cir. 1974).
Bauer v. Estate of Bauer, 687 S.W.2d 410 (Tex. Ct. App. 1985).
Bell, State v., 471 So. 2d 277 (La. Ct. App. 1985).
Bethea v. United States, 365 A.2d 64 (D.C. 1976).
Bishop, State v., 753 P.2d 439 (Utah 1988).

Blake v. United States, 407 F.2d 908 (5th Cir. 1969).
Blocker, United States v., 288 F.2d 853, (D.C. Cir. 1961).
Bock, State v., 288 N.C. 145, 217 S.E.2d 513 (1975).
Boone, State v., 307 N.C. 198, 297 S.E.2d 585 (1982).
Bradley v. State, 102 Tex. Crim. 41, 277 S.W. 147 (1925).
Bratty v. Attorney-General for Northern Ireland, [1961] 3 All E.R. 523.
Brawner, United States v., 471 F.2d 969 (D.C. Cir. 1972).
Bray, Regina v., 24 C.C.C.2d 366 (1976).
Breen v. State, 53 Ala. App. 588, 302 So. 2d 562 (1974).
Brennan, Commonwealth v., 399 Mass. 358, 504 N.E.2d 612 (1987).
Brown, State v., 38 Kan. 390, 16 P. 259 (1888).
Burge, State v., 195 Conn. 232, 487 A.2d 532 (1985).
Burnett v. Commonwealth, 284 S.W.2d 654 (Ky. 1955).
Burnim, United States v., 576 F.2d 236 (9th Cir. 1978).
Burns, 58 Crim. App. 364 (1974).
Burrows v. State, 38 Ariz. 99, 297 P. 1029 (1931).
Bushnell v. Bushnell, 103 Conn. 583, 131 A. 432 (1925).
Butterfield v. State, 317 S.W.2d 943 (Tex. Crim. App. 1958).

Caddell, State v., 287 N.C. 266, 215 S.E.2d 348 (1975).
Caldwell, People v., 102 Cal. App. 3d 461, 162 Cal. Rptr. 397 (1980).
Caldwell, Regina v., [1981] 1 All E.R. 961.
Calendar of Close Rolls, Edward I, 7 Edw. I 518 (1278).
Cameron, State v., 104 N.J. 42, 514 A.2d 1302 (1986).
Carter v. United States, 252 F.2d 608 (D.C. Cir. 1957).
Carter v. State, 376 P.2d 351 (Okla. Crim. App. 1962).
Casassa, People v., 49 N.Y.2d 668, 427 N.Y.S.2d 769, 404 N.E.2d 1310 (1980).
Castillo, People v., 70 Cal. 2d 264, 74 Cal. Rptr. 385, 449 P.2d 449 (1969).
Chapman, People v., 261 Cal. App. 2d 149, 67 Cal. Rptr. 601 (1968).
Chapman v. State, 136 Tex. Crim. 285, 124 S.W.2d 112 (1938).
Charlson, Regina v., [1955] 1 All E.R. 859.
Choate v. State, 19 Okla. Crim. 169, 197 P. 1060 (1921).
Choice v. State, 31 Ga. 424 (1860).
City of Minneapolis v. Altimus, 306 Minn. 462, 238 N.W.2d 851 (1976).
Cockerell, United States v., 49 C.M.R. 567 (1974).
Codarre, People v., 20 A.D.2d 98, 245 N.Y.S.2d 81 (1963).
Coleman, United States v., 475 F. Supp. 422 (E.D. Pa. 1979).
Collier v. State, 17 Okla. Crim. 139, 186 P. 963 (1920).
Collier, State v., 474 So. 2d 529 (La. Ct. App. 1985).
Conley, People v., 64 Cal. 2d 310, 49 Cal. Rptr. 815, 411 P.2d 911 (1966).
Conrad, People v., 148 Mich. App. 433, 385 N.W.2d 277 (1986).
Cook v. State, 271 So. 2d 232 (Fla. Dist. Ct. App. 1973).
Cooley v. Commonwealth, 459 S.W.2d 89 (Ky. 1970).
Cooper, State v., 111 Ariz. 332, 529 P.2d 231 (1974).

Cooper, United States v., 465 F.2d 451 (9th Cir. 1972).
Corder v. Commonwealth, 278 S.W.2d 77 (Ky. 1955).
Cox, People v., 67 Cal. App. 2d 166, 153 P.2d 362 (1944).
Coyle, State v., 86 S.C. 81, 67 S.E. 24 (1910).
Cram, People v., 12 Cal. App. 3d 37, 90 Cal. Rptr. 393 (1970).
Crews, People v., 122 Ill. 2d 266, 522 N.E.2d 1167 (1988).
Crittle, People v., 390 Mich. 367, 212 N.W.2d 196 (1973).
Croscup, State v., 604 S.W.2d 69 (Tenn. Crim. App. 1980).
Cruse v. State, 125 Tex. Crim. 123, 66 S.W.2d 324 (1933).
Crutchfield v. State, 627 P.2d 196 (Alaska 1980).
Cullum, Regina v., 14 C.C.C.2d 294 (1973).
Cummins, People v., 47 Mich. 334, 11 N.W. 184 (1882).
Currens, United States v., 290 F.2d 751 (3d Cir. 1961).
Curry, State v., 127 Ariz. 1, 617 P.2d 785 (1980).

D.P.P. v. Majewski, [1976] 2 All E.R. 142.
Davis, State v., 653 S.W.2d 167 (Mo. 1983).
Davis v. State, 161 Tenn. 23, 28 S.W.2d 993 (1930).
Davis, Regina v., 14 Cox C.C. 563 (1881).
Decina, People v., 2 N.Y.2d 133, 157 N.Y.S.2d 558, 138 N.E.2d 799 (1956).
DelGuidice, People v., 199 Colo. 41, 606 P.2d 840 (1979).
De Moss, State v., 244 Kan. 387, 770 P.2d 441 (1989).
Doepel v. United States, 434 A.2d 449 (D.C. 1981).
Doepel v. United States, 510 A.2d 1044 (D.C. 1986).
Dowd v. District of Columbia Police & Firefighters' Retirement & Relief Bd., 485 A.2d 212 (D.C. 1984).
Drew, People v., 22 Cal. 3d 333, 149 Cal. Rptr. 275, 583 P.2d 1318 (1978).
Drew, United States v., 25 F. Cas. 913 (C.C.D. Mass. 1828) (No. 14,993).
Dunigan, People v., 96 Ill. App. 3d 799, 421 N.E.2d 1319 (1981).
Durham v. United States, 214 F.2d 862 (D.C. Cir. 1954).

Egnor, People v., 175 N.Y. 419, 67 N.E. 906 (1903).
Ellenburg v. State, 353 So. 2d 810 (Ala. Crim. App. 1977).
Elliot, State v., 177 Conn. 1, 411 A.2d 3 (1979).
Estelle v. Smith, 451 U.S. 454, 101 S. Ct. 1866, 68 L. Ed. 2d 359 (1981).
Evans v. State, 645 P.2d 155 (Alaska 1982).
Evers v. State, 31 Tex. Crim. 318, 20 S.W. 744 (1892).
Evilsizer v. State, 487 S.W.2d 113 (Tex. Crim. App. 1972).

Fain v. Commonwealth, 78 Ky. 183 (1879).
Fendler v. Roy, 331 Mo. 1083, 58 S.W.2d 459 (1932).
Fenton, 61 Crim. App. 261 (1975).
Ferrer's Case, 19 How. St. Tr. 886 (1760).
Fields, State v., 324 N.C. 204, 376 S.E.2d 740 (1989).
Finkey, People v., 105 Ill. App. 3d 230, 434 N.E.2d 18 (1982).

Fisher v. United States, 80 U.S. App. D.C. 96, 149 F.2d 28 (D.C. Cir. 1945).
Fitzpatrick, Regina v., [1977] No. Irel. 20 (Ct. Crim. App.).
Fox, State v., 112 Ariz. 375, 542 P.2d 800 (1975).
Freeman, People v., 61 Cal. App. 2d 110, 142 P.2d 435 (1943).
Frisbee, United States v., 623 F. Supp. 1217 (N.D. Cal. 1985).
Frye v. United States, 293 F. 1013 (D.C. Cir. 1923).
Fulcher v. State, 633 P.2d 142 (Wyo. 1981).
Furlong, People v., 187 N.Y. 198, 79 N.E. 978 (1907).

Gaines, People v., 93 Ill. App. 3d 71, 416 N.E.2d 1156 (1981).
Garbutt, People v., 17 Mich. 9 (1868).
Gertson, United States v., 15 M.J. 990 (1983).
Gilcrist, State v., 552 P.2d 690 (Wash. Ct. App. 1976).
Gish, State v., 87 Idaho 341, 393 P.2d 342 (1964).
Glass, Commonwealth v., 401 Mass. 799, 519 N.E.2d 1311 (1988).
Gold, United States v., 661 F. Supp. 1127 (D.D.C. 1987).
Gooze, State v., 14 N.J. Super. 277, 81 A.2d 811 (1951).
Goza, State v., 317 S.W.2d 609 (Mo. 1958).
Grant, People v., 46 Ill. App. 3d 125, 360 N.E.2d 809 (1977).
Grant, People v., 71 Ill. 2d 551, 377 N.E.2d 4 (1978).
Grant v. State, 250 Ala. 164, 33 So. 2d 466 (1948).
Granville House, Inc. v. Dept. of Health & Human Services, 550 F. Supp. 628 (D. Minn. 1982).
Gray v. Commonwealth, 247 Ky. 282, 57 S.W.2d 6 (1933).
Guerra v. Workers' Comp. Appeals Bd., 168 Cal. App. 3d 195, 214 Cal. Rptr. 58 (1985).
Guillett, People v., 342 Mich. 1, 69 N.W.2d 140 (1955).

Hall, State v., 214 N.W.2d 205 (Iowa 1974).
Hallock, People v., 208 Cal. App. 3d 595, 256 Cal. Rptr. 264 (1989).
Hancock v. State, 741 P.2d 1210 (Alaska Ct. App. 1987).
Hanks v. State, 542 S.W.2d 413 (Tex. Crim. App. 1976).
Harrison-Owen, 35 Crim. App. 108 (1951).
Hawkins, Commonwealth v., 3 Gray 463 (1855).
Heffington, People v., 32 Cal. App. 3d 1, 107 Cal. Rptr. 859 (1973).
Helmick, State v., 112 Ariz. 166, 540 P.2d 638 (1975).
Hendershott v. People, 653 P.2d 385 (Colo. 1982).
Henderson, United States v., 680 F.2d 659 (9th Cir. 1982).
Hernandez, United States v., 20 C.M.A. 219, 43 C.M.R 59 (1970).
Heyward v. State, 470 N.E.2d 63 (Ind. 1984).
Hicklin v. State, 535 P.2d 743 (Wyo. 1975).
Hicks, Commonwealth v., 483 Pa. 305, 396 A.2d 1183 (1979).
Hicks v. State, 256 Ga. 715, 352 S.E.2d 762 (1987).
Higgins, People v., 5 N.Y.2d 607, 186 N.Y.S.2d 623, 159 N.E.2d 179 (1959).
Hill v. Baxter, [1958] 1 Q.B. 277.

Hinckley, United States v., 525 F. Supp. 1342 (D.D.C. 1981), *clarified and reconsid. denied,* 529 F. Supp. 520 (D.D.C.)(per curiam), *aff'd,* 672 F.2d 115 (D.C. Cir. 1982)(for the pre-trial rulings); Crim. No. 81-306 (D.D.C. 1981)(for the trial record).
Holden, State v., 85 N.M. 397, 512 P.2d 970 (1973).
Holota, State v., 194 A.2d 69 (Conn. Cir. Ct. 1963).
Holzman, State v., 176 N.J. Super. 590, 424 A.2d 454 (1980).
Hopt v. Utah, 104 U.S. 631, 26 L. Ed. 873 (1882).
Hoyt, State v., 21 Wis. 2d 284, 128 N.W.2d 645 (1964).
Hudson, State v., 152 Ariz. 121, 730 P.2d 830 (1986).
Hurley v. Commonwealth, 451 S.W.2d 838 (Ky. 1970).

In re Rosenfield, 157 F. Supp. 18 (D.D.C. 1957).
In Interest of A.M.S., 419 N.W.2d 723 (Iowa 1988).
In Interest of Palmer, 363 N.W.2d 401 (N.D. 1985).
In re Conservatorship of Torres, 180 Cal. App. 3d 1159, 226 Cal. Rptr. 142 (1986).
In re Winship, 397 U.S. 358, 90 S. Ct. 1068, 25 L. Ed. 2d 368 (1970).
In re S.P.W., 707 S.W.2d 814 (Mo. Ct. App. 1986).

J. Roth Builders, Inc. v. Aetna Life & Casualty Co., 151 Ill. App. 3d 572, 503 N.E.2d 782 (1987).
Jackson v. Denno, 378 U.S. 368, 84 S. Ct. 1774, 12 L. Ed. 2d 908 (1964).
Jackson, People v., 10 N.Y.2d 510, 225 N.Y.S.2d 200, 180 N.E.2d 561 (1962).
Jackson, People v., 14 N.Y.2d 5, 196 N.E.2d 887, 247 N.Y.S.2d 481 (1964).
Jackson, People v., 42 Ill. App. 3d 919, 356 N.E.2d 979 (1976).
Jandelli, People v., 116 Misc. 2d 384, 455 N.Y.S.2d 728 (1982).
Jandelli, People v., 118 A.D.2d 656, 499 N.Y.S.2d 962 (1986).
Jensen, State v., 282 N.W.2d 55 (N.D. 1979).
Jerrett, State v., 309 N.C. 239, 307 S.E.2d 339 (1983).
Jewett, United States v., 438 F.2d 495 (8th Cir. 1971).
Johnson, State v., 40 Conn. 136 (1873).
Johnson v. Commonwealth, 135 Va. 524, 115 S.E. 673 (1923).
Jones, People v., 225 Cal. App. 2d 598, 37 Cal. Rptr. 454 (1964).
Jones, State v., 50 N.H. 369 (1871).
Jones v. State, 648 P.2d 1251 (Okla. Crim. App. 1982).
Jones v. United States, 463 U.S. 354, 103 S. Ct. 3043, 77 L. Ed. 2d 694 (1983).

Kane v. United States, 399 F.2d 730 (9th Cir. 1968).
Kavanaugh, State v., 20 Del. 131, 53 A. 335 (1902).
Keeling, People v., 152 Cal. App. 2d 4, 312 P.2d 407 (1957).
Keenan v. Commonwealth, 44 Pa. 55 (1863).
Kelley, People v., 21 Mich. App. 612, 176 N.W.2d 435 (1970).
Kelly, People v., 10 Cal. 3d 565, 111 Cal. Rptr. 171, 516 P.2d 875 (1973).
Kemp, Regina v., [1956] 3 All E.R. 249.

Kilbride v. Lake, 1962 N.Z.L.R. 590.
King, Regina v., 35 D.L.R.2d 386 (1962).
Kitt, People v., 83 Cal. App. 3d 834, 148 Cal. Rptr. 447 (1978).
Knight, People v., 18 A.D.2d 890, 237 N.Y.S.2d 846 (1963).
Koon, State v., 285 S.C. 1, 328 S.E.2d 625 (1985).
Korell, State v., 213 Mont. 316, 690 P.2d 992 (1984).
Kowal, United States v., 596 F. Supp. 375 (D. Conn. 1984).
Kramer, United States v., 579 F. Supp. 314 (D. Md. 1984).

Laing, Commonwealth v., 310 Pa. Super. 105, 456 A.2d 204 (1983).
Lambert v. California, 355 U.S. 225, 78 S. Ct. 240, 2 L. Ed. 2d 228 (1957).
Larsonneur, 24 Crim. App. 74 (1933).
Lautzenheiser v. State, 481 N.E.2d 113 (Ind. 1985).
Leary v. R., [1978] 1 S.C.R. 29, 74 D.L.R.3d 103.
Lee, State v., 108 Wis. 2d 1, 321 N.W.2d 108 (1982).
Leggett v. State, 21 Tex. App. 382, 17 S.W. 159 (1886).
Lester v. State, 212 Tenn. 338, 370 S.W.2d 405 (1963).
Lewis, State v., 136 Mo. 84, 37 S.W. 806 (1896).
Lewis v. State, 196 Ga. 755, 27 S.E.2d 659 (1943).
Limp v. State, 228 Ind. 361, 92 N.E.2d 549 (1950).
Low, People v., 732 P.2d 622 (Colo. 1987).
Loretta, Commonwealth v., 386 Mass. 794, 438 N.E.2d 56 (1982).
Lyons, United States v., 731 F.2d 243 (5th Cir. 1984).

M'Naghten's Case, 8 Eng. Rep. 718 (1843).
Magnus, People v., 92 Misc. 80, 155 N.Y.S. 1013 (1915).
Maher v. People, 10 Mich. 212 (1862).
Martin v. State, 31 Ala. App. 334, 17 So. 2d 427 (1944).
Martin, State v., 213 N.J. Super. 426, 517 A.2d 513 (1986).
Martinez v. People, 124 Colo. 170, 235 P.2d 810 (1951).
Massey v. State, 222 Ga. 143, 149 S.E.2d 118 (1966).
Massey, State v., 242 Kan. 252, 747 P.2d 802 (1987).
Matter of Welfare of J.A., 417 N.W.2d 696 (Minn. Ct. App. 1988).
Matter of Welfare of N.C.K., 411 N.W.2d 577 (Minn. Ct. App. 1987).
Matthews, People v., 717 P.2d 970 (Colo. App. 1985).
Mayole v. B. Crystal & Son, Inc., 266 A.D. 1008, 44 N.Y.S.2d 411 (1943).
McCracken, United States v., 488 F.2d 406 (5th Cir. 1974).
McDonald v. United States, 312 F.2d 847 (D.C. Cir. 1962).
McIntyre v. State, 379 P.2d 615 (Alaska 1963).
McKinney v. State, 566 P.2d 653 (Alaska 1977).
McMahon, State v., 49 R.I. 107, 140 A. 359 (1928).
McNally, State v., 336 So. 2d 713 (Fla. Dist. Ct. App. 1976).
McNerlin, People v., 11 N.Y.2d 738, 226 N.Y.S.2d 443, 181 N.E.2d 456 (1962).
McNerlin, People v., 44 Misc. 2d 340, 253 N.Y.S.2d 912 (1964).

McVey, State v., 376 N.W.2d 585 (Iowa 1985).
Mercer, State v., 275 N.C. 108, 165 S.E.2d 328 (1969).
Middleton, State v., 295 Or. 485, 668 P.2d 371 (1983).
Miles v. State, 688 S.W.2d 219 (Tex. Ct. App. 1985).
Miller v. U.S. Fidelity & Guar. Co., 478 So. 2d 200 (La. Ct. App. 1985).
Molnar, State v., 81 N.J. 475, 410 A.2d 37 (1980).
Monie v. State Personnel Bd., 229 Neb. 27, 424 N.W.2d 874 (1988).
Mozingo v. Craven, 341 F. Supp. 296 (C.D. Cal. 1972).
Mriglot, State v., 88 Wash. 2d 573, 564 P.2d 784 (1977).
Murphy, State v., 185 N.J. Super. 72, 447 A.2d 219 (1982).
Murtishaw, People v., 48 Cal. 3d 1001, 258 Cal. Rptr. 821, 773 P.2d 172 (1989).
Myers v. State, 174 P.2d 395 (Okla. Crim. App. 1946).

Newsome v. Commonwealth, 287 Ky. 649, 154 S.W.2d 737 (1941).
Newton, People v., 8 Cal. App. 3d 359, 87 Cal. Rptr. 394 (1970).

O'Brien, Regina v., 56 D.L.R.2d 65 (1966).
O'Connor, Regina v., 29 A.L.R. 449 (1980).
O'Leary v. State, 604 P.2d 1099 (Alaska 1979).
Oborn v. State, 143 Wis. 249, 126 N.W. 737 (1910).
Olsen, State v., 108 Utah 377, 160 P.2d 427 (1945).
Olson, State v., 356 N.W.2d 110 (N.D. 1984).
Olvera, United States v., 4 C.M.A. 134, 15 C.M.R. 134 (1954).
Ott, State v., 297 Or. 375, 686 P.2d 1001 (1984).

Parelius, United States v., 83 F. Supp. 617 (D. Haw. 1949).
Parker v. State, 7 Md. App. 167, 254 A.2d 381 (1969).
Parker, State v., 416 So. 2d 545 (La. 1982).
Parmes, People v., 114 Misc. 2d 503, 451 N.Y.S.2d 1015 (N.Y. Sup. Ct. 1982).
Parmes, People v., 121 A.D.2d 658, 504 N.Y.S.2d 50 (1986).
Parsons v. State, 81 Ala. 577, 2 So. 854 (1886).
Pate, State v., 1984 W.L. 7066 (Ohio Ct. App. 1984).
Pauling v. State, 276 S.C. 92, 275 S.E.2d 881 (1981).
Pearson's Case, 2 Lew. C.C. 144, 168 Eng. Rep. 1108 (1835).
Penman, People v., 271 Ill. 82, 110 N.E. 894 (1915).
Perkins v. United States, 228 F. 408 (4th Cir. 1915).
Perrotta, People v., 224 Cal. App. 2d 498, 36 Cal. Rptr. 813 (1964).
Pettay, State v., 216 Kan. 555, 532 P.2d 1289 (1975).
Pike, State v., 49 N.H. 399 (1870).
Plank, Commonwealth v., 329 Pa. Super. 446, 478 A.2d 872 (1984).
Plummer, State v., 117 N.H. 320, 374 A.2d 431 (1977).
Polston v. State, 685 P.2d 1 (Wyo. 1984).
Poulsen, State v., 45 Wash. App. 706, 726 P.2d 1036 (1986).

Powell v. Texas, 392 U.S. 514, 88 S. Ct. 2145, 20 L. Ed. 2d 1254 (1968).
Prickett, United States v., 604 F. Supp. 407 (S.D. Ohio 1985).
Prince, Regina v., L.R. 2 Cr. Cas. Res. 154 (1875).

Quick, Regina v., 1973 Q.B. 910.

Rabey, Regina v., 79 D.L.R.3d 414 (1978).
Ray, People v., 14 Cal. 3d 20, 120 Cal. Rptr. 377, 533 P.2d 1017 (1975).
Read v. People, 119 Colo. 506, 205 P.2d 233 (1949).
Reeves v. State, 196 Ga. 604, 27 S.E.2d 375 (1943).
Reniger v. Feogossa, 1 Plowd. 1, 75 Eng. Rep. 1 (1551).
Roberts v. People, 19 Mich. 401 (1870).
Robey v. State, 54 Md. App. 60, 456 A.2d 953 (1983).
Robinson v. California, 370 U.S. 660, 82 S. Ct. 1417, 8 L. Ed. 2d 758 (1962).

Robinson, People v., 2 Park. Crim. R. 235 (N.Y. 1855).
Rodriguez, People v., 103 A.D.2d 121, 479 N.Y.S.2d 25 (N.Y. App. Div. 1984).
Roerman, People v., 189 Cal. App. 2d 150, 10 Cal. Rptr. 870 (1961).
Romaine, People v., 79 Ill. App. 3d 1089, 399 N.E.2d 319 (1979).
Rose v. State, 506 So. 2d 467 (Fla. Dist. Ct. App. 1987).
Rumsey, Commonwealth v., 309 Pa. Super. 137, 454 A.2d 1121 (1983).
Rush, United States v., 13 C.M.R. 594 (1953).

Saldiveri v. State, 217 Md. 412, 143 A.2d 70 (1958).
Salzman v. United States, 405 F.2d 358 (D.C. Cir. 1968).
Sam, People v., 71 Cal. 2d 194, 77 Cal. Rptr. 804, 454 P.2d 700 (1969).
Sanders v. State, 449 S.W.2d 262 (Tex. Crim. App. 1969).
Sandstrom v. Montana, 442 U.S. 510, 99 S. Ct. 2450, 61 L. Ed. 2d 39 (1979).
Santiago-Vargas, United States v., 5 M.J. 41 (C.M.A. 1978).
Savoie, People v., 419 Mich. 118, 349 N.W.2d 139 (1984).
Schlomann, United States v., 16 C.M.A. 414, 37 C.M.R. 34 (1966).
Schlomann, United States v., 36 C.M.R. 622 (1966).
Schlomann v. Ralston, 691 F.2d 401 (8th Cir. 1982), *cert. denied*, 459 U.S. 1221, 103 S. Ct. 1229, 75 L. Ed. 2d 463 (1983).
Schultz, People v., 173 Ill. App. 3d 738, 527 N.E.2d 984 (1988).
Scott, People v., 146 Cal. App. 3d 823, 194 Cal. Rptr. 633 (1983).
Sedeno, People v., 10 Cal. 3d 703, 112 Cal. Rptr. 1, 518 P.2d 913 (1974).
Seely, State v., 212 Kan. 195, 510 P.2d 115 (1973).
Sheehan, Commonwealth v., 376 Mass. 765, 383 N.E.2d 1115 (1978).
Shelley, Commonwealth v., 381 Mass. 340, 409 N.E.2d 732 (1980).
Shelton, People v., 88 Misc. 2d 136, 385 N.Y.S.2d 708 (1976).
Shields, State v., 444 So. 2d 287 (La. Ct. App. 1983).
Sikora, State v., 44 N.J. 453, 210 A.2d 193 (1965).
Sirbaugh, Commonwealth v., 347 Pa. Super. 154, 500 A.2d 453 (1985).

Skorka, People v., 147 Ill. App. 3d 976, 498 N.E.2d 607 (1986).
Smith, United States v., 404 F.2d 720 (6th Cir. 1968).
Smith v. Commonwealth, 268 S.W.2d 937 (Ky. 1954).
Smith v. Commonwealth, 282 S.W.2d 840 (Ky. 1955).
Smith, Gov't of the Virgin Islands v., 278 F.2d 169 (3d Cir. 1960).
Smith, State v., 59 N.C. App. 227, 296 S.E.2d 315 (1982).
Snowden, People v., 147 Ill. App. 3d 763, 498 N.E.2d 612 (1986).
Snyder, State v., 70 N.C. App. 335, 319 S.E.2d 668 (1984).
Spingola, United States v., 464 F.2d 909 (7th Cir. 1972).
Spragney, People v., 24 Cal. App. 3d 333, 100 Cal. Rptr. 902 (1972).
Sprague v. State, 52 Wis. 2d 89, 187 N.W.2d 784 (1971).
Spriggs, Regina v., [1958] 1 All E.R. 300.
Spurlin, People v., 156 Cal. App. 3d 119, 202 Cal. Rptr. 663 (1984).
Stewart, Commonwealth v., 377 Pa. Super. 530, 547 A.2d 1189 (1988).
Strickland v. State, 137 Ga. 115, 72 S.E. 922 (1911).
Stripp, 69 Crim. App. 318 (1978).
Sullivan, Regina v., [1983] 2 All E.R. 673.

Taylor, Commonwealth v., 263 Mass. 356, 161 N.E. 245 (1928).
Taylor v. United States, 7 App. D.C. 27 (1895).
Terrill v. State, 74 Wis. 278, 42 N.W. 243 (1889).
The Trial of Hadfield, 27 How. St. Tr. 1281 (1800).
Thomas v. State, 105 Ga. App. 754, 125 S.E.2d 679 (1962).
Thompson, State v., Wright's Ohio Rep. 617 (1834).
Thurman, State v., 10 Conn. App. 302, 523 A.2d 891 (1987).
Tibbs v. Commonwealth, 138 Ky. 558, 128 S.W. 871 (1910).
Todaro, Commonwealth v., 301 Pa. Super. 1, 446 A.2d 1305 (1982).
Toner, People v., 217 Mich. 640, 187 N.W. 386 (1922).
Traynor v. Turnage, 485 U.S. 535, 108 S. Ct. 1372, 99 L. Ed. 2d 618 (1988).

Upstone v. People, 109 Ill. 169 (1883).
Utter, State v., 4 Wash. App. 137, 479 P.2d 946 (1971).

Van Ermen v. Percy, 489 F. Supp. 791 (E.D. Wis. 1980).
Velez, People v., 175 Cal. App. 3d 785, 221 Cal. Rptr. 631 (1985).
Venegas, State v., 137 Ariz. 171, 669 P.2d 604 (1983).

Wade v. United States, 426 F.2d 64 (9th Cir. 1970).
Walker, People v., 33 Ill. App. 3d 681, 338 N.E.2d 449 (1975).
Walker, United States v., 12 C.M.A. 658, 31 C.M.R 244 (1962).
Wallace, Commonwealth v., 439 N.E.2d 848 (Mass. App. Ct. 1982).
Washington, People v., 71 Cal. 2d 1061, 80 Cal. Rptr. 567, 458 P.2d 479 (1969).
Watkins v. Commonwealth, 378 S.W.2d 614 (Ky. 1964).
Watkins v. People, 158 Colo. 485, 408 P.2d 425 (1965).

Watson, State v., 211 Mont. 401, 686 P.2d 879 (1984).
Watts v. State, 680 S.W.2d 667 (Tex. Ct. App. 1984).
Webb, Commonwealth v., 252 Pa. 187, 97 A. 189 (1916).
Wells, People v., 33 Cal. 2d 330, 202 P.2d 53 (1949).
Welsh, State v., 8 Wash. App. 719, 508 P.2d 1041 (1973).
West v. State, 511 So. 2d 258 (Ala. Crim. App. 1987).
Weston v. State, 28 Wis. 2d 136, 135 N.W.2d 820 (1965).
Wetmore, People v., 22 Cal. 3d 318, 149 Cal. Rptr. 265, 583 P.2d 1308 (1978).
Whalem v. United States, 346 F.2d 812 (D.C. Cir. 1965).
White, State v., 110 Ariz. 508, 520 P.2d 1132 (1974).
Wicks, State v., 98 Wash. 2d 620, 657 P.2d 781 (1983).
Wilburn, People v., 49 Cal. 2d 714, 321 P.2d 452 (1958).
Willard, State v., 292 N.C. 567, 234 S.E.2d 587 (1977).
Williams, People v., 22 Cal. App. 3d 34, 99 Cal. Rptr. 103 (1971).
Williams, State v., 296 N.C. 693, 252 S.E.2d 739 (1979).
Williams, People v., 44 Cal. 3d 883, 245 Cal. Rptr. 336, 751 P.2d 395 (1988).
Wilson, State v., 104 N.C. 868, 10 S.E. 315 (1889).
Wilson v. State, 60 N.J.L. 171, 37 A. 954 (1897).
Wilson, People v., 66 Cal. 2d 749, 59 Cal. Rptr. 156, 427 P.2d 820 (1967).
Wimer, State v., 168 W. Va. 417, 284 S.E.2d 890 (1981).
Wirth, People v., 77 Ill. App. 3d 253, 395 N.E.2d 1106 (1979).
Witty v. State, 75 Tex. Crim. 440, 171 S.W. 229 (1914).
Wolff, People v., 61 Cal. 2d 795, 40 Cal. Rptr. 271, 394 P.2d 959 (1964).
Woolmington v. D.P.P., 1935 A.C. 462.
Wright v. State, 374 A.2d 824 (Del. 1977).

Index

About the Authors

LAWRENCE P. TIFFANY is Professor of Law at the University of Denver College of Law where he teaches in the areas of Criminal Law and Criminal Procedure.

MARY TIFFANY is a free-lance Nurse Anesthetist (CRNA) and Chair of the Chemical Dependency Committee of the Colorado Association of Nurse Anesthetists.